THE COMPLETE
AIR FRYER
COOKBOOK

1000 Flavorful and Effortless Recipes for Everyday Air Fryer Cooking

2022 EDITION

JEREMY J. POPP

Copyright© 2021By Jeremy J. PoppAll Rights Reserved

This book is copyright protected. It is only for personal use. You cannot amend, distribute, sell, use, quote or paraphrase any part of the content within this book, without the consent of the author or publisher.

Under no circumstances will any blame or legal responsibility be held against the publisher, or author, for any damages, reparation, or monetary loss due to the information contained within this book, either directly or indirectly.

Disclaimer Notice:

Please note the information contained within this document is for educational and entertainment purposes only. All effort has been executed to present accurate, up to date, reliable, complete information. No warranties of any kind are declared or implied. Readers acknowledge that the author is not engaged in the rendering of legal, financial, medical or professional advice. The content within this book has been derived from various sources. Please consult a licensed professional before attempting any techniques outlined in this book.

By reading this document, the reader agrees that under no circumstances is the author responsible for any losses, direct or indirect, that are incurred as a result of the use of the information contained within this document, including, but not limited to, errors, omissions, or inaccuracies.

Table of Contents

Introduction 1

Chapter 1 Vegetables and Sides 2

1	Herbed Shiitake Mushrooms	2
2	Citrus Sweet Potatoes and Carrots	2
3	Sweet and Crispy Roasted Pearl Onions	2
4	Curry Roasted Cauliflower	2
5	Buttery Mushrooms	2
6	Mushroom and Rice Balls	2
7	Remoulade Tomato Slices	3
8	Cheesy Parsley Tomatoes	3
9	Garlicky Brussels Sprouts	3
10	Sweet Feta Carrots	3
11	Authentic Spanish Patatas Bravas	3
12	Delicious Potato Patties	3
13	Cheesy Potatoes and Asparagus	3
14	Easy Sweet Potato Fries	4
15	Curly Fries with Gochujang Ketchup	4
16	Rosemary and Parsley Potatoes	4
17	Zesty Bell Pepper Bites	4
18	Quick Beetroot Chips	4
19	Brussels Sprouts with Garlic Aioli	4
20	Crispy Bell Peppers with Tartare Sauce	4
21	Easy Cabbage Steaks	5
22	Green Cabbage with Blue Cheese Sauce	5
23	Indian Fried Okra	5
24	Zucchini Fries with Tabasco Dip	5
25	Bulgarian "Burek" Pepper with Yogurt Sauce	5
26	Green Pea Arancini with Tomato Sauce	5
27	Parmesan Zucchini Boats	6
28	Aunt's Roasted Carrots with Cilantro Sauce	6
29	Involtini di Melanzane (Eggplant Rollups)	6
30	Mediterranean Eggplant Burgers	6
31	Avocado Fries with Pico de Gallo	6
32	Cheesy Eggplant Schnitzels	6
33	Sesame Balsamic Asparagus	7
34	Air Fried Eggplant Bruschetta	7
35	Easy Eggplant and Zucchini Chips	7
36	Homemade Blooming Onion	7
37	Breaded Italian Green Beans	7
38	Cheese and Cauliflower Tater Tots	7
39	Russian-Style Eggplant Caviar	8
40	Tasty Balsamic Beets	8
41	Teriyaki Cauliflower	8
42	Easy Cauliflower Popcorn	8
43	Almond-Crusted Cauliflower Florets	8
44	Chili Corn on the Cob	8
45	Cholula Seasoned Broccoli	8
46	Parmesan Broccoli Bites	9
47	Catalan-Style "Escalivada" Veggie Spread	9
48	Zucchini and Turnip Bake	9
49	Black Beans and Veggie Burgers	9
50	Roasted Pumpkin with Goat Cheese	9
51	Sweet Butternut Squash with Walnuts	9
52	Crispy Fried Tofu	9
53	Spicy Vegetable Skewers	10
54	Tempura Veggies with Sesame Soy Sauce	10
55	Party Crispy Nachos	10
56	Middle Eastern Veggie Kofta	10
57	Indian Aloo Tikki	10
58	Roasted Balsamic Veggies	10
59	Classic French Ratatouille	11
60	Charred Broccolini with Lemon-Caper Sauce	11
61	Winter Vegetable Traybake	11
62	Winter Root Vegetable Medley	11
63	Turmeric Crispy Chickpeas	11
64	Air Fried Cheesy Ravioli	11
65	Cashew and Chickpea Balls	11
66	Chili Falafel with Cheesy Sauce	12
67	Quinoa and Veggie Stuffed Peppers	12
68	Fava Bean Falafel with Tzatziki	12
69	Green Vegetable Rotini Pasta Bake	12
70	Easy Vegetable Croquettes	12
71	Greek Halloumi Cheese with Veggies	13
72	Asian-Style Spring Rolls	13
73	Italian-Style Stuffed Mushrooms	13
74	Poblano and Tomato Stuffed Squash	13
75	Egg and Cauliflower Rice Casserole	13
76	Eggplant Gratin with Mozzarella Crust	13
77	Chili Roasted Pumpkin with Orzo	14
78	Greek-Style Stuffed Bell Peppers	14
79	Portuguese-Style Veggies with Cheese	14
80	Cheesy English Muffins	14
81	Roasted Veggies with Penne Pasta	14
82	Southern-Style Corn Cakes	14
83	Vegetable and Goat Cheese Tian	15
84	Chickpea and Spinach Casserole	15
85	Dill Zucchini Egg Cakes	15
86	Tomato Sandwiches with Feta and Pesto	15
87	Cheesy Green Beans and Egg Cups	15
88	Jalapeño and Bean Tacos	15
89	Cheesy Vegetable Quesadilla	16
90	Air Fried Veggie Sushi	16

91	Potato Filled Bread Rolls	16
92	Mexican Chile Relleno	16
93	Vegetable Tortilla Pizza	16
94	Spanish-Style Huevos Rotos (Broken Eggs)	16
95	Crispy Mozzarella Sliders	17
96	Easy Greek Briami (Ratatouille)	17
97	Baked Mediterranean Shakshuka	17
98	Brussels Sprouts with Raisins and Pine Nuts	17
99	Hasselback Potatoes with Chive Pesto	17
100	Roasted Brussels Sprouts with Bacon	17
101	Plantain Fritters	18
102	Lemon-Garlic Mushrooms	18
103	Brussels Sprouts with Pecans and Gorgonzola	18
104	Homemade Pie with Root Vegetables	18
105	"Faux-Tato" Hash	18
106	Indian Eggplant Bharta	18
107	Golden Garlicky Mushrooms	19
108	Crispy Green Beans	19
109	Creamed Asparagus	19
110	Lemon-Thyme Asparagus	19
111	Simple Zucchini Crisps	19
112	Crispy Garlic Sliced Eggplant	19
113	Air Fried Potatoes with Olives	19
114	Parmesan Herb Focaccia Bread	20
115	Garlic-Parmesan Crispy Baby Potatoes	20
116	Broccoli-Cheddar Twice-Baked Potatoes	20
117	Fried Zucchini Salad	20
118	Super Cheesy Gold Eggplant	20
119	Grits Casserole	21
120	Roasted Sweet Potatoes	21
121	Air-Fried Okra	21
122	Baked Jalapeño and Cheese Cauliflower Mash	21
123	Shishito Pepper Roast	21
124	Maple-Roasted Tomatoes	21
125	Fig, Chickpea, and Arugula Salad	22
126	Spinach and Cheese Stuffed Tomatoes	22
127	Potato with Creamy Cheese	22
128	Bacon-Wrapped Asparagus	22
129	Roasted Garlic	22
130	Citrus-Roasted Broccoli Florets	22
131	Buttery Green Beans	22
132	Easy Potato Croquettes	23
133	Hawaiian Brown Rice	23
134	Parsnip Fries with Romesco Sauce	23
135	Stuffed Red Peppers with Herbed Ricotta and Tomatoes	23
136	Dill-and-Garlic Beets	23
137	Lemony Broccoli	23
138	Flatbread	24
139	Tofu Bites	24
140	Cheddar Broccoli with Bacon	24
141	Parmesan-Rosemary Radishes	24
142	Tingly Chili-Roasted Broccoli	24
143	Golden Pickles	24
144	Ricotta Potatoes	24

Chapter 2 Vegetarian Mains 25

145	Pesto Spinach Flatbread	25
146	Spinach-Artichoke Stuffed Mushrooms	25
147	Zucchini-Ricotta Tart	25
148	Garlic White Zucchini Rolls	25
149	Almond-Cauliflower Gnocchi	26
150	Cheese Stuffed Zucchini	26
151	Crispy Eggplant Rounds	26
152	Cauliflower, Chickpea, and Avocado Mash	26
153	Air Fryer Veggies with Halloumi	26
154	Black Bean and Tomato Chili	26
155	Spinach Cheese Casserole	27
156	Basmati Risotto	27
157	Broccoli-Cheese Fritters	27
158	Baked Turnip and Zucchini	27
159	Mushroom and Pepper Pizza Squares	27
160	Sweet Potatoes with Zucchini	27
161	Super Veg Rolls	28
162	Quiche-Stuffed Peppers	28
163	Parmesan Artichokes	28
164	Cheese Stuffed Peppers	28

Chapter 3 Breakfasts 29

165	Breakfast Potatoes with Pepper and Onion	29
166	Classic Hash Brown Potatoes	29
167	Austrian Torn Pancake	29
168	Bacon Cheddar Potato Skins	29
169	Salami, Prosciutto and Sausage Omelet	29
170	Indian Omelet	30
171	Tamagoyaki	30
172	Cheesy Egg-Kale Omelet	30
173	Ham and Cheddar Omelet	30
174	Bacon Omelet Cups	30
175	Spinach and Tomato Frittata	30
176	Potato Chorizo Frittata with Manchego	30
177	Parmesan Sausage Frittata	31
178	Air Fried Shirred Eggs	31
179	Breakfast Shrimp and Egg Muffins	31
180	Prosciutt Eggs Cups	31
181	Egg-Pumpkin Bread	31
182	Ham and Hash Brown Cups	31
183	Egg in a Hole	32
184	Turkey and Mushroom Sandwich	32
185	Sourdough Sandwiches	32
186	Crisp Pepper Rings with Cherry Tomatoes	32
187	Cheesy Sausage Casserole	32
188	Tofu and Cabbage Sandwich	32
189	Vanilla French Toast	32
190	French Brioche Toast	33
191	Bacon and Egg Sandwich	33
192	Classic Avocado Toast	33
193	Very Berry Breakfast Puffs	33

#	Recipe	Page
194	Traditional Romanian Polenta	33
195	Soppressata Pizza	33
196	Tomato, Prosciutto and Basil Bruschetta	33
197	Easy Calzone	34
198	Vanilla Banana Bread with Walnuts	34
199	Greek Feta Cheese Triangles	34
200	Herb Toasted Bagel	34
201	Apple Sandwich with Brie Cheese	34
202	Corn Blueberry Toast	34
203	Bacon Tortilla Wraps with Salsa	34
204	Basic Welsh Rarebit	35
205	Simple Mango Bread	35
206	Tomato and Olive Quiche	35
207	Cheesy Mushroom-Broccoli Pie	35
208	Peanut Butter Porridge	35
209	Cinnamon Zucchini Muffins	35
210	Banana Muffins with Hazelnuts and Chocolates	35
211	Crisp Sausage Patties	36
212	Orange Cupcakes	36
213	Coconut and Oat Cookies	36
214	Cherry and Almond Scones	36
215	Blueberry Oat Bars	36
216	Kiwi Pecan Muffins	36
217	Raisin Bread Pudding with Hazelnuts	37
218	Super Easy Croutons	37
219	Golden Avocado	37
220	Baked Eggs in Avocado	37
221	Roasted Asparagus with Serrano Ham	37
222	Egg White Cups	37
223	Turkey Sausage Breakfast Pizza	37
224	Hearty Banana Pastry	38
225	Breakfast Cobbler	38
226	Mexican Breakfast Pepper Rings	38
227	Air Fried Bacon	38
228	Vegetable Frittata	38
229	Denver Omelet	38
230	Cheesy Cauliflower "Hash Browns"	39
231	Three-Berry Dutch Pancake	39
232	Sausage and Egg Breakfast Burrito	39
233	Cheddar Eggs	39
234	Breakfast Hash	39
235	Fried Cheese Grits	39
236	Hearty Cheddar Biscuits	40
237	Creamy Cinnamon Rolls	40
238	Cheddar Soufflés	40
239	Scotch Eggs	40
240	Baked Potato Breakfast Boats	40
241	Pancake for Two	41
242	Spinach and Feta Egg Bake	41
243	Apple Cider Doughnut Holes	41
244	Classic British Breakfast	41
245	Jalapeño and Bacon Breakfast Pizza	41
246	Cheesy Scrambled Eggs	41
247	Baked Egg and Mushroom Cups	42
248	Easy Buttermilk Biscuits	42
249	Drop Biscuits	42
250	Parmesan Ranch Risotto	42
251	Italian Egg Cups	42
252	Meritage Eggs	42
253	Red Pepper and Feta Frittata	43
254	Tomato and Mozzarella Bruschetta	43
255	Southwestern Ham Egg Cups	43
256	Breakfast Pita	43
257	Golden Avocado Tempura	43
258	Mexican Shakshuka	43
259	Gluten-Free Granola Cereal	43
260	Keto Quiche	44
261	Whole Wheat Blueberry Muffins	44
262	Canadian Bacon Muffin Sandwiches	44
263	Fried Chicken Wings with Waffles	44
264	Egg Muffins	44
265	Bacon Eggs on the Go	45
266	Strawberry Toast	45
267	Breakfast Sausage and Cauliflower	45
268	New York Strip Steaks with Eggs	45
269	Spaghetti Squash Fritters	45
270	Breakfast Meatballs	45
271	Pita and Pepperoni Pizza	45
272	Hole in One	46
273	Spinach and Bacon Roll-ups	46

Chapter 4 Beef, Pork, and Lamb — 47

#	Recipe	Page
274	Barbecue Pork Ribs	47
275	Asian Pork Noddle Bowl with Vegetables	47
276	Dill Pork Meatballs	47
277	St. Louis–style Pork Ribs	47
278	Roasted Pork Rack with Macadamia Nuts	47
279	Char Siew Pork Ribs	48
280	Chinese Pork Ribs	48
281	Basil-Mustard Pork Burgers	48
282	Pork Sausage with Best Ratatouille	48
283	Sausage Sticks Rolled in Bacon	48
284	Marinara Pork Balls	48
285	Pork and Mushroom Pinchos	49
286	Greek Pork Skewers with Walnuts	49
287	Pork Sausage Balls with Fennel and Sage	49
288	Pear and Pork Patties	49
289	Pork, Zucchini and Onion Kebabs	49
290	Creamy Spinach-Stuffed Pork	49
291	Pork, Pepper and Squash Kebabs	50
292	Orange-Flavored Pork Tenderloin	50
293	Pork, Radish and Lettuce in a Cup	50
294	Southeast-Asian Pork Chops	50
295	Pork Chops with Mustard-Apricot Glaze	50
296	Sage-Rubbed Pork Tenderloin	50
297	Lemony Pork Chops	51
298	Hungarian-Style Pork Chops	51
299	Mexican Pork Chops with Black Beans	51

#	Recipe	Page
300	Roasted Pork Chops with Mushrooms	51
301	Spicy-Sweet Pork Chops	51
302	Thyme Pork Escalopes	51
303	Italian-Style Apple Pork Chops	52
304	Sweet French Pork Chops with Blue Cheese	52
305	Stuffed Pork Chops	52
306	Juicy Double Cut Pork Chops	52
307	Pork Escalopes with Beet and Cabbage Salad	52
308	Bavarian-Style Crispy Pork Schnitzel	52
309	Italian Pork Scallopini	53
310	Provencal Pork Medallions	53
311	Beef Steak Strips with Tomato Sauce	53
312	Pork Belly the Philippine Style	53
313	Pork Sandwiches with Bacon and Cheddar	53
314	Herbed Pork Belly	53
315	Effortless Beef Short Ribs	54
316	Greek-Style Beef Meatballs	54
317	Mexican Beef Cabbage Wraps	54
318	Ginger-Garlic Beef Ribs with Hot Sauce	54
319	Beef Koftas in Tomato Sauce	54
320	Beef Meatballs with Cranberry Sauce	54
321	California-Style Street Beef Taco Rolls	55
322	Smoked Beef Burgers with Hoisin Sauce	55
323	South American Arepas with Cilantro Sauce	55
324	Healthy Burgers	55
325	Classic Beef Meatloaf	55
326	Cheesy Italian Beef Meatloaf	55
327	"Stefania" Beef Meatloaf	56
328	Homemade Hot Beef Satay	56
329	Beef Steak with Mustard Sauce	56
330	Chimichurri New York Steak	56
331	Argentinian Beef Empanadas	56
332	Mexican Chorizo and Beef Empanadas	56
333	Mini Beef Sausage Rolls	57
334	Garlic Steak with Mexican Salsa	57
335	Chipotle Rib-Eye Steak with Avocado Salsa	57
336	Gorgonzola Rib Eye Steak	57
337	Tender Rib Eye Steak	57
338	Parsley Crumbed Beef Strips	57
339	Pesto Beef Steaks	57
340	Delicious Beef with Rice and Broccoli	58
341	Spicy Sweet Beef with Veggie Topping	58
342	Sausage Beef Rolls	58
343	French-Style Entrecote with Bordelaise Sauce	58
344	Thai Roasted Beef	58
345	Bloody Mary Beef Steak with Avocado	58
346	Mexican Beef Quesadillas	59
347	Korean Beef Bulgogi	59
348	Beef Veggie Mix with Hoisin Sauce	59
349	Beef Roast with Red Potatoes	59
350	Beef Steak Au Poivre	59
351	Fusion Flank Steak with Mexican Dressing	60
352	Pesto Beef Rolls with Spinach	60
353	Air Fried Beef with Veggies and Oyster Sauce	60
354	Beer-Dredged Corned Beef	60
355	Simple Roasted Beef with Herbs	60
356	Yummy London Broil with Parsley Butter	60
357	Herby Roast Beef	61
358	Lamb Meatballs with Roasted Veggie Bake	61
359	Traditional Lamb Kebabs	61
360	Wiener Beef Schnitzel	61
361	Crunchy Beef Escalopes	61
362	Greek Stuffed Tenderloin	61
363	Beef Liver with Onions	62
364	African Minty Lamb Kofta	62
365	Bulgogi Burgers	62
366	Lamb Chops with Lemony Couscous	62
367	Easy Lamb Chop Bites	62
368	Sweet and Sour Lamb Strips	62
369	Thyme Lamb Chops with Asparagus	63
370	Lamb Taquitos	63
371	Lamb and Cucumber Burgers	63
372	Peppercorn-Crusted Beef Tenderloin	63
373	Spicy Lamb Sirloin Chops	63
374	Bacon and Cheese Stuffed Pork Chops	63
375	Goat Cheese-Stuffed Flank Steak	64
376	Beef and Broccoli Stir-Fry	64
377	Rosemary Ribeye Steaks	64
378	Simple Ground Beef with Zucchini	64
379	Steaks with Walnut-Blue Cheese Butter	64
380	Beef and Goat Cheese Stuffed Peppers	64
381	Buttery Pork Chops	65
382	Cantonese BBQ Pork	65
383	Greek Pork with Tzatziki Sauce	65
384	Pork Butt with Garlicky Coriander-Parsley Sauce	65
385	London Broil with Herb Butter	65
386	Teriyaki Rump Steak with Broccoli and Capsicum	66
387	Kheema Meatloaf	66
388	Beef and Pork Sausage Meatloaf	66
389	Sausage-Stuffed Peppers	66
390	Italian Lamb Chops with Avocado Mayo	66
391	Sweet and Spicy Country-Style Ribs	66
392	Swedish Meatloaf	67
393	Rosemary Roast Beef	67
394	Kale and Beef Omelet	67
395	Blue Cheese Steak Salad	67
396	Mongolian-Style Beef	67
397	Pepper Steak	68
398	Herbed Beef	68
399	Beef Steak Fingers	68
400	Pork Schnitzels with Sour Cream and Dill Sauce	68
401	Red Curry Flank Steak	68
402	Super Bacon with Meat	69
403	Ham Hock Mac and Cheese	69
404	Indian Mint and Chile Kebabs	69
405	Caraway Crusted Beef Steaks	69
406	Marinated Steak Tips with Mushrooms	69
407	Bacon-Wrapped Cheese Pork	69

408	Steak, Broccoli, and Mushroom Rice Bowls	70
409	Rack of Lamb with Pistachio Crust	70
410	Sausage and Pork Meatballs	70
411	Herb-Crusted Lamb Chops	70
412	Sumptuous Pizza Tortilla Rolls	70
413	Beef Burger	71
414	Onion Pork Kebabs	71
415	Spicy Flank Steak with Zhoug	71
416	Spice-Coated Steaks with Cucumber and Snap Pea Salad	71
417	Crescent Dogs	71
418	Herb-Roasted Beef Tips with Onions	72
419	Lebanese Malfouf (Stuffed Cabbage Rolls)	72
420	Lemony Pork Loin Chop Schnitzel	72
421	Korean Beef Tacos	72
422	Cheesy Low-Carb Lasagna	72
423	Lamb Chops with Horseradish Sauce	73
424	Bean and Beef Meatball Taco Pizza	73
425	Ham with Sweet Potatoes	73
426	Pork Loin Roast	73
427	Beef Burgers with Mushroom	73
428	Beefy Poppers	73

Chapter 5 Poultry — 74

429	Whole Cornish Hen with Lemon and Herbs	74
430	Pomegranate Chicken Wings	74
431	Sweet Chili and Ginger Chicken Wings	74
432	Hot Chicken Wings	74
433	Italian-Style Chicken Wings	74
434	A-Little-Sour Chicken Wings	75
435	Greek Parsley Wings	75
436	Sesame Chicken Wings	75
437	Chili Ginger Chicken Wings	75
438	Spinach and Chicken Meatballs with Marinara Farfalle	75
439	Honey-Vinegar Chicken Wings	75
440	Dijon Chicken Wings	76
441	Basic Chicken Patties	76
442	Chicken Fingers with Red Mayo Dip	76
443	Thai Tom Yum Wings	76
444	Oregano Chicken Kebabs with Mayonnaise Sauce	76
445	South Asian Chicken Strips	76
446	Panko-Crusted Chicken Bites	77
447	Buffalo Cheese-Chicken Tacos	77
448	Chicken Skewers with Yogurt Dip	77
449	Manchego Chicken Fingers	77
450	Jalapeño and Chicken Quesadillas	77
451	Chicken Pinchos with Salsa Verde	77
452	Quinoa Chicken Nuggets	78
453	Rice Krispies Chicken Goujons	78
454	Juicy Chicken Fillets with Peppers	78
455	San Antonio Taco Chicken Strips	78
456	Crispy Chicken Tenders with Hot Aioli	78
457	Balsamic Chicken with Green Beans	78
458	Harissa Chicken Sticks	79
459	Crunchy Coconut Chicken Dippers	79
460	Popcorn Chicken Tenders	79
461	Ranch Cheesy Chicken Tenders	79
462	Crispy Chicken Tenderloins	79
463	Almond-Fried Crispy Chicken	79
464	Effortless Chicken Scallopini	79
465	Chicken Schnitzel with Gypsy Sauce	80
466	Cajun Chicken Tenders	80
467	Jerusalem Matzah and Chicken Schnitzels	80
468	Gluten-Free Crunchy Chicken	80
469	Chicken Teriyaki	80
470	Sweet Curried Chicken Cutlets	80
471	Chicken Fillets with Sweet Chili Adobo	81
472	Texas BBQ Chicken Thighs	81
473	Greek Chicken Gyros	81
474	Swiss-Style Breaded Chicken	81
475	Chicken Breasts with Avocado-Mango Salsa	81
476	Lemony Chicken Breast	81
477	Chicken Breasts "En Papillote"	81
478	Jamaican Chicken Fajitas	82
479	Prosciutto-Wrapped Chicken Breasts	82
480	Chicken Parmigiana with Fresh Rosemary	82
481	Apricot Mustard Chicken Breasts	82
482	Ham and Cheese Chicken Breasts	82
483	Chicken Tikka Masala	82
484	Creamy Asiago Chicken	83
485	Sweet Wasabi Chicken	83
486	Easy Chicken Enchiladas	83
487	Caprese Chicken with Balsamic Sauce	83
488	Italian Chicken Breasts	83
489	Pineapple Sherry Chicken	83
490	French-Style Chicken Thighs	83
491	Air Fried Chicken Bowl with Black Beans	84
492	Chicken Cheesy Divan Casserole	84
493	Tasty Kiev-Style Chicken	84
494	Creamy Onion Chicken	84
495	Tropical Coconut Chicken Thighs	84
496	Rosemary and Oyster Chicken Breasts	84
497	Cheesy Marinara Chicken	84
498	Restaurant-Style Chicken with Yogurt Sauce	85
499	Garlicky Chicken Cubes On A Green Bed	85
500	Southern-Style Fried Chicken Drumsticks	85
501	Chicken Thighs with Herby Tomatoes	85
502	Enchilada Chicken Thighs	85
503	Crispy Drumsticks with Blue Cheese Sauce	85
504	Chicken Thighs with Parmesan Crust	86
505	Traditional Chicken Mole	86
506	Chicken Drumsticks with Garlic-Butter Sauce	86
507	Classic Buttermilk Chicken Thighs	86
508	Whole Chicken with Sage and Garlic	86
509	Spanish Roasted Whole Chicken	86
510	Cauli-Oat Crusted Drumsticks	87
511	BBQ Whole Chicken	87
512	Indonesian Sambal Chicken Drumsticks	87

#	Title	Page
513	Chicken and Baby Potato Traybake	87
514	Peri-Peri Chicken Legs	87
515	Thyme Fried Chicken Legs	87
516	Thai Chicken Satay	87
517	Chicken Asian Lollipop	88
518	Honey and Lemon-Glazed Stuffed Chicken	88
519	Asian Sticky Chicken Wingettes	88
520	Roasted Chicken with Pancetta and Thyme	88
521	Greek-Style Whole Chicken	88
522	Mediterranean-Style Whole Chicken	88
523	Chicken Quarters with Broccoli and Carrots	89
524	Whole Chicken with Fresno Chili Sauce	89
525	Moroccan Turkey Meatballs	89
526	Turkey Tenderloins with Fattoush Salad	89
527	Herb-Buttermilk Chicken Breast	89
528	Honey-Glazed Turkey	90
529	Turkey Burgers with Cabbage Slaw	90
530	Tex-Mex Chicken Roll-Ups	90
531	Parmesan Turkey Meatballs	90
532	Thyme Turkey Nuggets	90
533	Turkey and Veggie Skewers	90
534	Turkey Strips with Cranberry Glaze	91
535	Greek Chicken Souvlaki	91
536	Roasted Turkey with Brussels Sprouts	91
537	Mediterranean-Rubbed Turkey Tenderloins	91
538	Chipotle Buttered Turkey	91
539	Wild Rice and Kale Stuffed Chicken Thighs	91
540	Mini Turkey Meatloaves with Hot Sauce	92
541	Turkey Stuffed Bell Peppers	92
542	Cilantro Chicken Kebabs	92
543	Crisp Paprika Chicken Drumsticks	92
544	Easy Cajun Chicken Drumsticks	92
545	Sesame Chicken	92
546	Cranberry Curry Chicken	93
547	Cracked-Pepper Chicken Wings	93
548	Tandoori Chicken	93
549	African Piri-Piri Chicken Drumsticks	93
550	Spicy Chicken Thighs and Gold Potatoes	93
551	Lemon Thyme Roasted Chicken	94
552	Lemon Chicken	94
553	Coconut Chicken Wings with Mango Sauce	94
554	Bell Pepper Stuffed Chicken Roll-Ups	94
555	Pickle Brined Fried Chicken	94
556	Air Fried Chicken Potatoes with Sun-Dried Tomato	95
557	Lemon-Basil Turkey Breasts	95
558	Stuffed Turkey Roulade	95
559	Greek Chicken Stir-Fry	95
560	Fajita Chicken Strips	95
561	Cajun-Breaded Chicken Bites	95
562	Chicken Thighs with Cilantro	96
563	Pork Rind Fried Chicken	96
564	Buttermilk-Fried Drumsticks	96
565	Chicken Kiev	96
566	Chicken Croquettes with Creole Sauce	96
567	Lemon-Dijon Boneless Chicken	97
568	Buffalo Chicken Cheese Sticks	97
569	Chicken Hand Pies	97
570	Air Fried Chicken Wings with Buffalo Sauce	97
571	Easy Turkey Tenderloin	97
572	Cornish Hens with Honey-Lime Glaze	97
573	Lettuce-Wrapped Turkey and Mushroom Meatballs	98
574	Broccoli Cheese Chicken	98
575	Barbecue Chicken	98
576	Pecan-Crusted Chicken Tenders	98
577	Yellow Curry Chicken Thighs with Peanuts	98
578	Italian Flavor Chicken Breasts with Roma Tomatoes	99
579	Broccoli and Cheese Stuffed Chicken	99
580	Chicken Schnitzel Dogs	99
581	Korean Flavor Glazed Chicken Wings	99
582	Gold Livers	99
583	Barbecued Chicken with Creamy Coleslaw	100
584	Thai Tacos with Peanut Sauce	100
585	Golden Chicken Cutlets	100
586	Chicken Burgers with Ham and Cheese	100
587	Thai-Style Cornish Game Hens	100
588	Blackened Cajun Chicken Tenders	101
589	Yakitori	101
590	Ham Chicken with Cheese	101
591	Chicken Nuggets	101
592	Ethiopian Chicken with Cauliflower	101
593	Crispy Dill Chicken Strips	101
594	Almond-Crusted Chicken	102
595	Jerk Chicken Thighs	102
596	Chicken Patties	102

Chapter 6 Fish and Seafood 103

#	Title	Page
597	Crustless Shrimp Quiche	103
598	Cilantro Lime Baked Salmon	103
599	Ginger Chili Crab Fritters	103
600	Old Bay Crab Sticks	103
601	Dijon Crabmeat and Veggie Patties	103
602	Crabmeat Croquettes with Herbs	104
603	Garlicky Chili Prawns	104
604	Chinese-Style Prawns with Garlic	104
605	Bacon-Wrapped Prawns	104
606	Sesame Prawns with Firecracker Sauce	104
607	Ale Beer Prawns with Tartare Sauce	104
608	Orange and Coconut Shrimp	105
609	Spicy Shrimp with Coconut-Avocado Dip	105
610	Asian Shrimp Medley	105
611	Spicy Shrimp Skewers	105
612	Rosemary Cashew Shrimp	105
613	Buttered Lobster with Herbs	105
614	Mediterranean Squid Rings with Couscous	106
615	Greek Mussels with Hazelnuts	106
616	Old Bay Shrimp	106
617	Cajun Lemon Shrimp	106
618	Buttered Crab Legs	106

619	Breaded Scallops	106
620	Calamari Rings with Olives	106
621	Cod Fillets with Ginger-Cilantro Sauce	107
622	Lemon White Fish Nuggets	107
623	Bread-Crusted Seafood Mix	107
624	Crispy Cod Fillets	107
625	Cod Finger Pesto Sandwich	107
626	Cod Cornflake Nuggets with Avocado Dip	107
627	Soy Sauce-Glazed Cod	107
628	Gourmet Black Cod with Fennel and Pecans	108
629	Pistachio-Crusted Salmon Fillets	108
630	Ale-Battered Fish with Tartar Sauce	108
631	Korean Kimchi-Spiced Salmon	108
632	Tandoori-Style Crispy Salmon	108
633	Delicious Seafood Casserole	108
634	Easy Salmon with Greek Sauce	109
635	Salmon Cakes	109
636	Salmon and Spring Onion Balls	109
637	Smoked Salmon and Cheddar Taquitos	109
638	Salmon Fillets with Broccoli	109
639	Wild Salmon with Creamy Parsley Sauce	109
640	Sweet Caribbean Salmon Fillets	109
641	Classic Mediterranean Salmon	110
642	French Trout Meunière	110
643	Easy Creole Trout	110
644	Smoked Trout Frittata	110
645	Baked Trout en Papillote with Herbs	110
646	Lovely "Blackened" Catfish	110
647	Golden Batter Fried Catfish Fillets	110
648	Rosemary Catfish	111
649	Jamaican Fish Fillets	111
650	Parmesan Tilapia Fillets	111
651	Air-Fried Broiled Tilapia	111
652	Air Fried Tilapia Bites	111
653	Peppery and Lemony Haddock	111
654	Savory Shrimp	111
655	Crumbly Haddock Patties	112
656	Barramundi Fillets in Lemon Sauce	112
657	Garlic Shrimp	112
658	Hot Sardine Cakes	112
659	Air Fried Tuna Sandwich	112
660	Smoked Fish Quiche	112
661	Effortless Tuna Fritters	113
662	Sesame Halibut Fillets	113
663	Italian-Style White Fish	113
664	Oaty Fishcakes	113
665	Ponzu Marinated Tuna	113
666	Roasted Salmon Fillets	113
667	Bacon Halibut Steak	113
668	Peach Salsa and Beer Halibut Tacos	114
669	Lemony Salmon	114
670	Cucumber and Salmon Salad	114
671	Mackerel with Spinach	114
672	Panko-Crusted Fish Sticks	114
673	Butter-Wine Baked Salmon	114
674	Cajun Catfish Cakes with Cheese	115
675	Browned Shrimp Patties	115
676	Steamed Tuna with Lemongrass	115
677	Parmesan Lobster Tails	115
678	Miso Salmon	115
679	Golden Shrimp	115
680	Cod with Jalapeño	116
681	Salmon Burgers	116
682	Fish Croquettes with Lemon-Dill Aioli	116
683	Crunchy Air Fried Cod Fillets	116
684	Blackened Fish	116
685	Shrimp Bake	117
686	Cod with Creamy Mustard Sauce	117
687	Tortilla Shrimp Tacos	117
688	Crunchy Fish Sticks	117
689	Honey-Glazed Salmon	117
690	Cajun Salmon	117
691	Paprika Shrimp	118
692	Coconut Shrimp with Pineapple-Lemon Sauce	118
693	Panko Catfish Nuggets	118
694	Chili Tilapia	118
695	Rainbow Salmon Kebabs	118
696	Scallops and Spinach with Cream Sauce	118
697	Trout Amandine with Lemon Butter Sauce	119
698	Parmesan Mackerel with Coriander	119
699	Fried Catfish Fillets	119
700	Baked Tilapia with Garlic Aioli	119
701	Fried Shrimp	119
702	Lemony Shrimp	119
703	Cod with Avocado	120
704	Friday Night Fish Fry	120
705	Crab Cakes with Lettuce and Apple Salad	120
706	Almond Catfish	120
707	Cayenne Flounder Cutlets	120
708	Bacon-Wrapped Scallops	120
709	Panko Crab Sticks with Mayo Sauce	121
710	Sesame-Crusted Tuna Steak	121
711	Seasoned Breaded Shrimp	121
712	Tandoori Shrimp	121
713	Tuna-Stuffed Tomatoes	121
714	Lemon Mahi-Mahi	121
715	Crab Cakes	122
716	Tuna Casserole	122
717	Crab Cake Sandwich	122
718	Sweet Tilapia Fillets	122
719	Catfish Bites	122
720	Salmon with Cauliflower	122
721	Baked Grouper with Tomatoes and Garlic	123
722	Roasted Fish with Almond-Lemon Crumbs	123

Chapter 7 Snacks and Appetizers — 124

| 723 | Ranch Oyster Snack Crackers | 124 |
| 724 | Spicy Chicken Wings | 124 |

#	Recipe	Page
725	Sweet-Sour Chicken Wings	124
726	Alfredo Wings	124
727	Crunchy Ranch Chicken Wings	124
728	Lemony Chicken Wings	124
729	Chicken Wings with Gorgonzola Dip	125
730	Paprika Chicken Wings	125
731	Oregano Chicken Thighs	125
732	Sweet and Spicy Chicken Thighs	125
733	Panko Chicken Bites	125
734	Golden Chicken	125
735	Corn-Crusted Chicken Tenders	125
736	Oat-Crusted Chicken Croquettes	126
737	Cabbage Chicken Rolls	126
738	Mushroom Carrot Spring Rolls with Noddles	126
739	Mediterranean Beef Meatballs	126
740	Potato Cheese Balls	126
741	Crunchy Nachos	126
742	Thai-Style Cheesy Sticks	127
743	Garlicky Potato Chips	127
744	Rosemary Potato Chips	127
745	Spicy Carrot Chips	127
746	Sweet Pickle Chips	127
747	Root Vegetable Chips	127
748	Breaded Artichoke Hearts	127
749	Sage Brussels Sprouts	127
750	Simple Kale Chips	128
751	Buffalo Cauliflower	128
752	Parmesan Squash Chips with Greek Yogurt Dressing	128
753	Easy Empanadas with Spinach and Mushroom	128
754	Greek Avocado Wedges	128
755	Golden Asparagus with Romesco Sauce	128
756	Italian Cauliflower	129
757	Air Fried Green Olives	129
758	One-Step Radish Chips	129
759	Garlicky Green Bean	129
760	Kielbasa and Mushroom Pierogi	129
761	Mackerel and Rice Balls	129
762	Cheesy Salmon Mini Tarts with Dill	129
763	Crispy Shrimp	130
764	Prawn and Cabbage Egg Rolls	130
765	Corn-Crusted Cod Fingers	130
766	Italian Salmon Croquettes	130
767	Parsley and Lemon Fried Shrimp	130
768	Cheesy Bacon Fries	130
769	Air Fried Beef Sticks	131
770	Crispy Bacon with Butter Bean Dip	131
771	Bacon-Wrapped Avocados	131
772	Cheese-Stuffed Jalapeños	131
773	Black Bean and Corn Flatbreads	131
774	Parmesan Chicken Burgers	131
775	Barbecue Sausage Pizza	132
776	Italian Pork Sausage Pizza	132
777	Chorizo and Mushroom Pizza	132
778	Mozzarella Pepperoni Pizza	132
779	Bacon-Wrapped Dates	132
780	Greek Chicken Tortillas with Mozzarella	132
781	Lemony Meatballs	132
782	Cajun Beef Fajitas	133
783	South Asian Pork Momos	133
784	Feta French Fries	133
785	Spanish Chorizo with Brussels Sprouts	133
786	Cheddar Pork Balls	133
787	Baked Potatoes with Bacon	133
788	Buttered Red Potatoes	133
789	Crispy Hasselback Potatoes	134
790	Sweet Potato Boats	134
791	Horse Carrots Chips	134
792	Spiced Sweet Potato Wedges	134
793	Prosciutto and Cheese Stromboli	134
794	Fava Bean Falafel Bites	134
795	Plum and Pancetta Bombs	134
796	Fried Sausage Ravioli	135
797	Parsley Butternut Squash	135
798	Cayenne Chickpeas	135
799	Parmesan Parsnips with Cilantro and Paprika	135
800	Butter-Fried Broccoli	135
801	Balsamic-Lime Pumpkin	135
802	Italian Cheesy Mushrooms	135
803	Walnut-Stuffed Mushrooms	136
804	Ricotta-Stuffed Peppers	136
805	Garlicky Edamame	136
806	Lebanese Muhammara	136
807	Herbed Brie Croutons	136
808	Super Cabbage Canapes	136
809	Egg and Broccoli Quiche	136
810	Easy Parmesan Sandwich	137
811	Salty Carrot Cookies	137
812	Mini Cheese Scones	137
813	Cheese and Buttermilk Biscuits	137
814	Cauliflower and Tofu Croquettes	137
815	Panko Veggie Balls	137
816	Spicy Cheese Lings	137
817	Beef, Pork and Bacon balls	138
818	French Beans with Toasted Almonds	138
819	Cheddar Black Bean Burritos	138
820	Smoky Almonds	138
821	Spiced Almonds	138
822	Sweet Pumpkin Seeds	138
823	Masala Cashew Nuts	138
824	Mixed Nut Snacks	138
825	Cheesy Steak Fries	139
826	Sea Salt Potato Chips	139
827	Cinnamon Apple Chips	139
828	Zucchini Feta Roulades	139
829	Carrot Chips	139
830	Lemon-Pepper Chicken Drumsticks	139
831	Air Fried Pot Stickers	139
832	Vegetable Pot Stickers	140

833	Crispy Mozzarella Sticks	140
834	Pork and Cabbage Egg Rolls	140
835	Bacon-Wrapped Shrimp and Jalapeño	140
836	Sweet Potato Fries with Mayonnaise	140
837	Veggie Shrimp Toast	141
838	Crispy Breaded Beef Cubes	141
839	Spiced Roasted Cashews	141
840	Air Fryer Popcorn with Garlic Salt	141
841	Cheese Wafers	141
842	Apple Wedges	141
843	Tangy Fried Pickle Spears	141
844	Crunchy Tex-Mex Tortilla Chips	142
845	Parmesan Cauliflower	142
846	Crispy Green Bean Fries with Lemon-Yogurt Sauce	142
847	Crispy Phyllo Artichoke Triangles	142
848	Sausage Balls with Cheese	142
849	Homemade Sweet Potato Chips	142
850	Shrimp Toasts with Sesame Seeds	143
851	Artichoke and Olive Pita Flatbread	143
852	Kale Chips with Sesame	143
853	Skinny Fries	143
854	Parmesan French Fries	143
855	Egg Roll Pizza Sticks	143
856	Crunchy Chickpeas	144
857	Pepperoni Pizza Dip	144
858	Asian Five-Spice Wings	144
859	Stuffed Fried Mushrooms	144
860	Greens Chips with Curried Yogurt Sauce	144
861	Caramelized Onion Dip	144
862	Garlic-Roasted Tomatoes and Olives	145
863	Cream Cheese Stuffed Jalapeño Poppers	145
864	Lemon Shrimp with Garlic Olive Oil	145
865	Garlic Edamame	145
866	Spicy Tortilla Chips	145
867	Roasted Mushrooms with Garlic	145
868	Lemony Endive in Curried Yogurt	146
869	String Bean Fries	146
870	Cheese Drops	146
871	Greek Potato Skins with Olives and Feta	146
872	Eggplant Fries	146

Chapter 8 Fast and Easy Everyday Favorites 147

873	Classic French Fries	147
874	Curly Fries with Paprika	147
875	Perfect Air Fryer Eggs	147
876	Simple Baked Potatoes	147
877	Avocado Egg Rolls	147
878	Balsamic Brussels Sprouts	147
879	Zucchini-Parmesan Chips	147
880	Onion Rings	148
881	Breaded Mushrooms	148
882	Herb and Cheese Stuffed Mushrooms	148
883	Hot Air Fried Green Tomatoes	148
884	Classic Zucchini Fries	148

885	Corn on the Cob	148
886	Homemade Arancini (Rice Balls)	148
887	Air Fried Mac and Cheese	149
888	Morning Frittata	149
889	Mediterranean Bruschetta	149
890	Mozzarella Cheese Sticks	149
891	"Bikini" Ham and Cheese Sandwich	149
892	Cheddar Hash Browns	149
893	Bacon-Wrapped Chicken Breasts	149
894	Air-Fried Chicken Popcorn	150
895	Sweet Garlicky Chicken Wings	150
896	Effortless Chicken Drumsticks	150
897	Hot Chicken Wingettes	150
898	Turkey Scotch Eggs	150
899	Air Fried Pork Popcorn Bites	150
900	Sesame Pork Skewers	150
901	Spicy Buffalo Chicken Wings	151
902	Teriyaki Pork Ribs	151
903	Gorgonzola Cheese Burgers	151
904	Beef Steak Fingers	151
905	Easy Salmon Fillets	151
906	Air Fried Cinnamon Apples	151
907	Classic Fish and Chips	152
908	Chipotle-Lime Prawn Bowls	152
909	Simple Calamari Rings	152
910	Gambas al Ajillo (Garlic Shrimp)	152
911	Crispy Fish Finger Sticks	152
912	Raspberry and Vanilla Pancakes	152
913	Cinnamon French Toast Sticks	152

Chapter 9 Desserts 153

914	Shortcut Spiced Apple Butter	153
915	S'mores	153
916	Chocolate Cake	153
917	Honeyed Roasted Apples with Walnuts	153
918	Ricotta Lemon Poppy Seed Cake	153
919	Olive Oil Cake	153
920	Spanish Churros con Chocolate	154
921	Dark Chocolate Fondants	154
922	Mock Blueberry Pie	154
923	Maple Oat-Walnut Granola with Blueberries	154
924	French Sour Cherry Clafoutis	154
925	Apple Caramel Relish	154
926	Vanilla Crème Brûlée	155
927	Chocolate-Butter Brownies with Walnuts	155
928	Easy Lemony Cheesecake	155
929	Soft Buttermilk Biscuits	155
930	Mix-Berry Almond Crumble	155
931	Vanilla Orange Cake	155
932	Pineapple and Dark Chocolate Cake	156
933	White Chocolate Pudding	156
934	Chocolate Fudge Squares	156
935	Mini Peanut Butter Tarts	156
936	White Chocolate Cookies	156

#	Recipe	Page
937	Lemon Almond Meringues with Dark Chocolate	157
938	Chocolate and Raspberry Cake	157
939	Cinnamon Pecan Pie	157
940	Lemon-Glazed Cupcakes	157
941	Cinnamon Grilled Pineapples	157
942	Pineapple Galette	157
943	15-Minute Coffee Cake	158
944	Vanilla Peach Cake	158
945	Dark Rum Pear Pie	158
946	Yummy Moon Pie	158
947	Air Fried Donuts	158
948	Cheat Apple Pie	158
949	Chocolate Soufflé	158
950	Tropical Pineapple Fritters	159
951	Honey and Plum Homemade Rice	159
952	No Flour Lime Cupcakes	159
953	Apricot and Lemon Flapjacks	159
954	Five-Fruit Skewers with Caramel Sauce	159
955	Lemon Curd	159
956	New York Cheesecake	159
957	Molten Lava Mini Cakes	160
958	Snickerdoodle Poppers	160
959	Blueberry Muffins	160
960	Lime Bars	160
961	Apple Fries	160
962	Chocolate Lava Cakes	160
963	Chocolate Croissants	160
964	Oatmeal Raisin Bars	161
965	Berry Crumble	161
966	Baked Peaches with Yogurt and Blueberries	161
967	Coconut Flour Cake	161
968	Bourbon Bread Pudding	161
969	Air Fryer Apple Fritters	161
970	Lemon Curd Pavlova	162
971	Lemon Poppy Seed Macaroons	162
972	Coconut Macaroons	162
973	Boston Cream Donut Holes	162
974	White Chocolate Cookies	163
975	Bourbon and Spice Monkey Bread	163
976	Old-Fashioned Fudge Pie	163
977	Pecan and Cherry Stuffed Apples	163
978	Pecan Butter Cookies	163
979	Protein Powder Doughnut Holes	163
980	Almond-Roasted Pears	164
981	Lush Chocolate Chip Cookies	164
982	Strawberry Shortcake	164
983	Cinnamon-Sugar Almonds	164
984	Coconut Muffins	164
985	Vanilla Scones	164
986	Brownies for Two	164
987	Nutty Pear Crumble	165
988	Peach Cobbler	165
989	Gluten-Free Spice Cookies	165
990	Crustless Peanut Butter Cheesecake	165
991	Simple Pineapple Sticks	165
992	Pecan Clusters	165
993	Pumpkin Pudding with Vanilla Wafers	166
994	Rhubarb and Strawberry Crumble	166
995	Cream Cheese Danish	166
996	Crumbly Coconut-Pecan Cookies	166
997	Blueberry-Cream Cheese Bread Pudding	166
998	Blackberry Cobbler	167
999	Pineapple Wontons	167
1000	Simple Apple Turnovers	167

Appendix 1 Measurement Conversion Chart — 168

Appendix 2 Air Fryer Cooking Chart — 169

Appendix 3 Air Fryer Cooking Chart — 170

Appendix 4 Recipes Index — 171

Introduction

The fried foods I ate when we were out became some of my favorites, but it wasn't until years later I realized my eating habits were causing my weight to continue to creep up.

One area that often fell through the cracks for me was cooking healthy, balanced meals. It seemed to take a lot of time, effort, and energy to meal plan and prepare healthy dinners every night.

I tried different deprivation-themed diets, but I always ended up back at square one. I knew that these fad diets weren't the answer and I needed to start more simply. I needed to find ways to make foods I love healthier. The air fryer has been a game changer for me. I can make so many of my favorite recipes significantly healthier, and they taste as good and some are even better than before.

This cult-worthy countertop appliance cooks by circulating hot air around fries, chicken wings, and other fried favorites at a high speed, turning out crisp results with significantly less fat than what's used when cooking with a deep fryer. Technically, air fryers are mini convection ovens, though they work in a fraction of the time it would take your conventional oven and without heating up the whole house. With the turn of a dial, this trendy tool can fry up everything from bite-sized appetizers to weeknight main dishes in minutes—with all the flavor.

There is a whole new world of opportunities available when it comes to making delicious vegetables that I look forward to eating. Protein is no longer limited to a few boring basics. The air fryer delivers a crispy texture to many of my favorite foods, and there is no guilt involved because only an insignificant amount of olive oil is required.

Limiting my fat intake and reducing the calories on many recipes can make a difference on the scale. It also makes a difference inside my body and for my overall health.

This cookbook shows everyday families how to make easy and classic recipes a little bit healthier using the air fryer. This cookbook has recipes for real people. The ingredients are common and can easily be found at any grocery store. I adapted recipes my family has been eating for years, and my family is even more excited to come to the table when they see I am cooking their favorite meals with the air fryer!

As you begin to use your air fryer, I think you will quickly see how easy it is to adapt regular recipes into healthier versions by cooking them this way.

This book delivers 1000 foolproof recipes you will want to make at home.

Get ready for quick and easy recipes for breakfast and brunch, like Classic Avocado Toast, Tofu and Cabbage Sandwich, and Soppressata Pizza. Make snacks including Ranch Oyster Snack Crackers, Spicy Chicken Wings, and Oregano Chicken Thighs, or doable weeknight dinners, such as Lettuce-Wrapped Turkey and Mushroom Meatballs, and Pork Chops with Green Beans and Scalloped Potatoes. And let's not forget dessert, like these addicting Sweet and Salty Bars, Shortcut Spiced Apple Butter, and Ricotta Lemon Poppy Seed Cake. All made in one pot!

With the Air Fryer, be proud of what you cook!

Chapter 1 Vegetables and Sides

Herbed Shiitake Mushrooms

Prep time: 10 minutes | Cook time: 5 minutes | Serves 4

8 ounces (227 g) shiitake mushrooms, stems removed and caps roughly chopped
1 tablespoon olive oil
½ teaspoon salt
Freshly ground black pepper, to taste
1 teaspoon chopped fresh thyme leaves
1 teaspoon chopped fresh oregano
1 tablespoon chopped fresh parsley

1. Preheat the air fryer to 400ºF (204ºC). 2. Toss the mushrooms with the olive oil, salt, pepper, thyme and oregano. Air fry for 5 minutes, shaking the basket once or twice during cooking. 3. Once cooked, add the parsley to the mushrooms and toss. Season again to taste and serve.

Citrus Sweet Potatoes and Carrots

Prep time: 5 minutes | Cook time: 20 to 25 minutes | Serves 4

2 large carrots, cut into 1-inch chunks
1 medium sweet potato, peeled and cut into 1-inch cubes
½ cup chopped onion
2 garlic cloves, minced
2 tablespoons honey
1 tablespoon freshly squeezed orange juice
2 teaspoons butter, melted

1. Preheat the air fryer to 400ºF (204ºC). 2. In a 6-by-2-inch round pan, toss together the carrots, sweet potato, onion, garlic, honey, orange juice, and melted butter to coat. 3. Roast for 25 minutes, shaking the basket after 15 minutes, until the vegetables are tender and glazed. 4. Serve immediately.

Sweet and Crispy Roasted Pearl Onions

Prep time: 5 minutes | Cook time: 18 minutes | Serves 3

1 (14½-ounce / 411-g) package frozen pearl onions (do not thaw)
2 tablespoons extra-virgin olive oil
2 tablespoons balsamic vinegar
2 teaspoons finely chopped fresh rosemary
½ teaspoon kosher salt
¼ teaspoon black pepper

1. In a medium bowl, combine all the ingredients until well coated. 2. Air fry the onions at 400ºF (204ºC) for 18 minutes, or until the onions are tender and lightly charred, stirring once or twice during the cooking time.

Curry Roasted Cauliflower

Prep time: 10 minutes | Cook time: 20 minutes | Serves 4

¼ cup olive oil
2 teaspoons curry powder
½ teaspoon salt
¼ teaspoon freshly ground black pepper
1 head cauliflower, cut into bite-size florets
½ red onion, sliced
2 tablespoons freshly chopped parsley, for garnish (optional)

1. Preheat the air fryer to 400ºF (204ºC). 2. In a bowl, toss the cauliflower and onion with olive oil, curry powder, salt, and pepper. Arrange them to the frying basket. 3. Air fry for 20 minutes, shaking halfway through, until the cauliflower is tender and begins to brown. Top with parsley, if desired, before serving.

Buttery Mushrooms

Prep time: 10 minutes | Cook time: 10 minutes | Serves 4

8 ounces (227 g) cremini mushrooms, halved
2 tablespoons salted butter, melted
¼ teaspoon salt
¼ teaspoon ground black pepper

1. In a medium bowl, toss mushrooms with butter, then sprinkle with salt and pepper. Place into ungreased frying basket. Air fry at 400ºF (204ºC) for 10 minutes, shaking the basket halfway through cooking. Mushrooms will be tender when done. Serve warm.

Mushroom and Rice Balls

Prep time: 15 minutes | Cook time: 24 minutes | Serves 4

⅓ cup cooked rice
1 pound (454 g) mushrooms, chopped
½ onion, chopped
½ green bell pepper, chopped
Celery salt to taste
1 tablespoon Worcestershire sauce
1 garlic clove, minced
2 cups tomato juice
1 teaspoon oregano

1. Preheat the air fryer to 370ºF (188ºC). In a food processor, blend the mushrooms until they resemble large crumbs. In a bowl, combine the rice, ground mushrooms, onion, celery salt, green pepper, and garlic. Shape into balls, and arrange them in the greased frying basket. Air fry for 18 minutes, turning once. 2. Meanwhile, place a saucepan over medium heat and pour in tomato juice, oregano, celery salt, and Worcestershire sauce. Cook until reduced by half, 6 minutes. Drizzle the sauce over the balls to serve.

Remoulade Tomato Slices

Prep time: 10 minutes | Cook time: 5 to 6 minutes | Serves 2

2 green tomatoes, sliced
¼ tablespoon creole seasoning
¼ cup flour
1 egg, beaten
1 cup bread crumbs
1 cup remoulade sauce

1. Add flour to one bowl and the egg to another. Make a mix of creole seasoning and bread crumbs in a third bowl. Coat the tomato slices in the flour, then dip in the egg, and then in the crumbs. Air fry in the greased frying basket for 5 to 6 minutes at 400°F (204°C), turning once. Serve with remoulade sauce.

Cheesy Parsley Tomatoes

Prep time: 10 minutes | Cook time: 5 to 6 minutes | Serves 4

½ cup Cheddar cheese, shredded
¼ cup Parmesan cheese, grated
4 tomatoes, cut into ½ inch slices
2 tablespoons fresh parsley, chopped
Salt and black pepper to taste

1. Preheat the air fryer to 380°F (193°C). Lightly salt the tomato slices and put them in the greased frying basket in a single layer. Top with Cheddar and Parmesan cheeses and sprinkle with black pepper. Air fry for 5 to 6 minutes until the cheese is melted and bubbly. Serve topped with fresh parsley and enjoy!

Garlicky Brussels Sprouts

Prep time: 10 minutes | Cook time: 15 minutes | Serves 4

1 pound (454 g) Brussels sprouts
1 teaspoon garlic powder
2 tablespoons olive oil
Salt and black pepper to taste

1. Preheat the air fryer to 380°F (193°C). Trim off the outer leaves, keeping only the head of each sprout. In a bowl, mix olive oil, garlic powder, salt, and black pepper. Coat in the Brussels sprouts and transfer them to the greased frying basket. Air fry for 15 minutes, shaking once halfway through cooking.

Sweet Feta Carrots

Prep time: 10 minutes | Cook time: 12 to 14 minutes | Serves 4

1 pound (454 g) baby carrots
1 teaspoon dried dill
2 tablespoons olive oil
1 tablespoon honey
1 cup feta cheese, crumbled
Salt and black pepper to taste

1. Preheat the air fryer to 350°F (177°C). In a bowl, mix olive oil, carrots, and honey, and stir to coat. Season with dill, black pepper, and salt. Place the coated carrots in the greased frying basket and air fry for 12 to 14 minutes, shaking once or twice. Serve warm or chilled topped with feta cheese.

Authentic Spanish Patatas Bravas

Prep time: 15 minutes | Cook time: 31 to 38 minutes | Serves 4

1 pound (454 g) waxy potatoes, into bite-size chunks
4 tablespoons olive oil
1 teaspoon smoked paprika
1 shallot, chopped
2 tomatoes, chopped
1 tablespoon tomato paste
1 tablespoon flour
2 tablespoons sriracha hot chili sauce
1 teaspoon sugar
2 tablespoons fresh parsley, chopped
Salt to taste

1. Heat 2 tablespoons of olive oil in a skillet over medium heat and sauté the shallot for 3 minutes until fragrant. Stir in the flour for 2 more minutes. Add in the remaining ingredients and 1 cup of water. Bring to a boil, reduce the heat, and simmer for 6 to 8 minutes until the sauce becomes pulpy. Remove to a food processor and blend until smooth. Let cool completely. 2. Preheat the air fryer to 400°F (204°C). Coat the potatoes in the remaining olive oil and air fry in the fryer for 20 to 25 minutes, shaking once halfway through. Sprinkle with salt and spoon over the sauce to serve.

Delicious Potato Patties

Prep time: 10 minutes | Cook time: 14 to 16 minutes | Serves 4

4 potatoes, shredded
1 onion, chopped
1 egg, beaten
¼ cup milk
2 tablespoons butter
½ teaspoon garlic powder
Salt and black pepper to taste
3 tablespoons flour

1. Preheat the air fryer to 390°F (199°C). In a bowl, add the egg, potatoes, onion, milk, butter, black pepper, flour, garlic powder, and salt and mix well to form a batter. Mold the mixture into four patties. Place them in the greased frying basket and air fry for 14 to 16 minutes, flipping once. Serve warm with garlic mayo.

Cheesy Potatoes and Asparagus

Prep time: 10 minutes | Cook time: 21 to 23 minutes | Serves 4

4 potatoes, cut into wedges
1 bunch of asparagus, trimmed
2 tablespoons olive oil
¼ cup buttermilk
¼ cup cottage cheese,
crumbled
1 tablespoon whole-grain mustard
Salt and black pepper to taste

1. Preheat the fryer to 400°F (204°C). Place the potatoes in the greased frying basket and bake for 14 to 16 minutes. Drizzle the asparagus with olive oil and season with salt and pepper. Slide the frying basket out and shake the potatoes. Spread the asparagus all over and bake for 7 minutes, turning the spears once. 2. In a bowl, mix well the cottage cheese, buttermilk, and whole-grain mustard. Arrange potatoes and asparagus on a serving platter and drizzle with the cheese sauce. Serve and enjoy!

Easy Sweet Potato Fries

Prep time: 10 minutes | Cook time: 20 minutes | Serves 4

½ teaspoon salt
½ teaspoon garlic powder
½ teaspoon chili powder
¼ teaspoon cumin
3 tablespoons olive oil
4 sweet potatoes, cut into thick strips

1. Preheat the air fryer to 380ºF (193ºC). In a bowl, whisk olive oil, salt, garlic, chili powder, and cumin. Coat the strips in the mixture and place them in the frying basket. Air fry for 20 minutes, shaking once, until crispy.

Curly Fries with Gochujang Ketchup

Prep time: 10 minutes | Cook time: 20 to 25 minutes | Serves 2

2 potatoes, spiralized
Salt and black pepper to taste
2 tablespoons coconut oil
1 tablespoon Gochujang chili paste
½ cup tomato ketchup
2 teaspoons soy sauce
¼ teaspoon ginger powder

1. In a small bowl, whisk together the ketchup, Gochujang paste, soy sauce, and ginger powder; reserve. 2. Preheat the air fryer to 390ºF (199ºC). In a bowl, coat the potatoes in coconut oil, salt, and pepper. Place in the frying basket and air fry for 20 to 25 minutes, shaking once. Serve with Gochujang ketchup and enjoy!

Rosemary and Parsley Potatoes

Prep time: 5 minutes | Cook time: 23 to 25 minutes | Serves 4

1 pound (454 g) potatoes
2 garlic cloves, minced
Salt and black pepper to taste
1 tablespoon fresh rosemary, chopped
1 tablespoon fresh parsley, chopped
2 teaspoons butter, melted

1. Preheat the air fryer to 360ºF (182ºC). Prick the potatoes with a fork. Place them in the greased frying basket and bake for 23 to 25 minutes, turning once halfway through. Remove and cut a cross on top. Squeeze the sides and drizzle with melted butter. Sprinkle with garlic, rosemary, parsley, salt, and pepper. Serve.

Zesty Bell Pepper Bites

Prep time: 15 minutes | Cook time: 12 to 15 minutes | Serves 4

1 red bell pepper, cut into small portions
1 yellow pepper, cut into small portions
1 green bell pepper, cut into small portions
3 tablespoons balsamic vinegar
2 tablespoons olive oil
1 garlic clove, minced
½ teaspoon dried basil
½ teaspoon dried parsley
Salt and black pepper to taste
½ cup garlic mayonnaise

1. Preheat the air fryer to 390ºF (199ºC). In a bowl, mix bell peppers, olive oil, garlic, balsamic vinegar, basil, and parsley and season with salt and black pepper. Transfer to the greased frying basket and bake in the air fryer for 12 to 15 minutes, tossing once or twice. Serve with garlic mayonnaise.

Quick Beetroot Chips

Prep time: 5 minutes | Cook time: 12 minutes | Serves 2

2 golden beetroots, thinly sliced
2 tablespoons olive oil
1 tablespoon yeast flakes
1 teaspoon Italian seasoning

1. Preheat the air fryer to 360ºF (182ºC). In a bowl, add olive oil, beetroot slices, Italian seasoning, and yeast and mix well. Dump the coated chips in the greased frying basket and air fry for 12 minutes, shaking once.

Brussels Sprouts with Garlic Aioli

Prep time: 10 minutes | Cook time: 8 minutes | Serves 4

3 garlic cloves, minced
1 pound (454 g) Brussels sprouts, trimmed and halved
Salt and black pepper to taste
2 tablespoons olive oil
2 teaspoons lemon juice
¾ cup mayonnaise

1. Place a pot with water over medium heat; bring to a boil. Blanch in the sprouts for 3 minutes; drain. 2. Preheat the air fryer to 350ºF (177ºC). Drizzle the Brussels sprouts with olive oil and season to taste. Pour them into the frying basket and air fry for 5 minutes, shaking once. In a bowl, whisk the mayonnaise, garlic, lemon juice, salt and black pepper to taste, to make aioli. Serve the sprouts with aioli.

Crispy Bell Peppers with Tartare Sauce

Prep time: 10 minutes | Cook time: 4 to 7 minutes | Serves 4

1 egg, beaten
2 bell peppers, cut into ½-inch-thick slices
⅔ cup panko bread crumbs
½ teaspoon paprika
½ teaspoon garlic powder
Salt to taste
1 teaspoon lime juice
½ cup mayonnaise
2 tablespoons capers, chopped
2 dill pickles, chopped

1. Preheat the air fryer to 390ºF (199ºC). Mix the bread crumbs, paprika, garlic powder, and salt in a shallow bowl. In a separate bowl, whisk the egg with 1½ teaspoons of water to make an egg wash. Coat the bell pepper slices in the egg wash, then roll them up in the crumbs mixture until fully covered. 2. Put the peppers in the greased frying basket in a single layer and spray with olive oil, Air fry for 4 to 7 minutes until light brown. Meanwhile, in a bowl, mix the mayonnaise, lime juice, capers, pickles, and salt. Remove the peppers from the fryer and serve with the tartare sauce. Enjoy!

Easy Cabbage Steaks

Prep time: 5 minutes | Cook time: 14 to 16 minutes | Serves 3

1 cabbage head
1 tablespoon garlic paste
2 tablespoons olive oil
Salt and black pepper to taste
2 teaspoons fennel seeds

1. Preheat the air fryer to 350ºF (177ºC). Cut the cabbage into 1½-inch thin slices. In a small bowl, combine all the other ingredients and brush the cabbage with the mixture. Arrange the steaks in the greased frying basket and bake for 14 to 16 minutes, flipping once halfway through cooking. Serve warm or chilled.

Green Cabbage with Blue Cheese Sauce

Prep time: 10 minutes | Cook time: 18 to 20 minutes | Serves 4

1 head green cabbage, cut into wedges
1 cup Mozzarella cheese, shredded
4 tablespoons butter, melted
½ cup blue cheese sauce

1. Preheat the air fryer to 380ºF (193ºC). Brush the wedges with butter and sprinkle with Mozzarella. Transfer to the greased frying basket and bake in the air fryer for 18 to 20 minutes. Serve with blue cheese sauce.

Indian Fried Okra

Prep time: 10 minutes | Cook time: 11 to 13 minutes | Serves 4

1 tablespoon chili powder
2 tablespoons garam masala
1 cup cornmeal
¼ cup flour
Salt and black pepper to taste
½ pound (227 g) okra, trimmed and halved lengthwise
1 egg
1 cup Cholula hot sauce

1. Preheat the air fryer to 380ºF (193ºC). In a bowl, mix cornmeal, flour, chili powder, garam masala, salt, and black pepper. In another bowl, whisk the egg and season with salt and pepper. 2. Dip the okra in the egg and then coat in the cornmeal mixture. Spray with cooking spray and place in the frying basket. Air fry for 6 minutes, shake, and cook for another 5 to 7 minutes or until golden brown. Serve with hot sauce.

Zucchini Fries with Tabasco Dip

Prep time: 10 minutes | Cook time: 13 to 15 minutes | Serves 4

2 zucchinis, sliced
2 egg whites
½ cup seasoned bread crumbs
2 tablespoons Parmesan cheese, grated
¼ teaspoon garlic powder
Salt and black pepper to taste
1 cup mayonnaise
¼ cup heavy cream
1 tablespoon Tabasco sauce
1 teaspoon lime juice

1. Preheat the air fryer to 400ºF (204ºC). In a bowl, beat egg whites with salt and black pepper. In another bowl, mix garlic powder, Parmesan cheese, and bread crumbs. Dip zucchini strips in the egg whites, then in the crumbs and spray them with cooking oil. Air fry them for 13 to 15 minutes, turning once. 2. Meanwhile, in a bowl, mix mayonnaise, heavy cream, Tabasco sauce, and lime juice. Serve as a dip for the strips.

Bulgarian "Burek" Pepper with Yogurt Sauce

Prep time: 15 minutes | Cook time: 10 to 12 minutes | Serves 4

4 red bell peppers, roasted
1 cup feta cheese, crumbled
4 eggs
1 cup bread crumbs
4 garlic cloves, chopped
1 tomato, peeled and chopped
1 teaspoon fresh dill, chopped
1 tablespoon fresh parsley, chopped
Salt and black pepper to taste
1 tablespoon olive oil
½ cup flour
1 cup Greek yogurt

1. In a small bowl, mix yogurt, olive oil, half of the garlic, and dill. Keep the sauce in the fridge. 2. Preheat the air fryer to 350ºF (177ºC). In a bowl, beat 3 eggs with salt and black pepper. Add in feta cheese, the remaining garlic, tomato, and parsley and mix to combine. Fill the peppers with the mixture. 3. Beat the remaining egg with salt and pepper in a bowl. Coat the peppers first in flour, then dip in the egg, and finally in the crumbs. Arrange them in the greased frying basket and air fry for 10 to 12 minutes until golden brown, turning once. Serve the peppers with the yogurt sauce on the side and enjoy!.

Green Pea Arancini with Tomato Sauce

Prep time: 20 minutes | Cook time: 34 to 38 minutes | Serves 4

1 cup rice, rinsed
½ green peas
1 tablespoon butter
1 onion, chopped
2 garlic cloves, minced
1 egg
3 tablespoons Parmesan cheese, shredded
½ cup bread crumbs
2 tablespoons olive oil
Salt and black pepper to taste
1 pound (454 g) Roma tomatoes, chopped
2 tablespoons fresh basil, chopped

1. Fill a shallow saucepan with water and place over medium heat. Bring to a boil and add in the rice, salt, and pepper. Cook for 20 to 22 minutes, stirring often. Drain and transfer to a bowl; mix in the green peas. 2. Mix in the onion, garlic, Parmesan cheese, and egg. Mold the mixture into golf-size balls and roll them in bread crumbs. Place them in a baking sheet and refrigerate for 1 hour. Preheat the air fryer to 360ºF (182ºC). Remove the arancini from the fridge and arrange them in the greased frying basket. Air fry for 14 to 16 minutes, shaking from time to time until nicely browned. 3. Meanwhile, heat the olive oil in the skillet and stir-fry the tomatoes for 6 to 8 minutes until the sauce thickens. Season with salt and black pepper. Scatter basil on top and serve with the arancini.

Parmesan Zucchini Boats

Prep time: 10 minutes | Cook time: 12 minutes | Serves 4

4 small zucchinis, cut lengthwise
½ cup Parmesan cheese, grated
½ cup bread crumbs
¼ cup melted butter
¼ cup fresh parsley, chopped
4 garlic cloves, minced
Salt and black pepper to taste

1. Preheat the air fryer to 370ºF (188ºC). Scoop out the insides of the zucchini halves with a spoon. In a bowl, mix bread crumbs, garlic, and parsley. Season with salt and pepper and stir in the zucchini flesh. Spoon the mixture into the zucchini "boats" and sprinkle with Parmesan cheese. Drizzle with melted butter. Arrange the boats on the greased frying basket and bake for 12 minutes or until the cheese is golden.

Aunt's Roasted Carrots with Cilantro Sauce

Prep time: 15 minutes | Cook time: 15 to 20 minutes | Serves 4

¼ cup olive oil
2 shallots, cut into wedges
4 carrots, halved lengthways
4 garlic cloves, lightly crushed
¼ teaspoon nutmeg
¼ teaspoon allspice
¼ cup cilantro, chopped
¼ lime, zested and juiced
1 tablespoon Parmesan cheese, grated
1 tablespoon pine nuts

1. Preheat the air fryer to 370ºF (188ºC). Coat the carrots and shallots with allspice, nutmeg, and some olive oil. Put in the frying basket. Sprinkle with garlic and bake for 15 to 20 minutes, shaking halfway through. 2. In a food processor, blitz the remaining olive oil, cilantro, lime zest and juice, Parmesan cheese, and pine nuts until the mixture forms a paste. Remove and serve on the side of the roasted veggies.

Involtini di Melanzane (Eggplant Rollups)

Prep time: 15 minutes | Cook time: 15 to 18 minutes | Serves 4

2 eggplants, thinly sliced
1 teaspoon Italian seasoning
1 cup wheat flour
1 cup ricotta cheese, crumbled
Salt to taste
2 tablespoons Parmesan cheese, grated

1. Preheat the air fryer to 390ºF (199ºC). Season the eggplant slices with salt and dust them in the flour, shaking off the excess. Place them in the greased frying basket and air fry for 5 to 6 minutes, turning once. Remove to a kitchen paper to remove any excess moisture. Then spread them with the ricotta cheese. 2. Sprinkle with Italian seasoning and roll them up. Coat in the Parmesan cheese and transfer the rolls to the greased frying basket. Bake for 10 to 12 minutes or until the cheese is lightly browned. Serve warm.

Mediterranean Eggplant Burgers

Prep time: 15 minutes | Cook time: 7 minutes | Serves 2

2 hamburger buns, halved
2 (2-inch) eggplant slices, cut along the round axis
2 Mozzarella slices
1 red onion, cut into rings
2 lettuce leaves
1 tablespoon tomato sauce
1 pickle, sliced
Salt to taste

1. Preheat the air fryer to 360ºF (182ºC). Season the eggplant slices with salt and place them in the greased frying basket. Bake for 6 minutes, flipping once. Top with Mozzarella slices and cook for 30 more seconds. 2. Spread the tomato sauce on the bun bottoms. Top with the cheesy eggplant slices followed by the red onion rings, sliced pickle, and lettuce leaves. Finish with the bun tops and serve immediately.

Avocado Fries with Pico de Gallo

Prep time: 20 minutes | Cook time: 8 to 10 minutes | Serves 6

3 eggs, beaten in a bowl
4 avocados, cut in half, pits removed
2 tablespoons olive oil
1½ cups panko bread crumbs
1½ teaspoons paprika
Salt and black pepper to taste
2 tablespoons fresh cilantro, chopped
2 tomatoes, chopped
1 jalapeño pepper, minced
¼ cup red onions, finely chopped
1 lime, juiced
6 corn tortillas

1. In a mixing bowl, thoroughly combine the cilantro, tomatoes, jalapeño pepper, red onion, lime juice, and salt. Place in the fridge to allow the flavors to incorporate; until pico de gallo is ready to use. 2. Preheat the air fryer to 360ºF (182ºC). Remove the skin from the avocado, leaving the flesh intact. Cut the halves into 5 to 6 lengthwise slices. Mix the bread crumbs, salt, pepper, and paprika in a bowl. Dip each avocado slice in the eggs, then in the crumbs mixture, pressing gently into the avocado, so it sticks. 3. Put the avocado slices in a single layer on the greased fryer basket and brush with some olive oil. Air fry for 8 to 10 minutes, turning once, until light brown and crispy. Serve with pico de gallo on the side.

Cheesy Eggplant Schnitzels

Prep time: 10 minutes | Cook time: 10 to 12 minutes | Serves 4

2 eggplants
½ cup Mozzarella cheese, grated
2 tablespoons milk
1 egg, beaten
2 cups bread crumbs
2 tomatoes, sliced

1. Preheat the air fryer to 400ºF (204ºC). Cut the eggplants lengthways into ½-inch thick slices. In a bowl, mix the egg and milk. In another bowl, combine the bread crumbs and Mozzarella cheese. Dip the eggplant slices in the egg mixture, followed by the crumbs mixture and place them in the greased frying basket. Air fry for 10 to 12 minutes, turning once halfway through. Top with tomato slices and serve.

6 | Chapter 1 Vegetables and Sides

Sesame Balsamic Asparagus

Prep time: 15 minutes | Cook time: 10 to 12 minutes | Serves 4

1½ pounds (680 g) asparagus, trimmed
4 tablespoons balsamic vinegar
4 tablespoons olive oil
2 tablespoons fresh rosemary, chopped
Salt and black pepper to taste
2 tablespoons sesame seeds

1. Preheat the air fryer to 360°F (182°C). Whisk the olive oil, sesame seeds, balsamic vinegar, salt, and pepper to make a marinade. Place the asparagus on a baking dish and pour the marinade all over. Toss to coat and let them sit for 10 minutes. Transfer the asparagus to the frying basket and air fry for 10 to 12 minutes, shaking once, or until tender and lightly charred. Serve the asparagus topped with rosemary.

Air Fried Eggplant Bruschetta

Prep time: 15 minutes | Cook time: 12 to 15 minutes | Serves 2

2 large eggplant slices
1 large spring onion, finely sliced
½ cup sweet corn
1 egg white, whisked
1 tablespoon black sesame seeds
Salt to taste

1. Preheat the air fryer to 380°F (193°C). Salt the eggplant slices on both sides and place them in the greased frying basket. Air fry for 8 to 10 minutes, flipping once. In a bowl, place the corn, spring onion, egg white, and sesame seeds and mix well. Spread the mixture over the eggplant slices and place them in the air fryer again. Bake for 4 to 5 minutes or until the top is golden. Serve immediately.

Easy Eggplant and Zucchini Chips

Prep time: 15 minutes | Cook time: 10 to 12 minutes | Serves 4

1 large eggplant, cut into strips
1 zucchini, cut into strips
½ cup cornstarch
3 tablespoons olive oil
Salt to season

1. Preheat the fryer to 390°F (199°C). In a bowl, mix cornstarch, salt, pepper, oil, eggplant and zucchini strips. Place the coated veggies in the greased frying basket and air fry for 10 to 12 minutes, shaking once.

Homemade Blooming Onion

Prep time: 5 minutes | Cook time: 22 to 25 minutes | Serves 4

2 eggs
½ cup milk
1 large yellow onions
1 cup flour
1 teaspoon garlic powder
Salt and black pepper to taste
1 teaspoon paprika
1 teaspoon cayenne pepper
1 cup garlic or chili mayonnaise

1. Cut the top of the onion (not root) about half inch down to make it flat. Peel the onion and trim just the tip of the root. Lay the onion flat side down and make 4 vertical cuts, leaving the root intact. Make 3 more cuts between each of the 4 original cuts, so you have 12 to 16 cuts in total. Turn around and separate the petals resembling a flower. Place the onion in a deep bowl. Preheat the air fryer to 360°F (182°C). 2. In another bowl, mix flour, garlic powder, salt, pepper, paprika, and cayenne pepper. In a third bowl, whisk the eggs with the milk. Pour the flour mixture over the onion and thoroughly coat it with hands, making sure there is enough flour between the petals. Pick the onion up, turn it and shake it off. Place the onion in a clean bowl and pour the egg mixture over. Coat well and transfer the onion to another clean bowl. Dust the flour over and coat again. Spray generously with cooking oil and air fry for 22 to 25 minutes until golden and crispy. Serve with garlic or chili mayonnaise, and enjoy!

Breaded Italian Green Beans

Prep time: 10 minutes | Cook time: 14 to 16 minutes | Serves 4

1 cup panko bread crumbs
2 eggs, beaten
½ cup Parmesan cheese, grated
½ cup flour
1 teaspoon cayenne pepper
1½ pounds (680 g) green beans
1 cup tomato pasta sauce
Salt and black pepper to taste

1. Preheat the air fryer to 400°F (204°C). In a bowl, mix bread crumbs, Parmesan cheese, cayenne pepper, salt, and black pepper. Coat the beans in the flour, then dip them in the beaten egg and finally in the crumbs. Air fry in the fryer for 14 to 16 minutes, turning once halfway through. Serve with tomato sauce.

Cheese and Cauliflower Tater Tots

Prep time: 15 minutes | Cook time: 20 minutes | Serves 4

1 large egg
¼ cup Pecorino cheese, grated
¼ cup sharp Cheddar cheese, shredded
1 pound (454 g) cauliflower florets
1 garlic clove, minced
½ cup bread crumbs
1 tablespoon olive oil
2 tablespoons scallions, chopped
Salt and black pepper to taste

1. Cook the florets in boiling salted water until al dente. Drain well and let dry on absorbent paper for 10 minutes. Then finely chop the florets and place into a bowl. Add in the egg, garlic, Pecorino cheese, Cheddar cheese, bread crumbs, salt, and black pepper; stir to combine. Refrigerate for 10 minutes. 2. Preheat the air fryer to 380°F (193°C). Shape the cauliflower mixture into bite-sized oval 'tater tots.' Lay them into the greased frying basket, giving them plenty of space. Brush the tots with oil and air fry for 14 to 16 minutes, turning once, until crispy and browned. Top with scallions and serve with your favorite sauce.

Russian-Style Eggplant Caviar

Prep time: 5 minutes | Cook time: 20 minutes | Serves 4

2 eggplants
½ red onion, chopped
2 tablespoons balsamic vinegar
½ cup olive oil
Salt to taste
1 baguette, sliced

1. Preheat the air fryer to 380ºF (193ºC). Place the eggplants in the greased frying basket and bake for 20 minutes, turning every 5 minutes. Remove and let them cool. Then, peel the skin, and transfer the flesh to a food processor. Add in red onion and olive oil; process until pureed. Season with balsamic vinegar and a bit of salt. Serve at room temperature with sliced baguette.

Tasty Balsamic Beets

Prep time: 10 minutes | Cook time: 13 to 15 minutes | Serves 2

2 beets, cubed
⅓ cup balsamic vinegar
2 tablespoons olive oil
1 tablespoon honey
Salt and black pepper to taste
2 springs rosemary, chopped

1. Preheat the air fryer to 400ºF (204ºC). In a bowl, mix beets, olive oil, rosemary, black pepper, and salt and toss to coat. Air fry the beets in the frying basket for 13 to 15 minutes, shaking once halfway through. 2. Meanwhile, pour the vinegar and honey into a pan over medium heat. Bring to a boil and cook until reduced by half. Drizzle the beets with balsamic sauce and serve.

Teriyaki Cauliflower

Prep time: 15 minutes | Cook time: 13 to 15 minutes | Serves 4

1 big cauliflower head, cut into florets
½ cup soy sauce
1 tablespoon brown sugar
1 teaspoon sesame oil
½ chili powder
2 cloves garlic, chopped
1 teaspoon cornstarch

1. In a bowl, whisk soy sauce, brown sugar, sesame oil, ⅓ cup of water, chili powder, garlic, and cornstarch until smooth. In a bowl, add the cauliflower and pour teriyaki sauce over; toss to coat. 2. Place the cauliflower in the greased frying basket and air fry for 13 to 15 minutes at 380ºF (193ºC), turning once halfway through. When ready, check if the cauliflower is cooked but not too soft. Serve warm.

Easy Cauliflower Popcorn

Prep time: 10 minutes | Cook time: 20 minutes | Serves 4

1 head cauliflower, cut into florets
1 teaspoon garlic powder
1 teaspoon turmeric
1 teaspoon cumin
1 tablespoon olive oil
Salt and black pepper to taste

1. Preheat the air fryer to 390ºF (199ºC). In a mixing bowl, thoroughly combine the turmeric, cumin, garlic powder, salt, and black pepper. Add in the cauliflower florets and toss to coat well. 2. Add the florets to the greased frying basket and brush with olive oil. Air fry until browned and crispy, about 20 minutes, shaking the basket every 4 to 6 minutes. Serve hot.

Almond-Crusted Cauliflower Florets

Prep time: 10 minutes | Cook time: 8 to 10 minutes | Serves 4

1 head of cauliflower, cut into florets
2 eggs
1 cup ground almonds
4 tablespoons Parmesan cheese, grated
Garlic salt and black pepper to taste
2 tablespoons fresh cilantro, chopped

1. Preheat the air fryer to 380ºF (193ºC). In a bowl, mix the Parmesan cheese, ground almonds, garlic salt, and black pepper. In another bowl, whisk the eggs. Dip the florets into the eggs, then roll them up in the almond crumbs. Lay the florets in the greased frying basket and spritz with cooking spray. Air fry for 8 to 10 minutes, shaking once, until crispy. Serve sprinkled with fresh cilantro.

Chili Corn on the Cob

Prep time: 10 minutes | Cook time: 14 to 16 minutes | Serves 4

4 ears of sweet corn, shucked
1 clove garlic, minced
1 green chili, minced
1 lemon, zested
2 tablespoons olive oil
2 tablespoons butter, melted
Fine salt to taste

1. Preheat the air fryer to 380ºF (193ºC). in a bowl, mix olive oil, garlic, lemon zest, and green chili. Rub the mixture on all sides of the corn ears. Place the ears in the greased frying basket (work in batches). Air fry for 14 to 16 minutes, turning once, until lightly browned. Remove to a platter and drizzle with melted butter. Scatter with salt and serve.

Cholula Seasoned Broccoli

Prep time: 15 minutes | Cook time: 15 to 20 minutes | Serves 4

1 pound (454 g) broccoli florets
½ teaspoon lemon zest
1 garlic clove, minced
1 teaspoon olive oil
1½ tablespoons soy sauce
1 teaspoon lemon juice
1 teaspoon Cholula hot sauce
Salt and black pepper to taste

1. Preheat the air fryer to 390ºF (199ºC). Put the broccoli florets, olive oil, and garlic in a bowl and season with salt. Toss well, then transfer the florets to the greased frying basket. Air fry for 15 to 20 minutes or until light brown and crispy. Shake the basket every 5 minutes. 2. Meanwhile, whisk the soy sauce, hot sauce, and lemon juice in a bowl. Toss the broccoli and sauce mixture into a large bowl and mix well. Sprinkle with lemon zest, salt, and pepper, and serve.

Parmesan Broccoli Bites

Prep time: 10 minutes | Cook time: 12 to 14 minutes | Serves 4

1 small head broccoli
3 eggs
1 carrot, shredded
½ cup roasted red pepper, chopped
Salt and black pepper to taste
2 tablespoons Parmesan cheese, grated

1. Blanch the broccoli in salted boiling water for 4 to 5 minutes until just tender. Drain and let cool slightly. 2. Preheat the air fryer to 340°F (171°C). In a bowl, mix all the remaining ingredients. Cut the cooled broccoli into florets and mix in the egg mixture. Spoon the mixture into greased muffin cups and place in the air fryer. Bake for 12 to 14 minutes or until set and just turning golden. Let cool completely before serving.

Catalan-Style "Escalivada" Veggie Spread

Prep time: 15 minutes | Cook time: 13 to 15 minutes | Serves 6

1 pound (454 g) green peppers
1 pound (454 g) tomatoes
1 medium onion
3 tablespoons olive oil
½ tablespoon salt
4 garlic cloves, peeled

1. Preheat the air fryer to 360°F (182°C). Place green peppers, tomatoes, and onion in the greased frying basket and bake for 5 minutes, flip, and cook for 8 to 10 more minutes. Remove and peel the skin. Place the vegetables in a blender and add garlic, olive oil, and salt and pulse until smooth. Serve warm or cooled.

Zucchini and Turnip Bake

Prep time: 15 minutes | Cook time: 18 to 20 minutes | Serves 4

1 pound (454 g) turnips, sliced
1 large red onion, cut into rings
1 large zucchini, sliced
Salt and black pepper to taste
2 cloves garlic, crushed
2 tablespoons olive oil

1. Preheat the air fryer to 360°F (182°C). Place turnips, red onion, garlic, and zucchini in the greased frying basket. Drizzle with olive oil and season with salt and pepper. Bake in the fryer for 18 to 20 minutes, turning once.

Black Beans and Veggie Burgers

Prep time: 20 minutes | Cook time: 23 to 25 minutes | Serves 4

1 parsnip, chopped
1 carrot, chopped
½ pound (227 g) mushrooms, chopped
1 (15-ounce / 425-g) can black beans, drained and rinsed
2 tablespoons olive oil
1 egg, beaten
2 tablespoons tomato paste
2 garlic cloves, minced
½ teaspoon onion powder
½ cup bread crumbs
Salt and black pepper to taste
4 hamburger buns

1. Preheat the air fryer to 360°F (182°C). Put the parsnip and carrot in the greased frying basket, drizzle with some olive oil, and season with salt and pepper. Air fry for 8 minutes. Toss the mushrooms in the frying basket, spray with oil, and season with salt and black pepper. Air fry for 5 more minutes. 2. Mash the black beans in a bowl. Mix in the egg, tomato paste, garlic, onion powder, salt, cooked veggies and mash the veggies with a fork. Add the bread crumbs and stir to combine. Make 4 patties out of the mixture. Put the patties in the greased frying basket, giving each patty plenty of room. Air fry for 5 minutes, flip, spray with oil, and fry for 5 to 7 more minutes. Serve on buns.

Roasted Pumpkin with Goat Cheese

Prep time: 10 minutes | Cook time: 18 to 20 minutes | Serves 2

1 pound (454 g) pumpkin, cut into wedges
2 tablespoons olive oil
½ teaspoon red pepper flakes
1 tablespoon fresh sage, chopped
1 cup goat cheese, crumbled
Salt and garlic powder to taste

1. Preheat the air fryer to 390°F (199°C). Brush the pumpkin wedges with olive oil and arrange them on the frying basket. Sprinkle with salt, red pepper flakes, and garlic powder. Roast for 18 to 20 minutes, tossing once halfway through, or until browned and crisp. Top with goat cheese and sage and serve warm.

Sweet Butternut Squash with Walnuts

Prep time: 10 minutes | Cook time: 14 to 18 minutes | Serves 4

1 pound (454 g) butternut squash, halved and seeded
2 tablespoons sugar
⅓ cup walnuts, chopped
2 teaspoons olive oil
1 teaspoon ground cinnamon

1. Preheat the air fryer to 390°F (199°C). Cut the squash into large pieces similar in size, leaving the skin on, and arrange them on the greased frying basket. Drizzle with olive oil and roast for 8 to 10 minutes. Slide the basket out, and sprinkle with sugar. Cook until the sugar is caramelized, and the squash is lightly charred, 6 to 8 minutes. Top with walnuts and dust with cinnamon and serve.

Crispy Fried Tofu

Prep time: 10 minutes | Cook time: 13 to 15 minutes | Serves 4

14 ounces (397 g) firm tofu, cut into ½-inch thick strips
2 tablespoons olive oil
½ cup flour
½ cup crushed cornflakes
Salt and black pepper to taste

1. On a plate, mix flour, cornflakes, salt, and black pepper. Dip each tofu strip to coat, spray with olive oil, and arrange them on the frying basket. Air fry for 13 to 15 minutes at 360°F (182°C), turning once, until golden.

Spicy Vegetable Skewers

Prep time: 10 minutes | Cook time: 18 to 20 minutes | Serves 2

2 large sweet potatoes	½ teaspoon turmeric
1 beetroot	¼ teaspoon garlic powder
1 green bell pepper	¼ teaspoon paprika
1 teaspoon chili flakes	1 tablespoon olive oil
Salt and black pepper to taste	½ cup tomato chili sauce

1. Preheat the air fryer to 350ºF (177ºC). Peel the veggies and cut them into bite-sized chunks. Place the chunks in a bowl along with the remaining ingredients and mix until completely coated. Thread the vegetables, alternately, onto skewers in this order: potato, pepper, and beetroot. Place in the greased frying basket and air fry for 18 to 20 minutes, turning once. Serve with tomato chili sauce on the side.

Tempura Veggies with Sesame Soy Sauce

Prep time: 15 minutes | Cook time: 10 to 12 minutes | Serves 4

2 pounds (907 g) chopped veggies: carrot, parsnip, green beans, zucchini, onion rings, asparagus, cauliflower	Dipping Sauce:
	4 tablespoons soy sauce
	Juice of 1 lemon
1½ cups plain flour	½ teaspoon sesame oil
Salt and black pepper to taste	½ teaspoon sugar
1½ tablespoons cornstarch	½ garlic clove, chopped
¾ cup cold water	½ teaspoon sweet chili sauce

1. Line the frying basket with baking paper. In a bowl, mix flour, salt, pepper, and cornstarch; whisk to combine. Keep whisking as you add in cold water, so a smooth batter is formed. Dip each veggie piece into the batter and place it into the greased frying basket. Air fry for 10 to 12 minutes at 360ºF (182ºC), turning once; cook until crispy. Mix all dipping ingredients in a bowl. Serve with the crispy veggies.

Party Crispy Nachos

Prep time: 5 minutes | Cook time: 9 to 12 minutes | Serves 2

1 cup sweet corn	½ teaspoon chili powder
1 cup all-purpose flour plus some more	Salt to taste
	½ cup guacamole
1 tablespoon butter	

1. Add a small amount of water to the sweet corn and grind until you obtain a very fine paste. In a bowl, mix flour, salt, chili powder, and butter; stir into the corn. Knead with your palm until you obtain a stiff dough. 2. Preheat the air fryer to 350ºF (177ºC). On a working surface, dust a little bit of flour and spread the dough with a rolling pin. Make it around ¼-inch thickness. Cut into triangle shapes, as many as you can. Air fry the nachos in the greased frying basket for 9 to 12 minutes, shaking once, until crispy. Serve with guacamole.

Middle Eastern Veggie Kofta

Prep time: 20 minutes | Cook time: 10 to 12 minutes | Serves 4

2 tablespoons cornflour	2 tablespoons pine nuts
1 cup canned white beans	½ cup fresh Mozzarella, chopped
⅓ cup carrots, grated	
2 potatoes, boiled and mashed	3 garlic cloves, chopped
¼ cup fresh mint leaves, chopped	A bunch of skewers, soaked in water
½ teaspoon ras el hanout powder	Salt to taste

1. Preheat the air fryer to 390ºF (199ºC). Place the beans, carrots, pine nuts, garlic, Mozzarella cheese, and mint in a food processor. Blend until smooth, then transfer to a bowl. Add in the mashed potatoes, cornflour, salt, and ras el hanout and mix until fully incorporated. Divide the mixture into equal shaped-patties, about 3 inches long by 1 inch thick. Thread shapes on skewers and bake in the greased frying basket for 10 to 12 minutes, turning once halfway through. Serve warm.

Indian Aloo Tikki

Prep time: 15 minutes | Cook time: 14 to 16 minutes | Serves 2

4 boiled potatoes, shredded	2 tablespoons ginger-garlic paste
3 tablespoons lemon juice	
1 roasted bell pepper, chopped	1 tablespoon mint leaves, chopped
Salt to taste	
2 onions, chopped	1 tablespoon fresh cilantro, chopped
¼ cup fennel, chopped	
5 tablespoons flour	

1. Preheat the air fryer to 360ºF (182ºC). In a bowl, mix cilantro, mint, fennel, ginger-garlic paste, flour, salt, and lemon juice. Add in the potatoes, bell pepper, and onions, and mix to combine. Make balls from the mixture and flatten them to form patties. Place them into the greased frying basket and air fry them for 14 to 16 minutes, flipping once. Serve with mint chutney if desired.

Roasted Balsamic Veggies

Prep time: 10 minutes | Cook time: 18 to 22 minutes | Serves 4

2 pounds (907 g) chopped veggies: potatoes, parsnips, zucchini, pumpkin, carrot, leeks	3 tablespoons olive oil
	1 tablespoon balsamic vinegar
	1 tablespoon agave syrup
	Salt and black pepper to taste

1. In a bowl, add olive oil, balsamic vinegar, agave syrup, salt, and black pepper; mix well. Arrange the veggies on a baking tray and place them in the frying basket. Drizzle with the dressing and massage with hands until well-coated. Air fry for 18 to 22 minutes at 360ºF (182ºC), tossing once halfway through. Serve.

Classic French Ratatouille

Prep time: 15 minutes | Cook time: 15 to 20 minutes | Serves 2

2 tablespoons olive oil
2 Roma tomatoes, thinly sliced
2 garlic cloves, minced
1 zucchini, thinly sliced
2 yellow bell peppers, sliced
1 tablespoon vinegar
2 tablespoons herbs de Provence
Salt and black pepper to taste

1. Preheat the fryer to 390ºF (199ºC). Place all ingredients in a bowl and stir to coat. Transfer them to the greased frying basket and bake in the fryer for 15 to 20 minutes, shaking every 5 minutes, until slightly charred.

Charred Broccolini with Lemon-Caper Sauce

Prep time: 10 minutes | Cook time: 10 minutes | Serves 4

1 pound (454 g) broccolini
2 tablespoons olive oil
2 garlic cloves, sliced
½ teaspoon red chili flakes
2 teaspoons lemon juice
2 tablespoons capers
Salt and black pepper to taste
1 tablespoon fresh parsley, chopped

1. Preheat the air fryer to 380ºF (193ºC). Season the broccolini with salt and black pepper. Place them in the frying basket and drizzle with some olive oil. Air fry until tender and charred, 8 to 10 minutes. 2. Meanwhile, warm the remaining oil in a pan and sauté the garlic for 35 seconds; remove from heat. Stir in lemon juice, capers, and chili flakes. Pour the sauce over the broccolini and top with parsley.

Winter Vegetable Traybake

Prep time: 15 minutes | Cook time: 14 to 16 minutes | Serves 2

1 potato, cut into ½-inch half-moons
6 ounces (170 g) sliced butternut squash
1 small red onion, cut into wedges
1 carrot, sliced into rounds
1 teaspoon Italian seasoning
2 teaspoons olive oil

1. Preheat the air fryer to 380ºF (193ºC). Coat the vegetables with olive oil and Italian seasoning in a bowl. Transfer them to the frying basket and air fry for 14 to 16 minutes, tossing once, or until golden brown.

Winter Root Vegetable Medley

Prep time: 20 minutes | Cook time: 18 to 20 minutes | Serves 4

8 shallots, halved
2 carrots, sliced
1 turnip, cut into chunks
1 rutabaga, cut into chunks
2 potatoes, cut into chunks
1 beet, cut into chunks
Salt and black pepper to taste
2 tablespoons fresh thyme, chopped
2 tablespoons olive oil
2 tablespoons pesto sauce

1. Preheat the air fryer to 400ºF (204ºC). 2. In a bowl, combine all the root vegetables, salt, pepper, and olive oil. Toss to coat and transfer to the frying basket. Air fry for 10 minutes, shake, and cook for 8 to 10 more minutes or until crispy. Meanwhile, mix the pesto with 2 tablespoons water and drizzle over the vegetables, and serve sprinkled with thyme.

Turmeric Crispy Chickpeas

Prep time: 5 minutes | Cook time: 10 to 12 minutes | Serves 4

1 (15-ounce / 425-g) can chickpeas, rinsed
1 tablespoon salted butter, melted
½ teaspoon dried rosemary
¼ teaspoon turmeric

1. Preheat the air fryer to 380ºF (193ºC). In a bowl, combine together chickpeas, salted butter, rosemary, and turmeric; toss to coat. Place them in the greased frying basket and air fry for 6 minutes. Shake, and cook for 4 to 6 more minutes or until golden and crispy.

Air Fried Cheesy Ravioli

Prep time: 5 minutes | Cook time: 7 to 9 minutes | Serves 4

1 package cheese ravioli
2 cup Italian bread crumbs
¼ cup Pecorino cheese, grated
1 cup buttermilk
2 teaspoons olive oil
¼ teaspoon garlic powder

1. Preheat the air fryer to 390ºF (199ºC). In a small bowl, combine bread crumbs, Pecorino cheese, garlic powder, and olive oil. Dip the ravioli in the buttermilk and then coat them in the breadcrumb mixture. 2. Line the frying basket with parchment paper and arrange the ravioli inside. Bake for 7 to 9 minutes, turning once halfway through cooking, until nice and golden. Serve with marinara or carbonara sauce.

Cashew and Chickpea Balls

Prep time: 10 minutes | Cook time: 14 to 16 minutes | Serves 4

¼ cup rolled oats
½ cup cashews
15 ounces (425 g) canned chickpeas, drained
2 eggs
½ cup sweet onions, chopped
1 teaspoon cumin
1 teaspoon garlic powder
1 cup horseradish sauce

1. Preheat the air fryer to 380ºF (193ºC). Ground the oats and cashews in a food processor. Add in the chickpeas and process until mostly smooth. Transfer to a bowl and mix in the eggs, onions, garlic powder, and cumin. Make falafel-sized balls out of the mixture. Place the balls in the greased frying basket and air fry for 14 to 16 minutes, shaking once, until golden and crispy. Serve warm with horseradish sauce.

Chili Falafel with Cheesy Sauce

Prep time: 15 minutes | Cook time: 14 to 16 minutes | Serves 4

1 (14-ounce / 397-g) can chickpeas, drained
2 tablespoons fresh parsley, chopped
6 spring onions, sliced
1 teaspoon garlic powder
Salt to taste
¼ teaspoon chili powder
1 cup cream cheese, softened
1 clove garlic, finely chopped
½ teaspoon dried dill
1 teaspoon hot paprika
2 tablespoons olive oil
2 tablespoons plain yogurt
1 teaspoon apple cider vinegar

1. Place the cream cheese, chopped garlic, dill, hot paprika, olive oil, yogurt, and vinegar in a bowl and whisk until you obtain a smooth and homogeneous sauce consistency. Keep covered in the fridge. 2. In a blender, place chickpeas, parsley, spring onions, garlic powder, chili powder, and salt and process until crumbly. Transfer the mixture to a bowl and refrigerate covered for 20 minutes. For each falafel, take 2 tablespoons to form a round ball, flattened around the edges. 3. Preheat the air fryer to 370ºF (188ºC) and arrange falafel on the greased frying basket. Air fry for 14 to 16 minutes, flipping once, until lightly browned and cooked through. Serve with the cream cheese sauce.

Quinoa and Veggie Stuffed Peppers

Prep time: 15 minutes | Cook time: 12 to 15 minutes | Serves 2

1 cup cooked quinoa
2 red bell peppers, cored and cleaned
½ onion, diced
½ cup tomatoes, diced
¼ teaspoon smoked paprika
Salt and black pepper to taste
1 teaspoon olive oil
¼ teaspoon dried basil

1. Preheat the air fryer to 350ºF (177ºC). In a bowl, mix quinoa, onion, basil, tomatoes, smoked paprika, salt, and pepper and stir. Stuff the peppers with the filling and brush them with olive oil. Place the peppers in the greased frying basket and bake for 12 to 15 minutes until cooked through and slightly charred. Serve.

Fava Bean Falafel with Tzatziki

Prep time: 20 minutes | Cook time: 13 to 15 minutes | Serves 4

2 cups cooked fava beans
½ cup flour
2 tablespoons fresh parsley, chopped
Juice of 1 lemon
2 garlic cloves, chopped
1 onion, chopped
½ teaspoon ground cumin
1 cup tzatziki sauce
4 pita wraps, warm
Salt and black pepper to taste

1. In a blender, add fava beans, flour, parsley, lemon juice, garlic, onion, cumin, salt, and pepper; blend until well-combined but not too battery; there should be some lumps. Shape the mixture into balls. 2. Press them with hands, making sure they are still around. Spray with olive oil and arrange in the paper-lined frying basket. Air fry for 13 to 15 minutes at 360ºF (182ºC), turning once halfway through, until crunchy and golden. Serve in the pita wraps drizzled with tzatziki sauce.

Green Vegetable Rotini Pasta Bake

Prep time: 15 minutes | Cook time: 15 to 17 minutes | Serves 4

1 cup green peas
1 pound (454 g) broccoli florets, steamed
1 cup kale, chopped
1 garlic clove, minced
2 tablespoons flour
2 cups milk
¼ cup Mozzarella cheese, grated
16 ounces (454 g) rotini pasta
3 tablespoons butter
1 tablespoon fresh basil, chopped
Salt and black pepper to taste

1. Bring a large saucepan of salted water to a boil. Add in the rotini pasta and cook following the package instructions. Drain and set aside. Melt butter in a skillet over medium heat and sauté garlic for 1 minute. Stir in the flour for 1 minute. Gradually add in the milk and simmer until slightly thickened, 3 minutes. 2. Preheat the air fryer to 350ºF (177ºC). Transfer the milk mixture to a baking dish and add in the pasta, broccoli, kale, green peas, salt, and pepper; stir to combine. Top with the Mozzarella cheese and sprinkle with basil. Place in the air fryer and bake for 10 to 12 minutes or until the cheese is golden. Serve warm.

Easy Vegetable Croquettes

Prep time: 25 minutes | Cook time: 30 to 35 minutes | Serves 4

1 pound (454 g) red potatoes
1¼ cups milk
Salt to taste
3 tablespoons butter
2 teaspoons olive oil
1 red bell pepper, chopped
½ cup baby spinach, chopped
½ pound (227 g) mushrooms, chopped
½ pound (227 g) broccoli florets, chopped
1 green onion, sliced
1 red onion, chopped
2 garlic cloves, minced
1 cup flour
2 eggs, beaten
1½ cups bread crumbs

1. Cover the potatoes with salted water in a pot over medium heat and cook for 18 to 20 minutes until fork-tender. Drain and place them in a bowl. Add in 2 tablespoons of butter, 1 cup of milk, and salt. Mash with a potato masher. In a food processor, place red onion, garlic, bell pepper, broccoli, mushrooms, green onion, baby spinach, olive oil, salt, and the remaining milk and pulse until a crumbs texture is formed. 2. Mix in the mashed potatoes' bowl. Using your hands, create oblong balls out of the mixture and place them on a baking sheet in a single layer. Refrigerate for 30 minutes. 3. Preheat the air fryer to 390ºF (199ºC). Take 3 separate bowls, pour the bread crumbs in one, flour in another, and eggs in a third bowl. Remove the croquettes from the fridge and dredge them first in flour, then in the eggs, and finally in the crumbs. Arrange them in the greased frying basket without overlapping. Air fry for 12 to 15 minutes, flipping once. Remove to a wire rack to let cool a bit and serve.

Greek Halloumi Cheese with Veggies

Prep time: 15 minutes | Cook time: 15 to 18 minutes | Serves 2

6 ounces (170 g) halloumi cheese, grated
2 zucchinis, cut into even chunks
1 carrot, cut into chunks
1 eggplant, peeled, cut into chunks
2 teaspoons olive oil
1 teaspoon dried Greek seasoning
Salt and black pepper to taste

1. Preheat the air fryer to 350ºF (177ºC). In a bowl, add zucchinis, carrot, eggplant, olive oil, Greek seasoning, salt, and pepper. Transfer to the greased frying basket and air fry for 12 to 14 minutes, shaking once. Sprinkle with halloumi cheese and bake for 3 to 4 more minutes until the cheese is melted. Serve.

Asian-Style Spring Rolls

Prep time: 15 minutes | Cook time: 20 minutes | Serves 4

½ pound (227 g) shiitake mushrooms, chopped
2 tablespoons canola oil
1 clove garlic, minced
1-inch piece ginger, grated
2 cups green cabbage, shredded
1 carrot, shredded
1 green onion, thinly sliced
1 tablespoon soy sauce
1 tablespoon hoisin sauce
12 wonton wrappers

1. Warm 1 tablespoon of the canola oil in a pan over medium heat and sauté green onion, garlic, and ginger for 30 seconds. Add in shiitake mushrooms, carrot, and cabbage and stir-fry until tender, about 4 minutes. Stir in soy sauce and hoisin sauce. Preheat the air fryer to 390ºF (199ºC). 2. Distribute the mixture across the wrappers and roll them up. Place the rolls in the greased frying basket and air fry for 14 to 16 minutes, turning once, until golden and crispy. Serve warm with sweet chili sauce.

Italian-Style Stuffed Mushrooms

Prep time: 15 minutes | Cook time: 7 to 10 minutes | Serves 4

4 ounces (113 g) mascarpone cheese, softened
1 egg
1 cup fresh baby spinach
12 large mushrooms, stems removed
¾ cup shredded Italian blend cheese
¼ cup bread crumbs
1 tablespoon olive oil
Salt and black pepper to taste

1. Preheat the air fryer to 375ºF (191ºC). Whisk the mascarpone cheese, Italian blend cheese, bread crumbs, egg, salt, and pepper with an electric mixer. Stir in the spinach with a spoon until everything is well combined. Divide the mixture between the mushrooms, leaving some of it popping out of the top. 2. Put the mushrooms in the greased frying basket and drizzle them with olive oil. Bake for 7 to 10 minutes, until the mushrooms have begun to brown and the cheese on top is a light brown color. Serve warm.

Poblano and Tomato Stuffed Squash

Prep time: 15 minutes | Cook time: 30 minutes | Serves 4

1 butternut squash
6 grape tomatoes, halved
1 poblano pepper, cut into strips
¼ cup Mozzarella cheese, grated
2 teaspoons olive oil
Salt and black pepper to taste

1. Preheat the air fryer to 350ºF (177ºC). Trim the ends and cut the squash lengthwise. You'll only need half of the squash for this recipe. Scoop the flesh out to make room for the filling. Brush the squash with olive oil. 2. Place in the air fryer and bake for 15 minutes. Combine the remaining olive oil with tomatoes and poblano pepper, season with salt and pepper. Fill the squash half with the mixture and bake for 12 more minutes. Top with Mozzarella cheese and cook further for 3 to 5 minutes or until the cheese melts.

Egg and Cauliflower Rice Casserole

Prep time: 15 minutes | Cook time: 12 to 14 minutes | Serves 4

1 head cauliflower, cut into florets
2 tablespoons olive oil
1 yellow bell pepper, chopped
1 cup okra, chopped
½ onion, chopped
Salt and black pepper to taste
1 tablespoon soy sauce
2 eggs, beaten

1. Preheat the air fryer to 380ºF (193ºC). Grease a baking dish with cooking spray. 2. Pulse cauliflower in a food processor until it resembles rice. Add the cauli rice to the baking dish and mix in bell pepper, okra, onion, soy sauce, salt, and black pepper. Pour the beaten eggs over and drizzle with olive oil. Place the dish in the air fryer and bake for 12 to 14 minutes until golden. Serve.

Eggplant Gratin with Mozzarella Crust

Prep time: 25 minutes | Cook time: 17 to 23 minutes | Serves 2

1 cup eggplants, cubed
¼ cup red peppers, chopped
¼ cup green peppers, chopped
¼ cup onion, chopped
⅓ cup tomatoes, chopped
1 garlic clove, minced
1 tablespoon sliced pimiento-stuffed olives
1 teaspoon capers
¼ teaspoon dried basil
¼ teaspoon dried marjoram
Salt and black pepper to taste
¼ cup Mozzarella cheese, grated
1 tablespoon bread crumbs

1. Preheat the air fryer to 300ºF (149ºC). In a bowl, add eggplants, green peppers, red peppers, onion, tomatoes, olives, garlic, basil, marjoram, capers, salt, and pepper; mix well. Spoon the eggplant mixture into a greased baking dish and level it using the vessel. Sprinkle Mozzarella cheese on top and cover with bread crumbs. Place the dish in the air fryer and bake for 17 to 23 minutes until golden. Serve warm.

Chili Roasted Pumpkin with Orzo

Prep time: 15 minutes | Cook time: 24 to 29 minutes | Serves 4

1 pound (454 g) pumpkin, peeled and cubed
2 red bell peppers, diced
2 shallots, quartered
1 red chili pepper, minced
1 teaspoon ground caraway seeds
1 cup orzo
Salt and black pepper to taste

1. Preheat the air fryer to 380ºF (193ºC). In a bowl, place the pumpkin, bell peppers, shallots, chili pepper, ground caraway seeds, salt, and pepper; toss to coat. Transfer to the greased frying basket. Bake for 20 to 25 minutes, shaking once, until golden. 2. Place a pot filled with salted water over medium heat and bring to a boil. Add in the orzo and cook for 4 minutes. Drain and place on a serving platter. Spread the baked veggies all over and serve.

Greek-Style Stuffed Bell Peppers

Prep time: 15 minutes | Cook time: 15 to 18 minutes | Serves 4

4 red bell peppers, tops sliced off
2 cups cooked rice
1 onion, chopped
1 tablespoon Greek seasoning
¼ cup Kalamata olives, pitted and sliced
¾ cup tomato sauce
Salt and black pepper to taste
1 cup feta cheese, crumbled
2 tablespoons fresh dill, chopped

1. Preheat the air fryer to 360ºF (182ºC). Microwave the bell peppers for 1 to 2 minutes to soften. 2. In a bowl, combine rice, onion, Greek seasoning, feta cheese, olives, tomato sauce, salt, and pepper. Divide the mixture between the bell peppers and arrange them on the greased frying basket. Bake for 14 to 16 minutes. When ready, remove to a serving plate, scatter with dill and serve with yogurt if desired.

Portuguese-Style Veggies with Cheese

Prep time: 15 minutes | Cook time: 18 to 20 minutes | Serves 4

2 tablespoons olive oil
1 teaspoon paprika
2 teaspoons ground cumin
1 tablespoon tomato purée
1 lemon, juiced
2 yellow bell peppers, cut into chunks
1 zucchini, sliced
1 eggplant, cut into chunks
1 red onion, cut into wedges
2 garlic cloves, minced
6 ounces (170 g) fontina cheese, grated
10 green olives

1. Preheat the air fryer to 370ºF (188ºC). In a small bowl, combine paprika, garlic, cumin, tomato purée, lemon juice, and olive oil. Add in the bell peppers, zucchini, eggplant, and red onion and mix well. 2. Transfer to the greased frying basket. Bake for 18 to 20 minutes, shaking once, until golden. Sprinkle with fontina cheese and olives and bake for another 5 minutes or until the cheese is melted.

Cheesy English Muffins

Prep time: 15 minutes | Cook time: 7 to 10 minutes | Serves 2

2 English muffins, halved and toasted
½ cup Cheddar cheese, shredded
1 ripe avocado, mashed
2 tablespoons ranch-style salad dressing
½ cup alfalfa sprouts
1 tomato, chopped
½ sweet onion, chopped
1 tablespoon sesame seeds, toasted

1. Preheat the air fryer to 350ºF (177ºC). Arrange the muffins open-faced on the greased frying basket. Spread the mashed avocado on each half of the cupcakes. Top with sprouts, tomato, onion, ranch dressing, and Cheddar cheese. Bake in the air fryer for 7 to 10 minutes. Serve sprinkled with sesame seeds.

Roasted Veggies with Penne Pasta

Prep time: 20 minutes | Cook time: 25 minutes | Serves 4

1 pound (454 g) penne pasta
1 zucchini, sliced
1 bell pepper, sliced
½ pound (227 g) acorn squash, sliced
½ cup mushrooms, sliced
½ cup Kalamata olives, pitted and halved
¼ cup olive oil
1 teaspoon Italian seasoning
1 cup grape tomatoes, halved
3 tablespoons balsamic vinegar
2 tablespoons fresh basil, chopped
Salt and black pepper to taste

1. Fill a pot with salted water and bring to a boil over medium heat. Add in the penne pasta and cook until al dente, about 8 to 10 minutes. Drain and place in a bowl; set aside. Preheat the air fryer to 380ºF (193ºC). 2. In the frying basket, combine bell pepper, zucchini, acorn squash, mushrooms, and olive oil. Season with salt and pepper. Bake in the air fryer for 15 minutes, shaking once. Remove the veggies to the pasta bowl. Mix in tomatoes, olives, Italian seasoning, and balsamic vinegar. Sprinkle with basil to serve.

Southern-Style Corn Cakes

Prep time: 15 minutes | Cook time: 10 to 12 minutes | Serves 6

2 cups corn kernels, canned, drained
2 eggs, lightly beaten
⅓ cup green onions, finely chopped
¼ cup parsley, chopped
1 cup flour
½ teaspoon baking powder
Salt and black pepper to taste
⅓ cup sour cream

1. Preheat the air fryer to 380ºF (193ºC). In a bowl, add corn kernels, eggs, parsley, and green onions and season with salt and pepper; mix well. Sift flour and baking powder into the bowl and stir. Line the frying basket with parchment paper and spoon batter dollops, making sure they are separated by at least one inch. Bake in the fryer for 10 to 12 minutes, turning once halfway through, until golden. Serve with sour cream.

Vegetable and Goat Cheese Tian

Prep time: 15 minutes | Cook time: 25 to 31 minutes | Serves 4

2 tablespoons butter
1 garlic clove, minced
2 tomatoes, sliced
1 cup canned chickpeas, drained
¼ cup black olives, pitted and chopped
1 fennel bulb, sliced
1 zucchini, sliced into rounds
4 ounces (113 g) goat cheese, sliced into rounds
1 teaspoon dried thyme
Salt and black pepper to taste

1. Preheat the air fryer to 360ºF (182ºC). Melt the butter in a skillet over medium heat and sauté the fennel, garlic, and chickpeas for 5 to 6 minutes, stirring often until soft. Season with thyme, salt, and black pepper. 2. Transfer to a baking dish and arrange tomato, zucchini, and cheese slices on top. Scatter with black olives. Place the dish in the air fryer and bake for 20 to 25 minutes until the cheese is melted and golden in color. Remove and let sit for a few minutes before serving.

Chickpea and Spinach Casserole

Prep time: 15 minutes | Cook time: 21 to 23 minutes | Serves 4

2 tablespoons olive oil
1 onion, chopped
Salt and black pepper to taste
2 garlic cloves, minced
1 can coconut milk
1 tablespoon ginger, minced
1 pound (454 g) spinach
½ cup dried tomatoes, chopped
1 (14-ounce / 397-g) can chickpeas, drained
1 chili pepper, minced

1. Heat olive oil in a saucepan over medium heat and sauté onion, garlic, chili pepper, ginger, salt, and black pepper for 3 minutes. Add in spinach and stir for 4 minutes or until wilted. 2. Transfer to a baking dish and mix in the remaining ingredients. Preheat the air fryer to 370ºF (188ºC). Place the baking dish in the air fryer and bake for 14 to 16 minutes or until golden on top. Serve warm.

Dill Zucchini Egg Cakes

Prep time: 10 minutes | Cook time: 13 to 15 minutes | Serves 4

12 ounces (340 g) thawed puff pastry
4 large eggs
1 medium zucchini, chopped
4 ounces (113 g) feta cheese, drained and crumbled
2 tablespoons fresh dill, chopped
Salt and black pepper to taste

1. Preheat the air fryer to 360ºF (182ºC). In a bowl, whisk the eggs with salt and black pepper. Stir in zucchini, dill, and feta cheese. Grease a muffin tin tray with cooking spray. Roll the pastry out and arrange them to cover the sides of the muffin holes. Divide the egg mixture evenly between the holes. Place the muffin tray in the frying basket and bake for 13 to 15 minutes, until golden. Let cool a bit and serve warm.

Tomato Sandwiches with Feta and Pesto

Prep time: 10 minutes | Cook time: 6 to 8 minutes | Serves 2

1 heirloom tomato
1 (4-ounce / 113-g) block feta cheese
1 small red onion, thinly sliced
1 garlic clove
Salt to taste
2 teaspoons plus ¼ cup olive oil
1½ tablespoons pine nuts, toasted
2 tablespoons fresh parsley, chopped
¼ cup Parmesan cheese, grated
¼ cup fresh basil, chopped

1. Add basil, pine nuts, garlic, Parmesan cheese, and salt to a food processor. Pulse while slowly adding ¼ cup of olive oil. Preheat the air fryer to 390ºF (199ºC). Slice feta cheese and the tomato into ½-inch slices. 2. Spread the obtained pesto sauce on the tomato slices. Top with feta cheese and onion and drizzle with olive oil. Place the tomato in the greased frying basket and bake for 6 to 8 minutes. Remove to a serving platter, sprinkle lightly with salt, and top with fresh parsley. Serve chilled.

Cheesy Green Beans and Egg Cups

Prep time: 10 minutes | Cook time: 12 to 14 minutes | Serves 4

1 pound (454 g) green beans, steamed and chopped
4 eggs, beaten
1 cup sharp cheese, shredded
1 cup heavy cream
½ teaspoon nutmeg
½ teaspoon ginger powder
Salt and black pepper to taste

1. Place the green beans in a bowl and mix in the eggs, heavy cream, nutmeg, ginger powder, salt, and black pepper. Divide the mixture between 4 greased ramekins. Top with the cheese and bake in the air fryer for 12 to 14 minutes at 330ºF (166ºC). Remove and let cool for a few minutes before serving.

Jalapeño and Bean Tacos

Prep time: 15 minutes | Cook time: 12 to 14 minutes | Serves 4

4 soft taco shells, warm
½ cup kidney beans, drained
½ cup black beans, drained
1 tablespoon tomato puree
1 fresh jalapeño pepper, chopped
2 tablespoons fresh cilantro, chopped
1 cup corn kernels
½ teaspoon cumin
½ teaspoon cayenne pepper
Salt and black pepper to taste
1 cup Mozzarella cheese, grated
Guacamole to serve

1. In a bowl, add the beans, tomato puree, jalapeño, cilantro, corn, cumin, cayenne, salt, and black pepper and stir. Fill the taco shells with the bean mixture and sprinkle with Mozzarella. Lay the tacos in the greased frying basket and bake for 12 to 14 minutes at 360ºF (182ºC), turning once. Serve with guacamole.

Cheesy Vegetable Quesadilla

Prep time: 10 minutes | Cook time: 10 minutes | Serves 1

2 flour tortillas
¼ cup gouda cheese, shredded
¼ yellow bell pepper, sliced
¼ zucchini, sliced
½ green onion, sliced
1 tablespoon fresh cilantro, chopped
1 teaspoon olive oil

1. Preheat the air fryer to 390ºF (199ºC). Place a flour tortilla in the greased frying basket and top with gouda cheese, bell pepper, zucchini, cilantro, and green onion. Cover with the other tortilla and brush with olive oil. Bake for 10 minutes or until lightly browned. Cut into 4 wedges and serve.

Air Fried Veggie Sushi

Prep time: 15 minutes | Cook time: 11 to 13 minutes | Serves 4

2 cups cooked sushi rice
4 nori sheets
1 carrot, sliced lengthways
1 red bell pepper, sliced
1 avocado, sliced
1 tablespoon sesame oil
1 tablespoon rice wine vinegar
1 cup panko crumbs
2 tablespoons sesame seeds
Soy sauce, wasabi, and pickled ginger to serve

1. Prepare a clean working board, a small bowl of lukewarm water, and a sushi mat. Wet your hands, and lay a nori sheet onto the sushi mat, and spread half cup of sushi rice, leaving a half-inch of nori clear, so you can seal the roll. Place carrot, bell pepper, and avocado sideways of the rice. Roll the sushi tightly and rub warm water along the clean nori strip to seal. In a bowl, mix sesame oil and vinegar. 2. In another bowl, mix the crumbs and sesame seeds. Roll each sushi log in the vinegar mixture and then into the sesame bowl to coat. Arrange the sushi in the greased frying basket and bake for 11 to 13 minutes at 360ºF (182ºC), turning once. Slice and serve with soy sauce, pickled ginger, and wasabi.

Potato Filled Bread Rolls

Prep time: 15 minutes | Cook time: 11 to 14 minutes | Serves 4

8 slices sandwich bread
4 large potatoes, boiled and mashed
½ teaspoon turmeric
2 green chilies, seeded and chopped
1 onion, finely chopped
½ teaspoon mustard seeds
1 tablespoon olive oil
Salt to taste

1. Preheat the air fryer to 350ºF (177ºC). In a skillet over medium heat, warm the olive oil and stir-fry onion and mustard seeds, 3 minutes. Remove to a bowl and add in potatoes, chilies, turmeric, and salt; mix well. 2. Trim the crust sides of the bread, and roll out with a rolling pin. Spread a spoonful of the potato mixture on each bread sheet, and roll the bread over the filling, sealing the edges. Place the rolls in the greased frying basket and bake for 11 to 14 minutes until golden and crispy. Serve warm.

Mexican Chile Relleno

Prep time: 10 minutes | Cook time: 8 to 10 minutes | Serves 4

2 (8-ounce / 227-g) cans whole green chiles, drained
2 cups Mexican cheese, shredded
1 cup all-purpose flour
2 whole eggs
½ cup milk

1. Preheat the air fryer to 380ºF (193ºC). Lay the green chilies on a plate, cut them open at the top and fill them with cheese. In a bowl, whisk the eggs, milk, and half of the flour. Pour the remaining flour on a flat plate. Dip the chilies in the flour first, then in the egg mixture, and arrange them in the greased frying basket. Air fry for 8 to 10 minutes, flipping once halfway through. Serve with slices of avocado if desired.

Vegetable Tortilla Pizza

Prep time: 15 minutes | Cook time: 10 to 12 minutes | Serves 1

¼ tablespoon tomato paste
1 tablespoon Cheddar cheese, grated
1 tablespoon Mozzarella cheese, grated
1 tablespoon canned sweet corn
4 zucchini slices
4 eggplant slices
4 red onion rings
½ green bell pepper, chopped
1 large tortilla
A few fresh basil leaves, chopped

1. Preheat the air fryer to 350ºF (177ºC). Spread the tomato paste on the tortilla. Arrange zucchini and eggplant slices first, then green bell peppers and onion rings. Sprinkle the corn all over. Top with Cheddar and Mozzarella cheeses. Place the pizza in the frying basket and bake in the fryer for 10 to 12 minutes until nice and lightly browned on top. Sprinkle with freshly chopped basil leaves and serve.

Spanish-Style Huevos Rotos (Broken Eggs)

Prep time: 15 minutes | Cook time: 25 to 30 minutes | Serves 2

½ teaspoon salt
½ teaspoon garlic powder
3 tablespoons olive oil
1 teaspoon sweet paprika
2 russet potatoes, cut into wedges
2 eggs

1. Preheat the air fryer to 390ºF (199ºC). In a bowl, mix salt, garlic powder, and 1 tablespoon of olive oil. Add in the potatoes and toss to coat. Arrange them in the greased frying basket without overcrowding. 2. Air fry for 20 to 25 minutes, shaking regularly to get crispy on all sides. Heat the remaining olive oil in a pan over medium heat and fry the eggs until the whites are firm and the yolks are still runny, about 5 minutes. Place the potatoes on a serving bowl and top with the fried eggs and paprika. Break the eggs with a fork, and stir a bit. Serve with cold beer.

Crispy Mozzarella Sliders

Prep time: 10 minutes | Cook time: 13 to 16 minutes | Serves 4

8 Mozzarella cheese slices
8 Pepperidge farm rolls, halved
1 tablespoon butter, softened
1 teaspoon mustard seeds
1 teaspoon poppy seeds
1 small onion, chopped

1. Preheat the air fryer to 350°F (177°C). In a bowl, mix butter, mustard seeds, onion, and poppy seeds. Spread the mixture on-farm roll bottoms, top with a slice of Mozzarella cheese, and cover with the farm roll tops. Arrange the sliders in the greased frying basket and bake 13 to 16 minutes until golden. Serve.

Easy Greek Briami (Ratatouille)

Prep time: 15 minutes | Cook time: 40 minutes | Serves 6

2 russet potatoes, cubed
½ cup Roma tomatoes, cubed
1 eggplant, cubed
1 zucchini, cubed
1 red onion, chopped
1 red bell pepper, chopped
2 garlic cloves, minced
1 teaspoon dried mint
1 teaspoon dried parsley
1 teaspoon dried oregano
½ teaspoon salt
½ teaspoon black pepper
¼ teaspoon red pepper flakes
⅓ cup olive oil
1 (8-ounce) can tomato paste
¼ cup vegetable broth
¼ cup water

1. Preheat the air fryer to 320°F (160°C). 2. In a bowl, combine the first thirteen ingredients. In a bowl, mix together the olive oil, tomato paste, broth, and water. 3. Pour the oil-and-tomato-paste mixture over the vegetables and toss until coated. Arrange them to the frying basket. 4. Roast for 20 minutes. Stir well and spread out again and roast for an additional 10 minutes, then repeat the process and cook for another 10 minutes.

Baked Mediterranean Shakshuka

Prep time: 15 minutes | Cook time: 30 minutes | Serves 4

1 onion, sliced
2 garlic cloves, minced
2 tablespoons olive oil
1 teaspoon ground cumin
2 teaspoons paprika
¼ teaspoon chili powder
1 red bell pepper, seeded and diced
2 (14½-ounce / 411-g) cans tomatoes, diced
4 eggs
2 tablespoons fresh parsley, chopped
4 tablespoons feta cheese, crumbled
Salt and black pepper to taste

1. Preheat the air fryer to 390°F (199°C). Heat olive oil in a skillet over medium heat and sauté bell pepper, onion, and garlic for 5 minutes until tender. Stir in paprika, parsley, chili, cumin, salt, and pepper and pour in the tomatoes. Simmer for 10 minutes; transfer to a baking dish. Crack in the eggs. Bake in the air fryer for 12 to 15 minutes or until the egg whites are set but the yolks are still runny. Top with feta to serve.

Brussels Sprouts with Raisins and Pine Nuts

Prep time: 10 minutes | Cook time: 14 to 16 minutes | Serves 4

1 pound (454 g) Brussels sprouts, stems cut off and halved
2 tablespoons olive oil
1¾ ounce (50 g) raisins, soaked and drained
Juice of 1 orange
Salt to taste
2 tablespoons pine nuts, toasted

1. Preheat the air fryer to 390°F (199°C). In a bowl, toss the Brussels sprouts with olive oil and salt and stir to combine. Place them in the frying and air fry for 14 to 16 minutes, shaking once halfway through, until slightly charred. Top with toasted pine nuts and raisins. Drizzle with orange juice and serve.

Hasselback Potatoes with Chive Pesto

Prep time: 10 minutes | Cook time: 40 minutes | Serves 2

2 medium russet potatoes
5 tablespoons olive oil
Kosher salt and freshly ground black pepper, to taste
¼ cup roughly chopped fresh chives
2 tablespoons packed fresh flat-leaf parsley leaves
1 tablespoon chopped walnuts
1 tablespoon grated Parmesan cheese
1 teaspoon fresh lemon juice
1 small garlic clove, peeled
¼ cup sour cream

1. Thinly slice the potatoes crosswise and stop ½ inch short of each end of the potato. Rub the potatoes with 1 tablespoon olive oil and season with salt and pepper. 2. Air fry the potatoes at 375°F (191°C) for 40 minutes, until golden brown and crisp on the outside and tender inside, drizzling the insides with 1 tablespoon olive oil and seasoning with salt and pepper halfway through. 3. Meanwhile, in a blender, purée the remaining ingredients except sour cream until smooth. Season with salt and pepper. 4. Remove from the air fryer drizzle the potatoes with the pesto, letting it drip down into the grooves, then dollop with sour cream and serve hot.

Roasted Brussels Sprouts with Bacon

Prep time: 10 minutes | Cook time: 20 minutes | Serves 4

4 slices thick-cut bacon, chopped (about ¼ pound / 113 g)
1 pound (454 g) Brussels sprouts, halved (or quartered if large)
Freshly ground black pepper, to taste

1. Preheat the air fryer to 380°F (193°C). 2. Air fry the bacon for 5 minutes, shaking the basket once or twice. 3. Add the Brussels sprouts to the basket and drizzle a little bacon fat from the bottom of the air fryer drawer into the basket. Toss the sprouts to coat with the bacon fat. Air fry for 15 minutes until the Brussels sprouts are tender to a knifepoint. 4. Season with black pepper.

Plantain Fritters

Prep time: 5 minutes | Cook time: 8 to 10 minutes | Serves 4

3 ripe plantains, sliced diagonally
2 tablespoons cornflour
1 egg white
¼ cup bread crumbs
Salt and black pepper to taste

1. Preheat the air fryer to 340ºF (171ºC). Pour the bread crumbs into a plate; season with salt and pepper. Coat the plantain slices in the cornflour, brush with the egg white, and roll in the crumbs. Arrange on the greased frying basket and lightly spray with oil. Bake for 8 to 10 minutes, flipping once, until golden.

Lemon-Garlic Mushrooms

Prep time: 10 minutes | Cook time: 10 to 15 minutes | Serves 6

12 ounces (340 g) sliced mushrooms
1 tablespoon avocado oil
Sea salt and freshly ground black pepper, to taste
3 tablespoons unsalted butter
1 teaspoon minced garlic
1 teaspoon freshly squeezed lemon juice
½ teaspoon red pepper flakes
2 tablespoons chopped fresh parsley

1. Toss the mushrooms with the oil and season to taste with salt and pepper. 2. Place the mushrooms in a single layer in the frying basket. Roast at 375ºF (191ºC) for 10 to 15 minutes, until the mushrooms are tender. 3. Meanwhile, melt the butter in a small pot over medium-low heat. Stir in the garlic and cook for 30 seconds. Remove the pot from the heat and stir in the lemon juice and red pepper flakes. 4. Toss the mushrooms with the lemon-garlic butter and garnish with the parsley before serving.

Brussels Sprouts with Pecans and Gorgonzola

Prep time: 10 minutes | Cook time: 25 minutes | Serves 4

½ cup pecans
1½ pounds (680 g) fresh Brussels sprouts, trimmed and quartered
2 tablespoons olive oil
Salt and freshly ground black pepper, to taste
¼ cup crumbled Gorgonzola cheese

1. Spread the pecans in a single layer of the air fryer and air fry at 350ºF (177ºC) for 3 to 5 minutes until the pecans are lightly browned and fragrant. Remove the pecans and increase the heat to 400ºF (204ºC). 2. In a bowl, toss the Brussels sprouts with the olive oil and season with salt and black pepper to taste. 3. Arrange the Brussels sprouts in a single layer in the frying basket and air fry for 20 to 25 minutes until the sprouts are tender and starting to brown on the edges, shaking halfway. 4. Top with the toasted pecans and Gorgonzola. Serve warm or at room temperature.

Homemade Pie with Root Vegetables

Prep time: 15 minutes | Cook time: 30 minutes | Serves 4

1 pound (454 g) potatoes, cubed
1 parsnip, chopped
½ cup Parmesan cheese, grated
1 cup crème fraiche
1 bread slice, diced
½ teaspoon dried sage
2 tablespoons butter
1 teaspoon yellow mustard
Salt and black pepper to taste

1. Boil the potatoes and parsnip in a pot filled with salted water over medium heat for 15 minutes. Drain and transfer to a bowl. Add in mustard, crème fraiche, sage, butter, salt, and pepper and mash them with a masher. Mix in the bread and Parmesan cheese. Preheat the air fryer to 360ºF (182ºC). Add the resulting batter to the greased frying basket and place it in the fryer. Bake for 14 to 16 minutes until golden. Serve.

"Faux-Tato" Hash

Prep time: 10 minutes | Cook time: 12 minutes | Serves 4

1 pound (454 g) radishes, ends removed, quartered
¼ medium yellow onion, peeled and diced
½ medium green bell pepper, seeded and chopped
2 tablespoons salted butter, melted
½ teaspoon garlic powder
¼ teaspoon ground black pepper

1. In a bowl, combine radishes, onion, and bell pepper. Toss with butter. 2. Sprinkle garlic powder and black pepper over mixture in bowl, then spoon into ungreased frying basket. 3. Air fry at 320ºF (160ºC) for 12 minutes, shaking halfway through cooking. Radishes will be tender when done. Serve warm.

Indian Eggplant Bharta

Prep time: 15 minutes | Cook time: 20 minutes | Serves 4

1 medium eggplant
2 tablespoons vegetable oil
½ cup finely minced onion
½ cup finely chopped fresh tomato
2 tablespoons fresh lemon juice
2 tablespoons chopped fresh cilantro
½ teaspoon kosher salt
⅛ teaspoon cayenne pepper

1. Rub the eggplant all over with the vegetable oil. Place the eggplant in the frying basket. Air fry at 400ºF (204ºC) for 20 minutes, or until the eggplant skin is blistered and charred. 2. Transfer the eggplant to a resealable plastic bag, seal, and set aside for 15 to 20 minutes (the eggplant will finish cooking in the residual heat trapped in the bag). 3. Peel off and discard the charred skin of eggplant. Roughly mash the eggplant flesh. Add the onion, tomato, lemon juice, cilantro, salt, and cayenne. Stir to combine.

Golden Garlicky Mushrooms

Prep time: 10 minutes | Cook time: 10 minutes | Serves 4

6 small mushrooms
1 tablespoon bread crumbs
1 tablespoon olive oil
1 ounce (28 g) onion, peeled and diced
1 teaspoon parsley
1 teaspoon garlic purée
Salt and ground black pepper, to taste

1. Preheat the air fryer to 350ºF (177ºC). 2. Combine the bread crumbs, oil, onion, parsley, salt, pepper and garlic in a bowl. Cut out the mushrooms' stalks and stuff each cap with the crumb mixture. 3. Air fry for 10 minutes. 4. Serve hot.

Crispy Green Beans

Prep time: 5 minutes | Cook time: 8 minutes | Serves 4

2 teaspoons olive oil
½ pound (227 g) fresh green beans, ends trimmed
¼ teaspoon salt
¼ teaspoon ground black pepper

1. In a bowl, drizzle olive oil over green beans and sprinkle with salt and pepper. 2. Place green beans into ungreased frying basket. Air fry at 350ºF (177ºC) for 8 minutes, shaking the basket two times. Green beans will be dark golden and crispy at the edges when done. Serve warm.

Creamed Asparagus

Prep time: 10 minutes | Cook time: 18 minutes | Serves 4

½ cup heavy whipping cream
½ cup grated Parmesan cheese
2 ounces (57 g) cream cheese, softened
1 pound (454 g) asparagus, ends trimmed, chopped into 1-inch pieces
¼ teaspoon salt
¼ teaspoon ground black pepper

1. In a baking dish, whisk together heavy cream, Parmesan, and cream cheese until combined. Pour cheese mixture over top and sprinkle with salt and pepper. 2. Place dish into frying basket. Air fry at 350ºF (177ºC) for 18 minutes. Asparagus will be tender when done. Serve warm.

Lemon-Thyme Asparagus

Prep time: 5 minutes | Cook time: 4 to 8 minutes | Serves 4

1 pound (454 g) asparagus, woody ends trimmed off
1 tablespoon avocado oil
½ teaspoon dried thyme or ½ tablespoon chopped fresh thyme
Sea salt and freshly ground
black pepper, to taste
2 ounces (57 g) goat cheese, crumbled
Zest and juice of 1 lemon
Flaky sea salt, for serving (optional)

1. In a medium bowl, toss together the asparagus, avocado oil, and thyme, and season with sea salt and pepper. 2. Place the asparagus in the frying basket in a single layer. Air fry at 400ºF (204ºC) for 4 to 8 minutes, to your desired doneness. 3. Transfer to a serving platter. Top with the goat cheese, lemon zest, and lemon juice. If desired, season with a pinch of flaky salt.

Simple Zucchini Crisps

Prep time: 5 minutes | Cook time: 14 minutes | Serves 4

2 zucchini, sliced into ¼- to ½-inch-thick rounds (about 2 cups)
¼ teaspoon garlic granules
⅛ teaspoon sea salt
Freshly ground black pepper, to taste (optional)
Cooking spray

1. Preheat the air fryer to 392ºF (200ºC). Spritz the frying basket with cooking spray. 2. Put the zucchini rounds in the frying basket, spreading them out as much as possible. Top with garlic granules, sea salt, and black pepper (if desired). Spritz the zucchini rounds with cooking spray. 3. Roast for 14 minutes, flipping once halfway through, until crisp-tender. 4. Let them rest for 5 minutes and serve.

Crispy Garlic Sliced Eggplant

Prep time: 5 minutes | Cook time: 25 minutes | Serves 4

1 egg
1 tablespoon water
½ cup whole wheat bread crumbs
1 teaspoon garlic powder
½ teaspoon dried oregano
½ teaspoon salt
½ teaspoon paprika
1 medium eggplant, sliced into ¼-inch-thick rounds
1 tablespoon olive oil

1. Preheat the air fryer to 360ºF (182ºC). 2. In a medium shallow bowl, beat together the egg and water until frothy. 3. In a separate medium shallow bowl, mix together bread crumbs, garlic powder, oregano, salt, and paprika. 4. Dip each eggplant slice into the egg mixture, then bread crumb mixture until coated. Place the slices in a single layer in the frying basket. 5. Drizzle the eggplant with olive oil, then fry for 15 minutes. Turn and cook for an additional 10 minutes.

Air Fried Potatoes with Olives

Prep time: 15 minutes | Cook time: 40 minutes | Serves 1

1 medium russet potatoes, scrubbed and peeled
1 teaspoon olive oil
¼ teaspoon onion powder
⅛ teaspoon salt
Dollop of butter
Dollop of cream cheese
1 tablespoon Kalamata olives
1 tablespoon chopped chives

1. Preheat the air fryer to 400ºF (204ºC). 2. In a bowl, coat the potatoes with the onion powder, salt, olive oil, and butter. 3. Air fry for 40 minutes, turning once at the halfway point. 4.Serve with the cream cheese, Kalamata olives and chives on top.

Parmesan Herb Focaccia Bread

Prep time: 10 minutes | Cook time: 10 minutes | Serves 6

1 cup shredded Mozzarella cheese
1 ounce (28 g) full-fat cream cheese
1 cup blanched finely ground almond flour
¼ cup ground golden flaxseed
¼ cup grated Parmesan cheese
½ teaspoon baking soda
2 large eggs
½ teaspoon garlic powder
¼ teaspoon dried basil
¼ teaspoon dried rosemary
2 tablespoons salted butter, melted and divided

1. Microwave Mozzarella, cream cheese, and almond flour into a large microwave-safe bowl for 1 minute. Add the flaxseed, Parmesan, and baking soda and stir until smooth ball forms. 2. Stir in eggs and keep stirring into the dough. 3. Sprinkle dough with garlic powder, basil, and rosemary and knead into dough. Grease a baking pan with 1 tablespoon melted butter. Press the dough evenly into the pan. Place into the frying basket. 4. Bake at 400ºF (204ºC) for 10 minutes. 5. At 7 minutes, cover with foil if bread begins to get too dark. 6. Let cool at least 30 minutes. Drizzle with remaining butter and serve.

Garlic-Parmesan Crispy Baby Potatoes

Prep time: 10 minutes | Cook time: 15 minutes | Serves 4

Oil, for spraying
1 pound (454 g) baby potatoes
½ cup grated Parmesan cheese, divided
3 tablespoons olive oil
2 teaspoons granulated garlic
½ teaspoon onion powder
½ teaspoon salt
¼ teaspoon freshly ground black pepper
¼ teaspoon paprika
2 tablespoons chopped fresh parsley, for garnish

1. Wash and dry the potatoes. In a bowl, mix together ¼ cup Parmesan cheese, olive oil, garlic, onion powder, salt, black pepper, and paprika. Pour the mixture over the potatoes and toss to coat. 2. Transfer the potatoes to the frying basket in an even layer, taking care to keep them from touching. Spray lightly with oil. 3. Air fry at 400ºF (204ºC) for 15 minutes, stirring after 7 to 8 minutes, until easily pierced with a fork. 4. Sprinkle with the parsley and the remaining Parmesan cheese and serve.

Broccoli-Cheddar Twice-Baked Potatoes

Prep time: 10 minutes | Cook time: 46 minutes | Serves 4

Oil, for spraying
2 medium russet potatoes
1 tablespoon olive oil
¼ cup broccoli florets
1 tablespoon sour cream
1 teaspoon granulated garlic
1 teaspoon onion powder
½ cup shredded Cheddar cheese

1. Wash and dry the potatoes. Rub with the olive oil and place them in the frying basket. 2. Air fry at 400ºF (204ºC) for 40 minutes, or until easily pierced with a fork. Allow to cool, then cut the potatoes in half lengthwise. 3. Meanwhile, microwave the broccoli on high for 5 to 8 minutes. Drain and set aside. 4. Scoop out most of the potato flesh. Add the sour cream, garlic, and onion powder and stir until the potatoes are mashed. 5. Spoon the potato mixture back into the hollowed potato skins. Top with the broccoli and cheese. Return to the basket. 6. Air fry at 400ºF (204ºC) for 3 to 6 minutes, or until the cheese has melted. Serve immediately.

Fried Zucchini Salad

Prep time: 10 minutes | Cook time: 5 to 7 minutes | Serves 4

2 medium zucchini, thinly sliced
5 tablespoons olive oil, divided
¼ cup chopped fresh parsley
2 tablespoons chopped fresh mint
Zest and juice of ½ lemon
1 clove garlic, minced
¼ cup crumbled feta cheese
Freshly ground black pepper, to taste

1. Preheat the air fryer to 400ºF (204ºC). 2. In a bowl, toss the zucchini with 1 tablespoon olive oil. 3. Arrange the zucchini slices in an even layer in the frying basket and air fry for 5 to 7 minutes until soft and lightly browned, shaking once halfway the cooking time. 4. Meanwhile, in a bowl, combine the remaining olive oil, parsley, mint, lemon zest, lemon juice, and garlic. 5. Arrange the zucchini on a plate and drizzle with the dressing. Sprinkle the feta and black pepper on top. Serve warm or at room temperature.

Super Cheesy Gold Eggplant

Prep time: 15 minutes | Cook time: 30 minutes | Serves 4

1 medium eggplant, peeled and cut into ½-inch-thick rounds
1 teaspoon salt, plus more for seasoning
½ cup all-purpose flour
2 eggs
¾ cup Italian bread crumbs
2 tablespoons grated Parmesan cheese
Freshly ground black pepper, to taste
Cooking oil spray
¾ cup marinara sauce
½ cup shredded Parmesan cheese, divided
½ cup shredded Mozzarella cheese, divided

1. Dry the eggplant with paper towels. 2. Place the flour in a shallow bowl. 3. In another shallow bowl, beat the eggs. 4. In a third shallow bowl, stir together the bread crumbs and grated Parmesan cheese and season with salt and pepper. 5. Dip eggplant in the flour, in the eggs, and into the bread crumbs to coat. 6. Preheat the air fryer to 400ºF (204ºC). Place the eggplant rounds into the basket in a single layer and spray with cooking oil. 7. Air fry at 400ºF (204ºC) for 10 minutes. After 7 minutes, top each round with 1 teaspoon marinara sauce and ½ tablespoon each of shredded Parmesan and Mozzarella cheese. Air fry for 2 to 3 minutes until the cheese melts. 8. Serve immediately.

Grits Casserole

Prep time: 5 minutes | Cook time: 28 to 30 minutes | Serves 4

- 10 fresh asparagus spears, cut into 1-inch pieces
- 2 cups cooked grits, cooled to room temperature
- 1 egg, beaten
- 2 teaspoons Worcestershire sauce
- ½ teaspoon garlic powder
- ¼ teaspoon salt
- 2 slices provolone cheese (about 1½ ounces / 43 g), cut into pieces
- Oil for misting or cooking spray

1. Mist asparagus spears with oil and air fry at 390ºF (199ºC) for 5 minutes, until crisp-tender. 2. In a medium bowl, mix together the grits, egg, Worcestershire, garlic powder, and salt. 3. Spoon half of grits mixture into a baking pan and top with asparagus. 4. Top asparagus with cheese pieces and then top with remaining grits. 5. Bake at 360ºF (182ºC) for 23 to 25 minutes until browned lightly on top with just a hint of crispiness. The casserole will rise a little as it cooks.

Roasted Sweet Potatoes

Prep time: 10 minutes | Cook time: 25 minutes | Serves 4

- Cooking oil spray
- 2 sweet potatoes, peeled and cut into 1-inch cubes
- 1 tablespoon extra-virgin olive oil
- Pinch salt
- Freshly ground black pepper, to taste
- ½ teaspoon dried thyme
- ½ teaspoon dried marjoram
- ¼ cup grated Parmesan cheese

1. Preheat the air fryer to 330ºF (166ºC). Spray the frying basket with cooking oil. 2. Put the sweet potato cubes into the basket and drizzle with olive oil. Toss gently to coat. Sprinkle with the salt, pepper, thyme, and marjoram and toss again. 3. Roast for 25 minutes, shaking the basket every 10 minutes. At last 5 minutes, sprinkle evenly with the Parmesan cheese. 4. When done, the potatoes should be tender. Serve immediately.

Air-Fried Okra

Prep time: 10 minutes | Cook time: 10 minutes | Serves 4

- 1 egg
- ½ cup almond milk
- ½ cup crushed pork rinds
- ¼ cup grated Parmesan cheese
- ¼ cup almond flour
- 1 teaspoon garlic powder
- ¼ teaspoon freshly ground black pepper
- ½ pound (227 g) fresh okra, stems removed and chopped into 1-inch slices

1. Preheat the air fryer to 400ºF (204ºC). 2. In a shallow bowl, whisk together the egg and milk. 3. In a second shallow bowl, combine the pork rinds, Parmesan, almond flour, garlic powder, and black pepper. 4. Dip the okra into the egg mixture followed by the crumb mixture until well coated. 5. Arrange the okra in a single layer in the frying basket and spray lightly with olive oil. Air fry for 10 minutes, turning once halfway the cooking time, until tender and golden brown. Serve warm.

Baked Jalapeño and Cheese Cauliflower Mash

Prep time: 10 minutes | Cook time: 15 minutes | Serves 6

- 1 (12-ounce / 340-g) steamer bag cauliflower florets, cooked according to package instructions
- 2 tablespoons salted butter, softened
- 2 ounces (57 g) cream cheese, softened
- ½ cup shredded sharp Cheddar cheese
- ¼ cup pickled jalapeños
- ½ teaspoon salt
- ¼ teaspoon ground black pepper

1. Place cooked cauliflower into a food processor with remaining ingredients. Pulse twenty times until cauliflower is smooth and all ingredients are combined. 2. Spoon mash into an ungreased round nonstick baking dish. Bake at 380ºF (193ºC) for 15 minutes until golden brown on top. Serve warm.

Shishito Pepper Roast

Prep time: 4 minutes | Cook time: 9 minutes | Serves 4

- Cooking oil spray (sunflower, safflower, or refined coconut)
- 1 pound (454 g) shishito or bell peppers, rinsed
- 1 tablespoon soy sauce
- 2 teaspoons freshly squeezed lime juice
- 2 large garlic cloves, pressed

1. Preheat the air fryer to 390ºF (199ºC). 2. Place the peppers into the basket and spray them with oil. 3. Roast for 9 minutes, shaking the basket and spray the peppers with more oil every 3 minutes. 4. Meanwhile, in a bowl, whisk the soy sauce, lime juice, and garlic until combined. Set aside. 5. When done, the peppers should have lots of nice browned spots on them. 6. Toss to coat the peppers in the bowl with sauce evenly and serve.

Maple-Roasted Tomatoes

Prep time: 15 minutes | Cook time: 20 minutes | Serves 2

- 10 ounces (283 g) cherry tomatoes, halved
- Kosher salt, to taste
- 2 tablespoons maple syrup
- 1 tablespoon vegetable oil
- 2 sprigs fresh thyme, stems removed
- 1 garlic clove, minced
- Freshly ground black pepper

1. Place the tomatoes in a colander and sprinkle liberally with salt. Let stand for 10 minutes to drain. 2. Transfer the tomatoes cut-side up to a cake pan, then drizzle with the maple syrup and oil. Sprinkle with the thyme leaves and garlic and season with pepper. Roast at 325ºF (163ºC) for 20 minutes until the tomatoes are soft, collapsed, and lightly caramelized on top. 3. Serve with the juices from the pan.

Fig, Chickpea, and Arugula Salad

Prep time: 15 minutes | Cook time: 20 minutes | Serves 4

8 fresh figs, halved
1½ cups cooked chickpeas
1 teaspoon crushed roasted cumin seeds
4 tablespoons balsamic vinegar
2 tablespoons extra-virgin olive oil, plus more for greasing
Salt and ground black pepper, to taste
3 cups arugula rocket, washed and dried

1. Preheat the air fryer to 375ºF (191ºC). 2. Cover the frying basket with aluminum foil and grease lightly with oil. Air fry the figs for 10 minutes. 3. In a bowl, combine the chickpeas and cumin seeds. 4. Remove the figs and replace with the chickpeas. Air fry for 10 minutes. Leave to cool. 5. Meanwhile, prepare the dressing. Mix the balsamic vinegar, olive oil, salt and pepper. 6. In a salad bowl, combine the arugula rocket with the cooled figs and chickpeas. 7. Toss with the sauce and serve.

Spinach and Cheese Stuffed Tomatoes

Prep time: 20 minutes | Cook time: 15 minutes | Serves 2

4 ripe beefsteak tomatoes
¾ teaspoon black pepper
½ teaspoon kosher salt
1 (10-ounce / 283-g) package frozen chopped spinach, thawed and squeezed dry
1 (5.2-ounce / 147-g) package garlic-and-herb Boursin cheese
3 tablespoons sour cream
½ cup finely grated Parmesan cheese

1. Cut the tops off the tomatoes, remove and discard the pulp. Season the insides with ½ teaspoon black pepper and ¼ teaspoon salt. Invert the tomatoes onto paper towels and drain while you make the filling. 2. Meanwhile, in a bowl, combine the spinach, Boursin cheese, sour cream, ¼ cup Parmesan, the remaining ¼ teaspoon salt and ¼ teaspoon pepper. Stir until well combined. Divide the filling among the tomatoes. Top with the remaining Parmesan. 3. Place the tomatoes in the frying basket. Bake at 350ºF (177ºC) for 15 minutes, until the filling is hot.

Potato with Creamy Cheese

Prep time: 5 minutes | Cook time: 15 minutes | Serves 2

2 medium potatoes
1 teaspoon butter
3 tablespoons sour cream
1 teaspoon chives
1½ tablespoons grated Parmesan cheese

1. Preheat the air fryer to 350ºF (177ºC). 2. Pierce the potatoes with a fork and boil them in water until they are cooked. 3. Transfer to the air fryer and air fry for 15 minutes. 4. In the meantime, combine the sour cream, cheese and chives in a bowl. Cut the potatoes halfway to open them up and fill with the butter and sour cream mixture. 5. Serve immediately.

Bacon-Wrapped Asparagus

Prep time: 10 minutes | Cook time: 10 minutes | Serves 4

8 slices reduced-sodium bacon, cut in half
16 thick (about 1 pound / 454 g) asparagus spears, trimmed of woody ends

1. Preheat the air fryer to 350ºF (177ºC). 2. Wrap a half piece of bacon around the center of each stalk of asparagus. 3. Arrange seam-side down in a single layer in the frying basket. Air fry for 10 minutes until the bacon is crisp and the stalks are tender.

Roasted Garlic

Prep time: 5 minutes | Cook time: 20 minutes | Makes 12 cloves

1 medium head garlic
2 teaspoons avocado oil

1. Remove any hanging excess peel from the garlic but leave the cloves covered. Cut off ¼ of the head of garlic, exposing the tips of the cloves. 2. Drizzle with avocado oil. Place the garlic head into a small sheet of aluminum foil, completely enclosing it. Place it into the frying basket. 3. Air fry at 400ºF (204ºC) for 20 minutes until golden brown and very soft.

Citrus-Roasted Broccoli Florets

Prep time: 5 minutes | Cook time: 12 minutes | Serves 6

4 cups broccoli florets (approximately 1 large head)
2 tablespoons olive oil
½ teaspoon salt
½ cup orange juice
1 tablespoon raw honey
Orange wedges, for serving (optional)

1. Preheat the air fryer to 360ºF (182ºC). 2. In a bowl, combine the broccoli, olive oil, salt, orange juice, and honey. Toss the broccoli in the liquid until well coated. 3. Pour the broccoli mixture into the frying basket and roast for 6 minutes. Stir and roast for 6 minutes more. 4. Serve alone or with orange wedges for additional citrus flavor, if desired.

Buttery Green Beans

Prep time: 5 minutes | Cook time: 8 to 10 minutes | Serves 6

1 pound (454 g) green beans, trimmed
1 tablespoon avocado oil
1 teaspoon garlic powder
Sea salt and freshly ground black pepper, to taste
¼ cup (4 tablespoons) unsalted butter, melted
¼ cup freshly grated Parmesan cheese

1. In a bowl, toss green beans with avocado oil, garlic powder and season with salt and pepper. Arrange the green beans in a single layer in the frying basket. 2. Air fry at 400ºF (204ºC) for 8 to 10 minutes, tossing halfway through. 3. Transfer the beans to a large bowl and toss with the melted butter. Top with the Parmesan cheese and serve warm.

Easy Potato Croquettes

Prep time: 15 minutes | Cook time: 15 minutes | Serves 10

¼ cup nutritional yeast
2 cups boiled potatoes, mashed
1 flax egg
1 tablespoon flour
2 tablespoons chopped chives
Salt and ground black pepper, to taste
2 tablespoons vegetable oil
¼ cup bread crumbs

1. Preheat the air fryer to 400ºF (204ºC). 2. In a bowl, combine the nutritional yeast, potatoes, flax egg, flour, and chives. Sprinkle with salt and pepper as desired. 3. In a separate bowl, mix the vegetable oil and bread crumbs to achieve a crumbly consistency. 4. Shape the potato mixture into small balls and dip into the bread crumb mixture. 5. Air fry for 15 minutes until golden brown. 6. Serve immediately.

Hawaiian Brown Rice

Prep time: 10 minutes | Cook time: 12 to 16 minutes | Serves 4 to 6

¼ pound (113 g) ground sausage
1 teaspoon butter
¼ cup minced onion
¼ cup minced bell pepper
2 cups cooked brown rice
1 (8-ounce / 227-g) can crushed pineapple, drained

1. Shape sausage into 3 or 4 thin patties. Air fry at 390ºF (199ºC) for 6 to 8 minutes or until well done. Remove, drain, and crumble. Set aside. 2. Place butter, onion, and bell pepper in baking pan. Roast at 390ºF (199ºC) for 1 minute and stir. Cook 3 to 4 minutes longer until vegetables are tender. 3. Add sausage, rice, and pineapple to vegetables and stir together. 4. Roast for 2 to 3 minutes, until heated through.

Parsnip Fries with Romesco Sauce

Prep time: 20 minutes | Cook time: 24 minutes | Serves 2

Romesco Sauce:
1 red bell pepper, halved and seeded
1 (1-inch) thick slice of Italian bread, torn into pieces (about 1 to 1½ cups)
1 cup almonds, toasted
Olive oil
½ jalapeño pepper, seeded
1 tablespoon fresh parsley leaves
1 clove garlic
2 Roma tomatoes, peeled and seeded (or ⅓ cup canned crushed tomatoes)
1 tablespoon red wine vinegar
¼ teaspoon smoked paprika
½ teaspoon salt
¾ cup olive oil
3 parsnips, peeled and cut into long strips
2 teaspoons olive oil
Salt and freshly ground black pepper, to taste

1. Preheat the air fryer to 400ºF (204ºC). 2. Place the red pepper halves, cut side down, in the frying basket and air fry for 8 to 10 minutes until the skin turns black all over. Peel the pepper after cooling down. 3. Toss the torn bread and almonds with a little olive oil and air fry for 4 minutes until nicely toasted, shaking the basket a couple times. Let cool for a minute or two. 4. Combine the bread, almonds, red pepper, jalapeño, parsley, garlic, tomatoes, vinegar, paprika and salt until smooth in a blender. With the processor running, add the olive oil through the feed tube until the sauce comes in a smooth paste that is barely pourable. 5. Toss the parsnip strips with the olive oil, salt and black pepper and air fry at 400ºF (204ºC) for 10 minutes, shaking the basket a couple times. Serve warm with the Romesco sauce.

Stuffed Red Peppers with Herbed Ricotta and Tomatoes

Prep time: 10 minutes | Cook time: 20 minutes | Serves 4

2 red bell peppers, cut in half and stem removed
1 cup cooked brown rice
2 Roma tomatoes, diced
1 garlic clove, minced
¼ teaspoon salt
¼ teaspoon black pepper
4 ounces ricotta
3 tablespoons fresh basil, chopped
3 tablespoons fresh oregano, chopped
¼ cup shredded Parmesan, for topping

1. Preheat the air fryer to 360ºF (182ºC). 2. In a medium bowl, combine the brown rice, tomatoes, garlic, salt, and pepper. 3. Distribute the rice filling evenly among the four bell pepper halves. 4. In a bowl, combine the ricotta, basil, and oregano. Pour over the top of the rice mixture in each bell pepper. 5. Place the bell peppers into the air fryer and roast for 20 minutes. 6. Serve with Parmesan on top.

Dill-and-Garlic Beets

Prep time: 10 minutes | Cook time: 30 minutes | Serves 4

4 beets, cleaned, peeled, and sliced
1 garlic clove, minced
2 tablespoons chopped fresh dill
¼ teaspoon salt
¼ teaspoon black pepper
3 tablespoons olive oil

1. Preheat the air fryer to 380ºF (193ºC). 2. In a bowl, mix together all of the ingredients so the beets are well coated with the oil. 3. Pour the beet mixture into the frying basket, and roast for 15 minutes before stirring, then continue roasting for 15 minutes more.

Lemony Broccoli

Prep time: 10 minutes | Cook time: 9 to 14 minutes per batch | Serves 4

1 large head broccoli, rinsed and patted dry
2 teaspoons extra-virgin olive oil
1 tablespoon freshly squeezed lemon juice
Olive oil spray

1. Cut off the broccoli florets and separate them. 2. Preheat the air fryer to 390ºF (199ºC). 3. In a bowl, toss together the broccoli, olive oil, and lemon juice until coated. Place half the broccoli into the frying basket. 4. Roast for 14 minutes until crisp-tender and slightly brown around the edges. Shake the basket and check the broccoli every 5 minutes. 5. Repeat the steps with remaining broccoli. Serve immediately.

Flatbread

Prep time: 5 minutes | Cook time: 7 minutes | Serves 2

1 cup shredded Mozzarella cheese
¼ cup blanched finely ground almond flour
1 ounce (28 g) full-fat cream cheese, softened

1. Melt Mozzarella in the microwave for 30 seconds. Stir in almond flour until smooth and then add cream cheese. Mix until dough forms. 2. Divide the dough into two pieces and roll out to ¼-inch thickness between two pieces of parchment. Cut another piece of parchment to fit your frying basket. 3. Place a piece of flatbread on parchment and into the basket. 4. Air fry at 320°F (160°C) for 7 minutes, flipping once halfway through the cooking time. Repeat with the remaining dough. Serve warm.

Tofu Bites

Prep time: 15 minutes | Cook time: 30 minutes | Serves 4

1 packaged firm tofu, cubed and pressed to remove excess water
1 tablespoon soy sauce
1 tablespoon ketchup
1 tablespoon maple syrup
½ teaspoon vinegar
1 teaspoon liquid smoke
1 teaspoon hot sauce
2 tablespoons sesame seeds
1 teaspoon garlic powder
Salt and ground black pepper, to taste
Cooking spray

1. Preheat the air fryer to 375°F (191°C). 2. Spritz a baking dish with cooking spray. 3. Combine all the ingredients to coat the tofu completely and allow the marinade to absorb for half an hour. 4. Transfer the tofu to the baking dish, then air fry for 30 minutes, flipping halfway through. 5. Serve immediately.

Cheddar Broccoli with Bacon

Prep time: 10 minutes | Cook time: 10 minutes | Serves 2

3 cups fresh broccoli florets
1 tablespoon coconut oil
½ cup shredded sharp Cheddar cheese
¼ cup full-fat sour cream
4 slices sugar-free bacon, cooked and crumbled
1 scallion, sliced on the bias

1. Place broccoli into the frying basket and drizzle it with coconut oil. 2. Roast at 350°F (177°C) for 10 minutes until broccoli begins to crisp at ends, tossing the basket two or three times. 3. Top with shredded cheese, sour cream, and crumbled bacon and garnish with scallion slices.

Parmesan-Rosemary Radishes

Prep time: 5 minutes | Cook time: 15 to 20 minutes | Serves 4

1 bunch radishes, stemmed, trimmed, and quartered
1 tablespoon avocado oil
2 tablespoons finely grated fresh Parmesan cheese
1 tablespoon chopped fresh rosemary
Sea salt and freshly ground black pepper, to taste

1. Place the radishes in a bowl and toss them with the avocado oil, Parmesan cheese, rosemary, salt, and pepper. 2. Arrange the radishes in a single layer in the frying basket. Roast at 375°F (191°C) for 15 to 20 minutes, until golden brown and tender. Let cool for 5 minutes before serving.

Tingly Chili-Roasted Broccoli

Prep time: 5 minutes | Cook time: 10 minutes | Serves 2

12 ounces (340 g) broccoli florets
2 tablespoons Asian hot chili oil
1 teaspoon ground Sichuan peppercorns (or black pepper)
2 garlic cloves, finely chopped
1 (2-inch) piece fresh ginger, peeled and finely chopped
Kosher salt and freshly ground black pepper, to taste

1. In a bowl, toss together the broccoli, chili oil, Sichuan peppercorns, garlic, ginger, and salt and black pepper to taste. 2. Transfer to the air fryer and roast at 375°F (191°C) for 10 minutes until lightly charred, shaking the basket halfway through. Serve warm.

Golden Pickles

Prep time: 10 minutes | Cook time: 15 minutes | Serves 4

14 dill pickles, sliced
¼ cup flour
⅛ teaspoon baking powder
Pinch of salt
2 tablespoons cornstarch plus
3 tablespoons water
6 tablespoons panko bread crumbs
½ teaspoon paprika
Cooking spray

1. Preheat the air fryer to 400°F (204°C). 2. Drain moisture out of the dill pickles on a paper towel. 3. In a bowl, combine the flour, baking powder, salt, cornstarch and water mixture and combine well with a whisk. 4. Mix bread crumbs and paprika in a shallow dish. 5. Dip the pickles in the flour batter, then bread crumbs. Spritz with the cooking spray. 6. Air fry for 15 minutes until golden brown. 7. Serve immediately.

Ricotta Potatoes

Prep time: 15 minutes | Cook time: 15 minutes | Serves 4

4 potatoes
2 tablespoons olive oil
½ cup Ricotta cheese, at room temperature
2 tablespoons chopped scallions
1 tablespoon roughly chopped fresh parsley
1 tablespoon minced coriander
2 ounces (57 g) Cheddar cheese, preferably freshly grated
1 teaspoon celery seeds
½ teaspoon salt
½ teaspoon garlic pepper

1. Preheat the air fryer to 350°F (177°C). 2. Pierce the skin of the potatoes with a knife. 3. Air fry for 13 minutes. If they are not cooked through, leave for 2 to 3 minutes longer. 4. Meanwhile, make the stuffing by combining all the other ingredients. 5. Cut halfway into the cooked potatoes to open them. 6. Spoon equal amounts of the stuffing into each potato and serve hot.

Chapter 2 Vegetarian Mains

Pesto Spinach Flatbread

Prep time: 10 minutes | Cook time: 8 minutes | Serves 4

1 cup blanched finely ground almond flour
2 ounces (57 g) cream cheese
2 cups shredded Mozzarella cheese
1 cup chopped fresh spinach leaves
2 tablespoons basil pesto

1. Microwave flour, cream cheese, and Mozzarella in a large microwave-safe bowl on high 45 seconds, then stir. 2. Fold in spinach and microwave an additional 15 seconds. Stir until a soft dough ball forms. 3. Cut two pieces of parchment paper to fit frying basket. Separate dough into two sections and press on parchment to create 6-inch rounds. 4. Spread 1 tablespoon pesto over each flatbread and place into basket. Bake at 350°F (177°C) for 8 minutes until golden, turning crusts halfway through cooking. 5. Let cool 5 minutes before slicing and serving.

Spinach-Artichoke Stuffed Mushrooms

Prep time: 10 minutes | Cook time: 10 to 14 minutes | Serves 4

2 tablespoons olive oil
4 large portobello mushrooms, stems removed and gills scraped out
½ teaspoon salt
¼ teaspoon freshly ground pepper
4 ounces (113 g) goat cheese, crumbled
½ cup chopped marinated artichoke hearts
1 cup frozen spinach, thawed and squeezed dry
½ cup grated Parmesan cheese
2 tablespoons chopped fresh parsley

1. Preheat the air fryer to 400°F (204°C). 2. Rub the portobello mushrooms with olive oil and sprinkle both sides with salt and black pepper. 3. In a bowl, combine the goat cheese, artichoke hearts, and spinach. Mash until thoroughly combined. Divide the cheese mixture among the mushrooms and sprinkle with the Parmesan cheese. 4. Air fry for 10 to 14 minutes until the mushrooms are tender and the cheese has begun to brown. Top with the fresh parsley before serving.

Zucchini-Ricotta Tart

Prep time: 15 minutes | Cook time: 60 minutes | Serves 6

½ cup grated Parmesan cheese, divided
1½ cups almond flour
1 tablespoon coconut flour
½ teaspoon garlic powder
¾ teaspoon salt, divided
¼ cup unsalted butter, melted
1 zucchini, thinly sliced (about 2 cups)
1 cup ricotta cheese
3 eggs
2 tablespoons heavy cream
2 cloves garlic, minced
½ teaspoon dried tarragon

1. Preheat the air fryer to 330°F (166°C). Coat a round pan with olive oil and set aside. 2. In a bowl, whisk ¼ cup Parmesan with the almond flour, coconut flour, garlic powder, and ¼ teaspoon salt. Stir in the melted butter until the dough resembles coarse crumbs. Press the dough firmly into the prepared pan. Air fry for 12 to 15 minutes until the crust begins to brown. Let cool to room temperature. 3. Meanwhile, place the zucchini in a colander and sprinkle with the remaining salt. Toss gently and let sit for 30 minutes. Use paper towels to pat the zucchini dry. 4. In a bowl, whisk together the ricotta, eggs, heavy cream, garlic, and tarragon. Gently stir in the zucchini slices. Pour the cheese mixture into the cooled crust and sprinkle with the remaining Parmesan. 5. Bake at 350°F (177°C) for 45 to 50 minutes until a tester inserted into the center of the tart comes out clean. Serve warm or at room temperature.

Garlic White Zucchini Rolls

Prep time: 20 minutes | Cook time: 20 minutes | Serves 4

2 medium zucchini, cut into long strips lengthwise
2 tablespoons unsalted butter
¼ white onion, peeled and diced
½ teaspoon finely minced roasted garlic
¼ cup heavy cream
2 tablespoons vegetable broth
⅛ teaspoon xanthan gum
½ cup full-fat ricotta cheese
¼ teaspoon salt
½ teaspoon garlic powder
¼ teaspoon dried oregano
2 cups spinach, chopped
½ cup sliced baby portobello mushrooms
¾ cup shredded Mozzarella cheese, divided

1. Place zucchini strips between paper towels to absorb moisture. Set aside. 2. In a medium saucepan over medium heat, melt butter. Add onion and sauté until fragrant. Add garlic and sauté 30 seconds. 3. Pour in heavy cream, broth, and xanthan gum. Turn off heat and whisk mixture until it begins to thicken, about 3 minutes. 4. In a medium bowl, mix ricotta, salt, garlic powder, and oregano. Fold in spinach, mushrooms, and ½ cup Mozzarella. 5. Pour half of the sauce into a round baking pan. To assemble the rolls, place two strips zucchini on a work surface. Spoon 2 tablespoons of ricotta mixture onto the slices and roll up. Place seam side down on top of sauce. Repeat with remaining ingredients. 6. Pour remaining sauce over the rolls and sprinkle with remaining Mozzarella. Cover with foil and place into the frying basket. 7. Bake at 350°F (177°C) for 20 minutes. In the last 5 minutes, remove the foil to brown the cheese. Serve immediately.

Almond-Cauliflower Gnocchi

Prep time: 5 minutes | Cook time: 25 to 30 minutes | Serves 4

5 cups cauliflower florets
⅔ cup almond flour
½ teaspoon salt
¼ cup unsalted butter, melted
¼ cup grated Parmesan cheese

1. Pulse the cauliflower in a food processor until finely chopped. Microwave the cauliflower for 5 minutes in a large microwave-safe bowl and cover with a paper towel. Spread the cauliflower on a towel to cool. 2. When cool enough to handle, completely dry the cauliflower. Pulse cauliflower again until creamy. Sprinkle in the flour and salt and pulse until a sticky dough comes together. 3. Transfer the dough to a workspace floured with almond flour. Divide the dough into 4 equal sections. Roll each section into a rope 1 inch thick and slice into squares with a sharp knife. 4. Place the gnocchi in a single layer in the basket and spray with olive oil. Air fry at 400ºF (204ºC) for 25 to 30 minutes until golden brown and crispy on the edges, turning the gnocchi halfway through the cooking time. Toss with the melted butter and Parmesan cheese to serve.

Cheese Stuffed Zucchini

Prep time: 20 minutes | Cook time: 10 minutes | Serves 4

1 large zucchini, cut into four pieces
2 tablespoons olive oil
1 cup Ricotta cheese, room temperature
2 tablespoons scallions, chopped
1 heaping tablespoon fresh parsley, roughly chopped
1 heaping tablespoon coriander, minced
2 ounces (57 g) Cheddar cheese, preferably freshly grated
1 teaspoon celery seeds
½ teaspoon salt
½ teaspoon garlic pepper

1. Bake the zucchini in frying basket at 350ºF (177ºC) for 10 minutes. Check for doneness and cook for 2 to 3 minutes longer if needed. 2. Meanwhile, make the stuffing by mixing the other items. Divide the stuffing among all zucchini pieces and bake an additional 5 minutes.

Crispy Eggplant Rounds

Prep time: 15 minutes | Cook time: 10 minutes | Serves 4

1 large eggplant, ends trimmed, cut into ½-inch slices
½ teaspoon salt
2 ounces (57 g) Parmesan 100% cheese crisps, finely ground
½ teaspoon paprika
¼ teaspoon garlic powder
1 large egg

1. Sprinkle eggplant with salt. Place on a kitchen towel for 30 minutes to draw out excess water. Pat rounds dry. 2. In a medium bowl, mix cheese crisps, paprika, and garlic powder. In a separate medium bowl, whisk egg. Dip eggplant round in egg, then into cheese crisps to coat both sides. 3. Place eggplant rounds into frying basket. Air fry at 400ºF (204ºC) for 10 minutes until golden and crispy, turning once halfway through cooking. Serve warm.

Cauliflower, Chickpea, and Avocado Mash

Prep time: 10 minutes | Cook time: 25 minutes | Serves 4

1 medium head cauliflower, cut into florets
1 can chickpeas, drained and rinsed
1 tablespoon extra-virgin olive oil
2 tablespoons lemon juice
Salt and ground black pepper, to taste
4 flatbreads, toasted
2 ripe avocados, mashed

1. Preheat the air fryer to 425ºF (218ºC). 2. In a bowl, mix the chickpeas, cauliflower, lemon juice and olive oil. Sprinkle salt and pepper as desired. 3. Put inside the frying basket and air fry for 25 minutes. 4. Spread on top of the flatbread along with the mashed avocado. Sprinkle with more pepper and salt and serve.

Air Fryer Veggies with Halloumi

Prep time: 5 minutes | Cook time: 14 minutes | Serves 2

2 zucchinis, cut into even chunks
1 large eggplant, peeled, cut into chunks
1 large carrot, cut into chunks
6 ounces (170 g) halloumi cheese, cubed
2 teaspoons olive oil
Salt and black pepper, to taste
1 teaspoon dried mixed herbs

1. Preheat the air fryer to 340ºF (171ºC). 2. Combine the zucchinis, eggplant, carrot, cheese, olive oil, salt, and pepper in a bowl and toss to coat well. 3. Spread the mixture evenly in the frying basket and air fry for 14 minutes until crispy and golden, shaking once during cooking. Serve topped with mixed herbs.

Black Bean and Tomato Chili

Prep time: 15 minutes | Cook time: 23 minutes | Serves 6

1 tablespoon olive oil
1 medium onion, diced
3 garlic cloves, minced
1 cup vegetable broth
3 cans black beans, drained and rinsed
2 cans diced tomatoes
2 chipotle peppers, chopped
2 teaspoons cumin
2 teaspoons chili powder
1 teaspoon dried oregano
½ teaspoon salt

1. Over a medium heat, fry the garlic and onions in the olive oil for 3 minutes. 2. Add the remaining ingredients, stirring constantly and scraping the bottom to prevent sticking. 3. Place the mixture in a baking dish. Put a sheet of aluminum foil on top. 4. Bake at 400ºF (204ºC) for 20 minutes. 5. Serve immediately.

Spinach Cheese Casserole

Prep time: 15 minutes | Cook time: 15 minutes | Serves 4

1 tablespoon salted butter, melted
¼ cup diced yellow onion
8 ounces (227 g) full-fat cream cheese, softened
⅓ cup full-fat mayonnaise
⅓ cup full-fat sour cream
¼ cup chopped pickled jalapeños
2 cups fresh spinach, chopped
2 cups cauliflower florets, chopped
1 cup artichoke hearts, chopped

1. In a round baking dish, combine all the ingredients. Cover with foil and place into the frying basket. 2. Bake at 370ºF (188ºC) for 15 minutes. In the last 2 minutes of cooking, remove the foil to brown the top. Serve warm.

Basmati Risotto

Prep time: 10 minutes | Cook time: 30 minutes | Serves 2

1 onion, diced
1 small carrot, diced
2 cups vegetable broth, boiling
½ cup grated Cheddar cheese
1 clove garlic, minced
¾ cup long-grain basmati rice
1 tablespoon olive oil
1 tablespoon unsalted butter

1. Preheat the air fryer to 390ºF (199ºC). 2. Grease a baking tin with oil and stir in the butter, garlic, carrot, and onion. Bake for 4 minutes. 3. Pour in the rice and bake for another 4 minutes, stirring three times throughout the baking time. 4. Add the vegetable broth and give the dish a gentle stir. Bake at 320ºF (160ºC) for 22 minutes, leaving the air fryer uncovered. 5. Pour in the cheese, stir once more and serve.

Broccoli-Cheese Fritters

Prep time: 5 minutes | Cook time: 20 to 25 minutes | Serves 4

1 cup broccoli florets
1 cup shredded Mozzarella cheese
¾ cup almond flour
½ cup flaxseed meal, divided
2 teaspoons baking powder
1 teaspoon garlic powder
Salt and freshly ground black pepper, to taste
2 eggs, lightly beaten
½ cup ranch dressing

1. Preheat the air fryer to 400ºF (204ºC). 2. Pulse the broccoli in a food processor until finely chopped. Combine the broccoli, Mozzarella, almond flour, ¼ cup flaxseed meal, baking powder, and garlic powder in a bowl. Season with salt and black pepper. Add eggs and stir to form a sticky dough. Shape the dough into 1¼-inch fritters. 3. Roll the fritters in the remaining ¼ cup flaxseed meal to form an even coating. 4. Arrange the fritters in a single layer in the basket and spray with olive oil. Air fry for 20 to 25 minutes until golden brown and crispy, shaking once halfway through the cooking time. Serve with the ranch dressing.

Baked Turnip and Zucchini

Prep time: 5 minutes | Cook time: 15 to 20 minutes | Serves 4

3 turnips, sliced
1 large zucchini, sliced
1 large red onion, cut into rings
2 cloves garlic, crushed
1 tablespoon olive oil
Salt and black pepper, to taste

1. Preheat the air fryer to 330ºF (166ºC). 2. Put the turnips, zucchini, red onion, and garlic in a baking pan. Drizzle the olive oil over the top and sprinkle with the salt and pepper. 3. Bake for 15 to 20 minutes until the vegetables are tender. 4. Serve.

Mushroom and Pepper Pizza Squares

Prep time: 10 minutes | Cook time: 10 minutes | Serves 10

1 pizza dough, cut into squares
1 cup chopped oyster mushrooms
1 shallot, chopped
¼ red bell pepper, chopped
2 tablespoons parsley
Salt and ground black pepper, to taste

1. Preheat the air fryer to 400ºF (204ºC). 2. In a bowl, combine the oyster mushrooms, shallot, bell pepper and parsley. Sprinkle some salt and pepper as desired. 3. Spread this mixture on top of the pizza squares. 4. Bake in the air fryer for 10 minutes. 5. Serve warm.

Sweet Potatoes with Zucchini

Prep time: 20 minutes | Cook time: 20 minutes | Serves 4

2 large-sized sweet potatoes, peeled and quartered
1 medium zucchini, sliced
1 Serrano pepper, deseeded and thinly sliced
1 bell pepper, deseeded and thinly sliced
1 to 2 carrots, cut into matchsticks
¼ cup olive oil
1½ tablespoons maple syrup
½ teaspoon porcini powder
¼ teaspoon mustard powder
½ teaspoon fennel seeds
1 tablespoon garlic powder
½ teaspoon fine sea salt
¼ teaspoon ground black pepper
Tomato ketchup, for serving

1. Put the sweet potatoes, zucchini, peppers, and carrot into the frying basket. Coat with a drizzling of olive oil. 2. Preheat the air fryer to 350ºF (177ºC). Air fry the vegetables for 15 minutes. 3. Meanwhile, prepare the sauce by combining the other ingredients, except for the tomato ketchup, with a whisk. 4. Transfer the vegetables to a greased baking dish, pour over the sauce and coat the vegetables well. 5. Air fry at 390ºF (199ºC) for 5 minutes. 6. Serve warm with ketchup.

Super Veg Rolls

Prep time: 20 minutes | Cook time: 10 minutes | Serves 6

2 potatoes, mashed
¼ cup peas
¼ cup mashed carrots
1 small cabbage, sliced
¼ cups beans
2 tablespoons sweetcorn
1 small onion, chopped
½ cup bread crumbs
1 packet spring roll sheets
½ cup cornstarch slurry

1. Preheat the air fryer to 390ºF (199ºC). 2. Boil all the vegetables in water over a low heat. Rinse and allow to dry. 3. Unroll the spring roll sheets and spoon equal amounts of vegetable onto the center of each one. Fold into spring rolls and coat each one with the slurry and bread crumbs. 4. Air fry for 10 minutes and serve warm.

Quiche-Stuffed Peppers

Prep time: 5 minutes | Cook time: 15 minutes | Serves 2

2 medium green bell peppers
3 large eggs
¼ cup full-fat ricotta cheese
¼ cup diced yellow onion
½ cup chopped broccoli
½ cup shredded medium Cheddar cheese

1. Cut the tops off of the peppers and remove the seeds and white membranes with a small knife. 2. In a medium bowl, whisk eggs and ricotta. Add onion and broccoli. Pour the egg and vegetable mixture evenly into each pepper. Top with Cheddar. Place peppers into a 4-cup round baking dish and place into the frying basket. 3. Bake at 350ºF (177ºC) for 15 minutes. 4. Serve immediately.

Parmesan Artichokes

Prep time: 10 minutes | Cook time: 10 minutes | Serves 4

2 medium artichokes, trimmed and quartered, center removed
2 tablespoons coconut oil
1 large egg, beaten
½ cup grated vegetarian Parmesan cheese
¼ cup blanched finely ground almond flour
½ teaspoon crushed red pepper flakes

1. In a bowl, toss artichokes in coconut oil and then dip into the egg. 2. Mix the Parmesan and almond flour in a bowl. Add artichoke pieces and toss well, sprinkle with pepper flakes. Place into the frying basket. 3. Air fry at 400ºF (204ºC) for 10 minutes, tossing the basket two times. Serve warm.

Cheese Stuffed Peppers

Prep time: 20 minutes | Cook time: 15 minutes | Serves 2

1 red bell pepper, top and seeds removed
1 yellow bell pepper, top and seeds removed
Salt and pepper, to taste
1 cup Cottage cheese
4 tablespoons mayonnaise
2 pickles, chopped

1. Arrange the peppers in the lightly greased frying basket. Roast at 400ºF (204ºC) for 15 minutes, turning once halfway through the cooking time. 2. Season with salt and pepper. In a mixing bowl, combine the cream cheese with the mayonnaise and chopped pickles. Stuff the pepper with the cream cheese mixture and serve. Enjoy!

Chapter 3 Breakfasts

Breakfast Potatoes with Pepper and Onion

Prep time: 10 minutes | Cook time: 20 minutes | Serves 6

4 large potatoes, cubed
2 bell peppers, cut into 1-inch chunks
½ onion, diced
2 teaspoons olive oil
1 garlic clove, minced
½ teaspoon dried thyme
½ teaspoon cayenne pepper
Salt to taste

1. Preheat the air fryer to 390°F (199°C). Place the potato cubes in a bowl and sprinkle with garlic, cayenne pepper, and salt. Drizzle with some olive oil and toss to coat. Arrange the potatoes in an even layer in the greased frying basket. Air fry for 10 minutes, shaking once halfway through cooking. 2. In the meantime, add the remaining olive oil, garlic, thyme, and salt in a mixing bowl. Add in the bell peppers and onion and mix well. Pour the veggies over the potatoes and continue cooking for 10 more minutes. At the 5-minute mark, shake the basket and cook for 5 minutes. Serve warm.

Classic Hash Brown Potatoes

Prep time: 15 minutes | Cook time: 12 minutes | Serves 4

1 pound (454 g) potatoes, peeled and shredded
Salt and black pepper to taste
1 teaspoon garlic powder
1 teaspoon chili flakes
1 teaspoon onion powder
1 egg, beaten
1 tablespoon olive oil

1. Heat olive oil in a skillet over medium heat and sauté potatoes for 10 minutes; transfer to a bowl to cool. When cooled, add in the egg, black pepper, salt, chili flakes, onion powder, and garlic powder; mix well. On a flat plate, spread the mixture and pat it firmly with your fingers. Refrigerate for 20 minutes. 2. Preheat the air fryer to 350°F (177°C). Shape the cooled mixture into patties. Arrange them on the greased frying basket and air fry for 12 minutes, flipping once halfway through. Serve warm.

Austrian Torn Pancake

Prep time: 10 minutes | Cook time: 6 to 8 minutes | Serves 4

3 eggs, whites and yolks separated
1 tablespoon sugar
2 tablespoons butter, melted
1 cup flour
2 tablespoons sugar, powdered
½ cup milk
2 tablespoons raisins, soaked in rum
1 cup plum sauce

1. Preheat the air fryer to 350°F (177°C). In a bowl, mix flour, milk, and egg yolks until fully incorporated; stir in the drained raisins. Beat the egg whites with sugar until stiff. Gently fold the whites into the yolk mixture. Grease a baking pan with butter and pour in the batter. Place the pan inside the frying basket. 2. Bake for 6 to 8 minutes until the pancake is fluffy and golden brown. Break the pancake into pieces using two forks and dust with powdered sugar. Serve with plum sauce and enjoy!

Bacon Cheddar Potato Skins

Prep time: 10 minutes | Cook time: 20 minutes | Serves 4

4 eggs
2 large russet potatoes, scrubbed
1 tablespoon olive oil
2 tablespoons cooked bacon, chopped
1 cup Cheddar cheese, shredded
1 tablespoon chopped chives
¼ teaspoon red pepper flakes
Salt and black pepper to taste

1. Preheat the air fryer to 360°F (182°C). Using a fork, poke holes all over the potatoes, then cook them in the microwave on high for 5 minutes. Flip them and cook in the microwave for another 3 to 5 minutes. Test with a fork to make sure they are tender. Halve the potatoes lengthwise and scoop out most of the 'meat,' leaving enough potato, so 'boat' sides don't collapse. 2. Coat the skin side of the potatoes with olive oil, salt, and black pepper for taste. Arrange the potatoes, skin down, in the lightly greased frying basket. Crack an egg and put it in the scooped potato, one egg for each half. Divide the bacon and Cheddar cheese between the potatoes and sprinkle with salt and pepper. For a runny yolk, Air fry for 5 to 6 minutes, and for a solid yolk, Air fry for 7 to 10 minutes. Sprinkle with red pepper flakes and chives to serve.

Salami, Prosciutto and Sausage Omelet

Prep time: 10 minutes | Cook time: 10 to 12 minutes | Serves 2

1 beef sausage, chopped
4 slices prosciutto, chopped
3 ounces (85 g) salami, chopped
1 cup Mozzarella cheese, grated
4 eggs
1 green onion, chopped
1 tablespoon ketchup
1 teaspoon fresh parsley, chopped

1. Preheat the air fryer to 350°F (177°C). Whisk the eggs with ketchup in a bowl. Stir in the green onion, Mozzarella, salami, and prosciutto. Air fry the sausage in a greased baking pan inside the fryer for 2 minutes. Slide out and pour the egg mixture over. Bake for 8 to 10 more minutes until golden. Serve topped with parsley.

Indian Omelet

Prep time: 10 minutes | Cook time: 8 minutes | Serves 1

1 garlic clove, crushed
1 green onion
½ chili powder
½ teaspoon garam masala
2 eggs
1 tablespoon olive oil
1 tablespoon fresh cilantro, chopped
Salt and black pepper to taste

1. Preheat the air fryer to 360ºF (182ºC). In a bowl, whisk the eggs with salt and black pepper. Add in the green onion, garlic, chili powder, and garam masala; stir well. Transfer to a greased baking pan. Bake in the fryer for 8 minutes until the top is golden and the eggs are set. Scatter with fresh cilantro and serve.

Tamagoyaki

Prep time: 10 minutes | Cook time: 8 minutes | Serves 1

½ cup cubed tofu
3 whole eggs
Salt and black pepper to taste
¼ teaspoon ground coriander
¼ teaspoon cumin
1 teaspoon soy sauce
1 tablespoon green onions, chopped
¼ onion, chopped

1. In a bowl, mix eggs, onion, soy sauce, ground coriander, cumin, black pepper, and salt. Add in the tofu and pour the mixture into a greased baking pan. Place in the preheated air fryer and bake for 8 minutes at 360ºF (182ºC). Remove, and let cool for 2 minutes. Sprinkle with green onions and serve.

Cheesy Egg-Kale Omelet

Prep time: 10 minutes | Cook time: 10 minutes | Serves 2

5 eggs
3 tablespoons cottage cheese, crumbled
1 cup kale, chopped
½ tablespoon fresh basil, chopped
½ tablespoon fresh parsley, chopped
Salt and black pepper to taste

1. Beat the eggs, salt, and black pepper in a bowl. Stir in the rest of the ingredients. Pour the mixture into a greased baking pan and fit in the air fryer. Bake for 10 minutes at 330ºF (166ºC) until slightly golden and set.

Ham and Cheddar Omelet

Prep time: 5 minutes | Cook time: 6 to 8 minutes | Serves 2

4 eggs
3 tablespoons Cheddar cheese, grated
1 teaspoon soy sauce
½ cup ham, chopped

1. Preheat the air fryer to 350ºF (177ºC). In a bowl, whisk the eggs with soy sauce. Fold in the chopped ham and mix well to combine. Spoon the egg mixture into a greased baking pan and pour into the frying basket. Bake for 6 to 8 minutes until golden on top. Sprinkle with the Cheddar cheese and serve warm.

Bacon Omelet Cups

Prep time: 15 minutes | Cook time: 6 to 8 minutes | Serves 4

4 crusty rolls
5 eggs, beaten
½ teaspoon thyme, dried
3 strips cooked bacon, chopped
2 tablespoons heavy cream
4 Gouda cheese thin slices

1. Preheat the air fryer to 330ºF (166ºC). Cut the tops off the rolls and remove the inside with your fingers. Line the rolls with a slice of cheese and press down, so the cheese conforms to the inside of the roll. 2. In a bowl, mix the eggs, heavy cream, bacon, and thyme. Stuff the rolls with the egg mixture. Lay them in the greased frying basket and bake for 6 to 8 minutes or until the eggs become puffy, and the roll shows a golden brown texture. Remove and let them cool for a few minutes before serving.

Spinach and Tomato Frittata

Prep time: 10 minutes | Cook time: 17 to 19 minutes | Serves 4

5 eggs
1 cup baby spinach
½ cup grape tomatoes, halved
½ cup feta cheese, crumbled
10 Kalamata olives, sliced
Salt and black pepper to taste
2 tablespoons fresh parsley, chopped

1. Preheat the air fryer to 360ºF (182ºC). Beat the eggs, salt, and black pepper in a bowl, until well combined. Add in the spinach and stir until well mixed. Pour half the mixture into a greased baking pan. 2. On top of the mixture, add half of the tomatoes, olives, and feta cheese. Cover the pan with foil, making sure to close it tightly around the edges, then place it inside the air fryer and bake for 12 minutes. 3. Remove the foil and cook for an additional 5 to 7 minutes, until the eggs are fully cooked. Place the finished frittata on a serving plate and repeat the above instructions for the remaining ingredients. Decorate with fresh parsley and cut into wedges. Serve hot or at room temperature.

Potato Chorizo Frittata with Manchego

Prep time: 10 minutes | Cook time: 8 to 10 minutes | Serves 2

4 eggs
1 large potato, boiled and cubed
¼ cup Manchego cheese, grated
1 tablespoon parsley, chopped
1 Spanish chorizo, chopped
½ small red onion, chopped
¼ teaspoon paprika
Salt and black pepper to taste

1. Preheat the air fryer to 330ºF (166ºC). In a bowl, beat the eggs with paprika, salt, and pepper. Stir in all of the remaining ingredients, except for the parsley. Spread the egg batter on the greased baking pan and insert it into the air fryer. Bake for 8 to 10 minutes until the top is golden. Garnish with parsley to serve.

Parmesan Sausage Frittata

Prep time: 10 minutes | Cook time: 8 minutes | Serves 2

2 Vienna sausages, sliced
Salt and black pepper to taste
1 tablespoon fresh parsley, chopped
½ cup milk
4 eggs
½ teaspoon red pepper flakes, crushed
4 cherry tomatoes, halved
2 tablespoons Parmesan cheese, shredded

1. Preheat the air fryer to 360ºF (182ºC). In a bowl, whisk the eggs and milk. Stir in the Parmesan cheese, red pepper flakes, salt, parsley, and black pepper. Add the mixture to a lightly greased baking pan and top with sausage slices and cherry tomatoes. Bake in the fryer for 8 minutes until the eggs are set. Serve hot.

Air Fried Shirred Eggs

Prep time: 10 minutes | Cook time: 10 to 12 minutes | Serves 2

2 teaspoons butter, melted
4 eggs
2 tablespoons heavy cream
4 smoked ham slices
3 tablespoons Parmesan
cheese, grated
¼ teaspoon paprika
Salt and black pepper to taste
2 teaspoons fresh chives, chopped

1. Preheat the air fryer to 320ºF (160ºC). Lightly grease 4 ramekins with butter. Line the bottom of each ramekin with a piece of smoked ham. Crack the eggs on top of the ham and season with salt and pepper. Drizzle with heavy cream and sprinkle with Parmesan cheese. Air fry for 10 to 12 minutes until the eggs are completely set. Garnish with paprika and fresh chives to serve.

Breakfast Shrimp and Egg Muffins

Prep time: 10 minutes | Cook time: 16 minutes | Serves 4

4 eggs, beaten
2 tablespoons olive oil
½ small red bell pepper, finely diced
1 garlic clove, minced
4 ounces (113 g) shrimp,
cooked, chopped
4 teaspoons ricotta cheese, crumbled
1 teaspoon dry dill
Salt and black pepper to taste

1. Preheat the air fryer to 360ºF (182ºC). Warm the olive oil in a skillet over medium heat. Sauté the bell pepper and garlic until the pepper is soft, then add the shrimp. Season with dill, salt, and pepper and cook for about 5 minutes. Remove from the heat and mix in the eggs. Grease 4 ramekins with cooking spray. 2. Divide the mixture between the ramekins. Place them in the air fryer and bake for 6 minutes. Remove and stir the mixture. Sprinkle with ricotta and return to the fryer. Bake for 5 more minutes until the eggs are set, and the top is lightly browned. Let sit for 2 minutes, invert on a plate while warm, and serve.

Prosciutt Eggs Cups

Prep time: 15 minutes | Cook time: 10 to 12 minutes | Serves 2

4 prosciutto slices
2 eggs
4 tomato slices
¼ teaspoon balsamic vinegar
2 tablespoons Mozzarella
cheese, grated
¼ teaspoon maple syrup
2 tablespoons mayonnaise
Salt and black pepper to taste

1. Preheat the air fryer to 350ºF (177ºC). Grease 2 cups with cooking spray. Line the bottom and sides of each cup with prosciutto, patching up any holes using little pieces if necessary. Place the tomato slices on top and divide the Mozzarella cheese between the cups. Crack the eggs over the Mozzarella cheese and drizzle with maple syrup and balsamic vinegar. Season with salt and pepper. Bake in the fryer until the egg whites are just set, about 10 to 12 minutes. Top with mayonnaise and serve.

Egg-Pumpkin Bread

Prep time: 15 minutes | Cook time: 25 minutes | Serves 6

1 cup pumpkin, peeled and shredded
1 cup flour
1 teaspoon ground nutmeg
½ teaspoon salt
¼ teaspoon baking powder
2 eggs
½ cup sugar
¼ cup milk
2 tablespoons butter, melted
½ teaspoon vanilla extract
2 tablespoons sultanas, soaked
1 tablespoon honey
1 tablespoon canola oil

1. Preheat the air fryer to 350ºF (177ºC). In a bowl, beat the eggs and add pumpkin, sugar, milk, canola oil, sultanas, and vanilla. In a separate bowl, sift the flour and mix in nutmeg, salt, butter, and baking powder. 2. Combine the 2 mixtures and stir until a thick cake mixture forms. Spoon the batter into a greased baking dish and place it in the air fryer. Bake for 25 minutes until a toothpick inserted in the center comes out clean and dry. Remove to a wire rack to cool completely. Drizzle with honey and serve.

Ham and Hash Brown Cups

Prep time: 10 minutes | Cook time: 8 to 10 minutes | Serves 6

4 eggs, beaten
1 tablespoon olive oil
½ cup Colby cheese, shredded
2¼ cups frozen hash browns,
thawed
1 cup smoked ham, chopped
½ teaspoon Cajun seasoning

1. Preheat the air fryer to 360ºF (182ºC). Gather 12 silicone muffin cups and coat with olive oil. Whisk the eggs, hash browns, smoked ham, Colby cheese, and Cajun seasoning in a large bowl and add a heaping spoonful into each muffin cup. Put the muffin cups in the frying basket and air fry 8 to 10 minutes until golden brown and the center is set. Transfer to a wire rack to cool completely. Serve.

Egg in a Hole

Prep time: 5 minutes | Cook time: 8 minutes | Serves 2

2 bread slices
2 eggs
Salt and black pepper to taste
1 tablespoon butter, softened

1. Preheat the air fryer to 360ºF (182ºC). Place a heatproof pan in the frying basket and brush with butter. Make a hole in the middle of the bread slices with a bread knife and place in the heatproof pan in 2 batches. Crack an egg into the center of each hole; adjust the seasoning. Bake in the air fryer for 4 minutes. Turn the bread with a spatula and cook for another 4 minutes. Serve warm.

Turkey and Mushroom Sandwich

Prep time: 10 minutes | Cook time: 5 to 8 minutes | Serves 1

⅓ cup leftover turkey, shredded
⅓ cup sliced mushrooms, sauteed
½ tablespoon butter, softened
2 tomato slices
½ teaspoon red pepper flakes
Salt and black pepper to taste
1 hamburger bun, halved

1. Preheat the air fryer to 350ºF (177ºC). Brush the bun bottom with butter and top with shredded turkey. Arrange the mushroom slices on top of the turkey. Cover with tomato slices and sprinkle with salt, black pepper, and red flakes. Top with the bun top and air fry for 5 to 8 minutes until crispy. Serve and enjoy!

Sourdough Sandwiches

Prep time: 5 minutes | Cook time: 12 minutes | Serves 2

4 slices sourdough bread
2 tablespoons mayonnaise
2 slices ham
2 lettuce leaves
1 tomato, sliced
2 slices Mozzarella cheese

1. Preheat the air fryer to 350ºF (177ºC). On a clean working board, lay the bread slices and spread them with mayonnaise. Top 2 of the slices with ham, lettuce leaves, tomato slices, and Mozzarella. Cover with the remaining bread slices to form two sandwiches. Air fry for 12 minutes, flipping once. Serve hot.

Crisp Pepper Rings with Cherry Tomatoes

Prep time: 5 minutes | Cook time: 6 to 9 minutes | Serves 4

4 eggs
1 bell pepper, cut into four ¾-inch rings
5 cherry tomatoes, halved
Salt and black pepper to taste

1. Preheat the air fryer to 360ºF (182ºC). Add the bell pepper rings to a greased baking pan and crack an egg into each one. Season with salt and black pepper. Top with the halved cherry tomatoes. Put the pan into the air fryer and air fry for 6 to 9 minutes, or until the eggs are have set. Serve and enjoy!

Cheesy Sausage Casserole

Prep time: 15 minutes | Cook time: 15 minutes | Serves 6

2 tablespoons olive oil
1 pound (454 g) Italian sausages
6 eggs
1 red pepper, diced
1 green pepper, diced
1 yellow pepper, diced
1 sweet onion, diced
1 cup Cheddar cheese, shredded
Salt and black pepper to taste
2 tablespoons fresh parsley, chopped

1. Warm the olive oil in a skillet over medium heat. Add the sausages and brown them slightly, turning occasionally, about 5 minutes. Once done, drain any excess fat derived from cooking and set aside. 2. Arrange the sausages on the bottom of a greased casserole dish that fits in your air fryer. Top with onion, red pepper, green pepper, and yellow pepper. Sprinkle with Cheddar cheese on top. 3. In a bowl, beat the eggs with salt and pepper. Pour the mixture over the cheese. Place the casserole dish in the frying basket and bake at 360ºF (182ºC) for 15 minutes. Serve warm garnished with fresh parsley.

Tofu and Cabbage Sandwich

Prep time: 10 minutes | Cook time: 13 minutes | Serves 1

2 slices of bread
1 tofu slice, 1-inch thick
¼ cup red cabbage, shredded
2 teaspoons olive oil
¼ teaspoon vinegar
Salt to taste

1. Preheat the air fryer to 350ºF (177ºC). Add the bread slices to the frying basket and air fry for 3 minutes; set aside. Brush the tofu with some olive oil and place in the air fryer. Air fry for 5 minutes on each side. 2. Mix the cabbage, remaining olive oil, and vinegar. Season with salt. Place the tofu on top of one bread slice, place the cabbage over, and top with the other bread slice. Serve with cream cheese-mustard dip.

Vanilla French Toast

Prep time: 10 minutes | Cook time: 10 minutes | Serves 3

6 white bread slices
2 eggs
¼ cup milk
3 tablespoons caramel sauce
⅓ cup cream cheese, softened
1 teaspoon vanilla extract
⅓ cup sugar mixed with 1 teaspoon ground cinnamon

1. In a bowl, mix the cream cheese, caramel sauce, and vanilla. Spread three of the bread slices with the cheese mixture around the center. Place the remaining three slices on top to form three sandwiches. 2. Whisk the eggs and milk in a bowl. Dip the sandwiches into the egg mixture. Arrange them in the greased frying basket and air fry for 10 minutes at 340ºF (171ºC), turning once. Dust with the cinnamon mixture.

French Brioche Toast

Prep time: 10 minutes | Cook time: 7 to 8 minutes | Serves 2

4 slices of brioche
3 eggs
4 tablespoons butter
6 ounces (170 g) Nutella spread
½ cup heavy cream
1 teaspoon vanilla extract
1 tablespoon icing sugar
½ cup fresh strawberries, sliced

1. Preheat the air fryer to 350ºF (177ºC). 2. Beat the eggs along with heavy cream and vanilla in a small bowl. Dip the brioche slices in the egg mixture and air fry in the greased frying basket for 7 to 8 minutes in total, shaking once or twice. Spread two pieces of the toast with a thin layer of Nutella and cover with the remaining toast pieces. Dust with icing sugar and top with strawberries. Serve and enjoy!

Bacon and Egg Sandwich

Prep time: 5 minutes | Cook time: 4 to 6 minutes | Serves 1

1 egg, fried
1 slice English bacon
Salt and black pepper to taste
2 bread slices
½ tablespoon butter, softened

1. Preheat the air fryer to 400ºF (204ºC). Spread butter on one side of the bread slices. Add the fried egg on top and season with salt and black pepper. Top with the bacon and cover with the other slice of the bread. Place in the frying basket and air fry for 4 to 6 minutes. Serve warm.

Classic Avocado Toast

Prep time: 5 minutes | Cook time: 3 minutes | Serves 2

2 slices thick whole grain bread
4 thin tomato slices
1 ripe avocado, pitted, peeled,
and sliced
1 tablespoon olive oil
1 tablespoon pinch of salt
½ teaspoon chili flakes

1. Preheat the air fryer to 370ºF (188ºC). Arrange the bread slices in the frying basket and toast them for 3 minutes. Add the avocado to a bowl and mash it up with a fork until smooth. Season with salt. 2. When the toasted bread is ready, remove it to a plate. Spread the avocado and cover with thin tomato slices. Drizzle with olive oil, sprinkle the toasts with chili flakes and serve.

Very Berry Breakfast Puffs

Prep time: 15 minutes | Cook time: 15 minutes | Serves 4

1 puff pastry sheet
1 tablespoon strawberries, mashed
1 tablespoon raspberries,
mashed
¼ teaspoon vanilla extract
1 cup cream cheese
1 tablespoon honey

1. Preheat the air fryer to 375ºF (191ºC). Roll the puff pastry out on a lightly floured surface into a 1-inch thick rectangle. Cut into 4 squares. Spread the cream cheese evenly on top of them. In a bowl, combine the berries, honey, and vanilla. Spoon the mixture onto the pastry squares. Fold in the sides over the filling. Pinch the ends to form a puff. Place the puffs in the greased frying basket. Bake in the air fryer for 15 minutes until the pastry is puffed and golden all over. Let it cool for 10 minutes before serving.

Traditional Romanian Polenta

Prep time: 10 minutes | Cook time: 14 to 16 minutes | Serves 4

2 cups milk
1 cup instant polenta
Salt and black pepper to taste
2 tablespoons fresh thyme, chopped

1. Line a baking dish with parchment paper. Pour 2 cups of milk and 2 cups of water into a saucepan and let simmer. Keep whisking as you pour in the polenta. Continue to whisk until the polenta thickens and bubbles; season to taste. Add polenta into the lined dish and spread out. Refrigerate for 45 minutes. 2. Preheat the air fryer to 380ºF (193ºC). Slice the polenta into batons. Arrange the chips in the greased frying basket and sprinkle with thyme. Air fry for 14 to 16 minutes, turning once, until the fries are crispy.

Soppressata Pizza

Prep time: 10 minutes | Cook time: 10 minutes | Serves 2

1 pizza crust
½ teaspoon dried oregano
½ cup passata
½ cup Mozzarella cheese,
shredded
4 ounces (113 g) soppressata, chopped
4 basil leaves

1. Preheat the air fryer to 370ºF (188ºC). Spread the passata over the pizza crust, sprinkle with oregano, m⅓zarella, and finish with soppressata. Bake in the fryer for 10 minutes. Top with basil leaves and serve.

Tomato, Prosciutto and Basil Bruschetta

Prep time: 5 minutes | Cook time: 4 minutes | Serves 2

½ cup tomatoes, finely chopped
3 ounces (85 g) Mozzarella cheese, grated
3 prosciutto slices, chopped
1 tablespoon olive oil
1 teaspoon dried basil
6 small French bread slices

1. Preheat the air fryer to 350ºF (177ºC). Add in the bread slices and fry for 3 minutes to toast them. Remove and top the slices with tomatoes, prosciutto, and Mozzarella cheese. Sprinkle basil all over and drizzle with olive oil. Return to the fryer and air fry for 1 more minute, just to heat through. Serve warm.

Easy Calzone

Prep time: 15 minutes | Cook time: 10 to 12 minutes | Serves 4

1 pizza dough
4 ounces (113 g) Cheddar cheese, grated
1 ounce (28 g) Mozzarella cheese, grated
1 ounce (28 g) bacon, diced
2 cups cooked turkey, shredded
1 egg, beaten
4 tablespoons tomato paste
½ teaspoon dried basil
½ teaspoon dried oregano
Salt and black pepper to taste

1. Preheat the air fryer to 350ºF (177ºC). Divide the pizza dough into 4 equal pieces, so you have the dough for 4 pizza crusts. Combine the tomato paste, basil, and oregano in a small bowl. Brush the mixture onto the crusts; make sure not to go all the way to avoid brushing near the edges of each crust. 2. Scatter half of the turkey on top and season with salt and black pepper. Top with bacon, Mozzarella and Cheddar cheeses. Brush the edges with the beaten egg. Fold the crusts and seal with a fork. Bake for 10 to 12 minutes until puffed and golden, turning it over halfway through cooking. Serve warm.

Vanilla Banana Bread with Walnuts

Prep time: 10 minutes | Cook time: 20 to 25 minutes | Serves 2

1 cup flour
¼ teaspoon baking soda
1 teaspoon baking powder
⅓ cup sugar
2 bananas, mashed
¼ cup vegetable oil
1 egg, beaten
1 teaspoon vanilla extract
¾ cup walnuts, chopped
¼ teaspoon salt
2 tablespoons peanut butter, softened
2 tablespoons sour cream

1. Preheat the air fryer to 350ºF (177ºC). Sift the flour into a large bowl and add salt, baking powder, and baking soda; stir to combine. In another bowl, combine bananas, vegetable oil, egg, peanut butter, vanilla, sugar, and sour cream; stir well. Mix both mixtures and fold in the walnuts. Pour the batter into a greased baking dish and place in the fryer. Bake for 20 to 25 minutes until nice and golden. Serve chilled.

Greek Feta Cheese Triangles

Prep time: 10 minutes | Cook time: 8 minutes | Serves 3

1 cup feta cheese
1 onion, chopped
½ teaspoon parsley dried
1 egg yolk
2 tablespoons olive oil
3 sheets filo pastry

1. Cut each of the filo sheets into 3 equal-sized strips. Brush the strips with some olive oil. 2. In a bowl, mix onion, feta cheese, egg yolk, and parsley. Divide the mixture between the strips and fold each diagonally to make triangles. Arrange them in the a greased frying basket and brush the tops with the remaining olive oil. Place in the fryer and bake for 8 minutes at 360ºF (182ºC). Serve warm.

Herb Toasted Bagel

Prep time: 5 minutes | Cook time: 6 minutes | Serves 1

1 tablespoon butter, softened
¼ teaspoon dried basil
¼ teaspoon dried parsley
¼ teaspoon garlic powder
1 tablespoon Parmesan cheese, grated
Salt and black pepper to taste
1 bagel, halved

1. Preheat the air fryer to 370 degrees. Place the bagel halves in the frying basket and air fry for 3 minutes. Mix butter, Parmesan cheese, garlic, basil, and parsley in a bowl. Season with salt and pepper. Spread the mixture onto the toasted bagel and return to the fryer to air fry for 3 more minutes.

Apple Sandwich with Brie Cheese

Prep time: 5 minutes | Cook time: 5 minutes | Serves 1

2 bread slices
½ apple, thinly sliced
2 teaspoons butter
2 ounces (57 g) brie cheese, thinly sliced

1. Spread butter on the outside of the bread slices and top with apple slices. Place the brie slices on top of the apple and cover with the other slice of bread. Bake in the air fryer for 5 minutes at 350ºF (177ºC). When ready, remove and cut diagonally to serve.

Corn Blueberry Toast

Prep time: 10 minutes | Cook time: 8 minutes | Serves 2

2 eggs, beaten
4 bread slices
1 tablespoon maple syrup
1½ cups corn flakes
⅓ cup milk
¼ teaspoon ground nutmeg
1 cup fresh blueberries

1. Preheat the air fryer to 390ºF (199ºC). In a bowl, mix the eggs, nutmeg, and milk. Dip the bread slices in the egg mixture, then thoroughly coat them in corn flakes. Air fry them in the greased frying basket for 8 minutes, turning once halfway through cooking. Drizzle with maple syrup and top blueberries. Serve.

Bacon Tortilla Wraps with Salsa

Prep time: 10 minutes | Cook time: 10 minutes | Serves 3

3 flour tortillas
2 eggs, scrambled
3 slices bacon, cut into strips
3 tablespoons salsa
3 tablespoons cream cheese
1 cup Pepper Jack cheese, grated

1. Preheat the air fryer to 390ºF (199ºC). Spread cream cheese on the tortillas. Add the eggs and bacon and top with salsa. Scatter with grated Pepper Jack cheese and roll up tightly. Place in the frying basket and air fry for 10 minutes or until golden. Cut in half and serve warm.

Basic Welsh Rarebit

Prep time: 10 minutes | Cook time: 10 minutes | Serves 2

4 toasted bread slices
1 teaspoon smoked paprika
2 eggs, beaten
1 teaspoon Dijon mustard
4½ ounces (128 g) Cheddar cheese, grated
Salt and black pepper to taste

1. Preheat the fryer to 360ºF (182ºC). In a bowl, combine the eggs, mustard, Cheddar, and paprika. Season with salt and pepper. Spread the mixture on the bread slices and air fry them for 10 minutes or until golden.

Simple Mango Bread

Prep time: 15 minutes | Cook time: 18 to 20 minutes | Serves 6

½ cup butter, melted
1 egg, lightly beaten
½ cup brown sugar
1 teaspoon vanilla extract
3 ripe mangoes, mashed
1½ cups flour
1 teaspoon baking powder
½ teaspoon grated nutmeg
½ teaspoon ground cinnamon

1. Line a loaf tin with baking paper. In a bowl, whisk melted butter, egg, sugar, vanilla, and mangoes. Sift in flour, baking powder, nutmeg, and ground cinnamon and stir without overmixing. Pour the batter into the tin and place it in the frying basket. Bake for 18 to 20 minutes at 330ºF (166ºC). Let cool before slicing. Serve.

Tomato and Olive Quiche

Prep time: 15 minutes | Cook time: 30 minutes | Serves 2

4 eggs
½ cup tomatoes, chopped
1 cup feta cheese, crumbled
½ tablespoon fresh basil, chopped
½ tablespoon fresh oregano, chopped
¼ cup Kalamata olives, sliced
¼ cup onions, chopped
½ cup milk
Salt and black pepper to taste

1. Preheat the air fryer to 340ºF (171ºC). Beat the eggs with the milk, salt, and pepper in a bowl. Stir in all the remaining ingredients. Pour the egg mixture into a greased baking pan that fits in your air fryer and bake for 30 minutes or until lightly golden. Serve warm with a green salad if desired.

Cheesy Mushroom-Broccoli Pie

Prep time: 10 minutes | Cook time: 11 to 14 minutes | Serves 4

4 eggs, beaten
1 cup mushrooms, sliced
1 cup broccoli florets, steamed
½ cup Cheddar cheese, shredded
½ cup Mozzarella cheese, shredded
2 tablespoons olive oil
¼ teaspoon ground allspice
Salt and black pepper to taste

1. Preheat the air fryer to 360ºF (182ºC). Warm the olive oil in a pan over medium heat. Sauté the mushrooms for 3 to 4 minutes or until soft. Stir the broccoli for 1 minute; set aside. 2. Place the eggs, Cheddar cheese, Mozzarella cheese, allspice, salt, and pepper in a medium bowl and whisk well. Pour the mushrooms' mixture into the egg mixture and gently fold it in. Transfer the batter to a greased baking pan and into the fryer. Air fry for 5 minutes, then stir the mixture and cook until the eggs are done, about 3 to 5 more minutes. Cut into wedges and serve.

Peanut Butter Porridge

Prep time: 5 minutes | Cook time: 10 minutes | Serves 4

1 cup steel-cut oats
1 tablespoon flax seeds
1 tablespoon peanut butter
1 tablespoon butter
1 cup milk
2 tablespoons honey

1. Preheat the air fryer to 350ºF (177ºC). Combine all ingredients in an ovenproof bowl. Place the bowl in the air fryer and bake for 10 minutes. Let cool for a few minutes before serving. Enjoy!

Cinnamon Zucchini Muffins

Prep time: 10 minutes | Cook time: 18 to 20 minutes | Serves 4

1½ cups flour
1 teaspoon cinnamon
3 eggs
2 teaspoons baking powder
½ teaspoon sugar
1 cup milk
2 tablespoons butter, melted
1 tablespoon yogurt
1 zucchini, shredded
A pinch of salt
2 tablespoons cream cheese

1. Preheat the air fryer to 350ºF (177ºC). In a bowl, whisk the eggs with sugar, salt, cinnamon, cream cheese, flour, and baking powder. In another bowl, combine the remaining ingredients, except for the zucchini. 2. Gently combine the dry and liquid mixtures. Stir in the zucchini. Grease 4 muffin tins with oil and pour the batter inside them. Place them in the air fryer and bake for 18 to 20 minutes until golden. Serve.

Banana Muffins with Hazelnuts and Chocolates

Prep time: 15 minutes | Cook time: 20 minutes | Serves 6

¼ cup butter, melted
¼ cup honey
1 egg, lightly beaten
2 ripe bananas, mashed
½ teaspoon vanilla extract
1 cup flour
½ teaspoon baking powder
½ teaspoon ground cinnamon
¼ cup hazelnuts, chopped
¼ cup dark chocolate chips

1. Spray a muffin tin that fits in your air fryer with cooking spray. In a bowl, whisk butter, honey, egg, bananas, and vanilla until well combined. Sift in flour, baking powder, and cinnamon without overmixing. 2. Stir in the hazelnuts and chocolate chips. Pour the batter into the muffin holes and place in the air fryer. Bake for 20 minutes at 350ºF (177ºC), checking them around the 15-minute mark. Serve chilled.

Crisp Sausage Patties

Prep time: 10 minutes | Cook time: 15 minutes | Serves 4

1 pound (454 g) ground Italian sausage
¼ cup bread crumbs
1 teaspoon red pepper flakes
Salt and black pepper to taste
¼ teaspoon garlic powder
1 egg, beaten

1. Preheat the air fryer to 350ºF (177ºC). Thoroughly mix all the ingredients in a large bowl. Make balls out of the mixture using your hands. Flatten the balls to make the patties. Arrange them on the greased frying basket. Place them in the fryer and air fry for 15 minutes, flipping once halfway through. Serve.

Orange Cupcakes

Prep time: 15 minutes | Cook time: 12 minutes | Serves 4

Orange Frosting:
1 cup plain yogurt
2 tablespoons sugar
1 orange, juiced
1 tablespoon orange zest
7 ounces (198 g) cream cheese
Cake:
1 teaspoon dark rum
⅔ cup flour
¼ teaspoon salt
½ cup sugar
1 teaspoon vanilla extract
2 eggs
½ cup butter, softened

1. In a bowl, add yogurt and cream cheese and mix until smooth. Add in orange juice and zest and whisk well. Gradually add the sugar and stir until smooth. Make sure the frosting is not runny. Set aside. 2. Preheat the air fryer to 360ºF (182ºC). 3. For the cake, in a bowl, put the flour, rum, softened butter, eggs, vanilla extract, sugar, and salt. Beat with a whisk until smooth. Spoon the batter into 4 cupcake cases, ¾ way up. Place them in the air fryer and bake for 12 minutes or until an inserted toothpick comes out clean. Once ready, remove and let cool. Design the cupcakes with the frosting and serve.

Coconut and Oat Cookies

Prep time: 15 minutes | Cook time: 18 minutes | Serves 4

¾ cup flour
4 tablespoons sugar
½ cup oats
1 egg
¼ cup coconut flakes
Filling:
1 tablespoon white chocolate, melted
4 tablespoons butter
½ cup powdered sugar
1 teaspoon vanilla extract

1. In a bowl, beat egg, sugar, oats, and coconut flakes with an electric hand mixer. Fold in the flour. Drop spoonfuls of the batter into a greased baking sheet and bake in the air fryer at 350ºF (177ºC) for 18 minutes. Let cool to firm up and to resemble cookies. Cook in batches if needed. 2. Meanwhile, prepare the filling by beating all filling ingredients together. Spread the filling on half of the cookies. Top with the other halves to make cookie sandwiches like oreo. Serve and enjoy!

Cherry and Almond Scones

Prep time: 15 minutes | Cook time: 12 to 14 minutes | Serves 4

2 cups flour plus some more
⅓ cup sugar
2 teaspoons baking powder
½ cup sliced almonds
¾ cup dried cherries, chopped
¼ cup cold butter, cut into cubes
½ cup milk
1 egg

1. Preheat the air fryer to 390ºF (199ºC). Line the frying basket with baking paper. Mix together flour, sugar, baking powder, sliced almonds, and dried cherries in a bowl. Rub the butter with hands into the dry ingredients to form a sandy, crumbly texture. Whisk together egg, and milk. 2. Pour into the dry ingredients and stir to combine. Sprinkle a working board with flour, lay the dough onto the board, and give it a few kneads. Shape into a rectangle and cut into 9 squares. Arrange the squares in the frying basket and air fry for 12 to 14 minutes at 390ºF (199ºC). Work in batches if needed. Serve.

Blueberry Oat Bars

Prep time: 10 minutes | Cook time: 10 minutes | Makes 12 bars

2 cups rolled oats
¼ cup ground almonds
¼ cup sugar
1 teaspoon baking powder
½ teaspoon ground cinnamon
2 eggs, lightly beaten
½ cup canola oil
½ cup milk
1 teaspoon vanilla extract
2 cups blueberries

1. Spray a baking pan that fits in your air fryer with oil. In a bowl, add oats, almonds, sugar, baking powder, and cinnamon; stir well. In another bowl, whisk eggs, canola oil, milk, and vanilla. Stir the wet ingredients into the oat mixture. Fold in the blueberries. Pour the mixture into the pan and place it inside the fryer. Bake for 10 minutes. Remove to a wire rack to cool and then cut into 12 bars.

Kiwi Pecan Muffins

Prep time: 10 minutes | Cook time: 15 minutes | Serves 4

1 cup flour
1 kiwi, mashed
¼ cup powdered sugar
1 tablespoon milk
1 tablespoon pecans, chopped
½ teaspoon baking powder
¼ cup oats
¼ cup butter, room temperature

1. Preheat the air fryer to 350ºF (177ºC). Place the sugar, pecans, kiwi, and butter in a bowl and mix well. In another bowl, mix the flour, baking powder, and oats and stir well. Combine the two mixtures and stir in the milk. Pour the batter into a greased muffin tin that fits in the fryer and bake for 15 minutes. Remove to a wire rack and leave to cool for a few minutes before removing the muffin from the tin. Enjoy!

Raisin Bread Pudding with Hazelnuts

Prep time: 10 minutes | Cook time: 25 minutes | Serves 4

8 bread slices, cubed
½ cup buttermilk
¼ cup honey
1 cup milk
2 eggs
½ teaspoon vanilla extract
2 tablespoons butter, softened
¼ cup sugar
4 tablespoons raisins
2 tablespoons chopped hazelnuts
Ground cinnamon for garnish

1. Preheat the air fryer to 350ºF (177ºC). Beat the eggs along with buttermilk, honey, milk, vanilla, sugar, and butter in a bowl. Stir in raisins and hazelnuts, then add in the bread to soak, about 10 minutes. Transfer to a greased tin and bake the pudding in the air fryer for 25 minutes. Dust with cinnamon. Serve.

Super Easy Croutons

Prep time: 5 minutes | Cook time: 6 to 8 minutes | Serves 4

2 cups bread cubes
2 tablespoons butter, melted
1 teaspoon dried parsley
Garlic salt and black pepper to taste

1. Mix the cubed bread with butter, parsley, garlic salt, and black pepper until well coated. Place them in the frying basket and air fry for 6 to 8 minutes at 380ºF (193ºC), shaking once until golden brown.

Golden Avocado

Prep time: 5 minutes | Cook time: 8 to 10 minutes | Serves 4

½ cup bread crumbs
½ teaspoon salt
1 avocado, pitted, peeled, and sliced
½ cup soda water (club soda)

1. Preheat the air fryer to 360ºF (182ºC). In a bowl, add the bread crumbs and salt and mix well. Sprinkle the avocado with soda water and then coat in the bread crumbs. Arrange the slices in the grease frying basket in one layer and air fry for 8 to 10 minutes, shaking once or twice. Serve warm.

Baked Eggs in Avocado

Prep time: 5 minutes | Cook time: 8 to 12 minutes | Serves 1

1 ripe avocado, pitted and halved
2 eggs
Salt and black pepper, to taste
1 teaspoon fresh cilantro, chopped

1. Preheat the air fryer to 400ºF (204ºC). Crack one egg into each avocado half and place in the air fryer. Bake for 8 to 12 minutes until the eggs are cooked through. Let cool slightly and season to taste. Top with freshly chopped cilantro and serve warm.

Roasted Asparagus with Serrano Ham

Prep time: 5 minutes | Cook time: 10 minutes | Serves 4

12 spears asparagus, trimmed
12 Serrano ham slices
¼ cup Parmesan cheese, grated
Salt and black pepper to taste

1. Preheat the air fryer to 350ºF (177ºC). Season asparagus with salt and black pepper. Wrap each ham slice around each asparagus spear from one end to the other end to cover completely. Arrange them on the greased frying basket and air fry for 10 minutes, shaking once or twice throughout cooking. When ready, scatter with Parmesan cheese and serve immediately.

Egg White Cups

Prep time: 10 minutes | Cook time: 15 minutes | Serves 4

2 cups 100% liquid egg whites
3 tablespoons salted butter, melted
¼ teaspoon salt
¼ teaspoon onion powder
½ medium Roma tomato, cored and diced
½ cup chopped fresh spinach leaves

1. In a bowl, whisk egg whites with butter, salt, and onion powder. Stir in tomato and spinach, then pour evenly into four ramekins greased with cooking spray. 2. Place ramekins into frying basket. Bake at 300ºF (149ºC) for 15 minutes until eggs are fully cooked and firm in the center. Serve warm.

Turkey Sausage Breakfast Pizza

Prep time: 15 minutes | Cook time: 24 minutes | Serves 2

4 large eggs, divided
1 tablespoon water
½ teaspoon garlic powder
½ teaspoon onion powder
½ teaspoon dried oregano
2 tablespoons coconut flour
3 tablespoons grated Parmesan cheese
½ cup shredded provolone cheese
1 link cooked turkey sausage, chopped (about 2 ounces / 57 g)
2 sun-dried tomatoes, finely chopped
2 scallions, thinly sliced

1. Preheat the air fryer to 400ºF (204ºC). Lightly coat a cake pan with olive oil. 2. In a bowl, whisk 2 of the eggs with the water, garlic powder, onion powder, and dried oregano. Stir the coconut flour into the egg mixture, mixing until smooth. Stir in the Parmesan cheese. Allow the mixture to rest until thick and dough-like. 3. Transfer the mixture to the prepared pan. Air fry for 10 minutes until the crust is set but still light in color. Top with the cheeses, sausage, and sun-dried tomatoes. 4. Break the remaining 2 eggs into a small bowl, then slide them onto the pizza. Air fry 10 to 14 minutes until the egg whites are set and the yolks are the desired doneness. Top with scallions and allow to rest for 5 minutes before serving.

Hearty Banana Pastry

Prep time: 10 minutes | Cook time: 12 minutes | Serves 2

3 bananas, sliced
3 tablespoons honey
2 puff pastry sheets, cut into thin strips
1 cup fresh berries to serve

1. Preheat the air fryer to 340°F (171°C). Place banana slices into a greased baking dish. Cover with pastry strips and drizzle with honey. Bake inside the air fryer for 12 minutes until golden. Serve with berries.

Breakfast Cobbler

Prep time: 20 minutes | Cook time: 30 minutes | Serves 4

Filling:
10 ounces (283 g) bulk pork sausage, crumbled
¼ cup minced onions
2 cloves garlic, minced
½ teaspoon fine sea salt
½ teaspoon ground black pepper
1 (8-ounce / 227-g) package cream cheese (or Kite Hill brand cream cheese style spread for dairy-free), softened
¾ cup beef or chicken broth
Biscuits:
3 large egg whites
¾ cup blanched almond flour
1 teaspoon baking powder
¼ teaspoon fine sea salt
2½ tablespoons very cold unsalted butter, cut into ¼-inch pieces
Fresh thyme leaves, for garnish

1. Preheat the air fryer to 400°F (204°C). 2. Place the sausage, onions, and garlic in a pie pan. Break up the sausage into small pieces and spread it evenly throughout the pan. Season with the salt and pepper. Bake for 5 minutes. 3. Meanwhile, purée the cream cheese and broth in a food processor until smooth. 4. Use a fork or metal spatula to crumble the pork. Pour the cream cheese mixture into the sausage and stir. Set aside. 5. **Make the Biscuits:** Place the egg whites in a stand mixer and whip until stiff peaks form. 6. In a separate bowl, whisk together the almond flour, baking powder, and salt, then cut in the butter. Gently fold the flour mixture into the egg whites with a rubber spatula. 7. Use a large spoon to scoop the dough into 4 equal-sized biscuits, making sure the butter is evenly distributed. Place the biscuits on top of the sausage and bake for 5 minutes, then bake at 325°F (163°C) for another 17 to 20 minutes, until the biscuits are golden brown. Serve garnished with fresh thyme leaves.

Mexican Breakfast Pepper Rings

Prep time: 5 minutes | Cook time: 10 minutes | Serves 4

Olive oil
1 large red, yellow, or orange bell pepper, cut into four ¾-inch rings
4 eggs
Salt and freshly ground black pepper, to taste
2 teaspoons salsa

1. Preheat the air fryer to 350°F (177°C). Lightly spray a baking pan with olive oil. 2. Place pepper rings on the pan. Crack one egg into each bell pepper ring. Season with salt and black pepper. 3. Spoon ½ teaspoon of salsa on top of each egg. 4. Place the pan in the frying basket. Air fry until the yolk is slightly runny, 5 to 6 minutes or until the yolk is fully cooked, 8 to 10 minutes. 5. Serve hot.

Air Fried Bacon

Prep time: 2 minutes | Cook time: 10 minutes | Serves 4

8 ounces (227 g) bacon, sliced

1. Preheat the fryer to 390°F (199°C). Place the bacon slices in the frying basket. Air fry for 10 minutes, flipping once.

Vegetable Frittata

Prep time: 10 minutes | Cook time: 19 minutes | Serves 1 to 2

½ red or green bell pepper, cut into ½-inch chunks
4 button mushrooms, sliced
½ cup diced zucchini
½ teaspoon chopped fresh oregano or thyme
1 teaspoon olive oil
3 eggs, beaten
½ cup grated Cheddar cheese
Salt and freshly ground black pepper, to taste
1 teaspoon butter
1 teaspoon chopped fresh parsley

1. Preheat the air fryer to 400°F (204°C). 2. Toss the peppers, mushrooms, zucchini and oregano with the olive oil and air fry for 6 minutes, shaking once or twice during the cooking process. 3. Meanwhile, beat the eggs well in a bowl, stir in cheese and season with salt and black pepper. Add the fried vegetables to this bowl. 4. Place a cake pan into the frying basket with the butter. Air fry for 1 minute at 380°F (193°C) to melt the butter. Rotate to grease the pan. Pour the egg mixture into the cake pan. 5. Air fry at 380°F (193°C) for 12 minutes, or until the frittata has puffed up and is lightly browned. Allow to cool for 5 minutes. Sprinkle with parsley and serve.

Denver Omelet

Prep time: 5 minutes | Cook time: 8 minutes | Serves 1

2 large eggs
¼ cup unsweetened, unflavored almond milk
¼ teaspoon fine sea salt
⅛ teaspoon ground black pepper
¼ cup diced ham (omit for vegetarian)
¼ cup diced green and red bell peppers
2 tablespoons diced green onions, plus more for garnish
¼ cup shredded Cheddar cheese (about 1 ounce / 28 g) (omit for dairy-free)
Quartered cherry tomatoes, for serving (optional)

1. Preheat the air fryer to 350°F (177°C). 2. In a bowl, use a fork to whisk together the eggs, almond milk, salt, and pepper. Add the ham, bell peppers, and green onions. Pour the mixture into a greased cake pan. Add the cheese on top (if using). 3. Bake for 8 minutes until the eggs are cooked to your liking. 4. Loosen the omelet from the sides of the pan with a spatula and place it on a serving plate. Garnish with green onions and serve with cherry tomatoes, if desired.

Cheesy Cauliflower "Hash Browns"

Prep time: 30 minutes | Cook time: 24 minutes | Makes 6 hash browns

2 ounces (57 g) 100% cheese crisps
1 (12-ounce / 340-g) steamer bag cauliflower, cooked and cooled
1 large egg
½ cup shredded sharp Cheddar cheese
½ teaspoon salt

1. Wring out excess moisture from cauliflower. 2. Pulse cheese crisps on low for 30 seconds in a food processor until finely ground. Add cauliflower, egg to food processor and sprinkle with Cheddar and salt. Pulse five times until mixture is mostly smooth. 3. Cut two pieces of parchment to fit frying basket. Separate mixture into six even scoops and place three on each piece of parchment, keeping at least 2 inch of space between each scoop. Press each into a hash brown shape, about ¼ inch thick. 4. Place one batch on parchment into frying basket. Air fry at 375°F (191°C) for 12 minutes until golden brown, turning once halfway through cooking. Repeat with second batch. 5. Serve warm.

Three-Berry Dutch Pancake

Prep time: 10 minutes | Cook time: 12 to 16 minutes | Serves 4

2 egg whites
1 egg
½ cup whole-wheat pastry flour
½ cup 2% milk
1 teaspoon pure vanilla extract
1 tablespoon unsalted butter, melted
1 cup sliced fresh strawberries
½ cup fresh blueberries
½ cup fresh raspberries

1. In a medium bowl, mix the egg whites, egg, pastry flour, milk, and vanilla well. 2. Grease the baking pan with the melted butter and pour in the batter. Bake at 330°F (166°C) for 12 to 16 minutes, or until the pancake is puffed and golden brown. 3. Top with the strawberries, blueberries, and raspberries. Serve immediately.

Sausage and Egg Breakfast Burrito

Prep time: 5 minutes | Cook time: 30 minutes | Serves 6

6 eggs
Salt and pepper, to taste
Cooking oil
½ cup chopped red bell pepper
½ cup chopped green bell pepper
8 ounces (227 g) ground chicken sausage
½ cup salsa
6 medium (8-inch) flour tortillas
½ cup shredded Cheddar cheese

1. In a medium bowl, whisk the eggs. Add salt and pepper to taste. 2. Spray a skillet with cooking oil. Scramble eggs on medium-high heat for 2 to 3 minutes, until the eggs are fluffy. Remove and set aside. 3. Cook chopped red and green bell peppers for 2 to 3 minutes until soft. 4. Add the sausage to the skillet and cook for 3 to 4 minutes until brown. Break the sausage into smaller pieces. 5. Add the salsa and scrambled eggs. Stir to combine. Remove the skillet from heat. 6. Spoon the mixture evenly onto the tortillas. Fold the sides of each tortilla in toward the middle and then roll up from the bottom. 7. Spray the burritos with cooking oil and place them in the air fryer. Air fry at 400°F (204°C) for 8 minutes. Flip and cook for 2 minutes more until crisp. 8. Sprinkle the Cheddar cheese over the burritos. Cool before serving.

Cheddar Eggs

Prep time: 5 minutes | Cook time: 15 minutes | Serves 2

4 large eggs
2 tablespoons unsalted butter, melted
½ cup shredded sharp Cheddar cheese

1. Crack eggs into a round baking dish and whisk. Place dish into the frying basket. 2. Air fry at 400°F (204°C) for 10 minutes. After 5 minutes, stir the eggs and add the butter and cheese. Cook for 3 more minutes and stir again. Allow eggs to finish cooking an additional 2 minutes or remove if they are to your desired liking. 3. Use a fork to fluff. Serve warm.

Breakfast Hash

Prep time: 10 minutes | Cook time: 30 minutes | Serves 6

Oil, for spraying
3 medium russet potatoes, diced
½ yellow onion, diced
1 green bell pepper, seeded and diced
2 tablespoons olive oil
2 teaspoons granulated garlic
1 teaspoon salt
½ teaspoon freshly ground black pepper

1. Line the frying basket with parchment and spray lightly with oil. 2. In a bowl, mix together all the ingredients and stir. Transfer the mixture to the prepared basket. 3. Air fry at 400°F (204°C) for 20 to 30 minutes, shaking and spraying a little oil every 10 minutes, until browned and crispy.

Fried Cheese Grits

Prep time: 10 minutes | Cook time: 10 to 12 minutes | Serves 4

⅔ cup instant grits
1 teaspoon salt
1 teaspoon freshly ground black pepper
¾ cup whole or 2% milk
3 ounces (85 g) cream cheese,
at room temperature
1 large egg, beaten
1 tablespoon butter, melted
1 cup shredded mild Cheddar cheese
Cooking spray

1. Mix the all the ingredients except cooking spray in a bowl and whisk to combine. 2. Preheat the air fryer to 400°F (204°C). Spray a baking pan with cooking spray. 3. Spread the grits mixture into the baking pan and place in the frying basket. 4. Air fry for 1o to 12 minutes, or until the grits are cooked and a knife inserted in the center comes out clean. Stir the mixture once halfway through the cooking time. 5. Rest for 5 minutes and serve warm.

Hearty Cheddar Biscuits

Prep time: 10 minutes | Cook time: 20 minutes | Makes 8 biscuits

2⅓ cups self-rising flour
2 tablespoons sugar
½ cup butter (1 stick), frozen for 15 minutes
½ cup grated Cheddar cheese,
plus more to melt on top
1⅓ cups buttermilk
1 cup all-purpose flour, for shaping
1 tablespoon butter, melted

1.. Combine the flour and sugar in a large mixing bowl. Grate the butter into the flour. Add the grated cheese and stir to coat the cheese and butter with flour. Then add the buttermilk and stir just until you can no longer see streaks of flour. The dough should be quite wet. 2. Spread the all-purpose (not self-rising) flour out on a small cookie sheet. With a spoon, scoop 8 evenly sized balls of dough into the flour, making sure they don't touch each other. With floured hands, coat each dough ball with flour and toss them gently from hand to hand to shake off any excess flour. Put each floured dough ball into a buttered pan, right up next to the other. 3. Preheat the air fryer to 380ºF (193ºC). 4. Transfer the cake pan to the basket. Air fry for 20 minutes, checking the biscuits twice. 5. Let for a minute before pulling apart.

Creamy Cinnamon Rolls

Prep time: 10 minutes | Cook time: 9 minutes | Serves 8

1 pound (454 g) frozen bread dough, thawed to room temperature
¼ cup butter, melted
¾ cup brown sugar
1½ tablespoons ground cinnamon

Cream Cheese Glaze:
4 ounces (113 g) cream cheese, softened
2 tablespoons butter, softened
1¼ cups powdered sugar
½ teaspoon vanilla extract

1. On a lightly floured surface, roll the dough into a 13-inch by 11-inch rectangle. Position the rectangle so the 13-inch side is facing you. Brush the melted butter all over the dough, leaving a 1-inch border uncovered along the edge farthest away from you. 2. Combine brown sugar and cinnamon in a bowl. Sprinkle the mixture evenly over the buttered dough, keeping the 1-inch border uncovered. Roll the dough into a log, starting with the edge closest to you. Roll the dough tightly, rolling evenly, and push out any air pockets. When you get to the uncovered edge of the dough, press the dough onto the roll to seal it together. 3. Cut the log into 8 pieces, slicing slowly with a sawing motion. Turn the slices on their sides and cover with a clean kitchen towel. Let the rolls sit in the warmest part of the kitchen for 1½ to 2 hours to rise. 4. **Make the Glaze:** microwave the cream cheese and butter in a microwave-safe bowl for 30 seconds at a time until it is easy to stir. Gradually add the powdered sugar and stir to combine. Add the vanilla extract and whisk until smooth. Set aside. 5. Preheat the air fryer to 350ºF (177ºC). 6. Air fry the rolls for 9 minutes, turning once. 7. Let cool for two minutes before glazing. Spread cream cheese glaze on top, allowing some glaze to drip down the side of the rolls. Serve warm.

Cheddar Soufflés

Prep time: 15 minutes | Cook time: 12 minutes | Serves 4

3 large eggs, whites and yolks separated
¼ teaspoon cream of tartar
½ cup shredded sharp Cheddar cheese
3 ounces (85 g) cream cheese, softened

1. In a bowl, beat egg whites together with cream of tartar until soft peaks form, about 2 minutes. 2. In a separate medium bowl, beat egg yolks, Cheddar, and cream cheese together until frothy, about 1 minute. Add egg yolk mixture to whites, gently folding until combined. 3. Pour mixture evenly into four ramekins greased with cooking spray. Place ramekins into frying basket. Bake at 350ºF (177ºC) for 12 minutes until eggs are browned on the top and firm in the center. Serve warm.

Scotch Eggs

Prep time: 10 minutes | Cook time: 20 to 25 minutes | Serves 4

2 tablespoons flour, plus extra for coating
1 pound (454 g) ground breakfast sausage
4 hard-boiled eggs, peeled
1 raw egg
1 tablespoon water
Oil for misting or cooking spray
Crumb Coating:
¾ cup panko bread crumbs
¾ cup flour

1. Mix flour with ground sausage thoroughly. Divide into 4 portions and mold each around a hard-boiled egg so the sausage completely covers the egg. 2. In a bowl, beat together the raw egg and water. Dip sausage-covered eggs in the remaining flour, then the egg mixture, then roll in the crumb coating. 3. Air fry at 360ºF (182ºC) for 10 minutes. Spray eggs, turn, and spray other side. Continue cooking for another 10 to 15 minutes until sausage is well done.

Baked Potato Breakfast Boats

Prep time: 10 minutes | Cook time: 20 minutes | Serves 4

2 large russet potatoes, scrubbed
Olive oil
Salt and freshly ground black pepper, to taste
4 eggs
2 tablespoons chopped, cooked bacon
1 cup shredded Cheddar cheese

1. Poke holes in the potatoes with a fork and microwave on full power for 8 to 10 minutes until fork-tender. 2. Cut the potatoes in half lengthwise and use a spoon to scoop out the inside of the potato. Leave a layer of potato so that it makes a sturdy "boat." 3. Preheat the air fryer to 350ºF (177ºC). Lightly spray the frying basket and potatoes with olive oil. Sprinkle with salt and pepper to taste. 4. Place the potato skins in the frying basket, skin-side down. Crack one egg into each potato skin. 5. Sprinkle ½ tablespoon bacon pieces and ¼ cup shredded cheese on top of each egg. Sprinkle with salt and pepper to taste. 6. Air fry until the yolk is slightly runny, 5 to 6 minutes, or until the yolk is fully cooked, 7 to 10 minutes.

Pancake for Two

Prep time: 5 minutes | Cook time: 30 minutes | Serves 2

1 cup blanched finely ground almond flour
2 tablespoons granular erythritol
1 tablespoon salted butter, melted
1 large egg
⅓ cup unsweetened almond milk
½ teaspoon vanilla extract

1. In a bowl, mix all ingredients together, then pour half the batter into a round nonstick baking dish. 2. Place dish into frying basket. Bake at 320ºF (160ºC) for 15 minutes until pancake is golden brown on top and firm, and a toothpick inserted in the center will come out clean. Repeat with remaining batter. Slice in half in dish and serve warm.

Spinach and Feta Egg Bake

Prep time: 7 minutes | Cook time: 23 to 25 minutes | Serves 2

Avocado oil spray
⅓ cup diced red onion
1 cup frozen chopped spinach, thawed and drained
4 large eggs
¼ cup heavy (whipping) cream
Sea salt and freshly ground black pepper, to taste
¼ teaspoon cayenne pepper
½ cup crumbled feta cheese
¼ cup shredded Parmesan cheese

1. Spray a deep pan with oil. Put the onion in the pan, and place the pan in the frying basket. Bake at 350ºF (177ºC) for 7 minutes. 2. Sprinkle the spinach over the onion. 3. In a medium bowl, beat the eggs, heavy cream, salt, black pepper, and cayenne. Pour this mixture over the vegetables. Top with the feta and Parmesan cheese. Bake for 16 to 18 minutes, until the eggs are set and lightly brown.

Apple Cider Doughnut Holes

Prep time: 10 minutes | Cook time: 6 minutes | Makes 10 mini doughnuts

Doughnut Holes:
1½ cups all-purpose flour
2 tablespoons granulated sugar
2 teaspoons baking powder
1 teaspoon baking soda
½ teaspoon kosher salt
Pinch of freshly grated nutmeg
¼ cup plus 2 tablespoons buttermilk, chilled
2 tablespoons apple cider (hard or nonalcoholic), chilled
1 large egg, lightly beaten
Vegetable oil, for brushing
Glaze:
½ cup powdered sugar
2 tablespoons unsweetened applesauce
¼ teaspoon vanilla extract
Pinch of kosher salt

1. **Make the Doughnut Holes:** In a bowl, whisk together the flour, granulated sugar, baking powder, baking soda, salt, and nutmeg until smooth. Add the buttermilk, cider, and egg and stir with a small rubber spatula or spoon until the dough just comes together. 2. Using a 1-ounce (28-g) ice cream scoop, scoop and drop 10 balls of dough into the frying basket, spaced evenly apart, and brush the tops lightly with oil. Air fry at 350ºF (177ºC) until the doughnut holes are golden brown and fluffy, about 6 minutes. Allow to cool completely. 3. **Make the Glaze:** In a bowl, stir together the glaze ingredients until smooth. 4. Dip the tops of the doughnuts holes in the glaze, then let stand until the glaze sets before serving.

Classic British Breakfast

Prep time: 5 minutes | Cook time: 25 minutes | Serves 2

1 cup potatoes, sliced and diced
2 cups beans in tomato sauce
2 eggs
1 tablespoon olive oil
1 sausage
Salt, to taste

1. Preheat the air fryer to 390ºF (199ºC). 2. Break the eggs onto a baking dish and sprinkle with salt. Lay the beans on the dish, next to the eggs. 3. In a bowl, coat the potatoes with the olive oil. Sprinkle with salt. 4. Transfer the bowl of potato slices to the air fryer and bake for 10 minutes. Swap out the bowl of potatoes for the dish containing the eggs and beans. Bake for another 10 minutes. Cover the potatoes with parchment paper. 5. Slice up the sausage and throw the slices on top of the beans and eggs. Bake for another 5 minutes. 6. Serve with the potatoes.

Jalapeño and Bacon Breakfast Pizza

Prep time: 5 minutes | Cook time: 10 minutes | Serves 2

1 cup shredded Mozzarella cheese
1 ounce (28 g) cream cheese, broken into small pieces
4 slices cooked sugar-free bacon, chopped
¼ cup chopped pickled jalapeños
1 large egg, whisked
¼ teaspoon salt

1. Place Mozzarella in a single layer on the bottom of a round nonstick baking dish. Scatter cream cheese pieces, bacon, and jalapeños over Mozzarella, then pour egg evenly around baking dish. Sprinkle with salt and place into frying basket. Bake at 330ºF (166ºC) for 10 minutes until the cheese is brown and egg is set. 2. Let cool for 5 minutes before serving.

Cheesy Scrambled Eggs

Prep time: 2 minutes | Cook time: 9 minutes | Serves 2

1 teaspoon unsalted butter
2 large eggs
2 tablespoons milk
2 tablespoons shredded Cheddar cheese
Salt and freshly ground black pepper, to taste

1. Preheat the air fryer to 300ºF (149ºC). Place the butter in a baking pan and bake for 1 to 2 minutes, until melted. 2. In a bowl, whisk together the eggs, milk, and cheese. Season with salt and black pepper. Transfer the mixture to the pan. 3. Bake for 3 minutes. Stir the eggs in the center of the pan. 4. Bake for another 2 minutes, then stir again. Cook for another 2 minutes, until the eggs are just cooked.

Baked Egg and Mushroom Cups

Prep time: 5 minutes | Cook time: 15 minutes | Serves 6

Olive oil cooking spray
6 large eggs
1 garlic clove, minced
½ teaspoon salt
½ teaspoon black pepper
Pinch red pepper flakes
8 ounces baby bella mushrooms, sliced
1 cup fresh baby spinach
2 scallions, white parts and green parts, diced

1. Preheat the air fryer to 320ºF (160ºC). Lightly coat six silicone muffin cups with olive oil cooking spray. 2. In a bowl, beat the eggs, garlic, salt, pepper, and red pepper flakes for 1 to 2 minutes, or until well combined. 3. Fold in the mushrooms, spinach, and scallions. 4. Divide the mixture evenly among the muffin cups. 5. Bake for 12 to 15 minutes, or until the eggs are set. 6. Allow to cool for 5 minutes before serving.

Easy Buttermilk Biscuits

Prep time: 5 minutes | Cook time: 18 minutes | Makes 16 biscuits

2½ cups all-purpose flour
1 tablespoon baking powder
1 teaspoon kosher salt
1 teaspoon sugar
½ teaspoon baking soda
8 tablespoons (1 stick) unsalted butter, at room temperature
1 cup buttermilk, chilled

1. Stir together the flour, baking powder, salt, sugar, and baking powder in a bowl. Add butter and stir to mix well. Pour in buttermilk and stir with a rubber spatula just until incorporated. 2. Place the dough onto a lightly floured surface and roll the dough out to a disk, ½ inch thick. Cut out the biscuits with a 2-inch round cutter and re-roll any scraps until you have 16 biscuits. 3. Preheat the air fryer to 325ºF (163ºC). 4. Arrange the biscuits in the frying basket in a single layer. Bake for about 18 minutes until the biscuits are golden brown. 5. Serve hot.

Drop Biscuits

Prep time: 10 minutes | Cook time: 9 to 10 minutes | Serves 5

4 cups all-purpose flour
1 tablespoon baking powder
1 tablespoon sugar (optional)
1 teaspoon salt
6 tablespoons butter, plus more for brushing on the biscuits (optional)
¾ cup buttermilk
1 to 2 tablespoons oil

1. In a bowl, whisk the flour, baking powder, sugar (if using), and salt until blended. 2. Add the butter. Using a pastry cutter, work the dough until pea-size balls of the butter-flour mixture appear. Stir in the buttermilk until the mixture is sticky. 3. Preheat the air fryer to 330ºF (166ºC). Line the frying basket with parchment paper and spritz it with oil. 4. Drop the dough by the tablespoonful onto the prepared basket, leaving 1 inch between each, to form 10 biscuits. 5. Bake for 5 minutes. Flip the biscuits and cook for 4 minutes more for a light brown top, or 5 minutes more for a darker biscuit. Brush the tops with melted butter, if desired.

Parmesan Ranch Risotto

Prep time: 10 minutes | Cook time: 30 minutes | Serves 2

1 tablespoon olive oil
1 clove garlic, minced
1 tablespoon unsalted butter
1 onion, diced
¾ cup Arborio rice
2 cups chicken stock, boiling
½ cup Parmesan cheese, grated

1. Preheat the air fryer to 390ºF (199ºC). 2. Grease a round baking tin with olive oil and stir in the garlic, butter, and onion. 3. Transfer the tin to the air fryer and bake for 4 minutes. Add the rice and bake for 4 more minutes. 4. Pour in the chicken stock. Cover and bake at 320ºF (160ºC) for 22 minutes. 5. Scatter with cheese and serve.

Italian Egg Cups

Prep time: 5 minutes | Cook time: 10 minutes | Serves 4

Olive oil
1 cup marinara sauce
4 eggs
4 tablespoons shredded Mozzarella cheese
4 teaspoons grated Parmesan cheese
Salt and freshly ground black pepper, to taste
Chopped fresh basil, for garnish

1. Lightly spray 4 ramekins with olive oil. Pour ¼ cup marinara sauce into each ramekin. Crack one egg into each ramekin on top of the sauce. Sprinkle 1 tablespoon Mozzarella and 1 tablespoon Parmesan on top of each egg. Season with salt and pepper. 2. Cover each ramekin with aluminum foil. Air fry at 350ºF (177ºC) for 5 minutes and remove the aluminum foil. Air fry 2 to 4 minutes more until the top is lightly browned and the egg white is cooked. If you prefer the yolk to be firmer, cook for 3 to 5 more minutes. 3. Garnish with basil and serve.

Meritage Eggs

Prep time: 5 minutes | Cook time: 8 minutes | Serves 2

2 teaspoons unsalted butter (or coconut oil for dairy-free), for greasing the ramekins
4 large eggs
2 teaspoons chopped fresh thyme
½ teaspoon fine sea salt
¼ teaspoon ground black pepper
2 tablespoons heavy cream (or unsweetened, unflavored almond milk for dairy-free)
3 tablespoons finely grated Parmesan cheese (or Kite Hill brand chive cream cheese style spread, softened, for dairy-free)
Fresh thyme leaves, for garnish (optional)

1. Preheat the air fryer to 400ºF (204ºC). Grease two (4-ounce / 113-g) ramekins with the butter. 2. Crack 2 eggs into each ramekin and divide the thyme, salt, and pepper between the ramekins. Pour 1 tablespoon of the heavy cream into each ramekin. Sprinkle each ramekin with 1½ tablespoons Parmesan cheese. 3. Bake for 8 minutes for soft-cooked yolks (longer if you desire a harder yolk). 4. Garnish with ground black pepper and thyme leaves, if desired.

42 | Chapter 1 Vegetables and Sides

Red Pepper and Feta Frittata

Prep time: 10 minutes | Cook time: 20 minutes | Serves 4

Olive oil cooking spray
8 large eggs
1 medium red bell pepper, diced
½ teaspoon salt
½ teaspoon black pepper
1 garlic clove, minced
½ cup feta, divided

1. Preheat the air fryer to 360°F (182°C). Spray a 6-inch round cake pan with cooking spray. 2. In a bowl, beat the eggs for 1 to 2 minutes, or until well combined. Add the bell pepper, salt, black pepper, and garlic, and mix together until the bell pepper is distributed throughout. Fold in ¼ cup the feta cheese. 3. Pour the egg mixture into the prepared cake pan, and sprinkle the remaining ¼ cup feta over the top. 4. Bake for 18 to 20 minutes until the eggs are set in the center. 5. Allow to cool for 5 minutes before serving.

Tomato and Mozzarella Bruschetta

Prep time: 5 minutes | Cook time: 4 minutes | Serves 1

6 small loaf slices
½ cup tomatoes, finely chopped
3 ounces (85 g) Mozzarella
cheese, grated
1 tablespoon fresh basil, chopped
1 tablespoon olive oil

1. Preheat the air fryer to 350°F (177°C). 2. Put the loaf slices inside the air fryer and air fry for about 3 minutes. 3. Add the tomato, Mozzarella, basil, and olive oil on top. 4. Air fry for an additional minute before serving.

Southwestern Ham Egg Cups

Prep time: 5 minutes | Cook time: 12 minutes | Serves 2

4 (1-ounce / 28-g) slices deli ham
4 large eggs
2 tablespoons full-fat sour cream
¼ cup diced green bell pepper
2 tablespoons diced red bell pepper
2 tablespoons diced white onion
½ cup shredded medium Cheddar cheese

1. Place one slice of ham on the bottom of four baking cups. 2. In a bowl, whisk eggs with sour cream. Stir in green pepper, red pepper, and onion. 3. Pour the egg mixture into ham-lined baking cups. Top with Cheddar. Place cups into the frying basket. 4. Bake at 320°F (160°C) for 12 minutes or until the tops are browned. 5. Serve warm.

Breakfast Pita

Prep time: 5 minutes | Cook time: 6 minutes | Serves 2

1 whole wheat pita
2 teaspoons olive oil
½ shallot, diced
¼ teaspoon garlic, minced
1 large egg
¼ teaspoon dried oregano
¼ teaspoon dried thyme
⅛ teaspoon salt
2 tablespoons shredded Parmesan cheese

1. Preheat the air fryer to 380°F (193°C). 2. Brush the top of the pita with olive oil, then spread the diced shallot and minced garlic over the pita. 3. Crack the egg into a small bowl or ramekin, and season it with oregano, thyme, and salt. 4. Place the pita into the frying basket, and gently pour the egg onto the top of the pita. Sprinkle with cheese over the top. 5. Bake for 6 minutes. Allow to cool for 5 minutes before cutting into pieces for serving.

Golden Avocado Tempura

Prep time: 5 minutes | Cook time: 10 minutes | Serves 4

½ cup bread crumbs
½ teaspoons salt
1 Haas avocado, pitted, peeled and sliced
Liquid from 1 can white beans

1. Preheat the air fryer to 350°F (177°C). 2. Mix the bread crumbs and salt in a bowl until well-incorporated. 3. Dip the avocado slices in the bean liquid, then the bread crumbs. 4. Put the avocados in the air fryer and air fry for 10 minutes, shaking at the halfway point. 5. Serve immediately.

Mexican Shakshuka

Prep time: 5 minutes | Cook time: 6 minutes | Serves 1

½ cup salsa
2 large eggs, room temperature
½ teaspoon fine sea salt
¼ teaspoon smoked paprika
⅛ teaspoon ground cumin
For Garnish:
2 tablespoons cilantro leaves

1. Preheat the air fryer to 400°F (204°C). 2. Place the salsa in a pie pan. Crack the eggs into the salsa and sprinkle them with the salt, paprika, and cumin. 3. Place the pan in the air fryer and bake for 6 minutes, or until the egg whites are set and the yolks are cooked to your liking. 4. Garnish with the cilantro before serving.

Gluten-Free Granola Cereal

Prep time: 7 minutes | Cook time: 30 minutes | Makes 3½ cups

Oil, for spraying
1½ cups gluten-free rolled oats
½ cup chopped walnuts
½ cup chopped almonds
½ cup pumpkin seeds
¼ cup maple syrup or honey
1 tablespoon toasted sesame oil or vegetable oil
1 teaspoon ground cinnamon
½ teaspoon salt
½ cup dried cranberries

1. Preheat the air fryer to 250°F (121°C). Line the frying basket with parchment and spray lightly with oil. 2. In a bowl, mix together the oats, walnuts, almonds, pumpkin seeds, maple syrup, sesame oil, cinnamon, and salt. 3. Spread the mixture in an even layer in the prepared basket. 4. Bake for 30 minutes, stirring every 10 minutes. 5. Transfer the granola to a bowl, add the dried cranberries, and toss to combine. 6. Let cool to room temperature before storing in an airtight container.

Keto Quiche

Prep time: 10 minutes | Cook time: 1 hour | Makes 1 (6-inch) quiche

Crust:
1¼ cups blanched almond flour
1¼ cups grated Parmesan or Gouda cheese
¼ teaspoon fine sea salt
1 large egg, beaten
Filling:
½ cup chicken or beef broth (or vegetable broth for vegetarian)
1 cup shredded Swiss cheese (about 4 ounces / 113 g)
4 ounces (113 g) cream cheese (½ cup)
1 tablespoon unsalted butter, melted
4 large eggs, beaten
⅓ cup minced leeks or sliced green onions
¾ teaspoon fine sea salt
⅛ teaspoon cayenne pepper
Chopped green onions, for garnish

1. Preheat the air fryer to 325ºF (163ºC). Grease a pie pan. Spray two large pieces of parchment paper with avocado oil and set them on the countertop. 2. **Make the Crust:** In a medium-sized bowl, combine the flour, cheese, and salt and mix well. Add the egg and mix until the dough is well combined and stiff. 3. Place the dough in the center of one of the greased pieces of parchment. Top with the other piece of parchment. Using a rolling pin, roll out the dough into a circle about 1/16 inch thick. 4. Press the pie crust into the prepared pie pan and bake for 12 minutes, or until it starts to lightly brown. 5. **Make the Filling:** Meanwhile, in a bowl, combine all the ingredients except green onions. When the crust is ready, pour the mixture into the crust and bake for 15 minutes. 6. Turn the heat down to 300ºF (149ºC) and bake for an additional 30 minutes, or until a knife inserted 1 inch from the edge comes out clean. 7. Allow to cool for 10 minutes before garnishing with green onions and cutting into wedges.

Whole Wheat Blueberry Muffins

Prep time: 10 minutes | Cook time: 15 minutes | Serves 6

Olive oil cooking spray
½ cup unsweetened applesauce
¼ cup raw honey
½ cup nonfat plain Greek yogurt
1 teaspoon vanilla extract
1 large egg
1½ cups plus 1 tablespoon whole wheat flour, divided
½ teaspoon baking soda
½ teaspoon baking powder
½ teaspoon salt
½ cup blueberries, fresh or frozen

1. Preheat the air fryer to 360ºF (182ºC). Spray six silicone muffin cups cooking spray. 2. In a bowl, mix the applesauce, honey, yogurt, vanilla, and egg until smooth. 3. Sift in 1½ cups flour, baking soda, baking powder, and salt into the wet mixture, then stir until combined. 4. In a bowl, toss the blueberries with the remaining flour, then fold the mixture into the muffin batter. 5. Divide the mixture evenly among the muffin cups and place into the basket. Bake for 12 to 15 minutes, or until golden brown on top and a toothpick inserted into the middle of one of the muffins comes out clean. 6. Allow to cool for 5 minutes before serving.

Canadian Bacon Muffin Sandwiches

Prep time: 5 minutes | Cook time: 8 minutes | Serves 4

4 English muffins, split
8 slices Canadian bacon
4 slices cheese
Cooking spray

1. Preheat the air fryer to 370ºF (188ºC). 2. Top each of 4 muffin halves with 2 slices of Canadian bacon, 1 slice of cheese, and finish with the remaining muffin half. 3. Put the sandwiches in the frying basket and spritz the tops with cooking spray. 4. Bake for 4 minutes. Flip the sandwiches and bake for another 4 minutes. 5. Divide the sandwiches among four plates and serve warm.

Fried Chicken Wings with Waffles

Prep time: 10 minutes | Cook time: 30 minutes | Serves 4

8 whole chicken wings
1 teaspoon garlic powder
Chicken seasoning, for preparing the chicken
Freshly ground black pepper, to taste
½ cup all-purpose flour
Cooking oil spray
8 frozen waffles
Pure maple syrup, for serving (optional)

1. In a medium bowl, combine the chicken and garlic powder and season with chicken seasoning and pepper. Toss to coat. 2. Transfer the chicken to a resealable plastic bag and add the flour. Seal the bag and shake it to coat the chicken thoroughly. 3. Preheat the air fryer to 400ºF (204ºC). 4. Transfer the chicken from the bag to the frying basket. Spray them with cooking oil. 5. Air fry 20 minutes, shaking the basket every 5 minutes until the chicken is fully cooked. When done, cover the chicken to keep warm. 6. Rinse the basket with warm water. Place the frozen waffles into the basket. Spray with cooking oil. 7. Air fry at 360ºF (182ºC) for 6 minutes. 8. Serve the waffles with the chicken and maple syrup, if desired.

Egg Muffins

Prep time: 10 minutes | Cook time: 11 to 13 minutes | Serves 4

4 eggs
Salt and pepper, to taste
Olive oil
4 English muffins, split
1 cup shredded Colby Jack cheese
4 slices ham or Canadian bacon

1. Preheat the air fryer to 390ºF (199ºC). 2. Beat together eggs and add salt and pepper to taste. Spray a baking pan lightly with oil and add eggs. Bake for 5 to 6 minutes, stirring every minute, until eggs are scrambled to your preference. Remove pan from air fryer. 3. Place bottom halves of English muffins in frying basket. Divide ½ cup cheese among the muffins. Top each with 1 slice ham and one-quarter of the eggs. Sprinkle remaining cheese on top. Use a fork to press the cheese into the egg a little. 4. Air fry at 360ºF (182ºC) for 1 minute. Add English muffin tops and cook for 2 to 4 minutes to heat through and toast the muffins.

Bacon Eggs on the Go

Prep time: 5 minutes | Cook time: 15 minutes | Serves 1

2 eggs
4 ounces (113 g) bacon, cooked
Salt and ground black pepper, to taste

1. Preheat the air fryer to 400°F (204°C). Put liners in a regular cupcake tin. 2. Crack an egg into each of the cups and add the bacon. Season with some pepper and salt. 3. Bake for 15 minutes, or until the eggs are set. Serve warm.

Strawberry Toast

Prep time: 10 minutes | Cook time: 8 minutes | Makes 4 toasts

4 slices bread, ½-inch thick
Butter-flavored cooking spray
1 cup sliced strawberries
1 teaspoon sugar

1. Spray one side of each bread slice with butter-flavored cooking spray. Lay slices sprayed side down. 2. Divide the strawberries among the bread slices. 3. Sprinkle evenly with the sugar and place in the frying basket in a single layer. 4. Air fry at 390°F (199°C) for 8 minutes until the bottom looks brown and top looks glazed.

Breakfast Sausage and Cauliflower

Prep time: 5 minutes | Cook time: 45 minutes | Serves 4

1 pound (454 g) sausage, cooked and crumbled
2 cups heavy whipping cream
1 head cauliflower, chopped
1 cup grated Cheddar cheese, plus more for topping
8 eggs, beaten
Salt and ground black pepper, to taste

1. Preheat the air fryer to 350°F (177°C). 2. In a bowl, mix the sausage, heavy whipping cream, chopped cauliflower, cheese and eggs. Sprinkle with salt and ground black pepper. 3. Pour the mixture into a greased casserole dish. Bake for 45 minutes until firm. 4. Top with more Cheddar cheese and serve.

New York Strip Steaks with Eggs

Prep time: 8 minutes | Cook time: 14 minutes per batch | Serves 4

Cooking oil spray
4 (4-ounce / 113-g) New York strip steaks
1 teaspoon granulated garlic, divided
1 teaspoon salt, divided
1 teaspoon freshly ground black pepper, divided
4 eggs
½ teaspoon paprika

1. Preheat the air fryer to 360°F (182°C. Spray the frying basket with cooking oil. 2. Air fry 2 steaks in the basket for 9 minutes. After 5 minutes, flip the steaks. Sprinkle each with ¼ teaspoon granulated garlic, ¼ teaspoon salt, and ¼ teaspoon pepper. Resume cooking until the steaks register at least 145°F (63°C) on a food thermometer. 3. Transfer the steaks to a plate and tent with aluminum foil to keep warm. Repeat with the remaining steaks. 4. Spray 4 ramekins with olive oil. Crack 1 egg into each ramekin. Sprinkle the eggs with the paprika and remaining ½ teaspoon each salt and pepper. 5. Bake at 330°F (166°C) for 5 minutes until the eggs are cooked to 160°F (71°C). 6. Serve the eggs with the steaks.

Spaghetti Squash Fritters

Prep time: 15 minutes | Cook time: 8 minutes | Serves 4

2 cups cooked spaghetti squash
2 tablespoons unsalted butter, softened
1 large egg
¼ cup blanched finely ground almond flour
2 stalks green onion, sliced
½ teaspoon garlic powder
1 teaspoon dried parsley

1. Remove excess moisture from the squash using a cheesecloth or kitchen towel. 2. Mix all ingredients in a bowl. Form into four patties. Place into the frying basket. 3. Air fry at 400°F (204°C) for 8 minutes, flipping halfway through the cooking time. Serve warm.

Breakfast Meatballs

Prep time: 10 minutes | Cook time: 15 minutes | Makes 18 meatballs

1 pound (454 g) ground pork breakfast sausage
½ teaspoon salt
¼ teaspoon ground black pepper
½ cup shredded sharp Cheddar cheese
1 ounce (28 g) cream cheese, softened
1 large egg, whisked

1. Combine all ingredients in a bowl. Form mixture into eighteen 1-inch meatballs. 2. Place meatballs into ungreased frying basket. Air fry at 400°F (204°C) for 15 minutes, shaking basket three times during cooking until the internal temperature reaches 145°F (63°C). Serve warm.

Pita and Pepperoni Pizza

Prep time: 10 minutes | Cook time: 6 minutes | Serves 1

1 teaspoon olive oil
1 tablespoon pizza sauce
1 pita bread
6 pepperoni slices
¼ cup grated Mozzarella cheese
¼ teaspoon garlic powder
¼ teaspoon dried oregano

1. Preheat the air fryer to 350°F (177°C). Grease the frying basket with olive oil. 2. Spread the pizza sauce on top of the pita bread. Put the pepperoni slices over the sauce, followed by the Mozzarella cheese. 3. Season with garlic powder and oregano. 4. Put the pita pizza inside the air fryer and place a trivet on top. 5. Bake for 6 minutes and serve.

Hole in One

Prep time: 5 minutes | Cook time: 6 to 7 minutes | Serves 1

1 slice bread
1 teaspoon soft butter
1 egg
Salt and pepper, to taste
1 tablespoon shredded Cheddar cheese
2 teaspoons diced ham

1. Preheat the air fryer to 330°F (166°C). 2. Using a 2½-inch-diameter biscuit cutter, cut a hole in center of bread slice. Spread softened butter on both sides of bread. 3. Lay bread slice in a baking dish and crack egg into the hole. Sprinkle with salt and pepper to taste. 4. Bake for 5 minutes. Turn toast over and top with cheese and ham. Cook for 1 to 2 more minutes or until yolk is done to your liking.

Spinach and Bacon Roll-ups

Prep time: 5 minutes | Cook time: 8 to 9 minutes | Serves 4

4 flour tortillas (6- or 7-inch size)
4 slices Swiss cheese
1 cup baby spinach leaves
4 slices turkey bacon
Special Equipment:
4 toothpicks, soak in water for at least 30 minutes

1. Preheat the air fryer to 390°F (199°C). 2. Top each tortilla with one slice of cheese and ¼ cup spinach, then tightly roll them up. 3. Wrap each tortilla with a strip of turkey bacon and secure with a toothpick. 4. Arrange in the frying basket, leaving space between each roll-up. 5. Air fry for 4 minutes. Flip the roll-ups and air fry for another 4 to 5 minutes until the bacon is crisp. 6. Rest for 5 minutes before serving.

Chapter 4 Beef, Pork, and Lamb

Barbecue Pork Ribs

Prep time: 15 minutes | Cook time: 20 to 22 minutes | Serves 4

1 rack pork spareribs, fat trimmed
½ teaspoon ginger powder
Salt and black pepper to taste
2 garlic cloves, minced
1 teaspoon olive oil
1 tablespoon honey plus for brushing
4 tablespoons barbecue sauce
1 teaspoon soy sauce

1. Chop the ribs into individual bones. In a large bowl, whisk all the remaining ingredients, reserving some of the honey. Add in the meat and mix to coat. Cover with a lid and place in the fridge for 1 hour. 2. Preheat the air fryer to 350ºF (177ºC). Place the ribs in the frying basket and air fry for 8 minutes. Slide the basket out and brush the ribs with the reserved honey. Air fry for 12 to 14 minutes until golden and crispy.

Asian Pork Noddle Bowl with Vegetables

Prep time: 20 minutes | Cook time: 12 to 15 minutes | Serves 4

2 pounds (907 g) ground pork
2 eggs, beaten
1 tablespoon cooking oil, for greasing
1 cup panko bread crumbs
1 shallot, chopped
2 teaspoons soy sauce
2 garlic cloves, minced
½ teaspoon ground ginger
2 cups rice noodles, cooked
1 gem lettuce, torn
1 carrot, shredded
1 cucumber, peeled, thinly sliced
1 cup Asian sesame dressing
1 lime, cut into wedges

1. Preheat the air fryer to 390ºF (199ºC). Mix the ground pork, eggs, bread crumbs, shallot, soy sauce, garlic, and ginger in a mixing bowl. Divide the mixture into 24 balls. Place them into the greased frying basket. 2. Air fry for 12 to 15 minutes, shaking the basket every 5 minutes to ensure even cooking. Cook until the meatballs are golden brown. Divide the rice noodles, lettuce, carrot, and cucumber between 4 bowls. Top with meatballs and drizzle with the sesame dressing. Serve with lime wedges and enjoy.

Dill Pork Meatballs

Prep time: 15 minutes | Cook time: 12 to 14 minutes | Serves 4

1 pound (454 g) ground pork
1 tablespoon fresh dill, chopped
½ teaspoon nutmeg
⅓ cup seasoned bread crumbs
1 egg, beaten
Salt and white pepper to taste
2 tablespoons butter
⅓ cup sour cream
2 tablespoons flour

1. Preheat the air fryer to 360ºF (182ºC). In a bowl, combine the ground pork, dill, nutmeg, bread crumbs, egg, salt, and pepper and mix well. Shape the mixture into small balls. Air fry them in the greased frying basket for 12 to 14 minutes, flipping once. 2. Meanwhile, melt butter in a saucepan over medium heat and stir in the flour until lightly browned, about 2 minutes. Gradually pour 1 cup of water and whisk until the sauce thickens. Stir in sour cream and cook for 1 minute. Pour the sauce over the meatballs to serve.

St. Louis–style Pork Ribs

Prep time: 20 minutes | Cook time: 30 minutes | Serves 4

1½ pounds (680 g) St. Louis–style pork spareribs
Salt and black pepper to taste
½ teaspoon sweet paprika
½ teaspoon dry mustard
1 tablespoon brown sugar
1 tablespoon cayenne pepper
1 teaspoon poultry seasoning
1 teaspoon shallot powder
1 teaspoon garlic powder
½ cup hot sauce

1. Preheat the air fryer to 370ºF (188ºC). Cut the ribs individually. In a bowl, mix all the remaining ingredients, except for the hot sauce. Add the ribs to the bowl and rub the seasoning onto the meat. Place the ribs in the greased frying basket and bake for 20 minutes, turn them over, and cook for 10 more minutes or until the ribs are tender inside and golden brown and crisp on the outside. Serve with hot sauce.

Roasted Pork Rack with Macadamia Nuts

Prep time: 10 minutes | Cook time: 35 to 38 minutes | Serves 2

1 pound (454 g) pork rack
2 tablespoons olive oil
1 clove garlic, minced
Salt and black pepper to taste
1 cup macadamia nuts, finely chopped
1 tablespoon bread crumbs
1 egg, beaten in a bowl
1 tablespoon rosemary, chopped

1. Mix the olive oil and garlic vigorously in a bowl to make garlic oil. Place the rack of pork on a chopping board and brush with the garlic oil. Sprinkle with salt and pepper. Preheat the fryer to 370ºF (188ºC). 2. In a bowl, add bread crumbs, macadamia nuts, and rosemary. Brush the meat with the beaten egg on all sides and generously sprinkle with the nut mixture. Place the coated pork in the frying basket and bake for 30 minutes. Flip over and cook further for 5 to 8 minutes. Remove the meat onto a chopping board and let it rest for 10 minutes before slicing. Serve with a salad or steamed rice.

Char Siew Pork Ribs

Prep time: 15 minutes | Cook time: 25 to 27 minutes | Serves 4

2 pounds (907 g) pork ribs
2 tablespoons char siew sauce
2 tablespoons minced ginger
2 tablespoons hoisin sauce
2 tablespoons sesame oil
1 teaspoon honey
4 garlic cloves, minced
1 tablespoon soy sauce

1. Whisk together all the ingredients, except for the ribs, in a large bowl. Add in the ribs and toss to coat. Cover with a lid. Place the bowl in the fridge to marinate for 2 hours. Preheat the air fryer to 390ºF (199ºC). 2. Put the ribs in the greased frying basket and place in the fryer; do not throw away the liquid from the bowl. Bake for 15 minutes. Pour in the marinade and cook for 10 to 12 more minutes. Serve hot.

Chinese Pork Ribs

Prep time: 15 minutes | Cook time: 25 to 30 minutes | Serves 4

1 tablespoon sesame oil
1½ pounds (680 g) pork ribs
½ teaspoon red chili flakes
2 tablespoons light brown sugar
1-inch piece ginger, grated
2 garlic cloves, minced
1 tablespoon balsamic vinegar
½ teaspoon onion powder
½ teaspoon Chinese Five spice powder
1 tablespoon sweet chili sauce
Salt and black pepper to taste
2 scallions, chopped

1. In a bowl, mix the red chili flakes, brown sugar, ginger, garlic, vinegar, onion powder, Five spice powder, chili sauce, salt, and black pepper. Add in the ribs and toss to coat. Chill for at least 1 hour. 2. Preheat the air fryer to 370ºF (188ºC). Remove the ribs from the fridge and place them in the greased frying basket. Brush with sesame oil and bake for 25 to 30 minutes, flipping once. Serve topped with scallions.

Basil-Mustard Pork Burgers

Prep time: 20 minutes | Cook time: 15 to 17 minutes | Serves 2

½ pound (227 g) ground pork
½ medium onion, chopped
½ teaspoon herbs de Provence
½ teaspoon garlic powder
½ teaspoon dried basil
½ teaspoon mustard
Salt and black pepper to taste
2 bread buns, halved
Assembling:
½ red onion, sliced in 2-inch rings
1 large tomato, sliced in 2-inch rings
½ lettuce leaves, torn
4 slices Cheddar cheese

1. In a bowl, combine the ground pork, onion, herbs de Provence, garlic powder, basil, mustard, salt, and pepper and mix evenly. Form 2 patties out of the mixture and place on a flat plate. 2. Preheat the air fryer to 370ºF (188ºC). Place the pork patties in the greased frying basket and bake for 10 to 12 minutes. Slid the basket out and turn the patties. Continue cooking for 5 more minutes. Lay lettuce on bun bottoms, add the patties, followed by a slice of onion, tomato, and Cheddar cheese, and cover with the bun tops. Serve with ketchup and french fries if desired.

Pork Sausage with Best Ratatouille

Prep time: 20 minutes | Cook time: 27 to 33 minutes | Serves 4

4 pork sausages
Ratatouille:
1 red bell pepper, chopped
2 zucchinis, chopped
1 eggplant, chopped
1 medium red onion, chopped
2 tablespoons olive oil
1 cup canned butter beans, drained
15 ounces (425 g) canned tomatoes, chopped
1 tablespoon balsamic vinegar
2 garlic cloves, minced
1 red chili, minced

1. Preheat the air fryer to 390ºF (199ºC). Add the sausages to the greased frying basket and air fry for 12 to 15 minutes, turning once halfway through. Cover with foil to keep warm. Mix all ratatouille ingredients in the frying basket and bake for 15 to 18 minutes, shaking once. Serve the sausages with ratatouille.

Sausage Sticks Rolled in Bacon

Prep time: 20 minutes | Cook time: 32 to 34 minutes | Serves 4

Sausage:
8 bacon strips
8 pork sausages
Relish:
8 large tomatoes, chopped
1 clove garlic, peeled
1 small onion, peeled
3 tablespoons fresh parsley, chopped
Salt and black pepper to taste
2 tablespoons sugar
1 teaspoon smoked paprika
1 tablespoon white wine vinegar

1. Pulse the tomatoes, garlic, and onion in a food processor until the mixture is pulpy. Transfer to a saucepan over medium heat and add vinegar, salt, and pepper; simmer for 10 minutes. Stir in the smoked paprika, parsley, and sugar and cook for 10 more minutes until it thickens. Let cool for 1 hour. 2. Neatly wrap each sausage in a bacon strip and stick in a bamboo skewer at the end of the sausage to secure the bacon ends. Place in a greased frying basket and air fry for 12 to 14 minutes at 350ºF (177ºC), turning once halfway through. Serve the sausages with the cooled relish.

Marinara Pork Balls

Prep time: 15 minutes | Cook time: 17 minutes | Serves 4

1 pound (454 g) ground pork
1 large onion, chopped
½ teaspoon maple syrup
1 teaspoon yellow mustard
½ cup basil leaves, chopped
Salt and black pepper to taste
2 tablespoons Cheddar cheese, grated
1 cup marinara sauce

1. In a bowl, add the ground pork, onion, maple syrup, mustard, basil leaves, salt, pepper, and Cheddar cheese; mix well and form small balls. Place in the greased air fryer and air fry for 12 minutes at 400ºF (204ºC). Slide the basket out and shake the meatballs. Cook further for 5 minutes. Serve with marinara sauce.

48 | Chapter 1 Vegetables and Sides

Pork and Mushroom Pinchos

Prep time: 20 minutes | Cook time: 15 minutes | Serves 4

1 pound (454 g) pork tenderloin, cubed
2 tablespoons olive oil
1 lime, juiced and zested
2 cloves garlic, minced
1 teaspoon chili powder
1 teaspoon ground fennel seeds
½ teaspoon ground cumin
Salt and white pepper to taste
1 red pepper, cut into chunks
½ cup mushrooms, quartered

1. In a bowl, mix half of the olive oil, lime zest and juice, garlic, chili, ground fennel, cumin, salt, and white pepper. Add in the pork and stir to coat. Cover with cling film and place in the fridge for 1 hour. 2. Preheat the air fryer to 380°F (193°C). Season the mushrooms and red pepper with salt and black pepper and drizzle with the remaining olive oil. Thread alternating the pork, mushroom and red pepper pieces onto short skewers. Place in the greased frying basket and air fry for 15 minutes, turning once. Serve hot.

Greek Pork Skewers with Walnuts

Prep time: 15 minutes | Cook time: 14 to 16 minutes | Serves 4

1 pound (454 g) pork sausage meat
Salt and black pepper to taste
1 onion, chopped
½ teaspoon garlic puree
1 teaspoon ground cumin
1 cup Greek yogurt
2 tablespoons walnuts, finely chopped
1 tablespoon fresh dill, chopped

1. Preheat the air fryer to 340°F (171°C). In a bowl, mix the sausage meat, onion, garlic puree, ground cumin, salt, and pepper. Knead until everything is well incorporated. Form patties out the mixture, about ½ inch thick, and thread them onto flat skewers. Lay them on the greased frying basket. 2. Air fry for 14 to 16 minutes, turning them over once or twice until golden. Whisk the yogurt, walnuts, garlic, dill, and salt in a small bowl to obtain a sauce. Serve the skewers with the yogurt sauce.

Pork Sausage Balls with Fennel and Sage

Prep time: 15 minutes | Cook time: 14 to 16 minutes | Serves 4

1 pound (454 g) pork sausage meat
1 whole egg, beaten
1 onion, chopped
2 tablespoons fresh sage, chopped
2 tablespoons ground almonds
¼ head fennel bulb, chopped
1 cup passata di pomodoro (tomato sauce)
Salt and black pepper to taste

1. Preheat the air fryer to 350°F (177°C). In a bowl, place the sausage meat, onion, almonds, fennel, egg, salt, and pepper. Mix with hands until well combined. Shape the mixture into balls. Add them to the greased frying basket and bake for 14 to 16 minutes, shaking once. Top with sage and serve with passata sauce.

Pear and Pork Patties

Prep time: 15 minutes | Cook time: 12 to 14 minutes | Serves 2

½ pound (227 g) ground pork
1 pear, peeled and grated
1 cup bread crumbs
2 ounces (57 g) blue cheese, crumbled
½ teaspoon ground cumin
Salt and black pepper to taste

1. In a bowl, add the ground pork, pear, bread crumbs, cumin, blue cheese, salt, and black pepper, and mix with your hands. Shape into 2 even-sized burger patties. Arrange the patties on the greased frying basket and air fry for 12 to 14 minutes at 380°F (193°C), turning once halfway through. Serve warm.

Pork, Zucchini and Onion Kebabs

Prep time: 15 minutes | Cook time: 15 to 18 minutes | Serves 4

1 pound (454 g) pork tenderloin, cubed
Salt and black pepper to taste
1 green bell pepper, cut into chunks
8 pearl onions, halved
½ teaspoon Italian seasoning mix
½ teaspoon smoked paprika
1 zucchini, cut into chunks

1. Preheat the air fryer to 350°F (177°C). In a bowl, mix the pork, paprika, salt, and pepper. Thread alternating the vegetables and the pork cubes onto bamboo skewers. Spray with cooking spray and transfer to the frying basket. Bake for 15 to 18 minutes, flipping once halfway through. Serve sprinkled with Italian mix.

Creamy Spinach-Stuffed Pork

Prep time: 15 minutes | Cook time: 20 minutes | Serves 4

16 bacon slices
1 pound (454 g) pork tenderloin, butterflied
Salt and black pepper to taste
1 cup spinach
3 ounces (85 g) cream cheese
1 small onion, sliced
1 tablespoon olive oil
1 clove garlic, minced
½ teaspoon dried thyme
½ teaspoon dried rosemary

1. Place the tenderloin on a chopping board, cover it with a plastic wrap and pound it using a kitchen hammer to a 2-inches flat and square piece. Trim the uneven sides with a knife to have a perfect square; transfer to a plate. On the same chopping board, place and weave the bacon slices into a square the size of the pork. Place the pork on the bacon weave and set aside. 2. Heat olive oil in a skillet over medium heat and sauté onion and garlic until transparent, 3 minutes. Add in the spinach, rosemary, thyme, salt, and pepper and cook until the spinach wilts. Stir in the cream cheese until the mixture is even. Turn the heat off. Preheat the air fryer to 360°F (182°C). 3. Spread the spinach mixture onto the pork loin. Roll up the bacon and the pork over the spinach stuffing. Secure the ends with toothpicks and place in the greased air fryer. Bake for 15 minutes, turn them over, and cook for 5 more minutes or until golden. Let cool slightly before slicing.

Pork, Pepper and Squash Kebabs

Prep time: 15 minutes | Cook time: 12 to 14 minutes | Serves 4

1 pound (454 g) pork steak, cut into cubes
¼ cup soy sauce
2 teaspoons smoked paprika
1 teaspoon chili powder
1 teaspoon garlic salt
1 teaspoon red chili flakes
1 tablespoon white wine vinegar
3 tablespoons steak sauce
Skewing:
1 green pepper, cut into cubes
1 red pepper, cut into cubes
1 yellow squash, seeded and cut into cubes
1 green squash, seeded and cut into cubes
Salt and black pepper to taste
A bunch of skewers

1. In a mixing bowl, add the pork cubes, soy sauce, smoked paprika, chili powder, garlic salt, red chili flakes, wine vinegar, and steak sauce. Mix with a spoon and marinate for 1 hour in the fridge. 2. Preheat the air fryer to 370ºF (188ºC). On each skewer, stick the pork cubes and vegetables alternating them. Arrange the skewers on the greased frying basket and bake them for 12 to 14 minutes, flipping once.

Orange-Flavored Pork Tenderloin

Prep time: 15 minutes | Cook time: 15 to 18 minutes | Serves 4

1 pound (454 g) pork tenderloin, sliced
2 tablespoons quince preserve
1 orange, juiced and zested
2 tablespoons olive oil
1 tablespoon soy sauce
Salt and black pepper to taste

1. Brush the sliced tenderloin with 1 tablespoon of olive oil and season with salt and black pepper. Put them into the greased frying basket and bake for 13 to 15 minutes at 380ºF (193ºC), turning once halfway through. 2. Heat the remaining olive oil in a skillet over low heat and add in orange juice, soy sauce, orange zest, and quince preserve. Simmer until the sauce thickens slightly, about 2 to 3 minutes. Season to taste. Arrange the sliced pork on a platter and pour the quince sauce over. Serve immediately.

Pork, Radish and Lettuce in a Cup

Prep time: 20 minutes | Cook time: 11 to 13 minutes | Serves 4

1 tablespoon sesame oil
1 pound (454 g) pork tenderloin, sliced
½ white onion, sliced
2 tablespoons sesame seeds, toasted
2 Little Gem lettuces, leaves
separated
1 cup radishes, cut into matchsticks
1 teaspoon red chili flakes
2 tablespoons teriyaki sauce
1 teaspoon honey
Salt and black pepper to taste

1. In a bowl, whisk teriyaki sauce, red chili flakes, honey, sesame oil, salt, and black pepper. Add in the pork and toss to coat. Cover with a lid and leave in the fridge to marinate for 30 minutes. 2. Preheat the air fryer to 360ºF (182ºC). Remove the pork from the marinade and place it in the greased frying basket, reserving the marinade liquid. Air fry for 11 to 13 minutes, turning once halfway through. 3. Arrange the lettuce leaves on a serving platter and divide the pork between them. Top with onion, radishes, and sesame seeds. Drizzle with the reserved marinade and serve.

Southeast-Asian Pork Chops

Prep time: 15 minutes | Cook time: 14 to 16 minutes | Serves 4

4 pork chops
2 garlic cloves, minced
½ tablespoon sugar
4 stalks lemongrass, trimmed and chopped
2 shallots, chopped
2 tablespoons olive oil
1¼ teaspoons soy sauce
1¼ teaspoons fish sauce
Salt and black pepper to taste

1. In a bowl, add garlic, sugar, lemongrass, shallots, olive oil, soy sauce, fish sauce, salt, and pepper; mix well. Add in the pork chops, coat them with the mixture and marinate for 2 hours in the fridge. 2. Preheat the air fryer to 400ºF (204ºC). Remove the chops from the marinade and place them in the frying basket. Bake for 14 to 16 minutes, flipping once, until golden.

Pork Chops with Mustard-Apricot Glaze

Prep time: 15 minutes | Cook time: 16 to 18 minutes | Serves 4

4 pork chops, ½-inch thick
Salt and black pepper to taste
1 tablespoon apricot jam
1½ tablespoons minced, finely
chopped
2 tablespoons wholegrain mustard

1. In a bowl, add apricot jam, garlic, mustard, salt, and black pepper; mix well. Add the pork chops and toss to coat. Place the chops in the greased frying basket and bake for 10 minutes at 350ºF (177ºC). Turn the chops with a spatula and cook further for 6 to 8 minutes until golden and crispy. Once ready, remove the chops to a serving platter and serve with a side of steamed green veggies if desired.

Sage-Rubbed Pork Tenderloin

Prep time: 15 minutes | Cook time: 20 to 22 minutes | Serves 4

1 pound (454 g) boneless pork tenderloin
1 tablespoon olive oil
1 tablespoon lime juice
½ tablespoon soy sauce
½ tablespoon chili powder
1 garlic clove, minced
2 tablespoons fresh sage, minced
½ teaspoon ground coriander

1. Combine the lime juice, olive oil, soy sauce, chili powder, garlic, sage, and ground coriander in a bowl. Add in the pork and toss to coat. Cover with foil and refrigerate for at least 1 hour. 2. Preheat the air fryer to 390ºF (199ºC). Remove the pork from the bag, shaking off any extra marinade. Place in the greased frying basket and air fry for 15 minutes. Flip it over and cook for another 5 to 7 minutes. Remove and let sit for 10 minutes or so before cutting. Serve warm with steamed veggies or rice.

Lemony Pork Chops

Prep time: 15 minutes | Cook time: 15 minutes | Serves 4

4 lean pork chops
Salt and black pepper to taste
2 eggs
1 cup bread crumbs
½ teaspoon garlic powder
1 teaspoon paprika
½ teaspoon dried oregano
½ teaspoon cayenne pepper
¼ teaspoon dry mustard
1 lemon, zested

1. In a bowl, whisk the eggs with 1 tablespoon of water. In another bowl, add the bread crumbs, salt, black pepper, garlic powder, paprika, oregano, cayenne pepper, lemon zest, and dry mustard and mix evenly. 2. Preheat the air fryer to 380ºF (193ºC). In the egg mixture, dip each pork chop and then dip in the crumb mixture. Place in a greased frying basket and air fry for 10 minutes. Flip and cook for another 5 minutes or until golden. Remove the chops to a chopping board and let them rest for 3 minutes before slicing.

Hungarian-Style Pork Chops

Prep time: 15 minutes | Cook time: 14 to 16 minutes | Serves 4

1 pound (454 g) boneless pork chops
2 tablespoons olive oil
2 teaspoons Hungarian paprika
¼ teaspoon ground bay leaf
½ teaspoon dried thyme
1 teaspoon garlic powder
Salt and black pepper to taste
¼ cup yogurt
2 garlic cloves, minced

1. Preheat the air fryer to 380ºF (193ºC). Spray the frying basket with non-stick cooking spray. Mix the Hungarian paprika, ground bay leaf, thyme, garlic powder, salt, and black pepper in a bowl. Rub the pork with the mixture, drizzle with some olive oil, and place the chops in the fryer to air fry for 14 to 16 minutes, turning once. Mix yogurt with the remaining oil, garlic, and salt. Serve the chops drizzled with the sauce.

Mexican Pork Chops with Black Beans

Prep time: 20 minutes | Cook time: 35 to 38 minutes | Serves 4

4 pork chops
1 lime, juiced
Salt and black pepper to taste
1 teaspoon garlic powder
1 teaspoon onion powder
2 tablespoons olive oil
½ cup tomato sauce
1 onion, chopped
3 garlic cloves, minced
½ teaspoon oregano
1 teaspoon chipotle chili pepper
1 cup long-grain rice
2 tablespoons butter
1 cup canned black beans, drained

1. In a bowl, whisk the onion powder, garlic powder, chipotle pepper, oregano, lime juice, olive oil, salt, and pepper. Coat the pork with the mixture. Cover and place in fridge and marinate for at least 1 hour. 2. Melt the butter in a saucepan over medium heat. Sauté the onion and garlic for 3 minutes. Stir in the rice for 1 minute and pour in the tomato sauce and 2 cups of water. Season with salt and pepper and bring to a boil. Reduce the heat and simmer for 16 minutes or until the rice is tender. Stir in the beans. 3. Preheat the air fryer to 350ºF (177ºC). Remove the meat from the marinade and place the chops in the greased air fryer. Bake for 15 to 18 minutes, flipping once halfway through. Serve with rice and black beans.

Roasted Pork Chops with Mushrooms

Prep time: 15 minutes | Cook time: 15 to 18 minutes | Serves 4

1 pound (454 g) boneless pork chops
2 carrots, cut into sticks
1 cup mushrooms, sliced
2 tablespoons olive oil
2 garlic cloves, minced
1 teaspoon cayenne pepper
1 teaspoon dried thyme
Salt and black pepper to taste

1. Preheat the air fryer to 360ºF (182ºC). Season the chops with cayenne pepper, thyme, salt, and black pepper. In a bowl, combine carrots, garlic, olive oil, mushrooms, and salt. Place the veggies in the greased frying basket, top with the pork chops, and bake for 15 to 18 minutes, turning the chops once. Serve hot.

Spicy-Sweet Pork Chops

Prep time: 15 minutes | Cook time: 12 to 15 minutes | Serves 4

4 thin boneless pork chops
3 tablespoons brown sugar
½ teaspoon cayenne pepper
½ teaspoon ancho chili powder
½ teaspoon garlic powder
1 tablespoon olive oil
½ cup Cholula hot sauce
Salt and black pepper to taste

1. Preheat your Air Fryer to 375ºF (191ºC). 2. To make the marinade, mix brown sugar, olive oil, cayenne pepper, garlic powder, salt, and pepper in a small bowl. Dip each pork chop into the marinade, shaking off, and placing them in the frying basket in a single layer. Air fry for 7 minutes. Slide the basket out, turn the chops, and brush them with marinade. Cook for another 5 to 8 minutes until golden brown. Plate and top with hot sauce to serve.

Thyme Pork Escalopes

Prep time: 10 minutes | Cook time: 16 to 18 minutes | Serves 4

4 pork loin steaks
2 tablespoons olive oil
Salt and black pepper to taste
2 eggs
1 cup bread crumbs
1 tablespoon fresh thyme, chopped

1. In a bowl, mix olive oil, salt, and pepper to form a marinade. Place the pork in the marinade and let sit for 15 minutes. Preheat the fryer to 400ºF (204ºC). Beat the eggs in a separate bowl and add the bread crumbs to a plate. Dip the meat into the eggs and then roll in the crumbs. Place the steaks in the greased frying basket and bake for 16 to 18 minutes, shaking every 5 minutes. Sprinkle with thyme to serve.

Italian-Style Apple Pork Chops

Prep time: 15 minutes | Cook time: 19 minutes | Serves 4

1 small onion, sliced
3 tablespoons olive oil
2 tablespoons apple cider vinegar
½ teaspoon thyme
¼ teaspoon brown sugar
1 apple, sliced
½ teaspoon rosemary
¼ teaspoon smoked paprika
4 pork chops
Salt and black pepper to taste

1. Preheat the air fryer to 350ºF (177ºC). Heat 2 tablespoons olive oil in a skillet over medium heat and stir-fry onion, apple slices, 1 tablespoon apple cider vinegar, brown sugar, thyme, and rosemary for 4 minutes; set aside. 2. In a bowl, mix remaining olive oil, remaining vinegar, paprika, salt, and pepper. Add in the chops and toss to coat. Place them in the air fryer and bake for 10 minutes, flipping once halfway through. When cooked, top with the sautéed apples, return to the fryer, and cook for 5 more minutes. Serve warm.

Sweet French Pork Chops with Blue Cheese

Prep time: 15 minutes | Cook time: 14 to 16 minutes | Serves 4

2 teaspoons olive oil
1 teaspoon butter, softened
¼ cup blue cheese, crumbled
2 tablespoons hot mango chutney
4 thin-cut pork chops
1 tablespoon fresh thyme, chopped

1. Preheat the air fryer to 390ºF (199ºC). In a bowl, whisk together butter, mango chutney, and blue cheese; set aside. Season the chops with salt and pepper and drizzle with olive oil. Place the chops in the frying basket and air fry for 14 to 16 minutes, flipping once. Remove to a plate and spread the blue cheese mixture on each pork chop. Let sit covered with foil for 5 minutes. Sprinkle with fresh thyme and serve.

Stuffed Pork Chops

Prep time: 15 minutes | Cook time: 22 to 25 minutes | Serves 4

4 thick pork chops
½ cup mushrooms, sliced
1 shallot, chopped
Salt and black pepper to taste
1 tablespoon olive oil
2 tablespoons butter
2 garlic cloves, minced
2 tablespoons sage, chopped

1. Melt the butter in a skillet over medium heat. Add and sauté the shallot, garlic, mushrooms, sage, salt, and black pepper for 4 to 5 minutes until tender. Preheat the air fryer to 350ºF (177ºC). 2. Cut a pocket into each pork chop to create a cavity. Fill the chops with the mushroom mixture and secure with toothpicks. Season the stuffed chops with salt and pepper and brush with olive oil. Place them in the frying basket and bake for 18 to 20 minutes, turning once. Remove the toothpicks and serve.

Juicy Double Cut Pork Chops

Prep time: 10 minutes | Cook time: 16 to 18 minutes | Serves 4

4 pork chops
½ cup green mole sauce
2 tablespoons tamarind paste
1 garlic clove, minced
2 tablespoons corn syrup
1 tablespoon olive oil
2 tablespoons molasses
4 tablespoons southwest seasoning
2 tablespoons ketchup
2 tablespoons water

1. In a bowl, mix all ingredients, except for the pork chops and mole sauce. Add in the pork chops and toss to coat. Let them marinate for 30 minutes. Preheat the air fryer to 350ºF (177ºC). Place the chops in the greased frying basket. Bake for 16 to 18 minutes, turning once. Serve the chops drizzled with mole sauce.

Pork Escalopes with Beet and Cabbage Salad

Prep time: 20 minutes | Cook time: 12 to 15 minutes | Serves 4

2 eggs, beaten
4 boneless pork chops
1 tablespoon olive oil
½ cup panko bread crumbs
½ teaspoon garlic powder
Salt and black pepper to taste
1 cup white cabbage, shredded
1 red beet, grated
1 apple, sliced into matchsticks
2 tablespoons Italian dressing

1. In a mixing bowl, combine the cabbage, beet, and apple. Pour the Italian dressing all over and toss to coat. Keep in the fridge until ready to use. Preheat the air fryer to 390ºF (199ºC). 2. Divide the pork chops between two sheets of plastic wrap. Pound with a meat mallet or rolling pin until thin, about ¼ inch in thickness. In a shallow bowl, combine the bread crumbs and garlic powder. In a second shallow bowl, whisk the eggs with salt and black pepper. First, coat the pork chop in the egg mixture. Shake off, dredge in the bread crumbs. Lay the chops in a single layer in the greased frying basket, spray them with a little bit of olive oil, and air fry for 8 minutes. Turn the chops over, spray again with some oil, and cook for another 4 to 7 minutes. Serve with the beet-cabbage salad.

Bavarian-Style Crispy Pork Schnitzel

Prep time: 10 minutes | Cook time: 13 to 15 minutes | Serves 4

4 pork chops, center-cut
1 egg, beaten
1 teaspoon chili powder
2 tablespoons flour
2 tablespoons sour cream
Salt and black pepper to taste
½ cup bread crumbs
2 tablespoons olive oil

1. Preheat the air fryer to 380ºF (193ºC). Using a meat tenderizer, pound the chops until ¼-inch thickness. Whisk the egg and sour cream in a bowl. Mix the bread crumbs with chili powder, salt, and pepper in another bowl. Coat the chops with flour, then egg mixture, and finally in bread crumbs. Brush with olive oil and arrange them on the frying basket. Air fry for 13 to 15 minutes, turning once until golden brown. Serve.

Italian Pork Scallopini

Prep time: 10 minutes | Cook time: 14 to 16 minutes | Serves 4

4 pork loin thin steaks
Salt and black pepper to taste
¼ cup Parmesan cheese, grated
2 tablespoons Italian bread crumbs

1. Preheat the air fryer to 390ºF (199ºC). Spritz the frying basket with cooking spray. 2. In a bowl, mix Italian bread crumbs and Parmesan cheese. Season the pork steaks with salt and black pepper. Roll them in the breadcrumb mixture and spray them with cooking spray. Transfer to the frying basket and air fry for 14 to 16 minutes, turning once halfway through. Serve immediately.

Provencal Pork Medallions

Prep time: 10 minutes | Cook time: 14 to 17 minutes | Serves 4

1 pound (454 g) pork medallions
1 tablespoon olive oil
1 tablespoon herbs de Provence
½ cup dry white wine
½ lemon, juiced and zested
Salt and black pepper to taste

1. Preheat the air fryer to 360ºF (182ºC). Season the pork medallions with salt and black pepper and drizzle with olive oil. Place them in the frying basket and air fry for 12 to 14 minutes, flipping once. 2. Place a saucepan over medium heat and add white wine and 2 tablespoons of water; bring to a boil. Reduce the heat and add in the lemon zest and juice and herbs de Provence; season with salt and pepper. Simmer until the sauce thickens, about 2 to 3 minutes. Pour the sauce over the medallions and serve.

Beef Steak Strips with Tomato Sauce

Prep time: 20 minutes | Cook time: 19 to 23 minutes | Serves 4

1 pound (454 g) beef steak, cut into strips
1 tablespoon olive oil
½ cup flour
½ cup panko bread crumbs
¼ teaspoon cayenne pepper
2 eggs, beaten
½ cup milk
Salt and black pepper to taste
1 pound (454 g) tomatoes, chopped
1 tablespoon tomato paste
1 teaspoon honey
1 tablespoon white wine vinegar

1. Place the tomatoes, tomato paste, honey, and vinegar in a deep skillet over medium heat. Cook for 6 to 8 minutes, stirring occasionally until the sauce thickens. Set aside to cool. Preheat the air fryer to 390ºF (199ºC). 2. Spray the frying basket with olive oil. In a shallow bowl, thoroughly combine the flour, salt, black pepper, and cayenne pepper. In a second shallow bowl, whisk the eggs and milk until well combined. 3. Dredge the steak strips in the flour mixture, then dip in the egg mixture, and finally turn in the bread crumbs until completely coated. Arrange the strips in a single layer in the frying basket and spray with olive oil. Air fry for 8 minutes. Turn them and spray with a little bit of olive oil. Continue to cook for another 5 to 7 minutes until golden and crispy. Spoon into paper cones and serve warm with the tomato sauce. Enjoy!

Pork Belly the Philippine Style

Prep time: 20 minutes | Cook time: 30 minutes | Serves 4

2 pounds (907 g) pork belly, cut in half, blanched
1 bay leaf, crushed
2 tablespoons soy sauce
3 garlic cloves, minced
1 tablespoon peppercorns
1 tablespoon peanut oil
½ teaspoon salt

1. Take a mortar and pestle and place in the bay leaf, garlic, salt, peppercorns, and peanut oil. Smash until paste-like consistency forms. Whisk the paste with soy sauce. Pierce the belly skin with a fork. 2. Rub the mixture onto the meat, wrap the pork with a plastic foil and refrigerate for 2 hours. Preheat the fryer to 350ºF (177ºC) and grease the basket. Air fry the pork for 30 minutes, flipping once halfway through.

Pork Sandwiches with Bacon and Cheddar

Prep time: 15 minutes | Cook time: 25 to 28 minutes | Serves 2

½ pound (227 g) pork steak
1 teaspoon steak seasoning
Salt and black pepper to taste
5 thick bacon slices
½ cup Cheddar cheese, grated
½ tablespoon Worcestershire sauce
2 burger buns, halved

1. Preheat the air fryer to 400ºF (204ºC). Season the pork steak with black pepper, salt, and steak seasoning. Place in the greased frying basket and bake for 20 minutes, turning at the 14-minute mark. 2. Remove the steak to a chopping board, let cool slightly, and using two forks, shred into small pieces. Place the bacon in the frying basket and air fry at 370ºF (188ºC) for 5 to 8 minutes. Chop the bacon and transfer to a bowl. Mix in the pulled pork, Worcestershire sauce, and Cheddar cheese. Adjust the seasoning and spoon the mixture into the halved buns. Serve and enjoy.

Herbed Pork Belly

Prep time: 15 minutes | Cook time: 29 to 31 minutes | Serves 4

1½ pounds (680 g) pork belly, boiled
½ teaspoon garlic powder
½ teaspoon coriander powder
Salt and black pepper to taste
½ teaspoon dried thyme
½ teaspoon dried oregano
½ teaspoon cumin powder
1 lemon, halved

1. In a bowl, add the garlic powder, coriander powder, salt, black pepper, thyme, oregano, and cumin powder. Poke holes all around the belly using a fork. Smear the herbs, rub thoroughly on all sides of the meat with your hands, and squeeze the lemon juice all over. Let sit for 5 minutes. 2. Preheat the air fryer to 330ºF (166ºC). Put the pork in the greased frying basket and bake for 15 minutes. Flip, increase the temperature to 350ºF (177ºC), and cook for 14 to 16 more minutes. Remove to a chopping board. Let sit for 4 to 5 minutes before slicing. Serve the pork with sautéed asparagus and hot sauce if desired.

Effortless Beef Short Ribs

Prep time: 15 minutes | Cook time: 20 minutes | Serves 4

1½ pounds (680 g) bone-in beef short ribs
½ cup soy sauce
¼ cup white wine vinegar
1 brown onion, chopped
1 tablespoon ginger powder
2 garlic cloves, minced
1 tablespoon olive oil
2 tablespoons chives, chopped
Salt and black pepper to taste

1. In a shallow bowl, mix the short ribs, soy sauce, wine vinegar, onion, ginger powder, garlic, olive oil, salt, and pepper. Cover and marinate in the fridge for at least 2 hours. Preheat the air fryer to 390°F (199°C). 2. Arrange the ribs on the frying basket and bake for 12 minutes. Slide the basket out, flip, and cook for another 7 to 8 minutes until browned and crispy. Serve sprinkled with freshly chopped chives.

Greek-Style Beef Meatballs

Prep time: 15 minutes | Cook time: 21 to 25 minutes | Serves 4

1 pound (454 g) ground beef
2 tablespoons olive oil
1 teaspoon ground cumin
¼ cup Kalamata olives, chopped
1 red onion, chopped
1 garlic clove, minced
1 egg, beaten
1 pound (454 g) tomatoes, chopped
½ cup feta cheese, crumbled
Salt and black pepper to taste

1. Preheat the air fryer to 350°F (177°C). Mix the ground beef, red onion, garlic, Kalamata olives, and egg in a bowl. Season with cumin, salt, and black pepper. Shape the meat mixture into golf-sized balls. Place them in the greased frying basket and air fry for 11 to 13 minutes, shaking once halfway through. 2. Warm the olive oil in a saucepan over medium heat and add in the tomatoes, salt, and pepper. Bring to a boil and simmer for 8 to 10 until the sauce starts to thicken. Reduce the heat to low and gently stir in the meatballs; cook for 2 minutes. Transfer to a plate and scatter with the feta cheese all over to serve.

Mexican Beef Cabbage Wraps

Prep time: 15 minutes | Cook time: 25 minutes | Serves 4

1 pound (454 g) ground beef
8 savoy cabbage leaves
1 small onion, chopped
1 teaspoon taco seasoning
1 tablespoon cilantro-lime rotel
⅔ cup Mexican cheese, shredded
2 tablespoons olive oil
Salt and black pepper to taste
2 garlic cloves, minced
1 tablespoon fresh cilantro, chopped

1. Preheat the air fryer to 400°F (204°C). Heat olive oil in a skillet over medium heat and sauté onion and garlic until fragrant, about 3 minutes. Add in the ground beef, salt, black pepper, and taco seasoning. Cook until the beef browns while breaking it with a vessel as it cooks. Add cilantro rotel and stir to combine. 2. Lay 4 savoy cabbage leaves on a flat surface and scoop ¼ of the beef mixture in the center; sprinkle with Mexican cheese. Wrap diagonally and double wrap with the remaining cabbage leaves. 3. Arrange the rolls on the greased frying basket and bake for 8 minutes. Flip the rolls and cook for 5 to 6 more minutes. Remove to a plate, garnish with cilantro, and let cool before serving.

Ginger-Garlic Beef Ribs with Hot Sauce

Prep time: 10 minutes | Cook time: 15 to 17 minutes | Serves 2

1 rack rib steak
Salt and white pepper to taste
½ teaspoon garlic powder
½ teaspoon red pepper flakes
½ teaspoon ginger powder
3 tablespoons hot sauce

1. Preheat the air fryer to 360°F (182°C). Season the rib rack with salt, garlic powder, ginger powder, white pepper, and red pepper flakes. Place in the greased frying basket and bake for 10 minutes, turn and cook further for 5 to 7 minutes. Let sit for 3 minutes before slicing. Drizzle with hot sauce and serve.

Beef Koftas in Tomato Sauce

Prep time: 15 minutes | Cook time: 14 to 16 minutes | Serves 4

1 pound (454 g) ground beef
1 medium onion, chopped
1 egg
4 tablespoons bread crumbs
1 tablespoon fresh parsley, chopped
½ tablespoon thyme leaves, chopped
10 ounces (283 g) tomato sauce
Salt and black pepper to taste

1. Preheat the air fryer to 380°F (193°C). Mix all the ingredients, except for the tomato sauce, into a bowl. Shape the mixture into palm sized balls. Place the meatballs in the greased frying basket and air fry for 12 to 14 minutes, shaking once. Pour the tomato sauce in a deep saucepan over medium heat and simmer for 2 minutes or until heated through. Add in the meatballs and stir with a wooden spoon to coat. Serve.

Beef Meatballs with Cranberry Sauce

Prep time: 15 minutes | Cook time: 10 to 11 minutes | Serves 4

1 small onion, chopped
1 pound (454 g) grounded beef
1 tablespoon fresh parsley, chopped
½ tablespoon fresh thyme leaves, chopped
1 whole egg, beaten
3 tablespoons bread crumbs
Salt and black pepper to taste
1 cup cranberry sauce

1. Preheat the air fryer to 390°F (199°C). In a bowl, mix all the ingredients, except for the cranberry sauce. Roll the mixture into 10 to 12 balls. Place the balls in the greased frying basket and bake in the fryer for 8 minutes. Place the cranberry sauce in a saucepan over medium heat and stir for 2 to 3 minutes until heated through. Pour the sauce over the meatballs and serve.

California-Style Street Beef Taco Rolls

Prep time: 15 minutes | Cook time: 25 minutes | Serves 4

2 tablespoons olive oil
1 pound (454 g) ground beef
1 onion, chopped
2 garlic cloves, minced
½ tablespoon chili powder
2 tablespoons creole seasoning
1 (15-ounce / 425-g) can diced tomatoes
4 taco shells
1 cup Cheddar cheese, shredded
Salt and black pepper to taste
½ cup Pico de gallo
2 tablespoons fresh cilantro, chopped

1. Heat the olive oil in a pan over medium heat. Sauté garlic and onion for 3 minutes until soft. Add the ground beef and stir-fry for 6 minutes until no longer pink. Season with chili powder, creole seasoning, salt, and pepper. Pour in the tomatoes and stir-fry for another 5 to 6 minutes. Mix in the Cheddar cheese. 2. Divide the meat mixture between taco shells and roll up them, sealing the edges. Spray each roll with cooking spray and place them in the greased frying basket. Bake for 10 to 12 minutes at 390ºF (199ºC), turning once halfway through. Garnish with Pico de gallo and fresh cilantro. Serve immediately.

Smoked Beef Burgers with Hoisin Sauce

Prep time: 15 minutes | Cook time: 15 to 16 minutes | Serves 4

1 pound (454 g) ground beef
Salt and black pepper to taste
¼ teaspoon liquid smoke
2 teaspoons onion powder
1 teaspoon garlic powder
1½ tablespoons hoisin sauce
4 buns, halved
4 trimmed lettuce leaves
4 tablespoons mayonnaise
1 large tomato, sliced
4 Cheddar cheese slices

1. Preheat the air fryer to 370ºF (188ºC). In a bowl, combine the ground beef, salt, pepper, liquid smoke, onion powder, garlic powder, and hoisin sauce and mix with your hands. Form 4 patties out of the mixture. 2. Place the patties in the greased frying basket, making sure to leave enough space between them. Bake for 10 minutes, turn and cook further for 5 to 6 minutes until cooked through. Assemble the burgers in the buns with lettuce, mayonnaise, Cheddar cheese, tomato slices, and the patties. Serve and enjoy!

South American Arepas with Cilantro Sauce

Prep time: 15 minutes | Cook time: 12 to 14 minutes | Serves 4

1½ pounds (680 g) ground beef
1 Fresno chili pepper, chopped
2 tablespoons fresh cilantro, chopped
Salt and black pepper to taste
4 cheese arepas (buns), halved
½ red onion, sliced
1 cup mayonnaise
2 tablespoons fresh lime juice

1. In a small bowl, mix the mayonnaise with lime juice and cilantro. Season with salt and set aside. 2. Preheat the air fryer to 350ºF (177ºC). In a bowl, combine the ground beef, Fresno chili, salt, and black pepper. Mold the mixture into 4 patties. Spray them lightly on both sides with cooking spray and place in the frying basket. Air fry for 8 minutes, flip them, and cook for another 4 to 6 minutes or until browned and cooked through. Serve on cheese arepas with red onion and cilantro lime mayo sauce.

Healthy Burgers

Prep time: 15 minutes | Cook time: 14 to 16 minutes | Serves 4

1½ pounds (680 g) ground beef
½ teaspoon onion powder
Salt and black pepper to taste
½ teaspoon dried oregano
1 tablespoon Worcestershire sauce
½ teaspoon garlic powder
1 teaspoon Maggi seasoning sauce
1 tablespoon olive oil

1. Preheat the air fryer to 350ºF (177ºC). In a bowl, combine Worcestershire and Maggi sauces, onion and garlic powders, oregano, salt, and pepper. Add in the ground beef and mix until well combined. Divide the meat mixture into 4 equal pieces and flatten to form patties. Brush with olive oil and place the patties in the frying basket. Air fry for 14 to 16 minutes, turning once halfway through. Serve immediately.

Classic Beef Meatloaf

Prep time: 10 minutes | Cook time: 25 minutes | Serves 4

1 pound (454 g) ground beef
2 eggs, lightly beaten
½ cup bread crumbs
2 garlic cloves, minced
1 onion, finely chopped
2 tablespoons ketchup
1 teaspoon mixed dried herbs

1. Line a loaf pan that fits in the air fryer with baking paper. In a bowl, mix ground beef, eggs, bread crumbs, garlic, onion, and mixed herbs. Gently press the mixture into the pan and top with ketchup. Place in the frying basket and bake for 25 minutes at 380ºF (193ºC). Let cool for 10 to 15 minutes before slicing. Serve warm.

Cheesy Italian Beef Meatloaf

Prep time: 10 minutes | Cook time: 15 to 18 minutes | Serves 4

1 pound (454 g) ground beef
2 tablespoons fresh basil, chopped
1 onion, diced
1 tablespoon Worcestershire sauce
2 tablespoons tomato paste
Salt and black pepper to taste
1 cup bread crumbs
3 tablespoons Mozzarella cheese, grated

1. Preheat the air fryer to 350ºF (177ºC). In a bowl, add all ingredients except for the cheese. Mix with hands until well combined. Place in a greased baking dish and shape into a loaf. Place in the frying basket and bake for 15 to 18 minutes. Top with the cheese 3 to 4 minutes before it's cooked. Let cool slightly and slice.

"Stefania" Beef Meatloaf

Prep time: 15 minutes | Cook time: 25 minutes | Serves 4

1 cup tomato basil sauce
1½ pounds (680 g) ground beef
1 diced onion
2 garlic cloves, minced
2 tablespoons ginger, minced
½ cup bread crumbs
3 hard-boiled eggs, peeled
Salt and black pepper to taste
1 teaspoon paprika
½ teaspoon dried basil
2 tablespoons fresh parsley, chopped
2 egg whites

1. Preheat the air fryer to 360ºF (182ºC). In a bowl, add the beef, onion, garlic, ginger, bread crumbs, paprika, salt, pepper, basil, parsley, and egg whites; mix well. Shape half of the mixture into a long oblong form. Arrange the boiled eggs in a row at the center. Cover the eggs with the remaining meat dough. Scoop the meat mixture into a greased baking pan. Shape the meat into the pan while pressing firmly. Brush the tomato sauce onto the meat. Place the pan in the frying basket and bake for 25 minutes.

Homemade Hot Beef Satay

Prep time: 15 minutes | Cook time: 12 minutes | Serves 4

2 pounds (907 g) flank steaks, cut into long strips
2 tablespoons fish sauce
2 tablespoons soy sauce
2 tablespoons sugar
1½ teaspoons garlic powder
1½ teaspoons ground ginger
2 teaspoons hot sauce
2 tablespoons fresh cilantro, chopped
½ cup roasted peanuts, chopped

1. Preheat the air fryer to 400ºF (204ºC). In a Ziploc bag, add the beef strips, fish sauce, sugar, garlic powder, soy sauce, ginger, and hot sauce. Seal the bag and shake thoroughly. 2. Open the bag, remove the beef strips, shake off the excess marinade, and place in the frying basket in a single layer. Avoid overlapping. Air fry for 6 minutes, turn the beef, and cook further for 6 minutes. Dish the meat and garnish with roasted peanuts and freshly chopped cilantro.

Beef Steak with Mustard Sauce

Prep time: 10 minutes | Cook time: 15 minutes | Serves 2

2 (8-ounce / 227-g) beef sirloin steaks
Garlic salt and black pepper to taste
1 tablespoon olive oil
½ cup sour cream
1 tablespoon Dijon mustard
½ lemon, juiced and zested

1. In a bowl, whisk the olive oil with garlic salt and black pepper. Add in the beef and toss to coat. Cover and let sit for 1 hour at room temperature. 2. Place a small saucepan over medium heat and add in the sour cream, Dijon mustard, lemon zest, salt, and pepper. Bring to a simmer for 2 to 3 minutes. Remove and pour in the lemon juice; stir and set aside. 3. Preheat the air fryer to 380ºF (193ºC). Place the beef in the greased frying basket and air fry the beef for 6 minutes, turn over, and cook further for 6 minutes or until medium-rare. For well-done, add 1 more minute per side. Spoon the sauce over the beef and serve.

Chimichurri New York Steak

Prep time: 10 minutes | Cook time: 12 to 14 minutes | Serves 4

½ cup chimichurri salsa
1 tablespoon olive oil
1½ pounds (680 g) New York strip steak
1 tablespoon smoked paprika
Salt and black pepper to taste
1 jar (16-ounce / 454-g) roasted peppers, sliced

1. Preheat the air fryer to 380ºF (193ºC). Rub the steak with smoked paprika, salt, and black pepper. Drizzle with olive oil and bake in the air fryer for 12 to 14 minutes, turning once halfway through. Transfer to a cutting board and let it sit for 5 minutes. Slice, drizzle with chimichurri salsa, and serve with roasted peppers.

Argentinian Beef Empanadas

Prep time: 15 minutes | Cook time: 15 to 18 minutes | Serves 4

1 pound (454 g) ground beef
½ onion, diced
1 garlic clove, minced
¼ cup tomato salsa
4 empanada shells
1 egg yolk
2 teaspoons milk
½ teaspoon cumin
Salt and black pepper to taste
2 tablespoons olive oil

1. Heat olive oil in a pan over medium heat and cook the ground beef, onion, cumin, garlic, salt, and black pepper for 5 to 6 minutes, stirring occasionally. Stir in tomato salsa and cook for 3 minutes; set aside. 2. Preheat the air fryer to 350ºF (177ºC). In a bowl, whisk the egg yolk with milk. Divide the beef mixture between empanada shells, fold the shells and seal the ends with a fork. Brush with the egg mixture. Place the empanadas in the greased frying basket and air fry for 10 to 12 minutes, flipping once. Serve warm.

Mexican Chorizo and Beef Empanadas

Prep time: 15 minutes | Cook time: 30 minutes | Serves 4

2 garlic cloves, minced
½ cup green bell peppers, chopped
1 red onion, chopped
4 ounces (113 g) chorizo, chopped
½ pound (227 g) ground beef
4 dough discs
1 cup Mexican blend cheese, shredded
2 tablespoons vegetable oil
¼ cup chunky salsa
Salt and black pepper to taste

1. Warm the vegetable oil in a pan over medium heat and sauté bell peppers, garlic, and onion for 4 minutes until tender. Add the ground beef and chorizo and stir-fry for 5 to 6 minutes. Season with salt and pepper. Pour in the chunky salsa and cook, stirring occasionally, until the sauce thickens, 5 minutes. 2. Preheat the air fryer to 390ºF (199ºC). Divide the meat mixture and cheese between the dough discs. Fold them in half over the filling; press and seal the edges with a fork. Spritz with cooking spray and transfer to the air fryer. Bake for 12 to 15 minutes, turning once until golden. Let cool slightly before serving.

Mini Beef Sausage Rolls

Prep time: 10 minutes | Cook time: 18 to 20 minutes | Serves 4

1 pound (454 g) beef sausage meat	8 mini puff pastry squares
3 green onions, thinly sliced	1 cup flour
	1 egg, beaten

1. Preheat the air fryer to 360ºF (182ºC). Grease the frying basket with cooking spray. 2. In a bowl, mix the meat with green onions. Lay the pastry squares on a floured surface and divide the sausage mixture at the center of the pastry squares. Brush the edges with some of the beaten egg. Fold the squares and seal them. Transfer to the frying basket and brush the top of the rolls with the remaining egg. Air fry for 18 to 20 minutes, flipping once, until crisp and golden. Serve warm.

Garlic Steak with Mexican Salsa

Prep time: 10 minutes | Cook time: 16 to 18 minutes | Serves 4

2 rib-eye steaks	½ red onion, sliced
1 tablespoon olive oil	10 cherry tomatoes, quartered
Garlic salt and black pepper to taste	2 tablespoons fresh cilantro, chopped
½ cup heavy cream	1 green chili, minced
1 avocado, roughly chopped	1 lime, zested and juiced
7 ounces (198 g) canned sweetcorn	½ cup heavy cream

1. Preheat your air fryer to 390ºF (199ºC). In a bowl, whisk the olive oil, garlic salt, and black pepper. Massage the mixture onto the rib-eye steaks to coat on all sides. Lay the steaks in the greased frying basket and air fry for 16 to 18 minutes, turning once halfway through. Remove to a plate. 2. In a bowl, mix the avocado, corn, cherry tomatoes, red onion, cilantro, chili, lime juice, and lime zest. Season to taste. Serve the steaks with the Mexican salsa and a dollop of heavy cream on the side.

Chipotle Rib-Eye Steak with Avocado Salsa

Prep time: 10 minutes | Cook time: 16 minutes | Serves 4

1½ pounds (680 g) rib-eye steak	pepper
2 teaspoons olive oil	Salt and black pepper to taste
1 tablespoon chipotle chili	1 avocado, diced
	Juice from ½ lime

1. Place the steak on a chopping board. Drizzle with olive oil and sprinkle with chipotle pepper, salt, and black pepper. Rub the spices onto the meat. Let it sit to incorporate flavors for 30 minutes. 2. Preheat the air fryer to 400ºF (204ºC). Pull out the frying basket and place the meat inside. Bake for 10 minutes. Turn the steak and continue cooking for 6 minutes. Remove the steak, cover with foil, and let it sit for 5 minutes before slicing. Mash avocado in a bowl and mix with the lime juice. Serve with the sliced beef.

Gorgonzola Rib Eye Steak

Prep time: 15 minutes | Cook time: 17 to 19 minutes | Serves 4

1½ pounds (680 g) rib-eye steak	crumbled
1 teaspoon garlic powder	2 tablespoons fresh chives, chopped
1 cup heavy cream	2 tablespoons olive oil
1 cup gorgonzola cheese,	Salt and black pepper to taste

1. Preheat the air fryer to 400ºF (204ºC). In a bowl, combine olive oil, garlic powder, salt, and pepper. Rub the steak with the seasoning and place it in the frying basket. Bake for 14 to 16 minutes, flipping once. 2. Warm the heavy cream in a skillet over medium heat. Add the gorgonzola cheese and chives; stir until you obtain a smooth sauce, and the cheese is melted, 3 minutes. Drizzle the sauce over the steaks.

Tender Rib Eye Steak

Prep time: 10 minutes | Cook time: 18 to 20 minutes | Serves 2

2 beef rib-eye steaks	2 tablespoons olive oil
1 tablespoon balsamic vinegar	Salt and black pepper to taste
½ tablespoon Italian seasoning	

1. In a bowl, combine all ingredients and toss to coat. Refrigerate for 30 minutes. Preheat the air fryer to 360ºF (182ºC). Transfer the beef to the frying basket and bake for 18 to 20 minutes, flipping once. Serve hot.

Parsley Crumbed Beef Strips

Prep time: 10 minutes | Cook time: 14 to 16 minutes | Serves 2

2 tablespoons vegetable oil	1 whole egg, whisked
½ teaspoon fresh parsley, chopped	1 thin beef sirloin steak, cut into strips
1 cup bread crumbs	1 lemon, juiced

1. Preheat the air fryer to 370ºF (188ºC). In a bowl, add bread crumbs, parsley, and vegetable oil and stir well to get a loose mixture. Dip the beef in the egg, then coat in the crumbs mixture. Place the strips in the greased frying basket and air fry for 14 to 16 minutes, flipping once. Serve with a drizzle of lemon juice.

Pesto Beef Steaks

Prep time: 10 minutes | Cook time: 14 to 16 minutes | Serves 4

4 boneless beef steaks	Salt and black pepper to taste
1 tablespoon smoked paprika	4 tablespoons pesto sauce

1. Season the steaks with paprika, salt, and black pepper, and let sit for 20 minutes. Preheat the air fryer to 390ºF (199ºC). Place the steaks in the greased frying basket and bake for 14 to 16 minutes, flipping once. Remove to a cutting board and let cool slightly before slicing. Top with pesto sauce and serve.

Chapter 1 Vegetables and Sides | 57

Delicious Beef with Rice and Broccoli

Prep time: 20 minutes | Cook time: 16 to 18 minutes | Serves 4

1 pound (454 g) beef steak, cut into strips
Salt and black pepper to taste
2 cups cooked rice
1½ tablespoons soy sauce
2 teaspoons sesame oil
2 teaspoons ginger, finely chopped
2 teaspoons vinegar
1 garlic clove, finely chopped
½ head steamed broccoli, chopped

1. Season the beef with salt and black pepper. Preheat the air fryer to 400ºF (204ºC) and grease the frying basket. Bake the beef for 12 to 14 minutes, turning once. Remove to a plate and cover with foil to keep it warm. 2. Warm sesame oil in a skillet over medium heat. Sauté the ginger and garlic for 3 minutes until tender. Add in vinegar, cooked rice, broccoli, garlic, and soy sauce. Stir-fry for 1 minute or until heated through. Serve the strips over a bed of the rice mixture.

Spicy Sweet Beef with Veggie Topping

Prep time: 15 minutes | Cook time: 12 to 14 minutes | Serves 4

2 beef steaks, sliced into thin strips
2 garlic cloves, minced
2 teaspoons maple syrup
1 teaspoon oyster sauce
1 teaspoon cayenne pepper
½ teaspoon olive oil
Juice of 1 lime
Salt and black pepper to taste
1 cauliflower, cut into florets
2 carrots, cut into chunks
1 cup green peas

1. Preheat the air fryer to 400ºF (204ºC). In a bowl, place the beef strips, garlic, maple syrup, oyster sauce, cayenne pepper, olive oil, lime juice, salt, and black pepper; stir to combine. Transfer the mixture to the frying basket. Top with the veggies. Transfer to the fryer and bake for 12 to 14 minutes, shaking once.

Sausage Beef Rolls

Prep time: 20 minutes | Cook time: 20 minutes | Serves 4

½ pound (227 g) beef sausage, sliced
1 tablespoon olive oil
1½ pounds (680 g) sirloin steaks, sliced
2 bell peppers, cut into thin strips
2 tablespoons Worcestershire sauce
½ tablespoon garlic powder
½ tablespoon onion powder
Salt and black pepper to taste

1. Pound the steaks very thin using a meat mallet. Mix the Worcestershire sauce, garlic powder, and onion powder in a bowl. Add in the steaks and stir to coat. Cover with foil and refrigerate for at least 30 minutes. While the steaks are marinating, soak 8 toothpicks in water, about 15 to 20 minutes. 2. Preheat the air fryer to 390ºF (199ºC). Remove the steaks from the fridge. Place the bell peppers and beef sausage in the middle of the steaks, then sprinkle with salt and black pepper. Roll up the beef tightly and secure using toothpicks. Generously spray the frying basket with olive oil. Place the beef rolls in the frying basket with the toothpick side down; do not overlap. Air fry for 10 minutes. Turn the rolls and cook for another 7 to 10 minutes or until nice and crispy. Serve warm.

French-Style Entrecote with Bordelaise Sauce

Prep time: 10 minutes | Cook time: 15 to 18 minutes | Serves 2

2 beef rib-eye steaks
1 tablespoon butter, softened
1 shallot, chopped
¼ cup Merlot wine
½ cup beef stock
Salt and black pepper to taste

1. Preheat the air fryer to 390ºF (199ºC). Rub the steaks with salt and pepper. Place them in the greased frying basket and bake for 12 to 15 minutes, turning once halfway through. Let cool slightly before slicing. 2. Melt the butter in a saucepan over medium heat and sauté the shallot for 3 minutes. Pour in the wine and stock and simmer until reduced by half. Pour the sauce over the beef and serve with french fries.

Thai Roasted Beef

Prep time: 25 minutes | Cook time: 12 to 14 minutes | Serves 4

1 pound (454 g) beef steak, sliced
Salt and black pepper to taste
2 tablespoons soy sauce
1 tablespoon fresh ginger, minced
2 chilies, seeded and chopped
2 garlic cloves, chopped
1 teaspoon brown sugar
Juice of 1 lime
2 tablespoons mirin
1 tablespoon fresh cilantro, chopped
1 tablespoon fresh basil, chopped
2 tablespoons sesame oil
2 tablespoons fish sauce

1. Place all ingredients, except for the beef, in a blender and process until smooth. Transfer to a zipper bag and add in the beef. Seal the bag, shake to combine, and refrigerate for 1 hour. 2. Preheat the air fryer to 350ºF (177ºC). Place the marinated beef in the greased frying basket and air fry for 12 to 14 minutes. Let sit for a couple of minutes before serving.

Bloody Mary Beef Steak with Avocado

Prep time: 10 minutes | Cook time: 14 to 16 minutes | Serves 4

1½ pounds (680 g) flank steaks
2 tablespoons tomato juice
1 lemon, juiced and zested
2 tablespoons vodka
1 teaspoon Worcestershire sauce
1 teaspoon hot sauce
Celery salt and black pepper to taste

1. Combine tomato juice, vodka, Worcestershire sauce, hot sauce, lemon juice and zest, celery salt, and black pepper in a bowl. Add in the flank steaks and toss to coat. Marinate for 30 minutes. 2. Preheat the air fryer to 360ºF (182ºC). Remove the steaks from the marinade and place them in the greased frying basket. Bake for 14 to 16 minutes, turning once halfway through. Let them cool slightly before serving.

Mexican Beef Quesadillas

Prep time: 15 minutes | Cook time: 20 minutes | Serves 4

2 tablespoons olive oil
8 soft round taco shells
1 pound (454 g) beef steak, sliced
1 cup Mozzarella cheese, grated
½ cup fresh cilantro, chopped
1 jalapeño chili, chopped
1 cup corn kernels, canned
Salt and black pepper to taste

1. Heat olive oil in a skillet over medium heat. Brown the beef for 6 minutes, stirring occasionally. Place the cooked beef on each taco shell, top with Mozzarella cheese, cilantro, jalapeño, corn, salt, and pepper. Fold in half and secure with toothpicks. Arrange the quesadillas in the greased frying basket. Bake in the preheated air fryer for 14 to 16 minutes at 380ºF (193ºC), turning once halfway through. Serve.

Korean Beef Bulgogi

Prep time: 20 minutes | Cook time: 13 minutes | Serves 4

1 pound (454 g) flank steak
2 cups cooked brown rice
2 cups steamed broccoli florets
½ cup soy sauce
1 tablespoon gochujang (hot pepper paste)
1 tablespoon fresh ginger, grated
2 spring onion, sliced diagonally
2 tablespoons brown sugar
2 tablespoons red wine vinegar
1 tablespoon olive oil
1 tablespoon sesame oil
3 teaspoons slurry (2 teaspoons cornstarch mixed with 1 teaspoon water)

1. Slice the flank steak across the grain into about ¼-inch strips. Whisk the soy sauce, gochujang, ginger, brown sugar, vinegar, olive oil, and sesame oil in a large bowl. Add in the beef strips and toss to coat. Cover the bowl with plastic wrap and refrigerate for 1 hour. 2. Preheat your Air Fryer to 390ºF (199ºC). Remove the steak from the marinade. Set any leftover marinade aside. Put the steak in the greased frying basket in a single layer and air fry for 10 minutes. Turn the meat pieces over and cook until they reach your desired level of doneness according to the internal temperature. Rare is 120ºF (49ºC), medium-rare is 130ºF (54ºC), the medium is 140ºF (60ºC), and medium well is 150ºF (66ºC). 3. Put the reserved marinade in a small saucepan over medium heat and bring to a boil. Pour the slurry into the saucepan and simmer until the sauce thickens, about 3 minutes. Add in the meat pieces and stir to coat. Remove from the heat. Divide the brown rice and steamed broccoli between 4 bowls. Top with the meat and sprinkle with spring onions. Serve immediately.

Beef Veggie Mix with Hoisin Sauce

Prep time: 30 minutes | Cook time: 30 minutes | Serves 4

Hoisin Sauce:
2 tablespoons soy sauce
1 tablespoon peanut butter
½ teaspoon sriracha sauce
1 teaspoon sugar
1 teaspoon rice vinegar
3 cloves garlic, minced
Beef Veggie Mix:
1½ pounds (680 g) beef sirloin steak, cut into strips
1 yellow pepper, cut into strips
1 green pepper, cut into strips
1 white onion, cut into strips
1 red onion, cut into strips
1 pound (454 g) broccoli, cut into florets
1 tablespoon soy sauce
2 teaspoons sesame oil
1 garlic clove, minced
1 teaspoon ground ginger
1 tablespoon olive oil

1. Place a pan over low heat and add all hoisin sauce ingredients. Bring to a simmer and cook until reduced, about 3 to 4 minutes; let cool. To the chilled hoisin sauce, add garlic, sesame oil, soy sauce, ginger, and ½ cup of water; mix well. Stir in the beef, cover, and refrigerate for 20 minutes to marinate. 2. Preheat the air fryer to 400ºF (204ºC). In the frying basket, combine broccoli, peppers, onions, and olive oil. Place in the fryer and bake for 10 minutes, shaking once. Transfer to a plate; cover with foil to keep warm. 3. Remove the meat from the fridge and drain the liquid into a bowl. Add the beef to the heated frying basket. Bake for 10 minutes, shake, and cook for 7 more minutes. Transfer to the veggie plate, season with salt and pepper, and pour the hoisin sauce over. Serve immediately.

Beef Roast with Red Potatoes

Prep time: 15 minutes | Cook time: 50 to 60 minutes | Serves 4

2 tablespoons olive oil
1 (2-pound / 907-g) top round roast beef
Salt and black pepper to taste
½ teaspoon dried thyme
1 teaspoon fresh rosemary, chopped
1 pound (454 g) red potatoes, halved

1. Preheat the air fryer to 360ºF (182ºC). In a bowl, mix rosemary, salt, pepper, half of the oil, and thyme; rub onto the beef. Place the meat in the frying basket and bake for 20 minutes. Give the meat a turn and cook for 10 to 15 more minutes until browned. Remove the meat to a plate and cover with foil to keep warm. 2. Season the potatoes with the remaining olive oil, salt, and black pepper. Bake in the air fryer for 20 to 25 minutes at 400ºF (204ºC), shaking the basket occasionally. Slice the beef and serve with potatoes.

Beef Steak Au Poivre

Prep time: 15 minutes | Cook time: 15 to 17 minutes | Serves 4

2 tablespoons butter
1 pound (454 g) beef tenderloin steaks, 1½-inch thick
Salt to taste
2 tablespoons whole peppercorns, crushed
1 teaspoon Dijon mustard
1 teaspoon olive oil
½ cup brandy
1 cup heavy cream

1. Preheat air fryer to 400ºF (204ºC). Season the beef with salt and coat in the peppercorns. Transfer them to the greased frying basket. Drizzle with olive oil and air fry the beef for 12 to 14 minutes, turning once. 2. Warm butter in a pan over medium heat. Remove the pan, add in the brandy, and shake the pan until it evaporates. Stir in mustard and heavy cream and return to the heat, 3 minutes. Pour over the beef to serve.

Fusion Flank Steak with Mexican Dressing

Prep time: 10 minutes | Cook time: 12 to 14 minutes | Serves 4

2 tablespoons sesame oil
5 tablespoons tamari sauce
3 teaspoons honey
1 tablespoon grated fresh ginger
2 green onions, minced
2 garlic cloves, minced
¼ teaspoon crushed red pepper flakes
1¼ pounds (567 g) flank steak
Salt to taste
1 Jalapeño pepper, minced
2 tablespoons fresh cilantro, roughly chopped
2 tablespoons chives, finely chopped
1 lime, juiced
3 tablespoons olive oil

1. In a bowl, combine the jalapeño pepper with the cilantro, chives, lime juice, olive oil, and salt; set aside. 2. In another shallow bowl, mix the sesame oil, tamari sauce, honey, ginger, green onions, garlic, and pepper flakes. Stir until the honey is dissolved. Put the steak into the bowl and massage the marinade onto the meat to coat well. Cover the bowl with a lid and marinate for 2 hours in the fridge. 3. Preheat the air fryer to 390ºF (199ºC). Remove the steak from the marinade and place it in the air fryer. Bake for 6 minutes, flip, and cook further until it is done to your preference, 6 to 8 minutes. Let the steak rest for a few minutes and slice thinly against the grain. Serve topped with the Mexican dressing.

Pesto Beef Rolls with Spinach

Prep time: 10 minutes | Cook time: 14 to 16 minutes | Serves 4

4 beefsteak slices
Salt and black pepper to taste
3 tablespoons pesto
4 Cheddar cheese slices
¾ cup spinach, chopped
1 bell pepper, seeded and sliced

1. Preheat the air fryer to 400ºF (204ºC). Spread the steak slices with pesto and top with Cheddar cheese, spinach, and bell pepper. Roll the slices up and secure them with toothpicks. Season with salt and pepper. Place the rolls in the greased frying basket and air fry for 14 to 16 minutes, turning once halfway through. Serve.

Air Fried Beef with Veggies and Oyster Sauce

Prep time: 15 minutes | Cook time: 17 to 20 minutes | Serves 4

1 pound (454 g) circular beef steak, cut into strips
½ cauliflower head, cut into florets
2 carrots, sliced into rings
⅓ cup oyster sauce
2 tablespoons sesame oil
⅓ cup sherry
1 teaspoon soy sauce
1 teaspoon white sugar
1 teaspoon cornstarch
1 tablespoon olive oil
1 garlic clove, minced
2 tablespoons pine nuts, toasted

1. Preheat the air fryer to 390ºF (199ºC). In a bowl, mix all ingredients, except for the beef, cauliflower, and carrots. Add in the beef and stir to coat. Bake in the fryer for 14 to 16 minutes, shaking once or twice. Blanch the cauliflower and carrots in salted water in a pot over medium heat for 3 to 4 minutes. Drain and place on a serving plate. Top with pine nuts. When the beef is ready, place it on the side of the veggies and serve.

Beer-Dredged Corned Beef

Prep time: 10 minutes | Cook time: 20 minutes | Serves 4

2 tablespoons olive oil
1 white onion, chopped
2 carrots, julienned
1 (12- to 15-ounce / 340- to 425-g) bottle beer
1 cup chicken broth
1 pound (454 g) corned beef

1. Preheat the air fryer to 380ºF (193ºC). Cover the beef with beer and let sit for 20 minutes. Heat olive oil in a pot over medium heat and sauté the carrots and onion for 3 minutes. Add in the drained beef and broth and bring to a boil. Then simmer for 5 minutes. Remove the meat with a slotted spoon and place it in the greased frying basket. Air fry for 12 minutes or until nicely browned. Serve with veggies and sauce.

Simple Roasted Beef with Herbs

Prep time: 10 minutes | Cook time: 15 minutes | Serves 2

2 teaspoons olive oil
1 pound (454 g) beef roast
½ teaspoon dried rosemary
½ teaspoon dried thyme
½ teaspoon dried oregano
Salt and black pepper to taste

1. Preheat the air fryer to 400ºF (204ºC). Drizzle olive oil all over the beef and sprinkle with salt, black pepper, and herbs. Massage the meat with your hands. Place in the air fryer and bake for 15 minutes for medium-rare and 18 minutes for well-done. Check halfway through cooking and flip to ensure it cooks evenly. Remove from the fryer, wrap in foil for 10 minutes, to reabsorb the juices and serve sliced.

Yummy London Broil with Parsley Butter

Prep time: 20 minutes | Cook time: 12 to 15 minutes | Serves 4

2 London broil steaks, cut into strips
1 tablespoon brown sugar
½ teaspoon onion powder
2 garlic cloves, minced
½ sweet paprika
½ teaspoon mustard powder
1 tablespoon Worcestershire sauce
2 tablespoons canola oil
½ lemon, juiced
Salt and black pepper to taste
2 tablespoons butter, softened
2 tablespoons parsley, chopped

1. In a bowl, mix brown sugar, onion powder, garlic, paprika, mustard powder, Worcestershire sauce, canola oil, lemon juice, salt, and pepper. Add in the steaks and toss to coat. Refrigerate for 1 hour. Preheat the air fryer to 400ºF (204ºC). Place the beef in the greased frying basket and air fry for 12 to 15 minutes, shaking once. Mix the butter with parsley, salt, and pepper. Spread on the beef slices and serve hot.

Herby Roast Beef

Prep time: 10 minutes | Cook time: 15 to 18 minutes | Serves 4

2 pounds (907 g) beef loin
Salt and black pepper to taste
½ teaspoon dried thyme
½ teaspoon dried rosemary
½ teaspoon dried oregano
½ teaspoon garlic powder
1 teaspoon onion powder
2 tablespoons olive oil

1. Preheat the air fryer to 380ºF (193ºC). In a bowl, combine all the ingredients, except for the beef. Rub the mixture onto the meat. Place it in the air fryer and bake for 8 to 10 minutes. Turn the meat over and cook for 7 to 8 more minutes until well roasted. Let cool before slicing. Serve with steamed veggies if desired.

Lamb Meatballs with Roasted Veggie Bake

Prep time: 15 minutes | Cook time: 22 to 24 minutes | Serves 2

½ pound (227 g) ground lamb
1 shallot, chopped
½ teaspoon garlic powder
1 egg, beaten
1 potato, chopped
¼ red onion, sliced
1 carrot, sliced diagonally
½ small beetroot, sliced
1 cup cherry tomatoes, halved
2 tablespoons olive oil
Salt and black pepper to taste
Parmesan shavings

1. Preheat the air fryer to 370ºF (188ºC). In a bowl, mix red onion, potato, cherry tomatoes, carrot, beetroot, salt, and olive oil. Transfer to the frying basket and bake for 10 minutes, shaking once. In another bowl, mix the ground lamb, egg, shallot, garlic powder, salt, and black pepper. Shape the mixture into balls. Place them over the vegetables in the air fryer, and air fry for 12 to 14 minutes, flipping once. Remove the dish and top with Parmesan shavings to serve.

Traditional Lamb Kebabs

Prep time: 15 minutes | Cook time: 14 to 16 minutes | Serves 4

1½ pounds (680 g) ground lamb
1 green onion, chopped
2 tablespoons mint leaves, chopped
3 garlic cloves, minced
1 teaspoon paprika
2 teaspoons coriander seeds
½ teaspoon cayenne pepper
1 teaspoon salt
1 tablespoon fresh parsley, chopped
1 teaspoon cumin
½ teaspoon ground ginger
1 red bell pepper, cut into 2-inch pieces
1 sweet onion, cut into wedges
1 cup whole small mushrooms

1. Preheat the air fryer to 380ºF (193ºC). Combine all ingredients, except for the bell pepper, sweet onion, and mushrooms, in a bowl. Mix well with your hands until the herbs and spices are evenly distributed. Form the mixture into sausage shapes. Thread the shapes and vegetables onto the skewers, alternately, and place them in the greased frying basket. Air fry for 14 to 16 minutes, turning once. Serve hot.

Wiener Beef Schnitzel

Prep time: 15 minutes | Cook time: 12 minutes | Serves 1

1 (½ inch thick) top sirloin steak
1 egg, beaten
2 ounces (57 g) panko bread crumbs
2 tablespoons flour, sifted
Lemon slices
¼ teaspoon garlic powder
1 parsley butter slice
Salt and black pepper to taste

1. Preheat the air fryer to 350ºF (177ºC). Combine the bread crumbs, garlic, salt, and pepper in a bowl. Dredge the steak in the flour, then dip in the egg, and finally toss it into the crumbs mixture. Place in the greased frying basket and air fry for 12 minutes, turning once. Top with parsley butter and lemon slices.

Crunchy Beef Escalopes

Prep time: 15 minutes | Cook time: 16 minutes | Serves 4

4 beef bottom round steaks, thinly cut
½ cup flour, sifted
2 eggs, beaten
Salt and black pepper to taste
1 cup bread crumbs
2 tablespoons olive oil
2 butter slices

1. Preheat the air fryer to 360ºF (182ºC). Coat the steaks in the sifted flour and shake off any excess. Dip into the beaten eggs, season with salt and black pepper, and toss into the bread crumbs to coat well. Brush with olive oil and air fry for 16 minutes, turning once halfway through. Serve topped with butter slices.

Greek Stuffed Tenderloin

Prep time: 10 minutes | Cook time: 10 minutes | Serves 4

1½ pounds (680 g) venison or beef tenderloin, pounded to ¼ inch thick
3 teaspoons fine sea salt
1 teaspoon ground black pepper
2 ounces (57 g) creamy goat cheese
½ cup crumbled feta cheese
(about 2 ounces / 57 g)
¼ cup finely chopped onions
2 cloves garlic, minced
For Garnish/Serving (Optional):
Prepared yellow mustard
Halved cherry tomatoes
Extra-virgin olive oil
Sprigs of fresh rosemary
Lavender flowers

1. Spray the frying basket with avocado oil. Preheat the air fryer to 400ºF (204ºC). 2. Season the tenderloin on all sides with the salt and pepper. 3. In a mixing bowl, combine the goat cheese, feta, onions, and garlic. Place the mixture in the center of the tenderloin. Tightly roll the tenderloin like a jelly roll. Tie the rolled tenderloin tightly with kitchen twine. 4. Air fry the meat for 5 minutes. Flip over and cook for another 5 minutes, or until the internal temperature reaches 135ºF (57ºC) for medium-rare. 5. To serve, smear a line of yellow mustard on a platter, then place the meat next to it and add halved cherry tomatoes on the side, if desired. Drizzle with olive oil and garnish with rosemary sprigs and lavender flowers, if desired.

Beef Liver with Onions

Prep time: 15 minutes | Cook time: 17 to 19 minutes | Serves 2

1 pound (454 g) beef liver, sliced
2 onions, sliced
1 tablespoon black truffle oil
Salt and black pepper to taste
1 garlic clove, minced
1 tablespoon fresh parsley, chopped

1. Preheat the air fryer to 360ºF (182ºC). Season the liver with salt and pepper; brush with the oil. Spread the onion slices on a greased frying basket. Bake in the fryer for 5 minutes. Arrange the liver on top of the onions and bake further for 12 to 14 minutes, turning once halfway through cooking. Serve with garlic and parsley.

African Minty Lamb Kofta

Prep time: 15 minutes | Cook time: 10 to 12 minutes | Serves 4

1 pound (454 g) ground lamb
1 teaspoon cumin
2 tablespoons mint, chopped
1 teaspoon garlic powder
1 teaspoon onion powder
1 tablespoon ras el hanout
½ teaspoon dried coriander
4 bamboo skewers
Salt and black pepper to taste

1. In a bowl, mix ground lamb, cumin, garlic and onion powders, mint, ras el hanout, coriander, salt, and black pepper. Mold into sausage shapes and place onto skewers. Let sit for 15 minutes in the fridge. 2. Preheat the air fryer to 380ºF (193ºC). Grease the frying basket with cooking spray. Arrange the skewers in the basket and air fry for 10 to 12 minutes, turning once halfway through. Serve with yogurt dip if desired.

Bulgogi Burgers

Prep time: 30 minutes | Cook time: 10 minutes | Serves 4

Burgers:
1 pound (454 g) 85% lean ground beef
¼ cup chopped scallions
2 tablespoons gochujang (Korean red chile paste)
1 tablespoon dark soy sauce
2 teaspoons minced garlic
2 teaspoons minced fresh ginger
2 teaspoons sugar
1 tablespoon toasted sesame oil
½ teaspoon kosher salt
Gochujang Mayonnaise:
¼ cup mayonnaise
¼ cup chopped scallions
1 tablespoon gochujang (Korean red chile paste)
1 tablespoon toasted sesame oil
2 teaspoons sesame seeds
4 hamburger buns

1. Mix all the burger ingredients in a bowl. Marinate at room temperature, or refrigerate for up to 24 hours. 2. Divide the meat into four portions and form into round patties. Make a slight depression in the middle of each patty with your thumb to prevent them from puffing up into a dome shape while cooking. 3. Roast in the air fryer at 350ºF (177ºC) for 10 minutes until the internal temperature reaches 160ºF / 71ºC (medium). 4. Meanwhile, stir together the mayonnaise, scallions, gochujang, sesame oil, and sesame seeds. 5. To serve, place the burgers on the buns and top with the mayonnaise.

Lamb Chops with Lemony Couscous

Prep time: 10 minutes | Cook time: 14 to 16 minutes | Serves 4

4 lamb chops
2 tablespoons olive oil
2 garlic cloves, minced
Salt and black pepper to taste
2 tablespoons fresh thyme, chopped
1 cup couscous
1 lemon, zested and juiced

1. Preheat the air fryer to 400ºF (204ºC). Rub the lamb chops with olive oil, garlic, salt, and black pepper. Place them in the greased frying basket. Air fry for 14 to 16 minutes, turning once halfway through cooking. 2. Meanwhile, place the couscous in a heatproof bowl and pour over 1½ cups of salted boiling water. Cover and let it sit for 8 to 12 minutes until all the water is absorbed. Gently stir in the lemon juice and lemon zest and fresh thyme with a fork. Serve the lamb on a bed of couscous and enjoy!

Easy Lamb Chop Bites

Prep time: 10 minutes | Cook time: 12 to 16 minutes | Serves 4

1 pound (454 g) lamb loin chops
1 egg
¼ cup buttermilk
1 cup corn flakes, crushed
Salt and black pepper to taste

1. In a bowl, whisk the egg with buttermilk. Add in the lamb and stir to coat. On a plate, spread the corn flakes and mix them with salt and pepper. Coat the lamb chops in the cornflakes and arrange them on the greased frying basket. Air fry for 12 to 16 minutes at 360ºF (182ºC), turning once halfway through. Serve.

Sweet and Sour Lamb Strips

Prep time: 15 minutes | Cook time: 14 to 16 minutes | Serves 4

1 cup cornflour
1 teaspoon garlic powder
1 teaspoon allspice
Salt and black pepper to taste
2 eggs
1 pound (454 g) lean lamb, cut into strips
Sauce:
6 tablespoons ketchup
½ lemon, juiced
1 teaspoon honey
2 tablespoons soy sauce

1. Preheat the air fryer to 350ºF (177ºC). In a bowl, whisk all the sauce ingredients with ½ cup of water until smooth; reserve. In another bowl, mix the garlic powder, cornflour, allspice, salt, and black pepper. 2. In a third bowl, beat the eggs with a pinch of salt. Coat the lamb in the cornflour mixture, then dip in the eggs, then again in the cornflour mixture. Spray with cooking spray and place in the frying basket. Air fry for 14 to 16 minutes, shaking once halfway through. Serve drizzled with the prepared sauce.

Thyme Lamb Chops with Asparagus

Prep time: 15 minutes | Cook time: 14 to 16 minutes | Serves 4

1 pound (454 g) lamb chops
2 tablespoons olive oil
2 teaspoons fresh thyme, chopped
1 garlic clove, minced
Salt and black pepper to taste
1 pound (454 g) asparagus spears, trimmed

1. Preheat the air fryer to 400°F (204°C). Drizzle the asparagus with some olive oil and sprinkle with salt. Season the chops with salt and pepper. Brush with the remaining olive oil and place in the frying basket. Air fry for 10 minutes, turn and add the asparagus. Cook for another 4 to 6 minutes. Serve topped with thyme.

Lamb Taquitos

Prep time: 15 minutes | Cook time: 13 to 14 minutes | Serves 4

1 pound (454 g) lamb meat, sliced into strips
2 tablespoons olive oil
2 teaspoons fresh cilantro, chopped
2 teaspoons fire-roasted green chilies
2 tablespoons queso fresco, crumbled
4 corn tortillas

1. Warm olive oil in a skillet over medium heat and stir-fry the lamb for 5 to 6 minutes. Remove and stir in green chilies. Preheat the air fryer to 400°F (204°C). Divide the mixture between tortillas and roll up them. Spritz with cooking spray and air fry for 8 minutes, turning once. Top with queso fresco and cilantro to serve.

Lamb and Cucumber Burgers

Prep time: 8 minutes | Cook time: 15 to 18 minutes | Serves 4

1 teaspoon ground ginger
½ teaspoon ground coriander
¼ teaspoon freshly ground white pepper
½ teaspoon ground cinnamon
½ teaspoon dried oregano
¼ teaspoon ground allspice
¼ teaspoon ground turmeric
½ cup low-fat plain Greek yogurt
1 pound (454 g) ground lamb
1 teaspoon garlic paste
¼ teaspoon salt
¼ teaspoon freshly ground black pepper
Cooking oil spray
4 hamburger buns
½ cucumber, thinly sliced

1. In a bowl, stir together the ginger, coriander, white pepper, cinnamon, oregano, allspice, and turmeric. Put the yogurt in a bowl and add half the spice mixture. Mix well and refrigerate. 2. Preheat the air fryer to 360°F (182°C). Spray the frying basket with cooking oil. 3. In a bowl, combine the lamb, garlic paste, remaining spice mix, salt, and pepper. Gently but thoroughly mix the ingredients with your hands and form into 4 patties. 4. Air fry for 18 minutes, or until a food thermometer inserted into the burgers registers 160°F (71°C). Assemble the burgers on the buns with cucumber slices and a dollop of the yogurt dip.

Peppercorn-Crusted Beef Tenderloin

Prep time: 10 minutes | Cook time: 25 minutes | Serves 6

2 tablespoons salted butter, melted
2 teaspoons minced roasted garlic
3 tablespoons ground 4-peppercorn blend
1 (2-pound / 907-g) beef tenderloin, trimmed of visible fat

1. In a bowl, mix the butter and roasted garlic. Brush it over the beef tenderloin. 2. Place the ground peppercorns onto a plate and roll the tenderloin through them, creating a crust. Place tenderloin into the frying basket. 3. Roast at 400°F (204°C) for 25 minutes, turning once halfway through the cooking time. 4. Allow to rest 10 minutes before slicing.

Spicy Lamb Sirloin Chops

Prep time: 30 minutes | Cook time: 15 minutes | Serves 4

½ yellow onion, coarsely chopped
4 coin-size slices peeled fresh ginger
5 garlic cloves
1 teaspoon garam masala
1 teaspoon ground fennel
1 teaspoon ground cinnamon
1 teaspoon ground turmeric
½ to 1 teaspoon cayenne pepper
½ teaspoon ground cardamom
1 teaspoon kosher salt
1 pound (454 g) lamb sirloin chops

1. Pulse the onion, ginger, garlic, garam masala, fennel, cinnamon, turmeric, cayenne, cardamom, and salt in a blender until the onion is finely minced and the mixture forms a thick paste. 2. Place the lamb chops in a bowl. Slash the meat and fat with a sharp knife several times to allow the marinade to penetrate better. Add the spice paste to the bowl and toss the lamb to coat. Marinate for 30 minutes or cover and refrigerate for up to 24 hours. 3. Place the lamb chops in a single layer in the frying basket. Roast at 325°F (163°C) for 15 minutes, turning the chops halfway through the cooking time, until internal temperature reaches 145°F (63°C) (medium-rare).

Bacon and Cheese Stuffed Pork Chops

Prep time: 10 minutes | Cook time: 12 minutes | Serves 4

½ ounce (14 g) plain pork rinds, finely crushed
½ cup shredded sharp Cheddar cheese
4 slices cooked sugar-free bacon, crumbled
4 (4-ounce / 113-g) boneless pork chops
½ teaspoon salt
¼ teaspoon ground black pepper

1. In a bowl, mix pork rinds, Cheddar, and bacon. 2. Make a 3-inch slit in the side of each pork chop and stuff with ¼ pork rind mixture. Sprinkle each side of pork chops with salt and pepper. Place pork chops into ungreased frying basket, stuffed side up. Air fry at 400°F (204°C) for 12 minutes until pork chops are browned and the internal temperature reaches 145°F (63°C). Serve warm.

Chapter 1 Vegetables and Sides | 63

Goat Cheese-Stuffed Flank Steak

Prep time: 10 minutes | Cook time: 14 minutes | Serves 6

1 pound (454 g) flank steak
1 tablespoon avocado oil
½ teaspoon sea salt
½ teaspoon garlic powder
¼ teaspoon freshly ground black pepper
2 ounces goat cheese, crumbled
1 cup baby spinach, chopped

1. Place the steak in a large zip-top bag. Using a meat mallet pound the steak to an even ¼-inch thickness. 2. Brush the steak with the avocado oil. 3. Mix the salt, garlic powder, and pepper in a small dish. Sprinkle this mixture over the steak. 4. Sprinkle the goat cheese over top, and top that with the spinach. 5. Starting at one of the long sides, roll the steak up tightly. Tie the rolled steak with kitchen string at 3-inch intervals. 6. Roast at 400ºF (204ºC) for 14 minutes, flipping once, until an instant-read thermometer reads 120ºF (49ºC) for medium-rare.

Beef and Broccoli Stir-Fry

Prep time: 30 minutes | Cook time: 20 minutes | Serves 2

½ pound (227 g) sirloin steak, thinly sliced
2 tablespoons coconut aminos
¼ teaspoon grated ginger
¼ teaspoon finely minced garlic
1 tablespoon coconut oil
2 cups broccoli florets
¼ teaspoon crushed red pepper
⅛ teaspoon xanthan gum
½ teaspoon sesame seeds

1. Place the beef into a large bowl and add coconut aminos, ginger, garlic, and coconut oil. Marinate for 1 hour in refrigerator. 2. Remove beef from marinade, reserving marinade, and place beef into the frying basket. 3. Air fry at 320ºF (160ºC) for 20 minutes. After 10 minutes, add broccoli and sprinkle red pepper and shake. 4. Pour the marinade into a skillet over medium heat and bring to a boil, then reduce to simmer. Stir in xanthan gum and allow to thicken. 5. Transfer the cooked beef to skillet and toss. Sprinkle with sesame seeds. Serve immediately.

Rosemary Ribeye Steaks

Prep time: 10 minutes | Cook time: 15 minutes | Serves 2

¼ cup butter
1 clove garlic, minced
Salt and ground black pepper, to taste
1½ tablespoons balsamic vinegar
¼ cup rosemary, chopped
2 ribeye steaks

1. Melt the butter in a skillet over medium heat. Add the garlic and fry until fragrant. 2. Remove the skillet from the heat and add the salt, pepper, and vinegar. Allow it to cool. 3. Add the rosemary, then pour the mixture into a Ziploc bag. 4. Put the ribeye steaks in the bag and shake well, coating the meat well. Refrigerate for an hour, then allow to sit for a further twenty minutes. 5. Air fry the ribeye steaks at 400ºF (204ºC) for 15 minutes. 6. Serve immediately.

Simple Ground Beef with Zucchini

Prep time: 5 minutes | Cook time: 12 minutes | Serves 4

1½ pounds (680 g) ground beef
1 pound (454 g) chopped zucchini
2 tablespoons extra-virgin olive oil
1 teaspoon dried oregano
1 teaspoon dried basil
1 teaspoon dried rosemary
2 tablespoons fresh chives, chopped

1. Preheat the air fryer to 400ºF (204ºC). 2. In a bowl, combine all the ingredients, except for the chives, until well blended. 3. Place the beef and zucchini mixture in the baking pan. Air fry for 12 minutes, or until the beef is browned and the zucchini is tender. 4. Top with fresh chives and serve hot.

Steaks with Walnut-Blue Cheese Butter

Prep time: 30 minutes | Cook time: 10 minutes | Serves 6

½ cup unsalted butter, at room temperature
½ cup crumbled blue cheese
2 tablespoons finely chopped walnuts
1 tablespoon minced fresh rosemary
1 teaspoon minced garlic
¼ teaspoon cayenne pepper
Sea salt and freshly ground black pepper, to taste
1½ pounds (680 g) New York strip steaks, at room temperature

1. In a medium bowl, combine the butter, blue cheese, walnuts, rosemary, garlic, and cayenne pepper and salt and black pepper to taste. Form the mixture into a log. Wrap it tightly in plastic wrap. Refrigerate for at least 2 hours or freeze for 30 minutes. 2. Season the steaks generously with salt and pepper. Air fry at 400ºF (204ºC) for 10 minutes, flipping once, until an instant-read thermometer reads 120ºF (49ºC) for medium-rare (or as desired). 3. Transfer the steaks to a plate. Cut the butter into pieces and place the desired amount on top of the steaks. Tent a piece of aluminum foil over the steaks and allow to sit for 10 minutes before serving.

Beef and Goat Cheese Stuffed Peppers

Prep time: 10 minutes | Cook time: 30 minutes | Serves 4

1 pound lean ground beef
½ cup cooked brown rice
2 Roma tomatoes, diced
3 garlic cloves, minced
½ yellow onion, diced
2 tablespoons fresh oregano, chopped
1 teaspoon salt
½ teaspoon black pepper
¼ teaspoon ground allspice
2 bell peppers, halved and seeded
4 ounces goat cheese
¼ cup fresh parsley, chopped

1. Preheat the air fryer to 360ºF (182ºC). 2. In a bowl, mix the ground beef, rice, tomatoes, garlic, onion, oregano, salt, pepper, and allspice well. 3. Divide the beef mixture equally into the halved bell peppers and top each with about 1 ounce (a quarter of the total) goat cheese. 4. Place the peppers into the frying basket in a single layer. Bake for 30 minutes. 5. Top with fresh parsley before serving.

64 | Chapter 1 Vegetables and Sides

Buttery Pork Chops

Prep time: 5 minutes | Cook time: 12 minutes | Serves 4

4 (4-ounce / 113-g) boneless pork chops
½ teaspoon salt
¼ teaspoon ground black pepper
2 tablespoons salted butter, softened

1. Sprinkle pork chops on all sides with salt and pepper. Place chops into ungreased frying basket in a single layer. Air fry at 400ºF (204ºC) for 12 minutes. until pork chops are golden and have an internal temperature of at least 145ºF (63ºC). 2. Transfer pork chops to a large plate. Top each chop with ½ tablespoon butter and let sit 2 minutes to melt. Serve warm.

Cantonese BBQ Pork

Prep time: 30 minutes | Cook time: 15 minutes | Serves 4

¼ cup honey
2 tablespoons dark soy sauce
1 tablespoon sugar
1 tablespoon Shaoxing wine (rice cooking wine)
1 tablespoon hoisin sauce
2 teaspoons minced garlic
2 teaspoons minced fresh ginger
1 teaspoon Chinese five-spice powder
1 pound (454 g) fatty pork shoulder, cut into long, 1-inch-thick pieces

1. In a small microwave-safe bowl, combine the honey, soy sauce, sugar, wine, hoisin, garlic, ginger, and five-spice powder. Microwave in 10-second intervals, stirring in between, until the honey has dissolved. 2. Use a fork to pierce the pork slices to allow the marinade to penetrate better. Place the pork in a bowl and pour in half the marinade. Marinate the pork at room temperature for 30 minutes. 3. Place the pork in a single layer in the frying basket. Roast at 400ºF (204ºC) for 15 minutes, turning and basting the pork halfway through the cooking time. 4. Meanwhile, microwave the reserved marinade on high for 45 to 60 seconds, stirring every 15 seconds, to thicken it slightly to the consistency of a sauce. 5. Allow to cool for 10 minutes. Brush with the sauce and serve.

Greek Pork with Tzatziki Sauce

Prep time: 30 minutes | Cook time: 50 minutes | Serves 4

Greek Pork:
2 pounds (907 g) pork sirloin roast
Salt and black pepper, to taste
1 teaspoon smoked paprika
½ teaspoon mustard seeds
½ teaspoon celery seeds
1 teaspoon fennel seeds
1 teaspoon Ancho chili powder
1 teaspoon turmeric powder
½ teaspoon ground ginger
2 tablespoons olive oil
2 cloves garlic, finely chopped
Tzatziki:
½ cucumber, finely chopped and squeezed
1 cup full-fat Greek yogurt
1 garlic clove, minced
1 tablespoon extra-virgin olive oil
1 teaspoon balsamic vinegar
1 teaspoon minced fresh dill
A pinch of salt

1. Toss all ingredients for Greek pork in a large mixing bowl until the meat is well coated. 2. Roast at 360ºF (182ºC) for 30 minutes; turn over and cook another 20 minutes. 3. Meanwhile, prepare the tzatziki by mixing all the tzatziki ingredients. Refrigerate until ready to use. 4. Serve with the chilled tzatziki on the side.

Pork Butt with Garlicky Coriander-Parsley Sauce

Prep time: 1 hour 15 minutes | Cook time: 30 minutes | Serves 4

1 teaspoon golden flaxseed meal
1 egg white, well whisked
1 tablespoon soy sauce
1 teaspoon lemon juice, preferably freshly squeezed
1 tablespoon olive oil
1 pound (454 g) pork butt, cut into pieces 2-inches long
Salt and ground black pepper, to taste
Garlicky Coriander-Parsley Sauce:
3 garlic cloves, minced
⅓ cup fresh coriander leaves
⅓ cup fresh parsley leaves
1 teaspoon lemon juice
½ tablespoon salt
⅓ cup extra-virgin olive oil

1. Combine the flaxseed meal, egg white, soy sauce, lemon juice, salt, black pepper, and olive oil in a bowl. Dunk the pork strips in and press to submerge. 2. Wrap the bowl in plastic and refrigerate for at least an hour. 3. Air fry the pork strips at 380ºF (193ºC) for 30 minutes until cooked through and well browned. Flip the strips halfway through. 4. Meanwhile, mix well the ingredients for the sauce in a bowl. Refrigerate until ready to serve. 6. Serve the strips with the chilled sauce.

London Broil with Herb Butter

Prep time: 30 minutes | Cook time: 20 to 25 minutes | Serves 4

1½ pounds (680 g) London broil top round steak
¼ cup olive oil
2 tablespoons balsamic vinegar
1 tablespoon Worcestershire sauce
4 cloves garlic, minced
Herb Butter:
6 tablespoons unsalted butter, softened
1 tablespoon chopped fresh parsley
¼ teaspoon salt
¼ teaspoon dried ground rosemary or thyme
¼ teaspoon garlic powder
Pinch of red pepper flakes

1. In a bowl, whisk together the olive oil, balsamic vinegar, Worcestershire sauce, and garlic. Add beef and toss to coat. Let sit at room temperature for an hour or refrigerate overnight. 2. **Make the Herb Butter:** In a bowl, mix all the ingredients until smooth. Cover and refrigerate until ready to use. 3. Preheat the air fryer to 400ºF (204ºC). 4. Remove the beef from the marinade and place the beef in the frying basket. Air fry for 20 to 25 minutes, turning halfway through the cooking time, until a thermometer inserted into the thickest part indicates the desired doneness, 125ºF / 52ºC (rare) to 150ºF / 66ºC (medium). Allow to cool for 10 minutes before slicing. Serve topped with herb butter.

Teriyaki Rump Steak with Broccoli and Capsicum

Prep time: 5 minutes | Cook time: 13 minutes | Serves 4

½ pound (227 g) rump steak
⅓ cup teriyaki marinade
1½ teaspoons sesame oil
½ head broccoli, cut into florets
2 red capsicums, sliced
Fine sea salt and ground black pepper, to taste
Cooking spray

1. Toss the rump steak in a bowl with teriyaki marinade. Wrap the bowl in plastic and refrigerate for at least an hour. 2. Preheat the air fryer to 400ºF (204ºC). 3. Spritz the steak with cooking spray. Air fry for 13 minutes or until well browned. Flip the steak halfway through. 4. Meanwhile, heat the sesame oil in a nonstick skillet over medium heat. Add the broccoli and capsicum. Sprinkle with salt and pepper. Sauté for 5 minutes or until the broccoli is tender. 5. Transfer the steak on a plate and top with the broccoli and capsicum. Serve hot.

Kheema Meatloaf

Prep time: 10 minutes | Cook time: 15 minutes | Serves 4

1 pound (454 g) 85% lean ground beef
2 large eggs, lightly beaten
1 cup diced yellow onion
¼ cup chopped fresh cilantro
1 tablespoon minced fresh ginger
1 tablespoon minced garlic
2 teaspoons garam masala
1 teaspoon kosher salt
1 teaspoon ground turmeric
1 teaspoon cayenne pepper
½ teaspoon ground cinnamon
⅛ teaspoon ground cardamom

1. In a bowl, gently mix the ground beef, eggs, onion, cilantro, ginger, garlic, garam masala, salt, turmeric, cayenne, cinnamon, and cardamom until thoroughly combined. 2. Place the seasoned meat in a baking pan. Air fry at 350ºF (177ºC) for 15 minutes. Use a meat thermometer to ensure the meat loaf has reached an internal temperature of 160ºF / 71ºC (medium). 3. Drain the fat and liquid from the pan and let stand for 5 minutes before slicing. 4. Slice and serve hot.

Beef and Pork Sausage Meatloaf

Prep time: 20 minutes | Cook time: 25 minutes | Serves 4

¾ pound (340 g) ground chuck
4 ounces (113 g) ground pork sausage
1 cup shallots, finely chopped
2 eggs, well beaten
3 tablespoons plain milk
1 tablespoon oyster sauce
1 teaspoon porcini mushrooms
½ teaspoon cumin powder
1 teaspoon garlic paste
1 tablespoon fresh parsley
Salt and crushed red pepper flakes, to taste
1 cup crushed saltines
Cooking spray

1. Preheat the air fryer to 360ºF (182ºC). Spritz a baking dish with cooking spray. 2. Mix all the ingredients in a large bowl, combining everything well. 3. Transfer to the baking dish and bake in the air fryer for 25 minutes. 4. Serve hot.

Sausage-Stuffed Peppers

Prep time: 15 minutes | Cook time: 28 to 30 minutes | Serves 6

Avocado oil spray
8 ounces (227 g) Italian sausage, casings removed
½ cup chopped mushrooms
¼ cup diced onion
1 teaspoon Italian seasoning
Sea salt and freshly ground black pepper, to taste
1 cup keto-friendly marinara sauce
3 bell peppers, halved and seeded
3 ounces (85 g) provolone cheese, shredded

1. Spray a large skillet with oil and cook the sausage over medium-high heat for 5 minutes, breaking up the meat with a wooden spoon. Add the mushrooms, onion, and Italian seasoning, and season with salt and pepper. Cook for 5 minutes more. Stir in the marinara sauce and cook until heated through. 2. Scoop the sausage filling into the bell pepper halves and air fry for 15 minutes. 3. Top the stuffed peppers with the cheese and air fry for 3 to 5 minutes more, until the cheese is melted and the peppers are tender.

Italian Lamb Chops with Avocado Mayo

Prep time: 5 minutes | Cook time: 12 minutes | Serves 2

2 lamp chops
2 teaspoons Italian herbs
2 avocados
½ cup mayonnaise
1 tablespoon lemon juice

1. Season the lamb chops with the Italian herbs, then set aside for 5 minutes. 2. Air fry the chops at 400ºF (204ºC) for 12 minutes. 3. Meanwhile, halve the avocados and open to remove the pits. Spoon the flesh into a blender. Add the mayonnaise and lemon juice and pulse until a smooth consistency is achieved. 4. Serve the chops with the avocado mayo.

Sweet and Spicy Country-Style Ribs

Prep time: 10 minutes | Cook time: 25 minutes | Serves 4

2 tablespoons brown sugar
2 tablespoons smoked paprika
1 teaspoon garlic powder
1 teaspoon onion powder
1 teaspoon dry mustard
1 teaspoon ground cumin
1 teaspoon kosher salt
1 teaspoon black pepper
¼ to ½ teaspoon cayenne pepper
1½ pounds (680 g) boneless country-style pork ribs
1 cup barbecue sauce

1. In a bowl, mix the first nine ingredients until well combined. 2. Pat the ribs dry with a paper towel. Generously sprinkle the rub evenly over the ribs. 3. Place the ribs in the frying basket and roast at 350ºF (177ºC) for 15 minutes. Turn the ribs and brush with half the barbecue sauce. Cook for 10 minutes more until the pork reaches an internal temperature of 145ºF (63ºC). 4. Serve with remaining barbecue sauce.

Swedish Meatloaf

Prep time: 10 minutes | Cook time: 35 minutes | Serves 8

1½ pounds (680 g) ground beef (85% lean)
¼ pound (113 g) ground pork
1 large egg (omit for egg-free)
½ cup minced onions
¼ cup tomato sauce
2 tablespoons dry mustard
2 cloves garlic, minced
2 teaspoons fine sea salt
1 teaspoon ground black pepper, plus more for garnish

Sauce:
½ cup (1 stick) unsalted butter
½ cup shredded Swiss or mild Cheddar cheese (about 2 ounces / 57 g)
2 ounces (57 g) cream cheese (¼ cup), softened
⅓ cup beef broth
⅛ teaspoon ground nutmeg
Halved cherry tomatoes, for serving (optional)

1. Preheat the air fryer to 390°F (199°C). 2. In a bowl, mix the first nine ingredients until well combined. 3. Place the meatloaf mixture in a loaf pan and place it in the air fryer. Bake for 35 minutes, or until the internal temperature reaches 145°F (63°C). 4. Make the Sauce: Meanwhile, Heat the butter in a saucepan over medium-high heat until it sizzles and brown flecks appear, stirring constantly to keep the butter from burning. Turn the heat down to low and whisk in the Swiss cheese, cream cheese, broth, and nutmeg. Simmer for at least 10 minutes. 5. When the meatloaf is done, transfer to a serving tray and pour the sauce over it. Garnish with black pepper and serve with cherry tomatoes, if desired. Allow to cool for 10 minutes before slicing.

Rosemary Roast Beef

Prep time: 30 minutes | Cook time: 30 to 35 minutes | Serves 8

1 (2-pound / 907-g) top round beef roast, tied with kitchen string
Sea salt and freshly ground black pepper, to taste
2 teaspoons minced garlic
2 tablespoons finely chopped fresh rosemary
¼ cup avocado oil

1. Season the roast generously with salt and pepper. 2. In a bowl, rub the roast with garlic, rosemary, and avocado oil. Cover loosely with aluminum foil and refrigerate for at least 12 hours or up to 2 days. 3. Remove from the refrigerator and allow to sit at room temperature for about 1 hour. 4. Place the roast in the frying basket and roast at 325°F (163°C) for 15 minutes. Flip and cook for 15 to 20 minutes more, until the meat reaches 120°F (49°C) at the thickest part (for medium-rare). 5. Let it rest for 15 minutes before thinly slicing and serving.

Kale and Beef Omelet

Prep time: 15 minutes | Cook time: 16 minutes | Serves 4

½ pound (227 g) leftover beef, coarsely chopped
2 garlic cloves, pressed
1 cup kale, torn into pieces and wilted
1 tomato, chopped
¼ teaspoon sugar
4 eggs, beaten
4 tablespoons heavy cream
½ teaspoon turmeric powder
Salt and ground black pepper, to taste
⅛ teaspoon ground allspice
Cooking spray

1. Preheat the air fryer to 360°F (182°C). Spritz four ramekins with cooking spray. 2. Put equal amounts of each of the ingredients into each ramekin and mix well. 3. Air fry for 16 minutes. Serve immediately.

Blue Cheese Steak Salad

Prep time: 30 minutes | Cook time: 22 minutes | Serves 4

2 tablespoons balsamic vinegar
2 tablespoons red wine vinegar
1 tablespoon Dijon mustard
1 tablespoon Swerve
1 teaspoon minced garlic
Sea salt and freshly ground black pepper, to taste
¾ cup extra-virgin olive oil
1 pound (454 g) boneless sirloin steak
Avocado oil spray
1 small red onion, cut into ¼-inch-thick rounds
6 ounces (170 g) baby spinach
½ cup cherry tomatoes, halved
3 ounces (85 g) blue cheese, crumbled

1. In a blender, process balsamic vinegar, red wine vinegar, Dijon mustard, Swerve, garlic, salt and pepper until smooth. With the blender running, drizzle in the olive oil. Process until well combined. Refrigerate in a jar until ready to serve. 2. Season the steak with salt and pepper and let sit at room temperature for at least 45 minutes. 3. Spray the steak with oil and air fry in the frying basket at 400°F (204°C) for 12 minutes, flipping and spray with more oil halfway. 4. Spray the onion slices with oil and place in the frying basket. Cook at 400°F (204°C) for 10 minutes, flipping and spray with more oil halfway. 5. Slice the steak diagonally into thin strips. Place the spinach, cherry tomatoes, onion slices, and steak in a bowl. Toss with dressing,. sprinkle with crumbled blue cheese and serve.

Mongolian-Style Beef

Prep time: 10 minutes | Cook time: 10 minutes | Serves 4

Oil, for spraying
¼ cup cornstarch
1 pound (454 g) flank steak, thinly sliced
¾ cup packed light brown sugar
½ cup soy sauce
2 teaspoons toasted sesame oil
1 tablespoon minced garlic
½ teaspoon ground ginger
½ cup water
Cooked white rice or ramen noodles, for serving

1. Line the frying basket with parchment and spray lightly with oil. 2. Place the cornstarch in a bowl and dredge the steak until evenly coated. 3. Place the steak into basket and spray lightly with oil. 4. Roast at 390°F (199°C) for 10 minutes, flipping halfway through. 5. In a small saucepan, combine the sugar, soy sauce, sesame oil, garlic, ginger, and water and bring to a boil over medium-high heat, stirring frequently. Remove. 6. Transfer the meat to the sauce and toss until evenly coated. Let sit for 5 minutes so the steak absorbs the flavors. Serve with rice or noodles.

Pepper Steak

Prep time: 30 minutes | Cook time: 16 to 20 minutes | Serves 4

1 pound (454 g) cube steak, cut into 1-inch pieces
1 cup Italian dressing
1½ cups beef broth
1 tablespoon soy sauce
½ teaspoon salt
¼ teaspoon freshly ground black pepper
¼ cup cornstarch
1 cup thinly sliced bell pepper, any color
1 cup chopped celery
1 tablespoon minced garlic
1 to 2 tablespoons oil

1. In a large resealable bag, combine the beef and Italian dressing. Refrigerate to for 8 hours. 2. In a bowl, whisk the beef broth, soy sauce, salt, and pepper until blended. 3. In another small bowl, whisk ¼ cup water and the cornstarch until dissolved. Stir the cornstarch mixture into the beef broth mixture until blended. 4. Preheat the air fryer to 375°F (191°C). 5. Pour the broth mixture into a baking pan. Bake for 8 to 9 minutes, stirring once. Remove and set aside. 6. Line the frying basket with parchment paper. Transfer the steak to a bowl. Discard the marinade. Stir in the bell pepper, celery, and garlic. Place the mixture on the parchment. Spritz with oil. 7. Roast at 400°F (204°C) for 8 to 11 minutes, shaking once halfway through, until the vegetables are tender and the meat reaches an internal temperature of 145°F (63°C). Serve with the gravy.

Herbed Beef

Prep time: 5 minutes | Cook time: 22 minutes | Serves 6

1 teaspoon dried dill
1 teaspoon dried thyme
1 teaspoon garlic powder
2 pounds (907 g) beef steak
3 tablespoons butter

1. Preheat the air fryer to 360°F (182°C). 2. Combine the dill, thyme, and garlic powder in a bowl, and massage into the steak. 3. Air fry the steak in the air fryer for 20 minutes, then remove, shred, and return to the air fryer. 4. Add the butter and air fry the shredded steak for a further 2 minutes at 365°F (185°C). Make sure the beef is coated in the butter before serving.

Beef Steak Fingers

Prep time: 5 minutes | Cook time: 8 minutes | Serves 4

4 small beef cube steaks, cut into 1-inch-wide strips
Salt and ground black pepper, to taste
½ cup flour
Cooking spray

1. Preheat the air fryer to 390°F (199°C). 2. Lightly sprinkle the beef with salt and pepper to taste. Roll in flour to coat all sides. Spritz frying basket with cooking spray. 3. Put steak strips in frying basket in a single layer. Spritz with cooking spray and air fry for 8 minutes, turning and spritzing with cooking spray halfway, until crispy outside with no red juices inside. 4. Serve immediately.

Pork Schnitzels with Sour Cream and Dill Sauce

Prep time: 5 minutes | Cook time: 24 minutes | Serves 4 to 6

½ cup flour
1½ teaspoons salt
Freshly ground black pepper, to taste
2 eggs
½ cup milk
1½ cups toasted bread crumbs
1 teaspoon paprika
6 boneless, center cut pork chops (about 1½ pounds / 680 g), fat trimmed, pound to ½-inch thick
2 tablespoons olive oil
3 tablespoons melted butter
Lemon wedges, for serving
Sour Cream and Dill Sauce:
1 cup chicken stock
1½ tablespoons cornstarch
⅓ cup sour cream
1½ tablespoons chopped fresh dill
Salt and ground black pepper, to taste

1. Preheat the air fryer to 400°F (204°C). 2. Mix the flour with salt and black pepper in a bowl. Whisk the egg with milk in a second bowl. Stir the bread crumbs and paprika in a third bowl. 3. Dredge the pork chops in the flour bowl, then the egg milk, and then bread crumbs bowl. Press to coat well. 4. Arrange one pork chop in the air fryer each time. Brush with olive oil and butter on all sides. Air fry for 4 minutes or until golden brown and crispy. Flip the chop halfway through. 5. Transfer the cooked pork to a baking pan in the oven and keep warm over low heat while air frying the remaining pork chops. 6. Meanwhile, combine the chicken stock and cornstarch in a small saucepan and bring to a boil over medium-high heat. Simmer for 2 more minutes. 7. Turn off the heat, then mix in the sour cream, dill, salt, and pepper. 8. Transfer the schnitzels to a plate and baste with sauce. Squeeze the lemon wedges over and slice to serve.

Red Curry Flank Steak

Prep time: 30 minutes | Cook time: 12 to 18 minutes | Serves 4

²3 tablespoons red curry paste
¼ cup olive oil
2 teaspoons grated fresh ginger
2 tablespoons soy sauce
2 tablespoons rice wine vinegar
3 scallions, minced
1½ pounds (680 g) flank steak
Fresh cilantro (or parsley) leaves

1. Mix the red curry paste, olive oil, ginger, soy sauce, rice vinegar and scallions together in a bowl. Place the flank steak in a shallow glass dish and pour half the marinade over the steak. Pierce the steak several times with a fork or meat tenderizer to let the marinade penetrate the meat. Turn the steak over, pour the remaining marinade over the top and pierce the steak several times again. Cover and marinate the steak in the refrigerator for 6 to 8 hours. 2. Remove the steak from the refrigerator and let it sit at room temperature for 30 minutes. 3. Preheat the air fryer to 400°F (204°C). 4. Cut the flank steak in half. Pour the marinade over the steak. Air fry for 12 to 18 minutes, flipping halfway through. 5. Let it rest for 5 minutes before slicing. Thinly slice the flank steak against the grain of the meat. Transfer the slices to a serving platter, pour any juice from the bottom of the air fryer over the steak and sprinkle the fresh cilantro on top.

Super Bacon with Meat

Prep time: 5 minutes | Cook time: 1 hour | Serves 4

30 slices thick-cut bacon
4 ounces (113 g) Cheddar cheese, shredded
12 ounces (340 g) steak
10 ounces (283 g) pork sausage
Salt and ground black pepper, to taste

1. Preheat the air fryer to 400°F (204°C). 2. Lay out 30 slices of bacon in a woven pattern and bake for 20 minutes until crisp. Put the cheese in the center of the bacon. 3. Combine the steak and sausage to form a meaty mixture. 4. Lay out the meat in a rectangle of similar size to the bacon strips. Season with salt and pepper. 5. Roll the meat into a tight roll and refrigerate. 6. Make a 7×7 bacon weave and roll the bacon weave over the meat, diagonally. 7. Bake at 400°F (204°C) for 60 minutes or until the internal temperature reaches 165°F (74°C). 9. Let rest for 5 minutes.

Ham Hock Mac and Cheese

Prep time: 20 minutes | Cook time: 25 minutes | Serves 4

2 large eggs, beaten
2 cups cottage cheese, whole milk or 2%
2 cups grated sharp Cheddar cheese, divided
1 cup sour cream
½ teaspoon salt
1 teaspoon freshly ground black pepper
2 cups uncooked elbow macaroni
2 ham hocks (about 11 ounces / 312 g each), meat removed and diced
1 to 2 tablespoons oil

1. In a bowl, stir together the eggs, cottage cheese, 1 cup Cheddar cheese, sour cream, salt, pepper, macaroni and the diced meat. 2. Preheat the air fryer to 360°F (182°C). Spritz a baking pan with oil. Pour the mixture into the pan. Bake for 12 minutes. Stir in the remaining Cheddar cheese and cook for 13 minutes more, until the noodles are tender. Let rest for 5 minutes before serving.

Indian Mint and Chile Kebabs

Prep time: 30 minutes | Cook time: 15 minutes | Serves 4

1 pound (454 g) ground lamb
½ cup finely minced onion
¼ cup chopped fresh mint
¼ cup chopped fresh cilantro
1 tablespoon minced garlic
½ teaspoon ground turmeric
½ teaspoon cayenne pepper
¼ teaspoon ground cardamom
¼ teaspoon ground cinnamon
1 teaspoon kosher salt

1. In the bowl of a stand mixer fitted with the paddle attachment, mix all the ingredients on low speed until you have a sticky mess of spiced meat. 2. Divide the meat into eight equal portions. Form each into a long sausage shape. Place the kebabs in a single layer in the frying basket. Bake at 350°F (177°C) for 10 minutes and at 400°F (204°C) 3 to 4 minutes more to brown the kebabs until the internal temperature reaches 160°F / 71°C (medium).

Caraway Crusted Beef Steaks

Prep time: 5 minutes | Cook time: 10 minutes | Serves 4

4 beef steaks
2 teaspoons caraway seeds
2 teaspoons garlic powder
Sea salt and cayenne pepper, to taste
1 tablespoon melted butter
⅓ cup almond flour
2 eggs, beaten

1. Preheat the air fryer to 355°F (179°C). 2. Toss the beef steaks with the caraway seeds, garlic powder, salt and pepper until well coated in a bowl. 3. Stir together the butter and flour in a bowl. Whisk the eggs in a different bowl. 4. Dredge the steaks in the eggs, then almond butter mixture. 5. Air fry in the frying basket for 10 minutes, or until the internal temperature reaches 145°F (63°C), flipping once halfway through. 6. Let cool for 5 minutes and serve hot.

Marinated Steak Tips with Mushrooms

Prep time: 30 minutes | Cook time: 10 minutes | Serves 4

1½ pounds (680 g) sirloin, trimmed and cut into 1-inch pieces
8 ounces (227 g) brown mushrooms, halved
¼ cup Worcestershire sauce
1 tablespoon Dijon mustard
1 tablespoon olive oil
1 teaspoon paprika
1 teaspoon crushed red pepper flakes
2 tablespoons chopped fresh parsley (optional)

1. Place the beef and mushrooms in a gallon-size resealable bag. In a bowl, whisk together the Worcestershire, mustard, olive oil, paprika, and red pepper flakes. Pour the marinade into the bag and massage to coat the beef and mushrooms well. Refrigerate for at least 4 hours. Remove from the refrigerator 30 minutes before cooking. 2. Preheat the air fryer to 400°F (204°C). 3. Arrange the steak and mushrooms in the frying basket. Air fry for 10 minutes, shaking halfway through. Serve topped with the parsley, if desired.

Bacon-Wrapped Cheese Pork

Prep time: 10 minutes | Cook time: 20 minutes | Serves 4

4 (1-inch-thick) boneless pork chops
2 (5.2-ounce / 147-g) packages Boursin cheese
8 slices thin-cut bacon

1. Spray the frying basket with avocado oil. Preheat the air fryer to 400°F (204°C). 2. Place one of the chops on a cutting board. With a sharp knife held parallel to the cutting board, make a 1-inch-wide incision on the top edge of the chop. Cut into the chop to form a large pocket, leaving a ½-inch border along the sides and bottom. Repeat with the other 3 chops. 3. Snip the corner of a large resealable plastic bag to form a ¾-inch hole. Place the Boursin cheese in the bag and pipe the cheese into the pockets in the chops, dividing the cheese evenly among them. 4. Wrap 2 slices of bacon around each chop and secure the ends with toothpicks. Air fry the bacon-wrapped chops for 20 minutes, flipping halfway, until the internal temperature reaches 145°F (63°C).

Steak, Broccoli, and Mushroom Rice Bowls

Prep time: 10 minutes | Cook time: 21 minutes | Serves 4

2 tablespoons cornstarch
½ cup low-sodium beef broth
1 teaspoon low-sodium soy sauce
12 ounces (340 g) sirloin strip steak, cut into 1-inch cubes
2½ cups broccoli florets
1 onion, chopped
1 cup sliced cremini mushrooms
1 tablespoon grated peeled fresh ginger
Cooked brown rice (optional), for serving

1. In a medium bowl, stir together the cornstarch, beef broth, and soy sauce until the cornstarch is completely dissolved. 2. Add the beef cubes and toss to coat. Let stand for 5 minutes at room temperature. 3. Preheat the air fryer to 400°F (204°C). Transfer the beef from the broth mixture into a medium metal bowl and reserve the broth. Add the broccoli, onion, mushrooms, and ginger to the beef. Place the bowl into the basket. Air fry for 18 minutes until the beef reaches 145°F (63°C) and the vegetables are tender, add the reserved broth and cook for about 3 minutes until the sauce boils. 4. Serve over rice, if desired.

Rack of Lamb with Pistachio Crust

Prep time: 10 minutes | Cook time: 19 minutes | Serves 2

½ cup finely chopped pistachios
3 tablespoons panko bread crumbs
1 teaspoon chopped fresh rosemary
2 teaspoons chopped fresh oregano
Salt and freshly ground black pepper, to taste
1 tablespoon olive oil
1 rack of lamb, bones trimmed of fat and frenched
1 tablespoon Dijon mustard

1. Preheat the air fryer to 380°F (193°C). 2. Combine the pistachios, bread crumbs, rosemary, oregano, salt and pepper in a bowl. Drizzle in the olive oil and stir to combine. 3. Season the lamb with salt and pepper and transfer to the frying basket. Air fry the lamb for 12 minutes. Brush the fat side of the lamb with the Dijon mustard. Coat the rack with the pistachio mixture. 4. Air fry for another 3 to 7 minutes or until an instant read thermometer reads 140°F (60°C) for medium. 5. Let the lamb rest for at least 5 minutes before slicing and serving.

Sausage and Pork Meatballs

Prep time: 15 minutes | Cook time: 8 to 12 minutes | Serves 8

1 large egg
1 teaspoon gelatin
1 pound (454 g) ground pork
½ pound (227 g) Italian sausage, casings removed, crumbled
⅓ cup Parmesan cheese
¼ cup finely diced onion
1 tablespoon tomato paste
1 teaspoon minced garlic
1 teaspoon dried oregano
¼ teaspoon red pepper flakes
Sea salt and freshly ground black pepper, to taste
Keto-friendly marinara sauce, for serving

1. Beat the egg in a bowl and sprinkle with the gelatin. Allow to sit for 5 minutes. 2. In a bowl, combine the ground pork, sausage, Parmesan, onion, tomato paste, garlic, oregano, and red pepper flakes. Season with salt and black pepper. 3. Stir the gelatin mixture, then add it to the other ingredients and mix well. Form into 1½-inch round meatballs. 4. Set the air fryer to . Place the meatballs in the frying basket in a single layer. Air fry at 400°F (204°C) for 5 minutes. Flip and cook for 3 to 7 minutes more.

Herb-Crusted Lamb Chops

Prep time: 10 minutes | Cook time: 5 minutes | Serves 2

1 large egg
2 cloves garlic, minced
¼ cup pork dust
¼ cup powdered Parmesan cheese
1 tablespoon chopped fresh oregano leaves
1 tablespoon chopped fresh rosemary leaves
1 teaspoon chopped fresh thyme leaves
½ teaspoon ground black pepper
4 (1-inch-thick) lamb chops
For Garnish/Serving (Optional):
Sprigs of fresh oregano
Sprigs of fresh rosemary
Sprigs of fresh thyme
Lavender flowers
Lemon slices

1. Spray the frying basket with avocado oil. Preheat the air fryer to 400°F (204°C). 2. Beat the egg in a bowl, add the garlic, and stir. In another bowl, mix together the pork dust, Parmesan, herbs, and pepper. 3. Dip the lamb chops into the egg mixture, and then Parmesan mixture. 4. Place the lamb chops in the frying basket, leaving space between them, and air fry for 5 minutes, or until the internal temperature reaches 145°F (63°C) for medium doneness. Allow to rest for 10 minutes before serving. 5. Garnish with sprigs of oregano, rosemary, and thyme, and lavender flowers, if desired. Serve with lemon slices, if desired.

Sumptuous Pizza Tortilla Rolls

Prep time: 10 minutes | Cook time: 6 minutes | Serves 4

1 teaspoon butter
½ medium onion, slivered
½ red or green bell pepper, julienned
4 ounces (113 g) fresh white mushrooms, chopped
½ cup pizza sauce
8 flour tortillas
8 thin slices deli ham
24 pepperoni slices
1 cup shredded Mozzarella cheese
Cooking spray

1. Preheat the air fryer to 390°F (199°C). 2. Put butter, onions, bell pepper, and mushrooms in a baking pan. Bake for 3 minutes. Stir and cook 3 to 4 minutes longer until just crisp and tender. 3. To assemble rolls, spread about 2 teaspoons pizza sauce on one half of each tortilla. Top with a slice ham and 3 slices pepperoni. Divide sautéed vegetables among tortillas and top with cheese. 4. Roll up tortillas and spray with oil. 5. Air fry for 8 minutes, turning halfway through. 6. Serve immediately.

70 | Chapter 1 Vegetables and Sides

Beef Burger

Prep time: 20 minutes | Cook time: 12 minutes | Serves 4

1¼ pounds (567 g) lean ground beef
1 tablespoon coconut aminos
1 teaspoon Dijon mustard
A few dashes of liquid smoke
1 teaspoon shallot powder
1 clove garlic, minced
½ teaspoon cumin powder
¼ cup scallions, minced
⅓ teaspoon sea salt flakes
⅓ teaspoon freshly cracked mixed peppercorns
1 teaspoon celery seeds
1 teaspoon parsley flakes

1. Mix all of the ingredients in a bowl; knead until everything is well incorporated. 2. Shape the mixture into four patties. Make a shallow dip in the center of each patty to prevent them puffing up during air frying. 3. Spritz the patties on all sides using nonstick cooking spray. Roast 12 minutes at 360°F (182°C) until an instant-read thermometer reads 160°F (71°C).

Onion Pork Kebabs

Prep time: 22 minutes | Cook time: 18 minutes | Serves 3

2 tablespoons tomato purée
½ fresh serrano, minced
⅓ teaspoon paprika
1 pound (454 g) pork, ground
½ cup green onions, finely chopped
3 cloves garlic, peeled and finely minced
1 teaspoon ground black pepper, or more to taste
1 teaspoon salt, or more to taste

1. Thoroughly combine all ingredients in a mixing dish. Then form your mixture into sausage shapes. Bake for 18 minutes at 355°F (179°C). Mound salad on a serving platter, top with air-fried kebabs and serve warm.

Spicy Flank Steak with Zhoug

Prep time: 30 minutes | Cook time: 8 minutes | Serves 4

Marinade and Steak:
½ cup dark beer or orange juice
¼ cup fresh lemon juice
3 cloves garlic, minced
2 tablespoons extra-virgin olive oil
2 tablespoons Sriracha
2 tablespoons brown sugar
2 teaspoons ground cumin
2 teaspoons smoked paprika
1 tablespoon kosher salt
1 teaspoon black pepper
1½ pounds (680 g) flank steak, trimmed and cut into 3 pieces
Zhoug:
1 cup packed fresh cilantro leaves
2 cloves garlic, peeled
2 jalapeño or serrano chiles, stemmed and coarsely chopped
½ teaspoon ground cumin
¼ teaspoon ground coriander
¼ teaspoon kosher salt
2 to 4 tablespoons extra-virgin olive oil

1. Place the steak in a large resealable plastic bag. In a bowl, whisk together the first ten ingredients. Pour the mixture over the steak, seal the bag, and massage the steak to coat. Marinate in the refrigerator for 1 hour or up to 24 hours. 2. Meanwhile, in a food processor, process the cilantro, garlic, jalapeños, cumin, coriander, and salt until finely chopped. Add 2 tablespoons olive oil and pulse to form a loose paste, adding up to 2 tablespoons more olive oil if needed. Transfer the zhoug to a glass container. Cover and store in the refrigerator until 30 minutes before serving if marinating more than 1 hour. 3. Remove the steak from the marinade and air fry at 400°F (204°C) for 8 minutes until the internal temperature reaches 150°F / 66°C (for medium). 4. Let rest for 5 minutes. Slice the steak and serve with the zhoug.

Spice-Coated Steaks with Cucumber and Snap Pea Salad

Prep time: 15 minutes | Cook time: 15 to 20 minutes | Serves 4

1 (1½-pound / 680-g) boneless top sirloin steak, trimmed and halved crosswise
1½ teaspoons chili powder
1½ teaspoons ground cumin
¾ teaspoon ground coriander
⅛ teaspoon cayenne pepper
⅛ teaspoon ground cinnamon
1¼ teaspoons plus ⅛ teaspoon salt, divided
½ teaspoon plus ⅛ teaspoon ground black pepper, divided
1 teaspoon plus 1½ tablespoons extra-virgin olive oil, divided
3 tablespoons mayonnaise
1½ tablespoons white wine vinegar
1 tablespoon minced fresh dill
1 small garlic clove, minced
8 ounces (227 g) sugar snap peas, strings removed and cut in half on bias
½ English cucumber, halved lengthwise and sliced thin
2 radishes, trimmed, halved and sliced thin
2 cups baby arugula

1. Preheat the air fryer to 400°F (204°C). 2. In a bowl, mix chili powder, cumin, coriander, cayenne pepper, cinnamon, 1¼ teaspoons salt and ½ teaspoon pepper until well combined. 3. Add the steaks to another bowl and pat dry with paper towels. Brush with 1 teaspoon oil and transfer to the bowl of spice mixture. Roll over to coat thoroughly. 4. Air fry for 15 to 20 minutes, flipping halfway through, or until the meat reaches 145°F (63°C). 5. Transfer to a clean work surface and wrap with aluminum foil. Let stand while preparing salad. 6. In a bowl, stir together 1½ tablespoons olive oil, mayonnaise, vinegar, dill, garlic, ⅛ teaspoon salt, and ⅛ teaspoon pepper. Add snap peas, cucumber, radishes and arugula. Toss to blend well. 7. Slice the steaks and serve with the salad.

Crescent Dogs

Prep time: 15 minutes | Cook time: 8 minutes | Makes 24 crescent dogs

Oil, for spraying
1 (8-ounce / 227-g) can refrigerated crescent rolls
8 slices Cheddar cheese, cut into thirds
24 cocktail sausages or 8 (6-inch) hot dogs, cut into thirds
2 tablespoons unsalted butter, melted
1 tablespoon sea salt flakes

1. Line the frying basket with parchment and spray lightly with oil. 2. Separate the dough into 8 triangles. Cut each triangle into 3 narrow triangles. 3. Top each triangle with 1 piece cheese and 1 cocktail sausage. 4. Roll up each piece of dough, starting at the wide end and rolling toward the point. 5. Air fry at 325°F (163°C) for 6 to 8 minutes, flipping halfway, or until golden brown. 6. Brush with butter and sprinkle with the sea salt flakes before serving.

Herb-Roasted Beef Tips with Onions

Prep time: 5 minutes | Cook time: 10 minutes | Serves 4

1 pound rib eye steak, cubed
2 garlic cloves, minced
2 tablespoons olive oil
1 tablespoon fresh oregano
1 teaspoon salt
½ teaspoon black pepper
1 yellow onion, thinly sliced

1. Preheat the air fryer to 380ºF (193ºC). 2. In a medium bowl, combine the steak, garlic, olive oil, oregano, salt, pepper, and onion. Mix until all of the beef and onion are well coated. 3. Put the seasoned steak mixture into the frying basket. Roast for 5 minutes. Stir and roast for 5 minutes more. 4. Let rest for 5 minutes before serving.

Lebanese Malfouf (Stuffed Cabbage Rolls)

Prep time: 15 minutes | Cook time: 33 minutes | Serves 4

12 large cabbage leaves
1 pound lean ground beef
½ cup long-grain brown rice
4 garlic cloves, minced
1 teaspoon salt
½ teaspoon black pepper
1 teaspoon ground cinnamon
2 tablespoons chopped fresh mint
Juice of 1 lemon
Olive oil cooking spray
½ cup beef broth
1 tablespoon olive oil

1. Bring a large pot of salted water to a boil, then drop the cabbage leaves into the water, boiling them for 3 minutes. Remove from the water and set aside. 2. In a bowl, combine the ground beef, rice, garlic, salt, pepper, cinnamon, mint, and lemon juice, and mix together until combined. Divide this mixture into 12 equal portions. 3. Preheat the air fryer to 360ºF (182ºC). Lightly coat a small casserole dish with olive oil cooking spray. 4. Place a spoonful of the beef mixture on one side of the cabbage leaf, leaving space on all other sides. Fold the two perpendicular sides inward and then roll forward, tucking tightly as rolled. Place the rolls into the baking dish. Pour the beef broth over the top of the cabbage rolls, and then brush the tops with the olive oil. 5. Place the casserole dish into the frying basket and bake for 30 minutes.

Lemony Pork Loin Chop Schnitzel

Prep time: 15 minutes | Cook time: 15 minutes | Serves 4

4 thin boneless pork loin chops
2 tablespoons lemon juice
½ cup flour
¼ teaspoon marjoram
1 teaspoon salt
1 cup panko bread crumbs
2 eggs
Lemon wedges, for serving
Cooking spray

1. Preheat the air fryer to 390ºF (199ºC) and spritz with cooking spray. 2. Drizzle the pork chops with lemon juice on both sides. 3. Combine the flour with marjoram and salt on a shallow plate. Pour the bread crumbs on a separate shallow dish. Beat the eggs in a bowl. 4. Dredge the pork chops in the flour, then dunk in the beaten eggs to coat well. Roll over the bread crumbs. Spritz with cooking spray. Air fry for 15 minutes or until the chops are golden and crispy, flipping halfway through. Squeeze the lemon wedges over the fried chops and serve immediately.

Korean Beef Tacos

Prep time: 30 minutes | Cook time: 12 minutes | Serves 6

2 tablespoons gochujang (Korean red chile paste)
2 cloves garlic, minced
2 teaspoons minced fresh ginger
2 tablespoons toasted sesame oil
1 tablespoon soy sauce
2 tablespoons sesame seeds
2 teaspoons sugar
½ teaspoon kosher salt
1½ pounds (680 g) thinly sliced beef (chuck, rib eye, or sirloin)
1 medium red onion, sliced
12 (6-inch) flour tortillas, warmed; or lettuce leaves
½ cup chopped green onions
¼ cup chopped fresh cilantro (optional)
½ cup kimchi (optional)

1. In a bowl, mix the first eight ingredients well. Place the beef and red onion in a resealable plastic bag and pour the marinade over. Seal the bag and massage to coat the meat and onion. Marinate at room temperature for 30 minutes. 2. Place the meat and onion in the frying basket. Air fry at 400ºF (204ºC) for 12 minutes, shaking halfway through the cooking time. 3. To serve, place meat and onion in the tortillas. Top with the green onions and the cilantro and kimchi, if using.

Cheesy Low-Carb Lasagna

Prep time: 10 minutes | Cook time: 10 minutes | Serves 4

Meat Layer:
Extra-virgin olive oil
1 pound (454 g) 85% lean ground beef
1 cup prepared marinara sauce
¼ cup diced celery
¼ cup diced red onion
½ teaspoon minced garlic
Kosher salt and black pepper, to taste
Cheese Layer:
8 ounces (227 g) ricotta cheese
1 cup shredded Mozzarella cheese
½ cup grated Parmesan cheese
2 large eggs
1 teaspoon dried Italian seasoning, crushed
½ teaspoon each minced garlic, garlic powder, and black pepper

1. Meat Layer: Grease a cake pan with 1 teaspoon olive oil. 2. In a bowl, combine the ground beef, marinara, celery, onion, garlic, salt, and pepper. Place the seasoned meat in the pan. 3. Bake at 375ºF (191ºC) for 10 minutes. 4. Cheese Layer: In a medium bowl, stir the ricotta, half the Mozzarella, the Parmesan, lightly beaten eggs, Italian seasoning, minced garlic, garlic powder, and pepper until well blended. 5. At the end of the cooking time, spread the cheese mixture over the meat mixture. Sprinkle with the remaining Mozzarella. Bake at 375ºF (191ºC) for 10 minutes, or until the cheese is browned and bubbling and the internal temperature reaches 160ºF (71ºC). 6. Drain the fat and liquid from the pan. Let stand for 5 minutes before serving.

Lamb Chops with Horseradish Sauce

Prep time: 30 minutes | Cook time: 13 minutes | Serves 4

Lamb:
4 lamb loin chops
2 tablespoons vegetable oil
1 clove garlic, minced
½ teaspoon kosher salt
½ teaspoon black pepper
Horseradish Cream

Sauce:
½ cup mayonnaise
1 tablespoon Dijon mustard
1 to 1½ tablespoons prepared horseradish
2 teaspoons sugar
Vegetable oil spray

1. Brush the lamb chops with oil and garlic. Sprinkle with salt and pepper. Marinate at room temperature for 30 minutes. 2. Meanwhile, in a medium bowl, mix well the mayonnaise, mustard, horseradish, and sugar. Set aside half of the sauce for serving. 3. Spray the frying basket with vegetable oil and place the chops in the basket. Roast at 325ºF (163ºC) for 10 minutes, turning halfway through. 4. Remove the chops to the bowl with the horseradish sauce to coat. Roast at 400ºF (204ºC) for 3 minutes until the internal temperature reaches 145ºF (63ºC) (for medium-rare). 5. Serve the chops with the reserved horseradish sauce.

Bean and Beef Meatball Taco Pizza

Prep time: 10 minutes | Cook time: 7 to 9 minutes per batch | Serves 4

¾ cup refried beans (from a 16-ounce / 454-g can)
½ cup salsa
10 frozen precooked beef meatballs, thawed and sliced
1 jalapeño pepper, sliced
4 whole-wheat pita breads
1 cup shredded pepper Jack cheese
½ cup shredded Colby cheese
Cooking oil spray
⅓ cup sour cream

1. In a medium bowl, stir together the refried beans, salsa, meatballs, and jalapeño. 2. Preheat the air fryer to 375ºF (191ºC). 3. Top the pitas with the refried bean mixture and sprinkle with the cheeses. 4. Spray the frying basket with cooking oil and bake for 9 minutes until the cheese is melted and starts to brown. 5. When the cooking is complete, top each pizza with sour cream and serve warm.

Ham with Sweet Potatoes

Prep time: 20 minutes | Cook time: 15 to 17 minutes | Serves 4

1 cup freshly squeezed orange juice
½ cup packed light brown sugar
1 tablespoon Dijon mustard
½ teaspoon salt
½ teaspoon freshly ground black pepper
3 sweet potatoes, cut into small wedges
2 ham steaks (8 ounces / 227 g each), halved
1 to 2 tablespoons oil

1. In a bowl, whisk the orange juice, brown sugar, Dijon, salt, and pepper until blended. Toss the sweet potato wedges with the brown sugar mixture. Spritz with oil. 2. Preheat the air fryer to 400ºF (204ºC). 3. Air fry the sweet potato wedges for 10 minutes. 3. Place ham steaks on top of the sweet potatoes and brush with more of the orange juice mixture. Cook for 5 to 7 minutes, flipping once, until the sweet potatoes are soft and the glaze has thickened. Cut the ham steaks in half to serve.

Pork Loin Roast

Prep time: 30 minutes | Cook time: 55 minutes | Serves 6

1½ pounds (680 g) boneless pork loin roast, washed
1 teaspoon mustard seeds
1 teaspoon garlic powder
1 teaspoon porcini powder
1 teaspoon shallot powder
¾ teaspoon sea salt flakes
1 teaspoon red pepper flakes, crushed
2 dried sprigs thyme, crushed
2 tablespoons lime juice

1. Score the meat using a small knife; make sure to not cut too deep. 2. In a small-sized mixing dish, mix to all seasonings combine well. 3. Massage the spice mix into the pork meat to evenly distribute. Drizzle with lemon juice. Place the pork in the frying basket; roast the pork at 360ºF (182ºC) for 25 to 30 minutes. Check for doneness and cook for 25 minutes more.

Beef Burgers with Mushroom

Prep time: 10 minutes | Cook time: 21 to 23 minutes | Serves 4

1 pound (454 g) ground beef, formed into 4 patties
Sea salt and freshly ground black pepper, to taste
1 cup thinly sliced onion
8 ounces (227 g) mushrooms, sliced
1 tablespoon avocado oil
2 ounces (57 g) Gruyère cheese, shredded (about ½ cup)

1. Season the patties on both sides with salt and pepper. Air fry at 375ºF (191ºC) for 5 minutes, flipping once. Remove the burgers and set aside. 2. Toss the onion and mushrooms with avocado oil and salt and pepper to taste. Air fry for 15 minutes, stirring occasionally. 3. Spoon the onions and mushrooms over the patties. Top with the cheese. Air fry the patties for another 1 to 3 minutes, until the cheese melts and the internal temperature reaches 160ºF (71ºC). Remove and let rest.

Beefy Poppers

Prep time: 15 minutes | Cook time: 15 minutes | Makes 8 poppers

8 medium jalapeño peppers, stemmed, halved, and seeded
1 (8-ounce / 227-g) package cream cheese (or Kite Hill brand cream cheese style spread for dairy-free), softened
2 pounds (907 g) ground beef (85% lean)
1 teaspoon fine sea salt
½ teaspoon ground black pepper
8 slices thin-cut bacon
Fresh cilantro leaves, for garnish

1. Spray the frying basket with avocado oil. Preheat the air fryer to 400ºF (204ºC). 2. Stuff each jalapeño half with a few tablespoons of cream cheese. Place the halves back together again to form 8 jalapeños. 3. Season the ground beef with the salt and pepper. Flatten about ¼ pound (113 g) of ground beef in the palm of your hand and place a stuffed jalapeño in the center. Fold the beef around the jalapeño, forming an egg shape. Wrap the beef-covered jalapeño with a slice of bacon and secure it with a toothpick. 4. Air fry the jalapeño for 15 minutes, or until the beef is cooked through and the bacon is crispy. Garnish with cilantro before serving.

Chapter 5 Poultry

Whole Cornish Hen with Lemon and Herbs

Prep time: 5 minutes | Cook time: 45 minutes | Serves 2

1 (1½- to 2-pound) Cornish hen
¼ cup olive oil
2 tablespoons lemon juice
2 tablespoons fresh rosemary, chopped
2 tablespoons fresh thyme, chopped
4 garlic cloves, roughly chopped
1 teaspoon salt
1 teaspoon fresh ground black pepper
1 celery stalk, roughly chopped
½ small onion
½ lemon
Chopped fresh parsley, for garnish
Fresh cracked black pepper, for garnish

1. Preheat the air fryer to 380ºF (193ºC). 2. In a bowl, combine the olive oil, lemon juice, rosemary, thyme, garlic, salt, and pepper. Brush the mixture over the tops and sides of the hen. Pour any excess inside the cavity of the bird. 3. Stuff the celery, onion, and ½ lemon into the cavity of the hen. 4. Roast for 40 to 45 minutes, or until the internal temperature reaches 165ºF (74ºC). 5. Cut the hen in half and serve with parsley and fresh cracked black pepper.

Pomegranate Chicken Wings

Prep time: 20 minutes | Cook time: 14 to 16 minutes | Serves 2

10 chicken wings
2 tablespoons hot chili sauce
½ tablespoon balsamic vinegar
1 tablespoon pomegranate molasses
1 teaspoon brown sugar
1 teaspoon tomato paste
Salt and black pepper to taste
4 tablespoons mayonnaise
½ cup yogurt
1 tablespoon lemon juice
½ white cabbage, shredded
1 carrot, grated
1 green onion, sliced
2 tablespoons fresh parsley, chopped

1. Mix hot chili sauce, balsamic vinegar, pomegranate molasses, brown sugar, tomato paste, salt, and pepper in a bowl. Coat the chicken wings with the mixture, cover, and refrigerate for 30 minutes. 2. In a salad bowl, combine the cabbage, carrot, green onion, and parsley; mix well. In another bowl, whisk the mayonnaise, yogurt, lemon juice, salt, and black pepper. Pour over the coleslaw and mix to combine. Keep in the fridge until ready to use. 3. Preheat the air fryer to 350ºF (177ºC). Put the chicken wings in the greased frying basket and air fry for 14 to 16 minutes, turning once halfway through. Serve with the chilled coleslaw and enjoy!

Sweet Chili and Ginger Chicken Wings

Prep time: 10 minutes | Cook time: 12 to 14 minutes | Serves 4

1 pound (454 g) chicken wings
1 teaspoon ginger root powder
1 tablespoon tamarind powder
¼ cup sweet chili sauce

1. Preheat the air fryer to 390ºF (199ºC). Rub the chicken wings with tamarind and ginger root powders. Spray with cooking spray and place in the fryer. Air fry for 6 minutes. Slide the basket out and cover the wings with sweet chili sauce; cook for 6 to 8 more minutes until nice and crispy. Serve warm.

Hot Chicken Wings

Prep time: 15 minutes | Cook time: 20 to 22 minutes | Serves 4

1 pound (454 g) chicken wings
Salt and white pepper to taste
1 teaspoon garlic powder
½ teaspoon chili powder
½ teaspoon ground nutmeg
2 tablespoons butter, melted
½ cup red hot sauce
1 tablespoon sugar

1. Preheat the air fryer to 390ºF (199ºC). In a bowl, add the garlic powder, chili powder, nutmeg, salt, and white pepper. Rub the chicken wings with the mixture and transfer them to the greased frying basket. Brush with some butter and air fry for 20 to 22 minutes, flipping once, or until crispy and golden brown. In a bowl, whisk the remaining butter, hot sauce, and sugar. Serve the wings with the sauce.

Italian-Style Chicken Wings

Prep time: 10 minutes | Cook time: 18 to 20 minutes | Serves 4

1 pound (454 g) chicken wings
¼ cup butter
¼ cup Parmesan cheese, grated
2 cloves garlic, minced
½ teaspoon dried oregano
½ teaspoon dried rosemary
Salt and black pepper to taste
¼ teaspoon paprika

1. Preheat the air fryer to 370ºF (188ºC). Season the wings with salt and pepper and place them in the greased frying basket. Air fry for 12 to 14 minutes, flipping once. Remove to a the greased frying basket. 2. Melt the butter in a skillet over medium heat and cook the garlic for 1 minute. Stir in paprika, oregano, and rosemary for another minute. Spread the mixture over the chicken wings, sprinkle with Parmesan cheese, and bake in the air fryer for 5 minutes or until the cheese is bubbling. Serve immediately.

A-Little-Sour Chicken Wings

Prep time: 20 minutes | Cook time: 16 minutes | Serves 4

2 pounds (907 g) chicken wings
2 tablespoons olive oil
3 garlic cloves, minced
1 tablespoon chili powder
½ tablespoon cinnamon powder
½ teaspoon allspice
1 habanero pepper, seeded
1 tablespoon soy sauce
½ tablespoon lemon pepper
¼ cup red wine vinegar
3 tablespoons lime juice
½ tablespoon ginger, grated
½ tablespoon fresh thyme, chopped
⅓ tablespoon sugar

1. In a bowl, add olive oil, garlic, chili powder, cinnamon powder, allspice, habanero pepper, soy sauce, lemon pepper, red wine vinegar, lime juice, ginger, thyme, and sugar; mix well. Add the chicken wings to the mixture and toss to coat. Cover and refrigerate for 1 hour. 2. Preheat the air fryer to 380ºF (193ºC). Remove the chicken from the fridge, drain all the liquid, and pat dry with paper towels. Working in batches, cook the wings in the greased frying basket for 16 minutes in total. Shake once halfway through. Remove to a serving platter and serve with a blue cheese dip if desired.

Greek Parsley Wings

Prep time: 15 minutes | Cook time: 19 to 21 minutes | Serves 4

1 pound (454 g) chicken wings
1 tablespoon fresh parsley, chopped
Salt and black pepper to taste
1 tablespoon cashew butter
1 garlic clove, minced
1 tablespoon yogurt
1 teaspoon honey
½ tablespoon vinegar
½ tablespoon garlic chili sauce

1. Preheat the air fryer to 360ºF (182ºC). Season the wings with salt and pepper and spritz with cooking spray. Air fry for 14 to 16 minutes, shaking once. In a bowl, mix the remaining ingredients. Transfer the wings to the greased frying basket, top with the sauce, and cook in the air fryer for 5 more minutes. Serve.

Sesame Chicken Wings

Prep time: 15 minutes | Cook time: 18 to 20 minutes | Serves 4

8 chicken wings
2 tablespoons sesame oil
1 tablespoon honey
3 tablespoons light soy sauce
2 crushed garlic clove
1 small knob fresh ginger, grated
2 tablespoons black sesame seeds, toasted
1 green onion, sliced

1. Add all ingredients to a Ziploc bag, except for the sesame seeds. Seal up and massage the ingredients until the wings are well coated. Let them marinate for 30 minutes in the fridge. 2. Preheat the air fryer to 400ºF (204ºC). Place the wings in the frying basket and air fry for 10 minutes, flip, and cook for 8 to 10 more minutes until golden. Sprinkle with sesame seeds and green onion and serve.

Chili Ginger Chicken Wings

Prep time: 10 minutes | Cook time: 14 to 16 minutes | Serves 2

8 chicken wings
1 cup cornflour
½ cup white wine
1 teaspoon chili paste
1-inch fresh ginger, grated
1 tablespoon olive oil

1. In a bowl, mix wine, chili paste, and ginger. Add in the chicken wings and marinate for 30 minutes. Preheat the air fryer to 360ºF (182ºC). Remove the chicken, drain, and coat in cornflour. Brush with olive oil and place in the frying basket. Air fry for 14 to 16 minutes, shaking once until crispy. Serve and enjoy!

Spinach and Chicken Meatballs with Marinara Farfalle

Prep time: 15 minutes | Cook time: 12 to 15 minutes | Serves 6

1½ pounds (680 g) ground chicken
3 tablespoons olive oil
4 ounces (113 g) fresh spinach, chopped
½ cup panko bread crumbs
¼ teaspoon garlic powder
1 egg, beaten
⅓ cup feta cheese, crumbled
8 ounces (227 g) farfalle pasta, cooked
2 cups marinara sauce
Salt and black pepper to taste

1. Preheat the air fryer to 360ºF (182ºC). Mix the bread crumbs, salt, black pepper, and garlic powder in a bowl. Add the egg, ground chicken, spinach, and feta and stir to combine. Shape the mixture into balls. 2. Arrange them in a single layer in the greased frying basket and spray with the remaining olive oil. Air fry for 7 minutes, flip them, and cook for another 5 to 8 minutes or until golden. Serve the chicken meatballs on farfalle pasta and spoon over the marinara sauce.

Honey-Vinegar Chicken Wings

Prep time: 15 minutes | Cook time: 19 to 23 minutes | Serves 4

1 pound (454 g) chicken wings
1 cup flour
1 cup bread crumbs
2 eggs, beaten
2 tablespoons canola oil
Salt and black pepper to taste
2 tablespoons sesame seeds
2 tablespoons red pepper paste
1 tablespoon apple cider vinegar
1 tablespoon honey
1 tablespoon soy sauce

1. Preheat the air fryer to 350ºF (177ºC). Separate the chicken wings into winglets and drummettes. In a bowl, mix the canola oil, salt, and black pepper. Coat the chicken with flour, dip in the beaten eggs, and then in the crumbs. Place the chicken in the greased frying basket. Air fry for 14 to 16 minutes, shaking once. 2. Whisk the red pepper paste, vinegar, soy sauce, honey, and ¼ cup of water in a saucepan over medium heat. Simmer for 5 to 7 minutes until the sauce thickens. Pour the sauce over the chicken and sprinkle with sesame seeds. Serve and enjoy!

Chapter 1 Vegetables and Sides | 75

Dijon Chicken Wings

Prep time: 10 minutes | Cook time: 14 to 16 minutes | Serves 4

8 chicken wings
1 teaspoon Dijon mustard
Salt and black pepper to taste
2 tablespoons olive oil
4 tablespoons Parmesan cheese, grated
2 teaspoons fresh parsley, chopped

1. Preheat the air fryer to 380ºF (193ºC). Season the wings with salt and pepper. Brush them with mustard. Coat the chicken wings with 2 tablespoons of Parmesan cheese, drizzle with olive oil, and place in the greased frying basket. Air fry for 14 to 16 minutes, turning once. When cooked, sprinkle with the remaining Parmesan cheese and top freshly chopped parsley.

Basic Chicken Patties

Prep time: 15 minutes | Cook time: 10 to 12 minutes | Serves 4

1 pound (454 g) ground chicken
½ onion, chopped
2 garlic cloves, chopped
1 egg, beaten
½ cup bread crumbs
½ teaspoon cumin
½ tablespoon paprika
½ tablespoon coriander seeds, crushed
Salt and black pepper to taste

1. Preheat the air fryer to 360ºF (182ºC). In a bowl, mix the ground chicken, onion, garlic, egg, bread crumbs, cumin, paprika, coriander seeds, salt, and black pepper. Shape the mixture into 4 patties. Arrange them on the greased frying basket and bake for 10 to 12 minutes, turning once halfway through. Serve.

Chicken Fingers with Red Mayo Dip

Prep time: 15 minutes | Cook time: 18 to 20 minutes | Serves 4

1 pound (454 g) chicken breasts, cut into finger-sized strips
1 tablespoon olive oil
½ teaspoon paprika
½ teaspoon garlic powder
½ cup seasoned bread crumbs
1 teaspoon dried parsley
Salt and black pepper to taste
½ cup mayonnaise
2 tablespoons ketchup
½ teaspoon garlic powder
½ teaspoon sweet chili sauce

1. Preheat the air fryer to 375ºF (191ºC). Add the chicken with salt, black pepper, paprika, and garlic powder in a bowl, mix to coat. Mix the bread crumbs and parsley in another bowl. Dredge the chicken strips in the crumbs mixture, brush them with olive oil and place them in the fryer. Air fry for 10 minutes. 2. Shake or toss the strips, spray with olive oil, and cook for 8 to 10 more minutes or until golden and crisp. In a bowl, whisk the mayonnaise, ketchup, garlic powder, sweet chili sauce, salt, and black pepper. Pour the dip into a serving bowl and serve with the chicken fingers. Enjoy!

Thai Tom Yum Wings

Prep time: 10 minutes | Cook time: 12 to 14 minutes | Serves 2

8 chicken wings
2 tablespoons tom yum paste
1 tablespoon water
½ cup flour
2 tablespoons cornstarch
½ tablespoon baking powder

1. Whisk the tom yum paste and water in a small bowl. Place the wings in a large bowl, pour the tom yum mixture over, and brush to coat well. Cover the bowl with foil and refrigerate for 2 hours. 2. Preheat the air fryer to 370ºF (188ºC). In a shallow bowl, mix the flour, baking powder, and cornstarch. Dredge the chicken wings in the flour mixture, shaking off, and place them in the greased frying basket. Spritz with cooking spray and air fry them for 7 to 8 minutes. Flip and cook for another 5 to 6 minutes until crispy.

Oregano Chicken Kebabs with Mayonnaise Sauce

Prep time: 15 minutes | Cook time: 15 minutes | Serves 4

1 pound (454 g) ground chicken
½ teaspoon garlic powder
Salt and black pepper to taste
1 tablespoon fresh oregano
¼ teaspoon cayenne powder
¼ teaspoon paprika
Sauce:
½ cup mayonnaise
1 lemon, juiced
2 teaspoons sriracha sauce
1 teaspoon ketchup

1. Preheat the air fryer to 390ºF (199ºC). Place ground chicken, garlic powder, cayenne powder, paprika, oregano, salt, and black pepper in a large bowl. Gently mix with hands until well combined. Form the mixture into cylinder shapes and air fry them in the greased frying basket for 15 minutes, flipping once, until evenly browned on the outside. Place all the sauce ingredients in a bowl and stir well. Taste and adjust the seasoning. Serve the chicken kebabs with the sauce on the side.

South Asian Chicken Strips

Prep time: 15 minutes | Cook time: 18 to 21 minutes | Serves 4

1 pound (454 g) chicken breasts, cut into strips
2 tomatoes, cubed
1 green chili pepper, cut into stripes
½ teaspoon cumin
2 green onions, sliced
2 tablespoons olive oil
1 tablespoon yellow mustard
½ teaspoon ginger powder
2 tablespoons fresh cilantro, chopped
Salt and black pepper to taste

1. Warm the olive oil in a pan over medium heat. Sauté the green onions and chili pepper for 2 to 3 minutes. Stir in tomatoes, mustard, ginger powder, cumin, cilantro, and salt for 2 minutes; set aside. 2. Preheat the air fryer to 380ºF (193ºC). Season the chicken with salt and pepper and place the strips in the greased frying basket. Air fry for 14 to 16 minutes, shaking once. Top with the tomato sauce and serve.

Panko-Crusted Chicken Bites

Prep time: 10 minutes | Cook time: 14 to 16 minutes | Serves 4

4 chicken breasts, sliced
1 cup panko bread crumbs
¼ cup grated Parmesan cheese
2 large eggs
¼ cup flour
½ cup ketchup

1. Preheat the fryer to 360ºF (182ºC). In a bowl, mix Parmesan with bread crumbs. Whisk the eggs in another bowl, and pour the flour in a third bowl. Dip the chicken slices into the flour, then into the eggs, and finally roll them in the cheese crumbs; press lightly to coat. Put the chicken in the greased frying basket and spritz with cooking oil. Bake for 14 to 16 minutes, flipping once until crispy. Serve with ketchup.

Buffalo Cheese-Chicken Tacos

Prep time: 15 minutes | Cook time: 8 to 10 minutes | Serves 6

1 tablespoon buffalo sauce
2 cups shredded cooked chicken
6 ounces (170 g) cream cheese, softened
2 ounces (57 g) sharp cheese, grated
1 tablespoon olive oil
1 teaspoon ground cumin
½ teaspoon smoked paprika
12 flour tortillas

1. Preheat air fryer to 360ºF (182ºC). Stir the cheeses and Buffalo sauce in a bowl, then add the chicken and stir some more. On a clean workspace, lay the tortillas and spoon 2 to 3 tablespoons of the chicken mixture at the center of each tortilla. Sprinkle with cumin and paprika. Roll them up and put them in the air fryer, seam side down. Spray each tortilla with olive oil and air fry for 8 to 10 minutes or until golden and crisp.

Chicken Skewers with Yogurt Dip

Prep time: 15 minutes | Cook time: 11 to 14 minutes | Serves 4

1 pound (454 g) chicken tenderloins
1 teaspoon ground ginger
¼ cup soy sauce
1 tablespoon white vinegar
1 tablespoon honey
1 tablespoon toasted sesame oil
1 lime, zested and juiced
2 teaspoons toasted sesame seeds
4 tablespoons Greek yogurt
2 tablespoons fresh cilantro, chopped
2 tablespoons sweet chili sauce
8 wooden skewer, soaked in water for 30 minutes

1. In a small bowl, combine the Greek yogurt, cilantro, sweet chili sauce, and lime zest. Keep in the fridge until ready to use. Combine the ginger, soy sauce, vinegar, honey, sesame oil, and lime juice in a zip-top bag. Place the chicken in the bag, seal it, and shake to coat. Put it in the fridge for at least 2 hours. 2. Preheat the air fryer to 380ºF (193ºC). Thread each tenderloin onto a wooden skewer and sprinkle with sesame seeds. Keep the excess marinade. Put the skewers in a single layer in the greased fryer basket and air fry for 6 minutes, flip the tenderloins, baste with more marinade, and cook for 5 to 8 more minutes or until golden brown. Serve the skewers with the yogurt dip.

Manchego Chicken Fingers

Prep time: 15 minutes | Cook time: 14 to 1 minutes | Serves 2

2 chicken breasts, cut into strips
Salt and black pepper to taste
1 teaspoon garlic powder
3 tablespoons cornstarch
4 tablespoons bread crumbs
4 tablespoons Manchego cheese, grated
1 egg, beaten

1. Combine salt, garlic, and black pepper in a bowl. Add in the chicken strips and stir to coat. Marinate for 1 hour in the fridge. Mix the bread crumbs with Manchego cheese in another bowl. 2. Preheat the air fryer to 350ºF (177ºC). Remove the chicken from the fridge, lightly toss in cornstarch, dip in egg and coat the strips in the cheese mixture. Place them in the greased frying basket and air fry for 14 to 16 minutes, shaking once, until nice and crispy. Serve with a side of vegetable fries. Yummy!

Jalapeño and Chicken Quesadillas

Prep time: 10 minutes | Cook time: 12 to 14 minutes | Serves 4

8 tortillas
2 cups Monterey Jack cheese, shredded
½ cup cooked chicken, shredded
1 cup canned fire-roasted jalapeño peppers, chopped
1 beaten egg, to seal tortillas

1. Preheat the air fryer to 390ºF (199ºC). Divide the chicken, Monterey Jack cheese, and jalapeño peppers between 4 tortillas. Seal the tortillas with the beaten egg. Grease with cooking spray. Bake the quesadillas in the air fryer for 12 to 14 minutes, turning once halfway through. Work in batches. Serve with green salsa.

Chicken Pinchos with Salsa Verde

Prep time: 20 minutes | Cook time: 20 minutes | Serves 4

4 chicken breasts, cut into large cubes
Salt to taste
1 teaspoon chili powder
1 tablespoon maple syrup
½ cup soy sauce
2 red peppers, cut into sticks
1 green pepper, cut into sticks
8 mushrooms, halved
2 tablespoons sesame seeds
Salsa Verde:
1 garlic clove
2 tablespoons olive oil
Zest and juice from 1 lime
¼ cup fresh parsley, chopped
A bunch of skewers

1. In a bowl, mix chili powder, salt, maple syrup, soy sauce, and sesame seeds and coat in the chicken. Start stacking up the ingredients, alternately, on skewers: red pepper, green pepper, a chicken cube, and a mushroom half until the skewer is fully loaded. Repeat the process for all the ingredients. 2. Preheat the air fryer to 330ºF (166ºC). Brush the pinchos with the soy sauce mixture and place them into the greased frying basket. Air fry for 20 minutes, flipping once halfway through. 3. Blend all salsa verde ingredients in a food processor until you obtain a chunky paste. Taste and season with salt. Arrange the pinchos on a platter and serve with the salsa verde

Chapter 1 Vegetables and Sides | 77

Quinoa Chicken Nuggets

Prep time: 15 minutes | Cook time: 14 to 16 minutes | Serves 4

2 chicken breasts, cut into large chunks
½ cup cooked quinoa, cooled
1 cup flour
2 eggs, beaten
½ teaspoon cayenne pepper
Salt and black pepper to taste

1. In a bowl, beat the egg with salt and black pepper. Spread the flour on a plate and mix in the cayenne pepper. Coat the chicken in the flour, then dip in the eggs, shake off, and coat in the quinoa. Press firmly so the quinoa sticks on the chunks. Spritz with cooking spray and air fry the nuggets in the fryer for 14 to 16 minutes at 360ºF (182ºC), turning once halfway through cooking. Serve hot.

Rice Krispies Chicken Goujons

Prep time: 10 minutes | Cook time: 12 to 14 minutes | Serves 2

2 chicken breasts, cut into strips
Salt and black pepper to taste
½ teaspoon dried tarragon
½ cup rice Krispies
1 egg, beaten
½ cup plain flour
1 tablespoon butter, melted

1. Preheat the air fryer to 390ºF (199ºC). Line the frying basket with baking paper. Season the chicken with salt and pepper. Roll the strips in flour, then dip in egg, and finally coat in the rice Krispies. Place the strips in the fryer, drizzle with butter, and air fry for 12 to 14 minutes, shaking once. Top with tarragon to serve.

Juicy Chicken Fillets with Peppers

Prep time: 20 minutes | Cook time: 30 minutes | Serves 2

2 chicken fillets, cubed
Salt and black pepper to taste
1 cup flour
2 eggs
½ cup apple cider vinegar
½ tablespoon ginger paste
½ tablespoon garlic paste
1 tablespoon sugar
1 red chili, minced
1 tablespoon tomato puree
1 tablespoon paprika
4 tablespoons water
1 red bell pepper, seeded, cut into strips
1 green bell pepper, seeded, cut into strips

1. Preheat the air fryer to 350ºF (177ºC). Sift the flour in a bowl and whisk in the eggs, salt, and pepper. Coat the chicken cubes in the flour mixture. Place them in the frying basket. Spray with cooking spray and air fry for 8 minutes. Shake the basket, and cook for 6 to 8 more minutes until golden and crispy. 2. In a bowl, add apple cider vinegar, ginger paste, garlic paste, sugar, red chili, tomato puree, paprika, and water and mix well with a fork. Place a skillet over medium heat and spritz with cooking spray. Stir in the pepper strips and stir-fry until sweaty but still crunchy. Pour the chili mixture over, stir, and simmer for 10 minutes. Serve the chicken drizzled with the pepper-chili sauce.

San Antonio Taco Chicken Strips

Prep time: 15 minutes | Cook time: 15 minutes | Serves 4

3 mixed bell peppers, cut into chunks
1 red onion, sliced
1 pound (454 g) chicken tenderloins, cut into strips
1 tablespoon olive oil
2 tablespoons cilantro, chopped
1 tablespoon taco seasoning

1. Preheat the air fryer to 375ºF (191ºC). Mix the strips, bell peppers, onion, olive oil, and taco seasoning in a large bowl and stir until the strips are coated. Place the strips and veggies in the greased fryer basket and air fry for 7 minutes. Shake the basket, and cook for 5 to 8 more minutes, until the chicken is thoroughly cooked, and the veggies are starting to char. Serve topped with cilantro.

Crispy Chicken Tenders with Hot Aioli

Prep time: 15 minutes | Cook time: 12 to 14 minutes | Serves 4

1 pound (454 g) chicken breasts, cut into strips
4 tablespoons olive oil
1 cup bread crumbs
Salt and black pepper to taste
½ tablespoon garlic powder
½ tablespoon cayenne pepper
½ cup mayonnaise
2 tablespoons lemon juice
½ tablespoon ground chili

1. Preheat the air fryer to 390ºF (199ºC). Mix the crumbs, salt, black pepper, garlic powder, and cayenne pepper in a bowl. Brush the strips with some olive oil. Coat them in the crumbs mixture and arrange them in the greased frying basket in an even layer. Air fry for 12 to 14 minutes, turning once halfway through. To prepare the hot aioli: add the mayo, lemon juice and ground chili in a small bowl and whisk to combine. Serve with the chicken tenders and enjoy!

Balsamic Chicken with Green Beans

Prep time: 20 minutes | Cook time: 30 minutes | Serves 4

1 pound (454 g) chicken breasts, sliced
¾ cup balsamic vinegar
1 pound (454 g) green beans, trimmed
1 garlic clove, minced
1 pound (454 g) cherry tomatoes, halved
2 tablespoons olive oil

1. In a bowl, add ½ cup of balsamic vinegar and the chicken; stir to coat. Refrigerate for at least 1 hour. 2. Preheat the air fryer to 375ºF (191ºC). Mix the green beans, garlic, cherry tomatoes, and the remaining balsamic vinegar in a bowl and toss to coat. Put the veggies in the greased frying basket and air fry for 8 minutes. Shake the basket and fry further for 5 to 7 minutes until the beans are crisp and tender and the tomatoes are soft and slightly charred. Remove and cover with foil to keep warm. 3. Spray the frying basket with olive oil. Add in the chicken in a single layer and air fry for 7 minutes. Turn and cook for 5 to 8 more minutes until golden. Serve the chicken with the veggies.

Harissa Chicken Sticks

Prep time: 15 minutes | Cook time: 14 to 16 minutes | Serves 4

4 chicken tenders, cut into strips
½ teaspoon ground cumin seeds
1 tablespoon harissa powder
Salt and black pepper to taste
4 cup panko bread crumbs
2 large eggs, beaten

1. Preheat the air fryer to 400ºF (204ºC). In a bowl, mix the bread crumbs, harissa powder, cumin, salt, and black pepper. Dip the chicken strips in eggs and dredge in the harissa-crumb mixture. Place in the greased frying basket and air fry for 14 to 16 minutes, flipping once halfway through. Serve immediately. Yummy!

Crunchy Coconut Chicken Dippers

Prep time: 10 minutes | Cook time: 14 to 16 minutes | Serves 4

2 cups coconut flakes
4 chicken breasts, cut into strips
½ cup cornstarch
Salt and black pepper to taste
2 eggs, beaten

1. Preheat the air fryer to 350ºF (177ºC). Mix salt, pepper, and cornstarch in a bowl. Dip the strips in the cornstarch, then into the eggs, and finally, coat in the coconut flakes. Place the chicken strips in the greased frying basket and air fry for 14 to 16 minutes, flipping once until crispy. Serve with berry sauce if desired.

Popcorn Chicken Tenders

Prep time: 15 minutes | Cook time: 12 to 14 minutes | Serves 4

1 pound (454 g) chicken tenders, cut into strips
½ cup cooked popcorn
½ cup panko bread crumbs
2 eggs
½ cup cornflour
½ teaspoon dried oregano
2 tablespoons butter, melted
Salt and black pepper to taste

1. Preheat the air fryer to 400ºF (204ºC). Pulse the popcorn in a blender until crumbs-like texture. In a bowl, combine the cornflour, oregano, salt, and black pepper. In another bowl, beat the eggs with some salt. 2. In a third bowl, mix the bread crumbs with the popcorn crumbs. Dip the chicken strips in the cornflour, then in the eggs, and then coat in the crumbs. Place in the greased frying basket. Drizzle with butter and air fry for 12 to 14 minutes, shaking once or twice during cooking, until nice and crispy. Serve hot.

Ranch Cheesy Chicken Tenders

Prep time: 10 minutes | Cook time: 14 to 18 minutes | Serves 4

2 tablespoons olive oil
¾ cup bread crumbs
2 tablespoons Ranch dressing
spice blend
½ cup Parmesan cheese, grated
2 tablespoons Cheddar cheese, grated
1 pound (454 g) chicken tenders

1. Preheat the air fryer to 390ºF (199ºC). In a bowl, mix Parmesan cheese, Cheddar cheese, bread crumbs, and ranch dressing. Add in the tenders and coat well. Drizzle with olive oil and transfer the tenders in the greased frying basket. Air fry for 8 to 10 minutes. Toss the tenders and cook for 6 to 8 minutes until crispy.

Crispy Chicken Tenderloins

Prep time: 10 minutes | Cook time: 14 to 16 minutes | Serves 4

8 chicken tenderloins
2 eggs, beaten
2 tablespoons butter, melted
1 cup seasoned bread crumbs

1. Preheat the air fryer to 380ºF (193ºC). Dip the chicken in the eggs, then coat in the seasoned crumbs. Drizzle the frying basket with some butter and place in the chicken. Brush it with the remaining butter and air fry for 14 to 16 minutes, shaking once halfway through. Serve with your favorite dip.

Almond-Fried Crispy Chicken

Prep time: 15 minutes | Cook time: 14 to 16 minutes | Serves 4

4 chicken breasts, cubed
2 cups almond meal
3 whole eggs
½ cup cornstarch
Salt and black pepper to taste
1 tablespoon cayenne pepper

1. Preheat the air fryer to 350ºF (177ºC). In a bowl, mix the cornstarch, salt, black pepper, and cayenne pepper and toss in the chicken. In another bowl, beat the eggs. In a third bowl, pour the almond meal. Dredge the chicken in the eggs, then in almond meal. Air fry for 14 to 16 minutes, shaking once or twice. Serve.

Effortless Chicken Scallopini

Prep time: 15 minutes | Cook time: 20 minutes | Serves 4

4 chicken breasts
3 ounces (85 g) bread crumbs
2 tablespoons Parmesan cheese, grated
1 cup plus 1 tablespoon flour
2 eggs, beaten
2 tablespoons fresh dill, chopped
2 tablespoons butter
2 tablespoons lemon juice
2 tablespoons capers
½ cup chicken broth

1. Preheat the air fryer to 370ºF (188ºC). Place some plastic wrap underneath and on top of the breasts. Using a rolling pin, beat the breasts until they become skinny. In a bowl, mix Parmesan and bread crumbs. Dip the chicken in the eggs, then in the flour, and finally in the crumbs. Air fry for 14 to 16 minutes, flipping once. 2. Melt the butter in a saucepan and stir in 1 tablespoon of flour for 1 to 2 minutes. Pour in the lemon juice and chicken broth and simmer for 2 to 3 minutes until the sauce thickens. Remove and stir in the capers and dill. Pour the sauce over the chicken and serve.

Chicken Schnitzel with Gypsy Sauce

Prep time: 15 minutes | Cook time: 15 minutes | Serves 2

2 chicken breasts
2 eggs, beaten
1 cup flour
1 cup bread crumbs
2 tablespoons olive oil
1 onion, sliced
1 cup canned tomatoes, diced
2 green and red bell peppers, sliced
½ cup red wine
1 cup chicken stock

1. Place the chicken between 2 plastic sheets; flatten out using a rolling pin. Place the eggs, flour, and crumbs in 3 different bowls. Coat the chicken in flour, then in the eggs, and finally in the crumbs. 2. Preheat the air fryer to 350ºF (177ºC). Place the chicken in the greased frying basket and air fry for 14 to 16 minutes, flipping once. Meanwhile, warm the olive oil in a saucepan over medium heat and sauté the onion and peppers until tender, 5 minutes. Pour in the wine to deglaze and add the stock and tomatoes. Bring to a boil and simmer for 6 to 8 minutes until it thickens slightly. Pour the sauce over the schnitzel and serve.

Cajun Chicken Tenders

Prep time: 15 minutes | Cook time: 12 to 14 minutes | Serves 4

1 pound (454 g) chicken breasts, sliced
3 eggs
1 cup flour
2 tablespoons olive oil
½ tablespoon garlic powder
Salt and black pepper to taste
1 tablespoon Cajun seasoning
¼ cup milk

1. Sprinkle the chicken slices with garlic powder and Cajun seasoning. Pour the flour on a plate. In a bowl, whisk the eggs along with milk and olive oil. Season with salt and black pepper. 2. Preheat the air fryer to 370ºF (188ºC). Dip the chicken slices into the egg mixture, and then coat in the flour. Arrange them on the greased frying basket and air fry for 12 to 14 minutes, flipping once until crispy.

Jerusalem Matzah and Chicken Schnitzels

Prep time: 10 minutes | Cook time: 14 to 16 minutes | Serves 4

4 chicken breasts
1 cup panko bread crumbs
2 tablespoons Parmesan cheese, grated
6 sage leaves, chopped
½ cup fine matzah meal
2 beaten eggs

1. Pound the chicken to ¼-inch thickness using a rolling pin. In a bowl, mix Parmesan cheese, sage, and bread crumbs. Coat the chicken in matzah meal, dip it in the eggs, then coat in the crumbs' mixture. 2. Preheat the air fryer to 390ºF (199ºC). Spritz the chicken breasts with cooking spray and air fry them for 14 to 16 minutes, turning once halfway through, until golden and crispy. Serve warm.

Gluten-Free Crunchy Chicken

Prep time: 15 minutes | Cook time: 18 to 20 minutes | Serves 4

2 garlic cloves, minced
1 pound (454 g) chicken breasts, sliced
½ teaspoon dried thyme
1 cup potato flakes
Salt and black pepper to taste
½ cup Cheddar cheese, grated
½ cup mayonnaise
1 lemon, zested

1. Preheat the air fryer to 350ºF (177ºC). In a bowl, mix the garlic, potato flakes, Cheddar cheese, thyme, lemon zest, salt, and pepper. Brush the chicken slices with mayonnaise, then roll in the potato mixture. Place in the greased frying basket and air fry for 18 to 20 minutes, flipping once halfway through. Serve warm.

Chicken Teriyaki

Prep time: 15 minutes | Cook time: 11 to 13 minutes | Serves 4

1 pound (454 g) chicken tenderloins
⅓ cup soy sauce
⅓ cup honey
3 tablespoons white vinegar
1½ teaspoons dried thyme
½ teaspoon cayenne pepper
½ teaspoon ground allspice
2 cups cooked brown rice
2 cups steamed broccoli florets
1 teaspoon ground black pepper
1 tablespoon fresh cilantro, chopped
2 green onions, chopped

1. Mix soy sauce, honey, white vinegar, thyme, black pepper, cayenne pepper, and allspice in a bowl to make a marinade. Toss the tenderloins in the marinade and coat. Cover and refrigerate for 30 minutes. 2. Preheat the air fryer to 380ºF (193ºC). Remove the chicken from the marinade; keep the marinade for later. Put the chicken in a single layer in the greased frying basket and air fry for 6 minutes. Turn the chicken and brush with the remaining marinade. Cook for 5 to 7 more minutes or until crispy. Divide the rice, broccoli, and chicken tenderloins between 4 bowls. Top with cilantro and green onions and serve.

Sweet Curried Chicken Cutlets

Prep time: 10 minutes | Cook time: 14 to 16 minutes | Serves 4

1 pound (454 g) chicken breasts, halved crosswise
2 tablespoons garlic mayonnaise
½ teaspoon chili powder
½ teaspoon curry powder
½ teaspoon brown sugar
2 tablespoons soy sauce

1. Put the chicken halves between 2 pieces of plastic wrap and gently pound them to ¼-inch thickness using a rolling pin. In a bowl, mix the chili powder, curry powder, brown sugar, and soy sauce. Add in the chicken and toss to coat. Cover with plastic wrap and refrigerate for 1 hour. 2. Preheat the air fryer to 350ºF (177ºC). Remove the chicken from the marinade and place it in the greased frying basket. Air fry for 8 minutes, flip, and cook further for 6 to 8 minutes until crispy. Serve with garlic mayo.

Chicken Fillets with Sweet Chili Adobo

Prep time: 10 minutes | Cook time: 12 to 14 minutes | Serves 4

2 chicken breasts, halved
Salt and black pepper to taste
¼ cup sweet chili sauce
1 teaspoon turmeric

1. Preheat the air fryer to 390°F (199°C). In a bowl, place the sweet chili sauce, salt, black pepper, and turmeric; mix well. Lightly brush the chicken with the mixture and place them in the greased frying basket. Air fry for 12 to 14 minutes, turning once halfway through. Serve with a side of steamed greens if desired.

Texas BBQ Chicken Thighs

Prep time: 10 minutes | Cook time: 14 to 16 minutes | Serves 4

8 chicken thighs
Salt and black pepper to taste
2 teaspoons Texas BBQ Jerky seasoning
1 tablespoon olive oil
2 tablespoons fresh cilantro, chopped

1. Preheat the air fryer to 380°F (193°C). Grease the frying basket with cooking spray. Drizzle the chicken with olive oil, season with salt and black pepper, and rub with BBQ seasoning. Place in the fryer and air fry for 14 to 16 minutes in total, flipping once. Top with fresh cilantro and serve.

Greek Chicken Gyros

Prep time: 15 minutes | Cook time: 12 to 14 minutes | Serves 4

2 chicken breasts, cut into strips
Salt and black pepper to taste
1 cup flour
1 egg, beaten
½ cup bread crumbs
4 flatbreads
2 cups white cabbage, shredded
3 tablespoons Greek yogurt dressing

1. Preheat the air fryer to 380°F (193°C). Season the chicken with salt and black pepper. Pour the bread crumbs in one bowl, the flour in another, and the egg in a third bowl. Dredge the strips in flour, then in the egg, and finally in the crumbs. Spray with cooking oil and transfer to the fryer. Air fry for 12 to 14 minutes, flipping once halfway through. Serve the "pitas" filled with the strips, cabbage, and yogurt dressing.

Swiss-Style Breaded Chicken

Prep time: 10 minutes | Cook time: 12 to 14 minutes | Serves 4

½ cup seasoned bread crumbs
¼ cup Gruyere cheese, grated
1 pound (454 g) chicken breasts
½ cup flour
2 eggs, beaten
Salt and black pepper to taste
4 lemon slices

1. Preheat the air fryer to 370°F (188°C). Spray the frying basket with cooking spray. 2. Mix the bread crumbs with Gruyere cheese in a bowl, beat the eggs in another bowl, and pour the flour into a third bowl. Toss the chicken in the flour, then in the eggs, and finally in the bread crumbs mixture. 3. Place in the frying basket and air fry for 12 to 14 minutes. Turn the chicken over at the 6-minute mark. Once golden brown, remove to a plate and serve topped with lemon slices.

Chicken Breasts with Avocado-Mango Salsa

Prep time: 15 minutes | Cook time: 12 to 14 minutes | Serves 2

½ pound (227 g) chicken breasts, sliced
2 tablespoons olive oil
½ teaspoon cayenne pepper powder
Salt and black pepper to taste
1 mango, chopped
1 avocado, chopped
1 red pepper, chopped
1 tablespoon balsamic vinegar

1. In a bowl, mix the olive oil, cayenne pepper, salt, and black pepper. Add in the breasts, toss to coat, and marinate for 1 hour. Preheat the air fryer to 360°F (182°C). Place the chicken in the frying basket and air fry for 12 to 14 minutes, flipping once. Meanwhile, mix the avocado, mango, red pepper, balsamic vinegar, and salt in a large bowl. Spoon the salsa over the chicken slices and serve.

Lemony Chicken Breast

Prep time: 10 minutes | Cook time: 14 to 16 minutes | Serves 2

1 chicken breast
2 lemon, juiced and rind reserved
1 tablespoon chicken
seasoning
1 tablespoon garlic puree
Salt and black pepper to taste

1. Preheat the air fryer to 350°F (177°C). Place a silver foil sheet on a flat surface. Add all seasonings along with the lemon rind. Lay the chicken breast onto a chopping board and trim any fat. 2. Season each side with the seasoning. Place in the silver foil sheet, seal, and flatten with a rolling pin. Place the breast in the frying basket and air fry for 14 to 16 minutes, flipping once halfway through.

Chicken Breasts "En Papillote"

Prep time: 10 minutes | Cook time: 15 minutes | Serves 4

1 pound (454 g) chicken breasts
2 tablespoons butter, melted
Salt and black pepper to taste
½ teaspoon dried marjoram

1. Preheat the air fryer to 380°F (193°C). Place each chicken breast on a 12x12 inches aluminum foil wrap, and season with salt and pepper. Top with marjoram and butter. Wrap the foil around the breasts in a loose way to create a flow of air. Bake the in the fryer for 15 minutes. Unwrap, let cool slightly, and serve.

Jamaican Chicken Fajitas

Prep time: 15 minutes | Cook time: 13 to 15 minutes | Serves 4

1 pound (454 g) chicken tenderloins
1 cup Jamaican jerk seasoning
2 tablespoons lime juice
2 tablespoons olive oil
4 large tortilla wraps
1 cup julienned carrots
1 cucumber, peeled, sliced
1 cup shredded lettuce
1 cup coleslaw mix
½ cup mango chutney

1. Whisk the olive oil, jerk seasoning, and lime juice in a bowl. Add in the chicken and toss to coat. Put in the fridge for 1 hour. Remove the chicken from the fridge, setting the leftover marinade aside. 2. Preheat the air fryer to 380ºF (193ºC). Arrange the chicken tenderloins in the greased frying basket in a single layer. Air fry for 8 minutes. Flip them and brush with some more marinade. Fry for 5 to 7 more minutes. 3. Divide the coleslaw mix, carrots, cucumber, lettuce, and mango chutney between the tortilla wraps. Add the chicken tenderloins on top and roll the tortillas up. Serve warm or cold and enjoy!

Prosciutto-Wrapped Chicken Breasts

Prep time: 15 minutes | Cook time: 14 to 16 minutes | Serves 2

2 chicken breasts
1 tablespoon olive oil
Salt and black pepper to taste
4 sun-dried tomatoes, sliced
2 brie cheese slices
4 thin prosciutto slices

1. Preheat the air fryer to 370ºF (188ºC). Put the chicken breasts on a chopping board and cut a small incision deep enough to make stuffing possible. Insert 1 slice of brie cheese and 4 to 5 tomato slices into each cut. 2. Lay the prosciutto on the chopping board. Put the chicken on one side and roll the prosciutto over the breast, making sure that both ends of the prosciutto meet under the chicken. 3. Brush with olive oil and sprinkle with salt and black pepper. Place the chicken in the frying basket and air fry for 14 to 16 minutes, turning once halfway through. Slice each chicken breast in half and serve.

Chicken Parmigiana with Fresh Rosemary

Prep time: 10 minutes | Cook time: 11 to 13 minutes | Serves 4

1 pound (454 g) chicken breasts, halved
1 cup seasoned bread crumbs
½ cup Parmesan cheese, grated
Salt and black pepper to taste
2 eggs
2 sprigs rosemary, chopped

1. Preheat the air fryer to 380ºF (193ºC). Put the chicken halves on a clean flat surface and cover with a clingfilm. Gently pound them to become thinner using a rolling pin. Beat the eggs in a bowl and season them with salt and black pepper. In a separate bowl, mix bread crumbs with Parmesan cheese. 2. Dip the chicken in the eggs, then in the crumbs and spray with cooking spray. Air fry them for 6 minutes, flip and cook for 5 to 7 more minutes or until golden and crispy. Sprinkle with rosemary to serve.

Apricot Mustard Chicken Breasts

Prep time: 10 minutes | Cook time: 15 to 16 minutes | Serves 4

1 teaspoon yellow mustard
1 tablespoon apricot jam
2 garlic cloves, minced
Salt and black pepper to taste
1 pound (454 g) chicken breasts
3 tablespoons butter, melted

1. Preheat the air fryer to 360ºF (182ºC). In a bowl, mix together mustard, butter, garlic, apricot jam, black pepper, and salt. Rub the chicken with the mixture and place them in the greased frying basket. Air fry for 10 minutes, flip, and cook them for 5 to 6 more minutes or until golden and crispy. Slice before serving.

Ham and Cheese Chicken Breasts

Prep time: 10 minutes | Cook time: 20 minutes | Serves 4

4 chicken breasts
4 ham slices
4 Swiss cheese slices
3 tablespoons all-purpose flour
4 tablespoons butter
½ tablespoon paprika
1 tablespoon chicken bouillon granules
¼ cup dry white wine
1 cup heavy cream

1. Preheat the air fryer to 380ºF (193ºC). Pound the chicken and put a slice of ham and cheese onto each one. Fold the edges over the filling and seal them with toothpicks. In a bowl, combine paprika and flour, and coat in the chicken. Transfer them to the greased frying basket and bake for 15 minutes, turning once. 2. In a large skillet over medium heat, melt the butter and add the bouillon granules, wine, and heavy cream. Bring to a boil, reduce the heat to low, and simmer for 5 minutes. Serve the chicken with sauce.

Chicken Tikka Masala

Prep time: 15 minutes | Cook time: 14 to 16 minutes | Serves 4

2 chicken breasts, sliced
Salt and black pepper to taste
¼ teaspoon garlic powder
1 tablespoon paprika
½ cup plain yogurt
1 teaspoon lemon juice
½ teaspoon ginger powder
1 teaspoon ground cumin
1 tablespoon garam masala
2 cups basmati rice, cooked
2 tablespoons fresh cilantro, chopped
1 cup red hot sauce

1. In a bowl, combine garlic powder, paprika, yogurt, lemon juice, ginger powder, cumin, garam masala, salt, and black pepper. Add in the chicken, toss to coat, cover and refrigerate for 1 hour. 2. Preheat the air fryer to 360ºF (182ºC). Line the frying basket with waxed paper and place in the chicken slices. Air fry them for 14 to 16 minutes, flipping once halfway through cooking. Remove the chicken to a bowl, and stir in the hot sauce. Sprinkle with fresh cilantro and serve over cooked basmati rice.

Creamy Asiago Chicken

Prep time: 10 minutes | Cook time: 14 to 16 minutes | Serves 4

4 chicken breasts, cubed
½ teaspoon garlic powder
1 cup mayonnaise
½ cup Asiago cheese, grated
Salt and black pepper to taste
2 tablespoons fresh basil, chopped

1. Preheat the air fryer to 380ºF (193ºC). In a bowl, mix Asiago cheese, mayonnaise, garlic powder, black pepper, and salt. Add in the chicken and toss to coat. Place the coated chicken in the greased frying basket. Air fry for 14 to 16 minutes, shaking once or twice. Serve sprinkled with freshly chopped basil.

Sweet Wasabi Chicken

Prep time: 10 minutes | Cook time: 14 to 16 minutes | Serves 2

2 tablespoons wasabi
1 tablespoon agave syrup
2 teaspoons black sesame seeds
Salt and black pepper to taste
2 chicken breasts, cut into large chunks

1. Preheat the air fryer to 380ºF (193ºC). In a bowl, mix all ingredients and season to taste. Rub the mixture onto the chicken and arrange the chunks in a greased frying basket. Bake for 14 to 16 minutes, turning once.

Easy Chicken Enchiladas

Prep time: 15 minutes | Cook time: 22 to 28 minutes | Serves 4

1 pound (454 g) chicken breasts, cut into strips
1 cup Mozzarella cheese, grated
½ cup salsa
1 can green chilies, chopped
8 flour tortillas
1 cup enchilada sauce

1. Preheat the air fryer to 400ºF (204ºC). In a bowl, mix salsa and enchilada sauce. Toss in the chicken cubes to coat. Place the chicken in the greased frying basket and bake for 14 to 18 minutes, shaking once. 2. Remove and divide between the tortillas. Top with Mozzarella and green chilies and roll the tortillas up. Place in the greased frying basket and bake for 8 to 10 minutes. Serve with guacamole if desired.

Caprese Chicken with Balsamic Sauce

Prep time: 10 minutes | Cook time: 14 to 16 minutes | Serves 4

4 chicken breasts, cubed
6 basil leaves, chopped
¼ cup balsamic vinegar
4 tomato slices
1 tablespoon butter, melted
4 fresh Mozzarella cheese slices

1. Preheat the air fryer to 400ºF (204ºC). Mix butter and balsamic vinegar and pour it over the chicken in a bowl. Let marinate for 30 minutes. Place the chicken in the greased frying basket and air fry for 14 to 16 minutes, shaking once or twice. Serve topped with basil, tomato, and fresh Mozzarella slices.

Italian Chicken Breasts

Prep time: 10 minutes | Cook time: 13 to 14 minutes | Serves 4

1 cup spinach, chopped
4 tablespoons cottage cheese, crumbled
2 chicken breasts
2 tablespoons Italian seasoning
2 tablespoons olive oil

1. Preheat the air fryer to 390ºF (199ºC). Grease the basket with cooking spray. Mix spinach and cottage cheese in a bowl. Halve the breasts with a knife and flatten them with a meat mallet. Season with Italian seasoning. Divide the spinach/cheese mixture between the chicken pieces. 2. Roll them up to form cylinders and use toothpicks to secure them. Brush with olive oil and place them in the frying basket. Bake for 7 to 8 minutes, turn, and cook for 6 minutes or until golden brown. Serve.

Pineapple Sherry Chicken

Prep time: 15 minutes | Cook time: 18 to 22 minutes | Serves 4

4 chicken breasts, cubed
2 tablespoons ketchup
½ tablespoon ginger, minced
½ cup soy sauce
2 tablespoons sherry
1 tablespoon sriracha sauce
½ cup pineapple juice
½ cup brown sugar

1. In a bowl, mix ketchup, pineapple juice, brown sugar, soy sauce, sriracha sauce, sherry, and ginger. Add in the chicken and toss to coat. Cover and refrigerate for 8 hours or overnight. 2. Preheat the air fryer to 360ºF (182ºC). Remove the chicken from the fridge, drain from the marinade and place in the greased frying basket. Air fry for 18 to 22 minutes, shaking occasionally and brushing with the marinade every 4 to 5 minutes. Serve the chicken with grilled pineapple slices if desired.

French-Style Chicken Thighs

Prep time: 10 minutes | Cook time: 18 minutes | Serves 4

1 tablespoon herbs de Provence
1 pound (454 g) bone-in, skinless chicken thighs
Salt and black pepper to taste
2 garlic cloves, minced
½ cup honey
¼ cup Dijon mustard
2 tablespoons butter

1. Preheat the air fryer to 390ºF (199ºC). In a bowl, mix herbs de Provence, salt, and pepper. Rub onto the chicken thighs. Transfer to the greased frying basket and bake for 15 minutes, flipping once, until golden. 2. Meanwhile, melt butter in a saucepan over medium heat. Stir in honey, mustard, and garlic; cook until reduced to a thick consistency, 3 minutes. Serve the chicken drizzled with the honey-mustard sauce.

Air Fried Chicken Bowl with Black Beans

Prep time: 15 minutes | Cook time: 14 to 16 minutes | Serves 4

4 chicken breasts, cubed
1 can sweet corn
1 can black beans, rinsed and drained
1 cup red and green peppers, stripes, cooked
2 tablespoons vegetable oil
1 teaspoon chili powder

1. Preheat the air fryer to 380ºF (193ºC). Sprinkle the chicken with salt, black pepper, and a bit of oil. Place in the greased frying basket and air fry for 14 to 16 minutes until golden and crispy. Meanwhile, in a deep skillet, pour the remaining oil and stir in chili powder, corn, peppers, and beans. Add a little bit of hot water and stir-fry for 3 minutes. Transfer the veggies to a serving platter and top with the fried chicken.

Chicken Cheesy Divan Casserole

Prep time: 10 minutes | Cook time: 23 to 25 minutes | Serves 4

4 chicken breasts
Salt and black pepper to taste
1 cup Cheddar cheese, shredded
1 broccoli head, cut into florets
½ cup cream of mushroom soup
½ cup croutons

1. Preheat the air fryer to 390ºF (199ºC). Rub the chicken breasts with salt and black pepper and place them in the greased frying basket. Bake for 15 minutes, flipping once. Let cool a bit and cut into bite-size pieces. 2. In a bowl, add chicken pieces, broccoli florets, Cheddar cheese, and mushroom soup cream; mix well. Scoop the mixture into a greased baking dish, add the croutons on top and spray with cooking spray. Put the dish in the frying basket and bake for 8 to 10 minutes until golden. Serve with rice if desired.

Tasty Kiev-Style Chicken

Prep time: 15 minutes | Cook time: 15 to 17 minutes | Serves 4

1 pound (454 g) chicken breasts
4 tablespoons butter, softened
1 tablespoon fresh dill, chopped
2 garlic cloves, minced
1 tablespoon lemon juice
Salt and black pepper to taste
1 cup plain flour
2 eggs, beaten in a bowl
1 cup panko bread crumbs

1. Preheat the air fryer to 390ºF (199ºC). In a bowl, mix butter, dill, garlic, lemon juice, salt, and pepper until a smooth paste is formed. Using a sharp knife, make a deep cut of each breast to create a large pocket. 2. Stuff with the butter mixture and secure with toothpicks. Coat the breasts in the flour, then dip in the eggs, and finally in the bread crumbs. Place the chicken in the greased frying basket and bake for 10 minutes. Turn over and cook for 5 to 7 more minutes or until golden. Serve sliced.

Creamy Onion Chicken

Prep time: 10 minutes | Cook time: 16 minutes | Serves 4

4 chicken breasts, cubed
1½ cups onion soup mix
1 cup mushroom soup
½ cup heavy cream

1. Preheat the fryer to 400ºF (204ºC). Warm the soup, soup mix, and the heavy cream in a pan over low heat for 1 minute. Pour over the chicken in a bowl, and let sit for 25 minutes. Remove the chicken to the greased frying basket and air fry for 15 minutes, shaking once. Drizzle with the remaining sauce to serve.

Tropical Coconut Chicken Thighs

Prep time: 10 minutes | Cook time: 12 to 14 minutes | Serves 4

1 tablespoon curry powder
4 tablespoons mango chutney
Salt and black pepper to taste
¾ cup coconut, shredded
1 pound (454 g) chicken thighs

1. Preheat the air fryer to 400ºF (204ºC). In a bowl, mix curry powder, mango chutney, salt, and black pepper. Brush the thighs with the glaze and roll the thighs in the shredded coconut. Bake them in the greased frying basket for 12 to 14 minutes, turning once, until golden brown. Serve and enjoy!

Rosemary and Oyster Chicken Breasts

Prep time: 15 minutes | Cook time: 14 to 16 minutes | Serves 2

2 chicken breasts
1 tablespoon ginger paste
1 tablespoon soy sauce
1 tablespoon olive oil
1 tablespoon oyster sauce
2 fresh rosemary sprigs, chopped
1 tablespoon brown sugar
2 lemon wedges

1. Place the ginger paste, soy sauce, and olive oil in a mixing bowl and stir well. Coat in the chicken breasts. Cover the bowl with a lid and refrigerate for 30 minutes. 2. Preheat the air fryer to 370ºF (188ºC). Transfer the marinated chicken to a baking dish and bake in the fryer for 6 minutes. Mix oyster sauce, rosemary, and brown sugar in a bowl. Pour the sauce over the chicken. Return to the air fryer and bake for 8 to 10 minutes. Remove the rosemary and serve with lemon wedges.

Cheesy Marinara Chicken

Prep time: 10 minutes | Cook time: 12 to 14 minutes | Serves 2

2 chicken fillets, ½-inch thick
2 eggs, beaten
½ cup bread crumbs
2 tablespoons marinara sauce
2 tablespoons Grana Padano cheese, grated
2 Mozzarella cheese slices
Salt and black pepper to taste

1. Season the chicken with salt and black pepper. Dip the fillets in the eggs, then in the crumbs, and arrange them in the greased frying basket. Air fry for 7 to 8 minutes at 400ºF (204ºC). Turn, top with marinara sauce, Grana Padano and Mozzarella cheeses, and bake further for 5 to 6 more minutes. Serve warm.

Restaurant-Style Chicken with Yogurt Sauce

Prep time: 10 minutes | Cook time: 15 minutes | Serves 4

½ cup bread crumbs
2 whole eggs, beaten
½ cup all-purpose flour
Salt and black pepper to taste
2 tablespoons olive oil
1¼ pounds (567 g) chicken tenders
1 cup Greek yogurt
1 tablespoon lemon juice
1 tablespoon fresh dill, chopped

1. Preheat the air fryer to 380ºF (193ºC). Pour the crumbs, eggs, and flour into 3 separate bowls. Season the tenders with salt and pepper and dredge them first in the flour, then in eggs, and finally in the crumbs. Air fry them in the greased frying basket for 10 minutes. Flip and cook for 5 more minutes or until golden. Mix the yogurt with lemon juice, dill, salt, and pepper until smooth. Serve with the tenders.

Garlicky Chicken Cubes On A Green Bed

Prep time: 15 minutes | Cook time: 14 minutes | Serves 2

1 chicken breast, cut into cubes
2 tablespoons olive oil
1 garlic clove, minced
½ cup baby spinach
½ cup romaine lettuce, shredded
3 large kale leaves, chopped
1 teaspoon balsamic vinegar
Salt and black pepper to taste

1. Preheat the air fryer to 390ºF (199ºC). In a bowl, add the chicken, 1 tablespoon of olive oil, garlic, salt, and pepper; mix well. Pour the mixture into a baking dish that fits in the fryer. Bake for 14 minutes, shaking once. In a bowl, mix the greens, 1 tablespoon of olive oil, and vinegar. Place the cooked chicken on top and serve.

Southern-Style Fried Chicken Drumsticks

Prep time: 15 minutes | Cook time: 18 to 22 minutes | Serves 4

1 pound (454 g) chicken drumsticks
1 tablespoon hot chili sauce
1 cup buttermilk
1 teaspoon turmeric
1 garlic clove, minced
1 teaspoon smoked paprika
½ cup flour
½ cup bread crumbs
Salt and black pepper to taste
1 lemon, cut into wedges

1. In a large bowl, combine the buttermilk, hot sauce, garlic, salt, and black pepper. Add the chicken and toss to coat. Let it marinate in the fridge for at least 2 hours. Preheat the air fryer to 400ºF (204ºC). 2. Mix the flour, bread crumbs, turmeric, and paprika into a large plate. Remove the chicken from the marinade and dip the chicken into the flour mixture to coat. Transfer to the greased frying basket. Spray with oil and air fry for 18 to 22 minutes, flipping once, until golden brown. Serve with lemon wedges.

Chicken Thighs with Herby Tomatoes

Prep time: 15 minutes | Cook time: 13 to 15 minutes | Serves 2

2 chicken thighs
2 ripe tomatoes, sliced
¼ teaspoon red pepper flakes
2 cloves garlic, minced
¼ tablespoon dried tarragon
¼ tablespoon olive oil
Salt and black pepper to taste

1. Preheat the air fryer to 390ºF (199ºC). Add the tomatoes, red pepper flakes, garlic, tarragon, and olive oil to a bowl. Mix well. Season the chicken with salt and pepper and place the thighs in the greased frying basket. Bake for 8 to 10 minutes, flipping once. Top with the tomato mixture and bake for 5 more minutes.

Enchilada Chicken Thighs

Prep time: 10 minutes | Cook time: 12 to 14 minutes | Serves 4

4 chicken thighs, boneless
2 garlic cloves, crushed
1 jalapeño pepper, finely chopped
4 tablespoons green enchilada sauce
Salt and black pepper to taste

1. Preheat the air fryer to 390ºF (199ºC). In a bowl, add the thighs, garlic, jalapeño pepper, enchilada sauce, salt, and pepper and stir to coat. Place the thighs in the greased frying basket in an even layer and air fry them for 12 to 14 minutes, turning once, until golden. Serve warm.

Crispy Drumsticks with Blue Cheese Sauce

Prep time: 20 minutes | Cook time: 20 minutes | Serves 4

Drumsticks:
1 pound (454 g) drumsticks
3 tablespoons butter
1 teaspoon paprika
¼ cup hot sauce
1 teaspoon onion powder
1 teaspoon garlic powder
Blue Cheese Sauce:
½ cup mayonnaise
1 cup blue cheese, crumbled
1 cup sour cream
½ teaspoon garlic powder
½ teaspoon onion powder
Salt and black pepper to taste
½ teaspoon cayenne pepper
1½ teaspoons white wine vinegar
2 tablespoons buttermilk
1½ teaspoons Worcestershire sauce

1. Melt the butter in a skillet over medium heat and stir in the remaining drumstick ingredients, except for the drumsticks. Cook the mixture for 5 minutes or until the sauce reduces; then let cool. Place the drumsticks in a bowl, pour the cooled sauce over, and coat well. Refrigerate for 2 hours. 2. In a jug, add sour cream, blue cheese, mayonnaise, garlic powder, onion powder, buttermilk, cayenne pepper, white wine vinegar, Worcestershire sauce, black pepper, and salt. Using a stick mixer, blend the ingredients until well mixed with no large lumps. Taste and adjust the seasoning if needed. 3. Preheat the air fryer to 350ºF (177ºC). Remove the drumsticks from the fridge and place them in the greased frying basket. Bake for 14 to 16 minutes. Turn the drumsticks with tongs every 5 minutes to ensure they cook evenly. Serve with blue cheese sauce and a side of celery sticks.

Chicken Thighs with Parmesan Crust

Prep time: 10 minutes | Cook time: 10 to 13 minutes | Serves 4

½ cup Italian bread crumbs
2 tablespoons Parmesan cheese, grated
1 tablespoon butter, melted
4 chicken thighs
½ cup marinara sauce
½ cup sharp Cheddar cheese, shredded

1. Preheat the air fryer to 380ºF (193ºC). In a bowl, mix the bread crumbs with Cheddar cheese. Brush the thighs with butter. Dip each thigh into the crumbs mixture. Arrange them in the greased frying basket. 2. Air fry for 6 to 7 minutes, flip them over, top with shredded Parmesan cheese, and cook for another 4 to 6 minutes until crispy. Serve immediately with marinara sauce on the side.

Traditional Chicken Mole

Prep time: 10 minutes | Cook time: 21 to 27 minutes | Serves 4

1 pound (454 g) chicken thighs, bone-in
Salt and garlic powder to taste
1 cup mole verde, Mexican sauce
2 cups long-grain rice, cooked
2 tablespoons pumpkin seeds
2 tablespoons fresh cilantro, chopped

1. Preheat the air fryer to 390ºF (199ºC). Season the chicken thighs with salt and garlic powder and spritz with cooking spray. Air fry them in the greased frying basket for 18 to 22 minutes, turning once, until golden brown. Pour the mole sauce over and cook until thoroughly warmed, about 3 to 5 minutes. Sprinkle with pumpkin seeds and cilantro. Serve warm with rice and enjoy!

Chicken Drumsticks with Garlic-Butter Sauce

Prep time: 15 minutes | Cook time: 20 minutes | Serves 4

1 pound (454 g) chicken drumsticks, skin removed
2 tablespoons canola oil
½ teaspoon paprika
½ teaspoon garlic powder
½ teaspoon onion powder
Salt and black pepper to taste
3 garlic cloves, minced
½ cup butter
1 tablespoon fresh lemon juice
2 tablespoons fresh parsley, chopped

1. In a resealable bag, mix canola oil, paprika, garlic powder, onion powder, salt, and pepper. Add in the chicken and massage until well-coated. Marinate for 30 minutes. Preheat the air fryer to 380ºF (193ºC). Add the chicken to the greased frying basket and air fry for 18 to 22 minutes, turning once halfway through. 2. Melt the butter in a saucepan over medium heat. Sauté the garlic for 1 minute, stirring constantly or until tender but not burn. Add the lemon juice and salt and stir-fry for 30 more seconds. Remove the butter from the heat and sprinkle with fresh parsley. Pour the sauce over the chicken and serve.

Classic Buttermilk Chicken Thighs

Prep time: 15 minutes | Cook time: 16 to 18 minutes | Serves 4

1½ pounds (680 g) chicken thighs
½ tablespoon cayenne pepper
Salt and black pepper to taste
1 cup flour
½ teaspoon paprika
½ teaspoon baking powder
2 cups buttermilk

1. Place the chicken thighs in a bowl. Stir in cayenne, salt, black pepper, and buttermilk. Refrigerate for 2 hours. Preheat the air fryer to 350ºF (177ºC). In another bowl, mix flour, paprika, salt, and baking powder. Dredge the chicken thighs in the flour and then place them in the greased frying basket. Bake them for 16 to 18 minutes, flipping once halfway through cooking. Serve hot.

Whole Chicken with Sage and Garlic

Prep time: 15 minutes | Cook time: 45 minutes | Serves 4

3 tablespoons butter
4 cloves garlic, crushed
1 onion, chopped
2 eggs, beaten
⅓ cup sage, chopped
1 (3-pound / 1.4-kg) whole chicken
Salt and black pepper to taste

1. Melt butter in a pan over medium heat and sauté garlic and onion until browned, about 5 minutes. Add in the eggs, sage, black pepper, and salt; mix well. Cook for 20 seconds and turn the heat off. 2. Fill the chicken cavity with the mixture. Tie the legs with a butcher's twine and brush with olive oil. Rub the top and sides of the chicken with salt and black pepper. Preheat the air fryer to 390ºF (199ºC). Place the chicken into the greased frying basket and bake for 25 minutes. 3. Turn the chicken over and cook for 10 to 15 more minutes, checking regularly to ensure it doesn't dry or overcook. When done, wrap in aluminum foil and let rest for 10 minutes. Carve and serve.

Spanish Roasted Whole Chicken

Prep time: 15 minutes | Cook time: 40 to 45 minutes | Serves 4

1 (3-pound / 1.4-kg) whole chicken
1 lime, juiced
Spanish Seasoning:
Salt and black pepper to taste
1 teaspoon cayenne chili
1 teaspoon paprika
powder
1 teaspoon garlic powder
1 teaspoon oregano
1 teaspoon ground coriander
1 teaspoon cumin
2 tablespoons olive oil

1. In a bowl, mix the oregano, garlic powder, cayenne chili powder, coriander, paprika, cumin, black pepper, salt, and olive oil. Rub onto the chicken and refrigerate it for 20 minutes to marinate. 2. Preheat the air fryer to 350ºF (177ºC). Remove the chicken from the fridge, place it breast side down in the greased frying basket, and bake for 30 minutes. Turn the chicken breast-side up and continue cooking for 10 to 15 minutes. When over, let it rest for 10 minutes, then drizzle with lime juice and serve.

Cauli-Oat Crusted Drumsticks

Prep time: 10 minutes | Cook time: 14 to 16 minutes | Serves 4

8 chicken drumsticks
½ teaspoon dried oregano
½ teaspoon dried thyme
2 ounces (57 g) oats
10 ounces (283 g) cauliflower florets, steamed
1 egg, beaten
1 teaspoon ground cayenne pepper
Salt and black pepper to taste

1. Preheat the air fryer to 350ºF (177ºC). Rub the drumsticks with salt and black pepper. Place all the remaining ingredients, except for the egg, in a food processor. Pulse until smooth. Dip each drumstick in the egg first and then in the oat mixture. Air fry in the greased frying basket for 14 to 16 minutes, turning once.

BBQ Whole Chicken

Prep time: 15 minutes | Cook time: 35 minutes | Serves 4

1 whole small chicken, cut into pieces
Salt to taste
½ teaspoon smoked paprika
½ teaspoon garlic powder
1 cup BBQ sauce

1. Rub the chicken pieces with salt, paprika, and garlic powder. Place in the greased frying basket and bake for 25 minutes at 400ºF (204ºC). Remove to a plate and brush with barbecue sauce. Wipe the fryer clean from the chicken fat, return the chicken to the fryer, skin-side up, and bake for 8 to 10 more minutes.

Indonesian Sambal Chicken Drumsticks

Prep time: 10 minutes | Cook time: 18 to 22 minutes | Serves 2

2 chicken drumsticks, skin removed
2 tablespoons sambal oelek chili paste
2 teaspoons honey
1 tablespoon fish sauce
1 tablespoon garlic paste
3 spring onions, finely sliced

1. Put the chicken drumsticks in a resealable bag and add sambal oelek, honey, garlic, and fish sauce; squish the bag until well-coated. Marinate in the fridge for at least 2 hours. 2. Preheat the air fryer to 400ºF (204ºC). Add the chicken drumsticks to the greased frying basket and bake for 18 to 22 minutes, flipping once, until crispy and golden. Scatter with spring onions and serve.

Chicken and Baby Potato Traybake

Prep time: 15 minutes | Cook time: 23 to 25 minutes | Serves 4

1 pound (454 g) chicken drumsticks, skin on and bone-in
3 shallots, quartered
Salt and black pepper to taste
1 tablespoon cayenne pepper
1 pound (454 g) baby potatoes, halved
½ teaspoon garlic powder
2 tablespoons olive oil
1 cup cherry tomatoes

1. Preheat the air fryer to 360ºF (182ºC). Place the chicken in a baking tray and add in shallots, potatoes, oil, garlic powder, cayenne, salt, and pepper; toss to coat. Place in the air fryer and bake for 18 to 20 minutes, turning once. Slide the basket out and add in the cherry tomatoes. Cook for 5 minutes until charred.

Peri-Peri Chicken Legs

Prep time: 5 minutes | Cook time: 18 to 22 minutes | Serves 4

1 pound (454 g) chicken legs
1 cup hot Peri-Peri Sauce
2 tablespoons olive oil
1 lemon, cut into wedges
2 tablespoons fresh parsley, chopped

1. In a large bowl, coat the chicken legs in Peri-Peri sauce. Cover and marinate in the fridge for 2 hours. 2. Preheat the air fryer to 360ºF (182ºC). Remove the chicken from the marinade and lay the legs in the greased frying basket. Air fry for 18 to 22 minutes, turning at least twice while brushing with the marinade. Cook until browned and charred. Sprinkle with fresh parsley and serve with lemon wedges.

Thyme Fried Chicken Legs

Prep time: 10 minutes | Cook time: 14 minutes | Serves 4

4 chicken legs
½ lemon, juiced
1 tablespoon garlic powder
½ teaspoon dried thyme
⅓ cup olive oil
Salt and black pepper to taste

1. Preheat the fryer to 350ºF (177ºC). In a bowl, mix olive oil, thyme, garlic, lemon juice, salt, and pepper. Brush the chicken legs with most of the mixture and arrange them in the frying basket. Bake the legs in the air fryer for 8 minutes, flip the legs and brush again. Bake for 6 more minutes or until crispy. Serve.

Thai Chicken Satay

Prep time: 15 minutes | Cook time: 18 to 20 minutes | Serves 4

1 pound (454 g) chicken drumsticks
2 cloves garlic, minced
2 tablespoons sesame oil
½ cup Thai peanut satay sauce
1 lime, zested and juiced
2 tablespoons sesame seeds, toasted
4 scallions, chopped
1 red chili, sliced

1. In a bowl, mix the satay sauce, sesame oil, garlic, lime zest, and lime juice. Add in the chicken and toss to coat. Place in the fridge for 2 hours to marinate. Preheat the air fryer to 380ºF (193ºC). Transfer the marinated chicken to the frying basket and air fry for 18 to 20 minutes, flipping once halfway through. Garnish with sesame seeds, scallions, and red chili and serve.

Chapter 1 Vegetables and Sides | 87

Chicken Asian Lollipop

Prep time: 15 minutes | Cook time: 10 to 14 minutes | Serves 4

1 pound (454 g) mini chicken drumsticks	½ tablespoon chili powder
½ tablespoon soy sauce	½ tablespoon garlic-ginger paste
1 tablespoon lime juice	1 tablespoon plain vinegar
Salt and black pepper to taste	1 egg, beaten
1 tablespoon cornstarch	1 tablespoon flour
1 garlic clove, minced	1 tablespoon maple syrup

1. Mix garlic-ginger paste, chili powder, maple syrup, soy sauce, vinegar, egg, garlic, salt, and black pepper in a bowl. Add the chicken and toss to coat. Mix cornstarch and flour in another bowl. Preheat the air fryer to 350ºF (177ºC). Roll the drumsticks into the flour mixture and air fry in the greased frying basket for 5 to 7 minutes. Turn and cook for 5 to 7 more minutes or until golden. Serve drizzled with lime juice.

Honey and Lemon-Glazed Stuffed Chicken

Prep time: 20 minutes | Cook time: 45 minutes | Serves 4 to 6

1 (3-pound / 1.4-kg) whole chicken	2 cloves finely chopped garlic
Stuffing:	4 tablespoons fresh thyme, chopped
2 red onions, chopped	Salt and black pepper to taste
2 tablespoons olive oil	**Glaze:**
2 dry apricots, soaked and chopped	5 ounces (142 g) honey
1 zucchini, chopped	Juice from 1 lemon
1 apple, peeled and chopped	2 tablespoons olive oil
	Salt and black pepper to taste

1. In a bowl, mix together all the stuffing ingredients. Fill the cavity of the chicken with the stuffing, without packing it tightly. Place the chicken, breast-side down, in the air fryer and bake for 30 minutes at 380ºF (193ºC). 2. Warm the olive oil, honey, and lemon juice in a large pan; season with salt and pepper. Slide the basket out and flip the chicken breast side up. Brush with some of the honey-lemon glaze and return to the fryer. Bake for another 13 to 15 minutes, brushing every 5 minutes with the glaze. Serve warm.

Asian Sticky Chicken Wingettes

Prep time: 15 minutes | Cook time: 14 to 16 minutes | Serves 4

1 ginger, minced	½ tablespoon apple cider vinegar
1 garlic clove, minced	1 pound (454 g) chicken wingettes
½ tablespoon chili sauce	
½ tablespoon honey	1 tablespoon roasted peanuts, chopped
1½ tablespoons soy sauce	
1 tablespoon fresh cilantro, chopped	Salt and black pepper to taste

1. Preheat the air fryer to 360ºF (182ºC). Season the wingettes with salt and black pepper. In a bowl, mix the ginger, garlic, chili sauce, honey, soy sauce, cilantro, and vinegar. Coat the chicken in the mixture. Air fry in the greased frying basket for 14 to 16 minutes, turning once. Serve sprinkled with peanuts.

Roasted Chicken with Pancetta and Thyme

Prep time: 15 minutes | Cook time: 45 minutes | Serves 4

1 (3½-pound / 1.6-kg) whole chicken	chopped
	1 onion, chopped
1 lemon	1 sprig fresh thyme, chopped
4 slices pancetta, roughly	Salt and black pepper to taste

1. In a bowl, mix pancetta, onion, thyme, salt, and black pepper. Insert the mixture into the chicken's cavity and press tight. Put the whole lemon in, and rub the top and sides of the chicken with salt and pepper. Transfer to the greased frying basket, breast side down, and bake for 30 minutes at 360ºF (182ºC). Turn the chicken breast side up, and cook for 12 to 15 more minutes or until golden brown and crisp.

Greek-Style Whole Chicken

Prep time: 15 minutes | Cook time: 40 to 45 minutes | Serves 4 to 6

1 (3-pound / 1.4-kg) whole chicken, cut into pieces	1 tablespoon fresh rosemary, chopped
3 garlic cloves, minced	1 tablespoon fresh Greek oregano, chopped
2 tablespoons olive oil	
1 tablespoon ouzo (anise-flavored aperitif)	Juice from 1 lemon
	Salt and black pepper to taste

1. Preheat the air fryer to 380ºF (193ºC). In a large bowl, combine garlic, ouzo, rosemary, olive oil, lemon juice, Greek oregano, salt, and black pepper. Mix well and rub the mixture onto the chicken. 2. Place the chicken in the frying basket, breast side down, and bake for 30 minutes. Turn the chicken, breast side up, and broil for 10 to 15 more minutes until golden. Let sit for a few minutes before carving.

Mediterranean-Style Whole Chicken

Prep time: 15 minutes | Cook time: 40 to 45 minutes | Serves 4

1 (3-pound / 1.4-kg) whole chicken	2 tablespoons red wine vinegar
½ cup prunes, pitted	2 tablespoons olive oil
3 garlic cloves, minced	1 tablespoon dried oregano
2 tablespoons capers	1 tablespoon brown sugar
2 bay leaves	Salt and black pepper to taste

1. Preheat the air fryer to 360ºF (182ºC). In a bowl, mix prunes, capers, garlic, olive oil, bay leaves, oregano, vinegar, salt, and pepper. Spread the mixture on the bottom of a baking dish and place the chicken breast side down on top. Bake for 30 minutes in the fryer, turn it breast side up, and sprinkle with brown sugar on top; bake further for 10 to 15 minutes until golden. Let sit for a few minutes before slicing.

Chicken Quarters with Broccoli and Carrots

Prep time: 10 minutes | Cook time: 14 to 16 minutes | Serves 4

4 chicken legs
1 carrot, sliced
1 cup broccoli florets
Salt and black pepper to taste
1 teaspoon red pepper flakes
2 tablespoons olive oil

1. Preheat the air fryer to 390ºF (199ºC). Season the legs with salt and black pepper and drizzle with some olive oil. Place them in the greased frying basket and air fry for 8 minutes. Slide the basket out, and flip the chicken. Pour the broccoli and carrot over and sprinkle with salt and pepper. Drizzle with the remaining olive oil and cook for 6 to 8 more minutes or until the vegetables are tender. Top with flakes and serve.

Whole Chicken with Fresno Chili Sauce

Prep time: 25 minutes | Cook time: 55 minutes | Serves 4

1 chicken (around 3 pounds / 1.4 kg)
2 teaspoons garlic powder
½ cup Greek yogurt
1 lemon, juiced
2 teaspoons tomato paste
2 teaspoons ancho chili powder
2 teaspoons ground cinnamon
2 teaspoons sumac
Fresno Chili Sauce:
2 tablespoons olive oil
2 Fresno peppers, chopped
1 garlic clove, peeled
2 tomatoes, chopped
1 Vidalia onion, halved
1 tablespoon lemon juice

1. Preheat the air fryer to 380ºF (193ºC). In a bowl, mix yogurt, garlic powder, lemon juice, tomato paste, ancho chili powder, cinnamon, and sumac. Brush the chicken with the mixture and place it in the greased frying basket. Bake for 50 to 55 minutes, turning once, or until cooked through and golden. 2. Warm the olive oil in a pan over medium heat and sauté the Fresno peppers, Vidalia onion, and garlic for 2 minutes. Add in the remaining ingredients and simmer for 2 to 3 more minutes. Transfer to a food processor and pulse until smooth. Remove the chicken from the fryer, cover and let it rest for 10 minutes. Then carve the chicken and serve with the chili sauce.

Moroccan Turkey Meatballs

Prep time: 15 minutes | Cook time: 12 to 15 minutes | Serves 6

½ cup couscous
1 cucumber, chopped
1 egg, beaten
1 pound (454 g) ground turkey
2 garlic cloves, minced
½ cup panko bread crumbs
1 tablespoon soy sauce
2 teaspoons harissa powder, divided
1 teaspoon sriracha sauce
Salt and black pepper to taste

1. In a bowl, mix couscous and 1 cup of boiling water. Cover and let sit for 8 to 10 minutes. Fluff with a fork. Preheat the air fryer to 360ºF (182ºC). In a bowl, mix the ground turkey, bread crumbs, egg, soy sauce, 1 tablespoon of harissa, garlic, salt, and black pepper. Make small balls with a tablespoon. Combine the remaining harissa powder and sriracha sauce in a small bowl to make a glaze; set aside. 2. Arrange the meatballs on the greased frying basket in a single later and air fry for 8 minutes. Slide the basket out and generously brush the meatballs with the glaze. Cook for 4 to 7 more minutes or to your liking. Season the couscous with salt and mix in the cucumber. Top with the meatballs and serve.

Turkey Tenderloins with Fattoush Salad

Prep time: 20 minutes | Cook time: 30 to 35 minutes | Serves 4

1½ pounds (680 g) turkey tenderloin
3 tablespoons olive oil
½ teaspoon paprika
½ teaspoon garlic powder
½ teaspoon cayenne pepper
Salt and black pepper to taste
1 tablespoon lemon juice
1 tablespoon pomegranate molasses
½ pound (227 g) Roma tomatoes, chopped
2 spring onions, sliced
2 tablespoons fresh mint, chopped
6 radishes, thinly sliced
1 cucumber, deseeded and diced
5 ounces (142 g) pita crackers

1. In a bowl, mix the lemon juice, 2 tablespoons of olive oil, pomegranate molasses, and salt and whisk with a fork. Add in the tomatoes, spring onions, radishes, cucumber, fresh mint and toss to coat. Set aside. 2. Preheat your Air Fryer to 375ºF (191ºC). Combine the paprika, garlic powder, salt, pepper, and cayenne pepper in a bowl, then rub the mixture all over the turkey. Place the turkey in the greased frying basket and spray with olive oil. Air fry for 30 to 35 minutes, turning once until golden. Remove and let it sit for 5 to 8 minutes before slicing. Divide the fattoush salad between pita crackers and top with turkey slices.

Herb-Buttermilk Chicken Breast

Prep time: 5 minutes | Cook time: 40 minutes | Serves 2

1 large bone-in, skin-on chicken breast
1 cup buttermilk
1½ teaspoons dried parsley
1½ teaspoons dried chives
¾ teaspoon kosher salt
½ teaspoon dried dill
½ teaspoon onion powder
¼ teaspoon garlic powder
¼ teaspoon dried tarragon
Cooking spray

1. Place the chicken breast in a bowl and pour over the buttermilk to cover completely. Let the chicken stand at room temperature for at least 20 minutes. 2. Meanwhile, in a bowl, stir together the parsley, chives, salt, dill, onion powder, garlic powder, and tarragon. 3. Preheat the air fryer to 300ºF (149ºC). 4. Remove the chicken from the buttermilk, then place in the air fryer, skin-side up. Sprinkle the seasoning mix all over the top of the chicken breast, then let stand until the herb mix soaks into the buttermilk, at least 5 minutes. 5. Spray the top of the chicken with cooking spray. Bake for 10 minutes, then bake at 350ºF (177ºC) for 30 to 35 until until the internal temperature reaches 160ºF (71ºC) and the chicken is deep golden brown. 6. Let rest for 10 minutes, then cut the meat off the bone and slice for serving.

Honey-Glazed Turkey

Prep time: 15 minutes | Cook time: 30 minutes | Serves 4

1 to 1½ pounds (680 g) turkey tenderloin
¼ cup honey
2 tablespoons Dijon mustard
½ teaspoon dried thyme
½ teaspoon garlic powder
½ onion powder
1 tablespoon olive oil
½ tablespoon spicy brown mustard
Salt and black pepper to taste

1. Preheat the air fryer to 375°F (191°C). Combine the honey, mustard, thyme, garlic powder, and onion powder in a bowl to make a paste. Season the turkey with salt and pepper, then brush the paste all over. 2. Put the turkey in the frying basket and spray with olive oil. Air fry for 15 minutes. Turn the tenderloin over and spray again before frying for 10 to 15 more minutes until golden brown. Remove the turkey, cover loosely with foil and let stand 10 minutes before slicing. Serve and enjoy!

Turkey Burgers with Cabbage Slaw

Prep time: 15 minutes | Cook time: 15 to 20 minutes | Serves 4

1 pound (454 g) ground turkey
¼ cup bread crumbs
1 tablespoon olive oil
¼ cup hoisin sauce
4 buns
2 green onions, sliced
1 cup cabbage slaw
1 cup cherry tomatoes, halved

1. Preheat the air fryer to 375°F (191°C). Mix the ground turkey, bread crumbs, and hoisin sauce in a bowl and create 4 equal patties. Put the patties in the greased frying basket, spray with olive oil, and air fry for 10 minutes. Turn the patties, spray with oil again, and cook for 5 to 10 more minutes or until golden. Lay the patties on the buns and top with cherry tomatoes, green onions, and cabbage slaw. Serve.

Tex-Mex Chicken Roll-Ups

Prep time: 10 minutes | Cook time: 14 to 17 minutes | Serves 8

2 pounds (907 g) boneless, skinless chicken breasts or thighs
1 teaspoon chili powder
½ teaspoon smoked paprika
½ teaspoon ground cumin
Sea salt and freshly ground black pepper, to taste
6 ounces (170 g) Monterey Jack cheese, shredded
4 ounces (113 g) canned diced green chiles
Avocado oil spray

1. Place the chicken in a large zip-top bag. Using a meat mallet, pound the chicken until it is about ¼ inch thick. 2. In a bowl, combine the chili powder, smoked paprika, cumin, and salt and pepper to taste. Sprinkle both sides of the chicken with the seasonings. 3. Sprinkle the chicken with the Monterey Jack cheese, then the diced green chiles. 4. Roll up each piece of chicken from the long side, tucking in the ends as you go. Secure the roll-up with a toothpick. 5. Spray the chicken with avocado oil. Place the chicken in a single layer in the basket and roast at 350°F (177°C) for 7 minutes. Flip and cook for another 7 to 10 minutes, until an instant-read thermometer reads 160°F (71°C). 6. Allow to rest for about 5 minutes before serving.

Parmesan Turkey Meatballs

Prep time: 10 minutes | Cook time: 12 to 14 minutes | Serves 4

1 pound (454 g) ground turkey
1 egg
½ cup bread crumbs
1 tablespoon garlic powder
1 tablespoon Italian seasoning
1 tablespoon onion powder
¼ cup Parmesan cheese, grated
Salt and black pepper to taste

1. Preheat the air fryer to 400°F (204°C). In a bowl, mix ground turkey, egg, bread crumbs, garlic powder, onion powder, Italian seasoning, Parmesan cheese, salt, and black pepper. Make bite-sized balls out of the mixture. Add the balls to the greased frying basket and air fry for 12 to 14 minutes, shaking once. Serve.

Thyme Turkey Nuggets

Prep time: 10 minutes | Cook time: 12 to 14 minutes | Serves 2

½ pound (227 g) ground turkey
1 egg, beaten
1 cup bread crumbs
½ teaspoon dried thyme
½ teaspoon fresh parsley, chopped
Salt and black pepper to taste

1. Preheat the air fryer to 350°F (177°C). In a bowl, mix ground turkey, thyme, parsley, salt, and pepper. Shape the mixture into nuggets. Dip them in the egg, and then in the bread crumbs. Place the nuggets in the frying basket, spray with cooking spray and air fry for 12 to 14 minutes, flipping once. Serve with garlic mayo.

Turkey and Veggie Skewers

Prep time: 15 minutes | Cook time: 25 to 30 minutes | Serves 4

1 pound (454 g) turkey breast, cubed
2 tablespoons fresh rosemary, chopped
Salt and black pepper to taste
1 green bell pepper, cut into chunks
1 red bell pepper, cut into chunks
1 cup cherry tomatoes
1 red onion, cut into wedges

1. Preheat the air fryer to 350°F (177°C). Spray the frying basket with cooking spray. 2. Season the turkey with salt and black pepper. Thread the bell peppers, cherry tomatoes, onion, and turkey cubes alternately onto skewers. Spray with cooking spray and place them in the frying basket. Bake for 25 to 30 minutes, turning once halfway through. Serve sprinkled with fresh rosemary.

Turkey Strips with Cranberry Glaze

Prep time: 10 minutes | Cook time: 25 to 30 minutes | Serves 4

1 pound (454 g) turkey breast, cut into strips
1 tablespoon chicken seasoning
Salt and black pepper to taste
½ cup cranberry sauce

1. Preheat the air fryer to 390ºF (199ºC). Season the turkey with chicken seasoning, salt, and black pepper. Spritz with cooking spray and air fry for 20 to 25 minutes, shaking once or twice throughout cooking. 2. Put a saucepan over low heat, and add the cranberry sauce and ¼ cup of water. Simmer for 5 minutes, stirring continuously. Serve the turkey drizzled with cranberry sauce. Yummy!

Greek Chicken Souvlaki

Prep time: 30 minutes | Cook time: 15 minutes | Serves 3 to 4

Chicken:
Grated zest and juice of 1 lemon
2 tablespoons extra-virgin olive oil
1 tablespoon Greek souvlaki seasoning
1 pound (454 g) boneless, skinless chicken breast, cut into 2-inch chunks
Vegetable oil spray
For Serving:
Warm pita bread or hot cooked rice
Sliced ripe tomatoes
Sliced cucumbers
Thinly sliced red onion
Kalamata olives
Tzatziki

1. In a gallon-size resealable plastic bag, combine chicken, lemon zest, lemon juice, olive oil, and souvlaki seasoning. Seal bag and massage to coat. Marinate for 30 minutes. 2. Place the chicken a single layer in the frying basket and roast at 350ºF (177ºC) for 10 minutes, turning the chicken and spraying with a little vegetable oil spray halfway through. Roast at 400ºF (204ºC) for 5 minutes to allow the chicken to crisp and brown a little. 3. Serve with pita bread or rice, tomatoes, cucumbers, onion, olives and tzatziki.

Roasted Turkey with Brussels Sprouts

Prep time: 15 minutes | Cook time: 36 to 40 minutes | Serves 4 to 6

1½ to 2 pounds (680 to 907 g) turkey breast
2 garlic cloves, minced
1 tablespoon olive oil
2 teaspoons Dijon mustard
½ teaspoon rosemary
½ teaspoon thyme
1 pound (454 g) Brussels sprouts, halved
Salt and black pepper to taste

1. Preheat the air fryer to 375ºF (191ºC). Mix the garlic, olive oil, Dijon mustard, rosemary, thyme, salt, and black pepper in a bowl to make a paste. Smear the paste all over the turkey breast. 2. Put the turkey breast in the greased frying basket and air fry for 20 minutes. Turn it over and baste it with any drippings from the bottom drawer. Add in Brussels sprouts and fry for 16 to 20 more minutes. Let the turkey sit for 10 minutes before slicing. Serve with Brussels sprouts and a bed of rice if desired.

Mediterranean-Rubbed Turkey Tenderloins

Prep time: 15 minutes | Cook time: 20 to 25 minutes | Serves 4

1 pound (454 g) turkey breast, sliced
2 tablespoons olive oil
½ teaspoon garlic powder
1 cup jellied cranberry sauce
Salt and black pepper to taste
2 teaspoons Mediterranean herb seasoning

1. Preheat the air fryer to 360ºF (182ºC). In a bowl, whisk the olive oil, garlic powder, Mediterranean herbs, salt, and pepper. Add the turkey and toss to coat. Air fry them for 20 to 25 minutes, flipping once. Transfer the turkey to a serving plate, cover with foil, and let stand for 5 minutes. Serve with cranberry sauce.

Chipotle Buttered Turkey

Prep time: 10 minutes | Cook time: 14 to 17 minutes | Serves 4

1 pound (454 g) turkey breast, sliced
2 cups panko bread crumbs
Salt and chipotle powder to taste
1 stick butter, melted

1. In a bowl, combine panko bread crumbs and chipotle chili pepper. Sprinkle turkey with salt and brush with some butter. Coat the turkey with the crumbs mixture. Transfer to the frying basket and grease with some butter. Air fry for 10 minutes at 390ºF (199ºC). Flip the slices, drizzle with the remaining butter, and bake for 4 to 7 more minutes, until nice and crispy. Serve and enjoy!

Wild Rice and Kale Stuffed Chicken Thighs

Prep time: 10 minutes | Cook time: 22 minutes | Serves 4

4 boneless, skinless chicken thighs
1 cup cooked wild rice
½ cup chopped kale
2 garlic cloves, minced
1 teaspoon salt
Juice of 1 lemon
½ cup crumbled feta
Olive oil cooking spray
1 tablespoon olive oil

1. Preheat the air fryer to 380ºF (193ºC). 2. Place the chicken thighs between two pieces of plastic wrap, and using a meat mallet, pound them out to about ¼-inch thick. 3. In a medium bowl, mix the rice, kale, garlic, salt, and lemon juice. 4. Place a quarter of the rice mixture into the middle of each chicken thigh, then sprinkle 2 tablespoons feta over the filling. 5. Spray the frying basket with olive oil cooking spray. 6. Fold the sides of the chicken thigh over the filling, and then gently place each of them seam-side down into the frying basket. Brush each thigh with olive oil. 7. Roast for 12 minutes, then turn and cook for 10 minutes more, or until the internal temperature reaches 165ºF (74ºC).

Mini Turkey Meatloaves with Hot Sauce

Prep time: 10 minutes | Cook time: 20 to 25 minutes | Serves 4

2 tablespoons olive oil
1 pound (454 g) ground turkey
¼ cup hot sauce
1 shallot, chopped
1 egg
Salt and black pepper to taste

1. Preheat the air fryer to 360°F (182°C). In a bowl, mix the ground turkey, shallot, egg, salt, and pepper. Divide the mixture between 4 greased muffin cups. Spoon the hot sauce over the meatloaves. Bake in the fryer for 20 to 25 minutes. Insert a meat thermometer and it should display at least 165°F (74°C). Serve hot.

Turkey Stuffed Bell Peppers

Prep time: 15 minutes | Cook time: 10 to 15 minutes | Serves 2

1 teaspoon fresh cilantro, chopped
1 green onion, chopped
½ pound (227 g) ground turkey
Salt and garlic powder to taste
4 mini bell peppers, halved lengthwise, seeded
2 tablespoons Mozzarella cheese, crumbled

1. Preheat the air fryer to 360°F (182°C). Combine the ground turkey, onion, Mozzarella cheese, garlic powder, and salt, then spoon the mixture into the bell peppers. Put the stuffed peppers in the greased frying basket and bake for 10 to 15 minutes or until cooked through. Garnish with fresh cilantro and serve.

Cilantro Chicken Kebabs

Prep time: 30 minutes | Cook time: 10 minutes | Serves 4

Chutney:
½ cup unsweetened shredded coconut
½ cup hot water
2 cups fresh cilantro leaves, roughly chopped
¼ cup fresh mint leaves, roughly chopped
6 cloves garlic, roughly chopped
1 jalapeño, seeded and roughly chopped
¼ to ¾ cup water, as needed
Juice of 1 lemon
Chicken:
1 pound (454 g) boneless, skinless chicken thighs, cut crosswise into thirds
Olive oil spray

1. **Make the Chutney:** In a blender, combine the coconut and hot water; set aside to soak for 5 minutes. 2. Add the cilantro, mint, garlic, and jalapeño, along with ¼ cup water and blend at low speed, stopping occasionally to scrape down the sides. Add the lemon juice. With the blender running, add only enough additional water to keep the contents moving. Turn the blender to high once the contents are moving freely and blend until the mixture is puréed. 3. **Make the Chicken:** Toss the chicken pieces with ¼ cup chutney. Marinate for 15 minutes at room temperature. 4. Spray the frying basket with olive oil spray. Air fry at 350°F (177°C) for 10 minutes until the internal temperature reaches 165°F (74°C). 5. Serve the chicken with the remaining chutney.

Crisp Paprika Chicken Drumsticks

Prep time: 5 minutes | Cook time: 22 minutes | Serves 2

2 teaspoons paprika
1 teaspoon packed brown sugar
1 teaspoon garlic powder
½ teaspoon dry mustard
½ teaspoon salt
Pinch pepper
4 (5-ounce / 142-g) chicken drumsticks, trimmed
1 teaspoon vegetable oil
1 scallion, green part only, sliced thin on bias

1. Preheat the air fryer to 400°F (204°C). 2. Combine paprika, sugar, garlic powder, mustard, salt, and pepper in a bowl. Pat drumsticks dry with paper towels. Using metal skewer, poke 10 to 15 holes in skin of each drumstick. Rub with oil and sprinkle evenly with spice mixture. 3. Air fry for 22 to 25 minutes until chicken is crisp and registers 195°F (91°C), flipping chicken halfway through cooking. 4. Sprinkle with scallion and serve.

Easy Cajun Chicken Drumsticks

Prep time: 5 minutes | Cook time: 40 minutes | Serves 5

1 tablespoon olive oil
10 chicken drumsticks
1½ tablespoons Cajun seasoning
Salt and ground black pepper, to taste

1. Preheat the air fryer to 390°F (199°C). Grease the frying basket with olive oil. 2. On a clean work surface, rub the chicken drumsticks with Cajun seasoning, salt, and ground black pepper. 3. Arrange the seasoned chicken drumsticks in a single layer in the air fryer. 4. Air fry for 18 minutes or until lightly browned. Flip the drumsticks halfway through. 5. Serve immediately.

Sesame Chicken

Prep time: 10 minutes | Cook time: 18 minutes | Serves 6

Oil, for spraying
2 (6-ounce / 170-g) boneless, skinless chicken breasts, cut into bite-size pieces
½ cup cornstarch, plus 1 tablespoon
¼ cup soy sauce
2 tablespoons packed light brown sugar
2 tablespoons pineapple juice
1 tablespoon molasses
½ teaspoon ground ginger
1 tablespoon water
2 teaspoons sesame seeds

1. Line the frying basket with parchment and spray lightly with oil. 2. Place the chicken and ½ cup cornstarch in a zip-top plastic bag, seal, and shake well until evenly coated. 3. Spray the chicken liberally with oil. Air fry at 390°F (199°C) for 9 minutes, flip, spray with more oil, and cook for another 8 to 9 minutes, or until the internal temperature reaches 165°F (74°C). 4. In a small saucepan, combine the soy sauce, brown sugar, pineapple juice, molasses, and ginger over medium heat and cook, stirring frequently, until the brown sugar has dissolved. 5. In a bowl, mix together the water and remaining cornstarch. Pour it into the soy sauce mixture. Bring the mixture to a boil, stirring frequently, until the sauce thickens. 6. Transfer the chicken to a large bowl, add the sauce, and toss until evenly coated. Sprinkle with the sesame seeds and serve.

Cranberry Curry Chicken

Prep time: 12 minutes | Cook time: 18 minutes | Serves 4

3 (5-ounce / 142-g) low-sodium boneless, skinless chicken breasts, cut into 1½-inch cubes
2 teaspoons olive oil
2 tablespoons cornstarch
1 tablespoon curry powder
1 tart apple, chopped
½ cup low-sodium chicken broth
⅓ cup dried cranberries
2 tablespoons freshly squeezed orange juice
Brown rice, cooked (optional)

1. Preheat the air fryer to 380ºF (193ºC). 2. In a bowl, mix the chicken, olive oil, cornstarch and curry powder. Toss to coat. Stir in the apple and transfer to a metal pan. Bake for 8 minutes, stirring once during cooking. 3. Add the chicken broth, cranberries, and orange juice. Bake for 10 minutes more, or until the sauce is slightly thickened and the chicken reaches an internal temperature of 165ºF (74ºC). Serve over hot cooked brown rice, if desired.

Cracked-Pepper Chicken Wings

Prep time: 15 minutes | Cook time: 20 minutes | Serves 4

1 pound (454 g) chicken wings
3 tablespoons vegetable oil
½ cup all-purpose flour
½ teaspoon smoked paprika
½ teaspoon garlic powder
½ teaspoon kosher salt
1½ teaspoons freshly cracked black pepper

1. Place the chicken wings in a bowl. Drizzle the vegetable oil over wings. 2. In a separate bowl, whisk together the flour, paprika, garlic powder, salt, and pepper until combined. 3. Dredge the wings in the flour mixture, coating them well, and place in the frying basket. Roast at 400ºF (204ºC) for 20 minutes, turning the wings halfway through the cooking time, until the breading is browned and crunchy.

Tandoori Chicken

Prep time: 30 minutes | Cook time: 20 minutes | Serves 4

1 pound (454 g) chicken tenders, halved crosswise
¼ cup plain Greek yogurt
1 tablespoon minced fresh ginger
1 tablespoon minced garlic
¼ cup chopped fresh cilantro or parsley
1 teaspoon kosher salt
½ to 1 teaspoon cayenne pepper
1 teaspoon ground turmeric
1 teaspoon garam masala
1 teaspoon sweet smoked paprika
1 tablespoon vegetable oil or melted ghee
2 teaspoons fresh lemon juice
2 tablespoons chopped fresh cilantro

1. In a bowl, toss together the chicken, yogurt, ginger, garlic, cilantro, salt, cayenne, turmeric, garam masala, and paprika to coat. Marinate at room temperature for 30 minutes. 2. Spray the chicken with oil. Air fry in the fryer basket at 350ºF (177ºC) for 15 minutes. Halfway through the cooking time, spray with more vegetable oil, and toss gently to coat. Cook for 5 minutes more. 3. Sprinkle with lemon juice and cilantro to serve.

African Piri-Piri Chicken Drumsticks

Prep time: 30 minutes | Cook time: 20 minutes | Serves 2

Chicken:
1 tablespoon chopped fresh thyme leaves
1 tablespoon minced fresh ginger
1 small shallot, finely chopped
2 garlic cloves, minced
⅓ cup piri-piri sauce or hot sauce
3 tablespoons extra-virgin olive oil
Zest and juice of 1 lemon
1 teaspoon smoked paprika
½ teaspoon kosher salt
½ teaspoon black pepper
4 chicken drumsticks
Glaze:
2 tablespoons butter or ghee
1 teaspoon chopped fresh thyme leaves
1 garlic clove, minced
1 tablespoon piri-piri sauce
1 tablespoon fresh lemon juice

1. **Make the Chicken:** In a bowl, stir together all the ingredients except the chicken. Place the chicken and the marinade in a gallon-size resealable plastic bag. Seal the bag and massage to coat. Refrigerate for at least 2 hours or up to 24 hours. 2. Place the chicken legs in the frying basket and roast at 400ºF (204ºC) for 20 minutes, turning the chicken halfway through. 3. **Make the Glaze:** Meanwhile, melt the butter in a small saucepan over medium-high heat. Add the thyme and garlic. Stir until the garlic just begins to brown, 1 to 2 minutes. Add the piri-piri sauce and lemon juice. Reduce the heat to medium-low and simmer for 1 to 2 minutes. 4. To serve, pour the glaze over the chicken.

Spicy Chicken Thighs and Gold Potatoes

Prep time: 5 minutes | Cook time: 25 minutes | Serves 4

4 bone-in, skin-on chicken thighs
½ teaspoon kosher salt or ¼ teaspoon fine salt
2 tablespoons melted unsalted butter
2 teaspoons Worcestershire sauce
2 teaspoons curry powder
1 teaspoon dried oregano leaves
½ teaspoon dry mustard
½ teaspoon granulated garlic
¼ teaspoon paprika
¼ teaspoon hot pepper sauce
Cooking oil spray
4 medium Yukon gold potatoes, chopped
1 tablespoon extra-virgin olive oil

1. Sprinkle the chicken thighs on both sides with salt. 2. In a medium bowl, stir together the melted butter, Worcestershire sauce, curry powder, oregano, mustard, garlic, paprika, and hot pepper sauce. Add the thighs and stir to coat. 3. Preheat the air fryer to 400ºF (204ºC). Spray the fryer basket with cooking oil. In the basket, combine the potatoes and olive oil and toss to coat. 4. Add the wire rack to the air fryer and place the chicken thighs on top. Air fry for 25 minutes until a food thermometer inserted into the chicken registers 165ºF (74ºC). 5. Shake the basket and resume cooking for 3 to 6 minutes, or until the potatoes are crisp and golden brown. 6. Serve the chicken with the potatoes.

Chapter 1 Vegetables and Sides | 93

Lemon Thyme Roasted Chicken

Prep time: 10 minutes | Cook time: 60 minutes | Serves 6

1 (4-pound / 1.8-kg) chicken
2 teaspoons dried thyme
1 teaspoon garlic powder
½ teaspoon onion powder
2 teaspoons dried parsley
1 teaspoon baking powder
1 medium lemon
2 tablespoons salted butter, melted

1. Rub chicken with thyme, garlic powder, onion powder, parsley, and baking powder. 2. Slice lemon and place four slices on top of chicken, breast side up, and secure with toothpicks. Place remaining slices inside of the chicken. 3. Roast in the fryer basket at 350ºF (177ºC) and air fry for 60 minutes, flipping halfway the cooking time, until internal temperature reaches 165ºF (74ºC) and the skin is golden and crispy. To serve, pour butter over chicken.

Lemon Chicken

Prep time: 5 minutes | Cook time: 20 to 25 minutes | Serves 4

8 bone-in chicken thighs, skin on
1 tablespoon olive oil
1½ teaspoons lemon-pepper seasoning
½ teaspoon paprika
½ teaspoon garlic powder
¼ teaspoon freshly ground black pepper
Juice of ½ lemon

1. Preheat the air fryer to 360ºF (182ºC). 2. Place the chicken in a bowl and drizzle with the olive oil. Top with the lemon-pepper seasoning, paprika, garlic powder, and freshly ground black pepper. Toss until thoroughly coated. 3. Air fry for 20 to 25 minutes, turning halfway through, until internal temperature reaches 165ºF (74ºC). 4. Squeeze the lemon juice over the top.

Coconut Chicken Wings with Mango Sauce

Prep time: 15 minutes | Cook time: 20 minutes | Serves 4

16 chicken drumettes (party wings)
¼ cup full-fat coconut milk
1 tablespoon sriracha
1 teaspoon onion powder
1 teaspoon garlic powder
Salt and freshly ground black pepper, to taste
⅓ cup shredded unsweetened coconut
½ cup all-purpose flour
Cooking oil spray
1 cup mango, cut into ½-inch chunks
¼ cup fresh cilantro, chopped
½ cup red onion, chopped
2 garlic cloves, minced
Juice of ½ lime

1. Place the drumettes in a resealable plastic bag. 2. In a bowl, whisk the coconut milk and sriracha. 3. Drizzle the drumettes with the sriracha–coconut milk mixture. Season the drumettes with the onion powder, garlic powder, salt, and pepper. Seal the bag. Shake to combine the seasonings and coat the chicken. Marinate for at least 30 minutes, preferably overnight, in the refrigerator. 4. In a bowl, stir together the shredded coconut and flour. 5. Dip the drumettes into the coconut-flour mixture. Press the flour mixture onto the chicken. 6. Preheat the air fryer to 400ºF (204ºC). Spray the frying basket and drumettes with cooking oil. Air fry for 20 minutes, shaking the basket every 5 minutes until internal temperature reaches 165ºF (74ºC). 7. Let the chicken cool for 5 minutes. 8. Meanwhile, make the salsa by combining the last five ingredients. Serve with the wings.

Bell Pepper Stuffed Chicken Roll-Ups

Prep time: 10 minutes | Cook time: 12 minutes | Serves 4

2 (4-ounce / 113-g) boneless, skinless chicken breasts, slice in half horizontally
1 tablespoon olive oil
Juice of ½ lime
2 tablespoons taco seasoning
½ green bell pepper, cut into strips
½ red bell pepper, cut into strips
¼ onion, sliced

1. Preheat the air fryer to 400ºF (204ºC). 2. Rub the chicken breast slices with olive oil, then drizzle with lime juice and sprinkle with taco seasoning. 3. Top the chicken slices with equal amount of bell peppers and onion. Roll them up and secure with toothpicks. 4. Air fry for 12 minutes or until the internal temperature reaches 165ºF (74ºC). Flip the chicken roll-ups halfway through. 5. Discard the toothpicks and serve immediately.

Pickle Brined Fried Chicken

Prep time: 30 minutes | Cook time: 47 minutes | Serves 4

4 bone-in, skin-on chicken legs, cut into drumsticks and thighs (about 3½ pounds / 1.6 kg)
Pickle juice from 1 (24-ounce / 680-g) jar kosher dill pickles
½ cup flour
Salt and freshly ground black pepper, to taste
2 eggs
1 cup fine bread crumbs
1 teaspoon salt
1 teaspoon freshly ground black pepper
½ teaspoon ground paprika
⅛ teaspoon ground cayenne pepper
Vegetable or canola oil

1. Place the chicken and pickle juice in a shallow. Cover and refrigerate for 3 to 8 hours. 2. Remove the chicken from the pickle brine to let it come to room temperature and gently dry it with a clean kitchen towel. Place the flour in a shallow dish and season with salt and black pepper. Whisk the eggs in a second shallow dish. In a third shallow dish, combine the bread crumbs, salt, pepper, paprika and cayenne pepper. 3. Preheat the air fryer to 370ºF (188ºC). 4. Dredge each piece of chicken in the flour, then egg mixture, and finally bread crumb mixture to coat well. Spray with vegetable oil. 5. Air fry the chicken in two batches. Air fry two chicken thighs and two drumsticks for 20 minutes, turning halfway through. Let them rest on plate. Repeat with the second batch of chicken. 6. Place the first batch of chicken on top of the second batch already in the basket and air fry at 340ºF (171ºC) for an additional 7 minutes. Serve warm and enjoy.

Air Fried Chicken Potatoes with Sun-Dried Tomato

Prep time: 15 minutes | Cook time: 25 minutes | Serves 2

2 teaspoons minced fresh oregano, divided
2 teaspoons minced fresh thyme, divided
2 teaspoons extra-virgin olive oil, plus extra as needed
1 pound (454 g) fingerling potatoes, unpeeled
2 (12-ounce / 340-g) bone-in split chicken breasts, trimmed
1 garlic clove, minced
¼ cup oil-packed sun-dried tomatoes, patted dry and chopped
1½ tablespoons red wine vinegar
1 tablespoon capers, rinsed and minced
1 small shallot, minced
Salt and ground black pepper, to taste

1. Preheat the air fryer to 350ºF (177ºC). 2. Combine 1 teaspoon oregano, 1 teaspoon thyme, ¼ teaspoon salt, ¼ teaspoon ground black pepper, 1 teaspoons olive oil in a bowl. Add the potatoes and toss to coat well. 3. Combine the chicken with remaining thyme, oregano, and olive oil. Sprinkle with garlic, salt, and pepper. Toss to coat well. 4. Place the potatoes in air fryer, then top with chicken. 5. Air fry for 25 minutes, flipping halfway through, or until the internal temperature reaches 165ºF (74ºC) and the potatoes are wilted. 6. Meanwhile, combine the sun-dried tomatoes, vinegar, capers, and shallot in a separate large bowl. Sprinkle with salt and ground black pepper. Toss to mix well. 7. Serve with the sun-dried tomato mix.

Lemon-Basil Turkey Breasts

Prep time: 30 minutes | Cook time: 58 minutes | Serves 4

2 tablespoons olive oil
2 pounds (907 g) turkey breasts, bone-in, skin-on
Coarse sea salt and ground black pepper, to taste
1 teaspoon fresh basil leaves, chopped
2 tablespoons lemon zest, grated

1. Rub olive oil on all sides of the turkey breasts; sprinkle with salt, pepper, basil, and lemon zest. 2. Place the turkey breasts skin side up on frying basket. 3. Bake at 330ºF (166ºC) for 58 minutes, turning halfway through cooking. Serve with lemon wedges, if desired.

Stuffed Turkey Roulade

Prep time: 10 minutes | Cook time: 45 minutes | Serves 4

1 (2-pound) boneless turkey breast, skin removed
1 teaspoon salt
½ teaspoon black pepper
4 ounces goat cheese
1 tablespoon fresh thyme
1 tablespoon fresh sage
2 garlic cloves, minced
2 tablespoons olive oil
Fresh chopped parsley, for garnish

1. Preheat the air fryer to 380ºF (193ºC). 2. Using a sharp knife, butterfly the turkey breast, and season both sides with salt and pepper. 3. In a bowl, mix together the goat cheese, thyme, sage, and garlic. 4. Spread the cheese mixture over the turkey breast, then roll it up tightly, tucking the ends underneath. 5. Bake for 30 minutes. Brush the top with oil, then cook for another 10 to 15 minutes, or until the outside has browned and the internal temperature reaches 165ºF (74ºC). 6. Cut into 1-inch-wide slices and serve with parsley on top.

Greek Chicken Stir-Fry

Prep time: 15 minutes | Cook time: 15 minutes | Serves 2

1 (6-ounce / 170-g) chicken breast, cut into 1-inch cubes
½ medium zucchini, chopped
½ medium red bell pepper, seeded and chopped
¼ medium red onion, peeled and sliced
1 tablespoon coconut oil
1 teaspoon dried oregano
½ teaspoon garlic powder
¼ teaspoon dried thyme

1. Place all ingredients into a mixing bowl and toss until the coconut oil coats the meat and vegetables. Pour into the frying basket. 2. Air fry at 375ºF (191ºC) for 15 minutes, shaking halfway through the cooking time. Serve immediately.

Fajita Chicken Strips

Prep time: 10 minutes | Cook time: 15 minutes | Serves 4

1 pound (454 g) boneless, skinless chicken tenderloins, cut into strips
3 bell peppers, any color, cut into chunks
1 onion, cut into chunks
1 tablespoon olive oil
1 tablespoon fajita seasoning mix
Cooking spray

1. Preheat the air fryer to 370ºF (188ºC). 2. In a bowl, mix together the chicken, bell peppers, onion, olive oil, and fajita seasoning mix until completely coated. 3. Spray the frying basket, chicken and vegetables lightly with cooking spray. 4. Air fry for 7 minutes. Shake and air fry for 5 to 8 minutes more, until the chicken is cooked through and the veggies are starting to char. 5. Serve warm.

Cajun-Breaded Chicken Bites

Prep time: 10 minutes | Cook time: 12 minutes | Serves 4

1 pound (454 g) boneless, skinless chicken breasts, cut into 1-inch cubes
½ cup heavy whipping cream
½ teaspoon salt
¼ teaspoon ground black pepper
1 ounce (28 g) plain pork rinds, finely crushed
¼ cup unflavored whey protein powder
½ teaspoon Cajun seasoning

1. Place chicken in a bowl and pour in cream. Stir to coat. Sprinkle with salt and pepper. 2. In a separate large bowl, combine pork rinds, protein powder, and Cajun seasoning. Remove chicken from cream and toss in dry mix until fully coated. 3. Air fry at 400ºF (204ºC) for 12 minutes, shaking twice during cooking until golden brown and the internal temperature reaches 165ºF (74ºC). Serve warm.

Chicken Thighs with Cilantro

Prep time: 15 minutes | Cook time: 25 minutes | Serves 4

1 tablespoon olive oil
Juice of ½ lime
1 tablespoon coconut aminos
1½ teaspoons Montreal chicken seasoning
8 bone-in chicken thighs, skin on
2 tablespoons chopped fresh cilantro

1. In a gallon-size resealable bag, combine the olive oil, lime juice, coconut aminos, and chicken seasoning. Add the chicken thighs, seal the bag, and massage to coat. Refrigerate for at least 2 hours, preferably overnight. 2. Preheat the air fryer to 400°F (204°C). 3. Remove the chicken from the marinade and air fry for 20 to 25 minutes, flipping halfway through until the internal temperature reaches 165°F (74°C). 4. Top with the cilantro before serving.

Pork Rind Fried Chicken

Prep time: 30 minutes | Cook time: 20 minutes | Serves 4

¼ cup buffalo sauce
4 (4-ounce / 113-g) boneless, skinless chicken breasts
½ teaspoon paprika
½ teaspoon garlic powder
¼ teaspoon ground black pepper
2 ounces (57 g) plain pork rinds, finely crushed

1. Pour buffalo sauce into a large sealabl bag. Add chicken and toss to coat. Place sealed bag into refrigerator to marinate at least 30 minutes. 2. Remove chicken from marinade and sprinkle with paprika, garlic powder, and pepper. 3. Place pork rinds into a bowl and press each chicken breast into pork rinds to coat evenly on both sides. 4. Roast at 400°F (204°C) for 20 minutes, turning chicken halfway through cooking until the internal temperature reaches 165°F (74°C). Serve warm.

Buttermilk-Fried Drumsticks

Prep time: 10 minutes | Cook time: 25 minutes | Serves 2

1 egg
½ cup buttermilk
¾ cup self-rising flour
¾ cup seasoned panko bread crumbs
1 teaspoon salt
¼ teaspoon ground black pepper (to mix into coating)
4 chicken drumsticks, skin on
Oil for misting or cooking spray

1. Beat together egg and buttermilk in shallow dish. 2. In a second shallow dish, combine the flour, panko crumbs, salt, and pepper. 3. Sprinkle chicken legs with additional salt and pepper to taste. 4. Dip legs in buttermilk mixture, then roll in panko mixture, pressing in crumbs to make coating stick. Mist with oil or cooking spray. 5. Spray the frying basket with cooking spray. 6. Roast at 360°F (182°C) for 20 minutes, turning once during cooking. If you have any white spots that haven't begun to brown, spritz them with oil. Continue cooking for 5 more minutes or until crust is golden brown and juices run clear.

Chicken Kiev

Prep time: 15 minutes | Cook time: 25 minutes | Serves 4

1 cup (2 sticks) unsalted butter, softened (or butter-flavored coconut oil for dairy-free)
2 tablespoons lemon juice
2 tablespoons plus 1 teaspoon chopped fresh parsley leaves, divided, plus more for garnish
2 tablespoons chopped fresh tarragon leaves
3 cloves garlic, minced
1 teaspoon fine sea salt, divided
4 (4-ounce / 113-g) boneless, skinless chicken breasts
2 large eggs
2 cups pork dust
1 teaspoon ground black pepper
Sprig of fresh parsley, for garnish
Lemon slices, for serving

1. Spray the frying basket with avocado oil. Preheat the air fryer to 350°F (177°C). 2. In a medium-sized bowl, combine the butter, lemon juice, 2 tablespoons parsley, the tarragon, garlic, and ¼ teaspoon salt. Cover and place in the fridge to harden for 7 minutes. 3. Place one of the chicken breasts on a cutting board. With a sharp knife held parallel to the cutting board, make a 1-inch-wide incision at the top of the breast. Carefully cut into the breast to form a large pocket, leaving a ½-inch border along the sides and bottom. Repeat with the other 3 breasts. 4. Stuff one-quarter of the butter mixture into each chicken breast and secure the openings with toothpicks. 5. Beat the eggs in a small shallow dish. In another shallow dish, combine the pork dust, the remaining parsley, the remaining salt, and the pepper. 6. Dip the chicken breasts in the egg, and the pork dust mixture. Press the pork dust onto each breast to form a nice crust. Spray with avocado oil and place it in the frying basket. 7. Roast for 15 minutes, flip the breasts, and cook for another 10 minutes, or until the internal temperature reaches 165°F (74°C) and the crust is golden brown. 8. Serve garnished with chopped fresh parsley and a parsley sprig, with lemon slices on the side.

Chicken Croquettes with Creole Sauce

Prep time: 30 minutes | Cook time: 10 minutes | Serves 4

2 cups shredded cooked chicken
½ cup shredded Cheddar cheese
2 eggs
¼ cup finely chopped onion
¼ cup almond meal
1 tablespoon poultry seasoning
Olive oil
Creole Sauce:
¼ cup mayonnaise
¼ cup sour cream
1½ teaspoons Dijon mustard
1½ teaspoons fresh lemon juice
½ teaspoon garlic powder
½ teaspoon Creole seasoning

1. In a bowl, stir the first six ingredients until thoroughly combined. Cover and refrigerate for 30 minutes. 2. **Make the Creole Sauce:** Meanwhile, in a bowl, whisk together the sauce ingredients until thoroughly combined. Cover and refrigerate until ready to serve. 3. Preheat the air fryer to 400°F (204°C). Shape the chicken mixture into 8 patties. Coat both sides with olive oil. Air fry for 10 minutes, flipping halfway through until lightly browned and the cheese is melted. Serve with Creole sauce.

Lemon-Dijon Boneless Chicken

Prep time: 30 minutes | Cook time: 13 to 16 minutes | Serves 6

½ cup sugar-free mayonnaise
1 tablespoon Dijon mustard
1 tablespoon freshly squeezed lemon juice (optional)
1 tablespoon coconut aminos
1 teaspoon Italian seasoning
1 teaspoon sea salt
½ teaspoon freshly ground black pepper
¼ teaspoon cayenne pepper
1½ pounds (680 g) boneless, skinless chicken breasts or thighs

1. In a bowl, combine the first eight ingredients. 2. Place the chicken in a shallow dish or large zip-top plastic bag. Add the marinade to coat well. Cover and refrigerate for at least 30 minutes or up to 4 hours. 3. Arrange the chicken in a single layer in the frying basket. Air fry at 400°F (204°C) for 13 to 16 minutes, flipping halfway through until the internal temperature reaches 160°F (71°C).

Buffalo Chicken Cheese Sticks

Prep time: 5 minutes | Cook time: 8 minutes | Serves 2

1 cup shredded cooked chicken
¼ cup buffalo sauce
1 cup shredded Mozzarella cheese
1 large egg
¼ cup crumbled feta

1. In a bowl, mix all ingredients except the feta. Cut a piece of parchment to fit your frying basket and press the mixture into a ½-inch-thick circle. 2. Sprinkle the mixture with feta and place into the frying basket. Air fry at 400°F (204°C) for 8 minutes. 3. After 5 minutes, flip over the cheese mixture. Allow to cool 5 minutes before cutting into sticks. Serve warm.

Chicken Hand Pies

Prep time: 30 minutes | Cook time: 10 minutes | Makes 8 pies

¾ cup chicken broth
¾ cup frozen mixed peas and carrots
1 cup cooked chicken, chopped
1 tablespoon cornstarch
1 tablespoon milk
Salt and pepper, to taste
1 (8-count) can organic flaky biscuits
Oil for misting or cooking spray

1. In a medium saucepan, bring chicken broth to a boil. Cook frozen peas and carrots for 5 minutes over medium heat. Stir in chicken. 2. Mix the cornstarch into the milk until it dissolves. Stir into the chicken broth mixture and cook just until thickened. 3. Remove from heat, add salt and pepper to taste, and let cool slightly. 4. Lay biscuits out on wax paper. Peel each biscuit apart in the middle to make 2 rounds so you have 16 rounds total. Flatten each biscuit round slightly to make it larger and thinner. 5. Divide chicken filling among 8 of the biscuit rounds. Place remaining biscuit rounds on top and press edges all around, making sure they are sealed well. 6. Spray both sides lightly with oil or cooking spray. 7. Bake at 330°F (166°C) for 10 minutes or until biscuit dough is cooked through and golden brown.

Air Fried Chicken Wings with Buffalo Sauce

Prep time: 10 minutes | Cook time: 20 minutes | Serves 6

16 chicken drumettes (party wings)
Chicken seasoning or rub, to taste
1 teaspoon garlic powder
Ground black pepper, to taste
¼ cup buffalo wings sauce
Cooking spray

1. Preheat the air fryer to 400°F (204°C). Spritz the frying basket with cooking spray. 2. Rub the chicken wings with chicken seasoning, garlic powder, and black pepper. Spritz with cooking spray. Air fry for 10 minutes or until lightly browned, shaking halfway through. 3. Transfer the chicken wings in a bowl, then pour in the buffalo sauce and toss to coat. 4. Air fry for an additional 7 minutes. 5. Serve immediately.

Easy Turkey Tenderloin

Prep time: 20 minutes | Cook time: 30 minutes | Serves 4

Olive oil
½ teaspoon paprika
½ teaspoon garlic powder
½ teaspoon salt
½ teaspoon freshly ground black pepper
Pinch cayenne pepper
1½ pounds (680 g) turkey breast tenderloin

1. Spray the frying basket lightly with olive oil. 2. In a bowl, combine the paprika, garlic powder, salt, black pepper, and cayenne pepper. Rub the mixture all over the turkey. 3. Lightly spray the turkey with olive oil. 4. Air fry at 370°F (188°C) for 15 minutes. Flip the turkey over and lightly spray with olive oil. Air fry until the internal temperature reaches 170°F (77°C) for an additional 10 to 15 minutes. 5. Letrest for 10 minutes before slicing and serving.

Cornish Hens with Honey-Lime Glaze

Prep time: 15 minutes | Cook time: 25 to 30 minutes | Serves 2 to 3

1 Cornish game hen (1½ to 2 pounds / 680 to 907 g)
1 tablespoon honey
1 tablespoon lime juice
1 teaspoon poultry seasoning
Salt and pepper, to taste
Cooking spray

1. To split the hen into halves, cut through breast bone and down one side of the backbone. 2. Mix the honey, lime juice, and poultry seasoning together and rub onto all sides of the hen. Season with salt and pepper. 3. Spray the frying basket with cooking spray and place hen halves in the basket, skin-side down. 4. Air fry at 330°F (166°C) for 25 to 30 minutes until juices run clear. Let hen rest for 5 to 10 minutes before cutting.

Lettuce-Wrapped Turkey and Mushroom Meatballs

Prep time: 10 minutes | Cook time: 15 minutes | Serves 6

Sauce:
2 tablespoons tamari
2 tablespoons tomato sauce
1 tablespoon lime juice
¼ teaspoon peeled and grated fresh ginger
1 clove garlic, smashed to a paste
½ cup chicken broth
⅓ cup sugar
2 tablespoons toasted sesame oil
Cooking spray
Meatballs:
2 pounds (907 g) ground turkey
¾ cup finely chopped button mushrooms
2 large eggs, beaten
1½ teaspoons tamari
¼ cup finely chopped green onions, plus more for garnish
2 teaspoons peeled and grated fresh ginger
1 clove garlic, smashed
2 teaspoons toasted sesame oil
2 tablespoons sugar
For Serving:
Lettuce leaves, for serving
Sliced red chiles, for garnish (optional)
Toasted sesame seeds, for garnish (optional)

1. Preheat the air fryer to 350ºF (177ºC). 2. Combine the ingredients for the sauce in a bowl. Stir to mix well. Set aside. 3. Combine the ingredients for the meatballs in a bowl. Stir to mix well, then shape the mixture in twelve 1½-inch meatballs. 4. Baste the meatballs with sauce. Spritz with cooking spray. Air fry for 15 minutes, flipping halfway through, or until golden brown. 5. Transfer the cooked meatballs on the letttuce leaves. Spread the red chiles and sesame seeds over the balls, then serve.

Broccoli Cheese Chicken

Prep time: 10 minutes | Cook time: 19 to 24 minutes | Serves 6

1 tablespoon avocado oil
¼ cup chopped onion
½ cup finely chopped broccoli
4 ounces (113 g) cream cheese, at room temperature
2 ounces (57 g) Cheddar cheese, shredded
1 teaspoon garlic powder
½ teaspoon sea salt, plus additional for seasoning, divided
¼ freshly ground black pepper, plus additional for seasoning, divided
2 pounds (907 g) boneless, skinless chicken breasts
1 teaspoon smoked paprika

1. Heat avocado oil in a medium skillet over medium-high heat. Add onion and broccoli and cook for 5 to 8 minutes, stirring occasionally until the onion is tender. 2. Transfer to a large bowl and stir in the cream cheese, Cheddar cheese, and garlic powder, and season to taste with salt and pepper. 3. Hold a sharp knife parallel to the chicken breast and cut a long pocket into one side. Stuff the chicken pockets with the broccoli mixture, using toothpicks to secure. 4. In a small dish, combine the paprika, ½ teaspoon salt, and ¼ teaspoon pepper. Sprinkle this over the outside of the chicken. 5. Roast at the chicken 400ºF (204ºC) for 14 to 16 minutes, until the internal temperature reaches 160ºF (71ºC). Tent a piece of aluminum foil over the chicken. Allow to rest for 5 to 10 minutes before serving.

Barbecue Chicken

Prep time: 10 minutes | Cook time: 18 to 20 minutes | Serves 4

⅓ cup no-salt-added tomato sauce
2 tablespoons low-sodium grainy mustard
2 tablespoons apple cider vinegar
1 tablespoon honey
2 garlic cloves, minced
1 jalapeño pepper, minced
3 tablespoons minced onion
4 (5-ounce / 142-g) low-sodium boneless, skinless chicken breasts

1. Preheat the air fryer to 370ºF (188ºC). 2. In a bowl, stir together the first seven ingredients. 3. Brush the chicken breasts with some sauce and air fry for 10 minutes. 4. Turn the chicken; brush with more sauce. Air fry for 5 minutes more. 5. Turn the chicken again; brush with more sauce. Air fry for 3 to 5 minutes more, or until the internal temperature reaches 165ºF (74ºC). Discard any remaining sauce. Serve.

Pecan-Crusted Chicken Tenders

Prep time: 10 minutes | Cook time: 12 minutes | Serves 4

2 tablespoons mayonnaise
1 teaspoon Dijon mustard
1 pound (454 g) boneless, skinless chicken tenders
½ teaspoon salt
¼ teaspoon ground black pepper
½ cup chopped roasted pecans, finely ground

1. In a bowl, whisk mayonnaise and mustard until combined. Brush mixture onto chicken tenders on both sides, then sprinkle tenders with salt and pepper. 2. Place pecans in a bowl and press each tender into pecans to coat each side. 3. Roast the tenders at 375ºF (191ºC) t for 12 minutes, turning halfway through cooking, until golden brown and the internal temperature reaches 165ºF (74ºC). Serve warm.

Yellow Curry Chicken Thighs with Peanuts

Prep time: 10 minutes | Cook time: 20 minutes | Serves 6

½ cup unsweetened full-fat coconut milk
2 tablespoons yellow curry paste
1 tablespoon minced fresh ginger
1 tablespoon minced garlic
1 teaspoon kosher salt
1 pound (454 g) boneless, skinless chicken thighs, halved crosswise
2 tablespoons chopped peanuts

1. In a bowl, stir together the coconut milk, curry paste, ginger, garlic, and salt until well blended. Add the chicken; toss well to coat. Marinate at room temperature for 30 minutes. 2. Preheat the air fryer to 375ºF (191ºC). 3. Place the chicken (along with marinade) in a baking pan. Bake for 20 minutes, turning halfway through, until the internal temperature reaches 165ºF (74ºC). 4. Sprinkle with peanuts and serve.

98 | Chapter 1 Vegetables and Sides

Italian Flavor Chicken Breasts with Roma Tomatoes

Prep time: 10 minutes | Cook time: 60 minutes | Serves 8

3 pounds (1.4 kg) chicken breasts, bone-in
1 teaspoon minced fresh basil
1 teaspoon minced fresh rosemary
2 tablespoons minced fresh parsley
1 teaspoon cayenne pepper
½ teaspoon salt
½ teaspoon freshly ground black pepper
4 medium Roma tomatoes, halved
Cooking spray

1. Preheat the air fryer to 370ºF (188ºC). Spritz the frying basket with cooking spray. 2. Combine all the ingredients, except for the chicken breasts and tomatoes, in a bowl. Stir to mix well. Toss the chicken with the mixture to coat well. 3. Air fry for 25 minutes, flipping halfway through until the internal temperature reaches 165ºF (74ºC). 4. Remove and place tomatoes in the air fryer. Spritz with cooking spray and sprinkle with a touch of salt. Bake at 350ºF (177ºC) for 10 minutes, shaking halfway through cooking, or until tender. 5. Serve the tomatoes with chicken breasts.

Broccoli and Cheese Stuffed Chicken

Prep time: 15 minutes | Cook time: 20 minutes | Serves 4

2 ounces (57 g) cream cheese, softened
1 cup chopped fresh broccoli, steamed
½ cup shredded sharp Cheddar cheese
4 (6-ounce / 170-g) boneless, skinless chicken breasts
2 tablespoons mayonnaise
¼ teaspoon salt
¼ teaspoon garlic powder
⅛ teaspoon ground black pepper

1. In a medium bowl, combine cream cheese, broccoli, and Cheddar. Cut a 4-inch pocket into each chicken breast. Evenly divide mixture between chicken breasts; stuff the pocket of each chicken breast with the mixture. 2. Spread ¼ tablespoon mayonnaise per side of each chicken breast, then sprinkle both sides of breasts with salt, garlic powder, and pepper. 3. Roast at 350ºF (177ºC) for 20 minutes, turning halfway through cooking until the chicken is golden and the internal temperature reaches 165ºF (74ºC). Serve warm.

Chicken Schnitzel Dogs

Prep time: 15 minutes | Cook time: 8 to 10 minutes | Serves 4

½ cup flour
½ teaspoon salt
1 teaspoon marjoram
1 teaspoon dried parsley flakes
½ teaspoon thyme
1 egg
1 teaspoon lemon juice
1 teaspoon water
1 cup bread crumbs
4 chicken tenders, pounded thin
Oil for misting or cooking spray
4 whole-grain hotdog buns
4 slices Gouda cheese
1 small Granny Smith apple, thinly sliced
½ cup shredded Napa cabbage
Coleslaw dressing

1. In a shallow dish, mix together the flour, salt, marjoram, parsley, and thyme. 2. In another shallow dish, beat together egg, lemon juice, and water. 3. Place bread crumbs in a third shallow dish. 4. Cut each of the flattened chicken tenders in half lengthwise. 5. Dip flattened chicken strips in flour mixture, then egg wash. Let excess egg drip off and roll in bread crumbs. Spray both sides with oil or cooking spray. 6. Air fry at 390ºF (199ºC) for 8 to 10 minutes, turning and spraying with oil halfway through, until well done and crispy brown. 7. Place 2 schnitzel strips on bottom of each hotdog bun. Top with cheese, apple, and cabbage. Drizzle with coleslaw dressing and top with other half of bun.

Korean Flavor Glazed Chicken Wings

Prep time: 10 minutes | Cook time: 25 minutes | Serves 4

Wings:
2 pounds (907 g) chicken wings
1 teaspoon salt
1 teaspoon ground black pepper
Sauce:
2 tablespoons gochujang
1 tablespoon mayonnaise
1 tablespoon minced ginger
1 tablespoon minced garlic
1 teaspoon agave nectar
2 packets Splenda
1 tablespoon sesame oil
For Garnish:
2 teaspoons sesame seeds
¼ cup chopped green onions

1. Preheat the air fryer to 400ºF (204ºC). 2. Rub the chicken wings with salt and black pepper. Air fry for 20 minutes or until the wings are well browned, flipping halfway through. 3. Meanwhile, combine the ingredients for the sauce in a bowl. Stir to mix well. Reserve half of the sauce in a separate bowl until ready to serve. 4. Toss the air fried wings with remaining half of the sauce to coat well. Air fry for 5 more minutes or until the internal temperature reaches 165ºF (74ºC). 5. Sprinkle with sesame seeds and green onions. Serve with reserved sauce.

Gold Livers

Prep time: 10 minutes | Cook time: 20 minutes | Serves 4

2 eggs
2 tablespoons water
¾ cup flour
2 cups panko bread crumbs
1 teaspoon salt
½ teaspoon ground black pepper
20 ounces (567 g) chicken livers
Cooking spray

1. Preheat the air fryer to 390ºF (199ºC). Spritz the frying basket with cooking spray. 2. Whisk the eggs with water in a bowl. Pour the flour in a separate bowl. Pour the panko on a shallow dish and sprinkle with salt and pepper. 3. Dredge the chicken livers in the flour, then the whisked eggs, and roll the livers over the panko to coat well. Spritz with cooking spray. Air fry for 10 minutes or until the golden and crispy. Flip the livers halfway through. 4. Serve immediately.

Barbecued Chicken with Creamy Coleslaw

Prep time: 10 minutes | Cook time: 20 minutes | Serves 2

3 cups shredded coleslaw mix
Salt and pepper
2 (12-ounce / 340-g) bone-in split chicken breasts, trimmed
1 teaspoon vegetable oil
2 tablespoons barbecue sauce, plus extra for serving
2 tablespoons mayonnaise
2 tablespoons sour cream
1 teaspoon distilled white vinegar, plus extra for seasoning
¼ teaspoon sugar

1. Preheat the air fryer to 350ºF (177ºC). 2. Toss coleslaw mix and ¼ teaspoon salt in a colander set over bowl. Let sit until wilted slightly. Rinse, drain, and dry with a dish towel. 3. Meanwhile, pat chicken dry with paper towels, rub with oil, and season with salt and pepper. Arrange breasts skin-side down in frying basket, spaced evenly apart, alternating ends. Bake for 10 minutes. Flip breasts and brush skin side with barbecue sauce. Bake for 10 to 15 minutes until well browned and chicken registers 160ºF (71ºC). 4. Let rest for 5 minutes. Meanwhile, whisk mayonnaise, sour cream, vinegar, sugar, and pinch pepper together in a bowl. Stir in coleslaw mix and season with salt, pepper, and additional vinegar to taste. Serve chicken with coleslaw, passing extra barbecue sauce separately.

Thai Tacos with Peanut Sauce

Prep time: 10 minutes | Cook time: 6 minutes | Serves 4

1 pound (454 g) ground chicken
¼ cup diced onions (about 1 small onion)
2 cloves garlic, minced
¼ teaspoon fine sea salt
Sauce:
¼ cup creamy peanut butter, room temperature
2 tablespoons chicken broth, plus more if needed
2 tablespoons lime juice
2 tablespoons grated fresh ginger
2 tablespoons wheat-free tamari or coconut aminos
1½ teaspoons hot sauce
5 drops liquid stevia (optional)
For Serving:
2 small heads butter lettuce, leaves separated
Lime slices (optional)
For Garnish (Optional):
Cilantro leaves
Shredded purple cabbage
Sliced green onions

1. Preheat the air fryer to 350ºF (177ºC). 2. Place the ground chicken, onions, garlic, and salt in a pie pan or a dish. Break up the chicken with a spatula. Bake for 5 minutes, or until the chicken is browned and cooked through. Break up the chicken again into small crumbles. 3. **Make the Sauce:** In a medium-sized bowl, stir together all the sauce ingredients until well combined. 4. Add half of the sauce to the pan with the chicken. Cook for another minute, until heated through, and stir well to combine. 5. Place several lettuce leaves on a serving plate. Place a few tablespoons chicken mixture in each lettuce leaf and garnish with cilantro leaves, purple cabbage, and sliced green onions, if desired. Serve the remaining sauce on the side. Serve with lime slices, if desired.

Golden Chicken Cutlets

Prep time: 15 minutes | Cook time: 15 minutes | Serves 4

2 tablespoons panko bread crumbs
¼ cup grated Parmesan cheese
⅛ tablespoon paprika
½ tablespoon garlic powder
2 large eggs
4 chicken cutlets
1 tablespoon parsley
Salt and ground black pepper, to taste
Cooking spray

1. Preheat air fryer to 400ºF (204ºC). Spritz the frying basket with cooking spray. 2. Combine the bread crumbs, Parmesan, paprika, garlic powder, salt, and ground black pepper in a bowl. Stir to mix well. Beat the eggs in a separate bowl. 3. Dredge the chicken cutlets in the beaten eggs, then roll over the bread crumbs mixture to coat well. Shake the excess off. Spritz with cooking spray. 4. Air fry for 15 minutes or until crispy and golden brown, flipping halfway through. 5. Serve with parsley on top.

Chicken Burgers with Ham and Cheese

Prep time: 12 minutes | Cook time: 13 to 16 minutes | Serves 4

⅓ cup soft bread crumbs
3 tablespoons milk
1 egg, beaten
½ teaspoon dried thyme
Pinch salt
Freshly ground black pepper, to taste
1¼ pounds (567 g) ground chicken
¼ cup finely chopped ham
⅓ cup grated Havarti cheese
Olive oil for misting

1. Preheat the air fryer to 350ºF (177ºC). 2. In a medium bowl, combine the bread crumbs, milk, egg, thyme, salt, and pepper. Add the chicken and mix gently but thoroughly. 3. Form the chicken into eight thin patties. 4. Top four patties with ham and cheese. Top with remaining four patties and gently press the edges together to seal. 5. Place the burgers in the basket and mist with oil. Bake for 13 to 16 minutes or until the the internal temperature reaches 165ºF (74ºC). Serve immediately.

Thai-Style Cornish Game Hens

Prep time: 30 minutes | Cook time: 20 minutes | Serves 4

1 cup chopped fresh cilantro leaves and stems
¼ cup fish sauce
1 tablespoon soy sauce
1 serrano chile, seeded and chopped
8 garlic cloves, smashed
2 tablespoons sugar
2 tablespoons lemongrass paste
2 teaspoons black pepper
2 teaspoons ground coriander
1 teaspoon kosher salt
1 teaspoon ground turmeric
2 Cornish game hens, giblets removed, split in half lengthwise

1. Blend the cilantro, fish sauce, soy sauce, serrano, garlic, sugar, lemongrass, black pepper, coriander, salt, and turmeric until smooth in a blender. 2. Toss the hen halves with cilantro mixture to coat. Marinate at room temperature for 30 minutes. 3. Roast at 400ºF (204ºC) for 20 minutes until the internal temperature reaches 165ºF (74ºC).

100 | Chapter 1 Vegetables and Sides

Blackened Cajun Chicken Tenders

Prep time: 10 minutes | Cook time: 17 minutes | Serves 4

2 teaspoons paprika
1 teaspoon chili powder
½ teaspoon garlic powder
½ teaspoon dried thyme
¼ teaspoon onion powder
⅛ teaspoon ground cayenne pepper
2 tablespoons coconut oil
1 pound (454 g) boneless, skinless chicken tenders
¼ cup full-fat ranch dressing

1. In a bowl, combine all seasonings. 2. Drizzle oil over chicken tenders and then generously coat each tender in the spice mixture. Place tenders into the frying basket. 3. Roast at 375°F (191°C) and air fry for 17 minutes until the tenders are 165°F (74°C) internally. Serve with ranch dressing.

Yakitori

Prep time: 10 minutes | Cook time: 15 minutes | Serves 4

½ cup mirin
¼ cup dry white wine
½ cup soy sauce
1 tablespoon light brown sugar
1½ pounds (680 g) boneless, skinless chicken thighs, cut into 1½-inch pieces, fat trimmed
4 medium scallions, trimmed, cut into 1½-inch pieces
Cooking spray
Special Equipment:
4 (4-inch) bamboo skewers, soaked in water for at least 30 minutes

1. Combine the mirin, dry white wine, soy sauce, and brown sugar in a saucepan. Bring to a boil over medium heat. Keep stirring. 2. Boil for another 2 minutes or until it has a thick consistency. Turn off the heat. 3. Preheat the air fryer to 400°F (204°C). Spritz the frying basket with cooking spray. 4. Run the bamboo skewers through the chicken pieces and scallions alternatively. Brush with mirin mixture on both sides. Spritz with cooking spray. 5. Air fry for 10 minutes or until the chicken and scallions are glossy, flipping halfway through. 6. Serve immediately.

Ham Chicken with Cheese

Prep time: 15 minutes | Cook time: 25 minutes | Serves 4

¼ cup unsalted butter, softened
4 ounces (113 g) cream cheese, softened
1½ teaspoons Dijon mustard
2 tablespoons white wine vinegar
¼ cup water
2 cups shredded cooked chicken
¼ pound (113 g) ham, chopped
4 ounces (113 g) sliced Swiss or Provolone cheese

1. Preheat the air fryer to 380°F (193°C). Lightly coat a casserole dish with olive oil. 2. In a bowl and using an electric mixer, combine the butter, cream cheese, Dijon mustard, and vinegar. With the motor running at low speed, slowly add the water and beat until smooth. Set aside. 3. Arrange an even layer of chicken in the bottom of the prepared pan, followed by the ham. Spread the butter and cream cheese mixture on top of the ham, followed by the cheese slices on the top layer. Air fry for 20 to 25 minutes until warmed through and the cheese has browned.

Chicken Nuggets

Prep time: 10 minutes | Cook time: 15 minutes | Serves 4

1 pound (454 g) ground chicken thighs
½ cup shredded Mozzarella cheese
1 large egg, whisked
½ teaspoon salt
¼ teaspoon dried oregano
¼ teaspoon garlic powder

1. In a bowl, combine all ingredients. Form mixture into twenty nugget shapes, about 2 tablespoons each. Place nuggets into frying basket and air fry at 375°F (191°C) for 15 minutes, turning halfway through cooking. Let cool 5 minutes before serving.

Ethiopian Chicken with Cauliflower

Prep time: 15 minutes | Cook time: 28 minutes | Serves 6

2 handful fresh Italian parsley, roughly chopped
½ cup fresh chopped chives
2 sprigs thyme
6 chicken drumsticks
1½ small-sized head cauliflower, broken into large-sized florets
2 teaspoons mustard powder
⅓ teaspoon porcini powder
1½ teaspoons berbere spice
⅓ teaspoon sweet paprika
½ teaspoon shallot powder
1 teaspoon granulated garlic
1 teaspoon freshly cracked pink peppercorns
½ teaspoon sea salt

1. Simply combine all items for the berbere spice rub mix. Coat the chicken with rub mix on all sides. Transfer them to the baking dish. 2. Lower the cauliflower onto the chicken drumsticks. Add thyme, chives and Italian parsley and spritz with a pan spray. Roast at 355°F (179°C) for 28 minutes, turning occasionally.

Crispy Dill Chicken Strips

Prep time: 30 minutes | Cook time: 10 minutes | Serves 4

2 whole boneless, skinless chicken breasts (about 1 pound / 454 g each), halved lengthwise
1 cup Italian dressing
3 cups finely crushed potato chips
1 tablespoon dried dill weed
1 tablespoon garlic powder
1 large egg, beaten
1 to 2 tablespoons oil

1. In a large resealable bag, combine the chicken and Italian dressing. Seal the bag and refrigerate to marinate at least 1 hour. 2. In a shallow dish, stir together the potato chips, dill, and garlic powder. Place the beaten egg in a second shallow dish. 3. Remove the chicken from the marinade. Roll the chicken pieces in the egg and the potato chip mixture, coating thoroughly. Spritz with oil. 4. Bake at 325°F (163°C) for 10 minutes, flipping and spritzing with oil until the outsides are crispy and the insides are no longer pink.

Almond-Crusted Chicken

Prep time: 15 minutes | Cook time: 25 minutes | Serves 4

¼ cup slivered almonds
2 (6-ounce / 170-g) boneless, skinless chicken breasts
2 tablespoons full-fat mayonnaise
1 tablespoon Dijon mustard

1. Pulse the almonds in a food processor until finely chopped. Place almonds evenly on a plate and set aside. 2. Completely slice each chicken breast in half lengthwise. 3. Mix the mayonnaise and mustard in a bowl and then coat chicken with the mixture. 4. Lay each piece of chicken in the almonds to coat. 5. Bake at 350°F (177°C) for 25 minutes until the internal temperature reaches 165°F (74°C) or more. Serve warm.

Jerk Chicken Thighs

Prep time: 30 minutes | Cook time: 15 to 20 minutes | Serves 6

2 teaspoons ground coriander
1 teaspoon ground allspice
1 teaspoon cayenne pepper
1 teaspoon ground ginger
1 teaspoon salt
1 teaspoon dried thyme
½ teaspoon ground cinnamon
½ teaspoon ground nutmeg
2 pounds (907 g) boneless chicken thighs, skin on
2 tablespoons olive oil

1. In a bowl, stir the first nine ingredients until thoroughly combined. 2. Place the chicken in a baking dish and use paper towels to pat dry. Thoroughly coat both sides of the chicken with the spice mixture. Cover and refrigerate for at least 2 hours, preferably overnight. 3. Preheat the air fryer to 360°F (182°C). 4. Lightly coat the chicken with the olive oil. Air fry for 15 to 20 minutes, flipping halfway through the cooking time until the internal temperature reaches 165°F (74°C).

Chicken Patties

Prep time: 15 minutes | Cook time: 12 minutes | Serves 4

1 pound (454 g) ground chicken thigh meat
½ cup shredded Mozzarella cheese
1 teaspoon dried parsley
½ teaspoon garlic powder
¼ teaspoon onion powder
1 large egg
2 ounces (57 g) pork rinds, finely ground

1. In a bowl, mix ground chicken, Mozzarella, parsley, garlic powder, and onion powder. Form into four patties. Freezer for 15 to 20 minutes until they begin to firm up. 2. Whisk egg in a bowl. Place the ground pork rinds into a large bowl. 3. Dip each chicken patty into the egg and then press into pork rinds to fully coat. 4. Bake at 360°F (182°C) for 12 minutes until the internal temperature reaches 165°F (74°C). Serve immediately.

Chapter 6 Fish and Seafood

Crustless Shrimp Quiche

Prep time: 15 minutes | Cook time: 20 minutes | Serves 2

Vegetable oil
4 large eggs
½ cup half-and-half
4 ounces (113 g) raw shrimp, chopped (about 1 cup)
1 cup shredded Parmesan or Swiss cheese
¼ cup chopped scallions
1 teaspoon sweet smoked paprika
1 teaspoon herbes de Provence
1 teaspoon black pepper
½ to 1 teaspoon kosher salt

1. Grease a baking pan with vegetable oil. 2. In a bowl, beat together the eggs and half-and-half. Add ¾ cup cheese and the rest ingredients. Stir to thoroughly combine. Pour the egg mixture into the prepared pan. 3. Bake at 300°F (149°C) for 20 minutes. After 17 minutes, sprinkle the remaining cheese on top and cook for the remaining 3 minutes, or until the cheese has melted, the eggs are set, and a toothpick inserted into the center comes out clean. 4. Serve.

Cilantro Lime Baked Salmon

Prep time: 10 minutes | Cook time: 12 minutes | Serves 2

2 (3-ounce / 85-g) salmon fillets, skin removed
1 tablespoon salted butter, melted
1 teaspoon chili powder
½ teaspoon finely minced garlic
¼ cup sliced pickled jalapeños
½ medium lime, juiced
2 tablespoons chopped cilantro

1. Place salmon fillets into a round baking pan. Brush each with butter and sprinkle with chili powder and garlic. 2. Place jalapeño slices on top and around salmon. Pour half of the lime juice over the salmon and cover with foil. 3. Bake at 370°F (188°C) and for 12 minutes until the salmon flakes easily with a fork and reaches an internal temperature of at least 145°F (63°C). 4. To serve, spritz with remaining lime juice and garnish with cilantro.

Ginger Chili Crab Fritters

Prep time: 15 minutes | Cook time: 14 to 16 minutes | Serves 4

1 pound (454 g) jumbo crabmeat
1 lime, zested and juiced
1 teaspoon ginger paste
1 teaspoon garlic puree
1 tablespoon fresh cilantro, chopped
1 red chili, roughly chopped
1 egg
¼ cup panko bread crumbs
1 teaspoon soy sauce sauce
3 tablespoons sweet chili sauce

1. Preheat the air fryer to 400°F (204°C). In a bowl, mix crabmeat, lime zest, egg, ginger paste, and garlic puree. Form small cakes out of the mixture and dredge them in the bread crumbs. Place in the greased frying basket and air fry for 14 to 16 minutes, shaking once until golden brown. In a small bowl, mix the sweet chili sauce with lime juice and soy sauce. Serve the fritters topped with cilantro and the chili sauce.

Old Bay Crab Sticks

Prep time: 10 minutes | Cook time: 12 to 14 minutes | Serves 4

1 pound (454 g) crab sticks
1 tablespoon old bay seasoning
⅓ cup panko bread crumbs
2 eggs
½ cup mayonnaise
2 garlic cloves, minced
1 lime, juiced
1 cup flour

1. Preheat the air fryer to 390°F (199°C). Beat the eggs in a bowl. In another bowl, mix the bread crumbs with old bay seasoning. Pour the flour into a third bowl. Dip the sticks in the flour, then in the eggs, and finally in the bread crumbs. Spray with cooking spray and air fry for 12 to 14 minutes, flipping once, until golden. Mix the mayonnaise with garlic and lime juice. Serve as a dip along with crab sticks.

Dijon Crabmeat and Veggie Patties

Prep time: 15 minutes | Cook time: 12 to 14 minutes | Serves 4

3 potatoes, boiled and mashed
1 cup cooked crabmeat
¼ cup red onions, chopped
1 tablespoon fresh basil, chopped
½ celery stalk, chopped
½ bell red pepper, chopped
1 tablespoon Dijon mustard
½ lemon, zested and juiced
¼ cup bread crumbs
1 teaspoon ground allspice
½ cup mayonnaise
Salt and black pepper to taste

1. Place the mashed potatoes, red onions, allspice, bread crumbs, celery, bell pepper, mustard, lemon zest, crabmeat, salt, and black pepper in a large bowl and mix well. Make patties from the mixture and refrigerate for 30 minutes. Mix the mayonnaise, lemon juice, basil, salt, and pepper and set aside. 2. Preheat the air fryer to 390°F (199°C). Remove the patties from the fridge and place them in the greased frying basket. Air fry for 12 to 14 minutes, flipping once until golden. Serve the patties with the basil-mayo dip.

Crabmeat Croquettes with Herbs

Prep time: 20 minutes | Cook time: 15 to 17 minutes | Serves 4

1½ pounds (680 g) lump crabmeat	chopped
⅓ cup sour cream	1 teaspoon fresh parsley, chopped
⅓ cup mayonnaise	1 teaspoon cayenne pepper
1 red pepper, finely chopped	1½ cups bread crumbs
⅓ cup red onion, chopped	2 teaspoons olive oil
½ celery stalk, chopped	1 cup flour
1 teaspoon fresh tarragon, chopped	2 eggs, beaten
	Salt to taste
1 teaspoon fresh chives,	Lemon wedges to serve

1. Heat olive oil in a skillet over medium heat and sauté the red pepper, onion, and celery for 5 minutes or until sweaty and translucent. Turn off the heat. Pour the bread crumbs and salt on a plate. In 2 separate bowls, add the flour and the beaten eggs, respectively, and set aside. 2. In a separate bowl, add crabmeat, mayonnaise, sour cream, tarragon, chives, parsley, cayenne pepper, and sautéed vegetables. Form bite-size oval balls out of the mixture and place the balls on a plate. 3. Preheat the air fryer to 390°F (199°C). Dip each crab meatball in the beaten eggs and press down in the breadcrumb mixture. Place the croquettes in the greased frying basket without overcrowding. Air fry for 10 to 12 minutes or until golden brown, turning once. Serve hot with lemon wedges.

Garlicky Chili Prawns

Prep time: 10 minutes | Cook time: 8 to 10 minutes | Serves 4

8 prawns, cleaned	½ teaspoon red chili flakes
Salt and black pepper to taste	½ teaspoon ground cumin
½ teaspoon ground cayenne pepper	½ teaspoon garlic powder

1. In a bowl, season the prawns with salt and black pepper. Sprinkle with cayenne pepper, chili flakes, cumin, and garlic, and stir to coat. Spray the frying basket with oil and lay the prawns in an even layer. Air fry for 8 to 10 minutes at 340°F (171°C), turning once halfway through. Serve with sweet chili sauce if desired.

Chinese-Style Prawns with Garlic

Prep time: 15 minutes | Cook time: 15 minutes | Serves 4

1 pound (454 g) prawns, peeled and deveined	2 tablespoons cornstarch
	2 scallions, chopped
Juice from 1 lemon	¼ teaspoon Chinese powder
1 teaspoon sugar	1 red chili pepper, minced
2 tablespoons peanut oil	Salt and black pepper to taste
	4 garlic cloves, minced

1. In a Ziploc bag, mix lemon juice, sugar, black pepper, 1 tablespoon of peanut oil, cornstarch, Chinese powder, and salt. Add in the prawns and massage gently to coat well. Let sit for 20 minutes. Heat the remaining peanut oil in a pan over medium heat and sauté garlic, scallions, and red chili pepper for 3 minutes. 2. Preheat the air fryer to 390°F (199°C). Place the marinated prawns in a baking dish and cover with the sautéed vegetables. Air fry for 10 to 12 minutes, shaking once halfway through, until nice and crispy. Serve warm.

Bacon-Wrapped Prawns

Prep time: 5 minutes | Cook time: 9 to 12 minutes | Serves 4

8 bacon slices
8 jumbo prawns, peeled and deveined

1. Preheat the air fryer to 400°F (204°C). Wrap each prawn from head to tail in each bacon slice. Make sure to overlap to keep the bacon in place. Secure the ends with toothpicks. Arrange the bacon-wrapped prawns in the greased frying basket and air fry for 9 to 12 minutes, turning once. Serve hot.

Sesame Prawns with Firecracker Sauce

Prep time: 15 minutes | Cook time: 10 to 12 minutes | Serves 4

1 pound (454 g) tiger prawns, peeled	¾ cup seasoned bread crumbs
	Firecracker Sauce:
Salt and black pepper to taste	⅓ cup sour cream
2 eggs	2 tablespoons buffalo sauce
½ cup flour	¼ cup spicy ketchup
¼ cup sesame seeds	1 green onion, chopped

1. Preheat the air fryer to 390°F (199°C). In a bowl, beat the eggs with a pinch of salt. In another bowl, mix the bread crumbs with sesame seeds. In a third bowl, mix flour with salt and pepper. Dip the prawns in the flour, then in the eggs, and finally in the crumbs. Spray with cooking spray. 2. Air fry for 10 to 12 minutes, flipping once. Meanwhile, in a bowl mix all sauce ingredients, except for the green onion. Serve the prawns with firecracker sauce and scatter with freshly chopped green onions.

Ale Beer Prawns with Tartare Sauce

Prep time: 15 minutes | Cook time: 10 to 12 minutes | Serves 4

1 pound (454 g) prawns, peeled and deveined	chopped
	2 tablespoons fresh dill, chopped
1 cup plain flour	
1 cup ale beer	1 pickled cucumber, finely chopped
Salt and black pepper to taste	
Tartare Sauce:	2 teaspoons lemon juice
½ cup mayonnaise	½ teaspoon Worcestershire sauce
2 tablespoons capers, roughly	

1. Preheat the air fryer to 380°F (193°C). In a bowl, mix all sauce ingredients and keep in the fridge. Mix flour, ale beer, salt, and pepper in a large bowl. Dip in the prawns and place them in the greased frying basket. Air fry for 10 to 12 minutes, turning them once halfway through cooking. Serve with the tartare sauce.

Orange and Coconut Shrimp

Prep time: 15 minutes | Cook time: 12 to 14 minutes | Serves 2

8 large shrimp, peeled and deveined
½ cup bread crumbs
8 ounces (227 g) coconut milk
½ cup coconut, shredded
Salt to taste
½ cup orange jam
1 teaspoon mustard
1 tablespoon honey
½ teaspoon cayenne pepper
¼ teaspoon hot sauce

1. Combine bread crumbs, cayenne pepper, shredded coconut, and salt in a bowl. Dip the shrimp in the coconut milk, and then in the coconut crumbs. Arrange them in the greased frying basket and air fry for 12 to 14 minutes at 350ºF (177ºC). Whisk jam, honey, hot sauce, and mustard in a bowl. Serve with the shrimp.

Spicy Shrimp with Coconut-Avocado Dip

Prep time: 15 minutes | Cook time: 8 to 10 minutes | Serves 4

1¼ pounds (567 g) tiger shrimp, peeled and deveined
2 garlic cloves, minced
¼ teaspoon red chili flakes
1 lime, juiced and zested
Salt to taste
1 tablespoon fresh cilantro, chopped
1 large avocado, pitted
¼ cup coconut cream
2 tablespoons olive oil

1. Blend avocado, lime juice, coconut cream, cilantro, olive oil, and salt in a food processor until smooth. Transfer to a bowl, cover, and keep in the fridge until ready to use. 2. Preheat the air fryer to 390ºF (199ºC). In a bowl, place garlic, chili flakes, lime zest, and salt and add in the shrimp; toss to coat. Place them in the greased frying basket and air fry for 8 to 10 minutes, turning them once halfway through cooking, until entirely pink. Serve with the chilled avocado dip.

Asian Shrimp Medley

Prep time: 15 minutes | Cook time: 16 to 19 minutes | Serves 4

1 pound (454 g) shrimp, peeled and deveined
2 whole onions, chopped
3 tablespoons butter
1 tablespoon sugar
2 tablespoons soy sauce
2 cloves garlic, chopped
2 teaspoons lime juice
1 teaspoon ginger paste

1. Melt butter in a frying pan over medium heat and stir-fry the onions for 3 minutes until translucent. Mix in the lime juice, soy sauce, ginger paste, garlic, and sugar and stir for 1 to 2 minutes. Let cool and then pour the mixture over the shrimp. Cover and let marinate for 30 minutes in the fridge. 2. Preheat the air fryer to 380ºF (193ºC). Transfer the shrimp along with the marinade to a baking dish and place the dish inside the frying basket. Air fry for 12 to 14 minutes, turning once halfway through. Serve hot.

Spicy Shrimp Skewers

Prep time: 15 minutes | Cook time: 10 to 12 minutes | Serves 4

20 small-sized shrimp, peeled and deveined
2 tablespoons olive oil
½ teaspoon garlic powder
1 teaspoon mango powder (or tamarind)
2 tablespoons fresh lime juice
Salt and black pepper to taste
2 tablespoons fresh cilantro, chopped
1 garlic clove, minced
1 green onion, finely sliced
1 tablespoon red chili flakes, crushed
2 tablespoons white wine vinegar

1. In a bowl, mix garlic powder, mango powder, lime juice, salt, and pepper. Add the shrimp and toss to coat. Cover and marinate for 20 minutes. Meanwhile, soak wooden skewers in water for 15 minutes. In a small dish, mix cilantro, minced garlic, green onion, chili flakes, olive oil, and vinegar; set aside. 2. Preheat the air fryer to 390ºF (199ºC). Thread the marinated shrimp onto the skewers and place in the greased frying. Air fry for 10 to 12 minutes, turn once, until golden. Serve the skewers with the cilantro sauce.

Rosemary Cashew Shrimp

Prep time: 10 minutes | Cook time: 8 to 12 minutes | Serves 4

3 ounces (85 g) cashews, chopped
1 tablespoon fresh rosemary, chopped
1 pound (454 g) shrimp
1 garlic clove, minced
1 tablespoon bread crumbs
1 egg, beaten
1 tablespoon olive oil
Salt and black pepper to taste

1. Preheat the air fryer to 390ºF (199ºC). Whisk oil with garlic, salt, and pepper and brush the shrimp with the mixture. Mix rosemary, cashews, and bread crumbs in a bowl. Dip the shrimp in the egg and coat in the crumbs. Place in the greased frying basket and air fry for 4 to 6 minutes. Turn the shrimp and fry for 4 to 6 more minutes or until golden and crispy. Cover with a foil and let sit for a few minutes before serving.

Buttered Lobster with Herbs

Prep time: 10 minutes | Cook time: 10 minutes | Serves 4

4 ounces (113 g) lobster tails, halved
1 garlic clove, minced
2 tablespoons butter, melted
Salt and black pepper to taste
½ tablespoon lemon juice
1 tablespoon fresh parsley, chopped
1 tablespoon fresh dill, chopped
1 tablespoon fresh thyme, chopped

1. Whisk the garlic, butter, lemon juice, salt, and pepper in a bowl until well mixed. Clean the skin of the lobster and cover it with the mixture. Preheat the air fryer to 380ºF (193ºC). Place the lobster in the greased frying basket and air fry for 10 minutes, turning once. Serve sprinkled with parsley, thyme, and dill.

Mediterranean Squid Rings with Couscous

Prep time: 10 minutes | Cook time: 13 to 15 minutes | Serves 4

1 cup couscous
1 pound (454 g) squid rings
2 large eggs
½ cup all-purpose flour
½ cup semolina
1 teaspoon ground coriander seeds
1 teaspoon cayenne pepper
Salt and black pepper to taste

1. Place the couscous in a large bowl and cover with boiling water (about 1½ cups). Season with salt and pepper and stir. Cover and set aside for 5 to 7 minutes until the water is absorbed. 2. Preheat the air fryer to 390ºF (199ºC). 3. Beat the eggs in one bowl. In another bowl, combine the flour, semolina, ground coriander, cayenne pepper, salt, and black pepper. Dip the squid rings in the eggs first, then in the flour mixture, and place them in the greased frying basket. Air fry for 13 to 15 minutes, until golden brown, flipping once. Transfer the couscous to a large platter and serve the squid rings on top.

Greek Mussels with Hazelnuts

Prep time: 10 minutes | Cook time: 15 to 17 minutes | Serves 4

4 pounds (1.8 kg) black mussels
4 tablespoons olive oil
1 cup white wine
Salt and black pepper to taste
1 teaspoon Greek seasoning
2 tablespoons white wine vinegar
5 garlic cloves
4 bread slices
½ cup hazelnuts

1. Add the olive oil, garlic, Greek seasoning, vinegar, salt, black pepper, hazelnuts and bread slices to a food processor and process until you obtain a creamy texture. In a skillet over medium heat, pour the wine and mussels. Bring to a boil, then lower the heat and simmer until the mussels have opened up, about 5 minutes. Then, drain and remove from the shells. Discard any unopened mussels. 2. Add them to the previously prepared hazelnut mixture and toss to coat. Preheat the fryer to 350ºF (177ºC). Place the mussels in a greased baking dish and bake in the air fryer for 10 to 12 minutes, shaking once or twice.

Old Bay Shrimp

Prep time: 10 minutes | Cook time: 8 to 10 minutes | Serves 2

1 pound (454 g) jumbo shrimp, deveined
Salt to taste
¼ teaspoon old bay seasoning
⅓ teaspoon smoked paprika
¼ teaspoon cayenne pepper
2 tablespoons olive oil

1. Preheat the air fryer to 390ºF (199ºC). In a bowl, add the shrimp, paprika, olive oil, salt, old bay seasoning, and cayenne pepper; mix well. Place the shrimp in the fryer and air fry for 8 to 10 minutes, shaking once.

Cajun Lemon Shrimp

Prep time: 10 minutes | Cook time: 8 to 10 minutes | Serves 4

1 pound (454 g) shrimp, peeled and deveined
2 eggs
1 cup flour
1 cup bread crumbs
2 tablespoons Cajun seasoning
Salt and black pepper to taste
1 lemon, cut into wedges

1. Preheat the air fryer to 390ºF (199ºC). Spray the basket with cooking oil. Beat the eggs in a bowl and season to taste. In a separate bowl, mix the crumbs and Cajun seasoning. In a third bowl, pour the flour. Dip the shrimp in flour, then in the eggs, and finally in the crumbs. Air fry the shrimp in the greased frying basket for 5 minutes. Flip and cook for 3 to 5 more minutes until crispy. Serve with lemon wedges.

Buttered Crab Legs

Prep time: 5 minutes | Cook time: 10 to 12 minutes | Serves 4

2 pounds (907 g) crab legs
2 tablespoons butter, melted
1 tablespoon fresh parsley

1. Preheat the air fryer to 380ºF (193ºC). Place the legs in the greased frying basket and air fry for 10 to 12 minutes, shaking once or twice. Pour the butter over crab legs, sprinkle with parsley, and serve. Work in batches.

Breaded Scallops

Prep time: 5 minutes | Cook time: 6 to 8 minutes | Serves 4

1 pound (454 g) fresh scallops
3 tablespoons flour
1 egg, lightly beaten
1 cup seasoned bread crumbs
2 tablespoons olive oil
½ teaspoon fresh parsley, chopped

1. Preheat the air fryer to 360ºF (182ºC). Coat the scallops in flour. Dip them in the egg, then into the crumbs. Spray with olive oil and air fry for 6 to 8 minutes, flipping once until golden. Serve topped with parsley.

Calamari Rings with Olives

Prep time: 10 minutes | Cook time: 15 minutes | Serves 4

1 pound (454 g) calamari rings
2 tablespoons fresh cilantro, chopped
1 chili pepper, finely chopped
2 tablespoons olive oil
1 cup pimiento-stuffed green olives
Salt and black pepper to taste

1. Preheat the air fryer to 400ºF (204ºC). In a bowl, mix the chili pepper, salt, black pepper, olive oil, and fresh cilantro. Add in the calamari rings and toss to coat. Marinate for 10 minutes. Then place the calamari in the air fryer and air fry for 15 minutes, flipping every 5 minutes. Serve with pimiento-stuffed olives.

Chapter 1 Vegetables and Sides

Cod Fillets with Ginger-Cilantro Sauce

Prep time: 10 minutes | Cook time: 14 to 16 minutes | Serves 4

1 pound (454 g) cod fillets
2 tablespoons fresh cilantro, chopped
Salt to taste
4 green onions, chopped
1 cup water
1 tablespoon ginger paste
5 tablespoons light soy sauce
2 tablespoons olive oil
1 teaspoon soy sauce
2 cubes rock sugar

1. Preheat the air fryer to 360ºF (182ºC). Season the fillets with salt and drizzle with olive oil. Place in the frying basket and air fry for 14 to 16 minutes, turning once. Meanwhile, heat the remaining oil in a pan over medium heat. Stir-fry the remaining ingredients for 5 minutes. Pour the sauce over the fish to serve.

Lemon White Fish Nuggets

Prep time: 10 minutes | Cook time: 14 to 16 minutes | Serves 4

1 pound (454 g) white fish fillets
1 lemon, juiced
Salt and black pepper to taste
1 teaspoon dried dill
4 tablespoons mayonnaise
2 eggs, beaten
1 tablespoon garlic powder
1 cup bread crumbs
1 teaspoon paprika

1. Preheat the air fryer to 400ºF (204ºC). Season the fish with salt and black pepper. In a bowl, mix the beaten eggs, lemon juice, and mayonnaise. In a separate bowl, mix the crumbs, paprika, dill, and garlic. 2. Dredge the fillets in the eggs and then in the crumbs. Place them in the greased frying basket and air fry for 14 to 16 minutes, flipping once halfway through cooking. Serve with tomato chutney if desired.

Bread-Crusted Seafood Mix

Prep time: 10 minutes | Cook time: 10 to 12 minutes | Serves 4

1 pound (454 g) fresh scallops, mussels, fish fillets, prawns, shrimp
2 eggs
Salt and black pepper to taste
1 cup bread crumbs mixed with the zest of 1 lemon

1. Beat the eggs with salt and black pepper in a bowl. Dip in each piece of seafood and then coat in the crumbs. Place them in the greased frying basket and air fry for 10 to 12 minutes at 400ºF (204ºC), turning once.

Crispy Cod Fillets

Prep time: 10 minutes | Cook time: 10 minutes | Serves 4

1 cup bread crumbs
2 tablespoons olive oil
2 eggs, beaten
4 cod fillets
A pinch of salt
1 cup flour

1. Preheat the air fryer to 390ºF (199ºC). Mix the crumbs, olive oil, and salt in a bowl. In another bowl, beat the eggs. Put the flour into a third bowl. Toss the cod fillets in the flour, then in the eggs, and finally in the crumbs mixture. Place them in the greased frying basket and air fry for 10 minutes. At the 6-minute mark, quickly turn the fillets. Remove to a plate and serve with dill-yogurt sauce if desired.

Cod Finger Pesto Sandwich

Prep time: 10 minutes | Cook time: 13 to 15 minutes | Serves 4

4 cod fillets
4 bread rolls
1 cup bread crumbs
4 tablespoons pesto sauce
4 lettuce leaves
Salt and black pepper to taste

1. Preheat the air fryer to 370ºF (188ºC). Season the fillets with salt and black pepper and coat them in bread crumbs. Arrange them on the greased frying basket and bake for 13 to 15 minutes, flipping once. 2. Cut the bread rolls in half. Divide lettuce leaves between the bottom halves and place the fillets over. Spread the pesto sauce on top of the fillets and cover with the remaining halves. Serve warm.

Cod Cornflake Nuggets with Avocado Dip

Prep time: 15 minutes | Cook time: 14 to 16 minutes | Serves 4

1¼ pounds (567 g) cod fillets, cut into 4 chunks each
½ cup flour
2 eggs, beaten
1 cup cornflakes
1 tablespoon olive oil
Salt and black pepper to taste
1 avocado, chopped
1 lime, juiced

1. Mash the avocado with a fork in a small bowl. Stir in the lime juice and salt and set aside. Pour the olive oil and cornflakes in a food processor and process until crumbed. 2. Season the fish with salt and pepper. Preheat the air fryer to 350ºF (177ºC). Place flour, eggs and cornflakes in 3 separate bowls. Coat the fish in flour, dip in the eggs, then coat in the cornflakes. Air fry in the greased frying basket for 14 to 16 minutes, shaking once or twice, until golden. Serve with the avocado dip.

Soy Sauce-Glazed Cod

Prep time: 5 minutes | Cook time: 9 to 14 minutes | Serves 2

2 cod fillets
1 tablespoon olive oil
Salt and black pepper to taste
1 tablespoon soy sauce
1 tablespoon sesame oil
¼ teaspoon ginger powder
¼ teaspoon honey

1. Preheat the air fryer to 370ºF (188ºC). In a bowl, combine olive oil, salt, and black pepper. Massage the fillets with the mixture. Place them on the greased frying basket and bake in the fryer for 6 minutes. 2. Meanwhile, combine the soy sauce, ginger powder, honey, and sesame oil in a small bowl. Flip the fillets and brush them with the glaze. Bake for 3 to 5 more minutes until golden and crispy. Serve warm.

Gourmet Black Cod with Fennel and Pecans

Prep time: 10 minutes | Cook time: 10 to 12 minutes | Serves 2

2 black cod fillets
Salt and black pepper to taste
1 small fennel bulb, sliced
½ cup pecans
2 teaspoons white balsamic vinegar
2 tablespoons olive oil

1. Preheat the air fryer to 400°F (204°C). Season the fillets with salt and pepper and drizzle with some olive oil. Place in them the frying basket and air fry for 10 to 12 minutes, flipping once, or until golden brown. 2. Meanwhile, warm the remaining olive oil in a skillet over medium heat. Stir-fry the fennel for 5 minutes. Add in the pecans and cook for 3 to 4 minutes until toasted. Drizzle with the balsamic vinegar and season with salt and pepper. Stir well and remove from heat. Pour the mixture over the black cod and serve.

Pistachio-Crusted Salmon Fillets

Prep time: 15 minutes | Cook time: 12 to 15 minutes | Serves 2

2 salmon fillets
1 teaspoon yellow mustard
4 tablespoons pistachios, chopped
Salt and black pepper to taste
1 teaspoon garlic powder
2 teaspoons lemon juice
2 tablespoons Parmesan cheese, grated
1 teaspoon olive oil

1. Preheat the air fryer to 350°F (177°C). Whisk together the mustard, olive oil, lemon juice, salt, black pepper, and garlic powder in a bowl. Rub the mustard mixture evenly onto the salmon fillets. 2. Lay the fillets on the greased frying basket, skin side down and spread the pistachios and Parmesan cheese all over; press down gently to make a crust. Bake the salmon for 12 to 15 minutes until golden.

Ale-Battered Fish with Tartar Sauce

Prep time: 10 minutes | Cook time: 10 to 12 minutes | Serves 4

4 lemon wedges
2 eggs
1 cup ale beer
1 cup flour
Salt and black pepper to taste
4 white fish fillets
½ cup light mayonnaise
½ cup Greek yogurt
2 dill pickles, chopped
1 tablespoon capers
1 tablespoon fresh dill, roughly chopped
Lemon wedges to serve

1. Preheat the air fryer to 390°F (199°C). Beat the eggs in a bowl along with the ale beer, salt, and pepper. Dredge the fillets in the flour and shake off the excess. Dip them into the egg mixture and then in the flour again. Spray with cooking spray and place in the frying basket. Air fry for 10 to 12 minutes, turning once. 2. In a bowl, mix the mayonnaise, Greek yogurt, capers, salt, and dill pickles. Sprinkle the fish with a little bit of dill and serve with the sauce and some freshly cut lemon wedges on the side.

Korean Kimchi-Spiced Salmon

Prep time: 10 minutes | Cook time: 10 to 12 minutes | Serves 4

2 tablespoons soy sauce
2 tablespoons sesame oil
2 tablespoons mirin
1 tablespoon ginger puree
1 teaspoon kimchi spice
1 teaspoon sriracha sauce
2 pounds (907 g) salmon fillets
1 lime, cut into wedges

1. Preheat the air fryer to 350°F (177°C). Grease the frying basket with cooking spray. In a bowl, mix together soy sauce, mirin, ginger puree, kimchi spice, and sriracha sauce. Add the salmon and toss to coat. 2. Place the fillets in the frying basket and drizzle with sesame oil. Bake for 10 to 12 minutes, flipping once halfway through. Garnish with lime wedges and serve.

Tandoori-Style Crispy Salmon

Prep time: 15 minutes | Cook time: 12 to 15 minutes | Serves 2

2 salmon fillets
1 teaspoon ginger powder
1 garlic clove, minced
½ green bell pepper, sliced
1 teaspoon sweet paprika, minced
1 teaspoon honey
1 teaspoon garam masala
1 tablespoon fresh cilantro, chopped
¼ cup yogurt
Juice and zest from 1 lime

1. In a bowl, mix all the ingredients, except for the fish. Coat the fillets in the mixture and let sit for 15 minutes. Preheat the air fryer to 400°F (204°C). Place the fillets in the greased frying basket and bake for 12 to 15 minutes, flipping once, or until golden and crispy. Serve on a bed of basmati rice if desired.

Delicious Seafood Casserole

Prep time: 15 minutes | Cook time: 38 to 45 minutes | Serves 4

1 cup seafood mix
1 pound (454 g) russet potatoes, peeled and quartered
1 carrot, grated
½ fennel bulb, sliced
2 tablespoons fresh parsley, chopped
10 ounces (283 g) baby spinach
1 small tomato, diced
½ celery stick, grated
2 tablespoons butter
4 tablespoons milk
½ cup Cheddar cheese, grated
1 small red chili, minced
Salt and black pepper to taste

1. Cover the potatoes with salted water in a pot and cook over medium heat for 18 to 20 minutes or until tender. Drain and mash them along with butter, milk, salt, and pepper. Mix until smooth and set aside. 2. In a bowl, mix celery, carrot, red chili, fennel, parsley, seafood mix, tomato, spinach, salt, and pepper. 3. Preheat the air fryer to 330°F (166°C). In a casserole baking dish, spread the seafood mixture. Top with the potato mash and level. Sprinkle with Cheddar cheese and place the dish in the air fryer. Bake for 20 to 25 minutes or until golden and bubbling at the edges. Let cool for 10 minutes, slice, and serve.

Easy Salmon with Greek Sauce

Prep time: 10 minutes | Cook time: 10 to 12 minutes | Serves 4

1 pound (454 g) salmon fillets
Salt and black pepper to taste
2 teaspoons olive oil
2 tablespoons fresh dill, chopped
1 cup sour cream
1 cup Greek yogurt

1. In a bowl, mix the sour cream, Greek yogurt, dill, and salt. Keep in the fridge until ready to use. Preheat the air fryer to 340ºF (171ºC). Drizzle the fillets with olive oil and sprinkle with salt and pepper. Place the fish in the frying basket and bake for 10 to 12 minutes, flipping once. Serve drizzled with the Greek sauce.

Salmon Cakes

Prep time: 15 minutes | Cook time: 12 to 14 minutes | Serves 4

12 ounces (340 g) cooked salmon
2 potatoes, boiled and mashed
½ cup flour
2 tablespoons capers, chopped
2 tablespoons fresh parsley, chopped
1 tablespoon olive oil
Zest of 1 lemon

1. Place the mashed potatoes in a bowl and flake the salmon over. Stir in capers, parsley, and lemon zest. Mix well and shape into 4 cakes. Roll them up in flour, shake off, and refrigerate for 1 hour. 2. Preheat the air fryer to 350ºF (177ºC). Remove the cakes and brush them with olive oil. Bake in the greased frying basket for 12 to 14 minutes, flipping once halfway through cooking. Serve warm.

Salmon and Spring Onion Balls

Prep time: 10 minutes | Cook time: 8 to 10 minutes | Serves 2

1 cup tinned salmon
¼ celery stalk, chopped
1 spring onion, sliced
4 tablespoons wheat germ
2 tablespoons olive oil
1 large egg
1 tablespoon fresh dill, chopped
½ teaspoon garlic powder

1. Preheat the air fryer to 390ºF (199ºC). In a large bowl, mix tinned salmon, egg, celery, onion, dill, and garlic. Shape the mixture into balls and roll them up in wheat germ. Carefully flatten and place them in the greased frying basket. Air fry for 8 to 10 minutes, flipping once halfway through, or until golden.

Smoked Salmon and Cheddar Taquitos

Prep time: 10 minutes | Cook time: 10 to 12 minutes | Serves 4

1 pound (454 g) smoked salmon, chopped
Salt to taste
1 tablespoon taco seasoning
1 cup Cheddar cheese, shredded
1 lime, juiced
½ cup fresh cilantro, chopped
8 corn tortillas
1 cup hot salsa

1. Preheat the air fryer to 390ºF (199ºC). 2. In a bowl, mix the salmon, taco seasoning, lime juice, Cheddar cheese, salt, and cilantro. Divide the mixture between the tortillas. Wrap the tortillas around the filling and place them in the greased frying basket. Bake for 10 to 12 minutes, turning once halfway through cooking. Serve with hot salsa.

Salmon Fillets with Broccoli

Prep time: 10 minutes | Cook time: 14 minutes | Serves 2

2 salmon fillets
2 teaspoons olive oil
Juice of 1 lime
1 teaspoon red chili flakes
(optional)
Salt and black pepper to taste
5 ounces (142 g) broccoli florets, steamed

1. In a bowl, add 1 tablespoon of olive oil, lime juice, salt, and pepper and rub the mixture onto the fillets. Transfer to them to the frying basket. Drizzle the florets with the remaining olive oil and arrange them around the salmon. Bake in the preheated at 340ºF (171ºC) air fryer for 14 minutes or until the salmon is fork-tender and crispy on top. Sprinkle the fillets with red chili flakes (optional) and serve with broccoli.

Wild Salmon with Creamy Parsley Sauce

Prep time: 10 minutes | Cook time: 14 to 16 minutes | Serves 4

4 Alaskan wild salmon fillets
2 teaspoons olive oil
Salt and black pepper to taste
½ cup heavy cream
½ cup milk
2 tablespoons fresh parsley, chopped

1. Preheat the air fryer to 380ºF (193ºC). Drizzle the fillets with olive oil and season with salt and black pepper. Place in them in the frying basket and bake for 14 to 16 minutes, turning once, until tender and crispy. In a bowl, mix the milk, parsley, salt, and heavy cream. Serve the salmon with the sauce and enjoy!

Sweet Caribbean Salmon Fillets

Prep time: 10 minutes | Cook time: 11 to 13 minutes | Serves 4

4 salmon fillets
½ teaspoon brown sugar
1 tablespoon Cajun seasoning
1 lemon, zested and juiced
1 tablespoon fresh parsley, chopped
2 tablespoons mango salsa

1. Preheat the air fryer to 350ºF (177ºC). In a bowl, mix the sugar, Cajun seasoning, lemon juice and zest, and coat the salmon in the mixture. Line the frying basket with parchment paper and grease it with oil. Place in the fish and bake for 11 to 13 minutes, turning once. Top with parsley and mango salsa to serve.

Classic Mediterranean Salmon

Prep time: 10 minutes | Cook time: 10 to 12 minutes | Serves 2

2 salmon fillets
Salt and black pepper to taste
1 lemon, cut into wedges
8 asparagus spears, trimmed

1. Preheat the air fryer to 350ºF (177ºC). Spritz the salmon with cooking spray. Season the fillets and asparagus with salt and pepper. Arrange the asparagus evenly in a single layer in the greased frying basket and top with the fillets. Air fry for 10 to 12 minutes at 350ºF (177ºC), turning the fish once. Serve with lemon wedges.

French Trout Meunière

Prep time: 10 minutes | Cook time: 13 to 16 minutes | Serves 4

4 trout pieces
½ cup flour
Salt to taste
2 tablespoons butter
1 lemon, juiced
2 tablespoons chervil (French parsley), chopped

1. Preheat the air fryer to 380ºF (193ºC). Season the trout with salt and dredge in the flour. Spritz with cooking oil and air fry for 12 to 14 minutes, flipping once, until crispy. Remove and tent with foil to keep warm. 2. Melt the butter in a skillet over medium heat. Stir for 1 to 2 minutes until the butter becomes golden brown. Turn off the heat and stir in chervil and lemon juice. Pour the sauce over the fish and serve.

Easy Creole Trout

Prep time: 5 minutes | Cook time: 10 to 12 minutes | Serves 4

4 skin-on trout fillets
2 teaspoons creole seasoning
2 tablespoons fresh dill,
chopped
1 lemon, sliced

1. Preheat the air fryer to 350ºF (177ºC). Season the trout with creole seasoning on both sides and spray with cooking spray. Place in the frying basket and bake for 10 to 12 minutes, flipping once. Serve sprinkled with dill and garnished with lemon slices.

Smoked Trout Frittata

Prep time: 10 minutes | Cook time: 17 minutes | Serves 4

2 tablespoons olive oil
1 onion, sliced
1 egg, beaten
6 tablespoons crème fraiche
½ tablespoon horseradish
sauce
1 cup smoked trout, diced
2 tablespoons fresh dill, chopped

1. Preheat the fryer to 350ºF (177ºC). Heat olive oil in a pan over medium heat and sauté the onion, 3 minutes. In a bowl, mix the egg with crème fraiche and horseradish sauce. Add the onion, dill, and trout; mix well. Pour the mixture into a greased baking dish and bake inside the fryer for 14 minutes or until golden.

Baked Trout en Papillote with Herbs

Prep time: 10 minutes | Cook time: 15 minutes | Serves 2

2 whole trouts, scaled and cleaned
¼ bulb fennel, sliced
½ brown onion, sliced
1 tablespoon fresh parsley, chopped
1 tablespoon fresh dill, chopped
1 tablespoon olive oil
1 lemon, sliced
Garlic salt and black pepper to taste

1. In a bowl, whisk the olive oil, brown onion, parsley, dill, fennel, garlic salt, and pepper. 2. Preheat the air fryer to 350ºF (177ºC). Open the cavity of the fish and fill with the spicy mixture. Wrap the fish completely in parchment paper and then in foil. Place the fish in the frying basket and bake for 15 minutes. Remove the foil and paper. Top with lemon slices and serve warm.

Lovely "Blackened" Catfish

Prep time: 10 minutes | Cook time: 14 to 16 minutes | Serves 2

2 catfish fillets
2 teaspoons blackening seasoning
Juice of 1 lime
2 tablespoons butter, melted
1 garlic clove, minced
2 tablespoons fresh cilantro, chopped

1. Preheat the air fryer to 360ºF (182ºC). In a bowl, mix garlic, lime juice, cilantro, and butter. Divide the sauce into two parts, rub 1 part of the sauce onto the fillets. Sprinkle with the seasoning. Place the fillets in the greased frying basket and bake for 14 to 16 minutes, flipping once. Serve with the remaining sauce.

Golden Batter Fried Catfish Fillets

Prep time: 10 minutes | Cook time: 10 to 12 minutes | Serves 2

4 catfish fillets, cut into strips
½ cup polenta
½ cup flour
¼ teaspoon cayenne pepper
1 tablespoon fresh parsley, chopped
Salt and black pepper to taste
1 teaspoon onion powder
1 (7-ounce / 198-g) bottle club soda
1 lemon, sliced

1. Preheat the fryer to 400ºF (204ºC). Sift the flour into a large bowl. Add in the onion powder, salt, black pepper, and cayenne pepper and stir to combine. Pour in the soda and whisk until a smooth batter is formed. 2. Lightly spray the fish with cooking spray. Dip the fish strips into the batter, then into the polenta. Put the fillets in the lightly greased frying basket and air fry for 6 to 7 minutes. Flip or shake and cook further for 4 to 5 minutes or until brown and crispy. Garnish with parsley and lemon slices and serve.

110 | Chapter 1 Vegetables and Sides

Rosemary Catfish

Prep time: 5 minutes | Cook time: 8 to 12 minutes | Serves 4

4 catfish fillets
¼ cup seasoned fish fry
1 tablespoon olive oil
1 tablespoon fresh rosemary, chopped

1. Preheat the air fryer to 400ºF (204ºC). Add the seasoned fish fry and the fillets to a large Ziploc bag; massage to coat. Place the fillets in the greased frying basket and air fry for 6 to 8 minutes. Flip the fillets and cook for 2 to 4 more minutes or until golden and crispy. Top with freshly chopped rosemary and serve.

Jamaican Fish Fillets

Prep time: 10 minutes | Cook time: 13 minutes | Serves 4

4 hoki fillets
1 tablespoon ground Jamaican allspice
1 teaspoon paprika
Salt and garlic powder to taste
½ red onion, sliced
2 tomatoes, chopped
½ cup canned corn, drained
½ lemon, juiced

1. In a bowl, mix the red onion, tomatoes, corn, salt, and lemon juice; toss to coat and set aside. 2. Preheat the air fryer to 390ºF (199ºC). In a bowl, mix paprika, garlic powder, and Jamaican seasoning. Rub the hoki fillets with the spices mixture. Spritz with cooking spray. Transfer to the frying basket and air fry for 8 minutes, turn the fillets, and cook further for 5 minutes or until crispy. Serve with the corn salsa.

Parmesan Tilapia Fillets

Prep time: 10 minutes | Cook time: 10 to 12 minutes | Serves 4

¾ cup Parmesan cheese, grated
2 tablespoons olive oil
2 teaspoons paprika
2 tablespoons fresh parsley, chopped
¼ teaspoon garlic powder
4 tilapia fillets

1. Preheat the air fryer to 350ºF (177ºC). Mix parsley, Parmesan cheese, garlic powder, and paprika in a shallow bowl. Coat fillets in the mixture and brush with olive oil. Place the fillets in the frying basket and air fry for 10 to 12 minutes, flipping once, until golden brown. Serve immediately.

Air-Fried Broiled Tilapia

Prep time: 5 minutes | Cook time: 10 to 12 minutes | Serves 4

1 pound (454 g) tilapia fillets
1 teaspoon old bay seasoning
2 tablespoons canola oil
2 tablespoons lemon pepper
Salt to taste
2 butter buds

1. Preheat the air fryer to 400ºF (204ºC). Drizzle the fillets with canola oil. In a bowl, mix salt, lemon pepper, butter buds, and old bay seasoning; spread onto the fish. Place the fillets in the frying basket and air fry for 10 to 12 minutes, turning once, until crispy. Serve with green salad.

Air Fried Tilapia Bites

Prep time: 10 minutes | Cook time: 11 minutes | Serves 4

1 pound (454 g) tilapia fillets, cut into chunks
½ cup cornflakes
1 cup flour
2 eggs, beaten
Salt to taste
Lemon wedges for serving

1. Preheat the fryer to 390ºF (199ºC). Pour the flour, eggs, and cornflakes each into 3 different bowls. Salt the fish and dip first in the flour, then in the eggs, and finally in the cornflakes. Put in the greased frying basket and air fry for 6 minutes. Shake or flip, and cook for 5 more minutes or until crispy. Serve with lemon.

Peppery and Lemony Haddock

Prep time: 10 minutes | Cook time: 14 to 16 minutes | Serves 4

4 haddock fillets
1 cup bread crumbs
2 tablespoons lemon juice
Salt and black pepper to taste
¼ cup potato flakes
2 eggs, beaten
¼ cup Parmesan cheese, grated
3 tablespoons flour

1. In a bowl, combine flour, salt, and pepper. In another bowl, mix bread crumbs, Parmesan, and potato flakes. Dip fillets in the flour first, then in the eggs, and coat them in the crumbs mixture. Place them in the greased frying basket and air fry for 14 to 16 minutes at 370ºF (188ºC), flipping once. Serve with lemon juice.

Savory Shrimp

Prep time: 5 minutes | Cook time: 8 to 10 minutes | Serves 4

1 pound (454 g) fresh large shrimp, peeled and deveined
1 tablespoon avocado oil
2 teaspoons minced garlic, divided
½ teaspoon red pepper flakes
Sea salt and freshly ground black pepper, to taste
2 tablespoons unsalted butter, melted
2 tablespoons chopped fresh parsley

1. Place the shrimp in a bowl and toss with the avocado oil, 1 teaspoon of minced garlic, and red pepper flakes. Season with salt and pepper. 2. Arrange the shrimp in a single layer in the frying basket. Air fry at 350ºF (177ºC) for 6 minutes. Flip the shrimp and cook for 2 to 4 minutes more, until the internal temperature reaches 120ºF (49ºC). 3. Meanwhile, melt the butter in a saucepan over medium heat and stir in the remaining garlic. 4. Toss the cooked shrimp with garlic butter in a bowl. Top with the parsley and serve warm.

Crumbly Haddock Patties

Prep time: 10 minutes | Cook time: 12 to 14 minutes | Serves 2

8 ounces (227 g) haddock, cooked and flaked
2 potatoes, cooked and mashed
2 tablespoons green olives, pitted and chopped
1 tablespoon fresh cilantro, chopped
1 teaspoon lemon zest
1 egg, beaten

1. Mix haddock, lemon zest, olives, cilantro, egg, and potatoes. Shape into patties and chill for 60 minutes. 2. Preheat the air fryer to 350°F (177°C). Place the patties in the greased frying basket and air fry for 12 to 14 minutes, flipping once, halfway through cooking until golden. Serve with green salad or steamed rice.

Barramundi Fillets in Lemon Sauce

Prep time: 10 minutes | Cook time: 21 to 23 minutes | Serves 4

4 barramundi fillets
1 lemon, juiced
Salt and black pepper to taste
2 tablespoons butter
½ cup white wine
8 black peppercorns
2 cloves garlic, minced
2 shallots, chopped

1. Preheat the air fryer to 390°F (199°C). Season the fillets with salt and black pepper. Place them in the greased frying basket. Air fry for 15 minutes, flipping once, until the edges are golden brown. Remove to a plate. 2. Melt the butter in a pan over low heat. Add in garlic and shallots and stir-fry for 3 minutes. Pour in the white wine, lemon juice, and peppercorns. Cook until the liquid is reduced by three quarters, about 3 to 5 minutes. Adjust the seasoning and strain the sauce. Drizzle the sauce over the fish and serve warm.

Garlic Shrimp

Prep time: 15 minutes | Cook time: 10 minutes | Serves 3

Shrimp:
Oil, for spraying
1 pound (454 g) medium raw shrimp, peeled and deveined
6 tablespoons unsalted butter, melted
1 cup panko bread crumbs
2 tablespoons granulated garlic
1 teaspoon salt
½ teaspoon freshly ground black pepper
Garlic Butter Sauce:
½ cup unsalted butter
2 teaspoons granulated garlic
¾ teaspoon salt (omit if using salted butter)

Make the Shrimp: 1. Preheat the air fryer to 400°F (204°C). Line the frying basket with parchment and spray lightly with oil. 2. Toss the shrimp with melted butter until evenly coated. 3. In a medium bowl, mix together the bread crumbs, garlic, salt, and black pepper. 4. Toss the shrimp to the panko mixture until evenly coated. Shake off any excess coating. Spray lightly with oil. 5. Air fry for 8 to 10 minutes, flipping and spraying with oil halfway through, until golden brown and crispy. **Make the Garlic Butter Sauce:** 6. Microwave the sauce ingredients in a microwave-safe bowl on 50% power for 30 to 60 seconds, stirring every 15 seconds, until completely melted. 7. Serve the shrimp with the garlic butter sauce.

Hot Sardine Cakes

Prep time: 10 minutes | Cook time: 8 to 10 minutes | Serves 4

2 (4-ounce / 113-g) tins sardines, chopped
2 eggs, beaten
½ cup bread crumbs
⅓ cup green onions, finely chopped
2 tablespoons fresh parsley, chopped
1 tablespoon mayonnaise
1 teaspoon sweet chili sauce
½ teaspoon paprika
Salt and black pepper to taste
2 tablespoons olive oil

1. In a bowl, add sardines, eggs, bread crumbs, green onions, parsley, mayonnaise, sweet chili sauce, paprika, salt, and black pepper. Mix well with hands. Shape into 8 cakes and brush them lightly with olive oil. Air fry them for 8 to 10 minutes at 390°F (199°C), flipping once halfway through cooking. Serve warm.

Air Fried Tuna Sandwich

Prep time: 10 minutes | Cook time: 7 to 10 minutes | Serves 2

4 white bread slices
1 (5-ounce / 142-g) can tuna, drained
½ onion, finely chopped
2 tablespoons mayonnaise
1 cup Mozzarella cheese, shredded
1 tablespoon olive oil

1. In a small bowl, mix tuna, onion, and mayonnaise. Spoon the mixture over two bread slices, top with Mozzarella cheese, and cover with the remaining bread slices. Brush with olive oil and arrange the sandwiches in the frying basket. Bake at 360°F (182°C) for 7 to 10 minutes, flipping once halfway through. Serve.

Smoked Fish Quiche

Prep time: 15 minutes | Cook time: 22 to 25 minutes | Serves 4

1 (16-ounce / 454-g) pie crust
4 eggs, lightly beaten
4 tablespoons heavy cream
¼ cup green onions, finely chopped
2 tablespoons fresh parsley, chopped
1 teaspoon baking powder
Salt and black pepper to taste
1 pound (454 g) smoked salmon, chopped
1 cup Mozzarella cheese, shredded

1. In a bowl, whisk eggs, heavy cream, green onions, parsley, baking powder, salt, and pepper. Stir in the salmon and Mozzarella cheese. Roll out the pie crust and press it gently into a greased quiche pan that fits in your air fryer. Prick the pie all over with a fork. Pour in the salmon mixture and place the pan inside the fryer. Bake for 22 to 25 minutes at 360°F (182°C). Let cool slightly before slicing. Serve and enjoy!

Effortless Tuna Fritters

Prep time: 10 minutes | Cook time: 13 to 15 minutes | Serves 2

5 ounces (142 g) canned tuna
1 teaspoon lime juice
½ teaspoon paprika
¼ cup flour
½ cup milk
1 small onion, diced
2 eggs
1 teaspoon chili powder, optional
½ teaspoon salt

1. Place all ingredients in a bowl and mix well. Make two large patties out of the mixture. Refrigerate them for 30 minutes. Then, remove and air fry the patties in the greased frying basket for 13 to 15 minutes at 350ºF (177ºC), flipping once halfway through cooking. Serve warm.

Sesame Halibut Fillets

Prep time: 10 minutes | Cook time: 12 to 13 minutes | Serves 4

1 pound (454 g) halibut fillets
4 biscuits, crumbled
3 tablespoons flour
1 egg, beaten
Salt and black pepper to taste
¼ teaspoon dried rosemary
3 tablespoons olive oil
2 tablespoons sesame seeds

1. Preheat the air fryer to 390ºF (199ºC). 2. In a bowl, combine flour, black pepper, and salt. In another bowl, combine sesame seeds, crumbled biscuits, olive oil, and rosemary. Dip the fish fillets into the flour mixture first, then into the beaten egg. 3. Finally, coat them in the sesame/biscuit mixture. Arrange them on the greased frying basket and air fry for 8 minutes. Flip the fillets and cook for 4 to 5 more minutes or until golden. Serve immediately.

Italian-Style White Fish

Prep time: 10 minutes | Cook time: 8 to 10 minutes | Serves 4

2 tablespoons fresh basil, chopped
1 teaspoon garlic powder
2 tablespoons Romano cheese, grated
Salt and black pepper to taste
4 white fish fillets

1. Preheat the air fryer to 350ºF (177ºC). Season fillets with garlic, salt, and pepper. Place them in the greased frying basket and air fry for 8 to 10 minutes, flipping once. Serve topped with Romano cheese and basil.

Oaty Fishcakes

Prep time: 15 minutes | Cook time: 15 to 21 minutes | Serves 4

4 potatoes, cooked and mashed
2 salmon fillets, cubed
1 haddock fillet, cubed
1 teaspoon Dijon mustard
½ cup oats
2 tablespoons fresh dill, chopped
2 tablespoons olive oil
Salt and black pepper to taste

1. Preheat the air fryer to 400ºF (204ºC). Boil salmon and haddock cubes in a pot filled with salted water over medium heat, for 5 to 8 minutes. Drain, cool, and pat dry. Flake or shred the fish and transfer to a bowl. 2. Let cool slightly and mix in the mashed potatoes, mustard, oats, dill, salt, and black pepper. Shape into balls and flatten to make patties. Brush with olive oil and arrange them in the greased frying basket. Bake for 10 to 13 minutes, flipping once halfway through, until golden. Let cool slightly before serving.

Ponzu Marinated Tuna

Prep time: 10 minutes | Cook time: 14 to 16 minutes | Serves 4

4 tuna steaks
1 cup Japanese ponzu sauce
2 tablespoons sesame oil
1 tablespoon red pepper flakes
2 tablespoons ginger paste
¼ cup scallions, sliced
Salt and black pepper to taste

1. In a bowl, mix the ponzu sauce, sesame oil, red pepper flakes, ginger paste, salt, and black pepper. Add in the tuna and toss to coat. Cover and marinate for 60 minutes in the fridge. 2. Preheat the air fryer to 380ºF (193ºC). Remove tuna from the marinade and arrange the steaks on the greased frying basket. Air fry for 14 to 16 minutes, turning once. Top with scallions and serve with fresh salad.

Roasted Salmon Fillets

Prep time: 5 minutes | Cook time: 10 minutes | Serves 2

2 (8-ounce / 227 -g) skin-on salmon fillets, 1½ inches thick
1 teaspoon vegetable oil
Salt and pepper, to taste
Vegetable oil spray

1. Preheat the air fryer to 400ºF (204ºC). 2. Lightly spray the frying basket with vegetable oil spray. 3. Pat salmon dry with paper towels, rub with oil, and season with salt and pepper. Arrange fillets skin side down in the basket, spaced evenly apart. Air fry salmon until center is still translucent when checked with the tip of a paring knife and registers 125ºF (52ºC) (for medium-rare), 10 to 14 minutes, rotating halfway through. 4. Transfer the fillets to serving plates, leaving skin behind. Serve.

Bacon Halibut Steak

Prep time: 15 minutes | Cook time: 10 minutes | Serves 4

24 ounces (680 g) halibut steaks (6 ounces / 170 g each fillet)
1 teaspoon avocado oil
1 teaspoon ground black pepper
4 ounces bacon, sliced

1. Sprinkle the halibut steaks with avocado oil and ground black pepper. 2. Then wrap the fish in the bacon slices and put in the air fryer. 3. Roast at 390ºF (199ºC) for 5 minutes per side.

Peach Salsa and Beer Halibut Tacos

Prep time: 15 minutes | Cook time: 8 to 10 minutes | Serves 4

4 corn tortillas
1 pound (454 g) halibut fillets, sliced into strips
2 tablespoons olive oil
1½ cups flour
1 (12-ounce / 340-g) can beer
A pinch of salt
4 tablespoons peach salsa
4 teaspoons fresh cilantro, chopped
1 teaspoon baking powder

1. Preheat the fryer to 390ºF (199ºC). In a bowl, mix flour, baking powder, and salt. Pour in 1 to 2 ounces (28 to 57 g) of beer, enough to form a batter-like consistency. Save the rest of the beer to gulp with the tacos. Dip the fish strips into the beer batter. Arrange them in the greased frying basket and air fry them for 8 to 10 minutes, shaking or flipping once. Spread the peach salsa on the tortillas. Serve topped with the strips and cilantro.

Lemony Salmon

Prep time: 30 minutes | Cook time: 10 minutes | Serves 4

1½ pounds (680 g) salmon steak
½ teaspoon grated lemon zest
Freshly cracked mixed peppercorns, to taste
⅓ cup lemon juice
Fresh chopped chives, for garnish
½ cup dry white wine
½ teaspoon fresh cilantro, chopped
Fine sea salt, to taste

1. To prepare the marinade, place all ingredients, except for salmon steak and chives, in a deep pan. Bring to a boil over medium-high flame until it has reduced by half. Allow it to cool down. 2. Marinate salmon steak in the refrigerator for 40 minutes. Discard the marinade and transfer to the air fryer. Air fry at 400ºF (204ºC) for 9 to 10 minutes. Brush hot fish steaks with the reserved marinade, garnish with fresh chopped chives, and serve right away!

Cucumber and Salmon Salad

Prep time: 10 minutes | Cook time: 8 to 10 minutes | Serves 2

1 pound (454 g) salmon fillet
1½ tablespoons olive oil, divided
1 tablespoon sherry vinegar
1 tablespoon capers, rinsed and drained
1 seedless cucumber, thinly sliced
¼ Vidalia onion, thinly sliced
2 tablespoons chopped fresh parsley
Salt and freshly ground black pepper, to taste

1. Preheat the air fryer to 400ºF (204ºC). 2. Lightly coat the salmon with ½ tablespoon olive oil. Air fry for 8 to 10 minutes until the fish is opaque and flakes easily with a fork. Let cool to room temperature. Remove the skin and carefully flake the fish into bite-size chunks. 3. In a bowl, whisk the remaining olive oil and the vinegar until well combined. Add the flaked fish, capers, cucumber, onion, and parsley. Season with salt and black pepper. Toss gently to coat. Serve immediately or cover and refrigerate for up to 4 hours.

Mackerel with Spinach

Prep time: 15 minutes | Cook time: 20 minutes | Serves 5

1 pound (454 g) mackerel, trimmed
1 bell pepper, chopped
½ cup spinach, chopped
1 tablespoon avocado oil
1 teaspoon ground black pepper
1 teaspoon keto tomato paste

1. In the mixing bowl, mix bell pepper with spinach, ground black pepper, and tomato paste. 2. Fill the mackerel with spinach mixture. 3. Then brush the fish with avocado oil and put it in the air fryer. 4. Bake at 365ºF (185ºC) for 20 minutes.

Panko-Crusted Fish Sticks

Prep time: 10 minutes | Cook time: 15 minutes | Serves 4

Tartar Sauce:
2 cups mayonnaise
2 tablespoons dill pickle relish
1 tablespoon dried minced onions
Fish Sticks:
Oil, for spraying
1 pound (454 g) tilapia fillets
½ cup all-purpose flour
2 cups panko bread crumbs
2 tablespoons Creole seasoning
2 teaspoons granulated garlic
1 teaspoon onion powder
½ teaspoon salt
¼ teaspoon freshly ground black pepper
1 large egg

Make the Tartar Sauce: 1. In a bowl, whisk together the mayonnaise, pickle relish, and onions. Cover with plastic wrap and refrigerate until ready to serve. Make the Fish Sticks: 2. Preheat the air fryer to 350ºF (177ºC). 3. Cut the fillets into equal-size sticks and place them in a zip-top plastic bag. 4. Add the flour to the bag, seal, and shakeuntil evenly coated. 5. In a shallow bowl, mix together the bread crumbs, Creole seasoning, garlic, onion powder, salt, and black pepper. In another bowl, whisk the egg. 6. Dip the fish sticks in the egg, then dredge in the bread crumb mixture until completely coated. Spray lightly with oil. 7. Air fry for 12 to 15 minutes, or until browned and cooked through. Serve with tartar sauce.

Butter-Wine Baked Salmon

Prep time: 5 minutes | Cook time: 10 minutes | Serves 4

4 tablespoons butter, melted
2 cloves garlic, minced
Sea salt and ground black pepper, to taste
¼ cup dry white wine
1 tablespoon lime juice
1 teaspoon smoked paprika
½ teaspoon onion powder
4 salmon steaks
Cooking spray

1. Place all the ingredients except the salmon and oil in a shallow dish and stir to mix well. 2. Add the salmon steaks to coat well. Refrigerator to marinate for 30 minutes. 3. Preheat the air fryer to 360ºF (182ºC). 4. Remove and spray the salmon steaks with cooking spray. 5. Air fry for about 10 minutes, flipping the salmon steaks halfway through, or until cooked to your preferred doneness. 6. Serve.

Cajun Catfish Cakes with Cheese

Prep time: 5 minutes | Cook time: 35 minutes | Serves 4

2 catfish fillets
3 ounces (85 g) butter
1 cup shredded Parmesan cheese
1 cup shredded Swiss cheese
½ cup buttermilk
1 teaspoon baking powder
1 teaspoon baking soda
1 teaspoon Cajun seasoning

1. In a pot, boil the catfish fillets in the boiling salted water for 5 minutes until they become opaque. 2. Transfer the fillets to a mixing bowl and flake them into small pieces. 3. Add the remaining ingredients to the bowl and stir until well incorporated. 4. Divide the fish mixture into 12 equal portions and shape each into a patty. 5. Preheat the air fryer to 380ºF (193ºC). 6. Air fry the patties in the frying basket for 15 minutes until golden brown and cooked through, flipping once halfway through. 7. Let sit for 5 minutes and serve.

Browned Shrimp Patties

Prep time: 15 minutes | Cook time: 10 to 12 minutes | Serves 4

½ pound (227 g) raw shrimp, shelled, deveined, and chopped finely
2 cups cooked sushi rice
¼ cup chopped red bell pepper
¼ cup chopped celery
¼ cup chopped green onion
2 teaspoons Worcestershire sauce
½ teaspoon salt
½ teaspoon garlic powder
½ teaspoon Old Bay seasoning
½ cup plain bread crumbs
Cooking spray

1. Preheat the air fryer to 390ºF (199ºC). 2. Put all the ingredients except the bread crumbs and oil in a bowl and stir to incorporate. 3. Scoop out the shrimp mixture and shape into 8 equal-sized patties, no more than ½-inch thick. Roll the patties in the bread crumbs and spray both sides with cooking spray. 4. Air fry for 10 to 12 minutes, flipping halfway through, or until the outside is crispy brown. 5. Serve warm.

Steamed Tuna with Lemongrass

Prep time: 10 minutes | Cook time: 10 minutes | Serves 4

4 small tuna steaks
2 tablespoons low-sodium soy sauce
2 teaspoons sesame oil
2 teaspoons rice wine vinegar
1 teaspoon grated peeled fresh ginger
⅛ teaspoon freshly ground black pepper
1 stalk lemongrass, bent in half
3 tablespoons freshly squeezed lemon juice

1. In a bowl, whisk the soy sauce, sesame oil, vinegar, and ginger until combined. Pour this mixture over the tuna and gently rub it into both sides. Sprinkle the fish with the pepper. Marinate for 10 minutes. 2. Preheat the air fryer to 390ºF (199ºC). Place the lemongrass into the basket and top with the tuna steaks. Drizzle the tuna with the lemon juice and 1 tablespoon water. 3. Bake for 10 minutes until the tuna reaches 145ºF (63ºC). Discard the lemongrass and serve.

Parmesan Lobster Tails

Prep time: 5 minutes | Cook time: 7 minutes | Serves 4

4 (4-ounce / 113-g) lobster tails
2 tablespoons salted butter, melted
1½ teaspoons Cajun seasoning, divided
¼ teaspoon salt
¼ teaspoon ground black pepper
¼ cup grated Parmesan cheese
½ ounce (14 g) plain pork rinds, finely crushed

1. Cut lobster tails open carefully with a pair of scissors and gently pull meat away from shells, resting meat on top of shells. 2. Brush lobster meat with butter and sprinkle with 1 teaspoon Cajun seasoning, ¼ teaspoon per tail. 3. In a bowl, mix remaining Cajun seasoning, salt, pepper, Parmesan, and pork rinds. Gently press ¼ mixture onto meat on each lobster tail. 4. Air fry the tails at 400ºF (204ºC) for 7 minutesuntil lobster tails are crispy and golden on top and have an internal temperature of 145ºF (63ºC). Serve warm.

Miso Salmon

Prep time: 10 minutes | Cook time: 12 minutes | Serves 2

2 tablespoons brown sugar
2 tablespoons soy sauce
2 tablespoons white miso paste
1 teaspoon minced garlic
1 teaspoon minced fresh ginger
½ teaspoon freshly cracked black pepper
2 (5-ounce / 142-g) salmon fillets
Vegetable oil spray
1 teaspoon sesame seeds
2 scallions, thinly sliced, for garnish

1. In a bowl, whisk together the brown sugar, soy sauce, miso, garlic, ginger, and pepper to combine. 2. Coat both sides of the fillets with half the sauce on a plate. 3. Spray the frying basket with vegetable oil spray. Air fry the salmon in the basket for 12 minutes. Halfway through the cooking time, brush additional miso sauce on the salmon. 4. Sprinkle the salmon with the sesame seeds and scallions and serve.

Golden Shrimp

Prep time: 20 minutes | Cook time: 7 minutes | Serves 4

2 egg whites
½ cup coconut flour
1 cup Parmigiano-Reggiano, grated
½ teaspoon celery seeds
½ teaspoon porcini powder
½ teaspoon onion powder
1 teaspoon garlic powder
½ teaspoon dried rosemary
½ teaspoon sea salt
½ teaspoon ground black pepper
1½ pounds (680 g) shrimp, deveined

1. Whisk the egg with coconut flour and Parmigiano-Reggiano. Add in seasonings and mix to combine well. 2. Dip your shrimp in the batter and roll until covered on all sides. 3. Air fry at 390ºF (199ºC) for 5 to 7 minutes or until golden brown. Serve with lemon wedges if desired.

Cod with Jalapeño

Prep time: 5 minutes | Cook time: 14 minutes | Serves 4

4 cod fillets, boneless
1 jalapeño, minced
1 tablespoon avocado oil
½ teaspoon minced garlic

1. In the shallow bowl, mix minced jalapeño, avocado oil, and minced garlic. 2. Put the cod fillets in the frying basket in one layer and top with minced jalapeño mixture. 3. Bake at 365°F (185°C) for 7 minutes per side.

Salmon Burgers

Prep time: 15 minutes | Cook time: 12 minutes | Serves 5

Lemon-Caper Rémoulade:
½ cup mayonnaise
2 tablespoons minced drained capers
2 tablespoons chopped fresh parsley
2 teaspoons fresh lemon juice
Salmon Patties:
1 pound (454 g) wild salmon fillet, skinned and pin bones removed
6 tablespoons panko bread crumbs
¼ cup minced red onion plus ¼ cup slivered for serving
1 garlic clove, minced
1 large egg, lightly beaten
1 tablespoon Dijon mustard
1 teaspoon fresh lemon juice
1 tablespoon chopped fresh parsley
½ teaspoon kosher salt
For Serving:
5 whole wheat potato buns or gluten-free buns
10 butter lettuce leaves

1. Make the Lemon-Caper Rémoulade: In a bowl, mix all the rémoulade ingredients. 2. Make the Salmon Patties: Cut off a 4-ounce / 113-g piece salmon and pulse in a food processor until it becomes pasty. Chop the remaining salmon into small cubes. 3. In a bowl, combine the chopped and processed salmon with the panko, minced red onion, garlic, egg, mustard, lemon juice, parsley, and salt. Toss to combine. Form the mixture into 5 patties about ¾ inch thick. Refrigerate for at least 30 minutes. 4. Preheat the air fryer to 400°F (204°C). 5. Air fry the patties for 12 minutes, flipping halfway, until golden and cooked through. 6. Transfer each patty to a bun. Top each with 2 lettuce leaves, 2 tablespoons rémoulade, and slivered onions.

Fish Croquettes with Lemon-Dill Aioli

Prep time: 15 minutes | Cook time: 10 minutes | Serves 4

Croquettes:
3 large eggs, divided
12 ounces (340 g) raw cod fillet, flaked apart with two forks
¼ cup 1% milk
½ cup boxed instant mashed potatoes
2 teaspoons olive oil
⅓ cup chopped fresh dill
1 shallot, minced
1 large garlic clove, minced
¾ cup plus 2 tablespoons bread crumbs, divided
1 teaspoon fresh lemon juice
1 teaspoon kosher salt
½ teaspoon dried thyme
¼ teaspoon freshly ground black pepper
Cooking spray
Lemon-Dill Aioli:
5 tablespoons mayonnaise
Juice of ½ lemon
1 tablespoon chopped fresh dill

1. Make the Croquettes: In a medium bowl, lightly beat 2 of the eggs. Add the rest croquettes ingredients except for ¾ cup bread crumbs and mix well. 2. Make the Lemon-Dill Aioli: In a bowl, combine the mayonnaise, lemon juice, and dill. Set aside. 3. Measure out about 3½ tablespoons fish mixture and roll to form a log about 3 inches long. Repeat to make a total of 12 logs. 4. Beat the remaining egg in a bowl. Place the remaining bread crumbs in a separate bowl. Dip the croquettes in the egg, then coat in the bread crumbs. Spray with cooking spray. 5. Air fry at 350°F (177°C) for 10 minutes, flipping halfway, until golden. 6. Serve with the aioli for dipping.

Crunchy Air Fried Cod Fillets

Prep time: 10 minutes | Cook time: 12 minutes | Serves 2.

⅓ cup panko bread crumbs
1 teaspoon vegetable oil
1 small shallot, minced
1 small garlic clove, minced
½ teaspoon minced fresh thyme
Salt and pepper, to taste
1 tablespoon minced fresh parsley
1 tablespoon mayonnaise
1 large egg yolk
¼ teaspoon grated lemon zest, plus lemon wedges for serving
2 (8-ounce / 227-g) skinless cod fillets, 1¼ inches thick
Vegetable oil spray

1. Preheat the air fryer to 300°F (149°C). Lightly spray the frying basket with vegetable oil spray. 2. Toss the panko with the oil in a bowl until evenly coated. Stir in the shallot, garlic, thyme, ¼ teaspoon salt, and ⅛ teaspoon pepper. Microwave, stirring frequently, until the panko is light golden brown, about 2 minutes. Let cool slightly; stir in the parsley. Whisk the mayonnaise, egg yolk, lemon zest, and ⅛ teaspoon pepper together in another bowl. 3. Pat the cod dry with paper towels and season with salt and pepper. Arrange the fillets, skinned-side down, on plate and brush tops evenly with mayonnaise mixture. Dredge the coated side of fillets in panko mixture. Arrange the fillets, crumb-side up, in the prepared basket. 4. Bake for 12 to 16 minutes, rotating halfway through cooking. Serve with the lemon wedges.

Blackened Fish

Prep time: 15 minutes | Cook time: 8 minutes | Serves 4

1 large egg, beaten
Blackened seasoning, as needed
2 tablespoons light brown sugar
4 (4-ounce / 113-g) tilapia fillets
Cooking spray

1. In a shallow bowl, place the beaten egg. In another shallow bowl, stir together the Blackened seasoning and sugar. 2. Dip the fish fillets in the egg, then sugar mixture, coating thoroughly. 3. Preheat the air fryer to 300°F (149°C). 4. Spritz the fish with oil and bake for 8 to 10 minutes, flipping and spritzing with oil halfway through, until the fish is white inside and flakes easily with a fork. 5. Serve immediately.

Shrimp Bake

Prep time: 15 minutes | Cook time: 5 minutes | Serves 4

14 ounces (397 g) shrimp, peeled
1 egg, beaten
½ cup coconut milk
1 cup Cheddar cheese, shredded
½ teaspoon coconut oil
1 teaspoon ground coriander

1. In the mixing bowl, mix shrimps with egg, coconut milk, Cheddar cheese, coconut oil, and ground coriander. 2. Then put the mixture in the baking ramekins and put in the air fryer. 3. Air fry at 400ºF (204ºC) for 5 minutes.

Cod with Creamy Mustard Sauce

Prep time: 10 minutes | Cook time: 10 minutes | Serves 4

Fish:
Oil, for spraying
1 pound (454 g) cod fillets
2 tablespoons olive oil
1 tablespoon lemon juice
1 teaspoon salt
½ teaspoon freshly ground black pepper
Mustard Sauce:
½ cup heavy cream
3 tablespoons Dijon mustard
1 tablespoon unsalted butter
1 teaspoon salt

Make the Fish: 1. Spray the frying basket lightly with oil. 2. Rub the cod with the olive oil and lemon juice. Season with the salt and black pepper. 3. Roast at 350ºF (177ºC) for 5 minutes. Roast at 400ºF (204ºC) for another 5 minutes, until flaky and the internal temperature reaches 145ºF (63ºC). Make the Mustard Sauce: 4. Mix together and cook the heavy cream, mustard, butter, and salt over low heat in a small saucepan for 3 to 4 minutes, or until the sauce starts to thicken. 5. Drizzle with the mustard sauce and serve.

Tortilla Shrimp Tacos

Prep time: 10 minutes | Cook time: 6 minutes | Serves 4

Spicy Mayo:
3 tablespoons mayonnaise
1 tablespoon Louisiana-style hot pepper sauce
Cilantro-Lime Slaw:
2 cups shredded green cabbage
½ small red onion, thinly sliced
1 small jalapeño, thinly sliced
2 tablespoons chopped fresh cilantro
Juice of 1 lime
¼ teaspoon kosher salt
Shrimp:
1 large egg, beaten
1 cup crushed tortilla chips
24 jumbo shrimp (about 1 pound / 454 g), peeled and deveined
⅛ teaspoon kosher salt
Cooking spray
8 corn tortillas, for serving

1. Make the Spicy Mayo: In a bowl, mix the mayonnaise and hot pepper sauce. 2. Make the Cilantro-Lime Slaw: In a bowl, toss together all the slaw ingredients. Cover and refrigerate to chill. 3. Make the Shrimp: Place the egg in a shallow bowl and the crushed tortilla chips in another. Season the shrimp with the salt. Dip the shrimp in the egg, then in the crumbs, pressing gently to adhere. Spray both sides with oil. 4. Preheat the air fryer to 360ºF (182ºC). Air fry for 6 minutes, flipping halfway, until golden and cooked through in the center. 5. To serve, top each tortilla with 3 shrimp, ¼ cup slaw, then drizzle with spicy mayo.

Crunchy Fish Sticks

Prep time: 30 minutes | Cook time: 9 minutes | Serves 4

1 pound (454 g) cod fillets, cut into ¾-inch-wide strips
1½ cups finely ground blanched almond flour
2 teaspoons Old Bay seasoning
½ teaspoon paprika
Sea salt and freshly ground black pepper, to taste
¼ cup sugar-free mayonnaise
1 large egg, beaten
Avocado oil spray
Tartar sauce, for serving

1. In a shallow bowl, stir together the flour, Old Bay seasoning, paprika, salt and pepper to taste. In another shallow bowl, whisk together the mayonnaise and egg. 2. Dip the cod strips in the egg mixture, then the flour. 3. Freeze the fish on a sheet for 30 minutes. 4. Spray the frying basket with oil. Place the fish in the basket in a single layer, and spray each piece with oil. 5. Air fry at 400ºF (204ºC) for 5 minutes. Flip, spray with more oil and cook for 4 minutes, until the internal temperature reaches 140ºF (60ºC). Serve with tartar sauce.

Honey-Glazed Salmon

Prep time: 5 minutes | Cook time: 12 minutes | Serves 4

¼ cup raw honey
4 garlic cloves, minced
1 tablespoon olive oil
½ teaspoon salt
Olive oil cooking spray
4 (1½-inch-thick) salmon fillets

1. Preheat the air fryer to 380ºF (193ºC). 2. In a bowl, mix together the honey, garlic, olive oil, and salt. 3. Spray the frying basket with cooking spray, and place the salmon in a single layer in the frying basket. 4. Brush the top of each fillet with the honey-garlic mixture, and roast for 10 to 12 minutes, or until the internal temperature reaches 145ºF (63ºC).

Cajun Salmon

Prep time: 5 minutes | Cook time: 7 minutes | Serves 2

2 (4-ounce / 113-g) salmon fillets, skin removed
2 tablespoons unsalted butter, melted
⅛ teaspoon ground cayenne pepper
½ teaspoon garlic powder
1 teaspoon paprika
¼ teaspoon ground black pepper

1. Brush each fillet with butter. 2. Combine remaining ingredients in a bowl and then rub onto fish. Place fillets into the frying basket. Air fry at 390ºF (199ºC) for 7 minutes until the internal temperature reaches 145ºF (63ºC). Serve immediately.

Paprika Shrimp

Prep time: 5 minutes | Cook time: 6 minutes | Serves 2

8 ounces (227 g) medium shelled and deveined shrimp
2 tablespoons salted butter, melted
1 teaspoon paprika
½ teaspoon garlic powder
¼ teaspoon onion powder
½ teaspoon Old Bay seasoning

1. Toss all ingredients together in a bowl. Place shrimp into the frying basket. 2. Air fry at 400ºF (204ºC) for 6 minutes, turning halfway through the cooking time to ensure even cooking. Serve immediately.

Coconut Shrimp with Pineapple-Lemon Sauce

Prep time: 10 minutes | Cook time: 13 minutes | Serves 4

½ cup light brown sugar
2 teaspoons cornstarch
⅛ teaspoon plus ½ teaspoon salt, divided
4 ounces (113 g) crushed pineapple with syrup
2 tablespoons freshly squeezed lemon juice
1 tablespoon yellow mustard
1½ pounds (680 g) raw large shrimp, peeled and deveined
2 eggs
½ cup all-purpose flour
1 cup unsweetened shredded coconut
¼ teaspoon granulated garlic
Olive oil spray

1. In a medium saucepan over medium heat, combine the brown sugar, cornstarch, and ⅛ teaspoon salt. 2. Stir in the crushed pineapple with syrup, lemon juice, and mustard. Cook for about 4 minutes until the mixture thickens and begins to boil. Boil for 1 minute. Remove, set aside, and let cool. 3. Put the shrimp on a plate and pat them dry with paper towels. 4. In a bowl, whisk the eggs. In another bowl, stir together the flour, shredded coconut, the remaining salt, and garlic. 5. Preheat the air fryer to 400ºF (204ºC). Dip the shrimp into the egg and the coconut mixture to coat. 6. Spray the coated shrimp with oil. Air fry for 13 minutes, flipping and spraying with more oil halfway through. 7. Serve with the prepared pineapple sauce.

Panko Catfish Nuggets

Prep time: 10 minutes | Cook time: 7 to 8 minutes | Serves 4

2 medium catfish fillets, cut into chunks (approximately 1 × 2 inch)
Salt and pepper, to taste
2 eggs
2 tablespoons skim milk
½ cup cornstarch
1 cup panko bread crumbs
Cooking spray

1. Preheat the air fryer to 390ºF (199ºC). 2. In a medium bowl, season the fish chunks with salt and pepper to taste. 3. In a bowl, beat together the eggs with milk until well combined. 4. Place the cornstarch and bread crumbs into separate shallow dishes. 5. Dredge the fish chunks in the cornstarch, then egg mixture, finally the bread crumbs. Spritz the fish chunks with cooking spray. 6. Air fry the for 7 to 8 minutes, shaking once, until they are no longer translucent in the center and golden brown. 7. Repeat with the remaining fish chunks. 8. Serve warm.

Chili Tilapia

Prep time: 5 minutes | Cook time: 20 minutes | Serves 4

4 tilapia fillets, boneless
1 teaspoon chili flakes
1 teaspoon dried oregano
1 tablespoon avocado oil
1 teaspoon mustard

1. Rub the tilapia fillets with chili flakes, dried oregano, avocado oil, and mustard and put in the air fryer. 2. Bake at 360ºF (182ºC) for 10 minutes per side.

Rainbow Salmon Kebabs

Prep time: 10 minutes | Cook time: 8 minutes | Serves 2

6 ounces (170 g) boneless, skinless salmon, cut into 1-inch cubes
¼ medium red onion, peeled and cut into 1-inch pieces
½ medium yellow bell pepper, seeded and cut into 1-inch pieces
½ medium zucchini, trimmed and cut into ½-inch slices
1 tablespoon olive oil
½ teaspoon salt
¼ teaspoon ground black pepper

1. Using one (6-inch) skewer, skewer 1 piece salmon, then 1 piece onion, 1 piece bell pepper, and finally 1 piece zucchini. Repeat with additional skewers to make four kebabs. Drizzle with oil and sprinkle with salt and black pepper. 2. Air fry at 400ºF (204ºC) for 8 minutes, turning halfway through cooking until salmon easily flakes, has an internal temperature of 145ºF (63ºC) and vegetables are tender. Serve warm.

Scallops and Spinach with Cream Sauce

Prep time: 5 minutes | Cook time: 10 minutes | Serves 2

Vegetable oil spray
1 (10-ounce / 283-g) package frozen spinach, thawed and drained
8 jumbo sea scallops
Kosher salt and black pepper, to taste
¾ cup heavy cream
1 tablespoon tomato paste
1 tablespoon chopped fresh basil
1 teaspoon minced garlic

1. Spray a baking pan with vegetable oil. Spread the thawed spinach in an even layer in the bottom of the pan. 2. Spray both sides of the scallops with vegetable oil. Season lightly with salt and pepper. Arrange the scallops on top of the spinach. 3. In a bowl, whisk together the remaining ingredients. Pour the sauce over the scallops and spinach. 4. Bake at 350ºF (177ºC) for 10 minutes until the scallops have an internal temperature of 135ºF (57ºC).

Trout Amandine with Lemon Butter Sauce

Prep time: 20 minutes | Cook time: 8 minutes | Serves 4

Trout Amandine:
⅔ cup toasted almonds
⅓ cup grated Parmesan cheese
1 teaspoon salt
½ teaspoon freshly ground black pepper
2 tablespoons butter, melted
4 (4-ounce / 113-g) trout fillets, or salmon fillets
Cooking spray

Lemon Butter Sauce:
8 tablespoons (1 stick) butter, melted
2 tablespoons freshly squeezed lemon juice
½ teaspoon Worcestershire sauce
½ teaspoon salt
½ teaspoon freshly ground black pepper
¼ teaspoon hot sauce

1. In a blender, pulse the almonds for 5 to 10 seconds until finely processed. Transfer to a shallow bowl and whisk in the Parmesan cheese, salt, and pepper. Place the melted butter in another shallow bowl. 2. Dip the fish in the melted butter, then the almond mixture, coating thoroughly. 3. Preheat the air fryer to 300ºF (149ºC). 4. Place the coated fish in the frying basket and spritz with oil. 5. Bake for 8 minutes, flipping and spritzing with oil halfway through, until the fish flakes easily with a fork. 6. In a bowl, whisk the sauce ingredients until blended. 7. Serve with the fish.

Parmesan Mackerel with Coriander

Prep time: 10 minutes | Cook time: 7 minutes | Serves 2

12 ounces (340 g) mackerel fillet
2 ounces (57 g) Parmesan, grated
1 teaspoon ground coriander
1 tablespoon olive oil

1. Sprinkle the mackerel fillet with olive oil and put it in the frying basket. 2. Top the fish with ground coriander and Parmesan. 3. Roast at 390ºF (199ºC) for 7 minutes.

Fried Catfish Fillets

Prep time: 10 minutes | Cook time: 20 minutes | Serves 4

1 egg
⅔ cup finely ground cornmeal
¼ cup all-purpose flour
¾ teaspoon salt
1 teaspoon paprika
1 teaspoon Old Bay seasoning
¼ teaspoon garlic powder
¼ teaspoon freshly ground black pepper
4 (5-ounce / 142-g) catfish fillets, halved crosswise
Olive oil spray

1. In a shallow bowl, beat the egg with 2 tablespoons water. 2. On a plate, stir together the cornmeal, flour, salt, paprika, Old Bay, garlic powder, and pepper. 3. Dip the fish into the egg mixture and cornmeal mixture to coat. Press the cornmeal mixture into the fish and gently shake off any excess. 4. Preheat the air fryer to 400ºF (204ºC). Spray the fish with olive oil. Air fry for 20 minutes, flipping and spraying with oil halfway the cooking time, until golden and crispy and registers at least 145ºF (63ºC) on a food thermometer. 5. Serve.

Baked Tilapia with Garlic Aioli

Prep time: 5 minutes | Cook time: 15 minutes | Serves 4

Tilapia:
4 tilapia fillets
1 tablespoon extra-virgin olive oil
1 teaspoon garlic powder
1 teaspoon paprika
1 teaspoon dried basil
A pinch of lemon-pepper seasoning

Garlic Aioli:
2 garlic cloves, minced
1 tablespoon mayonnaise
Juice of ½ lemon
1 teaspoon extra-virgin olive oil
Salt and pepper, to taste

1. Preheat the air fryer to 400ºF (204ºC). 2. Brush both sides of each fillet with the olive oil. Sprinkle with the garlic powder, paprika, basil, and lemon-pepper seasoning. 3. Bake for 15 minutes, flipping the fillets halfway through, or until the fish flakes easily and is no longer translucent in the center. 4. **Make the Garlic Aioli:** Whisk together the aioli ingredients in a bowl until smooth. 5. Serve the fish with the garlic aioli on the side.

Fried Shrimp

Prep time: 15 minutes | Cook time: 5 minutes | Serves 4

½ cup self-rising flour
1 teaspoon paprika
1 teaspoon salt
½ teaspoon freshly ground black pepper
1 large egg, beaten
1 cup finely crushed panko bread crumbs
20 frozen large shrimp (about 1-pound / 907-g), peeled and deveined
Cooking spray

1. In a shallow bowl, whisk the flour, paprika, salt, and pepper until blended. Add the beaten egg to a second shallow bowl and the bread crumbs to a third. 2. Dip the shrimp into the flour, the egg, and the bread crumbs, coating thoroughly. 3. Preheat the air fryer to 400ºF (204ºC). 4. Place the shrimp in the frying basket and spritz with oil. 5. Air fry for 5 minutes, shaking and spritzing with oil until lightly browned and crispy. Serve hot.

Lemony Shrimp

Prep time: 10 minutes | Cook time: 7 to 8 minutes | Serves 4

1 pound (454 g) shrimp, deveined
4 tablespoons olive oil
1½ tablespoons lemon juice
1½ tablespoons fresh parsley, roughly chopped
2 cloves garlic, finely minced
1 teaspoon crushed red pepper flakes, or more to taste
Garlic pepper, to taste
Sea salt flakes, to taste

1. Preheat the air fryer to 385ºF (196ºC). 2. Toss all the ingredients in a bowl until the shrimp are coated on all sides. 3. Arrange the shrimp in the frying basket and air fry for 7 to 8 minutes, or until the shrimp are pink and cooked through. 4. Serve warm.

Cod with Avocado

Prep time: 30 minutes | Cook time: 10 minutes | Serves 2

1 cup shredded cabbage
¼ cup full-fat sour cream
2 tablespoons full-fat mayonnaise
¼ cup chopped pickled jalapeños
2 (3-ounce / 85-g) cod fillets
1 teaspoon chili powder
1 teaspoon cumin
½ teaspoon paprika
¼ teaspoon garlic powder
1 medium avocado, peeled, pitted, and sliced
½ medium lime

1. In a bowl, mix cabbage, sour cream, mayonnaise, and jalapeños until fully coated. Let sit for 20 minutes in the refrigerator. 2. Sprinkle cod fillets with chili powder, cumin, paprika, and garlic powder. 3. Air fry at 370ºF (188ºC) for 10 minutes, flipping halfway through the cooking time, until the fish has an internal temperature of at least 145ºF (63ºC). 4. To serve, divide slaw mixture into two serving bowls, break cod fillets into pieces and spread over the bowls, and top with avocado. Squeeze lime juice over each bowl.

Friday Night Fish Fry

Prep time: 10 minutes | Cook time: 10 minutes | Serves 4

1 large egg
½ cup powdered Parmesan cheese (about 1½ ounces / 43 g)
1 teaspoon smoked paprika
¼ teaspoon celery salt
¼ teaspoon ground black pepper
4 (4-ounce / 113-g) cod fillets
Chopped fresh oregano or parsley, for garnish (optional)
Lemon slices, for serving (optional)

1. Spray the frying basket with avocado oil. Preheat the air fryer to 400ºF (204ºC). 2. Crack the egg in a shallow bowl and beat it lightly with a fork. Combine the Parmesan cheese, paprika, celery salt, and pepper in a separate shallow bowl. 3. Dip the fillets into the egg, then Parmesan mixture. Press the Parmesan onto the fillets to form a nice crust. 4. Air fry the fish for 10 minutes, or until it is cooked through and flakes easily with a fork. Garnish with fresh oregano or parsley and serve with lemon slices, if desired.

Crab Cakes with Lettuce and Apple Salad

Prep time: 10 minutes | Cook time: 13 minutes | Serves 2

8 ounces (227 g) lump crab meat, picked over for shells
2 tablespoons panko bread crumbs
1 scallion, minced
1 large egg
1 tablespoon mayonnaise
1½ teaspoons Dijon mustard
Pinch of cayenne pepper
2 shallots, sliced thin
1 tablespoon extra-virgin olive oil, divided
1 teaspoon lemon juice, plus lemon wedges for serving
⅛ teaspoon salt
Pinch of pepper
½ (3-ounce / 85-g) small head Bibb lettuce, torn into bite-size pieces
½ apple, cored and sliced thinly

1. Preheat the air fryer to 400ºF (204ºC). 2. Pat crab meat dry with paper towels. Combine panko, scallion, egg, mayonnaise, mustard, and cayenne in a bowl. Using a rubber spatula, gently fold in crab meat until combined. Divide crab mixture into 4 tightly packed balls, then flatten each into 1-inch-thick cake. Refrigerate until firm, about 10 minutes. 3. Toss shallots with ½ teaspoon oil in separate bowl; transfer to frying basket. Air fry until shallots are browned, 5 to 7 minutes, tossing once halfway through cooking. Set aside. 4. Arrange crab cakes in frying basket and air fryer until light golden brown on both sides, 8 to 10 minutes, flipping and rotating cakes halfway through. 5. Meanwhile, whisk remaining 2½ teaspoons oil, lemon juice, salt, and pepper together in large bowl. Add lettuce, apple, and shallots and toss to coat. Serve crab cakes with salad, passing lemon wedges separately.

Almond Catfish

Prep time: 10 minutes | Cook time: 12 minutes | Serves 4

2 pounds (907 g) catfish fillet
½ cup almond flour
2 eggs, beaten
1 teaspoon salt
1 teaspoon avocado oil

1. Sprinkle the catfish fillet with salt and dip in the eggs. 2. Then coat the fish in the almond flour and put in the frying basket. Sprinkle the fish with avocado oil. 3. Bake the fish for 6 minutes per side at 380ºF (193ºC).

Cayenne Flounder Cutlets

Prep time: 15 minutes | Cook time: 10 minutes | Serves 2

1 egg
1 cup Pecorino Romano cheese, grated
Sea salt and white pepper, to taste
½ teaspoon cayenne pepper
1 teaspoon dried parsley flakes
2 flounder fillets

1. Whisk the egg until frothy. 2. In another bowl, mix Pecorino Romano cheese, and spices. 3. Dip the fish in the egg mixture and dredge in the cracker crumb mixture. 4. Air fry at 390ºF (199ºC) for 10 minutes, turning once. Enjoy!

Bacon-Wrapped Scallops

Prep time: 5 minutes | Cook time: 10 minutes | Serves 4

8 (1-ounce / 28-g) sea scallops, cleaned and patted dry
8 slices sugar-free bacon
¼ teaspoon salt
¼ teaspoon ground black pepper

1. Wrap each scallop in 1 slice bacon and secure with a toothpick. Sprinkle with salt and pepper. 2. Place scallops into frying basket. Air fry at 360ºF (182ºC) for 10 minutes until the scallops are opaque and firm, and reaches 135ºF (57ºC). Serve warm.

Panko Crab Sticks with Mayo Sauce

Prep time: 5 minutes | Cook time: 12 minutes | Serves 4

Crab Sticks:
2 eggs
1 cup flour
⅓ cup panko bread crumbs
1 tablespoon old bay seasoning
1 pound (454 g) crab sticks
Cooking spray
Mayo Sauce:
½ cup mayonnaise
1 lime, juiced
2 garlic cloves, minced

1. Preheat air fryer to 390ºF (199ºC). 2. In a bowl, beat the eggs. In a shallow bowl, place the flour. In another shallow bowl, thoroughly combine the panko bread crumbs and old bay seasoning. 3. Dredge the crab sticks in the flour, then the beaten eggs, finally press them in the bread crumb mixture to coat well. Spray with cooking spray. 4. Air fry for 12 minutes until golden brown, flipping halfway through the cooking time. 5. Meanwhile, make the sauce by whisking together the mayo, lime juice, and garlic in a bowl. 6. Serve the crab sticks with the mayo sauce.

Sesame-Crusted Tuna Steak

Prep time: 5 minutes | Cook time: 8 minutes | Serves 2

2 (6-ounce / 170-g) tuna steaks
1 tablespoon coconut oil, melted
½ teaspoon garlic powder
2 teaspoons white sesame seeds
2 teaspoons black sesame seeds

1. Brush tuna steaks with coconut oil and sprinkle with garlic powder. 2. In a bowl, toss the steak with sesame seeds until completely coated. 3. Air fry in the frying basket at 400ºF (204ºC) for 8 minutes, flipping halfway through the cooking time. Steaks will be well-done at 145ºF (63ºC). Serve warm.

Seasoned Breaded Shrimp

Prep time: 15 minutes | Cook time: 10 to 15 minutes | Serves 4

2 teaspoons Old Bay seasoning, divided
½ teaspoon garlic powder
½ teaspoon onion powder
1 pound (454 g) large shrimp, deveined, with tails on
2 large eggs
½ cup whole-wheat panko bread crumbs
Cooking spray

1. Preheat the air fryer to 380ºF (193ºC). 2. Spray the frying basket lightly with cooking spray. 3. In a medium bowl, mix together 1 teaspoon Old Bay seasoning, garlic powder, and onion powder. Add the shrimp and toss with the seasoning mix to lightly coat. 4. In a separate small bowl, whisk the eggs with 1 teaspoon water. 5. In a shallow bowl, mix together the remaining Old Bay seasoning and the panko bread crumbs. 6. Dip each shrimp in the egg mixture and bread crumb mixture to evenly coat. Lightly spray the shrimp with cooking spray. 7. Air fry for 10 to 15 minutes, or until the shrimp is cooked through and crispy, shaking the basket at 5-minute intervals to redistribute and evenly cook. 8. Serve immediately.

Tandoori Shrimp

Prep time: 25 minutes | Cook time: 6 minutes | Serves 4

1 pound (454 g) jumbo raw shrimp (21 to 25 count), peeled and deveined
1 tablespoon minced fresh ginger
3 cloves garlic, minced
¼ cup chopped fresh cilantro or parsley, plus more for garnish
1 teaspoon ground turmeric
1 teaspoon garam masala
1 teaspoon smoked paprika
1 teaspoon kosher salt
½ to 1 teaspoon cayenne pepper
2 tablespoons olive oil (for Paleo) or melted ghee
2 teaspoons fresh lemon juice

1. In a bowl, combine the first nine ingredients and toss to coat well. Add the oil or ghee and toss again. Marinate at room temperature for 15 minutes. 2. Air fry in the frying basket at 325ºF (163ºC) for 6 minutes. Transfer the shrimp to a serving platter. Cover and let the shrimp finish cooking in the residual heat, about 5 minutes. 3. Sprinkle the shrimp with the lemon juice and toss to coat. Garnish with additional cilantro and serve.

Tuna-Stuffed Tomatoes

Prep time: 5 minutes | Cook time: 5 minutes | Serves 2

2 medium beefsteak tomatoes, tops removed, seeded, membranes removed
2 (2.6-ounce / 74-g) pouches tuna packed in water, drained
1 medium stalk celery, trimmed and chopped
2 tablespoons mayonnaise
¼ teaspoon salt
¼ teaspoon ground black pepper
2 teaspoons coconut oil
¼ cup shredded mild Cheddar cheese

1. Scoop pulp out of each tomato, leaving ½-inch shell. 2. In a medium bowl, mix tuna, celery, mayonnaise, salt, and pepper. Drizzle with coconut oil. Spoon ½ mixture into each tomato and top each with 2 tablespoons Cheddar. 3. Bake at 320ºF (160ºC) for 5 minutes until cheese melts. Serve warm.

Lemon Mahi-Mahi

Prep time: 5 minutes | Cook time: 14 minutes | Serves 2

Oil, for spraying
2 (6-ounce / 170-g) mahi-mahi fillets
1 tablespoon lemon juice
1 tablespoon olive oil
¼ teaspoon salt
¼ teaspoon freshly ground black pepper
1 tablespoon chopped fresh dill
2 lemon slices

1. Line the frying basket with parchment and spray lightly with oil. 2. In a bowl, whisk together the lemon juice and olive oil. Brush the mixture evenly over the mahi-mahi. 3. Sprinkle the mahi-mahi with the salt and black pepper and top with the dill. 4. Air fry at 400ºF (204ºC) for 12 to 14 minutes until they flake easily. 5. Top with a lemon slices, and serve.

Crab Cakes

Prep time: 10 minutes | Cook time: 10 minutes | Serves 4

2 (6-ounce / 170-g) cans lump crab meat
¼ cup blanched finely ground almond flour
1 large egg
2 tablespoons full-fat mayonnaise
½ teaspoon Dijon mustard
½ tablespoon lemon juice
½ medium green bell pepper, seeded and chopped
¼ cup chopped green onion
½ teaspoon Old Bay seasoning

1. In a bowl, combine all ingredients. Form into four balls and flatten into patties. Place patties into the frying basket. 2. Bake at 350°F (177°C) for 10 minutes, flipping halfway through. Serve warm.

Tuna Casserole

Prep time: 15 minutes | Cook time: 15 minutes | Serves 4

2 tablespoons salted butter
¼ cup diced white onion
¼ cup chopped white mushrooms
2 stalks celery, finely chopped
½ cup heavy cream
½ cup vegetable broth
2 tablespoons full-fat mayonnaise
¼ teaspoon xanthan gum
½ teaspoon red pepper flakes
2 medium zucchini, spiralized
2 (5-ounce / 142-g) cans albacore tuna
1 ounce (28 g) pork rinds, finely ground

1. In a large saucepan over medium heat, melt butter. Add onion, mushrooms, and celery and sauté until fragrant, 3 to 5 minutes. 2. Pour in heavy cream, vegetable broth, mayonnaise, and xanthan gum. Reduce heat and continue cooking an additional 3 minutes, until the mixture begins to thicken. 3. Add red pepper flakes, zucchini, and tuna. Turn off heat and stir until zucchini noodles are coated. 4. Pour into a round baking dish. Top with ground pork rinds and cover the top of the dish with foil. 5. Bake at 370°F (188°C) for 15 minutes. Remove the foil to brown the top of the casserole at last 3 minutes. Serve warm.

Crab Cake Sandwich

Prep time: 15 minutes | Cook time: 10 minutes | Serves 4

Crab Cakes:
½ cup panko bread crumbs
1 large egg, beaten
1 large egg white
1 tablespoon mayonnaise
1 teaspoon Dijon mustard
¼ cup minced fresh parsley
1 tablespoon fresh lemon juice
½ teaspoon Old Bay seasoning
⅛ teaspoon sweet paprika
⅛ teaspoon kosher salt
Freshly ground black pepper, to taste
10 ounces (283 g) lump crab meat
Cooking spray
Cajun Mayo:
¼ cup mayonnaise
1 tablespoon minced dill pickle
1 teaspoon fresh lemon juice
¾ teaspoon Cajun seasoning
For Serving:
4 Boston lettuce leaves
4 whole wheat potato buns or gluten-free buns

1. **Make the Crab Cakes:** In a bowl, combine the first eleven ingredients and mix well. Fold in the crab meat, being careful not to over mix. Gently shape into 4 round patties, about ½ cup each, ¾ inch thick. Spray both sides with oil. 2. Preheat the air fryer to 370°F (188°C). 3. Air fry for about 10 minutes, flipping halfway, until the edges are golden. 4. **Make the Cajun Mayo:** Meanwhile, In a bowl, combine the mayonnaise, pickle, lemon juice, and Cajun seasoning. 5. Place a lettuce leaf on each bun bottom and top with a crab cake and a generous tablespoon Cajun mayonnaise. Add the bun top and serve.

Sweet Tilapia Fillets

Prep time: 5 minutes | Cook time: 14 minutes | Serves 4

2 tablespoons erythritol
1 tablespoon apple cider vinegar
4 tilapia fillets, boneless
1 teaspoon olive oil

1. Mix apple cider vinegar with olive oil and erythritol. 2. Then rub the tilapia fillets with the sweet mixture and put in the frying basket in one layer. Bake the fish at 360°F (182°C) for 7 minutes per side.

Catfish Bites

Prep time: 15 minutes | Cook time: 20 minutes | Serves 4

Oil, for spraying
1 pound (454 g) catfish fillets, cut into 2-inch pieces
1 cup buttermilk
½ cup cornmeal
¼ cup all-purpose flour
2 teaspoons Creole seasoning
½ cup yellow mustard

1. Place the catfish pieces and buttermilk in a zip-top plastic bag, seal, and refrigerate for about 10 minutes. 2. In a shallow bowl, mix together the cornmeal, flour, and Creole seasoning. 3. Remove the catfish from the bag and pat dry with a paper towel. 4. Spread the mustard on all sides of the catfish, then dip them in the cornmeal mixture until evenly coated. 6. Place the catfish in the prepared basket. Spray lightly with oil. 5. Air fry at 400°F (204°C) for 10 minutes, flip carefully, spray with oil, and cook for another 10 minutes. Serve immediately.

Salmon with Cauliflower

Prep time: 10 minutes | Cook time: 25 minutes | Serves 4

1 pound (454 g) salmon fillet, diced
1 cup cauliflower, shredded
1 tablespoon dried cilantro
1 tablespoon coconut oil, melted
1 teaspoon ground turmeric
¼ cup coconut cream

1. Mix salmon with cauliflower, dried cilantro, ground turmeric, coconut cream, and coconut oil. 2. Transfer the salmon mixture into the air fryer and cook at 350°F (177°C) for 25 minutes. Stir every 5 minutes to avoid the burning.

Baked Grouper with Tomatoes and Garlic

Prep time: 5 minutes | Cook time: 12 minutes | Serves 4

4 grouper fillets
½ teaspoon salt
3 garlic cloves, minced
1 tomato, sliced
¼ cup sliced Kalamata olives
¼ cup fresh dill, roughly chopped
Juice of 1 lemon
¼ cup olive oil

1. Preheat the air fryer to 380°F (193°C). 2. Season the grouper fillets on all sides with salt, then place into the fryer basket and top with minced garlic, tomato slices, olives, and dill. 3. Drizzle lemon juice and olive oil over the top of the grouper, then bake for 10 to 12 minutes, or until the internal temperature reaches 145°F (63°C).

Roasted Fish with Almond-Lemon Crumbs

Prep time: 10 minutes | Cook time: 7 to 8 minutes | Serves 4

½ cup raw whole almonds
1 scallion, finely chopped
Grated zest and juice of 1 lemon
½ tablespoon extra-virgin olive oil
¾ teaspoon kosher salt, divided
Freshly ground black pepper, to taste
4 (6 ounces / 170 g each) skinless fish fillets
Cooking spray
1 teaspoon Dijon mustard

1. In a food processor, pulse the almonds to coarsely chop. Transfer to a small bowl and add the scallion, lemon zest, and olive oil. Season with ¼ teaspoon salt and pepper to taste and mix to combine. 2. Spray the top of the fish with oil and squeeze the lemon juice over the fish. Season with the remaining salt and pepper to taste. Spread the mustard on top of the fish. Press the almond mixture evenly onto the top of the fillets to adhere. 3. Preheat the air fryer to 375°F (191°C). 4. Place the fillets in the frying basket in a single layer. Roast for 7 to 8 minutes, until the crumbs start to brown and the fish is cooked through. 5. Serve immediately.

Chapter 7 Snacks and Appetizers

Ranch Oyster Snack Crackers

Prep time: 3 minutes | Cook time: 12 minutes | Serves 6

Oil, for spraying
¼ cup olive oil
2 teaspoons dry ranch seasoning
1 teaspoon chili powder
½ teaspoon dried dill
½ teaspoon granulated garlic
½ teaspoon salt
1 (9-ounce / 255-g) bag oyster crackers

1. Preheat the air fryer to 325ºF (163ºC). Line the frying basket with parchment and spray lightly with oil. 2. In a bowl, mix together the olive oil, ranch seasoning, chili powder, dill, garlic, and salt. Add the crackers and toss until evenly coated. 3. Place the mixture in the prepared basket. 4. Bake for 10 to 12 minutes, shaking or stirring every 3 to 4 minutes, or until crisp and golden brown.

Spicy Chicken Wings

Prep time: 10 minutes | Cook time: 10 minutes | Serves 4

¼ teaspoon celery salt
¼ teaspoon bay leaf powder
Black pepper to taste
½ teaspoon cayenne pepper
¼ teaspoon allspice
1 tablespoon thyme leaves
1 pound (454 g) chicken wings

1. Preheat the air fryer to 360ºF (182ºC). In a bowl, mix celery salt, bay leaf powder, black pepper, paprika, thyme, cayenne pepper, and allspice. Coat the wings in the mixture. Arrange the wings on the greased frying basket and air fry for 10 minutes. Flip and cook for 6 to 8 more minutes until crispy on the outside.

Sweet-Sour Chicken Wings

Prep time: 15 minutes | Cook time: 20 minutes | Serves 4

1 pound (454 g) chicken wings
1 cup soy sauce
½ cup brown sugar
½ cup apple cider vinegar
2 tablespoons fresh ginger, minced
1 garlic clove, minced
Black pepper to taste
2 tablespoons cornstarch
2 tablespoons cold water
1 teaspoon sesame seeds

1. In a bowl, add the chicken wings and cover with half a cup of soy sauce. Refrigerate for 20 minutes. Drain and pat dry. Arrange them on the greased frying basket and air fry for 14 minutes at 380ºF (193ºC), turning once halfway through cooking. 2. In a skillet over medium heat, stir the sugar, remaining soy sauce, vinegar, ginger, garlic, and black pepper, for 4 minutes. Dissolve 2 tablespoons of cornstarch in cold water and stir in the sauce until it thickens, about 2 minutes. Pour the sauce over the wings and sprinkle with sesame seeds. Serve hot.

Alfredo Wings

Prep time: 5 minutes | Cook time: 17 minutes | Serves 4

1½ pounds (680 g) chicken wings, pat-dried
Salt to taste
½ cup Alfredo sauce

1. Preheat the air fryer to 370ºF (188ºC). Season the wings with salt. Arrange them in the greased frying basket, without overlapping, and air fry for 12 minutes until no longer pink in the center. Flip them, increase the heat to 390ºF (199ºC), and cook for 5 more minutes. Work in batches if needed. Plate the wings and drizzle with Alfredo sauce to serve.

Crunchy Ranch Chicken Wings

Prep time: 10 minutes | Cook time: 12 to 15 minutes | Serves 4

2 pounds (907 g) chicken wings
2 tablespoons olive oil
1 tablespoon ranch seasoning mix
Salt to taste

1. Preheat the air fryer to 390ºF (199ºC). Put the ranch seasoning, olive oil, and salt in a large, resealable bag and mix well. Add the wings, seal the bag, and toss until the wings are thoroughly coated. 2. Put the wings in the greased frying basket in one layer, spritz them with a nonstick cooking spray, and air fry for 7 minutes. Turn them over and fry for 5 to 8 more minutes until the wings are light brown and crispy. Test for doneness with a meat thermometer. Serve with your favorite dipping sauce and enjoy!

Lemony Chicken Wings

Prep time: 10 minutes | Cook time: 15 minutes | Serves 4

8 chicken wings
Salt to taste
1 teaspoon sesame oil
Juice from half lemon
¼ cup sriracha chili sauce
1-inch piece ginger, grated
1 teaspoon garlic powder
1 teaspoon sesame seeds

1. Preheat the air fryer to 370ºF (188ºC). Grease the air frying basket with cooking spray. In a bowl, mix salt, ginger, garlic, lemon juice, sesame oil, and chili sauce. Coat the wings in the mixture. Transfer the wings to the basket and air fry for 15 minutes, flipping once. Sprinkle with sesame seeds and serve.

Chicken Wings with Gorgonzola Dip

Prep time: 10 minutes | Cook time: 16 minutes | Serves 4

8 chicken wings
1 teaspoon cayenne pepper
Salt to taste
2 tablespoons olive oil
1 teaspoon red chili flakes
1 cup heavy cream
3 ounces (85 g) gorgonzola cheese, crumbled
½ lemon, juiced
½ teaspoon garlic powder

1. Preheat the air fryer to 380ºF (193ºC). Coat the wings with cayenne pepper, salt, and olive oil. Place in the fryer and air fry for 16 minutes until crispy and golden brown, flipping once. In a bowl, mix heavy cream, gorgonzola cheese, chili flakes, lemon juice, and garlic powder. Serve the wings with the cheese dip.

Paprika Chicken Wings

Prep time: 10 minutes | Cook time: 16 to 18 minutes | Serves 4

8 chicken wings
Salt and black pepper to taste
1 teaspoon smoked paprika
½ teaspoon ground ginger
½ teaspoon red chili powder
1 teaspoon ground cumin
1 cup mayonnaise mixed with 1 tablespoon lemon juice

1. Preheat the air fryer to 380ºF (193ºC). In a bowl, mix paprika, ginger, chili powder, cumin, salt, and pepper. Add the chicken wings and toss to coat. Place in the greased frying basket and air fry for 16 to 18 minutes, flipping once halfway through. Let cool for a few minutes. Serve with lemon mayonnaise.

Oregano Chicken Thighs

Prep time: 10 minutes | Cook time: 18 to 20 minutes | Serves 4

1½ pounds (680 g) chicken thighs
2 eggs, lightly beaten
1 cup seasoned bread crumbs
½ teaspoon oregano
Salt and black pepper to taste

1. Preheat the air fryer to 390ºF (199ºC). Season the thighs with oregano, salt, and black pepper. In a bowl, add the beaten eggs. In a separate bowl, add the bread crumbs. Dip the thighs in the egg wash. 2. Then roll them in the bread crumbs and press firmly, so the bread crumbs stick well. Spray the thighs with cooking spray and arrange them in the frying basket in a single layer, skin-side up. Air fry for 12 minutes, turn the thighs over, and cook for 6 to 8 more minutes until crispy. Serve and enjoy!

Sweet and Spicy Chicken Thighs

Prep time: 10 minutes | Cook time: 18 to 20 minutes | Serves 4

1 pound (454 g) chicken thighs
Salt and garlic powder to taste
2 tablespoons olive oil
1 teaspoon yellow mustard
1 teaspoon honey
¼ cup mayo mixed with 2 tablespoons hot sauce

2. Preheat the air fryer to 360ºF (182ºC). In a bowl, whisk the olive oil, honey, mustard, salt, and garlic powder. Add the thighs and stir to coat. Marinate for 10 minutes. Transfer the thighs to the greased frying basket, skin side down, and insert in the air fryer. Air fry for 18 to 20 minutes, flipping once until golden and crispy. Serve immediately with the hot mayo sauce. Enjoy!

Panko Chicken Bites

Prep time: 10 minutes | Cook time: 13 to 15 minutes | Serves 4

1 pound (454 g) chicken breasts, cut into large cubes
Salt and black pepper to taste
2 tablespoons olive oil
5 tablespoons plain bread crumbs
2 tablespoons panko bread crumbs
2 tablespoons grated Parmesan cheese

1. Preheat the air fryer to 380ºF (193ºC). Season the chicken with black pepper and salt. In a bowl, mix the bread crumbs and Parmesan cheese. Coat the chicken pieces with the olive oil. Then dip into the breadcrumb mixture, shake off the excess, and place in the greased frying basket. Lightly spray the nuggets with cooking spray and air fry for 13 to 15 minutes, flipping once. Serve warm

Golden Chicken

Prep time: 10 minutes | Cook time: 14 to 16 minutes | Serves 4

2 chicken breasts, cut into chunks
1 teaspoon paprika
2 tablespoons milk
2 eggs
1 teaspoon garlic powder
Salt and black pepper to taste
1 cup flour
2 cups bread crumbs

1. Preheat the air fryer to 370ºF (188ºC). In a bowl, mix paprika, garlic powder, salt, pepper, flour, and bread crumbs. In another bowl, beat eggs with milk. Dip the chicken in the egg mixture, then roll in the crumbs. Place in the frying basket and spray with cooking spray. Air fry for 14 to 16 minutes, flipping once. Yummy!

Corn-Crusted Chicken Tenders

Prep time: 5 minutes | Cook time: 12 to 14 minutes | Serves 4

2 chicken breasts, cut into strips
Salt and black pepper to taste
2 eggs
1 cup ground cornmeal

1. Preheat the air fryer to 390ºF (199ºC). In a bowl, mix cornmeal, salt, and black pepper. In another bowl, beat the eggs; season with salt and pepper. Dip the chicken in the eggs and then coat in the cornmeal. Spray the strips with cooking spray and place them in the frying basket in a single layer. Air fry for 6 minutes, slide the basket out, and flip the sticks. Cook for 6 to 8 more minutes until golden brown. Serve hot.

Oat-Crusted Chicken Croquettes

Prep time: 10 minutes | Cook time: 10 minutes | Serves 4

1 pound (454 g) ground chicken
2 eggs
Salt and black pepper to taste
1 cup oats, crumbled
½ teaspoon garlic powder
1 teaspoon dried parsley

1. Preheat the air fryer to 360ºF (182ºC). Mix the chicken with garlic, parsley, salt, and pepper. In a bowl, beat the eggs with a pinch of salt. In a third bowl, add the oats. Form croquettes out of the chicken mixture. Dip in the eggs and coat in the oats. Air fry them in the greased frying basket for 10 minutes, shaking once.

Cabbage Chicken Rolls

Prep time: 15 minutes | Cook time: 25 minutes | Serves 4

2 teaspoons olive oil
2 garlic cloves, minced
¼ cup soy sauce
1 teaspoon grated fresh ginger
1 pound (454 g) ground chicken
2 cups white cabbage, shredded
1 onion, chopped
1 egg, beaten
8 egg roll wrappers

1. Heat olive oil in a pan over medium heat and add garlic, onion, ginger, and ground chicken. Sauté for 5 minutes until the chicken is no longer pink. Pour in the soy sauce and shredded cabbage and stir-fry for another 5 to 6 minutes until the cabbage is tender. Remove from the heat and let cool slightly. 2. Fill each egg wrapper with the mixture, arranging it just below the center of the wrappers. Fold in both sides and roll up tightly. Use the beaten egg to seal the edges. Brush the tops with the remaining beaten egg. Place the rolls in the greased frying basket, spray them with cooking spray, and air fry for 12 to 14 minutes at 370ºF (188ºC) until golden, turning once halfway through. Let cool slightly and serve.

Mushroom Carrot Spring Rolls with Noddles

Prep time: 15 minutes | Cook time: 17 to 19 minutes | Serves 4

4 spring roll wrappers
½ cup cooked vermicelli noodles
1 garlic clove, minced
1 tablespoon fresh ginger, minced
1 tablespoon soy sauce
2 teaspoons sesame oil
½ red bell pepper, seeds removed, chopped
½ cup mushrooms, finely chopped
½ cup carrots, finely chopped
¼ cup scallions, finely chopped

1. Warm sesame oil in a saucepan over medium heat and add garlic, ginger, soy sauce, bell pepper, mushrooms, carrots, and scallions and stir-fry for 5 minutes. Stir in vermicelli noodles and set aside. 2. Place the wrappers onto a working board. Spoon the veggie-noodle mixture at the center of the roll wrappers. Roll and tuck in the corners and edges to create neat and secure rolls. Spray with oil and place them in the frying basket. Air fry for 12 to 14 minutes at 340ºF (171ºC), turning once or twice until golden.

Mediterranean Beef Meatballs

Prep time: 10 minutes | Cook time: 15 to 16 minutes | Serves 4

1 pound (454 g) ground beef
1 onion, finely chopped
2 garlic cloves, finely chopped
1 egg
1 cup bread crumbs
½ cup Mediterranean herbs
Salt and black pepper to taste
1 tablespoon olive oil

1. In a bowl, add the ground beef, onion, garlic, egg, bread crumbs, herbs, salt, and pepper and mix with your hands to combine. Shape into balls and brush them with olive oil. Arrange the meatballs in the frying basket and air fry for 15 to 16 minutes at 380ºF (193ºC), turning once halfway through. Serve immediately.

Potato Cheese Balls

Prep time: 10 minutes | Cook time: 14 to 16 minutes | Serves 4

2 cups cottage cheese, crumbled
2 cups Parmesan cheese, grated
2 red potatoes, boiled and mashed
1 medium onion, finely chopped
1½ teaspoons red chili flakes
1 green chili, finely chopped
Salt to taste
2 tablespoons fresh cilantro, chopped
1 cup flour
1 cup bread crumbs

1. In a bowl, combine the cottage and Parmesan cheeses, onion, chili flakes, green chili, salt, cilantro, flour, and mashed potatoes. Mold balls out of the mixture and roll them in bread crumbs. Place them in the greased frying basket and air fry for 14 to 16 minutes at 350ºF (177ºC), shaking once or twice. Serve warm.

Crunchy Nachos

Prep time: 5 minutes | Cook time: 4 to 6 minutes | Serves 4

8 corn tortillas, cut into wedges
1 tablespoon olive oil
½ teaspoon ground cumin
½ teaspoon chili powder
½ teaspoon paprika
½ teaspoon cayenne pepper
½ teaspoon salt
½ teaspoon ground coriander

1. Preheat the air fryer to 370ºF (188ºC). Brush the tortilla wedges with olive oil and arrange them in the frying basket in an even layer. Mix the spices thoroughly in a small bowl. Sprinkle the tortilla wedges with the spice mixture. Air fry for 2 to 3 minutes, shake the basket, and fry for another 2 to 3 minutes until crunchy and nicely browned. Serve the nachos immediately.

Thai-Style Cheesy Sticks

Prep time: 5 minutes | Cook time: 10 to 12 minutes | Serves 4

12 sticks Mozzarella cheese
2 cups bread crumbs
3 eggs
1 cup sweet Thai sauce
4 tablespoons skimmed milk

1. Pour the bread crumbs into a bowl. Beat the eggs with milk in another bowl. One after the other, dip the sticks in the egg mixture, in the crumbs, then in the egg mixture again, and lastly in the crumbs again. 2. Freeze for 1 hour. Preheat the air fryer to 380ºF (193ºC). Arrange the sticks in the greased frying basket and air fry for 10 to 12 minutes, flipping halfway through. Work in batches. Serve with sweet Thai sauce.

Garlicky Potato Chips

Prep time: 5 minutes | Cook time: 20 minutes | Serves 4

1 pound (454 g) potatoes, cut into thin slices
¼ cup olive oil
1 tablespoon garlic paste
2 tablespoons chives, chopped
A pinch of salt

1. Preheat the air fryer to 390ºF (199ºC). In a bowl, add olive oil, garlic paste, and salt and mix to obtain a marinade. Add the potatoes and let them sit for 30 minutes. Lay the potato slices into the frying basket and air fry for 20 minutes. At the 10-minute mark, give the chips a turn and sprinkle with freshly chopped chives.

Rosemary Potato Chips

Prep time: 5 minutes | Cook time: 18 to 20 minutes | Serves 2

2 potatoes, thinly sliced
1 tablespoon olive oil
1 garlic cloves, crushed
1 teaspoon each of fresh
rosemary, thyme, oregano, chopped
Salt and black pepper to taste

1. In a bowl, mix olive oil, garlic, herbs, salt, and pepper. Coat the potatoes thoroughly in the mixture. Arrange them in the frying basket and air fry for 18 to 20 minutes at 360ºF (182ºC), shaking every 4 to 5 minutes.

Spicy Carrot Chips

Prep time: 5 minutes | Cook time: 13 to 15 minutes | Serves 2

2 large carrots, cut into strips
½ teaspoon oregano
½ teaspoon hot paprika
½ teaspoon garlic powder
1 tablespoon olive oil
Salt to taste

1. Put the carrots in a bowl and stir in the remaining ingredients; toss to coat. Arrange the carrots in the greased frying basket and air fry for 13 to 15 minutes at 390ºF (199ºC), shaking once. Serve warm.

Sweet Pickle Chips

Prep time: 5 minutes | Cook time: 10 minutes | Serves 4

36 sweet pickle chips, drained
1 teaspoon cayenne pepper
1 cup flour
¼ cup cornmeal

1. Preheat the air fryer to 400ºF (204ºC). In a bowl, mix flour, cayenne pepper, and cornmeal. Dip the pickles in the flour mixture and spritz with cooking spray. Air fry for 10 minutes until golden brown, turning once.

Root Vegetable Chips

Prep time: 5 minutes | Cook time: 15 minutes | Serves 4

1 carrot, sliced
1 parsnip, sliced
1 potato, sliced
1 daikon, sliced
2 tablespoons olive oil
1 tablespoon soy sauce

1. Preheat the air fryer to 400ºF (204ºC). In a bowl, mix olive oil and soy sauce. Add in the veggies and toss to coat; marinate for 5 minutes. Transfer them to the fryer and air fry for 15 minutes, tossing once.

Breaded Artichoke Hearts

Prep time: 10 minutes | Cook time: 10 minutes | Serves 4

1 can (14-ounce / 397-g) artichoke hearts, drained
2 eggs
¼ cup flour
¼ Parmesan cheese, grated
⅓ cup panko bread crumbs
1 teaspoon garlic powder
Salt and black pepper to taste

1. Preheat the air fryer to 390ºF (199ºC). Pat dry the artichokes with a paper towel and cut them into wedges. In a bowl, whisk the eggs with a pinch of salt. In another bowl, combine Parmesan cheese, bread crumbs, and garlic powder. In a third bowl, pour the flour mixed with salt and black pepper. 2. Dip the artichokes in the flour, followed by a dip in the eggs, and finally coat with bread crumbs. Place them in the frying basket and air fry for 10 minutes, flipping once. Serve with mayo sauce if desired.

Sage Brussels Sprouts

Prep time: 10 minutes | Cook time: 15 minutes | Serves 4

1 pound (454 g) Brussels sprouts, halved
2 tablespoons canola oil
1 cup bread crumbs
1 tablespoon paprika
2 tablespoons Grana Padano cheese, grated
1 tablespoon sage, chopped

1. Preheat the air fryer to 400ºF (204ºC). Line the frying basket with parchment paper. 2. In a bowl, mix bread crumbs and paprika with Grana Padano cheese. Drizzle the Brussels sprouts with canola oil and add them to the crumbs/cheese mixture; toss to coat. Place in the frying basket and air fry for 15 minutes, shaking every 4 to 5 minutes. Serve sprinkled with chopped sage.

Chapter 1 Vegetables and Sides | 127

Simple Kale Chips

Prep time: 10 minutes | Cook time: 8 minutes | Serves 4

4 cups kale leaves, stems removed, chopped
2 tablespoons olive oil
1 teaspoon garlic powder
Salt and black pepper to taste
¼ teaspoon onion powder

1. In a bowl, mix kale and olive oil. Add in garlic and onion powders, salt, and black pepper; toss to coat. Arrange the kale in the frying basket and air fry for 8 minutes at 350ºF (177ºC), shaking once. Serve cool.

Buffalo Cauliflower

Prep time: 5 minutes | Cook time: 14 to 16 minutes | Serves 4

3 tablespoons butter, melted
3 tablespoons buffalo hot sauce
1 egg white
1 cup panko bread crumbs
Salt and black pepper to taste
½ head cauliflower, cut into florets

1. In a bowl, whisk butter, buffalo sauce, and egg white. In a separate bowl, mix bread crumbs with salt and black pepper. Toss the florets in the buffalo mixture and roll them in the bread crumbs to coat. Spritz with cooking spray and air fry them for 14 to 16 minutes at 340ºF (171ºC), shaking twice. Serve hot.

Parmesan Squash Chips with Greek Yogurt Dressing

Prep time: 15 minutes | Cook time: 10 minutes | Serves 4

2 yellow squash, sliced into rounds
½ cup flour
Salt and black pepper to taste
2 eggs
1 tablespoon soy sauce
¾ cup panko bread crumbs
¼ teaspoon dried dill
¼ cup Parmesan cheese, grated
Greek yogurt dressing, for serving

1. Preheat the air fryer to 380ºF (193ºC). Spray the frying basket with cooking spray. 2. In a bowl, mix the flour, dill, salt, and black pepper. In another bowl, beat the eggs with soy sauce. In a third, pour the bread crumbs and Parmesan cheese, mix well. 3. Dip the squash rounds in the flour, then in the eggs, and then coat with bread crumbs. Place in the frying basket and air fry for 10 minutes, flipping once halfway through. Serve with Greek yogurt dressing.

Easy Empanadas with Spinach and Mushroom

Prep time: 15 minutes | Cook time: 25 to 28 minutes | Serves 4

2 tablespoons olive oil
10 ounces (283 g) spinach, chopped
1 onion, chopped
2 garlic cloves, minced
¼ cup mushrooms, chopped
1 cup ricotta cheese, crumbled
1 (13-ounce / 369-g) pizza crust
1 tablespoon Italian seasoning
Salt and black pepper to taste
1½ cups marinara sauce

1. Heat olive oil in a pan over medium heat and sauté garlic, onion, and mushrooms for 4 minutes or until tender. Stir in spinach for 2 to 3 minutes. Season with Italian seasoning, salt, and pepper. Pour in marinara sauce and cook until the sauce thickens, about 5 minutes. Turn off and mix in ricotta cheese. 2. On a floured work surface, roll the pizza crust out. Slice into 4 rectangles. Divide the mixture between the rectangles and close them by folding in half. Seal the edges and lightly flatten. Spritz with cooking spray and transfer to the frying basket. Bake for 14 to 16 minutes, turning once halfway through. Serve.

Greek Avocado Wedges

Prep time: 15 minutes | Cook time: 8 minutes | Serves 4

2 avocados, peeled, stoned, cut into wedges
1 cup panko bread crumbs
2 egg, beaten
½ cup Greek yogurt
1 tablespoon fresh cilantro, chopped
½ teaspoon sriracha sauce
Salt and garlic powder to taste

1. Preheat the air fryer to 390ºF (199ºC). Add the yogurt, sriracha sauce, salt, garlic powder, and cilantro to a small bowl. Mix together until well incorporated. Place in the fridge to chill for 15 minutes. 2. In a bowl, whisk the eggs with a pinch of salt until frothy. In another bowl, mix the bread crumbs with garlic powder and salt. Dip the avocado wedges into the eggs and then dredge in the bread crumbs. Arrange the wedges in the greased frying basket. Spritz with cooking spray, Air fry for 4 minutes, flip, and cook for 3 to 4 more minutes until crispy. Serve the avocado wedges with yogurt sauce.

Golden Asparagus with Romesco Sauce

Prep time: 5 minutes | Cook time: 10 minutes | Serves 4

1 cup panko bread crumbs
Salt and black pepper to taste
½ cup almond flour
1 pound (454 g) asparagus spears, trimmed and washed
2 eggs
2 tomatoes, chopped
Romesco Sauce:
2 roasted peppers, chopped
½ cup almond flour
½ teaspoon garlic powder
1 tablespoon vinegar
2 slices toasted bread, torn into pieces
½ teaspoon paprika
1 teaspoon crushed red chili flakes
1 tablespoon tomato purée
½ cup extra-virgin olive oil

1. Preheat the air fryer to 390ºF (199ºC). On a plate, combine panko bread crumbs, salt, and black pepper. On another shallow plate, whisk the eggs with salt and black pepper. On a third plate, pour the almond flour. Dip asparagus in the almond flour, followed by a dip in the eggs, and finally, coat with bread crumbs. 2. Place in the greased frying basket and air fry for 10 minutes, turning once halfway. Pulse all romesco sauce ingredients in a food processor until smooth. Serve asparagus with romesco sauce.

Italian Cauliflower

Prep time: 5 minutes | Cook time: 12 minutes | Serves 4

1 tablespoon Italian seasoning
1 cup flour
1 cup milk
1 egg, beaten
1 head cauliflower, cut into florets

1. Preheat the air fryer to 390ºF (199ºC). Grease the frying basket with cooking spray. In a bowl, mix flour, milk, egg, and Italian seasoning. Coat the cauliflower in the mixture and drain the excess liquid. 2. Place the florets in the frying basket, spray with cooking spray, and air fry for 7 minutes. Shake and continue cooking for another 5 minutes. Allow to cool before serving.

Air Fried Green Olives

Prep time: 10 minutes | Cook time: 11 to 13 minutes | Serves 4

½ (13-ounce / 369-g) jar pimiento-stuffed green olives
¼ cup flour
¼ cup Parmesan cheese, grated
Salt and black pepper to taste
½ cup panko bread crumbs
1 egg, beaten
1 teaspoon cayenne pepper

1. Preheat the air fryer to 390ºF (199ºC). In a bowl, combine flour, cayenne pepper, salt, and black pepper. In another bowl, add the beaten egg. Mix the bread crumbs with Parmesan cheese in a third bowl. 2. Drain and pat dry the olives with a paper towel. Dredge the olives in flour, then in the egg, and finally in the bread crumbs. Place in the frying basket, spray them with cooking spray, and air fry for 8 to 10 minutes. Shake and cook for 3 more minutes. Let cool before serving.

One-Step Radish Chips

Prep time: 5 minutes | Cook time: 8 minutes | Serves 4

10 to 15 radishes, thinly sliced   Salt to season

1. Preheat the air fryer to 400ºF (204ºC). Grease the frying basket with cooking spray. Add in the sliced radishes and air fry for 8 minutes, flipping once halfway through. Season with salt and consume immediately.

Garlicky Green Bean

Prep time: 10 minutes | Cook time: 10 to 12 minutes | Serves 4

1 pound (454 g) green beans, trimmed
2 tablespoons olive oil
½ teaspoon garlic powder
½ teaspoon onion powder
½ teaspoon paprika
Salt and black pepper to taste

1. Preheat the air fryer to 390ºF (199ºC). In a bowl, mix olive oil, garlic and onion powders, paprika, salt, and black pepper. Coat the green beans in the mixture and place them in the greased frying basket. Air fry for 10 to 12 minutes, shaking once halfway through cooking. Serve warm.

Kielbasa and Mushroom Pierogi

Prep time: 10 minutes | Cook time: 12 to 14 minutes | Serves 4

½ package puff pastry dough, at room temperature
½ pound (227 g) Kielbasa smoked sausage, chopped
½ onion, chopped
½ pound (227 g) mushrooms, chopped
½ teaspoon ground cumin
¼ teaspoon paprika
Salt and black pepper to taste
1 egg, beaten

1. Preheat the air fryer to 360ºF (182ºC). In a bowl, mix Kielbasa sausage, onion, mushrooms, cumin, paprika, salt, and pepper. Place the pastry on a lightly floured surface. Using a glass, cut out 8 circles of the pastry. 2. Place 1 tablespoon of the sausage mixture on each pastry circle, brush the edges with the beaten egg, and fold over. Seal the edges with a fork. Brush the empanadas with the remaining egg and spray with cooking spray. Place in the greased frying basket and bake for 12 to 14 minutes until golden brown.

Mackerel and Rice Balls

Prep time: 10 minutes | Cook time: 14 to 16 minutes | Serves 4

1 cup smoked mackerel, flaked
2 cups cooked rice
2 eggs, lightly beaten
1 cup Grana Padano cheese, grated
¼ cup fresh thyme, chopped
Salt and black pepper to taste
1 cup panko bread crumbs
Cooking spray

1. In a bowl, add fish, rice, eggs, Grana Padano cheese, thyme, salt, and black pepper; stir to combine. Shape the mixture into 12 even-sized balls. Roll the balls in the crumbs, then spray with cooking spray. Place the balls in the frying basket and air fry for 14 to 16 minutes at 400ºF (204ºC), shaking once, until crispy.

Cheesy Salmon Mini Tarts with Dill

Prep time: 10 minutes | Cook time: 10 minutes | Serves 4 to 6

15 mini tart shells
4 eggs, lightly beaten
½ cup heavy cream
3 ounces (85 g) smoked salmon
6 ounces (170 g) cream cheese, divided into 15 pieces
2 tablespoons fresh dill, chopped

1. Mix together the eggs and heavy cream in a bowl. Arrange the tarts on a greased air fryer muffin tray. Pour the mixture into the tarts, about halfway up the side, and top with a piece of salmon and cheese. Bake in the fryer for 10 minutes at 340ºF (171ºC), regularly checking them to avoid overcooking. When ready, remove them from the tray and let cool. Sprinkle with freshly chopped dill and enjoy.

Crispy Shrimp

Prep time: 10 minutes | Cook time: 12 to 14 minutes | Serves 4

1 pound (454 g) jumbo shrimp, peeled and deveined
¾ cup coconut, shredded
1 teaspoon maple syrup
½ cup bread crumbs
⅓ cup cornstarch
½ cup milk

1. Pour the cornstarch and shrimp in a zipper bag and shake vigorously to coat. Mix maple syrup and milk in a bowl and set aside. In a separate bowl, mix the bread crumbs and shredded coconut. 2. Remove the shrimp from the bag while shaking off excess starch. Dip each piece in the milk mixture and then in the crumbs mixture. Lay the shrimp in the frying basket and air fry for 12 to 14 minutes at 350°F (177°C), flipping once halfway through. Serve with a coconut-based dip or sautéed green beans if desired.

Prawn and Cabbage Egg Rolls

Prep time: 15 minutes | Cook time: 16 minutes | Serves 4

2 tablespoons olive oil
1-inch piece fresh ginger, grated
1 tablespoon garlic paste
1 carrot, cut into strips
¼ cup chicken broth
2 tablespoons soy sauce
1 tablespoon sugar
1 cup Napa cabbage, shredded
1 tablespoon sesame oil
8 cooked prawns, chopped
1 egg
8 egg roll wrappers

1. Warm olive oil in a skillet over medium heat. Sauté ginger, carrot, and garlic paste for 2 minutes. Pour in the broth, soy sauce, and sugar and bring to a boil. Add the cabbage, lower the heat, and let simmer until softened, about 4 minutes. Remove from the heat and stir in sesame oil; let cool for 15 minutes. 2. Strain the cabbage mixture and add in the chopped prawns. Whisk an egg in a small bowl. Divide the prawn mixture between the wrappers. Fold the bottom part over the filling and tuck under. Fold in both sides and tightly roll-up. Use the whisked egg to seal the wrappers. Place the rolls into the greased frying basket, spray them with oil and air fry for 12 minutes at 370°F (188°C), turning once halfway through.

Corn-Crusted Cod Fingers

Prep time: 10 minutes | Cook time: 12 to 14 minutes | Serves 4

2 cups flour
Salt and black pepper to taste
1 teaspoon seafood seasoning
1 cup cornmeal
1 pound (454 g) cod fillets, cut into fingers
2 tablespoons milk
2 eggs, beaten
1 cup bread crumbs

1. Preheat the air fryer to 400°F (204°C). In a bowl, mix the eggs with milk, salt, and black pepper. In a separate bowl, mix the flour, cornmeal, and seafood seasoning. In a third bowl, pour the bread crumbs. 2. Roll the cod fingers in the flour mixture, then dip in the egg mixture, and finally coat with the bread crumbs. Place the fingers in the frying basket and air fry for 12 to 14 minutes, shaking once or twice. Serve hot.

Italian Salmon Croquettes

Prep time: 15 minutes | Cook time: 10 to 12 minutes | Serves 4

1 (15-ounce / 425-g) tinned salmon, flaked
1 cup onions, grated
1 cup carrots, grated
3 large eggs
1½ tablespoons fresh chives, chopped
4 tablespoons mayonnaise
4 tablespoons bread crumbs
2½ teaspoons Italian seasoning
Salt and black pepper to taste
2½ teaspoons lemon juice

1. In a bowl, mix well the salmon, onions, carrots, eggs, chives, mayonnaise, crumbs, Italian seasoning, salt, black pepper, and lemon juice. Form croquettes out of the mixture and refrigerate for 45 minutes. 2. Preheat the air fryer to 400°F (204°C). Grease the basket with cooking spray. Arrange the croquettes in a single layer and spray with cooking spray. Air fry for 10 to 12 minutes until golden, flipping once.

Parsley and Lemon Fried Shrimp

Prep time: 10 minutes | Cook time: 10 to 12 minutes | Serves 4

1½ pounds (680 g) shrimp, peeled and deveined
½ cup fresh parsley, chopped
Juice of 1 lemon
1 egg, beaten
½ cup flour
¾ cup seasoned bread crumbs
2 tablespoons chili garlic sauce

1. Add the shrimp, parsley, and lemon juice in a resealable bag and massage until well-coated. Place in the fridge to marinate for 20 minutes. Preheat the air fryer to 400°F (204°C). 2. Put beaten egg, flour, and bread crumbs each in a bowl. Dredge shrimp in the flour, then in the egg, and finally in the crumbs. Add to the frying basket and spray with cooking spray. Air fry for 10 to 12 minutes, shaking once. Remove to a serving plate and drizzle with chili garlic sauce to serve.

Cheesy Bacon Fries

Prep time: 10 minutes | Cook time: 30 to 32 minutes | Serves 4

2 russet potatoes, boiled and chopped
5 slices bacon
2 tablespoons olive oil
2 cups Cheddar cheese, shredded
3 ounces (85 g) softened cream cheese
Salt and black pepper to taste
¼ cup scallions, chopped

1. Preheat the air fryer to 400°F (204°C). Place the bacon in the frying basket and air fry for 5 minutes, turning once; set aside to cool. To the air fryer, add the potatoes and drizzle them with olive oil. Air fry for 20 to 22 minutes, shaking once. Remove and season with salt and black pepper. 2. In a bowl, mix Cheddar and cream cheeses. Pour over the potatoes and cook for 5 more minutes. Chop the fried bacon and scatter over the potatoes. Sprinkle with scallions and serve immediately.

130 | Chapter 1 Vegetables and Sides

Air Fried Beef Sticks

Prep time: 10 minutes | Cook time: 14 to 16 minutes | Serves 4

1 pound (454 g) ground beef
1 tablespoon thyme
½ teaspoon garlic powder
½ teaspoon chili powder
Salt to taste
1 teaspoon liquid smoke

1. Place the ground beef, thyme, garlic powder, chili powder, salt, and liquid smoke in a bowl; mix well. Mold out 4 sticks with your hands and place them on a plate to stand for 10 minutes. After, place them in the frying basket and air fry for 14 to 16 minutes at 350ºF (177ºC), flipping once halfway through. Serve warm.

Crispy Bacon with Butter Bean Dip

Prep time: 10 minutes | Cook time: 10 minutes | Serves 2

1 (14-ounce / 397-g) can butter beans
1 tablespoon scallions, chopped
½ cup feta cheese, crumbled
Black pepper to taste
3 tablespoons olive oil
2 ounces (57 g) bacon, sliced

1. Preheat the air fryer to 390ºF (199ºC). Arrange the bacon slices in the frying basket and air fry for 5 minutes. Flip and cook for 5 more minutes or until crispy. Remove to a paper towel-lined plate to drain. 2. Meanwhile, blend butter beans, olive oil, and black pepper in a blender. Add in the feta cheese and stir well. Serve the crispy bacon with the feta-bean dip and scatter fresh scallions on top.

Bacon-Wrapped Avocados

Prep time: 10 minutes | Cook time: 8 to 10 minutes | Serves 4

12 thick strips bacon
3 large avocados, sliced
⅓ teaspoon salt
⅓ teaspoon chili powder
⅓ teaspoon cumin

1. Stretch the bacon strips to elongate and cut in half to make 24 pieces. Wrap each bacon piece around a slice of avocado. Tuck the end of bacon into the wrap, and season with salt, chili powder, and cumin. 2. Arrange the wrapped pieces in the frying basket and air fry for 8 to 10 minutes at 350ºF (177ºC), flipping halfway through to cook evenly. Remove to a wire rack and repeat the process for the remaining avocados.

Cheese-Stuffed Jalapeños

Prep time: 15 minutes | Cook time: 11 to 13 minutes | Serves 4

8 jalapeño peppers, halved lengthwise and seeded
4 chicken breasts, halved and butterflied
6 ounces (170 g) cream cheese, softened
6 ounces (170 g) Cheddar cheese, grated
16 slices bacon
1 cup bread crumbs
Salt and black pepper to taste
2 eggs

1. Season the chicken with black pepper and salt on both sides. In a bowl, add cream and Cheddar cheeses, black pepper, and salt; mix well. Fill the jalapeños with the cheese mixture. 2. On a working board, flatten each piece of chicken and lay 2 bacon slices onto each one. Place a stuffed jalapeño on each laid out chicken and bacon set and wrap around the jalapeños. 3. Preheat the air fryer to 350ºF (177ºC). Add the eggs to a bowl and pour the bread crumbs into another bowl. Dip the wrappers into the eggs first and then in the bread crumbs. Arrange them on the greased frying basket and air fry for 7 to 8 minutes, turn and cook further for 4 to 5 minutes. Serve warm.

Black Bean and Corn Flatbreads

Prep time: 20 minutes | Cook time: 9 to 11 minutes | Serves 4

4 flatbreads, warm
2 ounces (57 g) cream cheese, softened
¼ cup Cheddar cheese, shredded
½ (15-ounce / 425-g) can corn, drained and rinsed
½ (15-ounce / 425-g) can black beans, drained and rinsed
¼ cup chunky salsa
½ teaspoon ground cumin
½ teaspoon paprika
Salt and black pepper to taste
2 tablespoons fresh cilantro, chopped

1. Preheat the air fryer to 320ºF (160ºC). Add the black beans, corn, chunky salsa, cream cheese, Cheddar cheese, cumin, paprika, salt, and pepper in a bowl. Mix well. 2. Spread the mixture out on a baking dish and insert in the air fryer. Air fry for 9 to 11 minutes until heated through. Divide the mixture among the flatbreads. Top with cilantro and serve warm.

Parmesan Chicken Burgers

Prep time: 15 minutes | Cook time: 16 to 18 minutes | Serves 4

1 pound (454 g) ground chicken
½ cup seasoned bread crumbs
¼ cup Parmesan cheese, grated
1 egg, beaten
1 tablespoon minced garlic
1 tablespoon olive oil
1 teaspoon horseradish sauce
4 tablespoons Greek yogurt
4 buns, halved
4 tomato slices

1. Preheat the air fryer to 380ºF (193ºC). In a bowl, combine ground chicken, bread crumbs, Parmesan, egg, and garlic. Mix well. Form balls and flatten to make patties. Brush them with olive oil and place in the greased frying basket. Air fry for 16 to 18 minutes, flipping once until nice and golden. 2. Mix the yogurt with horseradish sauce. Assemble the burgers by spreading the yogurt mixture on the bun bottoms, then add the patties and fresh tomato slices. Cover with the bun tops and serve. 3. Mix the yogurt with horseradish sauce. Assemble the burgers by spreading the yogurt mixture on the bun bottoms, then add the patties and fresh tomato slices. Cover with the bun tops and serve.

Barbecue Sausage Pizza

Prep time: 10 minutes | Cook time: 8 to 10 minutes | Serves 1

1 piece naan bread
¼ cup barbecue sauce
¼ cup Mozzarella cheese, shredded
¼ cup Monterrey Jack cheese, shredded
2 tablespoons red onions, thinly sliced
½ chicken sausage, sliced
½ tablespoon fresh cilantro, chopped

1. Spray naan's bread with cooking spray and place it on the greased frying basket. Brush with barbecue sauce, sprinkle with Mozzarella and Monterrey Jack cheeses, and red onions. Top with the chicken sausage. Bake in the preheated fryer for 8 to 10 minutes at 400ºF (204ºC). Sprinkle with cilantro to serve.

Italian Pork Sausage Pizza

Prep time: 10 minutes | Cook time: 10 minutes | Serves 2

1 piece pizza crust dough
½ teaspoon dried oregano
¼ cup tomato sauce
¼ cup Mozzarella cheese, shredded
1 shallot, thinly sliced
1 Italian pork sausage, sliced
4 fresh basil leaves
4 black olives

1. Preheat the air fryer to 390ºF (199ºC). Spread tomato sauce over the pizza dough and sprinkle with oregano. Top with Mozzarella cheese, shallot, and pork sausage slices. 2. Place the pizza dough on the greased frying basket. Bake for 10 minutes until the crust is golden and the cheese is melted. Scatter over basil leaves and olives to serve.

Chorizo and Mushroom Pizza

Prep time: 10 minutes | Cook time: 12 to 14 minutes | Serves 4

4 pita bread pieces
4 tablespoons marinara sauce
12 chorizo rounds
8 button mushrooms, sliced
8 fresh basil leaves
2 cups Cheddar cheese, grated
1 teaspoon chili flakes
Cooking oil

1. Spray the pitas with oil and scatter marinara sauce over. Top with chorizo rounds, mushrooms, basil, Cheddar cheese, and chili flakes. Bake in the fryer for 12 to 14 minutes at 360ºF (182ºC), checking regularly to ensure an even baking. Work in batches if needed. Serve warm with garlic mayo or yogurt dip.

Mozzarella Pepperoni Pizza

Prep time: 10 minutes | Cook time: 14 to 16 minutes | Serves 2

8 ounces (227 g) fresh pizza dough
⅓ cup tomato sauce
⅓ cup Mozzarella cheese, shredded
8 pepperonis, sliced
1 teaspoon oregano, dried
Flour to dust

1. On a floured surface, place pizza dough and dust with flour. Stretch with hands into greased frying basket. Spray the dish with cooking spray and place the pizza dough inside. 2. Spread the tomato sauce, leaving some space at the border. Scatter with Mozzarella cheese and oregano and top with pepperoni slices. Bake for 14 to 16 minutes or until crispy at 340ºF (171ºC). Serve sliced.

Bacon-Wrapped Dates

Prep time: 10 minutes | Cook time: 10 to 12 minutes | Serves 4

2 tablespoons maple syrup
16 dates, pits removed
⅓ cup blue cheese, softened
8 bacon slices, cut in half crosswise

1. Preheat the air fryer to 370ºF (188ºC). Grease the frying basket with cooking oil. Using a sharp knife, make a deep cut into each date to create a pocket. Stuff the dates with blue cheese and pinch to lock up. 2. Lay the bacon slices on the chopping board. Put a date on one side of each slice and roll up. Secure with toothpicks. Brush the wrapped dates with maple syrup and air fry for 10 to 12 minutes, turning halfway through cooking until the bacon is crispy. Let cool for 5 minutes and serve.

Greek Chicken Tortillas with Mozzarella

Prep time: 10 minutes | Cook time: 12 to 14 minutes | Serves 4

1 cup cooked chicken, shredded
1 cup Mozzarella cheese, shredded
¼ cup salsa
¼ cup Greek yogurt
Salt and black pepper to taste
8 flour tortillas

1. In a bowl, mix the chicken, Mozzarella, salsa, Greek yogurt, salt, and black pepper. Lay 2 tablespoons of the mixture at the center of the tortillas. Roll tightly around the mixture. Spray with cooking spray and arrange them in the frying basket. Air fry for 12 to 14 minutes at 380ºF (193ºC), turning once. Serve.

Lemony Meatballs

Prep time: 15 minutes | Cook time: 13 to 15 minutes | Serves 4

1 pound (454 g) ground beef
1 teaspoon grated ginger
1 tablespoon hot sauce
½ tablespoon white wine vinegar
½ teaspoon lemon juice
½ cup tomato ketchup
¼ teaspoon dry mustard
Salt and black pepper to taste

1. In a bowl, mix well ground beef, ginger, hot sauce, vinegar, lemon juice, ketchup, mustard, black pepper, and salt. With greased hands, shape the mixture into 2-inch sized balls. Add the balls to the fryer without overcrowding. Air fry at 370ºF (188ºC) for 13 to 15 minutes, shaking once. Serve with tomato dip if desired.

Cajun Beef Fajitas

Prep time: 15 minutes | Cook time: 10 minutes | Serves 4

1 pound (454 g) beef sirloin steak, cut into strips
2 garlic cloves, minced
1 teaspoon paprika
½ red bell pepper, sliced
½ orange bell pepper, sliced
2 shallots, sliced
2 tablespoons Cajun seasoning
2 tablespoons olive oil
8 tortilla wraps
½ cup Cheddar cheese, shredded
Salt and black pepper to taste

1. Preheat the air fryer to 360ºF (182ºC). In a bowl, combine the beef, shallots, bell peppers, and garlic. Season with Cajun seasoning, paprika, salt, and black pepper; toss to combine. Transfer the mixture to a greased frying basket and place it inside the frying basket. Bake for 10 minutes, shaking once or twice throughout cooking. Serve on the tortilla wraps, topped with Cheddar cheese.

South Asian Pork Momos

Prep time: 10 minutes | Cook time: 17 to 21 minutes | Serves 4

1 pound (454 g) ground pork
2 tablespoons olive oil
1 carrot, shredded
1 onion, chopped
1 teaspoon soy sauce
16 wonton wrappers
Salt and black pepper to taste

1. Preheat the air fryer to 320ºF (160ºC). Warm olive oil in a pan over medium heat and stir-fry ground pork, onion, carrot, soy sauce, salt, and black pepper for 8 to 10 minutes or until the meat is browned. 2. Divide the filling between the wrappers. Tuck them around the mixture to form momo shapes and seal the edges. Spritz the momos with cooking spray and air fry them for 9 to 11 minutes, flipping once.

Feta French Fries

Prep time: 10 minutes | Cook time: 20 minutes | Serves 4

6 russet potatoes, cut into strips
2 tablespoons olive oil
4 ounces (113 g) feta cheese, grated
Salt and black pepper to taste

1. Preheat the air fryer to 400ºF (204ºC). Drizzle the potatoes with olive oil and toss to coat. Place in the frying basket and air fry for 20 minutes, shaking once halfway through. Sprinkle the potatoes with freshly grated feta cheese and enjoy.

Spanish Chorizo with Brussels Sprouts

Prep time: 15 minutes | Cook time: 11 to 14 minutes | Serves 4

4 Spanish chorizo sausages, halved
1 pound (454 g) Brussels sprouts, trimmed and halved
2 tablespoons olive oil
Salt and black pepper to taste
1 teaspoon garlic puree
1 thyme sprig, chopped

1. Preheat the air fryer to 390ºF (199ºC). In a bowl, mix olive oil, garlic puree, salt, and black pepper. Add the Brussels sprouts and toss to coat. Arrange chorizo and Brussels sprouts on the greased frying basket and air fry for 11 to 14 minutes, tossing once halfway through cooking. Top with thyme to serve.

Cheddar Pork Balls

Prep time: 15 minutes | Cook time: 12 to 14 minutes | Serves 4

1 pound (454 g) ground pork sausage meat
1¼ cups Cheddar cheese, shredded
1 cup flour, sifted
¾ teaspoon baking soda
2 eggs
½ cup sour cream
½ teaspoon dried oregano
½ teaspoon smoked paprika
½ teaspoon garlic powder
2 tablespoons coconut oil

1. Heat coconut oil in a pan over medium heat and brown the sausage meat for 3 to 4 minutes. Mix flour with baking soda in a bowl. Whisk eggs, sour cream, oregano, paprika, and garlic in another bowl. 2. Combine egg and flour mixtures using a spatula. Mix in the cheese and sausage meat; let cool slightly. Mold out balls out of the batter and refrigerate for 15 minutes. Remove from the fridge and brush them with the sausage fat. Place the balls in the basket and air fry for 12 to 14 minutes at 400ºF (204ºC), shaking once.

Baked Potatoes with Bacon

Prep time: 10 minutes | Cook time: 12 to 15 minutes | Serves 4

4 potatoes, scrubbed, halved, cut lengthwise
1 tablespoon olive oil
Salt and black pepper to taste
4 ounces (113 g) bacon, chopped

1. Preheat the air fryer to 390ºF (199ºC). Brush the potatoes with olive oil and season with salt and black pepper. Arrange them in the greased frying basket, cut-side down. Bake for 15 minutes, flip them, top with bacon and bake for 12 to 15 minutes or until the potatoes are golden and the bacon is crispy. Serve.

Buttered Red Potatoes

Prep time: 10 minutes | Cook time: 20 to 22 minutes | Serves 4

4 red potatoes, cut into wedges
1 tablespoon garlic powder
Salt and black pepper to taste
2 tablespoons chives, chopped
3 tablespoons butter, melted

1. Preheat the air fryer to 380ºF (193ºC). In a bowl, mix butter, garlic powder, salt, and pepper. Add the potatoes and shake to coat. Place them in the frying basket and bake for 12 minutes, remove the basket, shake and continue to cook for another 8 to 10 minutes until golden brown. Serve warm topped with chives.

Crispy Hasselback Potatoes

Prep time: 15 minutes | Cook time: 25 to 30 minutes | Serves 4

2 tablespoons lard, melted
1 pound (454 g) russet potatoes
1 tablespoon olive oil
Salt and black pepper to taste
1 garlic clove, crushed
1 tablespoon fresh dill, chopped

1. Preheat the air fryer to 400ºF (204ºC). On the potatoes, make thin vertical slits, around 0.2 inch apart. Make sure to cut the potatoes ¾-the way down, so that they can hold together. Mix together the lard, olive oil, and garlic in a bowl. Brush the potatoes with some of the mixture. 2. Season with salt and pepper and place them in the greased frying basket. Air fry for 25 to 30 minutes, brushing once halfway through so they don't dry during cooking, until golden and crispy around the edges. Sprinkle with dill. Serve and enjoy!

Sweet Potato Boats

Prep time: 10 minutes | Cook time: 10 to 12 minutes | Serves 4

4 sweet potatoes, boiled and halved lengthwise
2 tablespoons olive oil
1 shallot, chopped
1 cup canned mixed beans
¼ cup Mozzarella cheese, grated
Salt and black pepper to taste

1. Preheat the air fryer to 400ºF (204ºC). Grease the frying basket with olive oil. 2. Scoop out the flesh from the potatoes, so shells are formed. Chop the potato flesh and put it in a bowl. Add in shallot, mixed beans, salt, and pepper; mix to combine. Fill the potato shells with the mixture and top with the cheese. Arrange on the basket and place inside the fryer. Bake for 10 to 12 minutes.

Horse Carrots Chips

Prep time: 10 minutes | Cook time: 12 minutes | Serves 4

1 tablespoon coconut oil, melted
1 pound (454 g) horse carrots, sliced
Salt and black pepper to taste
½ teaspoon chili powder

1. Preheat the air fryer to 400ºF (204ºC). 2. In a bowl, mix the carrots with coconut oil, chili powder, salt, and black pepper. Place them in the fryer and air fry for 7 minutes. Shake the basket and cook for another 5 minutes until golden brown. Serve.

Spiced Sweet Potato Wedges

Prep time: 10 minutes | Cook time: 23 to 25 minutes | Serves 2

½ pound (227 g) sweet potatoes, cut into wedges
1 tablespoon coconut oil
¼ teaspoon salt
¼ teaspoon chili powder
¼ teaspoon garlic powder
¼ teaspoon smoked paprika
¼ teaspoon dried thyme
¼ teaspoon cayenne pepper

1. In a bowl, mix coconut oil, salt, chili and garlic powders, paprika, thyme, and cayenne pepper. Toss in the potato wedges. Arrange the wedges on the frying basket and air fry for 23 to 25 minutes at 380ºF (193ºC), shaking a few times through cooking until golden. Serve and enjoy!

Prosciutto and Cheese Stromboli

Prep time: 10 minutes | Cook time: 15 minutes | Serves 4

1 (13-ounce / 369-g) pizza crust
4 (1-ounce / 28-g) fontina cheese slices
8 slices prosciutto
12 cherry tomatoes, halved
4 fresh basil leaves, chopped
½ teaspoon dried oregano
Salt and black pepper to taste

1. Roll out the pizza crust on a lightly floured work surface; slice into 4 squares. Top each one with a slice of fontina cheese, 2 slices of prosciutto, 3 halved cherry tomatoes, oregano, and basil. Season with salt and black pepper. Close the rectangles by folding in half, press, and seal the edges with a fork. Spritz with cooking spray and transfer to the greased frying basket. Bake for 15 minutes, turning once.

Fava Bean Falafel Bites

Prep time: 10 minutes | Cook time: 12 minutes | Serves 4

1 tablespoon olive oil
1 can (15½-ounce / 439-g) fava beans, drained
1 red onion, chopped
2 teaspoons chopped fresh cilantro
1 teaspoon ground cumin
Salt to taste
1 garlic clove, minced
3 tablespoons flour
4 lemon wedges to serve

1. Preheat the air fryer to 380ºF (193ºC). In a food processor, pulse all the ingredients until a thick paste is formed. Shape the mixture into ping pong-sized balls. Brush with olive oil and insert in the greased frying basket. Air fry for 12 minutes, turning once halfway through. Plate and serve with lemon wedges.

Plum and Pancetta Bombs

Prep time: 15 minutes | Cook time: 10 minutes | Serves 4 to 6

1¼ cups soft goat cheese, crumbled
1 tablespoon fresh rosemary, finely chopped
1 cup almonds, chopped
Salt and black pepper to taste
15 dried plums, soaked and chopped
15 pancetta slices

1. Line the frying basket with baking paper. In a bowl, add goat cheese, rosemary, almonds, salt, black pepper, and plums; stir well. Roll into balls and wrap with a pancetta slice. Place them into the fryer and air fry for 10 minutes at 400ºF (204ºC), shaking once. Let cool for a few minutes. Serve with toothpicks.

Fried Sausage Ravioli

Prep time: 10 minutes | Cook time: 10 to 12 minutes | Serves 6

2 (18-ounce / 510-g) packages of fresh sausage ravioli
1 cup flour
1 cup marinara sauce
4 eggs, beaten in a bowl
2 cups bread crumbs
2 tablespoons Parmesan cheese, grated

1. Preheat the air fryer to 400ºF (204ºC). In a bowl, mix bread crumbs with Parmesan cheese. Dip sausage ravioli into the flour, then into the eggs, and finally in the breadcrumb mixture. Arrange the coated ravioli on the greased frying basket in an even layer and spritz them with cooking spray. Air fry for 10 to 12 minutes, turning once halfway through cooking until nice and golden. Serve hot with the marinara sauce.

Parsley Butternut Squash

Prep time: 10 minutes | Cook time: 12 to 14 minutes | Serves 4

2 cups butternut squash, cubed
2 tablespoons olive oil
Salt and black pepper to taste
¼ teaspoon dried thyme
1 tablespoon fresh parsley, finely chopped

1. In a bowl, add squash, olive oil, salt, black pepper, and thyme; toss to coat. Place the squash in the air fryer and air fry for 12 to 14 minutes at 360ºF (182ºC), shaking once or twice. Serve sprinkled with fresh parsley.

Cayenne Chickpeas

Prep time: 15 minutes | Cook time: 15 to 20 minutes | Serves 4

1 (19-ounce / 539-g) can chickpeas, drained and rinsed
2 tablespoons olive oil
½ teaspoon ground cumin
¼ teaspoon mustard powder
¼ teaspoon onion powder
½ teaspoon chili powder
¼ teaspoon cayenne pepper
¼ teaspoon salt

1. Preheat the air fryer to 385ºF (196ºC). In a mixing bowl, thoroughly combine the olive oil, cumin, mustard powder, onion powder, chili powder, cayenne pepper, and salt. Add in the chickpeas. 2. Toss them until evenly coated. Transfer the chickpeas to the frying basket and air fry, shaking the basket every 2 to 3 minutes. Cook until they're as crunchy as you like them, about 15 to 20 minutes. Serve.

Parmesan Parsnips with Cilantro and Paprika

Prep time: 10 minutes | Cook time: 14 to 16 minutes | Serves 4

½ tablespoon paprika
1 pound (454 g) parsnips, peeled and halved
4 tablespoons avocado oil
2 tablespoons fresh cilantro, chopped
2 tablespoons Parmesan cheese, grated
1 teaspoon garlic powder
Salt and black pepper to taste

1. Preheat the air fryer to 390ºF (199ºC). 2. In a bowl, mix paprika, avocado oil, garlic, salt, and black pepper. Toss in the parsnips to coat. Arrange them on the greased frying basket and bake for 14 to 16 minutes, turning once halfway through cooking, until golden and crunchy. Remove and sprinkle with Parmesan cheese and cilantro. Serve.

Butter-Fried Broccoli

Prep time: 10 minutes | Cook time: 10 minutes | Serves 2

2 tablespoons butter, melted
1 egg white
1 garlic clove, grated
Salt and black pepper to taste
½ pound (227 g) broccoli florets
⅓ cup grated Parmesan cheese

1. In a bowl, whisk together butter, egg white, garlic, salt, and black pepper. Toss in the broccoli to coat. Arrange them in a single layer in the greased frying basket and air fry for 10 minutes at 360ºF (182ºC), shaking once. Remove to a plate and sprinkle with Parmesan cheese. Serve immediately.

Balsamic-Lime Pumpkin

Prep time: 10 minutes | Cook time: 15 to 17 minutes | Serves 4

1 pound (454 g) pumpkin, washed and cut into wedges
1 tablespoon paprika
2 tablespoons olive oil
1 lime, juiced
1 tablespoon balsamic vinegar
Salt and black pepper to taste
1 teaspoon turmeric

1. Preheat the air fryer to 400ºF (204ºC). Add the pumpkin wedges to the greased frying basket and air fry for 10 to 12 minutes, flipping once. In a bowl, mix olive oil, lime juice, balsamic vinegar, turmeric, salt, black pepper, and paprika. Drizzle the dressing over the pumpkin and fry for 5 more minutes. Serve warm.

Italian Cheesy Mushrooms

Prep time: 5 minutes | Cook time: 10 to 12 minutes | Serves 2

2 tablespoons olive oil
Salt and black pepper to taste
10 button mushroom caps
2 tablespoons Mozzarella cheese, grated
2 tablespoons Cheddar cheese, grated
1 teaspoon Italian seasoning

1. Preheat the air fryer to 390ºF (199ºC). In a bowl, mix olive oil, salt, black pepper, and Italian seasoning. Toss in the mushrooms to coat. Mix the cheeses in a separate bowl. Stuff the mushrooms with the cheese mixture and place them in the frying basket. Bake for 10 to 12 minutes until golden on top. Serve warm.

Chapter 1 Vegetables and Sides | 135

Walnut-Stuffed Mushrooms

Prep time: 10 minutes | Cook time: 10 to 12 minutes | Serves 4

4 large portobello mushroom caps
⅓ cup walnuts, finely chopped
1 tablespoon canola oil
½ cup Mozzarella cheese, shredded
2 tablespoons fresh parsley, chopped

1. Preheat the air fryer to 350°F (177°C). Grease the frying basket with cooking spray. 2. Rub the mushrooms with canola oil and fill them with Mozzarella cheese. Top with walnuts and arrange them in the greased frying basket. Bake for 10 to 12 minutes or until golden on top. Remove and let cool for a few minutes. Sprinkle with freshly chopped parsley and serve.

Ricotta-Stuffed Peppers

Prep time: 10 minutes | Cook time: 10 to 12 minutes | Serves 4

4 serrano peppers, halved and seeds removed
3 ounces (85 g) ricotta cheese, crumbled
1 cup bread crumbs
1 teaspoon paprika
1 tablespoon chives, chopped
1 tablespoon olive oil

1. Preheat the air fryer to 380°F (193°C). Grease the frying basket with cooking spray. In a bowl, combine ricotta cheese, paprika, and chives. Spoon the mixture into the pepper halves and top with bread crumbs. Drizzle with olive oil. Place in the basket and bake for 10 to 12 minutes. Serve warm.

Garlicky Edamame

Prep time: 10 minutes | Cook time: 10 minutes | Serves 4

1 (16-ounce / 454-g) bag frozen edamame in pods
1 red chili, finely chopped
1 tablespoon olive oil
½ teaspoon garlic salt
½ teaspoon red pepper flakes
Black pepper to taste

1. Preheat the air fryer to 380°F (193°C). In a mixing bowl, combine olive oil, garlic salt, red pepper flakes, and black pepper and mix well. Add in the edamame and toss to coat. 2. Transfer to the frying basket in a single layer and air fry for 10 minutes, shaking once. Cook until lightly browned and just crispy. Work in batches if needed. Serve topped with the red chili.

Lebanese Muhammara

Prep time: 15 minutes | Cook time: 15 minutes | Serves 6

2 large red bell peppers
¼ cup plus 2 tablespoons extra-virgin olive oil
1 cup walnut halves
1 tablespoon agave nectar or honey
1 teaspoon fresh lemon juice
1 teaspoon ground cumin
1 teaspoon kosher salt
1 teaspoon red pepper flakes
Raw vegetables (such as cucumber, carrots, zucchini slices, or cauliflower) or toasted pita chips, for serving

1. Drizzle the peppers with 2 tablespoons olive oil and place in frying basket. Roast at 400°F (204°C) for 10 minutes. Add walnuts around the peppers and roast for 5 minutes. 2. Remove the peppers, seal in a resealable plastic bag, and let rest for 5 to 10 minutes. Allow the walnuts cool on a plate. 3. Purée the softened peppers, walnuts, agave, lemon juice, cumin, salt, and ½ teaspoon pepper flakes in a food processor until smooth. 4. Transfer the dip to a serving bowl and make an indentation in the middle. Pour the remaining olive oil into the indentation. Garnish the dip with the remaining pepper flakes. 5. Serve with vegetables or pita chips.

Herbed Brie Croutons

Prep time: 5 minutes | Cook time: 10 to 12 minutes | Serves 2

2 tablespoons olive oil
1 tablespoon french herbs
6 ounces (170 g) brie cheese, chopped
2 slices bread, halved

1. Preheat the air fryer to 340°F (171°C). Brush the bread slices with olive oil and sprinkle with herbs. Top with brie cheese. Place in the greased frying basket and bake for 10 to 12 minutes. Let cool, then cut into cubes.

Super Cabbage Canapes

Prep time: 10 minutes | Cook time: 5 to 8 minutes | Serves 2

1 whole cabbage, cut into rounds
½ cup Mozzarella cheese, shredded
½ carrot, cubed
¼ onion, cubed
¼ bell pepper, cubed
1 tablespoon fresh basil, chopped

1. Preheat the air fryer to 360°F (182°C). In a bowl, mix onion, carrot, bell pepper, and Mozzarella cheese. Toss to coat evenly. Add the cabbage rounds to the greased frying basket, top with the cheese mixture, and bake for 5 to 8 minutes. Garnish with basil and serve.

Egg and Broccoli Quiche

Prep time: 10 minutes | Cook time: 10 to 12 minutes | Serves 3

1 head broccoli, cut into florets
½ cup Parmesan cheese, grated
¼ cup heavy cream
Salt and black pepper to taste
5 eggs

1. Preheat the air fryer to 340°F (171°C). Beat the eggs with the heavy cream. Season with salt and black pepper. In a greased baking dish, lay the florets and cover with the egg mixture. Spread Parmesan cheese on top and place inside the frying basket. Bake for 10 to 12 minutes until golden brown on top. Serve warm.

Easy Parmesan Sandwich

Prep time: 10 minutes | Cook time: 10 to 12 minutes | Serves 1

4 tablespoons Parmesan cheese, shredded
2 scallions
1 tablespoon butter, softened
2 bread slices

1. Preheat the air fryer to 360ºF (182ºC). Spread only one side of the bread slices with butter. Cover one of the buttered slices with Parmesan and scallions and top with the buttered side of the other slice to form a sandwich. Place in the frying basket and bake for 10 to 12 minutes. Cut into 4 triangles and serve.

Salty Carrot Cookies

Prep time: 10 minutes | Cook time: 14 to 16 minutes | Serves 4

6 carrots, boiled and mashed
Salt and black pepper to taste
½ teaspoon parsley
1¼ ounces (35 g) oats
1 whole egg, beaten
½ teaspoon thyme

1. Preheat the air fryer to 360ºF (182ºC). In a bowl, combine carrots, salt, black pepper, egg, oats, thyme, and parsley; mix well to form batter. Shape into cookie shapes. Place the cookies in the greased frying basket and bake for 14 to 16 minutes, flipping once halfway through. Serve.

Mini Cheese Scones

Prep time: 10 minutes | Cook time: 18 to 20 minutes | Serves 4

1 cup flour
A pinch of salt
1 teaspoon baking powder
2 ounces (57 g) butter, cubed
1 teaspoon fresh chives, chopped
1 egg
¼ cup milk
½ cup Cheddar cheese, shredded

1. Preheat the air fryer to 360ºF (182ºC). Stir the flour in a bowl and mix in butter, baking powder, and salt until a breadcrumb mixture is formed. Add cheese, chives, milk, and egg, and mix to get a sticky dough. 2. Roll the dough into small balls. Place the balls in the greased frying basket and air fry for 18 to 20 minutes, shaking once or twice. Serve warm.

Cheese and Buttermilk Biscuits

Prep time: 5 minutes | Cook time: 18 to 20 minutes | Serves 4

½ cup butter, softened
1 tablespoon melted butter
1 teaspoon salt
2 cups flour
½ cup buttermilk
½ cup Cheddar cheese, grated
1 egg, beaten

1. Preheat the air fryer to 360ºF (182ºC). In a bowl, mix salt, flour, butter, cheese, and buttermilk to form a batter. Shape into balls and flatten them into biscuits. Arrange them on a greased frying basket and brush with the beaten egg. Drizzle with melted butter and bake in the fryer for 18 to 20 minutes, flipping once.

Cauliflower and Tofu Croquettes

Prep time: 15 minutes | Cook time: 18 to 22 minutes | Serves 4

1 pound (454 g) cauliflower florets
2 eggs
½ cup tofu, crumbled
½ cup Mozzarella cheese
⅓ cup bread crumbs
1 teaspoon dried thyme
¼ teaspoon ground cumin
½ teaspoon onion powder
Salt and black pepper to taste
1 cup chipotle aioli

1. Place the cauliflower florets in your food processor and pulse until it resembles rice. Microwave the resulting "rice" in a heatproof dish for 4 to 6 minutes until it have softened completely. Let cool. 2. Preheat the air fryer to 390ºF (199ºC). Add the eggs, tofu, Mozzarella cheese, bread crumbs, thyme, cumin, onion powder, salt, and pepper to the cauliflower rice and mix to combine. Form the mixture into croquettes and arrange them on the greased frying basket. Spritz with cooking spray. Air fry for 14 to 16 minutes, turning once, until golden brown. Serve warm with the chipotle aioli.

Panko Veggie Balls

Prep time: 15 minutes | Cook time: 22 to 24 minutes | Serves 4

½ pound (227 g) mushrooms, diced
3 tablespoons olive oil plus some more for brushing
1 small red onion, chopped
3 garlic cloves, minced
3 cups cauliflower, chopped
1 cup bread crumbs
1 cup Grana Padano cheese, grated
2 sprigs fresh thyme, chopped
Salt and black pepper to taste

1. Heat 3 tablespoons olive oil in a skillet over medium heat and sauté garlic and onion for 3 minutes. Add in mushrooms and cauliflower and stir-fry for 5 minutes. Add in Grana Padano cheese, black pepper, thyme, and salt. Turn off and let cool. Make small balls out of the mixture and refrigerate for 30 minutes. 2. Preheat the air fryer to 350ºF (177ºC). Remove the balls from the refrigerator and roll in the bread crumbs. Brush with olive oil and place in the frying basket without overcrowding. Bake for 14 to 16 minutes, tossing every 4 to 5 minutes. Serve.

Spicy Cheese Lings

Prep time: 10 minutes | Cook time: 10 to 12 minutes | Serves 4

½ cup grated Cheddar cheese plus extra for rolling
1 cup flour plus extra for kneading
¼ teaspoon chili powder
½ teaspoon baking powder
3 teaspoons butter, melted
A pinch of salt

1. In a bowl, mix the cheese, flour, baking powder, chili powder, butter, and salt. Add some water and mix well to get a dough. Remove the dough onto a flat, floured surface. Using a rolling pin, roll out into a thin sheet and cut into lings' shape. Add the cheese lings to the greased frying basket and air fry for 10 to 12 minutes at 350ºF (177ºC), flipping once halfway through. Serve with ketchup if desired.

Beef, Pork and Bacon balls

Prep time: 15 minutes | Cook time: 8 to 10 minutes | Serves 4

½ pound (227 g) ground beef
½ pound (227 g) ground pork
2 ounces (57 g) bacon, chopped
1 egg
Salt and black pepper to taste
¼ teaspoon cayenne pepper
2 ounces (57 g) Cheddar cheese, shredded
1 cup jalapeño tomato ketchup

1. Preheat the air fryer to 400ºF (204ºC). In a bowl, thoroughly mix all ingredients. Form the mixture into 1-inch balls using an ice cream scoop. Place them into the greased frying basket and spray with cooking oil. Air fry for 8 to 10 minutes, turning once. Serve with toothpicks and jalapeño tomato ketchup on the side.

French Beans with Toasted Almonds

Prep time: 10 minutes | Cook time: 10 to 12 minutes | Serves 4

1 pound (454 g) French beans, trimmed
Salt and black pepper to taste
½ tablespoon onion powder
2 tablespoons olive oil
½ cup toasted almonds, chopped

1. Preheat air fryer to 400ºF (204ºC). In a bowl, drizzle the beans with olive oil. Add onion powder, salt, and pepper and toss to coat. Air fry for 10 to 12 minutes, shaking once. Sprinkle with almonds and serve.

Cheddar Black Bean Burritos

Prep time: 5 minutes | Cook time: 7 to 8 minutes | Serves 4

4 tortillas
1 cup Cheddar cheese, grated
1 can (8-ounce / 227-g) black beans, drained
1 teaspoon taco seasoning

1. Preheat the air fryer to 350ºF (177ºC). Mix the beans with the taco seasoning. Divide the bean mixture between the tortillas and top with Cheddar cheese. Roll the burritos and arrange them on the greased frying basket. Place in the air fryer and bake for 4 to 5 minutes, flip, and cook for 3 more minutes. Serve warm.

Smoky Almonds

Prep time: 5 minutes | Cook time: 5 to 8 minutes | Serves 4 to 6

2 cups almonds
2 tablespoons liquid smoke
Salt to taste
1 tablespoon molasses

1. Preheat the air fryer to 360ºF (182ºC). In a bowl, add salt, liquid smoke, molasses, and almonds; toss to coat. Place the hazelnuts in the greased frying basket and bake for 5 to 8 minutes, shaking once. Serve warm.

Spiced Almonds

Prep time: 5 minutes | Cook time: 12 to 14 minutes | Serves 4

½ teaspoon ground cinnamon
½ teaspoon smoked paprika
1 cup almonds
1 egg white
Sea salt to taste

1. Preheat the air fryer to 310ºF (154ºC). Grease the frying basket with cooking spray. In a bowl, whisk the egg white with cinnamon and paprika and stir in the almonds. Spread the almonds in the frying basket and air fry for 12 to 14 minutes, shaking once or twice. Remove and sprinkle with sea salt to serve.

Sweet Pumpkin Seeds

Prep time: 10 minutes | Cook time: 17 to 20 minutes | Serves 4

1 cup pumpkin seeds, pulp removed, rinsed
1 tablespoon butter, melted
1 tablespoon brown sugar
1 teaspoon orange zest
½ teaspoon cardamom
½ teaspoon salt

1. Preheat air fryer to 320ºF (160ºC). Place the pumpkin seeds in a greased baking dish and place the dish in the fryer. Air fry for 4 to 5 minutes to avoid moisture. In a bowl, whisk butter, sugar, zest, cardamom, and salt. 2. Add the seeds to the bowl and toss to coat well. Transfer the seeds to the baking dish inside the fryer and bake for 13 to 15 minutes, shaking the basket every 5 minutes, until lightly browned. Serve warm.

Masala Cashew Nuts

Prep time: 5 minutes | Cook time: 5 to 8 minutes | Serves 2

1 cup cashew nuts
Salt and black pepper to taste
½ teaspoon ground coriander
1 teaspoon garam masala

1. Preheat the air fryer to 360ºF (182ºC). In a bowl, mix coriander, garam masala, salt, and pepper. Add cashews and toss to coat. Place in a greased baking dish and air fry in the fryer for 5 to 8 minutes, shaking once.

Mixed Nut Snacks

Prep time: 10 minutes | Cook time: 9 to 12 minutes | Serves 5

½ cup pecans
½ cup walnuts
½ cup almonds
A pinch of cayenne pepper
1 tablespoon sugar
2 tablespoons egg whites
2 teaspoons ground cinnamon
Cooking spray

1. Add cayenne pepper, sugar, and cinnamon to a bowl and mix well; set aside. In another bowl, mix pecans, walnuts, almonds, and egg whites. Add in the spice mixture and stir. Grease a baking dish with cooking spray. Pour in the nuts and place the dish in the fryer. Bake for 5 to 7 minutes. Stir the nuts using a wooden spoon and cook for 4 to 5 more minutes. Pour the nuts into the bowl and let cool slightly.

Cheesy Steak Fries

Prep time: 5 minutes | Cook time: 20 minutes | Serves 5

1 (28-ounce / 794-g) bag frozen steak fries
Cooking spray
Salt and pepper, to taste
½ cup beef gravy
1 cup shredded Mozzarella cheese
2 scallions, green parts only, chopped

1. Preheat the air fryer to 400°F (204°C). 2. Air fry the frozen steak fries for 10 minutes. Shake the basket and spritz the fries with cooking spray. Sprinkle with salt and pepper. Air fry for an additional 8 minutes. 3. Microwave the beef gravy for 30 seconds in a microwave-safe bowl until warm. 4. Sprinkle the fries with the cheese. Air fry for an additional 2 minutes, until the cheese is melted. 5. To serve, drizzle the fries with gravy and sprinkle the scallions on top for a green garnish.

Sea Salt Potato Chips

Prep time: 30 minutes | Cook time: 27 minutes | Serves 4

Oil, for spraying
4 medium yellow potatoes, thinly sliced
1 tablespoon oil
⅛ to ¼ teaspoon fine sea salt

1. Place the potato slices in a bowl of cold water and let soak for about 20 minutes. Drain and pat dry with paper towels. 2. Drizzle the oil over the potatoes, sprinkle with the salt, and toss to combine. Transfer to the oil-greased basket. 3. Air fry at 200°F (93°C) for 20 minutes. Toss the chips and cook at 400°F (204°C) for another 5 to 7 minutes, until crispy.

Cinnamon Apple Chips

Prep time: 5 minutes | Cook time: 7 to 8 hours | Serves 4

4 medium apples, any type, cored and cut into ⅓-inch-thick slices (thin slices yield crunchy chips)
¼ teaspoon ground cinnamon
¼ teaspoon ground nutmeg

1. Place the apple slices in a bowl. Sprinkle the cinnamon and nutmeg onto the apple slices and toss to coat. 2. Place the apple chips into the frying basket and dehydrate at 135°F (57°C) for 7 or 8 hours. 3. Allow to cool before serve.

Zucchini Feta Roulades

Prep time: 10 minutes | Cook time: 10 minutes | Serves 6

½ cup feta
1 garlic clove, minced
2 tablespoons fresh basil, minced
1 tablespoon capers, minced
⅛ teaspoon salt
⅛ teaspoon red pepper flakes
1 tablespoon lemon juice
2 medium zucchini, cut into ⅛-inch strips lengthwise
12 toothpicks

1. Preheat the air fryer to 360°F (182°C). 2. In a bowl, combine the feta, garlic, basil, capers, salt, red pepper flakes, and lemon juice. 3. Spread 1 tablespoon cheese filling onto each slice of zucchini, then roll it up and secure with a toothpick. 4. Place the zucchini roulades into the frying basket in a single layer. Bake for 10 minutes. 5. Remove the toothpicks before serving.

Carrot Chips

Prep time: 15 minutes | Cook time: 8 to 10 minutes | Serves 4

1 tablespoon olive oil, plus more for greasing the basket
4 to 5 medium carrots, trimmed and thinly sliced
1 teaspoon seasoned salt

1. Preheat the air fryer to 390°F (199°C). Grease the frying basket with the olive oil. 2. Toss the carrot slices with olive oil and salt until thoroughly coated. 3. Arrange the carrot slices in the basket. Air fry for 8 to 10 minutes until the carrot slices are crisp-tender, shaking once during cooking. 4. Allow to cool for 5 minutes and serve.

Lemon-Pepper Chicken Drumsticks

Prep time: 30 minutes | Cook time: 30 minutes | Serves 2

2 teaspoons freshly ground coarse black pepper
1 teaspoon baking powder
½ teaspoon garlic powder
4 chicken drumsticks (4 ounces / 113 g each)
Kosher salt, to taste
1 lemon

1. In a bowl, stir together the pepper, baking powder, and garlic powder. Sprinkle the drumsticks evenly with the baking powder mixture until well coated. Refrigerate for at least 1 hour or up to overnight. 2. Sprinkle the drumsticks with salt, then transfer them to the air fryer. Air fry at 375°F (191°C) for 30 minutes until cooked through and crisp on the outside. 3. Finely grate the zest of the lemon and cut the lemon into wedges and serve with the warm drumsticks.

Air Fried Pot Stickers

Prep time: 10 minutes | Cook time: 18 to 20 minutes | Makes 30 pot stickers

½ cup finely chopped cabbage
¼ cup finely chopped red bell pepper
2 green onions, finely chopped
1 egg, beaten
2 tablespoons cocktail sauce
2 teaspoons low-sodium soy sauce
30 wonton wrappers
1 tablespoon water, for brushing the wrappers

1. Preheat the air fryer to 360°F (182°C). 2. In a bowl, combine the cabbage, pepper, green onions, egg, cocktail sauce, and soy sauce, and mix well. 3. Put about 1 teaspoon mixture in each wonton wrapper. Fold the wrapper in half, covering the filling; dampen the edges with water, and seal. Brush them with water. 4. Place the in the frying basket and air fry in 2 batches for 9 to 10 minutes, or until the bottoms are lightly browned. 5. Serve hot.

Vegetable Pot Stickers

Prep time: 12 minutes | Cook time: 11 to 18 minutes | Makes 12 pot stickers

1 cup shredded red cabbage
¼ cup chopped button mushrooms
¼ cup grated carrot
2 tablespoons minced onion
2 garlic cloves, minced
2 teaspoons grated fresh ginger
12 gyoza/pot sticker wrappers
2½ teaspoons olive oil, divided

1. In a baking pan, combine the red cabbage, mushrooms, carrot, onion, garlic, and ginger. Add 1 tablespoon water. Place in the air fryer and air fry at 370°F (188°C) for 3 to 6 minutes, until the vegetables are crisp-tender. Drain and set aside. 2. Top each wrapper with a scant 1 tablespoon the filling. Fold half of the wrapper over the other half to form a half circle. Dab one edge with water and press both edges together. 3. To another pan, add 1¼ teaspoons olive oil. Put half the pot stickers, seam-side up, in the pan. Air fry for 5 minutes, or until the bottoms are light golden brown. Add 1 tablespoon water and air fry for 4 to 6 minutes more, or until hot. Repeat with the remaining pot stickers, oil, and water. Serve immediately.

Crispy Mozzarella Sticks

Prep time: 8 minutes | Cook time: 5 minutes | Serves 4

½ cup all-purpose flour
1 egg, beaten
½ cup panko bread crumbs
½ cup grated Parmesan cheese
1 teaspoon Italian seasoning
½ teaspoon garlic salt
6 Mozzarella sticks, halved crosswise
Olive oil spray

1. Put the flour in a bowl. 2. Put the beaten egg in another small bowl. 3. In a medium bowl, stir together the panko, Parmesan cheese, Italian seasoning, and garlic salt. 4. Roll Mozzarella sticks in the flour, dip it into the egg, and then roll it in the panko mixture to coat. 5. Preheat the air fryer to 400°F (204°C). Spray the frying basket with olive oil. Place the Mozzarella sticks into the basket and lightly spray them with olive oil. Air fry at 400°F (204°C) for 5 minutes until golden and crispy. Let the sticks stand for 1 minute before serving.

Pork and Cabbage Egg Rolls

Prep time: 15 minutes | Cook time: 12 minutes | Makes 12 egg rolls

Cooking oil spray
2 garlic cloves, minced
12 ounces (340 g) ground pork
1 teaspoon sesame oil
¼ cup soy sauce
2 teaspoons grated peeled fresh ginger
2 cups shredded green cabbage
4 scallions, green parts (white parts optional), chopped
24 egg roll wrappers

1. Spray a skillet with the cooking oil and cook the garlic for 1 minute until fragrant over medium-high heat. Add the ground pork and break the pork into smaller chunks. 2. In a bowl, whisk the sesame oil, soy sauce, and ginger until combined. Add the sauce, stir and cook for about 5 minutes until the pork is browned and thoroughly cooked. 3. Stir in the cabbage and scallions. Transfer the pork mixture to a large bowl. 4. Lay the egg roll wrappers on a flat surface. Dip a basting brush in water and glaze each egg roll wrapper along the edges with the wet brush. 5. Stack 2 egg roll wrappers. Scoop 1 to 2 tablespoons pork mixture into the center of each wrapper stack. 6. Roll one long side of the wrappers up over the filling. Press firmly on the area with the filling, tucking it in lightly to secure it in place. Fold in the left and right sides. Continue rolling to close. Use the basting brush to wet the seam and seal the egg roll. Repeat with the remaining ingredients. 7. Preheat the air fryer to 400°F (204°C). Place the egg rolls into the basket. Spray them with cooking oil. Air fry for 12 minutes. After 8 minutes, flip the egg rolls. 8. Serve hot.

Bacon-Wrapped Shrimp and Jalapeño

Prep time: 20 minutes | Cook time: 26 minutes | Serves 8

24 large shrimp, peeled and deveined, about ¾ pound (340 g)
5 tablespoons barbecue sauce, divided
12 strips bacon, cut in half
24 small pickled jalapeño slices

1. Toss together the shrimp and 3 tablespoons barbecue sauce. Let stand for 15 minutes. Soak 24 wooden toothpicks in water for 10 minutes. Wrap 1 piece bacon around the shrimp and jalapeño slice, then secure with a toothpick. 2. Preheat the air fryer to 350°F (177°C). 3. Place half of the shrimp in the frying basket. Air fry for 10 minutes. Turn shrimp and air fry for 3 minutes more until bacon is golden brown and shrimp are cooked through. 4. Brush with the remaining sauce and serve.

Sweet Potato Fries with Mayonnaise

Prep time: 5 minutes | Cook time: 20 minutes | Serves 2 to 3

1 large sweet potato (about 1 pound / 454 g), scrubbed
1 teaspoon vegetable or canola oil
Salt, to taste
Dipping Sauce:
¼ cup light mayonnaise
½ teaspoon sriracha sauce
1 tablespoon spicy brown mustard
1 tablespoon sweet Thai chili sauce

1. Preheat the air fryer to 200°F (93°C). 2. Cut the sweet potato into ¼ inch wide and ¼ inch thick. 3. In a medium bowl, toss the sweet potato strips with the oil. 4. Transfer to the frying basket and air fry for 10 minutes, shaking twice during cooking. 5. Sprinkle with the salt and toss to coat. Air fry at 400°F (204°C) for an additional 10 minutes until crispy and tender. Shake the basket a few times during cooking. 6. Meanwhile, whisk together all the ingredients for the sauce in a bowl. 7. Serve warm alongside the dipping sauce.

Veggie Shrimp Toast

Prep time: 15 minutes | Cook time: 3 to 6 minutes | Serves 4

8 large raw shrimp, peeled and finely chopped
1 egg white
2 garlic cloves, minced
3 tablespoons minced red bell pepper
1 medium celery stalk, minced
2 tablespoons cornstarch
¼ teaspoon Chinese five-spice powder
3 slices firm thin-sliced no-sodium whole-wheat bread

1. Preheat the air fryer to 350ºF (177ºC). 2. In a bowl, stir together the shrimp, egg white, garlic, red bell pepper, celery, cornstarch, and five-spice powder. Top each slice of bread with one-third of the shrimp mixture, spreading it evenly to the edges. Cut each slice of bread into 4 strips. 3. Place the shrimp toasts in the frying basket in a single layer. Air fry for 3 to 6 minutes, until crisp and golden brown. 4. Serve hot.

Crispy Breaded Beef Cubes

Prep time: 10 minutes | Cook time: 12 to 16 minutes | Serves 4

1 pound (454 g) sirloin tip, cut into 1-inch cubes
1 cup cheese pasta sauce
1½ cups soft bread crumbs
2 tablespoons olive oil
½ teaspoon dried marjoram

1. Preheat the air fryer to 360ºF (182ºC). 2. In a medium bowl, toss the beef with the pasta sauce to coat. 3. In a shallow bowl, mix the bread crumbs, oil, and marjoram well. Drop the beef cubes into the bread crumb mixture to coat well. 4. Air fry the beef in two batches for 6 to 8 minutes, shaking once, until the beef is at least 145ºF (63ºC) and the outside is crisp and brown. 5. Serve hot.

Spiced Roasted Cashews

Prep time: 5 minutes | Cook time: 10 minutes | Serves 4

2 cups raw cashews
2 tablespoons olive oil
¼ teaspoon salt
¼ teaspoon chili powder
⅛ teaspoon garlic powder
⅛ teaspoon smoked paprika

1. Preheat the air fryer to 360ºF (182ºC). 2. In a bowl, toss all of the ingredients together. 3. Pour the cashews into the frying basket and roast for 10 minutes, shaking halfway the cooking time. 4. Serve immediately.

Air Fryer Popcorn with Garlic Salt

Prep time: 3 minutes | Cook time: 10 minutes | Serves 2

2 tablespoons olive oil
¼ cup popcorn kernels
1 teaspoon garlic salt

1. Preheat the air fryer to 380ºF (193ºC). 2. Spray the frying basket with olive oil. Pour in the popcorn kernels. Roast for 8 to 10 minutes until the popcorn stops popping. 3. Sprinkle with garlic salt before serving.

Cheese Wafers

Prep time: 30 minutes | Cook time: 5 to 6 minutes per batch | Makes 4 dozen

4 ounces (113 g) sharp Cheddar cheese, grated
¼ cup butter
½ cup flour
¼ teaspoon salt
½ cup crisp rice cereal
Oil for misting or cooking spray

1. Cream the butter and grated cheese together using a stand mixer. 2. Sift flour and salt together. Add to the cheese mixture and mix until well blended. Stir in cereal. 3. Place dough on wax paper and shape into a long roll about 1 inch in diameter. Wrap well with the wax paper and chill for at least 4 hours. 4. Preheat the air fryer to 360ºF (182ºC). Cut cheese roll into ¼-inch slices. 5. Spray the frying basket with oil or cooking spray and place slices in a single layer. Bake for 5 to 6 minutes or until golden brown. Allow them to cool before serving.

Apple Wedges

Prep time: 10 minutes | Cook time: 8 to 9 minutes | Serves 4

¼ cup panko bread crumbs
¼ cup pecans
1½ teaspoons cinnamon
1½ teaspoons brown sugar
¼ cup cornstarch
1 egg white
2 teaspoons water
1 medium apple, cored and cut into small wedges
Oil for misting or cooking spray

1. Process panko, pecans, cinnamon, and brown sugar into small crumbs in a food processor. 2. Place cornstarch in a plastic bag. In a shallow dish, beat together the egg white and water until slightly foamy. 3. Preheat the air fryer to 390ºF (199ºC). 4. Place apple wedges in cornstarch and shake to coat. Dip in egg wash and roll in crumb mixture. Spray with oil. 5. Place apples in frying basket in single layer and air fry for 5 minutes, shaking several times during cooking. Mist lightly with oil and cook 3 to 4 minutes longer until crispy.

Tangy Fried Pickle Spears

Prep time: 5 minutes | Cook time: 15 minutes | Serves 6

2 jars sweet and sour pickle spears, patted dry
2 medium-sized eggs
⅓ cup milk
1 teaspoon garlic powder
1 teaspoon sea salt
½ teaspoon shallot powder
⅓ teaspoon chili powder
⅓ cup all-purpose flour
Cooking spray

1. Preheat the air fryer to 385ºF (196ºC). Spritz the frying basket with cooking spray. 2. In a bowl, beat together the eggs with milk. In another bowl, combine garlic powder, sea salt, shallot powder, chili powder and flour until well blended. 3. Roll the pickle spears in the powder mixture, then dredge in the egg mixture. Dip them in the powder mixture a second time for additional coating. 4. Arrange the coated pickles in the basket. Air fry for 15 minutes until golden and crispy, shaking halfway through. 5. Let cool for 5 minutes before serving.

Crunchy Tex-Mex Tortilla Chips

Prep time: 5 minutes | Cook time: 5 minutes | Serves 4

Olive oil
½ teaspoon salt
½ teaspoon ground cumin
½ teaspoon chili powder
½ teaspoon paprika
Pinch cayenne pepper
8 (6-inch) corn tortillas, each cut into 6 wedges

1. Spray fryer basket lightly with olive oil. 2. In a bowl, combine the salt, cumin, chili powder, paprika, and cayenne pepper. 3. Place the tortilla wedges in the frying basket in a single layer. Spray the tortillas lightly with oil and sprinkle with some of the seasoning mixture. 4. Air fry at 375ºF (191ºC) for 2 to 3 minutes. Shake the basket and cook until the chips are light brown and crispy, an additional 2 to 3 minutes.

Parmesan Cauliflower

Prep time: 15 minutes | Cook time: 15 minutes | Makes 5 cups

8 cups small cauliflower florets (about 1¼ pounds / 567 g)
3 tablespoons olive oil
1 teaspoon garlic powder
½ teaspoon salt
½ teaspoon turmeric
¼ cup shredded Parmesan cheese

1. Preheat the air fryer to 390ºF (199ºC). 2. In a bowl, combine the cauliflower florets, olive oil, garlic powder, salt, and turmeric and toss to coat. 3. Transfer to the frying basket and air fry for 15 minutes, or until the florets are crisp-tender. Shake the basket twice during cooking. 4. To serve, sprinkle with the Parmesan cheese.

Crispy Green Bean Fries with Lemon-Yogurt Sauce

Prep time: 5 minutes | Cook time: 5 minutes | Serves 4

Green Beans:
1 egg
2 tablespoons water
1 tablespoon whole wheat flour
¼ teaspoon paprika
½ teaspoon garlic powder
½ teaspoon salt
¼ cup whole wheat bread crumbs
½ pound whole green beans
Lemon-Yogurt Sauce:
½ cup nonfat plain Greek yogurt
1 tablespoon lemon juice
¼ teaspoon salt
⅛ teaspoon cayenne pepper

Make the Green Beans: 1. Preheat the air fryer to 380ºF (193ºC). 2. In a medium shallow bowl, beat together the egg and water until frothy. 3. In a separate medium shallow bowl, whisk together the flour, paprika, garlic powder, and salt, then mix in the bread crumbs. 4. Spray the air fryer with cooking spray. 5. Dip each green bean into the egg mixture, the bread crumb mixture. Place the green beans in a single layer in the basket. 6. Air fry for 5 minutes, or until the breading is golden brown. **Make the Lemon-Yogurt Sauce:** 7. In a bowl, combine the yogurt, lemon juice, salt, and cayenne. 8. Serve the green bean fries with lemon-yogurt sauce.

Crispy Phyllo Artichoke Triangles

Prep time: 15 minutes | Cook time: 9 to 12 minutes | Makes 18 triangles

¼ cup Ricotta cheese
1 egg white
⅓ cup minced and drained artichoke hearts
3 tablespoons grated Mozzarella cheese
½ teaspoon dried thyme
6 sheets frozen phyllo dough, thawed
2 tablespoons melted butter

1. Preheat the air fryer to 400ºF (204ºC). 2. In a bowl, combine the Ricotta cheese, egg white, artichoke hearts, Mozzarella cheese, and thyme, and mix well. 3. Using one sheet at a time, place on the work surface and cut into thirds lengthwise. 4. Put about 1½ teaspoons filling on each strip at the base. Fold the bottom right-hand tip of phyllo over the filling to meet the other side in a triangle, then continue folding in a triangle. Brush each triangle with butter to seal the edges. Repeat with the remaining phyllo dough and filling. 5. Place the triangles in the frying basket. Bake, 6 at a time, for about 3 to 4 minutes, or until golden brown and crisp. 6. Serve hot.

Sausage Balls with Cheese

Prep time: 10 minutes | Cook time: 10 to 11 minutes | Serves 8

12 ounces (340 g) mild ground sausage
1½ cups baking mix
1 cup shredded mild Cheddar cheese
3 ounces (85 g) cream cheese, at room temperature
1 to 2 tablespoons olive oil

1. Preheat the air fryer to 325ºF (163ºC). Line the frying basket with parchment paper. 2. Mix together the ground sausage, baking mix, Cheddar cheese, and cream cheese in a bowl and stir to incorporate. 3. Divide the sausage mixture into 16 equal portions and roll them into 1-inch balls. 4. Arrange the sausage balls on the parchment. Spray with the olive oil and bake for 10 to 11 minutes, shaking the basket halfway through, or until the balls are firm and lightly browned on both sides. 5. Serve warm.

Homemade Sweet Potato Chips

Prep time: 5 minutes | Cook time: 15 minutes | Serves 2

1 large sweet potato, sliced thin
⅛ teaspoon salt
2 tablespoons olive oil

1. Preheat the air fryer to 380ºF (193ºC). 2. In a bowl, toss the sweet potatoes, salt, and olive oil together until the potatoes are well coated. 3. Put the sweet potato slices into the air fryer in a single layer. 4. Air fry for 10 minutes. Stir and fry for 3 to 5 minutes more, or until the chips reach the preferred level of crispiness.

Shrimp Toasts with Sesame Seeds

Prep time: 15 minutes | Cook time: 6 to 8 minutes | Serves 4 to 6

½ pound (227 g) raw shrimp, peeled and deveined
1 egg, beaten
2 scallions, chopped, plus more for garnish
2 tablespoons chopped fresh cilantro
2 teaspoons grated fresh ginger
1 to 2 teaspoons sriracha sauce
1 teaspoon soy sauce
½ teaspoon toasted sesame oil
6 slices thinly sliced white sandwich bread
½ cup sesame seeds
Cooking spray
Thai chili sauce, for serving

1. Preheat the air fryer to 400ºF (204ºC). Spritz the frying basket with cooking spray. 2. In a food processor, add the shrimp, egg, scallions, cilantro, ginger, sriracha sauce, soy sauce and sesame oil, and pulse until chopped finely. Transfer to a bowl. 3. Cut the crusts off the sandwich bread. Using a brush, generously brush one side of each slice of bread with shrimp mixture. 4. Place the sesame seeds on a plate. Press bread slices, shrimp-side down, into sesame seeds to coat evenly. Cut each slice diagonally into quarters. 5. Spread the coated slices in a single layer in the frying basket. 6. Air fry for 6 to 8 minutes, or until golden and crispy. Flip the bread slices halfway through. 7. Top with the chopped scallions and serve warm with Thai chili sauce.

Artichoke and Olive Pita Flatbread

Prep time: 5 minutes | Cook time: 10 minutes | Serves 4

2 whole wheat pitas
2 tablespoons olive oil, divided
2 garlic cloves, minced
¼ teaspoon salt
½ cup canned artichoke hearts, sliced
¼ cup Kalamata olives
¼ cup shredded Parmesan
¼ cup crumbled feta
Chopped fresh parsley, for garnish (optional)

1. Preheat the air fryer to 380ºF (193ºC). 2. Brush each pita with 1 tablespoon olive oil, then sprinkle the minced garlic and salt over the top. 3. Distribute the artichoke hearts, olives, and cheeses evenly between the two pitas, and place both into the air fryer to bake for 10 minutes. 4. Cut into 4 pieces each before serving. Sprinkle parsley over the top, if desired.

Kale Chips with Sesame

Prep time: 15 minutes | Cook time: 8 minutes | Serves 5

8 cups deribbed kale leaves, torn into 2-inch pieces
1½ tablespoons olive oil
¾ teaspoon chili powder
¼ teaspoon garlic powder
½ teaspoon paprika
2 teaspoons sesame seeds

1. Preheat air fryer to 350ºF (177ºC). 2. In a bowl, toss the kale with the olive oil, chili powder, garlic powder, paprika, and sesame seeds until well coated. 3. Put the kale in the frying basket and air fry for 8 minutes, flipping the kale twice during cooking, or until the kale is crispy. 4. Serve warm.

Skinny Fries

Prep time: 10 minutes | Cook time: 15 minutes | Serves 2

2 to 3 russet potatoes, peeled and cut into ¼-inch sticks
2 to 3 teaspoons olive or vegetable oil
Salt, to taste

1. Rinse the potatoes with cold water several times and let them soak in cold water for at least 10 minutes. 2. Preheat the air fryer to 380ºF (193ºC). 3. Drain and dry the potato sticks really well, using a clean kitchen towel. Toss the fries with the oil and air fry at 380ºF (193ºC) for 15 minutes, shaking a couple of times. 4. Season them with salt. Serve warm with ketchup or your favorite dip.

Parmesan French Fries

Prep time: 10 minutes | Cook time: 25 minutes | Serves 2 to 3

2 to 3 large russet potatoes, peeled and cut into ½-inch sticks
2 teaspoons vegetable or canola oil
¾ cup grated Parmesan cheese
½ teaspoon salt
Freshly ground black pepper, to taste
1 teaspoon fresh chopped parsley

1. Bring a large saucepan of salted water to a boil on the stovetop while you peel and cut the potatoes. Blanch the potatoes in water for 4 minutes while preheating the air fryer to 400ºF (204ºC). Strain the potatoes and rinse them with cold water. Dry with a clean kitchen towel. 2. Toss the dried potato sticks gently with the oil and place them in the frying basket. Air fry for 25 minutes, shaking the basket a few times. Combine the Parmesan cheese, salt and pepper. Sprinkle and toss the fries with the Parmesan cheese mixture in the last 2 minutes. Serve the finished fries with chopped parsley, a little more grated Parmesan cheese if you like.

Egg Roll Pizza Sticks

Prep time: 10 minutes | Cook time: 5 minutes | Serves 4

Olive oil
8 pieces reduced-fat string cheese
8 egg roll wrappers
24 slices turkey pepperoni
Marinara sauce, for dipping (optional)

1. Spray the frying basket lightly with olive oil. Fill a small bowl with water. 2. Place each egg roll wrapper diagonally on a work surface. It should look like a diamond. 3. Place 3 slices of turkey pepperoni in a vertical line down the center of the wrapper. 4. Place 1 Mozzarella cheese stick on top of the turkey pepperoni. 5. Fold the top and bottom corners of the egg roll wrapper over the cheese stick. 6. Fold the left corner over the cheese stick and roll the cheese stick up to resemble a spring roll. Dip a finger in the water and seal the edge of the roll 7. Repeat with the rest of the pizza sticks. 8. Place them in the frying basket in a single layer. Lightly spray with oil. 9. Air fry at 375ºF (191ºC) until lightly browned and crispy, about 5 minutes. 10. Serve hot with marinara sauce, if desired.

Crunchy Chickpeas

Prep time: 5 minutes | Cook time: 15 to 20 minutes | Serves 4

½ teaspoon chili powder
½ teaspoon ground cumin
¼ teaspoon cayenne pepper
¼ teaspoon salt
1 (19-ounce / 539-g) can chickpeas, drained and rinsed
Cooking spray

1. Preheat the air fryer to 390ºF (199ºC). Lightly spritz the frying basket and chickpeas with cooking spray. 2. Mix the chickpeas, chili powder, cumin, cayenne pepper, and salt in a bowl until the chickpeas are well coated. 3. Air fry in the basket for 15 to 20 minutes, or until the chickpeas are cooked to your preferred crunchiness, shaking three or four times during cooking. 4. Let cool for 5 minutes before serving.

Pepperoni Pizza Dip

Prep time: 10 minutes | Cook time: 10 minutes | Serves 6

6 ounces (170 g) cream cheese, softened
¾ cup shredded Italian cheese blend
¼ cup sour cream
1½ teaspoons dried Italian seasoning
¼ teaspoon garlic salt
¼ teaspoon onion powder
¾ cup pizza sauce
½ cup sliced miniature pepperoni
¼ cup sliced black olives
1 tablespoon thinly sliced green onion
Cut-up raw vegetables, toasted baguette slices, pita chips, or tortilla chips, for serving

1. In a bowl, mix the cream cheese, ¼ cup shredded cheese, the sour cream, Italian seasoning, garlic salt, and onion powder until smooth. 2. Spread the mixture in a baking pan. Top with the pizza sauce, spreading to the edges. Sprinkle with the remaining shredded cheese. Arrange the pepperoni slices on top of the cheese. Top with the black olives and green onion. 3. Bake in the fryer basket at 350ºF (177ºC) for 10 minutes until the pepperoni is beginning to brown on the edges and the cheese is bubbly and lightly browned. 4. Let stand for 5 minutes before serving with vegetables, toasted baguette slices, pita chips, or tortilla chips.

Asian Five-Spice Wings

Prep time: 30 minutes | Cook time: 13 to 15 minutes | Serves 4

2 pounds (907 g) chicken wings
½ cup Asian-style salad dressing
2 tablespoons Chinese five-spice powder

1. Cut off wing tips and discard or freeze for stock. Cut remaining wing pieces in two at the joint. 2. Place wing pieces and dressing in a large sealable plastic bag. Seal bag, and massage the marinade until well coated. Refrigerate for at least an hour. 3. Remove wings from bag, drain off excess marinade, and place wings in frying basket. 4. Air fry at 360ºF (182ºC) for 13 to 15 minutes or until juices run clear, shaking halfway through cooking. 5. To serve, sprinkle the Chinese five-spice powder on both sides of the wings.

Stuffed Fried Mushrooms

Prep time: 20 minutes | Cook time: 10 to 11 minutes | Serves 10

½ cup panko bread crumbs
½ teaspoon freshly ground black pepper
½ teaspoon onion powder
½ teaspoon cayenne pepper
1 (8-ounce / 227-g) package cream cheese, at room temperature
20 cremini or button mushrooms, stemmed
1 to 2 tablespoons oil

1. In a medium bowl, whisk the bread crumbs, black pepper, onion powder, and cayenne until blended. 2. Add the cream cheese and mix until well blended. Fill each mushroom top with 1 teaspoon of the cream cheese mixture 3. Preheat the air fryer to 360ºF (182ºC). 4. Place the mushrooms in the basket and spritz with oil. 5. Cook for 10 to 11 minutes, shaking once, until the filling is firm and the mushrooms are soft.

Greens Chips with Curried Yogurt Sauce

Prep time: 10 minutes | Cook time: 5 to 6 minutes | Serves 4

1 cup low-fat Greek yogurt
1 tablespoon freshly squeezed lemon juice
1 tablespoon curry powder
½ bunch curly kale, stemmed, ribs removed and discarded, leaves cut into 2- to 3-inch pieces
½ bunch chard, stemmed, ribs removed and discarded, leaves cut into 2- to 3-inch pieces
1½ teaspoons olive oil

1. In a bowl, stir together the yogurt, lemon juice, and curry powder. Set aside. 2. In a bowl, toss the kale and chard with the olive oil. 3. Air fry the greens at 390ºF (199ºC) for 5 to 6 minutes, until crisp, shaking the basket once during cooking. Serve with the yogurt sauce.

Caramelized Onion Dip

Prep time: 5 minutes | Cook time: 30 minutes | Serves 8 to 10

1 tablespoon butter
1 medium yellow onion, halved and thinly sliced
¼ teaspoon kosher salt, plus additional for seasoning
4 ounces (113 g) cream cheese, softened
½ cup sour cream
¼ teaspoon onion powder
1 tablespoon chopped fresh chives
Black pepper, to taste
Thick-cut potato chips or vegetable chips

1. Place the butter in a baking panand bake at 200ºF (93ºC) for 1 minute, or until the butter is melted. Add the onions and salt to the pan. Bake for 15 minutes, or until onions are softened. Bake at 375ºF (191ºC) for 15 minutes more, until onions are a deep golden brown, stirring two or three times. Let cool completely. 2. In a medium bowl, stir together the cooked onions, cream cheese, sour cream, onion powder, and chives. Season with salt and pepper. Cover and refrigerate for 2 hours. 3. Serve the dip with potato or vegetable chips.

Garlic-Roasted Tomatoes and Olives

Prep time: 5 minutes | Cook time: 20 minutes | Serves 6

2 cups cherry tomatoes
4 garlic cloves, roughly chopped
½ red onion, roughly chopped
1 cup black olives
1 cup green olives
1 tablespoon fresh basil, minced
1 tablespoon fresh oregano, minced
2 tablespoons olive oil
¼ to ½ teaspoon salt

1. Preheat the air fryer to 380ºF (193ºC). 2. In a bowl, combine all of the ingredients and toss until tomatoes and olives are coated well. 3. Pour the mixture into the frying basket, and roast for 20 minutes, stirring halfway through cooking. 4. Serve and enjoy.

Cream Cheese Stuffed Jalapeño Poppers

Prep time: 12 minutes | Cook time: 6 to 8 minutes | Serves 10

8 ounces (227 g) cream cheese, at room temperature
1 cup panko bread crumbs, divided
2 tablespoons fresh parsley, minced
1 teaspoon chili powder
10 jalapeño peppers, halved and seeded
Cooking oil spray

1. In a bowl, whisk the cream cheese, ½ cup panko, the parsley, and chili powder until combined. Stuff the cheese mixture into the jalapeño halves. 2. Sprinkle the tops of the stuffed jalapeños with the remaining panko and press it lightly into the filling. 3. Preheat the air fryer to 375ºF (191ºC). Spray the frying basket with cooking oil. Place the poppers into the basket. 4. Air fry for 8 minutes until poppers are softened and the cheese is melted. Serve warm.

Lemon Shrimp with Garlic Olive Oil

Prep time: 5 minutes | Cook time: 6 minutes | Serves 4

1 pound medium shrimp, cleaned and deveined
¼ cup plus 2 tablespoons olive oil, divided
Juice of ½ lemon
3 garlic cloves, minced and divided
½ teaspoon salt
¼ teaspoon red pepper flakes
Lemon wedges, for serving (optional)
Marinara sauce, for dipping (optional)

1. Preheat the air fryer to 380ºF (193ºC). 2. In a bowl, toss the shrimp with 2 tablespoons olive oil, lemon juice, ⅓ minced garlic, salt, and red pepper flakes. 3. In a small ramekin, combine the remaining ¼ cup olive oil and the remaining garlic. 4. Tear off a 12-by-12-inch sheet of aluminum foil. Pour the shrimp into the center of the foil, then fold the sides up and crimp the edges so that it forms an aluminum foil bowl that is open on top. Place this packet into the frying basket. 5. Roast the shrimp for 4 minutes, then open the air fryer and place the ramekin with oil and garlic in the basket beside the shrimp packet. Cook for 2 more minutes. 6. Serve the shrimp with oil-garlic dipping, lemon wedges and marinara sauce, if desired.

Garlic Edamame

Prep time: 5 minutes | Cook time: 10 minutes | Serves 4

Olive oil
1 (16-ounce / 454-g) bag frozen edamame in pods
½ teaspoon salt
½ teaspoon garlic salt
¼ teaspoon freshly ground black pepper
½ teaspoon red pepper flakes (optional)

1. Spray the frying basket lightly with olive oil. 2. In a medium bowl, add the frozen edamame and lightly spray with olive oil. Toss to coat. 3. In a bowl, mix together the salt, garlic salt, black pepper, and red pepper flakes (if using). Add the mixture to the edamame and toss until evenly coated. 4. Place edamame in the frying basket. Air fry at 375ºF (191ºC) for 8 to 10 minutes, shaking once halfway, until the edamame is starting to brown and get crispy. 5. Serve immediately.

Spicy Tortilla Chips

Prep time: 5 minutes | Cook time: 8 to 12 minutes | Serves 4

½ teaspoon ground cumin
½ teaspoon paprika
½ teaspoon chili powder
½ teaspoon salt
Pinch cayenne pepper
8 (6-inch) corn tortillas, each cut into 6 wedges
Cooking spray

1. Preheat the air fryer to 375ºF (191ºC). Lightly spritz the frying basket with cooking spray. 2. Stir together the cumin, paprika, chili powder, salt, and pepper in a bowl. 3. Arrange the tortilla wedges in the frying basket in a single layer. Lightly mist them with cooking spray. Sprinkle with some seasoning mixture. 4. Air fry for 4 to 6 minutes, shaking once halfway through, or until the chips are lightly browned and crunchy. 5. Let cool for 5 minutes and serve.

Roasted Mushrooms with Garlic

Prep time: 3 minutes | Cook time: 22 to 27 minutes | Serves 4

16 garlic cloves, peeled
2 teaspoons olive oil, divided
16 button mushrooms
½ teaspoon dried marjoram
⅛ teaspoon freshly ground black pepper
1 tablespoon white wine or low-sodium vegetable broth

1. In a baking pan, mix the garlic with 1 teaspoon of olive oil. Roast in the air fryer at 350ºF (177ºC) for 12 minutes. 2. Add the mushrooms, marjoram, and pepper. Stir to coat. Drizzle with the remaining olive oil and the white wine. 3. Roast for 10 to 15 minutes more, or until the mushrooms and garlic cloves are tender. Serve.

Lemony Endive in Curried Yogurt

Prep time: 5 minutes | Cook time: 10 minutes | Serves 6

6 heads endive, sliced in half lengthwise
½ cup plain and fat-free yogurt
3 tablespoons lemon juice
1 teaspoon garlic powder
½ teaspoon curry powder
Salt and ground black pepper, to taste

1. In a bowl, mix together the yogurt, lemon juice, garlic powder, curry powder, salt and pepper. 2. Brush the endive halves with the marinade, coating them completely. Allow to sit for at least 30 minutes or up to 24 hours. 3. Preheat the air fryer to 320°F (160°C). Air fry for 10 minutes. 4. Serve hot.

String Bean Fries

Prep time: 15 minutes | Cook time: 5 to 6 minutes | Serves 4

½ pound (227 g) fresh string beans, trimmed
2 eggs
4 teaspoons water
½ cup white flour
½ cup bread crumbs
¼ teaspoon salt
¼ teaspoon ground black pepper
¼ teaspoon dry mustard (optional)
Oil for misting or cooking spray

1. Preheat the air fryer to 360°F (182°C). 2. In a shallow dish, beat eggs and water together until well blended. Place flour in a second shallow dish. In a third shallow dish, stir together the bread crumbs, salt, pepper, and dry mustard if using. 3. Dip each string bean in egg mixture, flour, egg mixture again, then bread crumbs. Place them in basket. 4. Cook for 5 to 6 minutes until string beans are crispy and nicely browned, misting with oil halfway.

Cheese Drops

Prep time: 15 minutes | Cook time: 10 minutes per batch | Serves 8

¾ cup all-purpose flour
½ teaspoon kosher salt
¼ teaspoon cayenne pepper
¼ teaspoon smoked paprika
¼ teaspoon black pepper
Dash garlic powder (optional)
¼ cup butter, softened
1 cup shredded sharp Cheddar cheese, at room temperature
Olive oil spray

1. In a bowl, combine the flour, salt, cayenne, paprika, pepper, and garlic powder, if using. 2. Using a food processor, cream the butter and cheese until smooth. Gently add the seasoned flour and process until the dough is well combined, smooth, and no longer sticky. 3. Divide the dough into 32 equal-size pieces and roll each piece into a small ball. 4. Spray the frying basket with oil spray. Arrange 16 cheese drops in the basket. Bake at 325°F (163°C) for 10 minutes, or until drops are just starting to brown. Repeat with remaining dough, checking for doneness at 8 minutes. 5. Allow to cool and serve.

Greek Potato Skins with Olives and Feta

Prep time: 5 minutes | Cook time: 45 minutes | Serves 4

2 russet potatoes
3 tablespoons olive oil, divided, plus more for drizzling (optional)
1 teaspoon kosher salt, divided
¼ teaspoon black pepper
2 tablespoons fresh cilantro, chopped, plus more for serving
¼ cup Kalamata olives, diced
¼ cup crumbled feta
Chopped fresh parsley, for garnish (optional)

1. Preheat the air fryer to 380°F (193°C). 2. Using a fork, poke 2 to 3 holes in the potatoes, then coat each with about ½ tablespoon olive oil and ½ teaspoon salt. 3. Bake the potatoes into the frying basket for 30 minutes. 4. Slice in half. Using a spoon, scoop out the flesh of the potatoes, leaving a ½-inch layer of potato inside the skins, and set the skins aside. 5. In a medium bowl, mix the scooped potato middles well with the remaining olive oil, salt, black pepper, and cilantro. Divide into the potato skins evenly. Top each potato with olives and feta. Bake for 15 minutes. 6. Serve with additional cilantro or parsley and olive oil, if desired.

Eggplant Fries

Prep time: 10 minutes | Cook time: 7 to 8 minutes per batch | Serves 4

1 medium eggplant, peeled and sliced into ⅜- to ½-inch thick
1 teaspoon ground coriander
1 teaspoon cumin
1 teaspoon garlic powder
½ teaspoon salt
1 cup crushed panko bread crumbs
1 large egg
2 tablespoons water
Oil for misting or cooking spray

1. Preheat the air fryer to 390°F (199°C). 2. In a small cup, mix together the coriander, cumin, garlic, and salt. 3. Combine 1 teaspoon seasoning mix and panko crumbs in a shallow dish. 4. Sprinkle eggplant fries with remaining seasoning, and stir well. Beat eggs and water together and pour over eggplant fries. Stir to coat. 5. Remove eggplant from egg wash, shaking off excess, and roll in panko crumbs. Spray with oil. Place in frying basket. 6. Air fry for 5 minutes. Shake basket, mist lightly with oil, and cook 2 to 3 minutes longer, until browned and crispy.

Chapter 8 Fast and Easy Everyday Favorites

Classic French Fries

Prep time: 5 minutes | Cook time: 20 to 22 minutes | Serves 2

2 russet potatoes, peeled and cut into strips
1 tablespoon olive oil
Salt and black pepper to taste
½ cup garlic aioli (or garlic mayo)

1. Preheat the air fryer to 400°F (204°C). Spray the frying basket with cooking spray. 2. Place the potato strips in a bowl and toss with the olive oil, salt, and pepper. Arrange on the frying basket. Air fry for 20 to 22 minutes, turning once halfway through, until crispy. Serve with garlic aioli.

Curly Fries with Paprika

Prep time: 5 minutes | Cook time: 20 to 22 minutes | Serves 2

2 Yukon gold potatoes, spiralized
1 tablespoon olive oil
1 teaspoon all-purpose seasoning blend
1 teaspoon paprika

1. Coat the potatoes with olive oil. Place them in the frying basket and air fry for 20 to 22 minutes at 390°F (199°C), tossing them at the 10-minute mark. Sprinkle with the blend and paprika and serve immediately.

Perfect Air Fryer Eggs

Prep time: 5 minutes | Cook time: 10 to 15 minutes | Serves 6

6 large eggs
Salt and black pepper to taste

1. Preheat the air fryer to 270°F (132°C). Lay the eggs in the basket (or in a muffin tray) and cook for 10 minutes for runny or 15 minutes for hard. Using tongs, place the eggs in a bowl with cold water to cool for 5 minutes. When cooled, remove the shells, cut them in half, and sprinkle with salt and pepper. Serve.

Simple Baked Potatoes

Prep time: 15 minutes | Cook time: 30 minutes | Serves 4

4 Yukon gold potatoes, clean and dried
2 tablespoons olive oil
2 tablespoons butter
Salt and black pepper to taste

1. Preheat the air fryer to 400°F (204°C). Brush the potatoes with olive oil and season with salt and black pepper. Arrange them on the frying basket and air fry for 30 minutes at 400°F (204°C) until fork-tender, flipping once. 2. Let cool slightly, then cut slit down the center of each baked potato. Use a fork to fluff the insides of the potatoes. Top with butter, sprinkle with salt and black pepper. Serve immediately and enjoy!

Avocado Egg Rolls

Prep time: 10 minutes | Cook time: 10 minutes | Serves 4

2 ripe avocados, roughly chopped
8 egg roll wrappers
1 tomato, peeled and chopped
Salt and black pepper to taste

1. Place the avocados, tomato, salt, and black pepper in a bowl. Mash with a fork until somewhat smooth. Divide the mixture between the egg wrappers. Fold the edges in and over the filling, roll up tightly, and seal the wrappers with a bit of water. Arrange them on the greased frying basket. Spray the rolls with cooking spray and bake for 10 minutes at 350°F (177°C), turning halfway through until crispy and golden.

Balsamic Brussels Sprouts

Prep time: 5 minutes | Cook time: 10 to 14 minutes | Serves 2

½ pound (227 g) Brussels sprouts, trimmed and halved
1 tablespoon butter, melted
Salt and black pepper to taste
1 tablespoon balsamic vinegar

1. Preheat the air fryer to 380°F (193°C). In a bowl, mix Brussels sprouts with butter, salt, and black pepper. Place the sprouts in the greased frying basket and air fry for 5 to 7 minutes. Shake and cook until the sprouts are caramelized but tender on the inside, 5 to 7 more minutes. Drizzle with balsamic vinegar to serve.

Zucchini-Parmesan Chips

Prep time: 5 minutes | Cook time: 12 to 14 minutes | Serves 4

2 medium zucchinis, sliced
1 cup bread crumbs
2 eggs, beaten
1 cup Parmesan cheese, grated
Salt and black pepper to taste
1 teaspoon smoked paprika

1. Preheat the air fryer to 390°F (199°C). In a bowl, mix bread crumbs, salt, pepper, Parmesan, and paprika. Dip zucchini slices in the eggs and then in the cheese mix; press to coat well. Spray the coated slices with cooking spray and place them in the frying basket. Air fry for 12 to 14 minutes, flipping once. Serve hot.

Onion Rings

Prep time: 10 minutes | Cook time: 8 to 11 minutes | Serves 2

1 onion, sliced into 1-inch rings
1 egg, beaten
¼ cup milk
Salt and garlic powder to taste
½ cup all-purpose flour
¼ cup panko bread crumbs

1. Preheat the air fryer to 350ºF (177ºC). Dust the onion rings with some flour and set aside. In a bowl, mix the remaining flour, garlic powder, and salt. Stir in the egg and milk. Dip onion rings into the flour mixture, then coat them in the crumbs. Lay the rings into the frying basket and spray with cooking spray. Air fry for 8 to 11 minutes until golden and crispy, shaking once. Serve with honey-mustard dipping sauce.

Breaded Mushrooms

Prep time: 10 minutes | Cook time: 10 to 12 minutes | Serves 4

1 pound (454 g) white button mushrooms, cleaned
1 cup bread crumbs
2 eggs, beaten
Salt and black pepper to taste
1 cup Parmesan cheese, grated

1. Preheat the air fryer to 360ºF (182ºC). Pour bread crumbs into a bowl and add in the Parmesan cheese, salt, and pepper; mix well. Dip each mushroom into the eggs, then coat in the cheese mixture. Spray with cooking spray and bake in the fryer for 10 to 12 minutes, shaking once halfway through. Serve warm.

Herb and Cheese Stuffed Mushrooms

Prep time: 10 minutes | Cook time: 8 to 10 minutes | Serves 4

1 pound (454 g) brown mushrooms, stems removed
1 cup Grana Padano cheese, grated
½ teaspoon dried thyme
½ teaspoon dried rosemary
Salt and black pepper to taste
1 tablespoon olive oil

1. Preheat the air fryer to 360ºF (182ºC). In a bowl, mix Grana Padano cheese, herbs, salt, and black pepper. Spoon the mixture into the mushrooms and press down so that it sticks. Drizzle with olive oil and place in the air fryer. Bake for 8 to 10 minutes or until the cheese has melted. Serve warm.

Hot Air Fried Green Tomatoes

Prep time: 10 minutes | Cook time: 8 minutes | Serves 4

8 green tomato slices
2 egg whites
½ cup flour
1 cup bread crumbs
1 teaspoon cayenne pepper
½ teaspoon mustard powder
Salt and black pepper to taste

1. Preheat the air fryer to 390ºF (199ºC). In a bowl, beat the egg whites with a pinch of salt. In a separate bowl, mix the flour, mustard powder, cayenne pepper, salt, and black pepper. Add the bread crumbs to a third bowl. 2. Dredge the tomato slices in the flour mixture, then in the egg whites, and finally in the crumbs. Spray with oil and arrange in the greased frying basket. Air fry for 8 minutes, turning once. Serve warm.

Classic Zucchini Fries

Prep time: 10 minutes | Cook time: 10 to 12 minutes | Serves 2

1 zucchini, cut lengthways into strips
½ cup panko bread crumbs
½ cup all-purpose flour
1 egg
Salt and garlic powder to taste
½ cup garlic mayonnaise

1. Preheat the air fryer to 400ºF (204ºC). Sift the flour into a bowl with a pinch of salt. Whisk the egg in another bowl with some salt. Pour the bread crumbs in a third one and mix with garlic powder. Coat the zucchini strips in the flour, then in the beaten egg, and finally in the crumbs. Lightly spray the strips with cooking spray and air fry until crispy, 10 to 12 minutes, flipping once halfway through. Serve with garlic mayo.

Corn on the Cob

Prep time: 5 minutes | Cook time: 12 to 14 minutes | Serves 2

2 ears fresh corn, cut into halves
2 tablespoons fresh parsley, chopped
2 tablespoons butter, softened
Garlic salt to taste

1. Preheat the air fryer to 390ºF (199ºC). Spritz the corn with cooking spray and bake for 12 to 14 minutes, turning a few times until slightly charred. Brush the corn with the butter. Sprinkle with garlic salt and parsley.

Homemade Arancini (Rice Balls)

Prep time: 15 minutes | Cook time: 12 to 14 minutes | Serves 4

2 cups cooked rice
½ cup flour
1 green onion, chopped
2 garlic cloves, minced
2 eggs, lightly beaten
½ cup Parmesan cheese, grated
Salt and black pepper to taste
1 cup bread crumbs
1 teaspoon dried mixed herbs
1 cup arrabbiata sauce

1. Place the flour, beaten eggs, and bread crumbs into 3 separate bowls. Combine the cooked rice, onion, garlic, Parmesan cheese, herbs, salt, and pepper in a bowl. Shape into 10 balls. Roll them in the flour, shake off any excess, then dip in the eggs, and finally coat in the bread crumbs. Let chill for 20 minutes. 2. Preheat the air fryer to 390ºF (199ºC). Spray the arancini with cooking spray and air fry them for 12 to 14 minutes, turning once halfway through cooking, until golden and crispy. Serve with arrabbiata sauce.

148 | Chapter 1 Vegetables and Sides

Air Fried Mac and Cheese

Prep time: 5 minutes | Cook time: 16 minutes | Serves 2

8 ounces (227 g) elbow macaroni, cooked
1 cup Cheddar cheese, grated
1 cup warm milk
1 tablespoon Parmesan cheese, grated
Salt and black pepper to taste

1. Preheat the air fryer to 350ºF (177ºC). Add the macaroni to a baking dish and stir in Cheddar, milk, salt, and pepper. Place the dish in the fryer and bake for 16 minutes. Serve sprinkled with Parmesan cheese.

Morning Frittata

Prep time: 10 minutes | Cook time: 20 to 23 minutes | Serves 4

8 eggs
½ cup heavy cream
Salt and black pepper to taste
1 cup spinach, finely chopped
½ red onion, chopped
½ cup tomatoes, diced
1 cup Mozzarella cheese, shredded
2 teaspoons fresh parsley for garnishing

1. Preheat the air fryer to 330ºF (166ºC). Grease a baking dish that fits in your air fryer with cooking spray. 2. In a bowl, whisk the eggs and heavy cream until pale. Add in spinach, red onion, tomatoes, Mozzarella, salt, and pepper. Mix to combine. Pour the mixture into the baking dish and bake in the air fryer for 20 to 23 minutes, or until the eggs are set in the center. Sprinkle with parsley and cut into wedges to serve.

Mediterranean Bruschetta

Prep time: 10 minutes | Cook time: 8 to 10 minutes | Serves 4

8 French baguette slices
2 tablespoons olive oil
2 garlic cloves, haled
1 cup Mozzarella cheese, grated
1 teaspoon fresh basil, chopped
1 cup mixed cherry tomatoes, quartered

1. Brush the bread with olive oil and rub with garlic. Scatter Mozzarella cheese on top. Arrange the slices in the frying basket and bake for 8 to 10 minutes at 360ºF (182ºC). Top with cherry tomatoes and basil to serve.

Mozzarella Cheese Sticks

Prep time: 10 minutes | Cook time: 6 to 8 minutes | Serves 4

12 ounces (340 g) Mozzarella cheese sticks
½ cup flour
1 cup bread crumbs
2 eggs
¼ cup Parmesan cheese, grated
1 cup marinara sauce (optional)

1. Preheat the air fryer to 380ºF (193ºC). Pour the bread crumbs into a bowl. Beat the eggs in another bowl. In a third bowl, mix Parmesan cheese and flour. Dip each cheese stick in the flour, then in the eggs, and finally in bread crumbs. Place them in the greased frying basket and air fry until golden brown, about 6 to 8 minutes, shaking the basket once or twice. Serve with marinara sauce.

"Bikini" Ham and Cheese Sandwich

Prep time: 5 minutes | Cook time: 8 minutes | Serves 1

2 tablespoons butter
2 slices bread
2 slices Cheddar cheese
1 slice ham

1. Preheat the air fryer to 370ºF (188ºC). Spread 1 teaspoon of butter on the outside of each of the bread slices. Place the cheese on the inside of one bread slice. Top with ham and the other cheese slice. Close with the second bread slice. Air fry for 8 minutes, flipping once halfway through. Cut diagonally and serve.

Cheddar Hash Browns

Prep time: 10 minutes | Cook time: 20 to 22 minutes | Serves 4

4 russet potatoes, peeled and grated
1 brown onion, chopped
2 garlic cloves, minced
½ cup Cheddar cheese, grated
1 egg, lightly beaten
Salt and black pepper to taste
1 tablespoon fresh thyme, chopped

1. In a bowl, mix the potatoes, onion, garlic, Cheddar cheese, egg, salt, black pepper, and thyme. Spread the mixture in the greased frying basket and air fry in the preheated air fryer for 20 to 22 minutes at 400ºF (204ºC). Shake once halfway through cooking, until golden and crispy. Serve hot with ketchup (optional).

Bacon-Wrapped Chicken Breasts

Prep time: 10 minutes | Cook time: 16 to 18 minutes | Serves 4

2 chicken breasts
8 ounces (227 g) cream cheese
1 tablespoon butter
6 turkey bacon slices
Salt to taste
1 tablespoon fresh parsley, chopped

1. Preheat the air fryer to 390ºF (199ºC). Stretch out the bacon and lay the slices in 2 sets; 3 bacon strips together on each side. Place the chicken on each bacon set. Use a knife to smear the cream cheese on both. 2. Spread the butter on top and sprinkle with salt. Wrap the turkey bacon around the chicken and secure the ends into the wrap. Place the wrapped chicken in the greased frying basket and air fry for 16 to 18 minutes, turning halfway through. Top with fresh parsley and serve with steamed greens (optional).

Air-Fried Chicken Popcorn

Prep time: 10 minutes | Cook time: 16 to 18 minutes | Serves 4

2 chicken breasts, cut into small cubes
2 cups panko bread crumbs
Salt and black pepper to taste
1 teaspoon garlic powder

1. Preheat the air fryer to 360ºF (182ºC). Rub the chicken cubes with salt, garlic powder, and black pepper. Coat in the panko bread crumbs and place them in the greased frying basket. Spray with cooking spray and air fry for 16 to 18 minutes, flipping once until nice and crispy. Serve with tzatziki sauce if desired.

Sweet Garlicky Chicken Wings

Prep time: 10 minutes | Cook time: 15 minutes | Serves 4

16 chicken wings
¼ cup butter
1 teaspoon honey
½ tablespoon salt
4 garlic cloves, minced
¾ cup potato starch

1. Preheat the air fryer to 370ºF (188ºC). Coat the chicken with potato starch and place in the greased frying basket. Bake for 5 minutes. Whisk the rest of the ingredients in a bowl. Remove the wings from the fryer, pour the sauce over them, and bake for another 10 minutes, until crispy. Serve immediately.

Effortless Chicken Drumsticks

Prep time: 10 minutes | Cook time: 14 to 16 minutes | Serves 4

1 pound (454 g) chicken drumsticks
1 teaspoon garlic powder
1 teaspoon cayenne pepper
½ cup flour
¼ cup milk
Salt and black pepper to taste

1. Preheat the air fryer to 390ºF (199ºC). Spray the frying basket with cooking spray. In a small bowl, mix garlic powder, cayenne pepper, salt, and black pepper. Rub the chicken drumsticks with the mixture. 2. In a separate bowl, pour the flour. Dunk the chicken in the milk, then roll in the flour to coat. Place the drumsticks in the frying basket and spray with cooking spray. Air fry for 14 to 16 minutes, flipping once.

Hot Chicken Wingettes

Prep time: 10 minutes | Cook time: 15 to 18 minutes | Serves 4

1 pound (454 g) chicken wingettes
Salt and black pepper to taste
⅓ cup hot sauce
½ tablespoon white wine vinegar

1. Preheat the air fryer to 360ºF (182ºC). Season the wingettes with black pepper and salt and spray them with oil. Air fry them for 15 to 18 minutes, until golden, tossing every 5 minutes. In a bowl, mix vinegar with hot sauce. When the wingettes are ready, transfer them to a plate and pour the sauce over. Serve warm.

Turkey Scotch Eggs

Prep time: 10 minutes | Cook time: 12 to 14 minutes | Serves 4

4 hard-boiled eggs, peeled
1 cup panko bread crumbs
1 egg, beaten in a bowl
1 pound (454 g) ground turkey
½ teaspoon dried rosemary
Salt and black pepper to taste

1. Preheat the air fryer to 400ºF (204ºC). In a bowl, mix panko bread crumbs with rosemary. In another bowl, pour the ground turkey and mix it with salt and pepper. Shape into 4 balls. 2. Wrap the balls around the boiled eggs to form a large ball with the egg in the center. Dip in the beaten egg and coat with bread crumbs. Place in the greased frying basket and bake for 12 to 14 minutes, shaking once. Serve and enjoy!

Air Fried Pork Popcorn Bites

Prep time: 10 minutes | Cook time: 15 minutes | Serves 4

4 boneless pork chops, cut into 1-inch cubes
Salt and black pepper to taste
1 cup flour
¼ teaspoon garlic powder
¼ teaspoon onion powder
1 teaspoon paprika
2 eggs
1 cup ranch sauce

1. Preheat the Air fryer to 390ºF (199ºC). Spray the basket with cooking spray. In a bowl, combine the flour, garlic and onion powders, paprika, salt, and black pepper and mix well. In another bowl, whisk the eggs with a bit of salt. Dip the pork in the flour first, then in the eggs, and back again in the flour; coat well. 2. Spray with cooking spray and place in the frying basket. Air fry for 15 minutes, shaking once halfway through. Remove to a serving plate and serve with ranch sauce.

Sesame Pork Skewers

Prep time: 15 minutes | Cook time: 13 to 17 minutes | Serves 4

1 pound (454 g) pork tenderloin, cut into 1-inch chunks
1 red pepper, cut into 1-inch chunks
2 tablespoons sesame oil
1 garlic clove, minced
2 tablespoons soy sauce
Salt and black pepper to taste
1 tablespoon honey
1 teaspoon sesame seeds

1. In a bowl, mix the honey, sesame oil, soy sauce, salt, and black pepper. Coat the pork in the mixture. Cover with a lid and let sit for 30 minutes. Preheat the air fryer to 400ºF (204ºC). Thread the pork onto skewers, alternating the cubes of meat with chunks of red pepper. Place them in the greased frying basket. 2. Spritz them with cooking spray and air fry the skewers for 8 to 10 minutes. Flip them over and cook further for 5 to 7 minutes until golden brown. Top with sesame seeds and serve.

Chapter 1 Vegetables and Sides

Spicy Buffalo Chicken Wings

Prep time: 10 minutes | Cook time: 15 to 18 minutes | Serves 4

2 pounds (907 g) chicken wings
½ cup cayenne pepper sauce
2 tablespoons coconut oil
2 tablespoons Worcestershire sauce
Salt to taste
½ cup sour cream
¼ cup mayonnaise
1 tablespoon scallions, chopped
1 tablespoon fresh parsley, chopped
1 garlic clove, minced

1. In a mixing bowl, combine cayenne pepper sauce, coconut oil, Worcestershire sauce, and salt. Add in the chicken wings and toss to coat. Cover with a lid and marinate for 1 hour in the fridge. 2. Preheat the air fryer to 400ºF (204ºC). Place the chicken in a greased frying basket and air fry for 15 to 18 minutes or until the marinade becomes sticky and the wings are cooked through. 3. Meanwhile, in a small bowl, mix together sour cream, mayonnaise, garlic, parsley, and salt. Top the wings with scallions and serve with the prepared sauce on the side. Enjoy!

Teriyaki Pork Ribs

Prep time: 15 minutes | Cook time: 20 minutes | Serves 4

1 pound (454 g) pork ribs
2 tablespoons olive oil
Salt and black pepper to taste
1 teaspoon sugar
1 teaspoon ginger paste
1 teaspoon five-spice powder
1 tablespoon teriyaki sauce
1 tablespoon light soy sauce
1 garlic clove, minced
½ teaspoon honey
2 tablespoons water
1 tablespoon tomato sauce

1. In a bowl, mix teriyaki sauce, sugar, five-spice powder, ginger paste, salt, and black pepper. Add in the pork ribs and stir to coat. Cover with foil and marinate for 2 hours in the fridge. Preheat the air fryer to 350ºF (177ºC). Add the ribs to the greased frying basket and bake for 18 to 20 minutes, flipping once until crispy. 2. Heat the olive oil in a skillet over medium heat and stir in the soy sauce, garlic, honey, water, and tomato sauce. Cook the sauce for 1 to 2 minutes until it thickens slightly. Pour it over the ribs and serve.

Gorgonzola Cheese Burgers

Prep time: 15 minutes | Cook time: 20 minutes | Serves 4

1 pound (454 g) ground beef
½ cup Gorgonzola cheese, crumbled
1 tablespoon olive oil
1 teaspoon Worcestershire sauce
½ teaspoon hot sauce
½ garlic clove, minced
4 bread buns
4 yellow cheese slices
2 tablespoons mayonnaise
1 teaspoon ketchup
1 dill pickle, sliced
Salt and black pepper to taste

1. Preheat the air fryer to 360ºF (182ºC). In a mixing bowl, place the ground beef, Worcestershire sauce, hot sauce, gorgonzola cheese, garlic, salt, and pepper. Mix well. Shape the mixture into 4 burgers. 2. Grease the frying basket with a thin layer of olive oil. Add the burgers and air fry for 20 minutes, flipping once halfway through. On bread buns, spread the mayonnaise and add the dill pickles. Place the burgers over the top and lay the yellow cheese. Top with ketchup and serve.

Beef Steak Fingers

Prep time: 15 minutes | Cook time: 19 to 23 minutes | Serves 4

1 pound (454 g) beef steak, cut into strips
1 tablespoon olive oil
½ cup flour
½ cup panko bread crumbs
¼ teaspoon cayenne pepper
2 eggs, beaten
½ cup milk
Salt and black pepper to taste
1 pound (454 g) tomatoes, chopped
1 tablespoon tomato paste
1 teaspoon honey
1 tablespoon white wine vinegar

1. Place the tomatoes, tomato paste, honey, and vinegar in a deep skillet over medium heat. Cook for 6 to 8 minutes, stirring occasionally until the sauce thickens; set aside to cool. Grease the basket with oil. 2. Preheat the air fryer to 390ºF (199ºC). In a bowl, combine flour, salt, black pepper, and cayenne pepper. In a second bowl, whisk the eggs with the milk. Dredge the steak strips in the flour mixture, then coat with the egg mixture, and finally in the bread crumbs until completely coated. Air fry the dredged steak strips for 8 minutes. Turn them over and spray with a little bit of olive oil. Continue to cook for another 5 to 7 minutes until golden and crispy. Spoon into paper cones and serve with the tomato sauce.

Easy Salmon Fillets

Prep time: 5 minutes | Cook time: 8 minutes | Serves 2

2 salmon fillets
1 tablespoon olive oil
Salt to taste
1 lemon, cut into wedges

1. Preheat the air fryer to 380ºF (193ºC). Brush the salmon with olive oil and season with salt. Place the fillets in the greased frying basket and bake for 8 minutes until tender, turning once. Serve with lemon wedges.

Air Fried Cinnamon Apples

Prep time: 5 minutes | Cook time: 20 minutes | Serves 2

2 apples, cored, bottom intact
2 tablespoons butter, cold
3 tablespoons sugar
3 tablespoons crushed walnuts
2 tablespoons raisins
1 teaspoon cinnamon

1. Preheat the air fryer to 350ºF (177ºC). In a bowl, add butter, sugar, walnuts, raisins, and cinnamon. Mix well until you obtain a crumble. Stuff the apples with the filling mixture. Bake in the air fryer for 20 minutes.

Chapter 1 Vegetables and Sides | 151

Classic Fish and Chips

Prep time: 10 minutes | Cook time: 18 to 20 minutes | Serves 4

2 tablespoons olive oil	1 cup flour
4 potatoes, cut into thin slices	2 eggs, beaten
Salt and black pepper to taste	1 cup bread crumbs
4 white fish fillets	Salt and black pepper to taste

1. Preheat the air fryer to 400ºF (204ºC). Drizzle the potatoes with olive oil and season with salt and black pepper; toss to coat. Place them in the greased frying basket and air fry for 10 minutes. 2. Season the fillets with salt and black pepper. Coat them with flour, then dip in the eggs, and finally into the crumbs. Shake the potatoes and add in the fish; cook until the fish is crispy, 8 to 10 minutes. Serve.

Chipotle-Lime Prawn Bowls

Prep time: 10 minutes | Cook time: 10 to 15 minutes | Serves 4

1 pound (454 g) prawns, deveined, peeled	1 teaspoon chipotle powder
2 teaspoons olive oil	2 cups cooked brown rice
2 teaspoons lime juice	1 (15-ounce / 425-g) can black beans, warmed
1 teaspoon honey	1 large avocado, chopped
1 garlic clove, minced	1 cup sliced cherry tomatoes

1. Toss the lime juice, olive oil, honey, garlic, and chipotle powder in a bowl. Mix well to make a marinade. Add the prawns and toss to coat. Transfer them to the fridge for at least 30 minutes. 2. Preheat the air fryer to 390ºF (199ºC). Remove the prawns to the fryer and air fry them for 10 to 15 minutes, tossing once, until golden and cooked through. Divide the rice, beans, avocado, and tomatoes between 4 bowls and top with the prawns. Serve.

Simple Calamari Rings

Prep time: 15 minutes | Cook time: 12 minutes | Serves 4

1 pound (454 g) calamari rings	2 garlic cloves, minced
½ cup cornstarch	1 cup bread crumbs
2 large eggs, beaten	1 lemon, sliced

1. In a bowl, coat the calamari with cornstarch. In another bowl, mix the eggs with garlic. Dip the calamari in the egg and roll them up in the crumbs. Transfer to the fridge for 10 minutes. Remove calamari from the fridge and arrange them on the greased frying basket. Air fry for 12 minutes at 390ºF (199ºC), shaking once halfway through cooking. Serve with lemon slices.

Gambas al Ajillo (Garlic Shrimp)

Prep time: 10 minutes | Cook time: 12 to 13 minutes | Serves 4

1 pound (454 g) shrimp, peeled and deveined	1 tablespoon olive oil
½ teaspoon Cajun seasoning	¼ teaspoon garlic powder
10 lettuce leaves	2 tablespoons lemon juice, chopped

1. Mix the garlic powder, half of the lemon juice, olive oil, and Cajun seasoning in a bowl to make a marinade. Toss the shrimp to coat thoroughly. Cover with a plastic wrap and refrigerate for 30 minutes. 2. Preheat the air fryer to 400ºF (204ºC). Place the shrimp in the greased frying basket and air fry for 5 minutes. Shake the basket and cook for 7 to 8 more minutes, until cooked through. Arrange the lettuce leaves on a plate and top with the shrimp. Drizzle with the remaining lemon juice and serve.

Crispy Fish Finger Sticks

Prep time: 5 minutes | Cook time: 10 minutes | Serves 4

2 fresh white fish fillets, cut into 4 fingers each	½ cup buttermilk
1 egg	1 cup panko bread crumbs
	Salt and black pepper to taste
	1 cup aioli (or garlic mayo)

1. Preheat the air fryer to 380ºF (193ºC). In a bowl, beat the egg and buttermilk. On a plate, combine bread crumbs, salt, and pepper. Dip each finger into the egg mixture, roll it up in the crumbs, and spritz it with cooking spray. Arrange on the greased frying basket and air fry for 10 minutes, turning once. Serve with aioli.

Raspberry and Vanilla Pancakes

Prep time: 10 minutes | Cook time: 6 to 8 minutes | Serves 4

1½ cups all-purpose flour	2 tablespoons brown sugar
1 cup milk	1 teaspoon vanilla extract
3 eggs, beaten	½ cup frozen raspberries, thawed
1 teaspoon baking powder	2 tablespoons maple syrup

1. Preheat the air fryer to 370ºF (188ºC). In a bowl, mix the flour, baking powder, milk, eggs, vanilla, and brown sugar. Gently stir in the raspberries to avoid coloring the batter. Working in batches, drop the batter into a greased baking pan using a spoon. Bake for 6 to 8 minutes, flipping once. Repeat the process with the remaining batter. Serve the pancakes with maple syrup.

Cinnamon French Toast Sticks

Prep time: 10 minutes | Cook time: 5 minutes | Serves 2

4 white bread slices, cut them into strips	plus some for dusting
2 eggs	¼ nutmeg powder
1½ tablespoons butter	¼ clove powder
¼ teaspoon cinnamon powder	2 tablespoons brown sugar
	1 tablespoon icing sugar

1. Preheat the air fryer to 350ºF (177ºC). In a bowl, add the eggs, brown sugar, clove powder, nutmeg powder, and cinnamon powder. Beat the mixture using a whisk until well combined. Dip the strips into the egg mixture. Arrange them on the greased frying basket and spritz with cooking spray. Bake for 2 minutes. Flip the toasts and cook for 3 more minutes. Dust the toasts with cinnamon and icing sugar to serve.

Chapter 9 Desserts

Shortcut Spiced Apple Butter

Prep time: 5 minutes | Cook time: 1 hour | Makes 1¼ cups

Cooking spray
2 cups store-bought unsweetened applesauce
⅔ cup packed light brown sugar
3 tablespoons fresh lemon juice
½ teaspoon kosher salt
¼ teaspoon ground cinnamon
⅛ teaspoon ground allspice

1. Spray a cake pan with cooking spray. Whisk together all the ingredients in a bowl until smooth, then pour into the pan. Bake at 340°F (171°C) for 1 hour until the apple mixture is caramelized, reduced to a thick purée, and fragrant. 2. Stir to combine the caramelized bits at the edge with the rest, then let cool completely to thicken. Scrape the apple butter into a jar and store in the refrigerator for up to 2 weeks.

S'mores

Prep time: 5 minutes | Cook time: 30 seconds | Makes 8 s'mores

Oil, for spraying
8 graham cracker squares
2 (1½-ounce / 43-g) chocolate bars, cut in half
4 large marshmallows

1. Line the frying basket with parchment and spray with oil. 2. Place 4 graham cracker squares in basket. 3. Place 1 piece chocolate bars on top of each graham cracker. Top with 1 marshmallow. 4. Air fry at 370°F (188°C) for 30 seconds until the marshmallows are puffed and golden brown and slightly melted. 5. Top with the remaining graham cracker squares and serve.

Chocolate Cake

Prep time: 10 minutes | Cook time: 20 to 23 minutes | Serves 8

½ cup sugar
¼ cup flour, plus 3 tablespoons
3 tablespoons cocoa
½ teaspoon baking powder
½ teaspoon baking soda
¼ teaspoon salt
1 egg
2 tablespoons oil
½ cup milk
½ teaspoon vanilla extract

1. Preheat the air fryer to 330°F (166°C). Grease and flour a baking pan. 2. In a medium bowl, stir together the first six ingredients. Add all other ingredients and beat with a wire whisk until smooth. 3. Pour batter into pan and bake at 330°F (166°C) for 20 to 23 minutes, until toothpick inserted in center comes out clean or with crumbs clinging to it.

Honeyed Roasted Apples with Walnuts

Prep time: 5 minutes | Cook time: 12 to 15 minutes | Serves 4

2 Granny Smith apples
¼ cup certified gluten-free rolled oats
2 tablespoons honey
½ teaspoon ground cinnamon
2 tablespoons chopped walnuts
Pinch salt
1 tablespoon olive oil

1. Preheat the air fryer to 380°F (193°C). 2. Core the apples and slice them in half. 3. In a medium bowl, mix together the oats, honey, cinnamon, walnuts, salt, and olive oil. 4. Scoop a quarter of the oat mixture onto the top of each half apple. 5. Roast for 12 to 15 minutes until the apples are fork-tender.

Ricotta Lemon Poppy Seed Cake

Prep time: 10 minutes | Cook time: 55 minutes | Serves 4

Unsalted butter, at room temperature
1 cup almond flour
½ cup sugar
3 large eggs
¼ cup heavy cream
¼ cup full-fat ricotta cheese
¼ cup coconut oil, melted
2 tablespoons poppy seeds
1 teaspoon baking powder
1 teaspoon pure lemon extract
Grated zest and juice of 1 lemon, plus more zest for garnish

1. Generously butter a baking pan. 2. In a bowl, combine the remaining ingredient. Beat with a hand mixer on medium speed until well blended and fluffy. 3. Pour the batter into the prepared pan. Cover the pan tightly with aluminum foil. Bake at 325°F (163°C) for 45 minutes. Remove the foil and cook for 10 to 15 minutes more, until a knife (do not use a toothpick) inserted into the center of the cake comes out clean. Allow to cool before slicing. 4. Top with additional lemon zest, slice and serve.

Olive Oil Cake

Prep time: 10 minutes | Cook time: 30 minutes | Serves 8

2 cups blanched finely ground almond flour
5 large eggs, whisked
¾ cup extra-virgin olive oil
⅓ cup granular erythritol
1 teaspoon vanilla extract
1 teaspoon baking powder

1. In a bowl, mix all ingredients. Pour batter into a round nonstick baking dish. 2. Place dish into frying basket. Bake at 300°F (149°C) for 30 minutes until the cake is golden on top and firm in the center. 3. Let cool for 30 minutes before slicing and serving.

Spanish Churros con Chocolate

Prep time: 10 minutes | Cook time: 10 minutes | Serves 4

1 teaspoon vanilla extract
¼ cup butter
½ cup water
1 pinch of salt
½ cup all-purpose flour
2 eggs
¼ cup plus 1 tablespoon white sugar
½ teaspoon ground cinnamon
4 ounces (113 g) dark chocolate chips
¼ cup milk

1. In a skillet over medium heat, pour water, ¼ cup of sugar, butter, and salt; bring to a boil. Stir in the flour until the mixture thickens, about 3 minutes. Remove to a bowl, mix in vanilla, and let cool slightly. 2. Preheat the air fryer to 360ºF (182ºC). Gently stir the eggs in the cooled bowl, one at a time, until glossy and smooth. Place the dough in a piping bag and generously grease the frying basket with cooking spray. Pipe in the batter into long and thick strips. Air fry them for 8 to 10 minutes or until golden, flipping once. 3. Mix the chocolate with cinnamon in a heatproof bowl and microwave for 60 to 90 seconds or until the chocolate is melted. Stir in milk until smooth. Sprinkle the churros with sugar and serve with the hot chocolate as a dip and enjoy!

Dark Chocolate Fondants

Prep time: 10 minutes | Cook time: 12 to 13 minutes | Serves 4

¾ cup dark chocolate
½ cup peanut butter, crunchy
2 tablespoons butter
½ cup sugar, divided
4 eggs, room temperature
⅛ cup flour, sieved
1 teaspoon salt
¼ cup water

1. Make the praline by adding ¼ cup of sugar, 1 teaspoon of salt, and ¼ cup of water in a saucepan over low heat. Stir and bring to a boil. Simmer until the mixture reduces by half, about 5 minutes. 2. Spread on a baking tray to freeze up to harden. Then break into pieces and set the pralines aside. 3. Preheat the air fryer to 300ºF (149ºC). Place a pot of water over medium heat and place a heatproof bowl on top. Add in chocolate, butter, and peanut butter. Stir continuously until fully melted, combined, and smooth. Remove the bowl and let cool slightly. Whisk in the eggs, add flour and the remaining sugar; mix well. 4. Grease 4 small loaf pans with cooking spray and divide the chocolate mixture between them. Place them in the air fryer and bake for 7 to 8 minutes until browned. Remove and serve with a piece of praline.

Mock Blueberry Pie

Prep time: 5 minutes | Cook time: 20 to 25 minutes | Serves 6

2 store-bought pie crusts
21 ounces (595 g) blueberry pie filling
1 egg yolk, beaten
Powdered sugar, to dust

1. Preheat air fryer to 340ºF (171ºC). Place one pie crust into a greased pie pan. Poke holes into the crust and bake for 5 minutes in the air fryer. Remove the pan and spread the blueberry pie filling on top. Cut the other crust into strips and make a lattice over the filling. Brush the lattice with the yolk and bake the pie in the fryer for 15 to 20 minutes until golden. Dust with sugar and serve chilled.

Maple Oat-Walnut Granola with Blueberries

Prep time: 5 minutes | Cook time: 23 to 28 minutes | Serves 4

¼ cup walnuts, chopped
½ cup oats
3 tablespoons canola oil
½ cup maple syrup
2 tablespoons muscovado sugar
1 cup fresh blueberries

1. Preheat air fryer to 380ºF (193ºC). In a bowl, place oil, maple syrup, and muscovado sugar; mix well. Fold in the oats and walnuts. Spread out the mixture on a greased baking dish. Bake in the air fryer for 20 to 25 minutes. Sprinkle with blueberries and bake for 3 minutes. Let cool. Break it up and store it in a jar.

French Sour Cherry Clafoutis

Prep time: 15 minutes | Cook time: 25 to 30 minutes | Serves 4

½ pound (227 g) sour cherries, pitted
½ cup all-purpose flour
¼ teaspoon salt
2 tablespoons sugar
2 eggs plus 2 yolks
1 teaspoon vanilla extract
1 tablespoon lemon zest
2 tablespoons butter, melted
1¼ cups milk
Icing sugar to dust

1. Preheat air fryer to 380ºF (193ºC). In a bowl, mix the flour, sugar, and salt. Whisk in the eggs, egg yolks, vanilla extract, lemon zest, and melted butter until creamy. Gradually, add in the milk and stir until bubbly. 2. Spread the sour cherries on a greased baking dish and pour the batter over. Bake in the air fryer for 25 to 30 minutes or until a lovely golden crust is formed. Dust the top with icing sugar and serve warm.

Apple Caramel Relish

Prep time: 15 minutes | Cook time: 18 to 20 minutes | Serves 4

1 vanilla box cake mix
2 apples, peeled, sliced
3 ounces (85 g) butter, melted
½ cup brown sugar
1 teaspoon cinnamon
½ cup flour
1 cup caramel sauce

1. Line a cake tin with baking paper. In a bowl, mix butter, brown sugar, cinnamon, and flour until you obtain a crumbly texture. Prepare the cake mix according to the instructions (no baking). 2. Pour the obtained batter into the tin and arrange the apple slices on top. Spoon the caramel over the apples and pour the crumbly flour mixture over the sauce. Bake in the preheated air fryer for 18 to 20 minutes at 360ºF (182ºC). Check regularly to avoid overcooking. Serve chilled.

Vanilla Crème Brûlée

Prep time: 5 minutes | Cook time: 31 to 38 minutes | Serves 4

1 cup whipped cream
¾ cup milk
1 vanilla pod
5 egg yolks
⅓ cup plus 1 tablespoon sugar

1. Place a saucepan over low heat and add the milk and whipped cream. Cut the vanilla pods open and scrape the seeds into the saucepan along with the pods. Cook until almost boiled, stirring regularly, about 6 to 8 minutes. Turn off the heat and remove the vanilla pods. Preheat air fryer to 300ºF (149ºC). 2. Beat egg yolks in a bowl and whisk in ⅓ cup of sugar, but not too bubbly. Slowly pour in the egg yolk mixture and beat until combined. Fill 4 ramekins with the custard mix. Place the ramekins in a baking pan and pour in boiling water to reach halfway up ramekins. Bake in the fryer for 25 to 30 minutes. 3. Remove the ramekins and let them cool at room temperature, then refrigerate for 1 hour. Sprinkle the remaining sugar over the crème brûlée and use a torch to caramelize the top. Serve and enjoy!

Chocolate-Butter Brownies with Walnuts

Prep time: 15 minutes | Cook time: 20 to 25 minutes | Serves 6

6 ounces (170 g) dark chocolate
6 ounces (170 g) butter
¾ cup white sugar
3 eggs
2 teaspoons vanilla extract
¾ cup flour
¼ cup cocoa powder
1 cup walnuts, chopped
1 cup white chocolate chips

1. Preheat air fryer to 340ºF (171ºC). Line a baking dish with waxed paper. Melt the dark chocolate and butter in a saucepan over low heat, stirring constantly until a smooth mixture is obtained; let cool slightly. 2. In a bowl, whisk eggs, sugar, and vanilla. Fold in the flour and cocoa powder and mix to combine. Stir in the white chocolate chips and melted dark chocolate. Sprinkle the walnuts over. Spread the batter onto the baking dish and bake in the fryer for 20 to 25 minutes. Transfer to a wire rack to cool before slicing.

Easy Lemony Cheesecake

Prep time: 15 minutes | Cook time: 20 to 25 minutes | Serves 6

8 ounces (227 g) graham crackers, crushed
4 ounces (113 g) butter, melted
16 ounces (454 g) cream cheese, at room temperature
3 eggs
3 tablespoons sugar
1 tablespoon vanilla extract
Zest of 2 lemons

1. Line a cake tin that fits in your air fryer with baking paper. Mix together the crackers and butter and press them at the bottom of the tin. In a bowl, add cream cheese, eggs, sugar, vanilla, and lemon zest and beat with a hand mixer until well combined and smooth. Pour the mixture on top of the crackers. 2. Bake in the air fryer for 20 to 25 minutes at 350ºF (177ºC). Regularly check to ensure it's set but still a bit wobbly. Let cool, then refrigerate overnight. Serve at room temperature or chilled.

Soft Buttermilk Biscuits

Prep time: 10 minutes | Cook time: 16 to 18 minutes | Makes 10 Biscuits

1 cup all-purpose flour
¾ teaspoon salt
½ teaspoon baking powder
4 tablespoons butter, cubed
1 teaspoon sugar
¾ cup buttermilk

1. Preheat air fryer to 360ºF (182ºC). In a bowl, stir the flour, baking powder, sugar, and salt until well combined. Add in butter and rub it into the flour mixture until crumbed. Stir in the buttermilk until a dough is formed. 2. Flour a flat and dry surface and roll the dough out until half-inch thick. Cut out 10 rounds with a small cookie cutter. Arrange the biscuits on a greased baking tray. Working in batches, Bake in the air fryer for 16 to 18 minutes. Let cool for a few minutes before serving.

Mix-Berry Almond Crumble

Prep time: 10 minutes | Cook time: 11 to 16 minutes | Serves 4

2 tablespoons flaked almonds
1⅓ cups frozen mixed berries
1 teaspoon lemon zest
⅔ cup all-purpose flour
4 tablespoons caster sugar
2 tablespoons unsalted butter, softened

1. Preheat air fryer to 380ºF (193ºC). Spread the mixed berries on a 6-by-2-inch baking dish and sprinkle them with some sugar, lemon zest, and almonds. In a bowl, mix the remaining sugar and flour. Rub the butter into the mixture with your fingertips until it becomes crumbly. Pour the crumble topping on top of the almonds and bake in your air fryer for 11 to 16 minutes until golden and bubbling. Serve warm

Vanilla Orange Cake

Prep time: 10 minutes | Cook time: 15 minutes | Serves 4

1 cup white sugar
1 cup self-rising flour
3 eggs
1 teaspoon vanilla extract
Zest and juice from 1 orange
2 egg whites
4 tablespoons superfine sugar
½ cup ground walnuts

1. Preheat air fryer to 360ºF (182ºC). In a bowl, beat white sugar, flour, eggs, vanilla, and orange zest with an electric mixer until creamy and fluffy, about 8 minutes. Transfer half of the batter into a greased and floured cake pan and bake in the air fryer for 15 minutes. Repeat the process for the remaining batter. 2. Meanwhile, prepare the frosting by beating egg whites, orange juice, and superfine sugar together. Spread half of the frosting mixture on top of one cooled cake. Top with the other cake and spread the remaining frosting all over. Top with walnuts, slice, and serve.

Pineapple and Dark Chocolate Cake

Prep time: 15 minutes | Cook time: 20 to 25 minutes | Serves 4

2 ounces (57 g) dark chocolate, grated
8 ounces (227 g) self-rising flour
4 ounces (113 g) butter, melted
7 ounces (198 g) pineapple chunks
½ cup pineapple juice
1 egg
2 tablespoons milk
½ cup sugar

1. Preheat air fryer to 350°F (177°C). In a large bowl, combine the flour, sugar, and chocolate. In another bowl, beat the egg, butter, pineapple juice, and milk, without overmixing. Mix the wet ingredients with the dry ingredients, then fold in the pineapple chunks. Spread the batter on a greased cake pan. Bake in the air fryer for 20 to 25 minutes or until a toothpick comes out dry and clean. Let cool before serving.

White Chocolate Pudding

Prep time: 10 minutes | Cook time: 14 to 16 minutes | Serves 2

3 ounces (85 g) white chocolate
4 egg whites
2 egg yolks, at room temperature
¼ cup sugar
1 tablespoon melted butter
1 tablespoon cold butter
¼ teaspoon vanilla extract
1½ tablespoons flour

1. Brush two ramekins with melted butter. Swirl in 2 tablespoons of sugar to coat the butter. Melt the cold butter with the chocolate in a heatproof bowl, inside the microwave, then set aside. In another bowl, beat the egg yolks vigorously. Add the vanilla and the remaining sugar; beat to incorporate fully. Mix in the melted chocolate. Add the flour and mix until there are no lumps. 2. Preheat air fryer to 330°F (166°C). Whisk the egg whites in another bowl until the mixture holds stiff peaks. Fold in the chocolate mixture and divide the mixture between the ramekins. Place them in the frying basket, and bake for 14 to 16 minutes or until cooked through and golden.

Chocolate Fudge Squares

Prep time: 15 minutes | Cook time: 23 to 26 minutes | Serves 6

1 cup sugar
½ cup plain flour
1 tablespoon honey
1 teaspoon baking powder
1 teaspoon vanilla extract
1 tablespoon cocoa powder
3 eggs
½ cup butter, softened
1 orange, zested
½ cup dark chocolate, melted
Chocolate Topping:
2 tablespoons chocolate chips
2 tablespoons heavy cream

1. Preheat air fryer to 350°F (177°C). In a bowl, whisk the eggs with sugar and honey until pale and creamy. Sift the flour into another bowl and mix in the baking powder and cocoa powder. Gently stir in the egg mixture to combine. Stir in orange zest, melted chocolate, and vanilla extract, be careful not to overmix. 2. Transfer the batter to a greased cake pan and bake in the air fryer for 23 to 26 minutes, until set in the center and the top is slightly crusty. Remove and let cool completely. Microwave the chocolate chips and heavy cream in a heatproof bowl for 60 to 90 seconds. Remove and stir until smooth. Drizzle over the chilled cake. Cut into squares and enjoy!

Mini Peanut Butter Tarts

Prep time: 25 minutes | Cook time: 12 to 15 minutes | Serves 8

1 cup pecans
1 cup finely ground blanched almond flour
2 tablespoons unsalted butter, at room temperature
½ cup plus 2 tablespoons Swerve, divided
½ cup heavy (whipping) cream
2 tablespoons mascarpone cheese
4 ounces (113 g) cream cheese
½ cup sugar-free peanut butter
1 teaspoon pure vanilla extract
⅛ teaspoon sea salt
½ cup stevia-sweetened chocolate chips
1 tablespoon coconut oil
¼ cup chopped peanuts or pecans

1. Process the pecans in a food processor until finely ground. In a medium bowl, stir pecans, almond flour, butter and 2 tablespoons Swerve, until the mixture becomes wet and crumbly. Divide the mixture among 8 silicone muffin cups. 2. Arrange the muffin cups in the frying basket. Bake at 300°F (149°C) for 12 to 15 minutes until the crusts begin to brown. Allow to cool. 3. Combine the heavy cream and mascarpone cheese in a stand mixer and beat until peaks form. Transfer to a large bowl. 4. In the same stand mixer, combine the cream cheese, peanut butter, remaining Swerve, vanilla, and salt. Beat at medium-high speed until smooth. 5. Reduce the speed to low and add the heavy cream mixture back a spoonful at a time, beating after each addition. 6. Spoon the peanut butter mixture over the crusts, and freeze for 30 minutes. 7. Stir and melt chocolate chips and coconut oil in the top of a double boiler over high heat. 8. Drizzle the melted chocolate over the peanut butter tarts. Top with the nuts and freeze for another 15 minutes until set.

White Chocolate Cookies

Prep time: 20 minutes | Cook time: 18 to 20 minutes | Serves 4

1 cup self-rising flour
4 tablespoons brown sugar
1 egg
2 ounces (57 g) white chocolate chips
1 tablespoon honey
1½ tablespoons milk
1 teaspoon baking soda
½ cup butter, softened

1. Preheat air fryer to 350°F (177°C). In a bowl, beat butter and sugar until fluffy. Mix in honey, egg, and milk. In a separate bowl, mix flour and baking soda and gradually add the butter/egg mixture, stirring constantly. 2. Gently fold in the chocolate chips. Drop spoonfuls of the mixture onto a greased cookie sheet and press down slightly to flatten. Bake in the air fryer for 18 to 20 minutes. Remove to a wire rack to cool completely before serving.

Lemon Almond Meringues with Dark Chocolate

Prep time: 10 minutes | Cook time: 35 minutes | Serves 4

8 egg whites
½ teaspoon almond extract
1⅓ cups sugar
2 teaspoons lemon juice
1½ teaspoons vanilla extract
Melted dark chocolate, to drizzle

1. In a bowl, beat egg whites and lemon juice with an electric mixer until foamy. Slowly beat in the sugar until thoroughly combined. Add almond and vanilla extracts. Beat until glossy and stiff peaks form. 2. Line a baking dish that fits in the fryer with parchment paper. Fill a piping bag with the mixture and pipe as many mounds in the baking dish as you can, leaving 1½-inch spaces between each mound. 3. Place the baking dish inside the frying basket and bake at 250ºF (121ºC) for 5 minutes. Reduce the temperature to 220ºF (104ºC) and bake for 15 more minutes. Then, reduce the temperature to 190ºF (88ºC) and cook for 13 to 15 more minutes. Let the meringues cool. Drizzle with dark chocolate and serve.

Chocolate and Raspberry Cake

Prep time: 20 minutes | Cook time: 18 to 22 minutes | Serves 6

1 cup flour
⅓ cup cocoa powder
1 teaspoon baking powder
½ cup white sugar
¼ cup brown sugar
½ cup butter, melted
1 teaspoon vanilla extract
⅔ cup milk
2 eggs, beaten
1 cup raspberries
1 cup chocolate chips

1. Line a cake tin with baking paper. In a bowl, sift flour, cocoa powder, and baking powder. In another bowl, whisk butter, white and brown sugar, vanilla, and milk until creamy. Mix in the eggs. 2. Pour the wet ingredients into the dry ones, and whisk to combine. Add in the raspberries and chocolate chips. Pour the batter into the cake tin and bake in the fryer for 18 to 22 minutes at 350ºF (177ºC). Serve cooled.

Cinnamon Pecan Pie

Prep time: 15 minutes | Cook time: 30 to 35 minutes | Serves 4

¾ cup maple syrup
2 eggs
¼ teaspoon ground nutmeg
½ teaspoon cinnamon
2 tablespoons almond butter
2 tablespoons brown sugar
½ cup pecans, chopped
1 tablespoon butter, melted
1 (8-inch) pie dough
¾ teaspoon vanilla extract

1. Preheat air fryer to 360ºF (182ºC). 2. Coat the pecans with melted butter. Place them in the frying basket and air fry for 8 to 10 minutes, shaking once. Lay the pie crust into a 7-inch round pie pan and pour the pecans over. 3. Whisk together all the remaining ingredients in a bowl. Spread the mixture over the pecans. Set the air fryer to 320ºF (160ºC) and bake the pie for 22 to 25 minutes. Serve chilled.

Lemon-Glazed Cupcakes

Prep time: 15 minutes | Cook time: 12 to 14 minutes | Serves 6

1 cup flour
½ cup sugar
1 egg
1 teaspoon lemon zest
¾ teaspoon baking powder
2 tablespoons vegetable oil
½ cup milk
½ teaspoon vanilla extract
½ cup powdered sugar
2 teaspoons lemon juice

1. Preheat air fryer to 360ºF (182ºC). In a bowl, combine flour, sugar, lemon zest, and baking powder. In another bowl, whisk together egg, vegetable oil, milk, and vanilla extract. Gently combine the two mixtures to obtain a smooth batter. Divide the batter between greased muffin tins or a 6-hole muffin tray. 2. Place the muffin tins or tray in the air fryer and bake for 12 to 14 minutes. Remove the muffins and let cool. Whisk the sugar with lemon juice until smooth. Pour the glaze on top of the muffins and serve.

Cinnamon Grilled Pineapples

Prep time: 10 minutes | Cook time: 9 to 11 minutes | Serves 2

1 teaspoon cinnamon
5 pineapple slices
½ cup brown sugar
1 tablespoon mint, chopped
1 tablespoon honey

1. Preheat air fryer to 340ºF (171ºC). In a small bowl, mix the sugar and cinnamon. Drizzle the sugar mixture over the pineapple slices. Place them in the greased frying basket and bake for 5 minutes. Flip the pineapples and cook for 4 to 6 more minutes. Remove, drizzle with honey and sprinkle with fresh mint.

Pineapple Galette

Prep time: 15 minutes | Cook time: 40 minutes | Serves 2

¼ medium-size pineapple, peeled, cored, and cut crosswise into ¼-inch-thick slices
2 tablespoons dark rum
1 teaspoon vanilla extract
½ teaspoon kosher salt
Finely grated zest of ½ lime
1 store-bought sheet puff pastry, cut into an 8-inch round
3 tablespoons granulated sugar
2 tablespoons unsalted butter, cubed and chilled
Coconut ice cream, for serving

1. In a bowl, combine the pineapple, rum, vanilla, salt, and lime zest and let stand for at least 10 minutes. 2. Meanwhile, press the puff pastry round into the bottom and up the sides of a cake pan and use the tines of a fork to dock the bottom and sides. 3. Arrange the pineapple slices on the bottom of the pastry in a single layer, then sprinkle with the sugar and butter. Drizzle with the leftover juices. Bake at 310ºF (154ºC) until the pastry is puffed and golden brown and the pineapple is lightly caramelized on top, about 40 minutes. 4. Allow to cool for 15 minutes. Unmold the galette from the pan and serve warm with coconut ice cream.

15-Minute Coffee Cake

Prep time: 15 minutes | Cook time: 15 minutes | Serves 2

¼ cup butter
½ teaspoon instant coffee
1 tablespoon black coffee, brewed
1 egg
¼ cup sugar
¼ cup flour
1 teaspoon cocoa powder
Powdered sugar, for icing

1. Preheat air fryer to 320ºF (160ºC). In a bowl, beat sugar and egg until creamy. Mix in cocoa, instant and black coffees; and stir in the flour. Transfer the batter to a greased baking dish. Bake in the air fryer for 15 minutes. Let cool for at least 1 hour at room temperature. Dust with powdered sugar, slice and serve.

Vanilla Peach Cake

Prep time: 15 minutes | Cook time: 20 to 25 minutes | Serves 4

3 tablespoons butter, melted
1 cup peaches, chopped
3 tablespoons sugar
1 cup almond flour
1 cup heavy cream
1 teaspoon vanilla extract
2 eggs, whisked
1 teaspoon baking soda

1. Preheat air fryer to 360ºF (182ºC). In a bowl, mix all the ingredients and stir well. Pour the mixture into a greased baking dish and insert in the frying basket. Bake for 20 to 25 minutes. Let cool, slice, and serve.

Dark Rum Pear Pie

Prep time: 15 minutes | Cook time: 20 minutes | Serves 4

1 cup flour
5 tablespoons sugar
3 tablespoons butter, softened
1 tablespoon dark spiced rum
2 pears, sliced

1. Preheat air fryer to 370ºF (188ºC). In a bowl, place 3 tablespoons of the sugar, butter, and flour and mix to form a batter. Roll the butter out onto a floured surface and transfer to a greased baking dish. Arrange the pears slices on top and sprinkle with sugar and dark rum. Bake in the air fryer for 20 minutes. Serve cooled.

Yummy Moon Pie

Prep time: 15 minutes | Cook time: 5 minutes | Serves 4

4 graham cracker sheets, snapped in half
8 large marshmallows
8 squares each of dark, milk, and white chocolate

1. Arrange the crackers on a cutting board. Put 2 marshmallows onto half of the graham cracker halves. Place 2 squares of chocolate on top of the marshmallows. Place the remaining crackers on top to create 4 sandwiches. Wrap each one in baking paper, so it resembles a parcel. Bake in the preheated air fryer for 5 minutes at 340ºF (171ºC). Serve at room temperature or chilled.

Air Fried Donuts

Prep time: 15 minutes | Cook time: 10 to 12 minutes | Serves 4

2¼ cups self-rising flour, mixed with ¼ teaspoon salt
2¼ dry active yeast
⅓ cup lukewarm milk
¼ cup unsalted butter, softened
2 eggs, beaten
3 tablespoons brown sugar

1. In a bowl, stir eggs, butter, and milk until well mixed. Mix the flour, brown sugar, and yeast with a mixer on low speed. Slowly add the egg mixture, increase the speed and mix until a elastic, glossy dough forms. Transfer to a oiled bowl, cover, and let it rise for 1 hour. Preheat air fryer to 350ºF (177ºC).
2. Remove and knead for 3 to 4 minutes. Form donut shapes and cut off the center using cookie cutters. Arrange on a lined baking sheet and bake in the fryer for 10 to 12 minutes, flipping once. Serve with your favorite glaze.

Cheat Apple Pie

Prep time: 10 minutes | Cook time: 20 to 22 minutes | Serves 4

2 apples, diced
2 tablespoons butter, melted
2 tablespoons white sugar
1 tablespoon brown sugar
1 teaspoon cinnamon
1 egg, beaten
2 large puff pastry sheets
¼ teaspoon salt

1. In a bowl, whisk white sugar, brown sugar, cinnamon, salt, and butter. Place the apples in a greased baking dish and coat them with the mixture. Place the dish in the fryer and bake for 10 minutes at 350ºF (177ºC). Roll out the pastry on a floured flat surface and cut each sheet into 6 equal pieces. 2. Divide the apple filling between the pieces. Brush the edges of the pastry squares with the egg. Fold the squares and seal the edges with a fork. Place on a lined baking dish and bake in the fryer at 350ºF (177ºC) for 8 minutes. Flip over, and cook for 2 to 4 more minutes until golden. Serve chilled.

Chocolate Soufflé

Prep time: 20 minutes | Cook time: 14 minutes | Serves 2

2 eggs, whites and yolks separated
¼ cup butter, melted
2 tablespoons flour
3 tablespoons sugar
3 ounces (85 g) chocolate, melted
½ teaspoon vanilla extract

1. Preheat the air fryer to 320ºF (160ºC). In a bowl, beat the yolks along with sugar and vanilla extract until creamy. Stir in the butter, chocolate, and flour. In another bowl, whisk the egg whites until stiff peak forms. Working in batches, gently combine the egg whites with the chocolate mixture. Divide the batter between two greased ramekins and bake in the air fryer for 14 minutes. Serve warm or cooled.

158 | Chapter 1 Vegetables and Sides

Tropical Pineapple Fritters

Prep time: 10 minutes | Cook time: 14 to 16 minutes | Serves 5

1½ cups flour
1 pineapple, sliced into rings
3 tablespoons sesame seeds
2 eggs, beaten
1 teaspoon baking powder
½ tablespoon sugar

1. Preheat air fryer to 350°F (177°C). In a bowl, mix sesame seeds, flour, baking powder, eggs, sugar, and 1 cup of water. Dip pineapple slices into the flour mixture and arrange them in the greased frying basket. Air fry for 14 to 16 minutes, turning once, until golden. Serve and enjoy!

Honey and Plum Homemade Rice

Prep time: 10 minutes | Cook time: 20 minutes | Serves 4

1 cup long-grain rice
2 cups milk
½ cup plums, chopped
3 tablespoons honey
1 teaspoon vanilla extract
⅓ cup heavy cream

1. Preheat the air fryer to 360°F (182°C). In a baking dish, combine all the ingredients, except for the ch. Place the dish in the air fryer and bake for 20 minutes. Spoon into glass cups, top with plums and serve warm.

No Flour Lime Cupcakes

Prep time: 10 minutes | Cook time: 15 minutes | Serves 4

2 eggs plus 1 egg yolk
Juice and zest of 1 lime
1 cup yogurt
¼ cup superfine sugar
8 ounces (227 g) cream cheese
1 teaspoon vanilla extract

1. Preheat the fryer to 300°F (149°C). In a bowl, mix yogurt and cream cheese until uniform. In another bowl, beat the eggs, yolk, sugar, vanilla, lime juice, and zest. Gently fold the in the cheese mixture. Divide the batter between greased muffin tins and bake in the fryer for 15 minutes or until golden. Serve chilled.

Apricot and Lemon Flapjacks

Prep time: 10 minutes | Cook time: 20 minutes | Serves 4

¼ cup butter
2 tablespoons maple syrup
2 tablespoons pure cane sugar
1¼ cups rolled oats
2 teaspoons lemon zest
3 apricots, stoned and sliced

1. Preheat the air fryer to 350°F (177°C). Line a baking dish with parchment paper. 2. Melt the butter in a skillet over medium heat and stir in cane sugar and maple syrup until the sugar dissolves, about 2 minutes. Mix in the remaining ingredients and transfer to the baking dish. Bake for 18 to 20 minutes or until golden. Let cool for a few minutes before cutting into flapjacks.

Five-Fruit Skewers with Caramel Sauce

Prep time: 10 minutes | Cook time: 6 to 8 minutes | Serves 2

1 cup blueberries
1 banana, sliced
1 mango, peeled and cut into cubes
1 peach, cut into wedges
2 kiwi fruit, peeled and quartered
2 tablespoons caramel sauce (optional)

1, Preheat the air fryer to 340°F (171°C). Thread the fruit pieces alternately onto 4 to 6 previously soaked in water bamboo skewers. Place them in the greased frying basket and air fry for 6 to 8 minutes, turning once or until the fruit caramelize slightly. Drizzle with the caramel sauce (optional), let cool slightly and serve.

Lemon Curd

Prep time: 10 minutes | Cook time: 20 minutes | Serves 2

3 tablespoons butter
3 tablespoons sugar
1 whole egg
1 egg yolk
¾ lemon, juiced

1. Add sugar and butter to a medium-size ramekin and beat evenly. Slowly whisk in the whole egg and egg yolk until fresh yellow color is obtained. Mix in the lemon juice. Place the ramekin in the preheated air fryer and bake at 220°F (104°C) for 6 minutes. Increase the temperature to 320°F (160°C) and cook for 13 to 15 minutes until golden. Remove the ramekin and use a spoon to check for any lumps. Serve chilled.

New York Cheesecake

Prep time: 1 hour | Cook time: 37 minutes | Serves 8

1½ cups almond flour
3 ounces (85 g) Swerve
½ stick butter, melted
20 ounces (567 g) full-fat cream cheese
½ cup heavy cream
1¼ cups granulated Swerve
3 eggs, at room temperature
1 tablespoon vanilla essence
1 teaspoon grated lemon zest

1. Coat the sides and bottom of a baking pan with a little flour. 2. In a mixing bowl, combine the almond flour and Swerve. Add the butter and mix until looks like bread crumbs. 3. Press the mixture into the bottom of the pan to form an even layer. Bake at 330°F (166°C) for 7 minutes until golden brown. Allow it to cool completely. 4. Meanwhile, prepare the filling by mixing the soft cheese, heavy cream, and granulated Swerve in a mixer; beat until creamy and fluffy. 5. Crack the eggs into the mixing bowl, one at a time; add the vanilla and lemon zest and continue to mix until fully combined. 6. Pour the prepared topping over the cooled crust and spread evenly. 7. Bake at 330°F (166°C) for 25 to 30 minutes; leave it in the air fryer to keep warm for another 30 minutes. 8. Cover your cheesecake with plastic wrap. Place in your refrigerator and allow it to cool at least 6 hours or overnight. Serve well chilled.

Molten Lava Mini Cakes

Prep time: 15 minutes | Cook time: 10 to 12 minutes | Serves 4

2 tablespoons butter, melted
3½ tablesp0ons sugar
1½ tablespoons self-rising flour
3½ ounces dark chocolate, melted
2 eggs
½ teaspoon ground cinnamon

1. Preheat the fryer to 360ºF (182ºC). In a bowl, beat the eggs and sugar until frothy. Stir in butter, cinnamon, and chocolate and gently fold in the flour. Divide the mixture between 4 greased ramekins and bake in the air fryer for 10 to 12 minutes. Let cool for a few minutes before inverting the cakes onto serving plates.

Snickerdoodle Poppers

Prep time: 15 minutes | Cook time: 7 minutes | Serves 5

1 box instant vanilla Jell-O mix
1 can (5 pieces) Pillsbury
Grands Flaky Layers Biscuits
1½ cups cinnamon sugar
2 tablespoons butter, melted

1. Preheat the fryer to 340ºF (171ºC). Unroll the biscuits and cut them into fourths. Shape each into a ball. Arrange the balls on a paper-lined baking dish and bake in the air fryer for 7 minutes or until golden. 2. Prepare the Jell-O following the package's instructions. Using an injector, insert some of the vanilla pudding into each ball. Brush the balls with melted butter and then coat in cinnamon sugar. Serve cool.

Blueberry Muffins

Prep time: 20 minutes | Cook time: 10 to 12 minutes | Serves 6

1½ cups flour
½ teaspoon salt
½ cup sugar
¼ cup vegetable oil
2 teaspoons vanilla extract
1 cup fresh blueberries
2 eggs
1 teaspoon baking powder
1 lemon, zested
¼ cup sour cream

1. Preheat the air fryer to 340ºF (171ºC). In a bowl, combine flour, sugar, salt, lemon zest, and baking powder. In another bowl, add the vegetable oil, sour cream, vanilla extract, and eggs and whisk until fully incorporated. Combine the wet and dry ingredients, and gently fold in the blueberries. Divide the mixture between a greased 6-hole muffin tray or 4 muffin cups and bake in the air fryer for 10 to 12 minutes or until set and golden. Serve cooled.

Lime Bars

Prep time: 10 minutes | Cook time: 33 minutes | Makes 12 bars

1½ cups blanched finely ground almond flour, divided
¾ cup confectioners' erythritol, divided
4 tablespoons salted butter, melted
½ cup fresh lime juice
2 large eggs, whisked

1. In a medium bowl, mix together 1 cup flour, ¼ cup erythritol, and butter. Press mixture into bottom of a round nonstick cake pan. 2. Bake at 300ºF (149ºC) 13 minutes until crust is brown and set in the middle. 3. Allow to cool in pan 10 minutes. 4. In a medium bowl, combine remaining flour, remaining erythritol, lime juice, and eggs. Pour mixture over cooled crust and bake for 20 minutes more until browned and firm on top. 5. Let cool completely in pan, about 30 minutes, then chill covered in the refrigerator 1 hour. Serve chilled.

Apple Fries

Prep time: 10 minutes | Cook time: 7 minutes | Serves 8

Oil, for spraying
1 cup all-purpose flour
3 large eggs, beaten
1 cup graham cracker crumbs
¼ cup sugar
1 teaspoon ground cinnamon
3 large Gala apples, peeled, cored, and cut into wedges
1 cup caramel sauce, warmed

1. Preheat the air fryer to 380ºF (193ºC). 2. Place the flour and beaten eggs in separate bowls. In another bowl, mix together the graham cracker crumbs, sugar, and cinnamon. 3. Coat the apple wedges in the flour, egg, and graham cracker mix until evenly coated. Spray lightly with oil. 4. Air fry for 5 minutes, flip, spray with oil, and cook for another 2 minutes, until crunchy and golden brown. 5. Top with caramel sauce and serve.

Chocolate Lava Cakes

Prep time: 5 minutes | Cook time: 15 minutes | Serves 2

2 large eggs, whisked
¼ cup blanched finely ground almond flour
½ teaspoon vanilla extract
2 ounces (57 g) low-carb chocolate chips, melted

1. In a medium bowl, mix eggs with flour and vanilla. Fold in chocolate until fully combined. 2. Pour batter into two ramekins greased with cooking spray. Place ramekins into frying basket. Bake at 320ºF (160ºC) for 15 minutes until set at the edges and firm in the center. Let cool 5 minutes before serving.

Chocolate Croissants

Prep time: 5 minutes | Cook time: 8 minutes per batch | Serves 8

1 sheet frozen puff pastry, thawed
⅓ cup chocolate-hazelnut spread
1 large egg, beaten

1. On a lightly floured surface, roll puff pastry into a 14-inch square. Cut pastry into quarters to form 4 squares. Cut each square diagonally to form 8 triangles. 2. Spread 2 teaspoons chocolate-hazelnut spread on each triangle; from wider end, roll up pastry. Brush egg on top of each roll. 3. Air fry 4 rolls at a time, at 375ºF (191ºC) for 8 minutes, or until pastry is golden brown. 4. Serve warm or at room temperature.

Oatmeal Raisin Bars

Prep time: 15 minutes | Cook time: 15 minutes | Serves 8

⅓ cup all-purpose flour
¼ teaspoon kosher salt
¼ teaspoon baking powder
¼ teaspoon ground cinnamon
¼ cup light brown sugar, lightly packed
¼ cup granulated sugar
½ cup canola oil
1 large egg
1 teaspoon vanilla extract
1⅓ cups quick-cooking oats
⅓ cup raisins

1. Preheat the air fryer to 360ºF (182ºC). Spray a baking pan with nonstick cooking spray. 2. In the pan, combine all the ingredients and evenly distribute. Bake for 15 minutes or until golden brown. 3. Let cool for 20 minutes before slicing and serving.

Berry Crumble

Prep time: 10 minutes | Cook time: 15 minutes | Serves 4

Filling:
2 cups mixed berries
2 tablespoons sugar
1 tablespoon cornstarch
1 tablespoon fresh lemon juice
Topping:
¼ cup all-purpose flour
¼ cup rolled oats
1 tablespoon sugar
2 tablespoons cold unsalted butter, cut into small cubes
Whipped cream or ice cream (optional)

1. Preheat the air fryer to 400ºF (204ºC). 2. **Make the Filling:** In a round baking pan, gently mix the berries, sugar, cornstarch, and lemon juice until thoroughly combined. 3. **Make the Topping:** In a bowl, combine the flour, oats, and sugar. Stir the butter into the flour mixture until the mixture has the consistency of bread crumbs. 4. Sprinkle the topping over the berries. 5. Put the pan in the frying basket and air fry for 15 minutes. Let cool for 5 minutes on a wire rack. 6. Serve topped with whipped cream or ice cream, if desired.

Baked Peaches with Yogurt and Blueberries

Prep time: 10 minutes | Cook time: 7 to 11 minutes | Serves 6

3 peaches, peeled, halved, and pitted
2 tablespoons packed brown sugar
1 cup plain Greek yogurt
¼ teaspoon ground cinnamon
1 teaspoon pure vanilla extract
1 cup fresh blueberries

1. Preheat the air fryer to 380ºF (193ºC). 2. Arrange the peaches in the frying basket, cut-side up. Top with a generous sprinkle of brown sugar. 3. Bake for 7 to 11 minutes, or until the peaches are lightly browned and caramelized. 4. Meanwhile, whisk together the yogurt, cinnamon, and vanilla in a bowl until smooth. 5. Serve topped with the yogurt mixture and fresh blueberries.

Coconut Flour Cake

Prep time: 10 minutes | Cook time: 25 minutes | Serves 6

2 tablespoons salted butter, melted
⅓ cup coconut flour
2 large eggs, whisked
½ cup granular erythritol
1 teaspoon baking powder
1 teaspoon vanilla extract
½ cup sour cream

1. Mix all ingredients in a bowl. Pour batter into a round nonstick baking dish. 2. Place baking dish into frying basket. Bake at 300ºF (149ºC) for 25 minutes. The cake will be dark golden on top, and a toothpick inserted in the center should come out clean when done. 3. Let cool in dish 15 minutes before slicing and serving.

Bourbon Bread Pudding

Prep time: 10 minutes | Cook time: 20 minutes | Serves 4

3 slices whole grain bread, cubed
1 large egg
1 cup whole milk
2 tablespoons bourbon
½ teaspoons vanilla extract
¼ cup maple syrup, divided
½ teaspoons ground cinnamon
2 teaspoons sparkling sugar

1. Preheat the air fryer to 270ºF (132ºC). 2. Spray a baking pan with nonstick cooking spray, then place the bread cubes in the pan. 3. In a medium bowl, whisk together the egg, milk, bourbon, vanilla extract, 3 tablespoons maple syrup, and cinnamon. Pour the egg mixture over the bread and press down with a spatula to coat all the bread, then sprinkle the sparkling sugar on top and bake for 20 minutes. 4. Allow to cool for 10 minutes. Drizzle the remaining maple syrup on top. Slice and serve warm.

Air Fryer Apple Fritters

Prep time: 30 minutes | Cook time: 7 to 8 minutes | Serves 6

1 cup chopped, peeled Granny Smith apple
½ cup granulated sugar
1 teaspoon ground cinnamon
1 cup all-purpose flour
1 teaspoon baking powder
1 teaspoon salt
2 tablespoons milk
2 tablespoons butter, melted
1 large egg, beaten
Cooking spray
¼ cup confectioners' sugar (optional)

1. Mix together the apple, granulated sugar, and cinnamon in a bowl. Allow to sit for 30 minutes. 2. Combine the flour, baking powder, and salt in a bowl. Add the milk, butter, and egg and stir to incorporate. 3. Pour the apple mixture into the bowl of flour mixture and stir with a spatula until a dough forms. 4. Divide the dough into 12 equal portions and shape into 1-inch balls. Flatten them into patties. 5. Preheat the air fryer to 350ºF (177ºC). 6. Transfer the apple fritters in the fryer basket. Spray with cooking spray. Bake for 7 to 8 minutes until lightly browned. Flip halfway through the cooking time. 7. Serve topped with the confectioners' sugar, if desired.

Lemon Curd Pavlova

Prep time: 10 minutes | Cook time: 1 hour | Serves 4

Shell:
3 large egg whites
¼ teaspoon cream of tartar
¾ cup Swerve confectioners'-style sweetener or equivalent amount of powdered sweetener
1 teaspoon grated lemon zest
1 teaspoon lemon extract
Lemon Curd:
1 cup Swerve confectioners'-style sweetener or equivalent amount of liquid or powdered sweetener
½ cup lemon juice
4 large eggs
½ cup coconut oil
For Garnish (Optional):
Blueberries
Swerve confectioners'-style sweetener or equivalent amount of powdered sweetener

1. Preheat the air fryer to 275ºF (135ºC). Grease a pie pan with butter or coconut oil. 2. **Make the Shell:** In a bowl, use a hand mixer to beat the egg whites and cream of tartar until soft peaks form. With the mixer on low, slowly sprinkle in the sweetener and mix until completely incorporated. 3. Add the lemon zest and lemon extract and continue to beat with the hand mixer until stiff peaks form. 4. Spoon the mixture into the pie pan, then smooth it across the bottom, up the sides, and onto the rim to form a shell. Bake for 1 hour. Let the shell stand in the air fryer for 20 minutes. 5. **Make the Lemon Curd:** Meanwhile, in a saucepan, whisk together the sweetener, lemon juice, and eggs. Add the coconut oil and place the pan on the stovetop over medium heat. Once the oil is melted, whisk constantly until the mixture thickens and thickly coats the back of a spoon, about 10 minutes. Do not allow the mixture to come to a boil. 6. Pour the lemon curd mixture through a fine-mesh strainer into a medium-sized bowl. Place the bowl inside a larger bowl filled with ice water and whisk occasionally until the curd is completely cool. 7. Place the lemon curd on top of the shell and garnish with blueberries and powdered sweetener, if desired.

Lemon Poppy Seed Macaroons

Prep time: 10 minutes | Cook time: 14 minutes | Makes 1 dozen cookies

2 large egg whites, room temperature
⅓ cup Swerve confectioners'-style sweetener or equivalent amount of powdered sweetener
2 tablespoons grated lemon zest, plus more for garnish if desired
2 teaspoons poppy seeds
1 teaspoon lemon extract
¼ teaspoon fine sea salt
2 cups unsweetened shredded coconut
Lemon Icing:
¼ cup Swerve confectioners'-style sweetener or equivalent amount of powdered sweetener
1 tablespoon lemon juice

1. Preheat the air fryer to 325ºF (163ºC). Line a pie pan with parchment paper. 2. Place the egg whites in a medium-sized bowl and use a hand mixer on high to beat the whites until stiff peaks form. Add the sweetener, lemon zest, poppy seeds, lemon extract, and salt. Mix on low until combined. Gently fold in the coconut with a rubber spatula. 3. Use a 1-inch cookie scoop to place the cookies on the parchment, spacing them about ¼ inch apart. Bake for 12 to 14 minutes, until the cookies are golden and a toothpick inserted into the center comes out clean. 4. **Make the Lemon Icing:** Place the sweetener in a bowl. Add the lemon juice and stir well. 5. Allow to cool for about 10 minutes, then drizzle with the icing. Garnish with lemon zest, if desired.

Coconut Macaroons

Prep time: 5 minutes | Cook time: 8 to 10 minutes | Makes 12 macaroons

1⅓ cups shredded, sweetened coconut
4½ teaspoons flour
2 tablespoons sugar
1 egg white
½ teaspoon almond extract

1. Preheat the air fryer to 330ºF (166ºC). 2. Mix all ingredients together. Shape into 12 balls. Place into frying basket. 3. Air fry at 330ºF (166ºC) for 8 to 10 minutes, until golden.

Boston Cream Donut Holes

Prep time: 30 minutes | Cook time: 4 minutes per batch | Makes 24 donut holes

1½ cups bread flour
1 teaspoon active dry yeast
1 tablespoon sugar
¼ teaspoon salt
½ cup warm milk
½ teaspoon pure vanilla extract
2 egg yolks
2 tablespoons butter, melted
Vegetable oil
Custard Filling:
1 (3.4-ounce / 96-g) box French vanilla instant pudding mix
¾ cup whole milk
¼ cup heavy cream
Chocolate Glaze:
1 cup chocolate chips
⅓ cup heavy cream

1. Combine the flour, yeast, sugar and salt in the bowl of a stand mixer. Add the milk, vanilla, egg yolks and butter. Mix until the dough starts to come together in a ball. Shape the dough into a ball, place it in a large oiled bowl, cover the bowl and let the dough rise for 1 to 1½ hours. 2. When the dough has risen, punch it down and roll it into a 24-inch log. Cut the dough into 24 pieces and roll each piece into a ball. Place the dough balls on a baking sheet and let them rise for another 30 minutes. 3. Preheat the air fryer to 400ºF (204ºC). 4. Spray the dough balls lightly with vegetable oil and air fry eight at a time for 4 minutes, turning them over halfway through the cooking time. While donut holes are cooking, make the filling and chocolate glaze. 5. **Make the Filling:** Use an electric hand mixer to beat the French vanilla pudding, milk and ¼ cup heavy cream for 2 minutes. 6. **Make the Chocolate Glaze:** Place the chocolate chips in a bowl. Bring the heavy cream to a boil on the stovetop and pour it over the chocolate chips. Stir until the chips are melted and the glaze is smooth. 7. Poke a hole into the side of the donut hole with a small knife. Wiggle the knife around to make room for the filling. Transfer the custard into the center of the donut. Dip the top half of the donut into the chocolate glaze, letting any excess glaze drip back into the bowl. Let the glazed donut holes sit for a few minutes before serving.

162 | Chapter 1 Vegetables and Sides

White Chocolate Cookies

Prep time: 5 minutes | Cook time: 11 minutes | Serves 10

8 ounces (227 g) unsweetened white chocolate
2 eggs, well beaten
¾ cup butter, at room temperature
1⅔ cups almond flour
½ cup coconut flour
¾ cup granulated Swerve
2 tablespoons coconut oil
⅓ teaspoon grated nutmeg
⅓ teaspoon ground allspice
⅓ teaspoon ground anise star
¼ teaspoon fine sea salt

1. Preheat the air fryer to 350ºF (177ºC). Line the frying basket with parchment paper. 2. Combine all the ingredients in a mixing bowl and knead for about 3 to 4 minutes, or until a soft dough forms. Transfer to the refrigerator to chill for 20 minutes. 3. Roll the dough into 1-inch balls and transfer to basket, spacing 2 inches apart. Flatten each with the back of a spoon. 4. Bake for about 11 minutes until golden and firm to the touch. 5. Allow to cool completely. Serve immediately.

Bourbon and Spice Monkey Bread

Prep time: 5 minutes | Cook time: 25 minutes | Serves 6 to 8

1 (16.3-ounce / 462-g) can store-bought refrigerated biscuit dough
¼ cup packed light brown sugar
1 teaspoon ground cinnamon
½ teaspoon freshly grated nutmeg
½ teaspoon ground ginger
½ teaspoon kosher salt
¼ teaspoon ground allspice
⅛ teaspoon ground cloves
4 tablespoons (½ stick) unsalted butter, melted
½ cup powdered sugar
2 teaspoons bourbon
2 tablespoons chopped candied cherries
2 tablespoons chopped pecans

1. Cut each biscuit into quarters. Toss the biscuit quarters in a bowl with the brown sugar, cinnamon, nutmeg, ginger, salt, allspice, and cloves until evenly coated. Transfer the dough pieces and any sugar left in the bowl to a cake pan and drizzle evenly with the melted butter. bake at 310ºF (154ºC) until the monkey bread is golden brown and cooked through in the middle, about 25 minutes. Let cool completely. Unmold from the pan. 2. In a bowl, whisk the powdered sugar and the bourbon into a smooth glaze. Drizzle the glaze over the cooled monkey bread and, while the glaze is still wet, sprinkle with the cherries and pecans to serve.

Old-Fashioned Fudge Pie

Prep time: 15 minutes | Cook time: 25 to 30 minutes | Serves 8

1½ cups sugar
⅓ cup unsweetened cocoa powder
½ cup self-rising flour
3 large eggs, unbeaten
12 tablespoons (1½ sticks) butter, melted
1½ teaspoons vanilla extract
1 (9-inch) unbaked piecrust
¼ cup confectioners' sugar (optional)

1. In a medium bowl, stir together the sugar, cocoa powder, and flour. Stir in the eggs and melted butter. Stir in the vanilla. 2. Preheat the air fryer to 350ºF (177ºC). 3. Pour the chocolate filing into the crust. 4. Bake for 25 to 30 minutes, stirring every 10 minutes, until a knife inserted into the middle comes out clean. Let sit for 5 minutes before dusting with confectioners' sugar (if using) to serve.

Pecan and Cherry Stuffed Apples

Prep time: 10 minutes | Cook time: 20 minutes | Serves 4

4 apples (about 1¼ pounds / 567 g)
¼ cup chopped pecans
⅓ cup dried tart cherries
1 tablespoon melted butter
3 tablespoons brown sugar
¼ teaspoon allspice
Pinch salt
Ice cream, for serving

1. Cut off top ½ inch from each apple; reserve tops. With a melon baller, core through stem ends without breaking through the bottom. (Do not trim bases.) 2. Preheat the air fryer to 350ºF (177ºC). Combine pecans, cherries, butter, brown sugar, allspice, and a pinch of salt into the apples. Cover with apple tops. Put into frying basket. Air fry for 20 to 25 minutes until tender. 3. Serve warm with ice cream.

Pecan Butter Cookies

Prep time: 5 minutes | Cook time: 24 minutes | Makes 12 cookies

1 cup chopped pecans
½ cup salted butter, melted
½ cup coconut flour
¾ cup erythritol, divided
1 teaspoon vanilla extract

1. In a food processor, blend together pecans, butter, flour, ½ cup erythritol, and vanilla 1 minute until a dough forms. 2. Form dough into twelve individual cookie balls, about 1 tablespoon each. 3. Place four cookies on one piece ungreased parchment and place into frying basket. Bake at 325ºF (163ºC) for 8 minutes. Repeat with remaining batches. 4. Allow cookies to cool 5 minutes. While still warm, dust with remaining erythritol. Allow to cool completely before serving.

Protein Powder Doughnut Holes

Prep time: 25 minutes | Cook time: 6 minutes | Makes 12 holes

½ cup blanched finely ground almond flour
½ cup low-carb vanilla protein powder
½ cup granular erythritol
½ teaspoon baking powder
1 large egg
5 tablespoons unsalted butter, melted
½ teaspoon vanilla extract

1. Mix all ingredients in a bowl and freeze for 20 minutes. 2. Wet your hands with water and roll the dough into twelve balls. 3. Cut a piece of parchment to fit your frying basket. Place doughnut holes into the frying basket. 4. Air fry at 380ºF (193ºC) for 6 minutes, flipping halfway through the cooking time. 5. Let cool completely before serving.

Chapter 1 Vegetables and Sides | 163

Almond-Roasted Pears

Prep time: 10 minutes | Cook time: 15 to 20 minutes | Serves 4

Yogurt Topping:
1 container vanilla Greek yogurt (5 to 6 ounces / 142 to 170 g)
¼ teaspoon almond flavoring
2 whole pears, cored and halved
¼ cup crushed Biscoff cookies (approx. 4 cookies)
1 tablespoon sliced almonds
1 tablespoon butter, cut into 4 pieces

1. Stir almond flavoring into yogurt and set aside. 2. Place pear halves in frying basket. 3. Stir together the cookie and almonds. Place a quarter of this mixture into the hollow of each pear half. Place one piece butter on top of crumb mixture in each pear. 4. Roast at 360ºF (182ºC) for 15 to 20 minutes or until pears have cooked through but are still slightly firm. 5. Serve warm with yogurt topping.

Lush Chocolate Chip Cookies

Prep time: 7 minutes | Cook time: 9 minutes | Serves 4

3 tablespoons butter, at room temperature
⅓ cup plus 1 tablespoon light brown sugar
1 egg yolk
½ cup all-purpose flour
2 tablespoons ground white chocolate
¼ teaspoon baking soda
½ teaspoon vanilla extract
¾ cup semisweet chocolate chips
Nonstick flour-infused baking spray

1. In medium bowl, beat together the butter and brown sugar until fluffy. Stir in the egg yolk. 2. Add the flour, white chocolate, baking soda, and vanilla and mix well. Stir in the chocolate chips. 3. Line a 6-by-2-inch round baking pan with parchment paper. Spray with baking spray. 4. Preheat the air fryer to 300ºF (149ºC). Spread the batter into the prepared pan, leaving a ½-inch border on all sides. Bake for 9 minutes until the cookie is light brown and just barely set. Let cool completely and serve.

Strawberry Shortcake

Prep time: 10 minutes | Cook time: 25 minutes | Serves 6

2 tablespoons coconut oil
1 cup blanched finely ground almond flour
2 large eggs, whisked
½ cup granular erythritol
1 teaspoon baking powder
1 teaspoon vanilla extract
2 cups sugar-free whipped cream
6 medium fresh strawberries, hulled and sliced

1. In a bowl, combine coconut oil, flour, eggs, erythritol, baking powder, and vanilla. Pour batter into a round nonstick baking dish. 2. Bake at 300ºF (149ºC) for 25 minutes until the shortcake is golden and a toothpick inserted in the middle comes out clean. 3. Let cool and serve topped with whipped cream and strawberries.

Cinnamon-Sugar Almonds

Prep time: 5 minutes | Cook time: 8 minutes | Serves 4

1 cup whole almonds
2 tablespoons salted butter, melted
1 tablespoon sugar
½ teaspoon ground cinnamon

1. In a medium bowl, combine all the ingredients until the almonds are well coated. 2. Transfer the almonds to the frying basket in a single layer. Bake at 300ºF (149ºC) for 8 minutes, stirring halfway through the cooking time. 3. Let cool completely before serving.

Coconut Muffins

Prep time: 5 minutes | Cook time: 25 minutes | Serves 5

½ cup coconut flour
2 tablespoons cocoa powder
3 tablespoons erythritol
1 teaspoon baking powder
2 tablespoons coconut oil
2 eggs, beaten
½ cup coconut shred

1. In the mixing bowl, mix all ingredients and pour the mixture into the molds of the muffin and transfer in the frying basket. 2. Bake at 350ºF (177ºC) for 25 minutes.

Vanilla Scones

Prep time: 20 minutes | Cook time: 10 minutes | Serves 6

4 ounces (113 g) coconut flour
½ teaspoon baking powder
1 teaspoon apple cider vinegar
2 teaspoons mascarpone
¼ cup heavy cream
1 teaspoon vanilla extract
1 tablespoon erythritol
Cooking spray

1. In the mixing bowl, mix coconut flour with baking powder, apple cider vinegar, mascarpone, heavy cream, vanilla extract, and erythritol. 2. Knead the dough and cut into scones. 3. Then put them in the frying basket and sprinkle with cooking spray. 4. Bake at 365ºF (185ºC) for 10 minutes.

Brownies for Two

Prep time: 5 minutes | Cook time: 15 minutes | Serves 2

½ cup blanched finely ground almond flour
3 tablespoons granular erythritol
3 tablespoons unsweetened cocoa powder
½ teaspoon baking powder
1 teaspoon vanilla extract
2 large eggs, whisked
2 tablespoons salted butter, melted

1. In a medium bowl, combine flour, erythritol, cocoa powder, and baking powder. 2. Add in vanilla, eggs, and butter, and stir until a thick batter forms. 3. Pour batter into two ramekins greased with cooking spray and place ramekins into frying basket. Bake at 325ºF (163ºC) for 15 minutes. Let ramekins cool 5 minutes before serving.

Nutty Pear Crumble

Prep time: 10 minutes | Cook time: 30 minutes | Serves 2 to 4

2 ripe d'Anjou pears (1 pound / 454 g), peeled, cored, and roughly chopped
¼ cup packed light brown sugar
2 tablespoons cornstarch
1 teaspoon kosher salt
¼ cup granulated sugar
3 tablespoons unsalted butter, at room temperature
⅓ cup all-purpose flour
2½ tablespoons Dutch-process cocoa powder
¼ cup chopped blanched hazelnuts
Vanilla ice cream or whipped cream, for serving (optional)

1. In a cake pan, combine the pears, brown sugar, cornstarch, and ½ teaspoon salt and toss until the pears are evenly coated. 2. In a bowl, combine the remaining salt with the granulated sugar, butter, flour, and cocoa powder and pinch and press the butter into the other ingredients until a sandy, shaggy crumble dough forms. Stir in the hazelnuts. Sprinkle the topping evenly over the pears. 3. Bake at 320ºF (160ºC) until the crumble is crisp and the pears are bubbling in the center, about 30 minutes. 4. Serve hot topped with ice cream or whipped cream, if you like.

Peach Cobbler

Prep time: 15 minutes | Cook time: 12 to 14 minutes | Serves 4

16 ounces (454 g) frozen peaches, thawed, with juice (do not drain)
6 tablespoons sugar
1 tablespoon cornstarch
1 tablespoon water

Crust:
½ cup flour
¼ teaspoon salt
3 tablespoons butter
1½ tablespoons cold water
¼ teaspoon sugar

1. Mix peaches with juice, and sugar well in a baking pan. 2. In a small cup, dissolve cornstarch in the water. Stir into peaches. 3. In a medium bowl, combine the flour and salt. Cut in butter using knives and stir in the cold water to make a stiff dough. 4. Pat dough into a square or circle. Cut diagonally into 4 pieces. 5. Place dough pieces on top of peaches, leaving a tiny bit of space between the edges. Sprinkle very lightly with sugar, no more than about ¼ teaspoon. 6. Bake at 360ºF (182ºC) for 12 to 14 minutes, until fruit bubbles and crust browns.

Gluten-Free Spice Cookies

Prep time: 10 minutes | Cook time: 12 minutes | Serves 4

4 tablespoons (½ stick) unsalted butter, at room temperature
2 tablespoons agave nectar
1 large egg
2 tablespoons water
2½ cups almond flour
½ cup sugar
2 teaspoons ground ginger
1 teaspoon ground cinnamon
½ teaspoon freshly grated nutmeg
1 teaspoon baking soda
¼ teaspoon kosher salt

1. Line the bottom of the frying basket with parchment paper cut to fit. 2. In a bowl using a hand mixer, beat together the butter, agave, egg, and water on medium speed until light and fluffy. 3. Add the remaining ingredients and beat on low speed until well combined. 4. Roll the dough into 2-tablespoon balls and arrange them on the parchment paper in the basket. Bake at 325ºF (163ºC) for 12 minutes, or until the tops of cookies are lightly browned. 5. Let cool completely.

Crustless Peanut Butter Cheesecake

Prep time: 10 minutes | Cook time: 10 minutes | Serves 2

4 ounces (113 g) cream cheese, softened
2 tablespoons confectioners' erythritol
1 tablespoon all-natural, no-sugar-added peanut butter
½ teaspoon vanilla extract
1 large egg, whisked

1. In a medium bowl, mix cream cheese, erythritol, peanut butter and vanilla until smooth. Add egg and stir just until combined. 2. Spoon mixture into a springform pan and place into frying basket. Bake at 300ºF (149ºC) for 10 minutes. Edges will be firm, but center will be mostly set with only a small amount of jiggle when done. 3. Let cool at room temperature 30 minutes, cover with plastic wrap, then refrigerate at least 2 hours. Serve chilled.

Simple Pineapple Sticks

Prep time: 5 minutes | Cook time: 10 minutes | Serves 4

½ fresh pineapple, cut into sticks
¼ cup desiccated coconut

1. Preheat the air fryer to 400ºF (204ºC). 2. Coat the pineapple sticks in the desiccated coconut and put each one in the frying basket. 3. Air fry for 10 minutes. 4. Serve immediately

Pecan Clusters

Prep time: 10 minutes | Cook time: 8 minutes | Serves 8

3 ounces (85 g) whole shelled pecans
1 tablespoon salted butter, melted
2 teaspoons confectioners' erythritol
½ teaspoon ground cinnamon
½ cup low-carb chocolate chips

1. In a medium bowl, toss pecans with butter, then sprinkle with erythritol and cinnamon. 2. Place pecans into frying basket. Bake at 350ºF (177ºC) for 8 minutes, shaking the basket two times. 3. Line a large baking sheet with parchment paper. 4. Microwave chocolate on high in a medium microwave-safe bowl, heating in 20-second increments and stirring until melted. Place 1 teaspoon chocolate in a rounded mound on baking sheet, then press 1 pecan into top, repeating with remaining chocolate and pecans. 5. Place baking sheet into refrigerate at least 30 minutes.

Pumpkin Pudding with Vanilla Wafers

Prep time: 10 minutes | Cook time: 12 to 17 minutes | Serves 4

1 cup canned no-salt-added pumpkin purée (not pumpkin pie filling)
¼ cup packed brown sugar
3 tablespoons all-purpose flour
1 egg, whisked
2 tablespoons milk
1 tablespoon unsalted butter, melted
1 teaspoon pure vanilla extract
4 low-fat vanilla wafers, crumbled
Nonstick cooking spray

1. Preheat the air fryer to 350°F (177°C). Coat a baking pan with nonstick cooking spray. Set aside. 2. Mix the pumpkin purée, brown sugar, flour, whisked egg, milk, melted butter, and vanilla in a bowl and whisk to combine. Transfer the mixture to the baking pan. 3. Place the baking pan in the frying basket and bake for 12 to 17 minutes until set. 4. Allow to cool before dividing the pudding into four bowls and serve with the vanilla wafers sprinkled on top.

Rhubarb and Strawberry Crumble

Prep time: 10 minutes | Cook time: 12 to 17 minutes | Serves 6

1½ cups sliced fresh strawberries
¾ cup sliced rhubarb
⅓ cup granulated sugar
⅔ cup quick-cooking oatmeal
½ cup whole-wheat pastry flour, or all-purpose flour
¼ cup packed light brown sugar
½ teaspoon ground cinnamon
3 tablespoons unsalted butter, melted

1. Preheat the air fryer to 375°F (191°C). In a 6-by-2-inch round metal baking pan, combine the strawberries, rhubarb, and granulated sugar. 2. In a medium bowl, stir together the oatmeal, flour, brown sugar, and cinnamon. Stir the melted butter into this mixture until crumbly. Sprinkle the crumble mixture over the fruit. 3. Place the pan into the basket and bake at 375°F (191°C) for 12 to 17 minutes until golden brown. 4. When the cooking is complete, serve warm.

Cream Cheese Danish

Prep time: 20 minutes | Cook time: 15 minutes | Serves 6

¾ cup blanched finely ground almond flour
1 cup shredded Mozzarella cheese
5 ounces (142 g) full-fat cream cheese, divided
2 large egg yolks
¾ cup powdered erythritol, divided
2 teaspoons vanilla extract, divided

1. Mix and microwave the almond flour, Mozzarella, and 1 ounce (28 g) cream cheese in a large microwave-safe bowl for 1 minute. 2. Stir and add egg yolks to the bowl. Continue stirring until soft dough forms. Add ½ cup erythritol to dough and 1 teaspoon vanilla. 3. Cut a piece of parchment to fit your frying basket. Press the dough into a ¼-inch-thick rectangle. 4. In a medium bowl, mix remaining cream cheese, erythritol, and vanilla. Place this cream cheese mixture on the right half of the dough rectangle. Fold over the left side of the dough and press to seal. Place into the frying basket. 5. Bake at 330°F (166°C) for 15 minutes, flipping halfway the cooking. 6. Allow to completely cool before cutting.

Crumbly Coconut-Pecan Cookies

Prep time: 10 minutes | Cook time: 25 minutes | Serves 10

1½ cups coconut flour
1½ cups extra-fine almond flour
½ teaspoon baking powder
⅓ teaspoon baking soda
3 eggs plus an egg yolk, beaten
¾ cup coconut oil, at room temperature
1 cup unsalted pecan nuts, roughly chopped
¾ cup monk fruit
¼ teaspoon freshly grated nutmeg
⅓ teaspoon ground cloves
½ teaspoon pure vanilla extract
½ teaspoon pure coconut extract
⅛ teaspoon fine sea salt

1. Preheat the air fryer to 370°F (188°C). Line the frying basket with parchment paper. 2. Mix the coconut flour, almond flour, baking powder, and baking soda in a large mixing bowl. 3. In another mixing bowl, stir together the eggs and coconut oil. Add the wet mixture to the dry mixture. 4. Mix in the remaining ingredients and stir until a soft dough forms. 5. Drop about 2 tablespoons of dough on the parchment paper for each cookie and flatten each biscuit until it's 1 inch thick. 6. Bake for about 25 minutes until the cookies are golden and firm to the touch. Let the cookies cool to room temperature and serve.

Blueberry-Cream Cheese Bread Pudding

Prep time: 15 minutes | Cook time: 1 hour 10 minutes | Serves 6

1 cup light cream or half-and-half
4 large eggs
⅓ cup plus 3 tablespoons granulated sugar
1 teaspoon pure lemon extract
4 cups cubed croissants (4 to 5 croissants)
1 cup blueberries
4 ounces (113 g) cream cheese, cut into small cubes

1. In a bowl, combine the cream, eggs, the ⅓ cup sugar, and the extract. Whisk until well combined. Add the cubed croissants, blueberries, and cream cheese. Toss gently until everything is thoroughly combined; set aside. 2. Place a 3-cup Bundt pan in the frying basket. Preheat the air fryer to 400°F (204°C). 3. Sprinkle the remaining 3 tablespoons sugar in the bottom of the hot pan. Bake for 10 minutes, or until the sugar caramelizes. Tip the pan to spread the caramel evenly across the bottom of the pan. 4. Pour in the bread mixture, distributing it evenly across the pan. Bake at 350°F (177°C) for 60 minutes, or until the custard is set in the middle. Let stand for 10 minutes before unmolding onto a serving plate.

Blackberry Cobbler

Prep time: 15 minutes | Cook time: 25 to 30 minutes | Serves 6

3 cups fresh or frozen blackberries
1¾ cups sugar, divided
1 teaspoon vanilla extract

8 tablespoons (1 stick) butter, melted
1 cup self-rising flour
1 to 2 tablespoons oil

1. In a medium bowl, stir together the blackberries, 1 cup sugar, and vanilla. 2. In another medium bowl, stir together the melted butter, remaining ¾ cup sugar, and flour until a dough forms. 3. Spritz a baking pan with oil. Add the blackberry mixture. Crumble the flour mixture over the fruit. Cover the pan with aluminum foil. Transfer to the frying basket. 4. Bake at 350°F (177°C) for 20 to 25 minutes until the filling is thickened. 5. Uncover the pan and cook for 5 minutes more, depending on how juicy and browned you like your cobbler. Let sit for 5 minutes before serving.

Pineapple Wontons

Prep time: 15 minutes | Cook time: 15 to 18 minutes per batch | Serves 5

1 (8-ounce / 227-g) package cream cheese
1 cup finely chopped fresh pineapple

20 wonton wrappers
Cooking oil spray

1. ,Microwave the cream cheese in a small microwave-safe bowl on high power for 20 seconds to soften. 2. In a medium bowl, mix the cream cheese and pineapple well. 3. Lay out the wonton wrappers on a work surface. Spoon 1½ teaspoons cream cheese mixture onto each wrapper. Fold each wrapper diagonally across to form a triangle. Bring the 2 bottom corners up toward each other. Do not close the wrapper yet. Bring up the 2 open sides and push out any air. Squeeze the open edges together to seal. 4. Preheat the air fryer to 390°F (199°C). Spray the frying basket with cooking oil. 5. Place the wontons into the basket. Spray with the cooking oil. Air fry for 18 minutes. After 10 minutes, flip each wonton, and spray them with more oil. Resume cooking for 5 to 8 minutes more until the wontons are light golden brown and crisp. Cool for 5 minutes before serving.

Simple Apple Turnovers

Prep time: 10 minutes | Cook time: 10 minutes | Serves 4

1 apple, peeled, quartered, and thinly sliced
½ teaspoons pumpkin pie spice
Juice of ½ lemon

1 tablespoon granulated sugar
Pinch of kosher salt
6 sheets phyllo dough

1. Preheat the air fryer to 330°F (166°C). 2. In a medium bowl, combine the apple, pumpkin pie spice, lemon juice, granulated sugar, and kosher salt. 3. Cut the phyllo dough sheets into 4 equal pieces and place individual tablespoons of apple filling in the center of each piece, then fold in both sides and roll from front to back. 4. Spray the frying basket with nonstick cooking spray, then place the turnovers in the basket and bake for 10 minutes or until golden brown. 5. Allow to cool for 10 minutes before serving.

Appendix 1 Measurement Conversion Chart

VOLUME EQUIVALENTS(DRY)

US STANDARD	METRIC (APPROXIMATE)
1/8 teaspoon	0.5 mL
1/4 teaspoon	1 mL
1/2 teaspoon	2 mL
3/4 teaspoon	4 mL
1 teaspoon	5 mL
1 tablespoon	15 mL
1/4 cup	59 mL
1/2 cup	118 mL
3/4 cup	177 mL
1 cup	235 mL
2 cups	475 mL
3 cups	700 mL
4 cups	1 L

VOLUME EQUIVALENTS(LIQUID)

US STANDARD	US STANDARD (OUNCES)	METRIC (APPROXIMATE)
2 tablespoons	1 fl.oz.	30 mL
1/4 cup	2 fl.oz.	60 mL
1/2 cup	4 fl.oz.	120 mL
1 cup	8 fl.oz.	240 mL
1 1/2 cup	12 fl.oz.	355 mL
2 cups or 1 pint	16 fl.oz.	475 mL
4 cups or 1 quart	32 fl.oz.	1 L
1 gallon	128 fl.oz.	4 L

WEIGHT EQUIVALENTS

US STANDARD	METRIC (APPROXIMATE)
1 ounce	28 g
2 ounces	57 g
5 ounces	142 g
10 ounces	284 g
15 ounces	425 g
16 ounces (1 pound)	455 g
1.5 pounds	680 g
2 pounds	907 g

TEMPERATURES EQUIVALENTS

FAHRENHEIT(F)	CELSIUS(C) (APPROXIMATE)
225 °F	107 °C
250 °F	120 °C
275 °F	135 °C
300 °F	150 °C
325 °F	160 °C
350 °F	180 °C
375 °F	190 °C
400 °F	205 °C
425 °F	220 °C
450 °F	235 °C
475 °F	245 °C
500 °F	260 °C

Appendix 2 Air Fryer Cooking Chart

Beef

Item	Temp (°F)	Time (mins)	Item	Temp (°F)	Time (mins)
Beef Eye Round Roast (4 lbs.)	400 °F	45 to 55	Meatballs (1-inch)	370 °F	7
Burger Patty (4 oz.)	370 °F	16 to 20	Meatballs (3-inch)	380 °F	10
Filet Mignon (8 oz.)	400 °F	18	Ribeye, bone-in (1-inch, 8 oz)	400 °F	10 to 15
Flank Steak (1.5 lbs.)	400 °F	12	Sirloin steaks (1-inch, 12 oz)	400 °F	9 to 14
Flank Steak (2 lbs.)	400 °F	20 to 28			

Chicken

Item	Temp (°F)	Time (mins)	Item	Temp (°F)	Time (mins)
Breasts, bone in (1 ¼ lb.)	370 °F	25	Legs, bone-in (1 ¾ lb.)	380 °F	30
Breasts, boneless (4 oz)	380 °F	12	Thighs, boneless (1 ½ lb.)	380 °F	18 to 20
Drumsticks (2 ½ lb.)	370 °F	20	Wings (2 lb.)	400 °F	12
Game Hen (halved 2 lb.)	390 °F	20	Whole Chicken	360 °F	75
Thighs, bone-in (2 lb.)	380 °F	22	Tenders	360 °F	8 to 10

Pork & Lamb

Item	Temp (°F)	Time (mins)	Item	Temp (°F)	Time (mins)
Bacon (regular)	400 °F	5 to 7	Pork Tenderloin	370 °F	15
Bacon (thick cut)	400 °F	6 to 10	Sausages	380 °F	15
Pork Loin (2 lb.)	360 °F	55	Lamb Loin Chops (1-inch thick)	400 °F	8 to 12
Pork Chops, bone in (1-inch, 6.5 oz)	400 °F	12	Rack of Lamb (1.5 – 2 lb.)	380 °F	22

Fish & Seafood

Item	Temp (°F)	Time (mins)	Item	Temp (°F)	Time (mins)
Calamari (8 oz)	400 °F	4	Tuna Steak	400 °F	7 to 10
Fish Fillet (1-inch, 8 oz)	400 °F	10	Scallops	400 °F	5 to 7
Salmon, fillet (6 oz)	380 °F	12	Shrimp	400 °F	5
Swordfish steak	400 °F	10			

Appendix 3 Air Fryer Cooking Chart

Vegetables

INGREDIENT	AMOUNT	PREPARATION	OIL	TEMP	COOK TIME
Asparagus	2 bunches	Cut in half, trim stems	2 Tbsp	420°F	12-15 mins
Beets	1½ lbs	Peel, cut in ½-inch cubes	1Tbsp	390°F	28-30 mins
Bell peppers (for roasting)	4 peppers	Cut in quarters, remove seeds	1Tbsp	400°F	15-20 mins
Broccoli	1 large head	Cut in 1-2-inch florets	1Tbsp	400°F	15-20 mins
Brussels sprouts	1lb	Cut in half, remove stems	1Tbsp	425°F	15-20 mins
Carrots	1lb	Peel, cut in ¼-inch rounds	1 Tbsp	425°F	10-15 mins
Cauliflower	1 head	Cut in 1-2-inch florets	2 Tbsp	400°F	20-22 mins
Corn on the cob	7 ears	Whole ears, remove husks	1 Tbps	400°F	14-17 mins
Green beans	1 bag (12 oz)	Trim	1 Tbps	420°F	18-20 mins
Kale (for chips)	4 oz	Tear into pieces, remove stems	None	325°F	5-8 mins
Mushrooms	16 oz	Rinse, slice thinly	1 Tbps	390°F	25-30 mins
Potatoes, russet	1½ lbs	Cut in 1-inch wedges	1 Tbps	390°F	25-30 mins
Potatoes, russet	1lb	Hand-cut fries, soak 30 mins in cold water, then pat dry	½ -3 Tbps	400°F	25-28 mins
Potatoes, sweet	1lb	Hand-cut fries, soak 30 mins in cold water, then pat dry	1 Tbps	400°F	25-28 mins
Zucchini	1lb	Cut in eighths lengthwise, then cut in half	1 Tbps	400°F	15-20 mins

Appendix 4 Recipes Index

A

Acorn squash
Roasted veggies with penne pasta   14
Albacore tuna
Tuna casserole   122
Ale beer
Ale beer prawns with tartare sauce   104
All-purpose flour
Apple fries   160
Air fryer apple fritters   161
Mix-berry almond crumble   155
Easy buttermilk biscuits   42
Drop biscuits   42
Soft buttermilk biscuits   155
Lush chocolate chip cookies   164
Spanish churros con chocolate   154
Apple cider doughnut holes   41
Raspberry and vanilla pancakes   152
Party crispy nachos   10
Super cheesy gold eggplant   20
Cheese drops   146
French sour cherry clafoutis   154
Oatmeal raisin bars   161
Berry crumble   161
Nutty pear crumble   165
Almond
Smoky almonds   138
Spiced almonds   138
Cinnamon-sugar almonds   164
Almond-crusted cauliflower florets   8
Cherry and almond scones   36
Almond-crusted chicken   102
Trout amandine with lemon butter sauce   119
Roasted fish with almond-lemon crumbs   123
French beans with toasted almonds   138
Almond flour
Parmesan herb focaccia bread   20
Cream cheese danish   166
Chocolate lava cakes   160
Strawberry shortcake   164
New york cheesecake   159
Pancake for two   41
Ricotta lemon poppy seed cake   153
Olive oil cake   153
Lime bars   160
Keto quiche   44
Flatbread   24
Vanilla peach cake   158
Mini peanut butter tarts   156
White chocolate cookies   163
Protein powder doughnut holes   163
Gluten-free spice cookies   165
Zucchini-ricotta tart   25
Almond-cauliflower gnocchi   26
Crumbly coconut-pecan cookies   166
Apple
Apple sandwich with brie cheese   34
Pecan and cherry stuffed apples   163
Apple caramel relish   154
Honeyed roasted apples with walnuts   153
Apple wedges   141
Simple apple turnovers   167
Cheat apple pie   158
Cinnamon apple chips   139
Air fried cinnamon apples   151
Italian-style apple pork chops   52
Apple fries   160
Air fryer apple fritters   161
Applesauce
Shortcut spiced apple butter   153
Apricot
Apricot and lemon flapjacks   159
Arborio rice
Parmesan ranch risotto   42
Artichoke
Parmesan artichokes   28
Artichoke heart
Artichoke and olive pita flatbread   143
Breaded artichoke hearts   127
Crispy phyllo artichoke triangles   142
Asparagus
Creamed asparagus   19
Lemon-thyme asparagus   19
Roasted asparagus with serrano ham   37
Sesame balsamic asparagus   7
Cheesy potatoes and asparagus   3
Asparagus spear
Grits casserole   21
Golden asparagus with romesco sauce   128
Bacon-wrapped asparagus   22
Thyme lamb chops with asparagus   63
Classic mediterranean salmon   110
Avocado
Bacon-wrapped avocados   131
Baked eggs in avocado   37
Avocado egg rolls   147
Golden avocado   37
Greek avocado wedges   128
Avocado fries with pico de gallo   6
Cheesy english muffins   14
Air fried veggie sushi   16
Classic avocado toast   33
Chipotle rib-eye steak with avocado salsa   57
Italian lamb chops with avocado mayo   66
Chicken breasts with avocado-mango salsa   81
Spicy shrimp with coconut-avocado dip   105
Cod cornflake nuggets with avocado dip   107

B

Baby carrot
Sweet feta carrots   3
Baby potato
Garlic-parmesan crispy baby potatoes   20
Chicken and baby potato traybake   87
Baby spinach
Spinach and tomato frittata   30
Italian-style stuffed mushrooms   13
Baked egg and mushroom cups   42
Goat cheese-stuffed flank steak   64
Blue cheese steak salad   67
Bacon

Bacon-wrapped asparagus   22
Bacon omelet cups   30
Bacon eggs on the go   45
Jalapeño and bacon breakfast pizza   41
Super bacon with meat   69
Air fried bacon   38
Roasted brussels sprouts with bacon   17
Cheddar broccoli with bacon   24
Bacon tortilla wraps with salsa   34
Creamy spinach-stuffed pork   49
Pork sandwiches with bacon and cheddar   53
Bacon-wrapped cheese pork   69
Bacon-wrapped prawns   104
Bacon halibut steak   113
Bacon-wrapped scallops   120
Crispy bacon with butter bean dip   131
Bacon-wrapped avocados   131
Bacon-wrapped dates   132
Baked potatoes with bacon   133
Bacon strip
Sausage sticks rolled in bacon   48
Bagel
Herb toasted bagel   34
Baguette
Russian-style eggplant caviar   8
Banana
Hearty banana pastry   38
Banana muffins with hazelnuts and chocolates   35
Vanilla banana bread with walnuts   34
Five-fruit skewers with caramel sauce   159
Barramundi fillet
Barramundi fillets in lemon sauce   112
Basmati rice
Basmati risotto   27
Chicken tikka masala   82
Bean
Sweet potato boats   134
Beef
Beef and goat cheese stuffed peppers   64
Mexican beef cabbage wraps   54
South american arepas with cilantro sauce   55
Classic beef meatloaf   55
Korean beef tacos   72
Kale and beef omelet   67
Beef koftas in tomato sauce   54
Beef meatballs with cranberry sauce   54
Cheesy italian beef meatloaf   55
"stefania" Beef meatloaf   56
Argentinian beef empanadas   56
Swedish meatloaf   67
Greek-style beef meatballs   54
Beef roast with red potatoes   59
California-style street beef taco rolls   55
Smoked beef burgers with hoisin sauce   55
Kheema meatloaf   66
Simple ground beef with zucchini   64
Healthy burgers   55
Simple roasted beef with herbs   60
Bulgogi burgers   62
Mexican chorizo and beef empanadas   56
Beef bottom round steak
Crunchy beef escalopes   61
Beef cube steak
Beef steak fingers   68
Beef liver
Beef liver with onions   62
Beef loin
Herby roast beef   61
Beef meatball

Bean and beef meatball taco pizza   73
Beef rib-eye steaks
Tender rib eye steak   57
Beef sausage
Mini beef sausage rolls   57
Sausage beef rolls   58
Salami, prosciutto and sausage omelet   29
Beef short rib
Effortless beef short ribs   54
Beef sirloin steak
Beef steak with mustard sauce   56
Parsley crumbed beef strips   57
Beef veggie mix with hoisin sauce   59
Beef steak
Spicy sweet beef with veggie topping   58
Air fried beef with veggies and oyster sauce   60
Thai roasted beef   58
Mexican beef quesadillas   59
Delicious beef with rice and broccoli   58
Pesto beef rolls with spinach   60
Beef steak strips with tomato sauce   53
Beef steak fingers   151
Herbed beef   68
Caraway crusted beef steaks   69
Pesto beef steaks   57
Beef tenderloin
Greek stuffed tenderloin   61
Peppercorn-crusted beef tenderloin   63
Beef tenderloin steak
Beef steak au poivre   59
Beefsteak tomato
Tuna-stuffed tomatoes   121
Beer
Peach salsa and beer halibut tacos   114
Beet
Tasty balsamic beets   8
Dill-and-garlic beets   23
Beetroot
Spicy vegetable skewers   10
Bell pepper
Lebanese muhammara   136
Shishito pepper roast   21
Crispy bell peppers with tartare sauce   4
Cheese stuffed peppers   28
Breakfast potatoes with pepper and onion   29
Mexican breakfast pepper rings   38
San antonio taco chicken strips   78
Turkey stuffed bell peppers   92
Bell pepper stuffed chicken roll-ups   94
Fajita chicken strips   95
Cajun beef fajitas   133
Air fried pot stickers   139
Berries
Hearty banana pastry   38
Berry crumble   161
Mix-berry almond crumble   155
Bibb lettuce
Crab cakes with lettuce and apple salad   120
Biscuit dough
Bourbon and spice monkey bread   163
Black bean
Cheddar black bean burritos   138
Black bean and corn flatbreads   131
Black bean and tomato chili   26
Black beans and veggie burgers   9
Air fried chicken bowl with black beans   84
Chipotle-lime prawn bowls   152
Black cod fillet
Gourmet black cod with fennel and pecans   108

172 | Chapter 1 Vegetables and Sides

Black mussel
Greek mussels with hazelnuts   106
Blackberry
Blackberry cobbler   167
Blue cheese
Steaks with walnut-blue cheese butter   64
Blueberry
Five-fruit skewers with caramel sauce   159
Blueberry oat bars   36
Maple oat-walnut granola with blueberries   154
Whole wheat blueberry muffins   44
Corn blueberry toast   34
Blueberry muffins   160
Blueberry-cream cheese bread pudding   166
Blueberry pie filling
Mock blueberry pie   154
Bread
Herbed brie croutons   136
Easy parmesan sandwich   137
"bikini" Ham and cheese sandwich   149
Egg in a hole   32
Cinnamon french toast sticks   152
Raisin bread pudding with hazelnuts   37
Bourbon bread pudding   161
Super easy croutons   37
Veggie shrimp toast   141
Shrimp toasts with sesame seeds   143
Bread crumb
Parmesan chicken burgers   131
Bread dough
Creamy cinnamon rolls   40
Bread flour
Boston cream donut holes   162
Brie cheese
Apple sandwich with brie cheese   34
Brioche
French brioche toast   33
Broccoli
Parmesan broccoli bites   9
Egg and broccoli quiche   136
Lemony broccoli   23
Butter-fried broccoli   135
Teriyaki rump steak with broccoli and capsicum   66
Steak, broccoli, and mushroom rice bowls   70
Chicken cheesy divan casserole   84
Broccoli cheese chicken   98
Broccoli and cheese stuffed chicken   99
Salmon fillets with broccoli   109
Broccoli floret
Cheddar broccoli with bacon   24
Broccoli-cheese fritters   27
Green vegetable rotini pasta bake   12
Cholula seasoned broccoli   8
Citrus-roasted broccoli florets   22
Tingly chili-roasted broccoli   24
Broccoli-cheddar twice-baked potatoes   20
Cheesy mushroom-broccoli pie   35
Korean beef bulgogi   59
Beef and broccoli stir-fry   64
Broccolini
Charred broccolini with lemon-caper sauce   11
Brown mushroom
Herb and cheese stuffed mushrooms   148
Marinated steak tips with mushrooms   69
Brown onion
Effortless beef short ribs   54
Cheddar hash browns   149
Brown rice
Stuffed red peppers with herbed ricotta and tomatoes   23

Beef and goat cheese stuffed peppers   64
Lebanese malfouf (stuffed cabbage rolls)   72
Chicken teriyaki   80
Brown sugar
Mongolian-style beef   67
Brussels sprout
Roasted brussels sprouts with bacon   17
Brussels sprouts with pecans and gorgonzola   18
Brussels sprouts with raisins and pine nuts   17
Garlicky brussels sprouts   3
Brussels sprouts with garlic aioli   4
Sage brussels sprouts   127
Brussels sprouts
Roasted turkey with brussels sprouts   91
Spanish chorizo with brussels sprouts   133
Balsamic brussels sprouts   147
Butter bean
Crispy bacon with butter bean dip   131
Butter lettuce
Thai tacos with peanut sauce   100
Buttermilk
Air fried cheesy ravioli   11
Hearty cheddar biscuits   40
Easy buttermilk biscuits   42
Drop biscuits   42
Classic buttermilk chicken thighs   86
Herb-buttermilk chicken breast   89
Cheese and buttermilk biscuits   137
Soft buttermilk biscuits   155
Butternut squash
Winter vegetable traybake   11
Sweet butternut squash with walnuts   9
Parsley butternut squash   135
Poblano and tomato stuffed squash   13
Button mushroom
Italian cheesy mushrooms   135
Vegetable frittata   38
Roasted mushrooms with garlic   145
Breaded mushrooms   148
Lettuce-wrapped turkey and mushroom meatballs   98
Vegetable pot stickers   140

C

Cabbage
Air fried pot stickers   139
Super cabbage canapes   136
Super veg rolls   28
Easy cabbage steaks   5
Cod with avocado   120
Cabbage leaf
Mexican beef cabbage wraps   54
Calamari rings
Calamari rings with olives   106
Simple calamari rings   152
Canadian bacon
Canadian bacon muffin sandwiches   44
Egg muffins   44
Carrot
Salty carrot cookies   137
Root vegetable chips   127
Winter root vegetable medley   11
Citrus sweet potatoes and carrots   2
Aunt's roasted carrots with cilantro sauce   6
Spicy carrot chips   127
Horse carrots chips   134
Carrot chips   139
Jamaican chicken fajitas   82
Chicken quarters with broccoli and carrots   89
Chicken hand pies   97
Italian salmon croquettes   130

South asian pork momos   133
Super cabbage canapes   136
Cashew
Masala cashew nuts   138
Spiced roasted cashews   141
Rosemary cashew shrimp   105
Catfish fillet
Cajun catfish cakes with cheese   115
Golden batter fried catfish fillets   110
Lovely "blackened" Catfish   110
Rosemary catfish   111
Panko catfish nuggets   118
Fried catfish fillets   119
Almond catfish   120
Catfish bites   122
Cauliflower
Almond-crusted cauliflower florets   8
Cheesy cauliflower "hash browns"   39
Baked jalapeño and cheese cauliflower mash   21
Cauliflower, chickpea, and avocado mash   26
Cheese and cauliflower tater tots   7
Egg and cauliflower rice casserole   13
Cauliflower and tofu croquettes   137
Curry roasted cauliflower   2
Teriyaki cauliflower   8
Easy cauliflower popcorn   8
Buffalo cauliflower   128
Italian cauliflower   129
Parmesan cauliflower   142
Spicy sweet beef with veggie topping   58
Air fried beef with veggies and oyster sauce   60
Cauli-oat crusted drumsticks   87
Ethiopian chicken with cauliflower   101
Salmon with cauliflower   122
Panko veggie balls   137
Cauliflower floret
Almond-cauliflower gnocchi   26
Spinach cheese casserole   27
Celery
Pepper steak   68
Chard
Greens chips with curried yogurt sauce   144
Cheddar cheese
Cheddar eggs   39
Fried cheese grits   39
Basic welsh rarebit   35
Cheesy parsley tomatoes   3
Cheesy cauliflower "hash browns"   39
Cheddar soufflés   40
Baked potato breakfast boats   40
Cheese
Cheese drops   146
Thai-style cheesy sticks   127
Creamed asparagus   19
Parmesan herb focaccia bread   20
Baked jalapeño and cheese cauliflower mash   21
Easy calzone   34
Greek stuffed tenderloin   61
Cheesy low-carb lasagna   72
Tex-mex chicken roll-ups   90
Stuffed turkey roulade   95
Chicken croquettes with creole sauce   96
Chicken nuggets   101
Chicken patties   102
Smoked salmon and cheddar taquitos   109
Cajun catfish cakes with cheese   115
Shrimp bake   117
Parmesan mackerel with coriander   119
Potato cheese balls   126

Easy empanadas with spinach and mushroom   128
Cheesy bacon fries   130
Italian pork sausage pizza   132
Chorizo and mushroom pizza   132
Mozzarella pepperoni pizza   132
Greek chicken tortillas with mozzarella   132
Feta french fries   133
Cheddar pork balls   133
Italian cheesy mushrooms   135
Ricotta-stuffed peppers   136
Herbed brie croutons   136
Easy parmesan sandwich   137
Mini cheese scones   137
Spicy cheese lings   137
Cheddar black bean burritos   138
Cheesy steak fries   139
Zucchini feta roulades   139
Cheese wafers   141
Sausage balls with cheese   142
Egg roll pizza sticks   143
Air fried mac and cheese   149
"bikini" Ham and cheese sandwich   149
Gorgonzola cheese burgers   151
Cream cheese danish   166
Cheese arepas
South american arepas with cilantro sauce   55
Cheese ravioli
Air fried cheesy ravioli   11
Cherry
Cherry and almond scones   36
Pecan and cherry stuffed apples   163
Cherry tomato
Crisp pepper rings with cherry tomatoes   32
Garlic-roasted tomatoes and olives   145
Maple-roasted tomatoes   21
Parmesan sausage frittata   31
Turkey burgers with cabbage slaw   90
Turkey and veggie skewers   90
Prosciutto and cheese stromboli   134
Mediterranean bruschetta   149
Chicken
Chicken hand pies   97
Chicken croquettes with creole sauce   96
Greek chicken tortillas with mozzarella   132
Buffalo cheese-chicken tacos   77
Ham chicken with cheese   101
Roasted chicken with pancetta and thyme   88
Mediterranean-style whole chicken   88
Whole chicken with fresno chili sauce   89
Jalapeño and chicken quesadillas   77
Honey and lemon-glazed stuffed chicken   88
Whole chicken with sage and garlic   86
Spanish roasted whole chicken   86
Greek-style whole chicken   88
Lemon thyme roasted chicken   94
Buffalo chicken cheese sticks   97
Chicken breast
Almond-crusted chicken   102
Chicken breasts with avocado-mango salsa   81
Chicken tikka masala   82
Bell pepper stuffed chicken roll-ups   94
Air fried chicken bowl with black beans   84
Chicken cheesy divan casserole   84
Broccoli cheese chicken   98
Broccoli and cheese stuffed chicken   99
Herb-buttermilk chicken breast   89
Tex-mex chicken roll-ups   90
Barbecued chicken with creamy coleslaw   100
Corn-crusted chicken tenders   125

174 | Chapter 1 Vegetables and Sides

Cranberry curry chicken   93
Balsamic chicken with green beans   78
Easy chicken enchiladas   83
Ham and cheese chicken breasts   82
Lemony chicken breast   81
Chicken pinchos with salsa verde   77
Pork rind fried chicken   96
Air fried chicken potatoes with sun-dried tomato   95
Crispy dill chicken strips   101
Quinoa chicken nuggets   78
Italian flavor chicken breasts with roma tomatoes   99
Garlicky chicken cubes on a green bed   85
Italian chicken breasts   83
South asian chicken strips   76
Chicken schnitzel with gypsy sauce   80
Prosciutto-wrapped chicken breasts   82
Bacon-wrapped chicken breasts   149
Greek chicken gyros   81
Greek chicken stir-fry   95
Chicken fingers with red mayo dip   76
Panko-crusted chicken bites   77
Manchego chicken fingers   77
Rice krispies chicken goujons   78
Crispy chicken tenders with hot aioli   78
Crunchy coconut chicken dippers   79
Crispy chicken tenderloins   79
Almond-fried crispy chicken   79
Effortless chicken scallopini   79
Cajun chicken tenders   80
Jerusalem matzah and chicken schnitzels   80
Gluten-free crunchy chicken   80
Sweet curried chicken cutlets   80
Chicken fillets with sweet chili adobo   81
Swiss-style breaded chicken   81
Chicken breasts "en papillote"   81
Chicken parmigiana with fresh rosemary   82
Apricot mustard chicken breasts   82
Creamy asiago chicken   83
Sweet wasabi chicken   83
Caprese chicken with balsamic sauce   83
Pineapple sherry chicken   83
Tasty kiev-style chicken   84
Creamy onion chicken   84
Rosemary and oyster chicken breasts   84
Greek chicken souvlaki   91
Sesame chicken   92
Cajun-breaded chicken bites   95
Chicken kiev   96
Lemon-dijon boneless chicken   97
Barbecue chicken   98
Panko chicken bites   125
Golden chicken   125
Air-fried chicken popcorn   150
Cheese-stuffed jalapeños   131
Chicken cutlet
Golden chicken cutlets   100
Chicken drumettes
Coconut chicken wings with mango sauce   94
Air fried chicken wings with buffalo sauce   97
Chicken and baby potato traybake   87
Cauli-oat crusted drumsticks   87
Ethiopian chicken with cauliflower   101
Crispy drumsticks with blue cheese sauce   85
Southern-style fried chicken drumsticks   85
Chicken drumsticks with garlic-butter sauce   86
Indonesian sambal chicken drumsticks   87
Thai chicken satay   87
Chicken asian lollipop   88
Crisp paprika chicken drumsticks   92

Easy cajun chicken drumsticks   92
African piri-piri chicken drumsticks   93
Buttermilk-fried drumsticks   96
Lemon-pepper chicken drumsticks   139
Effortless chicken drumsticks   150
Chicken fillet
Juicy chicken fillets with peppers   78
Cheesy marinara chicken   84
Chicken legs
Chicken quarters with broccoli and carrots   89
Chicken legs
Peri-peri chicken legs   87
Thyme fried chicken legs   87
Pickle brined fried chicken   94
Chicken liver
Gold livers   99
Chicken sausage
Sausage and egg breakfast burrito   39
Barbecue sausage pizza   132
Chicken tender
Restaurant-style chicken with yogurt sauce   85
Chicken schnitzel dogs   99
Popcorn chicken tenders   79
Harissa chicken sticks   79
Ranch cheesy chicken tenders   79
Tandoori chicken   93
Pecan-crusted chicken tenders   98
Blackened cajun chicken tenders   101
Chicken tenderloin
San antonio taco chicken strips   78
Fajita chicken strips   95
Chicken teriyaki   80
Jamaican chicken fajitas   82
Chicken skewers with yogurt dip   77
Chicken thighs
Classic buttermilk chicken thighs   86
Chicken nuggets   101
Chicken patties   102
Cilantro chicken kebabs   92
Tropical coconut chicken thighs   84
Yellow curry chicken thighs with peanuts   98
Enchilada chicken thighs   85
Traditional chicken mole   86
Spicy chicken thighs and gold potatoes   93
Chicken thighs with herby tomatoes   85
Wild rice and kale stuffed chicken thighs   91
Texas bbq chicken thighs   81
French-style chicken thighs   83
Chicken thighs with parmesan crust   86
Lemon chicken   94
Chicken thighs with cilantro   96
Yakitori   101
Jerk chicken thighs   102
Oregano chicken thighs   125
Sweet and spicy chicken thighs   125
Chicken wing
Fried chicken wings with waffles   44
Chicken wings with gorgonzola dip   125
Spicy buffalo chicken wings   151
Pomegranate chicken wings   74
Sweet chili and ginger chicken wings   74
Hot chicken wings   74
Italian-style chicken wings   74
A-little-sour chicken wings   75
Greek parsley wings   75
Sesame chicken wings   75
Chili ginger chicken wings   75
Honey-vinegar chicken wings   75
Dijon chicken wings   76

Thai tom yum wings   76
Cracked-pepper chicken wings   93
Korean flavor glazed chicken wings   99
Spicy chicken wings   124
Sweet-sour chicken wings   124
Alfredo wings   124
Crunchy ranch chicken wings   124
Lemony chicken wings   124
Paprika chicken wings   125
Asian five-spice wings   144
Sweet garlicky chicken wings   150
Chicken wingettes
Asian sticky chicken wingettes   88
Hot chicken wingettes   150
Chickpea
Cashew and chickpea balls   11
Chili falafel with cheesy sauce   12
Turmeric crispy chickpeas   11
Cayenne chickpeas   135
Vegetable and goat cheese tian   15
Chickpea and spinach casserole   15
Fig, chickpea, and arugula salad   22
Cauliflower, chickpea, and avocado mash   26
Crunchy chickpeas   144
Chili
Thai roasted beef   58
Chocolate
Chocolate soufflé   158
Chocolate lava cakes   160
Boston cream donut holes   162
Lush chocolate chip cookies   164
Pecan clusters   165
Chorizo
Mexican chorizo and beef empanadas   56
Spanish chorizo with brussels sprouts   133
Chorizo and mushroom pizza   132
Chuck
Beef and pork sausage meatloaf   66
Cilantro
Spicy flank steak with zhoug   71
Cilantro chicken kebabs   92
Thai-style cornish game hens   100
Tandoori shrimp   121
Coconut
Lemon poppy seed macaroons   162
Coconut macaroons   162
Tropical coconut chicken thighs   84
Simple pineapple sticks   165
Coconut flour
Crumbly coconut-pecan cookies   166
Coconut flour cake   161
Coconut muffins   164
Vanilla scones   164
Pecan butter cookies   163
Coconut milk
Yellow curry chicken thighs with peanuts   98
Orange and coconut shrimp   105
Cod fillet
Cod cornflake nuggets with avocado dip   107
Cod with avocado   120
Cod with creamy mustard sauce   117
Cod with jalapeño   116
Cod finger pesto sandwich   107
Fish croquettes with lemon-dill aioli   116
Cod fillets with ginger-cilantro sauce   107
Crispy cod fillets   107
Soy sauce-glazed cod   107
Crunchy air fried cod fillets   116
Crunchy fish sticks   117

Friday night fish fry   120
Corn-crusted cod fingers   130
Coleslaw
Barbecued chicken with creamy coleslaw   100
Corn
Corn on the cob   148
Jamaican fish fillets   111
Black bean and corn flatbreads   131
Corn flake
Corn blueberry toast   34
Easy lamb chop bites   62
Corn kernel
Southern-style corn cakes   14
Jalapeño and bean tacos   15
Mexican beef quesadillas   59
Corn tortilla
Crunchy nachos   126
Crunchy tex-mex tortilla chips   142
Spicy tortilla chips   145
Lamb taquitos   63
Corned beef
Beer-dredged corned beef   60
Cornflour
Sweet and sour lamb strips   62
Cornish hen
Thai-style cornish game hens   100
Whole cornish hen with lemon and herbs   74
Cornish hens with honey-lime glaze   97
Cornmeal
Indian fried okra   5
Corn-crusted chicken tenders   125
Sweet pickle chips   127
Couscou
Lamb chops with lemony couscous   62
Moroccan turkey meatballs   89
Mediterranean squid rings with couscous   106
Crab legs
Buttered crab legs   106
Crab sticks
Old bay crab sticks   103
Panko crab sticks with mayo sauce   121
Crabmeat
Dijon crabmeat and veggie patties   103
Cranberry
Cranberry curry chicken   93
Cream
Vanilla crème brûlée   155
Gorgonzola rib eye steak   57
Strawberry shortcake   164
Cream cheese
Pepperoni pizza dip   144
No flour lime cupcakes   159
Crustless peanut butter cheesecake   165
Very berry breakfast puffs   33
Creamy cinnamon rolls   40
Cheesy salmon mini tarts with dill   129
Stuffed fried mushrooms   144
Caramelized onion dip   144
Cream cheese stuffed jalapeño poppers   145
New york cheesecake   159
Pineapple wontons   167
Cremini mushroom
Stuffed fried mushrooms   144
Buttery mushrooms   2
Crescent roll
Crescent dogs   71
Croissant
Blueberry-cream cheese bread pudding   166
Cube steak

176 | Chapter 1 Vegetables and Sides

Pepper steak   68
Cucumber
Lamb and cucumber burgers   63
Greek pork with tzatziki sauce   65
Cucumber and salmon salad   114

D

Dark chocolate
Dark chocolate fondants   154
Chocolate-butter brownies with walnuts   155
Molten lava mini cakes   160
Spanish churros con chocolate   154
Dates
Bacon-wrapped dates   132
Deli ham
Southwestern ham egg cups   43
Dill pickle
Crispy bell peppers with tartare sauce   4
Golden pickles   24

E

Edamame
Garlicky edamame   136
Garlic edamame   145
Egg
Avocado fries with pico de gallo   6
Baked egg and mushroom cups   42
Mexican breakfast pepper rings   38
Cheddar soufflés   40
Austrian torn pancake   29
Ham and cheddar omelet   30
Cheesy egg-kale omelet   30
Lemon curd   159
Red pepper and feta frittata   43
Morning frittata   149
Egg white cups   37
Tamagoyaki   30
Turkey sausage breakfast pizza   37
Denver omelet   38
Cheesy scrambled eggs   41
Italian egg cups   42
Meritage eggs   42
Mexican shakshuka   43
Hole in one   46
Perfect air fryer eggs   147
Lemon curd pavlova   162
Remoulade tomato slices   3
Zucchini fries with tabasco dip   5
Bulgarian "burek" Pepper with yogurt sauce   5
Breaded italian green beans   7
Cheese and cauliflower tater tots   7
Parmesan broccoli bites   9
Cashew and chickpea balls   11
Southern-style corn cakes   14
Cheesy green beans and egg cups   15
Spanish-style huevos rotos (broken eggs)   16
Baked mediterranean shakshuka   17
Plantain fritters   18
Air-fried okra   21
Quiche-stuffed peppers   28
Bacon cheddar potato skins   29
Indian omelet   30
Bacon omelet cups   30
Spinach and tomato frittata   30
Air fried shirred eggs   31
Breakfast shrimp and egg muffins   31

Egg in a hole   32
Crisp pepper rings with cherry tomatoes   32
Cheesy sausage casserole   32
Vanilla french toast   32
French brioche toast   33
Bacon and egg sandwich   33
Tomato and olive quiche   35
Crisp sausage patties   36
Baked eggs in avocado   37
Breakfast cobbler   38
Vegetable frittata   38
Three-berry dutch pancake   39
Sausage and egg breakfast burrito   39
Cheddar eggs   39
Scotch eggs   40
Pancake for two   41
Spinach and feta egg bake   41
Apple cider doughnut holes   41
Southwestern ham egg cups   43
Breakfast pita   43
Bacon eggs on the go   45
Breakfast sausage and cauliflower   45
New york strip steaks with eggs   45
Breakfast meatballs   45
Lemony pork chops   51
Thyme pork escalopes   51
Bavarian-style crispy pork schnitzel   52
Classic beef meatloaf   55
Crunchy beef escalopes   61
Crustless shrimp quiche   103
Ginger chili crab fritters   103
Salmon and spring onion balls   109
Smoked fish quiche   112
Egg and broccoli quiche   136
Turkey scotch eggs   150
Raspberry and vanilla pancakes   152
Cinnamon french toast sticks   152
Chocolate cake   153
Ricotta lemon poppy seed cake   153
Olive oil cake   153
Dark chocolate fondants   154
Chocolate-butter brownies with walnuts   155
Vanilla orange cake   155
White chocolate pudding   156
Chocolate fudge squares   156
Chocolate soufflé   158
Molten lava mini cakes   160
Lime bars   160
Chocolate croissants   160
Coconut flour cake   161
Old-fashioned fudge pie   163
Coconut muffins   164
Brownies for two   164
Egg white
Lemon almond meringues with dark chocolate   157
Lemon poppy seed macaroons   162
Coconut macaroons   162
Egg yolk
Vanilla crème brûlée   155
Eggplant
Super cheesy gold eggplant   20
Russian-style eggplant caviar   8
Mediterranean eggplant burgers   6

Chapter 1 Vegetables and Sides | 177

Air fried eggplant bruschetta   7
Indian eggplant bharta   18
Crispy eggplant rounds   26
Involtini di melanzane (eggplant rollups)   6
Cheesy eggplant schnitzels   6
Eggplant gratin with mozzarella crust   13
Easy greek briami (ratatouille)   17
Crispy garlic sliced eggplant   19
Eggplant fries   146
Easy eggplant and zucchini chips   7
Greek halloumi cheese with veggies   13
Vegetable tortilla pizza   16
Elbow macaroni
Air fried mac and cheese   149
Ham hock mac and cheese   69
Endive
Lemony endive in curried yogurt   146
English bacon
Bacon and egg sandwich   33
English muffin
Cheesy english muffins   14
Canadian bacon muffin sandwiches   44
Egg muffins   44

F

Farfalle pasta
Spinach and chicken meatballs with marinara farfalle   75
Fava bean
Fava bean falafel with tzatziki   12
Fava bean falafel bites   134
Fennel
Gourmet black cod with fennel and pecans   108
Baked trout en papillote with herbs   110
Feta cheese
Tomato and olive quiche   35
Greek feta cheese triangles   34
Sweet feta carrots   3
Fig
Fig, chickpea, and arugula salad   22
Firm tofu
Crispy fried tofu   9
Tofu bites   24
Fish fillet
Roasted fish with almond-lemon crumbs   123
Flank steak
Goat cheese-stuffed flank steak   64
Korean beef bulgogi   59
Mongolian-style beef   67
Spicy flank steak with zhoug   71
Fusion flank steak with mexican dressing   60
Homemade hot beef satay   56
Bloody mary beef steak with avocado   58
Red curry flank steak   68
Flounder fillet
Cayenne flounder cutlets   120
Flour
Blueberry muffins   160
Cheese and buttermilk biscuits   137
Mini cheese scones   137
Spicy cheese lings   137
Chocolate cake   153
Chocolate fudge squares   156
Lemon-glazed cupcakes   157
Coconut and oat cookies   36

Dark rum pear pie   158
Tropical pineapple fritters   159
Chocolate and raspberry cake   157
Cinnamon zucchini muffins   35
15-minute coffee cake   158
Homemade blooming onion   7
Crispy fried tofu   9
Austrian torn pancake   29
Egg-pumpkin bread   31
Simple mango bread   35
Banana muffins with hazelnuts and chocolates   35
Kiwi pecan muffins   36
Beef steak fingers   68
Pork schnitzels with sour cream and dill sauce   68
Effortless tuna fritters   113
Homemade arancini (rice balls)   148
Apple caramel relish   154
Peach cobbler   165
Flour tortilla
Bacon tortilla wraps with salsa   34
Cheesy vegetable quesadilla   16
Korean beef tacos   72
Buffalo cheese-chicken tacos   77
Fontina cheese
Portuguese-style veggies with cheese   14
French baguette
Mediterranean bruschetta   149
French bean
French beans with toasted almonds   138
French bread
Tomato, prosciutto and basil bruschetta   33

G

Garlic
Roasted mushrooms with garlic   145
Goat cheese
Roasted pumpkin with goat cheese   9
Lemon-thyme asparagus   19
Golden beetroot
Quick beetroot chips   4
Gouda cheese
Keto quiche   44
Graham cracker
Easy lemony cheesecake   155
S'mores   153
Yummy moon pie   158
Easy lemony cheesecake   155
Greek yogurt
Greek pork skewers with walnuts   49
Restaurant-style chicken with yogurt sauce   85
Ale-battered fish with tartar sauce   108
Easy salmon with greek sauce   109
Crispy green bean fries with lemon-yogurt sauce   142
Baked peaches with yogurt and blueberries   161
Almond-roasted pears   164
Green bean
Breaded italian green beans   7
Cheesy green beans and egg cups   15
Crispy green bean fries with lemon-yogurt sauce   142
Crispy green beans   19
Buttery green beans   22
Garlicky green bean   129
Balsamic chicken with green beans   78
Green bell pepper
Quiche-stuffed peppers   28
Zesty bell pepper bites   4
"faux-tato" Hash   18

Green cabbage
Green cabbage with blue cheese sauce   5
Asian-style spring rolls   13
Tortilla shrimp tacos   117
Pork and cabbage egg rolls   140
Green chile
Mexican chile relleno   16
Chili corn on the cob   8
Easy chicken enchiladas   83
Green olive
Air fried green olives   129
Calamari rings with olives   106
Green onion
Indian omelet   30
Spaghetti squash fritters   45
Mini beef sausage rolls   57
Fusion flank steak with mexican dressing   60
Onion pork kebabs   71
Green pepper
Catalan-style "escalivada" Veggie spread   9
Green tomato
Hot air fried green tomatoes   148
Grit
Grits casserole   21
Fried cheese grits   39
Ground beef
Lebanese malfouf (stuffed cabbage rolls)   72
Cheesy low-carb lasagna   72
Gorgonzola cheese burgers   151
Beef, pork and bacon balls   138
Beefy poppers   73
Beef burgers with mushroom   73
Mediterranean beef meatballs   126
Beef burger   71
Air fried beef sticks   131
Lemony meatballs   132
Ground chicken
Parmesan chicken burgers   131
Thai tacos with peanut sauce   100
Spinach and chicken meatballs with marinara farfalle   75
Chicken burgers with ham and cheese   100
Oat-crusted chicken croquettes   126
Cabbage chicken rolls   126
Basic chicken patties   76
Oregano chicken kebabs with mayonnaise sauce   76
Ground lamb
Indian mint and chile kebabs   69
Ground pork
South asian pork momos   133
Cheddar pork balls   133
Pork and cabbage egg rolls   140
Onion pork kebabs   71
Sausage and pork meatballs   70
Beef, pork and bacon balls   138
Ground sausage
Sausage balls with cheese   142
Ground turkey
Turkey stuffed bell peppers   92
Lettuce-wrapped turkey and mushroom meatballs   98
Turkey burgers with cabbage slaw   90
Moroccan turkey meatballs   89
Turkey scotch eggs   150
Parmesan turkey meatballs   90

Thyme turkey nuggets   90
Mini turkey meatloaves with hot sauce   92
Grouper fillet
Baked grouper with tomatoes and garlic   123

H

Haas avocado
Golden avocado tempura   43
Haddock
Crumbly haddock patties   112
Haddock fillet
Peppery and lemony haddock   111
Halibut fillet
Peach salsa and beer halibut tacos   114
Sesame halibut fillets   113
Halibut steak
Bacon halibut steak   113
Halloumi cheese
Air fryer veggies with halloumi   26
Ham
Ham and cheddar omelet   30
Sourdough sandwiches   32
Ham and cheese chicken breasts   82
Chicken burgers with ham and cheese   100
Ham chicken with cheese   101
Ham hocks
Ham hock mac and cheese   69
Ham steak
Ham with sweet potatoes   73
Hash brown
Ham and hash brown cups   31
Hazelnut
Greek mussels with hazelnuts   106
Heavy cream
Brownies for two   164
Beef steak au poivre   59
Wild salmon with creamy parsley sauce   109
Cod with creamy mustard sauce   117
Chicken wings with gorgonzola dip   125
Vanilla scones   164
Hoki fillet
Jamaican fish fillets   111
Honey
Cantonese bbq pork   65
Hot dog
Crescent dogs   71

I

Instant polenta
Traditional romanian polenta   33
Italian sausage
Sausage-stuffed peppers   66
Sausage and pork meatballs   70
Cheesy sausage casserole   32
Crisp sausage patties   36

J

Jalapeño
Cheese-stuffed jalapeños   131
Cream cheese stuffed jalapeño poppers   145
Beefy poppers   73
Enchilada chicken thighs   85
Cilantro lime baked salmon   103
Cod with jalapeño   116
Bacon-wrapped shrimp and jalapeño   140
Jumbo crabmeat
Ginger chili crab fritters   103

K

Kalamata olive
Artichoke and olive pita flatbread   143
Greek potato skins with olives and feta   146
Kale
Greens chips with curried yogurt sauce   144
Simple kale chips   128
Kale chips with sesame   143
Cheesy egg-kale omelet   30
Kale and beef omelet   67
Kiwi
Kiwi pecan muffins   36

L

Lamb
Lamb taquitos   63
Sweet and sour lamb strips   62
Lamb and cucumber burgers   63
Traditional lamb kebabs   61
Lamb meatballs with roasted veggie bake   61
African minty lamb kofta   62
Lamb chop
Thyme lamb chops with asparagus   63
Lamb chops with lemony couscous   62
Herb-crusted lamb chops   70
Lamb loin chop
Easy lamb chop bites   62
Lamb chops with horseradish sauce   73
Lamb sirloin chop
Spicy lamb sirloin chops   63
Lamp chop
Italian lamb chops with avocado mayo   66
Lemon
Provencal pork medallions   53
Herbed pork belly   53
Beef steak with mustard sauce   56
Parsley crumbed beef strips   57
Lemony chicken breast   81
Cajun lemon shrimp   106
Barramundi fillets in lemon sauce   112
Lemon curd   159
Lemongrass
Steamed tuna with lemongrass   115
Lettuce
Cod finger pesto sandwich   107
Salmon burgers   116
Gambas al ajillo (garlic shrimp)   152
Lobster tails
Parmesan lobster tails   115
Buttered lobster with herbs   105
London broil steak
Yummy london broil with parsley butter   60
London broil top round steak
London broil with herb butter   65
Long-grain rice
Honey and plum homemade rice   159
Mexican pork chops with black beans   51
Traditional chicken mole   86
Lump crab meat
Crab cakes with lettuce and apple salad   120
Crabmeat croquettes with herbs   104
Crab cake sandwich   122
Crab cakes   122

M

Macadamia nut
Roasted pork rack with macadamia nuts   47
Mackerel
Mackerel with spinach   114
Mackerel fillet
Parmesan mackerel with coriander   119
Mahi-mahi fillet
Lemon mahi-mahi   121
Mango
Simple mango bread   35
Coconut chicken wings with mango sauce   94
Marshmallow
S'mores   153
Yummy moon pie   158
Mashed potato
Fish croquettes with lemon-dill aioli   116
Mexican cheese
Mexican chile relleno   16
Milk
Traditional romanian polenta   33
Peanut butter porridge   35
Raisin bread pudding with hazelnuts   37
Lemon-glazed cupcakes   157
Air fried donuts   158
Honey and plum homemade rice   159
Bourbon bread pudding   161
Mozzarella
Mediterranean eggplant burgers   6
Mozzarella cheese
Crispy mozzarella sliders   17
Green cabbage with blue cheese sauce   5
Flatbread   24
Pesto spinach flatbread   25
Broccoli-cheese fritters   27
Jalapeño and bacon breakfast pizza   41
Tomato and mozzarella bruschetta   43
Pita and pepperoni pizza   45
Mozzarella stick
Crispy mozzarella sticks   140
Mozzarella cheese sticks   149
Mushroom
Black beans and veggie burgers   9
Cheesy mushroom-broccoli pie   35
Panko veggie balls   137
Mushroom and rice balls   2
Golden garlicky mushrooms   19
Lemon-garlic mushrooms   18
Easy vegetable croquettes   12
Italian-style stuffed mushrooms   13
Turkey and mushroom sandwich   32
Pork and mushroom pinchos   49
Roasted pork chops with mushrooms   51
Stuffed pork chops   52
Traditional lamb kebabs   61
Sausage-stuffed peppers   66
Beef burgers with mushroom   73
Chicken pinchos with salsa verde   77
Mushroom carrot spring rolls with noddles   126
Kielbasa and mushroom pierogi   129
Mussel
Bread-crusted seafood mix   107

N

Naan bread
Barbecue sausage pizza   132
Napa cabbage
Chicken schnitzel dogs   99
Napa cabbage
Prawn and cabbage egg rolls   130
New york strip steak
Steaks with walnut-blue cheese butter   64
New york strip steaks with eggs   45
Chimichurri new york steak   56

O

Oat
Oatmeal raisin bars 161
Apricot and lemon flapjacks 159
Peanut butter porridge 35
Gluten-free granola cereal 43
Coconut and oat cookies 36
Blueberry oat bars 36
Oat-crusted chicken croquettes 126
Salty carrot cookies 137
Honeyed roasted apples with walnuts 153
Maple oat-walnut granola with blueberries 154
Okra
Indian fried okra 5
Air-fried okra 21
Egg and cauliflower rice casserole 13
Olive
Garlic-roasted tomatoes and olives 145
Onion
Pork sausage balls with fennel and sage 49
Onion rings 148
Mushroom and rice balls 2
Delicious potato patties 3
Green pea arancini with tomato sauce 5
Air fried eggplant bruschetta 7
Indian aloo tikki 10
Chili falafel with cheesy sauce 12
Fava bean falafel with tzatziki 12
Cheesy vegetable quesadilla 16
Indian eggplant bharta 18
Golden garlicky mushrooms 19
Basmati risotto 27
Greek feta cheese triangles 34
Parmesan ranch risotto 42
Basil-mustard pork burgers 48
Marinara pork balls 48
Beef koftas in tomato sauce 54
Beef meatballs with cranberry sauce 54
Cheesy italian beef meatloaf 55
"stefania" Beef meatloaf 56
Argentinian beef empanadas 56
Beef liver with onions 62
Indian mint and chile kebabs 69
Asian shrimp medley 105
Mediterranean beef meatballs 126
Orange
Orange cupcakes 36
Orange-flavored pork tenderloin 50
Orzo
Chili roasted pumpkin with orzo 14
Oyster cracker
Ranch oyster snack crackers 124
Oyster mushroom
Mushroom and pepper pizza squares 27

P

Pancetta
Roasted chicken with pancetta and thyme 88
Plum and pancetta bombs 134
Parmesan cheese
Parmesan zucchini boats 6
Garlic-parmesan crispy baby potatoes 20
Crispy eggplant rounds 26
Parmesan artichokes 28
Italian pork scallopini 53
Parsnip
Parmesan parsnips with cilantro and paprika 135
Homemade pie with root vegetables 18
Parsnip fries with romesco sauce 23
Root vegetable chips 127
Peach
Peach cobbler 165
Baked peaches with yogurt and blueberries 161
Peache
Vanilla peach cake 158
Peanut
Homemade hot beef satay 56
Pear
Nutty pear crumble 165
Almond-roasted pears 164
Pear and pork patties 49
Dark rum pear pie 158
Pearl onion
Sweet and crispy roasted pearl onions 2
Pork, zucchini and onion kebabs 49
Pecan
Pecan clusters 165
Pecan butter cookies 163
Mixed nut snacks 138
Brussels sprouts with pecans and gorgonzola 18
Apple wedges 141
Mini peanut butter tarts 156
Cinnamon pecan pie 157
Pepper
Chimichurri new york steak 56
Beef veggie mix with hoisin sauce 59
Pepperidge farm roll
Crispy mozzarella sliders 17
Pepperoni
Mozzarella pepperoni pizza 132
Pita and pepperoni pizza 45
Sumptuous pizza tortilla rolls 70
Pepperoni pizza dip 144
Penne pasta
Roasted veggies with penne pasta 14
Phyllo dough
Crispy phyllo artichoke triangles 142
Simple apple turnovers 167
Pickle
Cheese stuffed peppers 28
Pickle spear
Tangy fried pickle spears 141
Pie crust
Mock blueberry pie 154
Pie dough
Cinnamon pecan pie 157
Pineapple
Simple pineapple sticks 165
Pineapple wontons 167
Pineapple galette 157
Cinnamon grilled pineapples 157
Hawaiian brown rice 23
Coconut shrimp with pineapple-lemon sauce 118
Pineapple and dark chocolate cake 156
Tropical pineapple fritters 159
Pistachio
Rack of lamb with pistachio crust 70
Pizza crust
Soppressata pizza 33
Pizza dough
Mushroom and pepper pizza squares 27
Plain flour
Tempura veggies with sesame soy sauce 10
Plantain
Plantain fritters 18
Plum
Plum and pancetta bombs 134
Polenta

Golden batter fried catfish fillets   110
Popcorn
Air fryer popcorn with garlic salt   141
Popcorn chicken tenders   79
Pork
Basil-mustard pork burgers   48
Marinara pork balls   48
Pear and pork patties   49
Asian pork noddle bowl with vegetables   47
Dill pork meatballs   47
Swedish meatloaf   67
Pork belly
Herbed pork belly   53
Pork belly the philippine style   53
Pork breakfast sausage
Breakfast meatballs   45
Pork butt
Pork butt with garlicky coriander-parsley sauce   65
Pork chop
Italian-style apple pork chops   52
Bacon-wrapped cheese pork   69
Lemony pork chops   51
Bavarian-style crispy pork schnitzel   52
Pork schnitzels with sour cream and dill sauce   68
Mexican pork chops with black beans   51
Roasted pork chops with mushrooms   51
Stuffed pork chops   52
Pork escalopes with beet and cabbage salad   52
Southeast-asian pork chops   50
Pork chops with mustard-apricot glaze   50
Hungarian-style pork chops   51
Spicy-sweet pork chops   51
Sweet french pork chops with blue cheese   52
Juicy double cut pork chops   52
Buttery pork chops   65
Air fried pork popcorn bites   150
Bacon and cheese stuffed pork chops   63
Pork loin chop
Lemony pork loin chop schnitzel   72
Pork loin roast
Pork loin roast   73
Pork loin steak
Thyme pork escalopes   51
Pork loin thin steak
Italian pork scallopini   53
Pork medallion
Provencal pork medallions   53
Pork rack
Roasted pork rack with macadamia nuts   47
Pork rib
Char siew pork ribs   48
Chinese pork ribs   48
Sweet and spicy country-style ribs   66
Teriyaki pork ribs   151
Pork rind
Bacon and cheese stuffed pork chops   63
Pork rind fried chicken   96
Parmesan lobster tails   115
Pork sausage
Italian pork sausage pizza   132
Breakfast cobbler   38
Greek pork skewers with walnuts   49
Pork sausage with best ratatouille   48
Sausage sticks rolled in bacon   48
Pork sausage balls with fennel and sage   49
Beef and pork sausage meatloaf   66
Pork shoulder
Cantonese bbq pork   65
Pork sirloin

Greek pork with tzatziki sauce   65
Pork sparerib
Barbecue pork ribs   47
St. Louis–style pork ribs   47
Pork steak
Pork sandwiches with bacon and cheddar   53
Pork, pepper and squash kebabs   50
Pork tenderloin
Creamy spinach-stuffed pork   49
Pork and mushroom pinchos   49
Orange-flavored pork tenderloin   50
Pork, zucchini and onion kebabs   49
Pork, radish and lettuce in a cup   50
Sesame pork skewers   150
Sage-rubbed pork tenderloin   50
Portobello mushroom
Walnut-stuffed mushrooms   136
Spinach-artichoke stuffed mushrooms   25
Potato
Cheesy potatoes and asparagus   3
Baked potatoes with bacon   133
Breakfast potatoes with pepper and onion   29
Cheddar hash browns   149
Cheesy bacon fries   130
Feta french fries   133
Greek potato skins with olives and feta   146
Delicious potato patties   3
Indian aloo tikki   10
Homemade pie with root vegetables   18
Ricotta potatoes   24
Potato filled bread rolls   16
Classic british breakfast   41
Potato chorizo frittata with manchego   30
Middle eastern veggie kofta   10
Easy sweet potato fries   4
Curly fries with gochujang ketchup   4
Rosemary and parsley potatoes   4
Potato with creamy cheese   22
Easy potato croquettes   23
Classic hash brown potatoes   29
Garlicky potato chips   127
Rosemary potato chips   127
Crispy hasselback potatoes   134
Sea salt potato chips   139
Skinny fries   143
Parmesan french fries   143
Classic french fries   147
Curly fries with paprika   147
Simple baked potatoes   147
Winter vegetable traybake   11
Winter root vegetable medley   11
Super veg rolls   28
Lamb meatballs with roasted veggie bake   61
Spicy chicken thighs and gold potatoes   93
Air fried chicken potatoes with sun-dried tomato   95
Dijon crabmeat and veggie patties   103
Delicious seafood casserole   108
Salmon cakes   109
Crumbly haddock patties   112
Oaty fishcakes   113
Classic fish and chips   152
Potato chip
Crispy dill chicken strips   101
Prawn
Ale beer prawns with tartare sauce   104

Bacon-wrapped prawns   104
Chipotle-lime prawn bowls   152
Prawn and cabbage egg rolls   130
Sesame prawns with firecracker sauce   104
Garlicky chili prawns   104
Chinese-style prawns with garlic   104
Prosciutto
Salami, prosciutto and sausage omelet   29
Prosciutto and cheese stromboli   134
Tomato, prosciutto and basil bruschetta   33
Prosciutt eggs cups   31
Prune
Mediterranean-style whole chicken   88
Puff pastry
Very berry breakfast puffs   33
Chocolate croissants   160
Dill zucchini egg cakes   15
Pineapple galette   157
Cheat apple pie   158
Pumpkin
Egg-pumpkin bread   31
Roasted pumpkin with goat cheese   9
Chili roasted pumpkin with orzo   14
Balsamic-lime pumpkin   135
Pumpkin purée
Pumpkin pudding with vanilla wafers   166
Pumpkin seeds
Sweet pumpkin seeds   138

Q

Quinoa
Quinoa and veggie stuffed peppers   12
Quinoa chicken nuggets   78

R

Rack of lamb
Rack of lamb with pistachio crust   70
Rack rib steak
Ginger-garlic beef ribs with hot sauce   54
Radish
"faux-tato" Hash   18
Parmesan-rosemary radishes   24
One-step radish chips   129
Pork, radish and lettuce in a cup   50
Raisin
Brussels sprouts with raisins and pine nuts   17
Raspberry
Chocolate and raspberry cake   157
Ravioli
Fried sausage ravioli   135
Red bell pepper
Bulgarian "burek" Pepper with yogurt sauce   5
Zesty bell pepper bites   4
Quinoa and veggie stuffed peppers   12
Greek-style stuffed bell peppers   14
Red pepper and feta frittata   43
Red cabbage
Vegetable pot stickers   140
Tofu and cabbage sandwich   32
Red onion
Tomato sandwiches with feta and pesto   15
Greek-style beef meatballs   54
Crabmeat croquettes with herbs   104
Fava bean falafel bites   134
Red pepper
Sesame pork skewers   150
Red potato

Potato cheese balls   126
Easy vegetable croquettes   12
Buttered red potatoes   133
Beef roast with red potatoes   59
Refried bean
Bean and beef meatball taco pizza   73
Rhubarb
Rhubarb and strawberry crumble   166
Rib eye steak
Herb-roasted beef tips with onions   72
Rosemary ribeye steaks   64
Chipotle rib-eye steak with avocado salsa   57
Gorgonzola rib eye steak   57
Garlic steak with mexican salsa   57
French-style entrecote with bordelaise sauce   58
Rice
Homemade arancini (rice balls)   148
Green pea arancini with tomato sauce   5
Greek-style stuffed bell peppers   14
Delicious beef with rice and broccoli   58
Mackerel and rice balls   129
Rice cereal
Cheese wafers   141
Rice noodle
Asian pork noddle bowl with vegetables   47
Ricotta cheese
Involtini di melanzane (eggplant rollups)   6
Ricotta potatoes   24
Cheese stuffed zucchini   26
Roma tomato
Parsnip fries with romesco sauce   23
Classic french ratatouille   11
Stuffed red peppers with herbed ricotta and tomatoes   23
Turkey tenderloins with fattoush salad   89
Italian flavor chicken breasts with roma tomatoes   99
Romaine lettuce
Garlicky chicken cubes on a green bed   85
Rotini pasta
Green vegetable rotini pasta bake   12
Rump steak
Teriyaki rump steak with broccoli and capsicum   66
Russet potato
Broccoli-cheddar twice-baked potatoes   20
Baked potato breakfast boats   40
Spanish-style huevos rotos (broken eggs)   16
Bacon cheddar potato skins   29
Breakfast hash   39
Hasselback potatoes with chive pesto   17
Air fried potatoes with olives   19

S

Salmon
Italian salmon croquettes   130
Salmon and spring onion balls   109
Salmon cakes   109
Rainbow salmon kebabs   118
Salmon fillet
Classic mediterranean salmon   110
Salmon fillets with broccoli   109
Salmon with cauliflower   122
Cucumber and salmon salad   114
Easy salmon with greek sauce   109
Cilantro lime baked salmon   103
Oaty fishcakes   113
Pistachio-crusted salmon fillets   108
Korean kimchi-spiced salmon   108
Tandoori-style crispy salmon   108
Sweet caribbean salmon fillets   109
Roasted salmon fillets   113
Miso salmon   115

Chapter 1 Vegetables and Sides | 183

Honey-glazed salmon   117
Cajun salmon   117
Easy salmon fillets   151
Salmon steak
Lemony salmon   114
Butter-wine baked salmon   114
Sandwich bread
Potato filled bread rolls   16
Sardines
Hot sardine cakes   112
Sausage
Breakfast sausage and cauliflower   45
Hawaiian brown rice   23
Classic british breakfast   41
Scallops
Bread-crusted seafood mix   107
Breaded scallops   106
Sea scallops
Bacon-wrapped scallops   120
Scallops and spinach with cream sauce   118
Seafood mix
Delicious seafood casserole   108
Self-rising flour
Hearty cheddar biscuits   40
Vanilla orange cake   155
Old-fashioned fudge pie   163
Air fried donuts   158
Pineapple and dark chocolate cake   156
White chocolate cookies   156
Blackberry cobbler   167
Serrano ham
Roasted asparagus with serrano ham   37
Serrano pepper
Ricotta-stuffed peppers   136
Shiitake mushroom
Asian-style spring rolls   13
Herbed shiitake mushrooms   2
Shrimp
Spicy shrimp with coconut-avocado dip   105
Veggie shrimp toast   141
Shrimp toasts with sesame seeds   143
Rosemary cashew shrimp   105
Shrimp bake   117
Orange and coconut shrimp   105
Breakfast shrimp and egg muffins   31
Crustless shrimp quiche   103
Tortilla shrimp tacos   117
Bacon-wrapped shrimp and jalapeño   140
Cajun lemon shrimp   106
Gambas al ajillo (garlic shrimp)   152
Asian shrimp medley   105
Coconut shrimp with pineapple-lemon sauce   118
Browned shrimp patties   115
Spicy shrimp skewers   105
Old bay shrimp   106
Savory shrimp   111
Garlic shrimp   112
Golden shrimp   115
Paprika shrimp   118
Fried shrimp   119
Lemony shrimp   119
Seasoned breaded shrimp   121
Crispy shrimp   130
Parsley and lemon fried shrimp   130
Lemon shrimp with garlic olive oil   145
Sirloin
Marinated steak tips with mushrooms   69
Sirloin steak
Blue cheese steak salad   67

Cajun beef fajitas   133
Steak, broccoli, and mushroom rice bowls   70
Beef and broccoli stir-fry   64
Spice-coated steaks with cucumber and snap pea salad   71
Sausage beef rolls   58
Sirloin tip
Crispy breaded beef cubes   141
Smoked ham
Air fried shirred eggs   31
Ham and hash brown cups   31
Smoked mackerel
Mackerel and rice balls   129
Smoked salmon
Smoked salmon and cheddar taquitos   109
Cheesy salmon mini tarts with dill   129
Smoked fish quiche   112
Smoked sausage
Kielbasa and mushroom pierogi   129
Smoked trout
Smoked trout frittata   110
Soppressata
Soppressata pizza   33
Sour cherry
French sour cherry clafoutis   154
Sour cream
Crispy drumsticks with blue cheese sauce   85
Sesame prawns with firecracker sauce   104
Spicy buffalo chicken wings   151
Sourdough bread
Sourdough sandwiches   32
Spaghetti squash
Spaghetti squash fritters   45
Spanish chorizo
Potato chorizo frittata with manchego   30
Spinach
Easy empanadas with spinach and mushroom   128
Chickpea and spinach casserole   15
Spinach and feta egg bake   41
Spinach-artichoke stuffed mushrooms   25
Spinach and cheese stuffed tomatoes   22
Garlic white zucchini rolls   25
Spinach cheese casserole   27
Pesto beef rolls with spinach   60
Italian chicken breasts   83
Mackerel with spinach   114
Scallops and spinach with cream sauce   118
Morning frittata   149
Spinach leaf
Pesto spinach flatbread   25
Egg white cups   37
Spinach and bacon roll-ups   46
Squash
Pork, pepper and squash kebabs   50
Squid rings
Mediterranean squid rings with couscous   106
Steak
Super bacon with meat   69
Steak fries
Cheesy steak fries   139
Strawberry
Rhubarb and strawberry crumble   166
Strawberry toast   45
String bean
String bean fries   146
Sugar snap pea
Spice-coated steaks with cucumber and snap pea salad   71
Sushi rice
Air fried veggie sushi   16
Browned shrimp patties   115

Sweet corn
Chili corn on the cob   8
Party crispy nachos   10
Sweet paprika
Yummy london broil with parsley butter   60
Sweet pickle chip
Sweet pickle chips   127
Sweet potato
Sweet potato boats   134
Spicy vegetable skewers   10
Sweet potatoes with zucchini   27
Roasted sweet potatoes   21
Spiced sweet potato wedges   134
Sweet potato fries with mayonnaise   140
Homemade sweet potato chips   142
Citrus sweet potatoes and carrots   2
Ham with sweet potatoes   73
Sweetcorn
Garlic steak with mexican salsa   57

T

Taco shell
Jalapeño and bean tacos   15
Three-berry
Three-berry dutch pancake   39
Tilapia fillet
Parmesan tilapia fillets   111
Air-fried broiled tilapia   111
Air fried tilapia bites   111
Panko-crusted fish sticks   114
Blackened fish   116
Chili tilapia   118
Baked tilapia with garlic aioli   119
Sweet tilapia fillets   122
Toasted bread
Basic welsh rarebit   35
Tofu
Tofu and cabbage sandwich   32
Tamagoyaki   30
Cauliflower and tofu croquettes   137
Tomato
Classic avocado toast   33
Poblano and tomato stuffed squash   13
Cheesy parsley tomatoes   3
Remoulade tomato slices   3
Baked mediterranean shakshuka   17
Tomato and mozzarella bruschetta   43
Tomato sandwiches with feta and pesto   15
Authentic spanish patatas bravas   3
Cheesy eggplant schnitzels   6
Catalan-style "escalivada" Veggie spread   9
Eggplant gratin with mozzarella crust   13
Spinach and cheese stuffed tomatoes   22
Black bean and tomato chili   26
Prosciutt eggs cups   31
Beef steak strips with tomato sauce   53
California-style street beef taco rolls   55
Smoked beef burgers with hoisin sauce   55
South asian chicken strips   76
Chicken schnitzel with gypsy sauce   80
Prosciutto-wrapped chicken breasts   82
Chicken thighs with herby tomatoes   85
Whole chicken with fresno chili sauce   89
Baked grouper with tomatoes and garlic   123
Golden asparagus with romesco sauce   128
Avocado egg rolls   147
Beef steak fingers   151
Top round beef
Rosemary roast beef   67
Top sirloin steak

Wiener beef schnitzel   61
Tortilla
Spinach and bacon roll-ups   46
Jalapeño and chicken quesadillas   77
Trout
Baked trout en papillote with herbs   110
French trout meunière   110
Trout fillet
Trout amandine with lemon butter sauce   119
Easy creole trout   110
Tuna
Tuna-stuffed tomatoes   121
Effortless tuna fritters   113
Air fried tuna sandwich   112
Tuna steak
Tandoori shrimp   121
Steamed tuna with lemongrass   115
Ponzu marinated tuna   113
Sesame-crusted tuna steak   121
Turkey
Easy calzone   34
Scotch eggs   40
Turkey and mushroom sandwich   32
Turkey bacon
Bacon-wrapped chicken breasts   149
Turkey breast
Roasted turkey with brussels sprouts   91
Stuffed turkey roulade   95
Turkey and veggie skewers   90
Turkey strips with cranberry glaze   91
Mediterranean-rubbed turkey tenderloins   91
Chipotle buttered turkey   91
Lemon-basil turkey breasts   95
Easy turkey tenderloin   97
Turkey pepperoni
Egg roll pizza sticks   143
Turkey sausage
Turkey sausage breakfast pizza   37
Turkey tenderloin
Turkey tenderloins with fattoush salad   89
Turkey tenderloin
Honey-glazed turkey   90
Turnip
Zucchini and turnip bake   9
Baked turnip and zucchini   27

V

Vanilla jell-o mix
Snickerdoodle poppers   160
Veggies
Tempura veggies with sesame soy sauce   10
Roasted balsamic veggies   10
Vermicelli noodles
Mushroom carrot spring rolls with noddles   126
Vienna sausages
Parmesan sausage frittata   31

W

Waffle
Fried chicken wings with waffles   44
Walnut
Sweet butternut squash with walnuts   9
Vanilla banana bread with walnuts   34
Gluten-free granola cereal   43
Walnut-stuffed mushrooms   136
Lebanese muhammara   136
Mixed nut snacks   138
Waxy potato

Chapter 1 Vegetables and Sides | 185

Authentic spanish patatas bravas   3
White bean
Middle eastern veggie kofta   10
Golden avocado tempura   43
White bread
Vanilla french toast   32
Air fried tuna sandwich   112
White cabbage
Pork escalopes with beet and cabbage salad   52
Pomegranate chicken wings   74
Greek chicken gyros   81
Cabbage chicken rolls   126
White chocolate
White chocolate pudding   156
White chocolate cookies   156
White chocolate cookies   163
White fish fillet
Ale-battered fish with tartar sauce   108
Classic fish and chips   152
Lemon white fish nuggets   107
Italian-style white fish   113
Crispy fish finger sticks   152
White mushroom
Sumptuous pizza tortilla rolls   70
White onion
Beer-dredged corned beef   60
Whole chicken
Bbq whole chicken   87
Whole wheat flour
Whole wheat blueberry muffins   44
Whole wheat pita
Breakfast pita   43
Whole wheat potato bun
Crab cake sandwich   122
Wild rice
Wild rice and kale stuffed chicken thighs   91
Wild salmon fillet
Wild salmon with creamy parsley sauce   109
Salmon burgers   116

Y

Yellow onion
Caramelized onion dip   144

Homemade blooming onion   7
Breakfast hash   39
Spicy lamb sirloin chops   63
Kheema meatloaf   66
Herb-roasted beef tips with onions   72
Yellow squash
Parmesan squash chips with greek yogurt dressing   128
Yogurt
Orange cupcakes   36
No flour lime cupcakes   159

Z

Zucchini
Zucchini-ricotta tart   25
Zucchini feta roulades   139
Vegetable and goat cheese tian   15
Zucchini fries with tabasco dip   5
Easy eggplant and zucchini chips   7
Greek halloumi cheese with veggies   13
Vegetable tortilla pizza   16
Portuguese-style veggies with cheese   14
Air fryer veggies with halloumi   26
Parmesan zucchini boats   6
Cheese stuffed zucchini   26
Classic french ratatouille   11
Garlic white zucchini rolls   25
Simple zucchini crisps   19
Fried zucchini salad   20
Zucchini-parmesan chips   147
Classic zucchini fries   148
Zucchini and turnip bake   9
Dill zucchini egg cakes   15
Easy greek briami (ratatouille)   17
Baked turnip and zucchini   27
Sweet potatoes with zucchini   27
Cinnamon zucchini muffins   35
Pork sausage with best ratatouille   48
Simple ground beef with zucchini   64
Honey and lemon-glazed stuffed chicken   88
Greek chicken stir-fry   95
Rainbow salmon kebabs   118
Tuna casserole   122

Printed in Great Britain
by Amazon